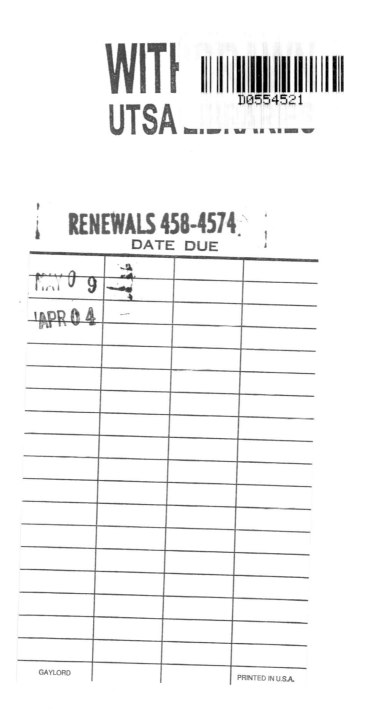

The publisher gratefully acknowledges the generous contribution to this book provided by Sukey and Gil Garcetti, Michael P. Roth, and the Roth Family Foundation.

Proof through the Night

Proof through the Night

Music and the Great War

GLENN WATKINS

University of California Press

BERKELEY   LOS ANGELES   LONDON

University of California Press
Berkeley and Los Angeles, California

University of California Press, Ltd.
London, England

Library of Congress Cataloging-in-Publication Data

Watkins, Glenn, 1927–
    Proof through the night : music and the great war / Glenn Watkins.
        p.   cm.
    Includes bibliographical references (p.   ) and index.
    ISBN 0-520-23158-9 (Cloth : alk. paper)
    1. World War, 1914–1918—Music and the war.   2. Music—20th century—History and criticism.   I. Title.
    ML197 .W436 2003
    780'.9'04—dc21

                                                    2002005967

Manufactured in the United States of America
11   10   09   08   07   06   05   04   03
10   9   8   7   6   5   4   3   2   1

The paper used in this publication is both acid-free and totally chlorine-free (TCF). It meets the minimum requirements of ANSI/NISO Z39.48-1992 (R 1997) (*Permanence of Paper*). ♾

To the Memory of
My Father, George Earl Watkins (1893–1986),
Peacetime educator who served as an officer
in both World Wars,
and of
My Mother, Orpha Andes (1900–1977),
Who waited for him in the First
and joined him wherever possible in the Second.

The cannon thunders . . . limbs fly in all directions . . . one can hear the groans of the victims and the howling of those performing the sacrifice . . . it's Humanity in search of happiness.

Charles Baudelaire

Contents

List of Illustrations

Figures

Musical Examples

Acknowledgments

The list of persons and institutions who provided assistance or encouragement in one way or another during the preparation of this book is too large to cite in its entirety, but the following were especially supportive: Calvin Elliker, Charles Reynolds, and Amy Marino of the University of Michigan, School of Music Library; Sam Perryman, Library of Congress; David Peter Coppen, Sibley Library of the Eastman School of Music; Judy Chou, University of California, Berkeley; David Seubert, Performing Arts Collections, University of California, Santa Barbara; Tim Gracyk; Perrin Stein, Metropolitan Museum of Art; and the librarians at the Chicago Symphony Orchestra Archive Library and the Bibliothèque nationale, Paris.

I owe a particular debt to the students in my final seminar on "Music and the Great War," who opened numerous lines of inquiry that proved indispensable to the final project: Benjamin Broening, Susanne Camino, Rohan De Livera, Amanda Eubanks, Luke Howard, Kevin March, and Duncan Neilson, and to Denise Pilmer Taylor in an earlier seminar.

Other colleagues and friends who offered perceptions, advice, and material support in various ways were: Bruce Adolphe, Lynne Bartholomew, Michael Beckerman, James Borders, Robert Craft, Richard Crawford, John Crayton, David Dennis, Marvin Eisenberg, David Gompper, Joseph Herter, Jeffrey Lyman, Craig Matteson, Scott Messing, Eric Saylor, Kenneth Silver, Gregory Vitarbo, Jay Winter, R. John Wiley, and Steven Whiting. Significant subventions were also received from the University of Michigan, including those provided by Paul Boylan, dean of the School of Music; the vice-president for research; and the International Institute's Center for European Studies. Without their combined support the accompanying compact disc and the inclusion of much of the artwork would not have been possible.

Between 1995 and 2002, several versions of chapters were delivered as lectures for the University of California, Santa Barbara, the State University of New York at Buffalo, the Eastman School of Music, the University of Iowa, the University of Chicago, the Peabody Conservatory of Music, the University of North Carolina, Northwestern University, the Chicago Museum of Contemporary Art and the Chicago Chamber Players, the Arts Club of Chicago, the Philadelphia Orchestra, the Historial de la Grand Guerre, Péronne, France, the College Band Directors National Association annual meeting in 1999, the 2001 Ethel V. Curry Lecture at the University of Michigan, and the 2001 Stravinsky Festival, sponsored by the Kansas City Symphony and the University of Missouri at Kansas City. Two lectures were also delivered for the Moscow Conservatory of Music in May 1999 and three for the Lincoln Center Chamber Music Society in 1998 and 2000.

I am also deeply indebted to the following artists who contributed to the accompanying compact disc that graces this book: Frederica von Stade, mezzo-soprano; Martin Katz, piano; John Browning, piano; Leslie Guinn, baritone; John Muriello, baritone; Susan Jones, soprano; Kristie Tigges, soprano; David Gompper, piano; Réne Lecuona, piano; Hu Ching-chu, piano; the Arizona State University Harmonie Ensemble, Jeffrey Lyman, director; and the University of Michigan Chamber Choir, Thomas Hilbish, director.

Three friends in particular went far beyond the call of friendship: Marvin Eisenberg, who read at least three different versions of the entire project; David Gompper, who coordinated various aspects of the recording project too numerous to mention; and Richard Grunow, who answered repeated calls to consult the stacks of the Sibley Library of the Eastman School of Music. Finally, I offer a special debt of gratitude to my editor, Lynne Withey, for her unwavering belief in a project that required more than the usual periodic reassurances; to Dore Brown, project editor, who guided the manuscript through its numerous stages and kept the author on track; and to Peter Dreyer and Rebecca Frazier, who helped in the difficult task of making large but necessary cuts to the initial text.

Introduction

Historians are to nationalism what poppy-growers in Pakistan are
to heroin-addicts: we supply the essential raw material for the
market.

> E. J. Hobsbawm, lecture to the American Anthropological
> Association, February 1992

Musicians, in their most idealistic moments, argue that their art is
an international language. But when nationalism is asserted, music
is rarely far behind.

> Allan Kozinn, *The New York Times*, 23 December 1997

War is a terrible thing. Yet the cadence of troops marching through the
streets, the ringing sound of national airs, the flapping of proudly hoisted
flags, and, in more modern times, the swoosh of aircraft racing overhead
typically send hearts pounding and aspirations soaring. Inevitably, it is in
the period following the cessation of hostilities, in times of so-called peace,
that the initially envisioned mission becomes increasingly difficult to identify. An awareness of the cohorts of war surfaces even more gradually, and
only in recent decades has the study of the Great War of 1914–1918 moved
beyond political and military tactics to a consideration of cultural issues.
This shift has in turn helped to illuminate the factors behind the call to
arms and has simultaneously driven the debate concerning the Great War's
role in the birth of modernism.

These are large questions that have necessarily been addressed piece-
meal. Paul Fussell has defined the Great War as a world calamity that un-
dermined traditional cultural sensibilities and promoted a language of dis-
illusionment and ironic skepticism. More recent studies have focused on
urban culture, the role of memory, and postwar commemorative rituals;
considered the religious imagination and the sometimes conflicting roles of
church and state in wartime; traced humankind's encounter with age-old
dreams of flight viewed in light of the conquest of the air on the eve of
world war; given sympathetic accounts of the child as symbolic participant
and unwitting victim; discussed the role of masculinity and the fallen soldier in the reshaping of memory of the Great War; argued the functions

1

of entertainment, propaganda, and popular culture not only in western Europe but also in Russia, where war abroad and revolution at home overlapped; and considered how views of gender and color in Europe and America changed as a result of the call to arms.

In the course of writing the present set of essays I came to realize that each of these topics has a musical counterpart. Indeed, music in every nation gave "proof through the night"—ringing evidence during the dark hours of the war—not only of its historic role in the definition of nationhood and of nationalist resolve but also of its power on distant battlefields to recall home and hearth and to commemorate loss long after the guns had been stilled. A somewhat grander argument, one clearly incapable of final resolution, centers on the suggestion that twentieth-century modernism was launched full force with the advent of the Great War. Yet modernism, both as term and concept, has resisted consensus definition to such a degree that the notion that it signals a manageable concept or even an identifiable chronology has had to be jettisoned.[1] No surer sign was ever given of the impossibility of viewing modernism as a progressive movement along a single continuum than during the period of the Great War, when Neoclassicism sounded not so much a full retreat into history as a necessary reclamation of it in the service of establishing national identities, and when Dada launched a brief and zany sideshow, signaling from another angle that prewar modernism was moribund and due for a facelift.

Both developments invite recall of Baudelaire's observation that "modernity is the transient, the fleeting, the contingent; it is one half of art, the other being the eternal and the immovable."[2] For just as in Germany an exhausted Expressionism found a resonating and essential converse in a "new objectivity," so in France a spent Impressionism and Primitivism transmuted into a seeming polar opposite, Neoclassicism.[3] Action and reaction thus often appeared as the operative coordinates, and ultimately none of the "isms" emerged as tidy affairs.

Clearly, then, there were numerous façades to the Great War, all haunted by the looming specter of personal sacrifice in the name of country. They ranged from the deliberately frivolous to the patently grisly, from boisterous rally to solemn rite. The present study of the music produced during this period of crisis must be read, therefore, as an anthology of somewhat arbitrary, if also central, test cases that are obliged to stand for a host of equally compelling stories. Because music is related to other cultural markers such as national institutions and international politics, as well as to other arts, these topics are periodically allowed to direct and occasionally even dominate the discussion of the music. The aim throughout is to present history not as indiscriminate static cling but as resonating interdisciplinary collage.

The impossibility of covering every aspect of music's relation to the Great War prompted the further decision to tilt the present study toward a consideration of responses by the Allies to the perceived threat of German hegemony in matters of intellectual and artistic accomplishment. As a result it will be noted that, although only three chapters are devoted primarily to Austro-Germany and its internal struggle with the politics of culture, the book's perspective takes that very culture as a continual point of reference from the first to the last chapters. Furthermore, the sectional organization of the book along lines of national identity and an approximate chronology should not conceal the fact that within this framework lies a series of broad topical essays intended to italicize the degree to which principles and values bled conspicuously between opposing camps and the extent to which they were frequently verbalized with similar language.

On 3 August 1914 the British statesman Lord Grey of Falloden sounded a dire warning that was to prove prophetic: "The lamps are going out all over Europe; we shall not see them lit again in our lifetime."[4] There can be no question that the wick sputtered in the world of music, but even though composer after composer complained of the struggle to keep the flame alive, it never expired. Fixation on the issue of national identity may have promoted a degree of self-consciousness that was little conducive to the writing of enduring masterworks, yet ultimately it did not preclude their emergence. At the same time, when placed in their proper context, the import of the slightest of these pieces is greater than an unannotated performance would suggest, and their role during the war was arguably no less powerful than that of wartime propaganda leaflets or political cartoons. It should be clear, therefore, that several chapters, which may initially appear to be close readings of minor works by a single composer, address issues well beyond the concept of the masterpiece or personal biography. The accompanying compact disc offers the opportunity to hear some of these less familiar works together with other more popular ones of special historical interest and to judge their collective impact.

Among the political, social, artistic, and literary personalities of both sides was surprising agreement on one thing: the power of music to establish national goals and to secure a spiritual or moral tone for society that seemed to be beyond the power of the written word or the visual image. One of the most forceful proponents of this credo was the controversial Romain Rolland, whose story serves not only as the opening gambit of this study but also as a recurrent foil for artists as diverse as Richard Strauss,

Maurice Ravel, Igor Stravinsky, Vincent d'Indy, Gerhart Hauptmann, and Gabriele D'Annunzio.

Another persistent figure was the mythic Ludwig van Beethoven—a paradoxical presence repeatedly summoned by Allied and Central powers alike under a rainbow of claims. He appears logically and positively in biographies written by Rolland and d'Indy, but under an even wider range of perspectives he is found in the writings of Stravinsky, Ravel, Claude Debussy, Alfredo Casella, George Bernard Shaw, Edward Elgar, and Ferruccio Busoni. And the inclusion of Beethoven's works throughout the war on orchestral programs from Chicago, Boston, and New York to Berlin, Rome, and London spoke of the capacity of his music to serve as a symbol of human aspiration for virtually all nations. Contrarily, the reputation of Richard Wagner among the Central powers as the standardbearer of some future glorious empire was countered in Allied quarters by redefining him as a composer whose purportedly bloated music matched the basest implications of the word *boche*. Such an appraisal represented a sea change in France, where during the period immediately following his death in 1883 Wagner had been viewed virtually as a god.

Of necessity, such a review forces the central question that lies behind all cultural studies devoted to the Great War. Was it really just a military operation after all? Was imperialist territorial conquest the ultimate goal, or was the more fundamental issue one of cultural identity? From the perspective of the Allied nations German *Kultur* was on the line and was being backed by a military machine. Contrarily, the French, repeatedly denying any and all aggressive intentions (with the obvious exception of a healthy *revanchisme* that promoted the prospect of national revenge through the recovery of Alsace-Lorraine), preached that it was engaged in an act of defense for its own *civilisation*. Although the judgment that World War I took place because "Britain owned the world and Germany wanted it"[5] may summarize the issue of maritime supremacy and colonial ambition with reasonable clarity, it barely hints at the deeper concerns regarding cultural stature and the attendant insecurity reflected in persistent patterns of global outreach by small patches of European real estate.

What was implied by the word *Kultur*? The admiration of the French and British for German philosophy, science, and literature, for example, could be counterbalanced by Germany's recognition of Anglo-French political stability and, among other things, France's dominance in the world of form and taste. Yet it was understood that under the appropriate sponsorship each of these positives could be transformed into a negative. Especially unsettling was the recognition that if the equivalent of *Kultur* in these countries were reduced to the prevailing state of music, the balance of power would shift dramatically.

Since the eighteenth century, German-speaking countries had produced such a sequence of commanding musical personalities (Mozart, Haydn, Beethoven, Schubert, Schumann, Bruckner, Brahms, Wagner, and Mahler among them) that their supremacy in that sphere could scarcely be questioned. With the principal exception of Berlioz, and to a lesser extent Gounod, Bizet, Chabrier, and the imported Meyerbeer, France's musical profile in the Romantic Age had been somewhat less glorious than that of Germany. At the turn of the century, however, Saint-Saëns, Fauré, Massenet, Charpentier, and d'Indy had been joined by Debussy and Ravel in signaling an impending era of preeminence. England's musical creativity, barely audible beyond its borders after the age of Purcell (except for the Anglo-German Handel), in no way matched the triumph of its colonial policies, even as Elgar was now claimed as a hopeful sign alongside the newly promoted notion of an English Renaissance. And Italy, a minor contributor to the war effort, had enjoyed an enviable and continuous history of musical achievement comparable to that of France from the time of the Middle Ages, including more recently two of the great masters of opera, Verdi and Puccini. Somewhat different from all of these countries was Russia, long dormant as a producer of art music, who through the course of the nineteenth century had gradually come of age and had begun to show signs of escalating authority, beginning with Glinka and continuing with The Five and Tchaikovsky.

More recently, the United States of America, savoring the first flush of colonial success in the wake of war with Spain in the Caribbean and then in the Philippines, and awakening to the proposition that its geographical horizons need no longer be "rooted in the territorial formation of the nation," began to imagine its frontier anew in relation to its destiny in the world.[6] As a consequence, the Great War saw American composers making a self-conscious effort to free their music from a pervasive German influence even as America's longstanding musical dependence upon Germany left it struggling to define what might qualify as truly American. Although the present study is not focused exclusively, or even largely, on American music, it does entail a broad consideration of the newly emergent status of the United States as not only an economic and military power but also a musical and cultural one with expanding musical aspirations in the post-Armistice period.

Of all the musical genres during the war, popular song offered both the largest repertoire and the broadest call to patriotism and humor in all countries, and by enlisting the willing participation of citizens in the war effort, it promoted the notion of "total" engagement. A cadre of popular tunes— like "Le chant du départ," "La Madelon," "Wacht am Rhein," "Over There," "Keep the Home Fires Burning," and "It's a Long Way to Tipperary"—by turns reinforced nostalgia for home, reflected the fleeting relaxation of moral constraints, and inspired feelings of national pride. Although French, German, and Italian wartime songs also figure in the pages that follow, the power of popular song will be considered primarily through a review of British and American pieces. Consequently, it should become clear that the sentiment behind a song like "Tipperary" not only transcended Irish national history, for example, but also summed up the feelings of displacement endured by soldiers everywhere and society's collective hopes for a brighter future. Soldier songs, both newly minted and recalled from earlier struggles, were joined in the battle by old-time hymns as well as new texts and melodies sponsored by religious institutions that readily exhibited their zeal alongside guarantees of the righteousness of their cause. The Church Militant, historic summoner of youth to join in holy alliance against the infidel, once again invoked music as a powerful cohort.

Yet the first question we are inclined to ask of much of the music written between 1914 and 1918 is "Where's the war?" Indeed, today many of these musical scores seem decidedly free of political entanglements. Arnold Schoenberg, for example, left only the torso of his most philosophical work in *Die Jakobsleiter,* and Strauss composed the metaphorical *Alpine Symphony.* Fortunately, the correspondence and essays of both clarify their feelings about the conflict and help us to contextualize the works that they wrote during the period. More pointedly, if obliquely, attuned to the issue of war were works like Ravel's *Tombeau de Couperin* and Alban Berg's *Wozzeck,* although in the process of becoming staples of the concert repertoire the implicit message of both works largely disappeared. Both Ravel and Berg were in uniform, an observation that merits further scrutiny.

Logically, the story concludes with a consideration of the postwar period when, on the classical music front, memory began to forge a response that was frequently more powerful than in wartime. Popular repertoires understandably now turned to newly sprung concerns surrounding the returning soldier: the first Armistice Day celebrations; the ensuing scenes of commemoration that attempted to fix for posterity an inevitably fading memory; the problems of readjustment to civilian life; and the attempts by veterans' movements to preserve the sense of comradeship experienced in the service. Numerous song texts from this period clearly attempted to perpetuate a social intimacy across class barriers that was largely illusory and difficult to maintain in postwar society.

More than a little paradoxically, the coda to this set of postwar reflections is given over to a work written in 1961 by a composer born in 1913. In attempting to resolve questions about its creator's pacifist convictions, Benjamin Britten's *War Requiem* challenged not only the notion of a sacred versus secular art in a period of relative calm but also the discrete categories of art and the isolating chronologies of history. Britten accomplished this not through the juxtaposition of popular war songs and ecclesiastical chant but through the conscription of World War I poems by the British poet Wilfred Owen as tropes to the Latin Requiem Mass. The series of glosses in turn served as an invitation to view the years from 1914 to 1945 as a continuous period.

If most of the British World War I poets knew the horrors of the front, while only a few of the major composers of any country during the period 1914–1918 could claim first-hand knowledge of battle, this distinction ultimately proved not to be the most crucial one in determining music's impact either in America or abroad. Instead, it was in the varying perspectives of combatants and noncombatants, jingoists and pacifists, Tin Pan Alley songsters and genteel composers alike, that music reminded us of its capacity to incite and to calm, to preach and to moralize, to jeer and to cheer, and finally to lament and to memorialize. Collectively, it offered a heady mixture that traversed the entire landscape between heaven and hell.

Today we have just begun to reassess the poignant, if faded, symbolism of numerous concert pieces—the left-hand concertos, oratorios, and requiems, the many incidental pieces penned for war relief, the telling dedications, the soldiers' tales, the art songs—and to protest their essential, if now muted, testimony. But we have also come to recognize how such concert fare is enhanced by assuming a position alongside the lingering popularity of poems like "In Flanders Fields" and songs such as "Over There" and "Goin' Home." There is a reciprocity there. The struggle to recall the original circumstances that spawned these collective repertoires is one of society's perennial exercises. And despite the irrefutable truth of Robert Wohl's cautionary judgment with respect to the generation of 1914 that "communication across generational boundaries will always be illusory,"[7] such illusions can and do surprise us with their immediacy and power.

Indeed, confronted with these gathered sonorities from the Great War, listeners are often surprised by the recognition of how many of them speak with a poignancy that can still break the heart. The innocent philosophy and simple wisdom of children lying on quilts under a starry night, so warmly evoked in James Agee's poem "Knoxville: Summer 1915," captures with rare poignancy a sense of those precious last months prior to a nation's journey to the battlefields of Europe. And the reverie and echoing lyrics of Charles Ives's "Tom Sails Away," set only two years later, barely disguises the price paid for that adventure—one that brought the loss of innocence not just for a child but for a nation.

The sense of epiphany that accrues from such encounters provides only partial redress, however, for the sense of powerlessness that inevitably follows all attempts to reconstitute the first meanings of so vast and variegated a repertoire. It is not just that the traps of writing history loom at every turn—of question-framing, factual verification, generalization, and authorial motivation.[8] Rather, more simply put, it is the frustrating recognition that, in recounting the stories and making an arrangement, "first meanings" invariably prove to be irretrievable; that despite the weight of our documentation and the purported clarity of our summons, we are all "doomed to be forever hailing someone who has just gone around the corner and out of earshot."[9]

· · ·

One of the most vivid memories of my childhood was of an oversized book bound in dark brown leather with a title on the front cover set in deeply embossed gold. Always on display in the living room of our home in Garnett, Kansas, it was a picture book of World War I. My father had been called into the service in February 1918 and quickly commissioned while a senior in college, and the volume still claimed pride of place in our home more than a decade following the Armistice. Many of the scenes contained therein were vivid color pictures of trench warfare—of tanks and machine guns, of gravely wounded and bandaged soldiers. The occasional family visit to Kansas City, where only two weeks after the Armistice a fund drive had been launched by civic leaders to create a war memorial, reinforced the message. The site dedication took place in 1921 before 200,000 people with General John J. Pershing in attendance, and amongst my most vivid boyhood memories was my father's description of this ceremony (which he had witnessed) as we both stood in front of the Union Station at the bottom of the knoll a decade or more later.[10]

The eventually completed tower—designed by the winner of a national competition, the Chicago architect H. Van Buren Magonigle, and dedicated in 1926 with President Calvin Coolidge as the principal speaker—soared some 217 feet high. No other monument to World War I in America approached it in size or grandeur, and Edward Durell Stone purportedly likened it to the Acropolis and the monuments of Paris.[11] When in 1998, over seventy years later, Kansas City undertook a vigorous campaign to restore its Liberty Memorial and accompanying Museum of World War I, both were in need of serious repair. As the American Century, the Century of Wars, approached its end, it suddenly seemed urgent—somehow more urgent than ever that the specter of the Great War not be allowed to dissolve.[12]

Little could my father have imagined when I was born, a year after this monument was dedicated, that only thirteen years later he would be called up a second time in December 1940, a year before Pearl Harbor, for what eventually became a seven-year tour of duty—or that three-and-a-half years after his recall his son would report for duty on D-Day. Trained as a Japanese linguist, I eventually joined the Allied Translator and Interpreter Section of General Douglas MacArthur's Headquarters in Tokyo nine months after the surrender. I had just turned nineteen. A few months later, my father, an American history teacher and secondary school administrator in civilian life, arrived in Osaka, where he served as the Information and Education Officer for the 25th Division. The story of our civilian family was not an unfamiliar one at the time. But for us the sense of continuity in what has come to be called the Thirty-One Years War (1914–1945) was not a historical ploy but a personal reality. It is to the memory of my parents during these unforgettable years that I dedicate this book.

Part 1

PROLOGUE

1 In Search of *Kultur*

> The fire smouldering in the forest of Europe was beginning to
> burst into flames. In vain did they try to put it out in one place;
> it only broke out in another. With gusts of smoke and a shower
> of sparks it swept from one point to another, burning the dry
> brushwood. Already in the East there were skirmishes as the
> prelude to the great war of the nations. All Europe, Europe that
> only yesterday was sceptical and apathetic, like a dead wood, was
> swept by the flames. All men were possessed by the desire for
> battle. War was ever on the point of breaking out.
>
> Romain Rolland, *Jean-Christophe*

In 1912 the future Nobel laureate Romain Rolland finished his grand
novel, *Jean-Christophe*, with a vivid premonition of war, yet the first entry of his wartime journal, dated 31 July 1914, suggests that he was almost
incredulous that it had arrived.

> A telegram of the federal council posted at the Vevey railroad station
> announces "complete mobilisation in Russia and a state of war pro-
> claimed in Germany." It is one of the most beautiful days of the year,
> a truly wondrous evening. The mountains undulate in a light haze, lu-
> minous and tinged with blue; the moonlight scatters a splash of crim-
> son gold on the lake. . . . The air is delicious, the perfume of wisterias
> floats in the night; and the stars shine with a brightness that is so clear.
> It is in this divine peace and this delicate beauty that the people of Eu-
> rope commence the grand slaughter.[1]

When Germany invaded Luxembourg a few days later, on 3 and 4 August
1914, and threw a final ultimatum at Belgium, the author was overcome. "I
wish I were dead," he remarked. "It is horrible to live in the midst of this
demented humanity and to be a powerless witness to the bankruptcy of civilization. This European war is the greatest catastrophe in history over the
centuries, the ruin of our most sacred hopes for the human fraternity."[2]

The winds of war had begun to blow well before the guns launched their
endless thunder in the fall of 1914, however, and *Jean-Christophe*, published between 1904 and 1912, provided only one of the more vivid testimonies. It was a tardy response to a sentiment that had been repeatedly
voiced by Rolland and others since 1880, namely that the Franco-Prussian

War had settled nothing and that another war was both certain and imminent. When the American editor and writer Thomas Bailey Aldrich observed in 1903 that "civilization is the lamb's skin in which barbarism masquerades,"[3] he articulated an awareness that was shared by virtually all observers of the international scene: Germany's military buildup had already commenced under the façade of *Kultur*. The Germans were not the only ones fanning a war psychology, however. The Futurists in Italy were calling for war as "the world's only hygiene," and the French artist Marcel Duchamp was heard shouting, "We need the great enema in Europe. And, if it's gonna be war, then if we need war, we need war. But, we need a great enema."[4]

Starting in the 1880s Friedrich Nietzsche had made dire Zarathustrian pronouncements that the cities—the melting pots of humanity—must inevitably explode in a great revolution. "The press, the machine, the railway, the telegraph," he said, "are premises whose thousand-year conclusion no one has yet dared to draw."[5] A developing corollary in the shadow of such industrial developments was the escalating concept of nationhood. Prior to the Franco-Prussian War of 1870 there had been no Germany as we know it today, only a collection of independent German states, of which Prussia was the largest. The ruler of Germany for the thirty years between 1888 and 1918 was Kaiser Wilhelm II, who longed for empire and coveted Britain's vast domain, which was ruled by his cousin King George V.

Britain had the largest and most widely dispersed empire in the world, and although she did not have the same border problems that were experienced by the Continental countries, a mounting desire for independence had split Ireland in two. Only the north expressed any appetite for continued loyalty to Britain, and civil war appeared imminent.

France, too, had suffered a severe blow to its national pride through the loss of Alsace and Lorraine during the Franco-Prussian War, and anti-German sentiment had escalated rapidly as a result. Complicating matters was the fact that, under the pretext of Encirclement, Germany had joined colonialist England and France in the "scramble for Africa" during the 1890s. Russia, having recently tested Japan in the east and intent upon acquiring Mediterranean seaports, was ruled by an autocratic monarchy that was loath to accede any power to democratic forces. Inevitably, the generally low standard of living led to popular demands for a rebellion against Tsar Nicholas, who, like Germany's Kaiser Wilhelm and England's King George, was a grandson of Queen Victoria.

A series of alliances involving pledges of mutual support in time of war set the pattern for the inevitable conflict that exploded in August 1914. Talk of war had been on lips everywhere for most of the previous decade. It could be heard not only in the science fiction of H. G. Wells's *The War of the Worlds* of 1898 and the war rooms of statesmen and generals but also in the daily conversation of the most ordinary citizens and lesser politicians. The assassination of Archduke Ferdinand on 28 June 1914 was simply the match that lit the fuse.

Some have argued retrospectively that the Great War was unnecessary and could have been avoided.[6] Even in 1910 the British internationalist and economist Norman Angell had forwarded the argument in his bestseller, *The Great Illusion,* that general war was in fact an impossibility given the prevailing economic interdependence among nations.[7] Such theorizing proved hollow, however, and years later Rolland pointed with some justification to his prescient forecast of war in *Jean-Christophe.*

> With Christophe I fought against the fate that I saw coming. And I called the younger generation to the struggle. Hope remained until 1914, the fateful year that sealed the destiny of the West, the year of the conflict that mowed down my young brothers, my spiritual sons, the flower of Europe.[8]

Essentially a literary figure with a strong passion for the arts and an unwavering social conscience, Rolland articulated with uncanny accuracy the power of music to sort out national priorities. His novels, historical studies, and biographies repeatedly focused on music as a societal barometer, bolstering the oft-repeated claim that during periods of growing national aspiration as well as in times of national crisis the arts invariably become political bellwethers.

Rolland knew this well, for artistic intrigue in France in the period between the Franco-Prussian War of 1870 and the Great War of 1914 was so labyrinthine and so politically motivated that aesthetic endorsements not only became increasingly reflective of developing social and national events but also stoked the fires of emergent controversy. An old order that held to the incontrovertible authority of army, church, and nation was defended by various leagues such as the Patrie Française and Action Française. Their rivals sought to uphold the egalitarian ideals of the French Revolution, and with the official separation of church and state in 1905 the whole issue of French national identity reached a point of crisis that even the ensuing war did not resolve. In this battle music in its many guises and disguises did not join the fray tentatively or tardily, but, instead, boldly manned the ramparts.[9]

Two of Rolland's publications achieved an ever more powerful resonance

as the Great War progressed. His mega-novel *Jean-Christophe* was ultimately translated into some thirty languages and awarded the Nobel Prize
for literature in 1915. The quasi-pacifist document *Au-dessus de la mêlée*
(Above the Battle) appeared in the same year and secured for Rolland a reputation as one of the most controversial moral figures of his age. Although
some might have argued that both volumes should have been awarded the
peace prize, others maintained that Rolland deserved to be tried as a traitor.

A reclusive intellectual who was as quixotic and volatile as he was be-
nevolent and thoughtful, Rolland transcended his parochial French base
and identified the cultural foundation of Europe's problem with amazing
clarity well before smoldering suspicions erupted in a clash of arms. His
initial attraction was to the music of France, Italy, and Germany from the
second half of the sixteenth century, a period marked by religious wars, and
to a new kind of historical writing based on personalities who had made a
striking impact upon the course of events. He believed strongly in the importance of trying to understand art within the context of a period, which
he felt could be achieved only by illuminating the social and political conditions of the time.

In the process of penning his numerous biographies—including those
of Beethoven (1903), Michelangelo (1908), Handel (1910), Tolstoy (1911),
and Gandhi (1924)—Rolland struggled to achieve a momentary union
with the personalities in question. This he hoped would in turn lead to the
possibility of a universal understanding that approached the concept of
"charity" as described by Tolstoy, who was his idol.[10] Rolland's honor roll
contained more musicians than persons from any other profession, and his
search for moral qualities in the sound of music as well as in its social and
philosophical contexts was unremitting. His early interest in music history
had few precedents in France: his doctoral thesis of 1895 was only the second in its field at the Sorbonne.[11] Titled *Les origines du théâtre lyrique
moderne,* the work took careful note of sources while limiting discussion
largely to biography and cultural context. Analytical scrutiny of the score
played no part. Indeed, the study of musical form was deemed suspect in
light of the author's search for the spirit of the composer and his times.

In 1902 Rolland delivered a series of lectures on the French revolutionary period at the newly formed École des Hautes Études Sociales. It was
a government-supported, Republican-oriented institution whose values
meshed in the main with Rolland's personal views. At the same time, Rolland also supported the formalist and historical curricular objectives at the
Schola Cantorum, a musical conservatory whose founder, d'Indy, was a
Catholic monarchist.[12] In 1903 Rolland was appointed to the faculty of the

history of art at the Sorbonne, and the following year he was appointed to the faculty of the history of music, where his lectures were said to have rivaled Henri Bergson's philosophy courses in popularity.[13] In his inaugural lecture, "De la place de la musique dans l'histoire générale," Rolland emphasized the personal moral view that dominated his later biographies of Beethoven and Handel. Whatever his failings as a researcher or writer of music history, as judged by today's standards, one cannot fail to note that Rolland's best pupils, including Henry Prunières, Louis Laloy, and Paul-Marie Masson, ultimately became the central figures in the establishment of the discipline of musicology in France.

THE STRASBOURG OLYMPIC GAMES IN MUSIC

War loves to come like a thief in the night; professions of eternal amity provide the night.

Samuel Taylor Coleridge

As a young man who had just come to Paris in the 1880s, Rolland had already started to configure his personal role of honor for European composers. It was a time when *revanchisme* against Germany for the loss of Alsace-Lorraine flourished. Nevertheless, in Rolland's pantheon Berlioz was soon joined by Wagner, and his discovery of Beethoven changed the course of his life forever. (Wagner, whose favor had escalated to cult status in fin-de-siècle France, was ultimately discarded by Rolland, as he was by most of his compatriots.)[14] Rolland had initially added Saint-Saëns to his constellation of favorites, but in 1887 Saint-Saëns began to charge that the Germans and Italians were much more attuned than were the French to extolling the virtues of their own countrymen, and he chastised Rolland for his support of foreign artists. Rolland countered that such a fear of foreigners could only signal a lack of confidence in French art, a perspective that echoed the ongoing debate regarding the necessarily cosmopolitan basis of all classic art.[15] Rolland was intent upon expanding the boundaries of a limited native expression, but he nonetheless simultaneously, and paradoxically, stressed the importance of developing a genuine French school of music.

His doctoral studies, which had given him a familiarity with seventeenth- and eighteenth-century French musical masters such as Lully, Campra, Destouches, and Rameau, expanded under the influence of his teacher, Henri Expert, who had made a study and prepared editions of the sixteenth-century composer Claude Le Jeune. In Rolland's view these early French masters had prepared the way for Berlioz, and he even anachronistically applied the term "Berliozienne" in praise of Rameau.[16] D'Indy, on the other hand, argued that Berlioz was not truly French, a fact underscored by his positive reception in Germany.[17] Nothing could have more vividly illustrated how the issue of national identity was being fought on musical terrain and especially how the revival of early music in the fin de siècle—often read simply as a preparation for the vigorous rise of Neoclassicism in the mid-1910s and the 1920s—was, in fact, deeply rooted in the nationalistic concerns of the prewar decades.

César Franck, although of Belgian birth, was also a central figure in the Parisian musical scene, and he was the first contemporary composer to win a place of honor alongside Berlioz and Beethoven in Rolland's pantheon. This was not so strange, for the French had always viewed Flemish art as more French than German, and in light of attempts by Rolland and others to claim that even Beethoven was of Flemish stock the choice of Franck was natural.[18] As the teacher of d'Indy, Albéric Magnard, Joseph Canteloube, and Charles-Marie Widor (who was the teacher of Edgard Varèse and Marcel Dupré, who in turn taught Olivier Messiaen, an early mentor of Pierre Boulez), Franck provided an indisputable legacy for French music well into the twentieth century. In his attempt to identify those traits that could be most readily identified as French, Rolland was guided by a sense of history as well as personal taste.[19]

Rolland noted with pride the French concern for musical declamation, as evidenced in their artful control of the recitative. In 1905, while a French translation of Strauss's *Salome* was being prepared, Rolland gently instructed Strauss in the art of prosody in a protracted correspondence. Extolling Claude Debussy's *Pelléas et Mélisande* (1902) over the works of Richard Wagner, Rolland provided Strauss, the most prominent German composer of the period, with detailed instructions on matters of stress and inflection. Although their letters reveal that Strauss was a willing and pliant pupil, Rolland ultimately concluded—one suspects not particularly reluctantly—that the nuances of the French language were probably beyond a German to comprehend.[20]

In May 1905, the year in which *Salome* premiered in Dresden, the city of Strasbourg scheduled the first musical festival of Alsace-Lorraine. The region had been a source of confrontation between France and Germany for centuries. France's loss of Alsace-Lorraine to the Germans was recent enough that its significance was undiminished on both sides, and attempts at mutual understanding after 1870 had been scarce. Shortly after the conclusion of the festival Rolland set down a critique, titled simply "French and German Music," that served as the final essay in his collection of essays, *Musiciens d'aujourd'hui,* published in 1908. No piece of criticism written in the immediate prewar years so succinctly summarized the musical aspirations as well as the doubts that existed between the two countries. Proclaiming the Strasbourg festival as a kind of European Olympic Games of music, Rolland reported that "in spite of good intentions, this meeting of nations resulted in a fight, on musical ground, between two civilisations and two arts—French art and German art."[21] Rolland had no doubt placed his hopes in Nietzsche's pronouncement, published in 1889, that whenever Germany rises as a great military and economic power, France inevitably gains new importance as a cultural power.[22]

Rolland was chagrined, however, that France had maintained an indifferent attitude toward the notion of a national music contest. He charged Parisian audiences with smugness, and judged that in the absence of a genuine capacity for criticism French music was destined to fall behind. Such events as the Strasbourg festival would, he thought, have allowed the opportunity for cultural encounter, or even "combat," as he phrased it, where one could judge the virility of one's own national art. Rolland announced that by making up a program of Beethoven's Ninth Symphony, the last scene from Wagner's *Die Meistersinger von Nürnberg,* Brahms's *Rhapsody,* Franck's *Les béatitudes,* Charpentier's *Impressions d'Italie,* Strauss's *Sinfonia domestica,* and Mahler's Fifth Symphony, "perfect eclecticism had been exercised."[23]

Rolland bitterly protested, however, that only five of the eight sections of Franck's *Béatitudes* had been played, that some of these were cut, that the work was not understood by the conductor, and, finally, that the work itself did not provide an ideal profile of the Franck of France. In the future, he argued, "French people must be allowed to choose the works that are to represent them," and he insisted that works should henceforth not be mutilated or cut in any way.[24] Nonetheless, recognizing that France in the future could ill afford such unfavorable comparisons, he also prescribed that a whole day should be set aside for French music and complained that the festival organizers "had carefully sandwiched the French pieces in between German works to weaken their effect, and lessen the probable (and actual) enthusiasm with which French music would be received . . . by a section of the Alsatian public."

Rolland virtually advertised his realization that Franck's piece had not measured up to expectations when placed against the German titans, but his most serious complaint centered on the fact that "the German work chosen to end the evening was the final scene from *Die Meistersinger*, with its ringing couplet from Hans Sachs, in which he denounces foreign insincerity and frivolity (*Wälschen Dunst mit wälschen Tand*)." Finally, Rolland acknowledged that

> Charpentier's *Impressions d'Italie* . . . , though a brilliantly clever work, is not of the first rank, and was too easily crushed by one of Wagner's most stupendous compositions. If people wish to institute a joust between French and German art, let it be a fair one, I repeat; let Wagner be matched with Berlioz, and Strauss with Debussy, and Mahler with Dukas or Magnard.[25]

The judgment, although not completely amiss, carries a curious ring today. Wagner matched with Berlioz, and Strauss with Debussy? Reasonable enough. But Paul Dukas vis-à-vis Mahler? If nothing else, the assertion verifies that the impact and influence of the composer of *L'apprenti sorcier* (1897) was much stronger at that time than it was ever to be again—a fact that one of Stravinsky's first orchestral pieces, *Fireworks*, from 1908, endorsed in its opening pages.[26] But who was Magnard? Although little remembered today, Magnard was indeed a fine, if conservative, composer, and one whose death at the hands of the Germans in the first weeks of the war made him something of a martyr.[27] More important for the present story, however, is the fact that his name belongs firmly alongside d'Indy and Rolland on the honor roll of those musicians who in the prewar years helped to identify a French musical spirit that commanded a solid sense of form and counterpoint and transcended parochial perspectives.

Although Rolland could hold up Debussy as an ideal representative for some future Strasbourg festival and as a consummate model for Strauss in matters of diction, he nonetheless worried about the power of Debussy's influence for future generations. Troubled that his art was excessively refined despite its indisputable originality, Rolland was concerned that it might lead to an elite Parisian school rather than a more broadly based one that would be representative of the true spirit of the French people.

BEETHOVEN AND *JEAN-CHRISTOPHE*

Rolland was anything but a blindly chauvinistic Frenchman. In *Jean-Christophe*, a work begun the year before the Strasbourg festival, he attempted to undertake an impartial assessment of the qualities of French musical life. His novel follows the development of a Beethoven figure, a musical genius of German birth, who lives in both Germany and France during the Belle Époque. The name of this protagonist, Jean-Christophe Krafft, advertised a bicultural sensibility. Appearing serially in seventeen issues of *Cahiers de la Quinzaine* between 1904 and 1912, it was a novel sequence, or *roman-fleuve,* comparable to a flowing river whose character was ever changing. Epic in conception and construction, the work quickly achieved renown throughout Europe and was received in England as the most influential novel of its time by such figures as H. G. Wells, Arnold Bennett, John Galsworthy, and E. M. Forster. Yet among his own countrymen, including André Gide and Marcel Proust, there was a pronounced disdain. While admiration was registered regarding its formal qualities, including the putative use of leitmotif and a symphonic structure that carried a decidedly musical resonance, Gide was predictably repulsed by Rolland's strong note of didacticism and judged the work categorically mediocre when weighed against the French ideals of clarity and economy.

Whatever its literary merits, as a witness to its epoch *Jean-Christophe* has few rivals. Rolland traces the development of a friendship between Krafft and a young Frenchman, Olivier, casting them as symbols of the "harmony of opposites" between nations as well as individuals. Krafft, as his name implies, signifies indefatigable dynamism and dash. He springs from peasant ancestry and has inherited Siegfried's belief in his own invincibility. If Krafft is the offspring of the best energies of Germany—an impetuous genius—then Olivier is the sentimental artist, embodying the essence of French culture and eschewing hatred in any form. Ultimately the two figures realize that despite their seemingly masculine and feminine polarity they are spiritual brothers. Through the course of the novel Krafft experiences a dramatic change in perspective and gradually develops an awareness of the subtleties and richness, even boldness, of French chamber music.

The necessity of transcending national barriers and discovering an international musical code that would speak to the people of all nations was paramount to Rolland. In the formation of a new art Rolland not surprisingly introduced alongside Beethoven-like features certain qualities that were inspired by the new musical prophet, Franck, who loomed as the one figure who might mediate German and French musical values. The necessity of transcending national barriers and discovering an international musical code that would speak to the people of all nations reigned paramount. Nevertheless, in an attempt to remain loyal to his native country, Rolland continuously preached that internationalism was to be pursued specifically from the perspective of a French national art.[28] The means by which such a goal could be achieved were less than clear, and the resolution of this dilemma was destined to concern French composers throughout the war years and beyond.

In 1903, just prior to beginning *Jean-Christophe*, Rolland wrote a work whose moral posture claimed the attention of a generation. His study of Beethoven was a slender volume with an appendix that contained letters and the composer's celebrated document of personal crisis, the Heiligenstadt Testament. Like Krafft, his fictional figure to come, Rolland's Beethoven indicts contemporary society and posits his compositions principally as moral testaments of a humanitarian crisis. Eschewing technical and formal analysis in *Vie de Beethoven,* as he had in his earlier works, Rolland underscored personal qualities that could point the way to moral regeneration for contemporary society. Viewed in this light, it is not surprising that reports circulated of the pocket version of *Vie de Beethoven* being carried into the trenches by soldiers of both sides.[29] The renowned Schubert scholar Otto Erich Deutsch, stung by Rolland's adoption of Beethoven, criticized his biography as filled with "poetic inaccuracies," thus joining the ranks of German nationalists who dismissed all such discussions of Beethoven's Flemish ancestry as products of a "war psychosis."[30]

There were other factors that conspired to make Rolland's study of Beethoven more than just another moral biography. Throughout the nineteenth century the Beethoven legacy was periodically documented and interpreted in numerous studies devoted to both art and politics, and this literature, in tandem with a developing portraiture and sculpture, propelled and escalated the Beethoven myth.[31] The unremitting and varied manipulation of Beethoven's music for different and sometimes diametrically opposing national purposes may be unique in all the arts. Concert halls in Paris, Berlin, Milan, Rome, London, Vienna, Chicago, Boston, and New York resounded with his symphonies and concertos throughout World War I. Beethoven's music was performed more frequently than the music of any other composer, regardless of nationality.

Although Beethoven was invoked by the Germans during the war in support of their nationalistic aims, one notable German also entertained notions of pacifism in the name of this very composer. At the very beginning of the struggle Hermann Hesse, who, like Rolland, was a novelist and avid devotee of music, decried the importation of music into the arena of world conflict and particularly the abuse of Beethoven's Ninth Symphony in this regard.[32] By August 1917, however, his view had shifted somewhat, as evidenced by an open letter addressed "To a Cabinet Minister," who had given an angry speech that seemed to preclude the prospect of a negotiated peace. Prompted by the hearing of a Beethoven sonata and a re-reading of the Sermon on the Mount, Hesse wrote that for him the two carried the same message and symbolized "the only spring from which man derives good."[33]

Destined many years later to become a Nobel laureate himself, Hesse was one of the few German literary figures to introduce a humanitarian perspective on the war and to endorse the basic implications of Rolland's Beethoven study. For decades, however, the French had been conditioned to hear in Beethoven's Fifth Symphony something close to a national manifesto, and the French socialist Edgar Quinet (1803–1875) had already borrowed Beethoven as a hero who challenged France to take revenge for her losses in the Franco-Prussian War. Although Quinet had spoken of the Ninth Symphony's joyous finale as "the Marseillaise of Humanity,"[34] in the Fifth Symphony he heard "an explosion of the public conscience," whose final movement he felt was "in fact a heroic act, a victory, something like the return of Alsace-Lorraine to the fatherland, to France," which represented "a free nation, a happy one that falls into a triumphal march and arouses patriotic enthusiasm."[35] Not surprisingly, Quinet's extraordinary French perspectives on Germany were collected and republished in Paris in 1917.[36] Thus the passionate adoption of Beethoven by Germany's World War II adversaries was historically well prepared when the Allies picked as their symbol of victory the Fifth Symphony's opening motif, whose short-short-short-long pattern (. . . _) was the Morse code equivalent of the letter *V*.[37]

As Rolland kept insisting, his veneration for Beethoven was for the man, not German music as a whole. Despite the power of the Beethoven cult, its influence was not sufficient—once war broke out—to blind him to what he now began to claim was the mediocrity of German music. Acknowledgment of the glories of German culture of the past was in fact rigorously compartmentalized. In his essay "The Lesser of Two Evils: Pangermanism, Panslavism," originally published in the *Journal de Genève*, 10 October 1914,[38] Rolland extolled his feelings for Tolstoy and Dostoyevsky, for whom he claimed Germany had no counterpart, and concluded that in the world of music

> Germany, so proud of its ancient glory, has only the successors of Wagner, neurotic jugglers with orchestral effects, like Richard Strauss, not a single sober and virile work of the quality of *Boris Godunov*. No German musician has opened up new roads. A single page of Moussorgsky or Stravinsky shows more originality, more potential greatness than the complete scores of Mahler and Reger.[39]

ROMAIN ROLLAND AND RICHARD STRAUSS

Tellingly, Rolland was a personal acquaintance of both Strauss and Stravinsky, the two principal living composers whom he had subjected to such an odious comparison. Yet Rolland's expressed antipathy for German music, especially for Richard Strauss, could scarcely disguise the fact that his opinion of German musicians was driven by strictly pragmatic concerns of the moment. The ongoing veneration of Beethoven in France, for example, was not viewed as an inconsistency. Under Rolland's guardianship the veneration of Beethoven had transcended myth and approached something very close to a religion for the better part of a decade. With the beginning of the war, however, Rolland's Beethoven cult began to suffer a series of fatal concussions. By the centennial of the composer's death in 1927 Rolland was still writing about Beethoven, but now it was with the bittersweet recognition that the composer's music could never again carry the hopes of the world as it had at the beginning of the century.[40]

In the letters that Strauss and Rolland exchanged in 1907, Strauss had admonished Rolland for his anti-German bias, stating "there you go, publishing books against German music! But you haven't got any French music. . . . The smallest town in Germany has a concert hall, an orchestra, choirs, organs, better than you have here in Paris." Rolland replied, "Yes, but you have bad music played in them." Rolland was capable of acknowledging the power of Strauss and Mahler, but he believed that both were subject to "the hypnotism of force which is driving all German artists crazy nowadays."[41] "There are morbid germs in present-day Germany," he stated at another time, "a mania of pride, a belief of itself and a contempt for others which are reminiscent of France in the seventeenth century."[42]

The Rolland-Strauss correspondence reveals that the two maintained a close relationship marked throughout by an extraordinary candor with respect to national issues. Rolland, for his part, made clear his feelings that Germany was awash in moral decay and that music like Strauss's *Salome* was symptomatic of it. He stated that "Oscar Wilde's *Salome* is not worthy of you. . . . It has a nauseous and sickly atmosphere about it: it exudes vice and literature."[43] Paradoxically, Wilde had been directly influenced by French works such as Joris-Karl Huysman's "breviary of the Decadence," *A rebours* (1884), and, significantly, the original language of Wilde's play was French. Yet, regardless of Rolland's moral posturing along dimly defined national lines, he could not ignore *Salome*'s success. "You have triumphed over the Europe of our time," he admitted to Strauss. "Now you must leave our Europe, raise yourself above it."[44]

On 12 February 1917 Strauss wrote to Rolland, expressing his disappointment that Rolland had not been able to come to Berne to see his new version of *Ariadne auf Naxos* (1916), which, he believed, might "rectify your judgement of German music such as I have seen exhibited in *Jean-Christophe.*" He also noted that he could see from reading Rolland's article that they had numerous points of agreement on humanistic issues and even a common admiration for the courageous armies on the field of battle. Noting persistent reports of French maltreatment of German prisoners, Strauss concluded:

> I have always held that men such as you can, by personal inquiry in enemy country, establish a more solid and convincing base for conducting their work in the interpretation of justice and truth. *Would you not like to do this?* I have not yet spoken to anyone of this idea, but I think that, given my connections, it would be possible to invite you this spring to Garmisch, and there arrange the opportunity to witness diverse impressions of our people in time of war.[45]

Rolland's astonished reaction to Strauss's letter is recorded in his journal.

> Richard Strauss writes me from Zurich (12 February), at the moment when he was about to leave Switzerland. He amicably proposed to me that I come spend some time with him at Garmisch in Bavaria! He felt confident of being able to obtain the proper authorisation. . . . How little these poor Germans suspect of the state of mind in Europe! Just reverse the situation: a German invited to France, it would be like one of Napoleon's soldiers in besieged Saragossa![46]

The reasonableness of Strauss's offer—or its utter naïveté—can be judged only from a consideration of Rolland's writings during the period. There can be little doubt that Strauss had read *Jean-Christophe* and, more especially, the essay "Au-dessus de la mêlée," and that he saw in his friendship with Rolland a parallel with the friendship of Krafft and Olivier. "I love my country," wrote Olivier to Krafft. "I love it just as you love yours. But am I for this reason to betray my conscience, to kill my soul? This would signify the betrayal of my country. I belong to the army of the spirit, not to the army of force."[47]

ABOVE THE BATTLE?

Two months into the war, on 13 October 1914, a document was published in the Paris daily *Le temps* titled "An Appeal to the Civilized World." The article, which came to be known as the Manifesto of 93, was signed by the German intellectual elite from the sciences and the arts, including novelist and playwright Gerhart Hauptmann and composer Engelbert Humperdinck. Strauss had been importuned to endorse the statement, but he had refused on the grounds that as a composer his business was to write music, not manifestos. The German manifesto was straightforward enough: it denied the legitimacy of the charges of barbarism that had been brought against the German army and charged willful misrepresentation on the part of the Allies. The arts were enlisted through the claim that as the intellectual heir of Goethe, Beethoven, and Kant, the German nation would obviously not be capable of dishonoring the principles of these great men. On a specific level the signatories claimed that the Germans and their emperor were peace-loving; that war had begun only because a numerically superior Allied force, "which had been laying in wait on the frontiers," had pushed Germany to the brink; and that all charges pertaining to the violation of Belgian neutrality and subsequent atrocities were false.

The reaction among the French in particular was swift and brought a stern reply to one of the most maligned documents to come out of Germany in the early war. Catholics and Republicans came together to fashion a response that immediately engaged France's intellectuals and artists. It was signed by Debussy, Gide, Saint-Saëns, Maurice Barrès, Paul Claudel, Georges Clemenceau, Anatole France, Henri Matisse, and Claude Monet.[48]

The most celebrated censure of such intellectual action tethered to national interests came from Rolland, who in 1915 published a collection of recently written articles under the title *Au-dessus de la mêlée* that included the famous eponymously titled essay. Here the moral arguments of *Vie de Beethoven* and *Jean-Christophe* were removed from the realms of biography and fiction and relocated in the realities of a world trapped in global conflagration. As its author no doubt foresaw, it created a storm of controversy. In the summer of 1914, two months before the outbreak of hostilities, Rolland traveled to Switzerland for a vacation. He stayed for the remainder of the war, a decision that would bring repeated charges in the years to come that he had fled to Switzerland to escape service at the front.[49] Rolland, who was forty-eight years of age, frail from childhood, rejected from military service as a young man, and recently retired from teaching at the Sorbonne because of poor health, would not have been accepted in any event. A man of such humanitarian inclinations could hardly have been expected to sit out the war, however, and by October 1914 Rolland was performing menial tasks for the Red Cross in its newly organized International Agency for Prisoners of War at Geneva.[50]

Even before the onset of war Rolland's choice of a German hero for his novel *Jean-Christophe* and its initial stinging and relentless attack on musical life in Paris had brought direct charges that he had defected to the Germans. Ostracized by friends and colleagues, he moved to neutral Switzerland, which he viewed as a haven in which French and German cultures readily coexisted. Indeed, Rolland seemed to be replicating in real life the role of his novel's hero, an archetypal artist-wanderer who looks abroad for an intellectual engagement that he cannot find at home. In Switzerland Rolland felt he "was in a position to listen to the confidences of both camps." "In Switzerland alone," he said, "I could judge impartially, from there and there alone I could assemble all the documents for the inquest."[51]

Rolland's flight to Switzerland mirrored the actions of more than one important figure in the history of music. Richard Wagner had been exiled to Switzerland in 1848, where he began work on his *Der Ring des Niebelungen*, a project that was to occupy him over the next twenty-two years. Similarly, Chopin, following revolution at home, left Poland for Paris and immediately began to showcase his native traditions in polonaises and mazurkas. And Stravinsky, who absolutely cringed at much of Rolland's moral and aesthetic philosophy and stated categorically that the Romantic mythologizing and posturing of *Jean-Christophe* and *Vie de Beethoven* "were and are exactly what I most abhor," also left his homeland when war and revolution broke out. Stravinsky's search for the language of a people, which was much like Krafft's, escalated precipitously at a moment of conflict and exile.[52]

Challenged to find his voice during his five years in Switzerland, Rolland reacted quickly and unapologetically to the events of the day. News of the destruction of the library of Louvain University and the cathedral at Rheims brought an especially impassioned cry of protest in an open letter to Hauptmann, dated 29 August 1914.[53] Their public exchange carried a particular poignancy because Hauptmann, Nobel laureate in 1912, was the foremost German writer of the day, and Rolland, Nobel laureate to be, was the literary sensation of the hour. Rolland not only protested against the brutal invasion of Belgium, the bombardment of Malines, and the destruction of Louvain and its art treasures, he also reminded the Germans of his lifelong labors at effecting rapprochement between the two nations. It was a sentiment that he repeated even more vehemently in another essay, "Pro aris." There Rolland reprimanded Hauptmann for adopting the slogan "Perish every *chef-d'oeuvre* rather than one German soldier!" then entered a resounding proclamation concerning the national importance of such a sacred edifice as Rheims cathedral.

> A piece of architecture like Rheims is much more than one life; it is
> a people—whose centuries vibrate like a symphony in this organ of
> tone. It is their memories of joy, of glory, and of grief; their medita-
> tions, ironies, dreams. It is the tree of the race, whose roots plunge to
> the profoundest depths of its soil, and whose branches stretch with a
> sublime *élan* towards the sky. . . . Whoever destroys this work, mur-
> ders more than a man; he murders the purest soul of a race. His crime
> is inexpiable, and Dante would have it punished with an eternal agony,
> eternally renewed.[54]

Rheims cathedral became a metaphor for numerous visions of the
war—even Sarah Bernhardt, the legendary actress who gave performances
at the front even after she had a leg amputated in February 1915, chose to
recite a monologue standing in front the cathedral's ruins. Literary depic-
tions of this renowned edifice in decay include a lapidary description by
Edith Wharton in *Fighting France* from the same year.

> The interweaving of colour over the whole blunted bruised surface re-
> calls the metallic tints, the peacock-and-pigeon iridescences, the incred-
> ible mingling of red, blue, umber and yellow of the rocks along the
> Gulf of Aegine. And the wonder of the impression is increased by the
> sense of its evanescence; the knowledge that this is the beauty of dis-
> ease and death, that every one of the transfigured statues must crumble
> under the autumn rains, that every one of the pink or golden stones is
> already eaten away to the core, that the Cathedral of Rheims is glowing
> and dying before us like a sunset.[55]

There are decidedly fewer sonic evocations, however.[56] A choice exception was the song "Cathédrale de Reims" by the writer-singer Gabriello,
which begins "O Rheims, You, whose cathedral was the pride of the entire
world" and which was to be sung to the tune "C'est si jolie la femme," much
in vogue at the time.[57] Another was "Davanti alle rovine della cattedrale di
Reims" (Before the Ruins of Rheims Cathedral) from Casella's *Pagine di
guerra* of 1915, a work for piano duet that makes explicit although inverted
reference to the parallel chordal motion of Debussy's piano prelude "La
cathédrale engloutie" (The Engulfed Cathedral). And Jacques Ibert captured a similar allusion in his "Le vent dans les ruines" for solo piano of
1914, whose title recalls a Debussy prelude, "Le vent dans le plaine."[58]

Auguste Rodin protested in a poignant letter of support to Rolland on
30 September that the meaning of such desecration could be truly understood only by the French.[59] Rheims, a Roman city that had been an archi-
episcopal see since the eighth century, had served as the traditional coronation site of French kings. Rolland's use of a musical metaphor to describe

Rheims was especially apt because of the city's political-architectural-musical tradition, which can be traced to at least the fourteenth century. Guillaume de Machaut, the most important French composer of the late Middle Ages, had worked in Rheims during the reign of two kings and composed a *Messe de Notre-Dame* (about 1360) that is remembered today as the first unified polyphonic setting of the Ordinary of the Mass. A century later Charles VII had been crowned in Rheims, with Joan of Arc at his side.

The destruction of this national shrine prompted indignant responses to the claim in the Manifesto of 93 that the Germans had committed no atrocities. In a direct counterattack on Rolland's condemnation of the German shelling, the Austrian satirist Karl Kraus provided an unsettlingly sober view of the situation. He bluntly claimed that guilt belonged to all parties: "all this halfpenny newspaper rubbish about Rheims. . . . If I were a military officer defending Rheims I should have to put an observation post on the cathedral roof; and if I were his opponent I should have to fire on it."[60]

Rolland sought no peace without victory for France, yet he refused to blame the German people as a whole for the crimes of war, and he tried to calm the growing hysteria against the enemy. Again summoning a musical imagery in "Au-dessus de la mêlée," Rolland summarized the current situation with a commanding resonance.

> Strange combats are being waged between metaphysicians, poets, historians—Eucken against Bergson; Hauptmann against Maeterlinck; Rolland against Hauptmann; Wells against Bernard Shaw. Kipling and D'Annunzio, Dehmel and de Régnier sing war hymns, Barrès and Maeterlinck chant paeans of hatred. Between a fugue of Bach and the organ which thunders *Deutschland über Alles,* Wundt, the aged philosopher of eighty-two, calls the students of Leipzig to holy war in his quavering voice. And each nation hurls at the other the name "Barbarians."[61]

Rolland failed to mention that Haydn's tune, used for "Deutschland über Alles," was well known to churches throughout France, where it was familiarly adapted to the "Tantum ergo."[62]

During the war "Au-dessus de la mêlée" had a mixed reception abroad and was even viewed somewhat favorably in England. It was not until many years later, however, especially after the publication of his wartime journal, that some degree of appreciation for Rolland's commitment became possible. His aspirations for music were recorded in a poem, "Ars pacis," written between late August and early September 1914 and first published in German translation in the *Neue Züricher Zeitung* of 24–

25 September 1915. Not surprisingly the concluding strophes invoke the world of sound: the cricket sings, the tempest arrives, the rain falls in torrents; scarcely does the anguish pass before the stubborn little musician commences again. At the conclusion the Four Horsemen of the Apocalypse gallop across the scorched earth as the poet lifts his head and resumes his sorrowful and persistent song.

Rolland claimed that the purpose behind this poem was similar to that of Friedrich von Schiller's "An die Freude"—that is, he was not arguing for a truce to the present conflict but attempting to pen a hymn in praise of peace that transcended the individual and the nation as well as the generation. As the war progressed and as feelings escalated following the conclusion of a separate Russian peace with the Germans in 1917, protestations against the author of *Jean-Christophe* intensified. As if by way of response, Ivan Goll, a French-born, German-trained, bilingual pacifist-poet who escaped to Switzerland to avoid conscription in the German army, dedicated his *Requiem für die Gefallenen von Europa* to Rolland.[63]

Rolland's journal entry for 26 September 1914 contains a notice that sums up a personal view that sustained him throughout the war. He noted that the Austrian writer Stefan Zweig had sent him an article that had appeared in the *Berliner Tageblatt* on 20 September, "An die Freunde in Fremdland," wherein Zweig bids adieu to his foreign friends in order to serve his country. Rolland responded by sending him a copy of his "Au-dessus de la mêlée," which was appended with the words "I am more faithful than you to our Europe, dear Stefan Zweig, and I say goodbye to none of my friends." Herein lies the essence of Rolland's belief: a commitment to European civilization over parochial nationhood and to the notion that the makers of imperialist policies in virtually all nations had to bear some of the responsibility for the war.[64] Significantly, Rolland had also come to believe, with Hesse, that only music was capable of pointing the way toward humankind's highest aspirations and consequently to a resolution of its current moral dilemma.

Part 2

GREAT BRITAIN

2   Pomp and Circumstance

Oh, the brave Music of a distant Drum!
Omar Khayyám, *The Rubáiyát*

When war broke out in August 1914 a number of British composers, some of whom had been vacationing or attending the Wagner festival at Bayreuth, found themselves in Germany. Over the next weeks and months some 4,000 English men were rounded up and incarcerated at a makeshift prisoner-of-war camp for civilians at Ruhleben, site of a racetrack near Berlin. In time an active educational program was launched, courses in composition and harmony were offered to a group of forty-two musicians, and a musical society, backed by an orchestra of some eighty musicians, was established. The oratorios of Handel and Mendelssohn, the music of Bach and Mozart, and evenings dedicated to Wagner comprised a series of concerts that openly emphasized German music, although later concerts included a variety of works by Byrd, Debussy, Holst, and Vaughan Williams as well.[1] Numerous songs were composed by a group of minor English composers during this internment, but Ernest MacMillan, who was later to become the doyen of Canadian music, completed an openly Straussian "Ode to England" for orchestra, soloists, and chorus on a text of Swinburne. It was eventually posted to Oxford University, where it was accepted as fulfillment of the requirements for the D.Mus. degree.[2]

Back home the London music critic Ernest Newman began to speak of the current state of affairs, including specifically the appeal of the Straussian dialect and the challenge he felt the war would pose. He predicted that music would be more profoundly affected by the conflict than the other arts would be, and that music performing and publishing—principal German enterprises—were bound to suffer. As early as September 1914 he asserted in *The Musical Times* that the daily interchange of compositions and performers had made Europe virtually a single country. "Musicians may well doubt the sanity of a world in which Kreisler is in arms against Ysaye and Thibaud, in which it is the business of those of us here who owe some of the finest moments of our life to the great living German composers to do all we can to prevent their pouring out any more of their genius upon us," he observed.[3] A month later, in an article in the same journal, Newman was more attuned to the war.

> Is it the fault of the composers or of the peoples that national songs are as a rule such poor stuff? Why should our soldiers in France go marching to the most wretched of music-hall songs when we have composers of the calibre of Elgar and Bantock in the country? Is it that the composers cannot write the sort of music that will satisfy at once the musician and the populace, or that the populace has no ear for any but the most obvious music? In his D major "Pomp and Circumstance" March, Elgar has given the soldiers an ideal piece of "popular" music in the best sense of that term. I wonder how many soldiers know it, and of those who do, how many realise how thoroughly good it is?[4]

The active recruitment of England's educated elite for war services was predictably conducted on a note of patriotic revival,[5] and despite their keen admiration for Germany's philosophy and educational system, British academics and intellectuals were reluctant to seem pro-German once their country had gone to war. Newman's monograph of Richard Strauss in 1908, which had been cautiously optimistic about his potential, concluded with these words: "His new opera, which is to be produced early next year, will probably show whether he is going to realize our best hopes or our worst fears." Newman's dismissal of German music and Strauss shortly after the outbreak of war left no mistake as to his final verdict.

> [With hindsight] we might perhaps say that some such war was necessary for the re-birth of music. For there is no denying that of late music has lacked truly commanding personalities and really vitalising forces. Now that Strauss has failed us there is no one of whom we can think as having the seeds of the future in him. German music as a whole has settled into a complacent tilling of an almost exhausted field: a few discontented spirits like Schoenberg have aspirations towards something new and more personal, but without the capacity to realise them.[6]

Newman went on to equivocate slightly, saying, "It will be interesting to watch the lines of development of German music during the next ten years. Will the older men such as Strauss find in this tremendous emotional shock the stimulus that their music has plainly been in need of for years if it was not to degenerate into mere *Musikmacherei,* or will some flaming new spirit be born out of the needs of the new time?"[7]

Yet even Russia, France, and Italy were censured by Newman with a surprising lack of goodwill.

> The French are all small people,—very interesting, but indubitably small. Italian music is strangling in the grip of a commercial octopus. Russia is divided between men who see the wisdom of building upon the classical tradition but are not quite big enough to give the tradition an unmistakably new life, and men who reject the past before they are sure of the future, or even of the present. In England Elgar is still the one figure of impressive stature; the men who are almost contemporary with him are not fulfilling their early promise, while in the crowd of younger men it is impossible to distinguish one who has the least chance of making history.[8]

In a tone reminiscent of Rolland, Newman then presciently warned against a bad political settlement at the end of hostilities and openly endorsed the end of provincialism amongst all European nations as the only sane path for the future. French music, he argued, was "so small because it is so bent on being exclusively French. By its refusal to fertilise itself with the great German tradition it deliberately cuts itself off from permanent spiritual elements in that tradition that would give it a wider range and a deeper humanity." He also maintained that "the German tradition in its turn would be all the better for some cross-fertilisation from modern France; but again Chauvinism intervenes, and new harmonic possibilities are not developed as they might be because they are associated primarily with French music."[9] Romain Rolland could not have put it better.

The *Musical Herald* solicited the opinion of several composers regarding the question "Do you, as a British composer, think that our wide sympathies check our national spirit in composition?" Holst's answer soberly confirmed an orientation completely in accord with the classical view that stressed cultural outreach. "In art everything matters except the subject," he declared, and he added that true nationality in the arts was attainable only when the range of subject matter was broad. Holst recalled the period of the late Renaissance, a time when England looked to Italy for its models and inspiration.

> When this breadth of outlook is most apparent in English history—as in the sixteenth century—English music flourishes. Contrast the Elizabethan, a brilliant linguist, poet and musician, with the Englishman of

the eighteenth century. No wonder there is so much difference between the madrigal and the glee.[10]

By the summer of 1916 it was common knowledge that the progressive trend in English letters and art had virtually dried up, and in music it had always been too weak to have much of an impact.[11] Wyndham Lewis's Vorticism, England's foremost attempt at avant-gardism during the war, did try to enlist the issue of nationalism in the cause of the avant-garde.[12] Embracing the shenanigans of Filippo Marinetti and company, the Vorticists had sponsored a "Grand Futurist Concert of Noises" at the Coliseum in June 1913 that featured a gaggle of Luigi Russolo's "noise makers" (which Pound decried as "a mimetic representation of dead cats on a fog-horn"), but it was ultimately viewed as a fleeting and zany sideshow.

Edward Elgar's legacy was primarily traceable to Germany, and Vaughan Williams, whose sights were currently set on English folksong, gave little hint of the modernist bent that would later become more evident in his music. Reflecting the perspective of Edith Sitwell's literary circle, Lord Berners did display a capacity for a Satie-like humor in works like "Fragments psychologiques" (1916). His "Le poisson d'or" (1915), dedicated to Stravinsky, also sported a cover design by Goncharova, and his "Trois petites marches funèbres" (1916) ultimately achieved a certain respectable popularity.[13] The iconoclasm of William Walton's *Façade* (1922), which would soon give momentary promise of a postwar avant-garde, was still out of view, however. Sir Thomas Beecham, who was the guiding force for new music in England, regularly performed the most recent scores of Stravinsky, Debussy, Ravel, Delius, and Bantock, but he generally ignored the music of Vaughan Williams and Holst during the war. When hostilities ceased, interest in the native sources of English music witnessed a resurgence, and as a consequence interest in the music of the latter two composers escalated.

As the Armistice came into view, Newman made a final call for the "unconscious assimilation" of the best values of both French and German music and for putting aside any belief "in the possibility of a 'national' music." He then risked the ruination of his argument by stating that he was a "strong believer in the possibility of our music becoming more truly British."[14] The question of a national musical identity had plagued Germany following the Franco-Prussian War; even Wagner, in his essay "What Is German?" (1878), had failed to answer it.[15] Newman now sensibly encouraged England's composers to look more seriously to their own literary tradition, much as the French had always done, and to take it as a point of inspiration. He argued that in England there was no comparable parallel to Debussy's relationship to Stéphane Mallarmé and Paul Verlaine and that from Delius to Elgar composers had looked to foreign literary sources or often to inferior local ones.

For all its equivocation, by promoting respect for the best of foreign cultures alongside an increased awareness and endorsement of native literary, artistic, and musical traditions, Newman made an attempt, however feeble, to discourage an isolated quest for national superiority in the arts.[16] Yet even as he rejected the increasingly xenophobic perspective of the Germans, which renounced all outside influences and the notion of a common classical heritage, he warned against the danger that younger English composers might be tempted "to reproduce traits of French music that they could well afford to pass by. The French, for instance—and Stravinsky with them—have declared war on what they call 'expression.'"[17] By cautioning against the lure of Neoclassicism, Newman had collided with an unresolvable dilemma: for Neoclassicism was paradoxically based upon cultural outreach, a perspective he heartily endorsed.

DEFINING POLAND AND BELGIUM

While England and other countries were struggling to define themselves musically in light of Germany's commanding presence, other sovereign states faced the even more fundamental problems of geographical and cultural identity. Poland, the principal battleground for Russian and German forces on the eastern front in the early phase of the war, had not been able to claim sovereignty as a nation for well over a century, having been partitioned by its three neighbors, Austro-Hungary, Prussia, and Russia. The likelihood that a Polish composer would be inspired to write a patriotic work was small, especially in light of the potential fratricide inherent in the fact that 725,000 Poles found themselves conscripted into the Russian army, 571,000 into the Austrian army, and another 250,000 into the Prussian army.[18]

Ignacy Paderewski came to London for the purpose of organizing a Polish Relief Fund (Elgar not only agreed to serve on his committee but also ultimately composed a fitting tribute to Poland, titled "Polonia," for a projected benefit concert at Queen's Hall in July).[19] Paderewski had spent the first months of the war in Switzerland, where Rolland and Stravinsky were living. Then, shortly after New Year's Day in 1915, he left for Paris, London, and eventually the United States, where he remained throughout the war years, touring the country, giving recitals, raising public conscience as well as funds, and preparing for the day when he could return to a free Poland.[20]

The notion of a Belgian national identity was even more crucial, not only because the German campaign had been initiated there but also because the country's independence as a constitutional monarchy was traceable only to 1830. Although in August 1914 Great Britain had no investment in Serbia and no explicit obligation to fight for Russia or for France, and although the Entente Cordiale of 1904 between Great Britain and France was only a loose agreement that fell far short of an alliance, an almost forgotten treaty expressly committed Great Britain to defending Belgium. In the opening phase of the war Liège and then Brussels fell quickly to the German war machine, and King Albert, refusing to surrender, retreated first to fortified Antwerp and then to La Panne on the coast just north of Ypres, where he remained with his troops to the end of the war. Left behind were Louvain and other devastated medieval cities, many of whose irreplaceable libraries and cathedrals now lay in ruins.[21]

Although attempts to promote Belgium as a country with a historically independent culture were repeatedly made by the Allies, internal attempts to make distinctions as to what constituted Belgium and Flanders only proved to highlight what the Germans claimed throughout the war, namely that the whole notion of "Belgium" was a fiction. It was equally difficult to sustain the contention that Flanders was essentially German, culturally speaking, and the view of Belgium as a country diplomatically created in the nineteenth century and lacking in genuine cultural identity was destined to persist.[22] Inevitably, Belgium's relatively new national anthem, "La brabançonne," was pressed into service in efforts to distinguish Belgium from its neighbors.

Despite some similarities, the situations of Poland and Belgium were quite different, and the entente nations deliberately set out to exaggerate the historical legacy of "brave little Belgium." That the British, in particular, were increasingly drawn to the image sprang from their concerns regarding the immediate threat of German troops as they pushed through Belgium and France to the shores of the English Channel.[23] English entertainers expressed sympathy for Belgium through popular songs and poetry, but the most conspicuous early signal of England's support for Belgium came with *King Albert's Book*, a project launched in London at Christmastide 1914 to support the Belgian Relief Program. Some of the most prominent statesmen of the period, including Winston Churchill and William Howard Taft, former president of the United States, contributed essays to the volume. They were joined by the archbishop of Canterbury,

Henri Bergson, and Andrew Carnegie, as well as by figures in the arts such as Edith Wharton, Sarah Bernhardt, Rudyard Kipling, and Romain Rolland. Among the several composers were Elgar, Stanford, Debussy, Mascagni, and Paderewski, who collectively provided a concrete signal that, at least for the moment, the goals of international politics and the world of art, literature, and music could be viewed as the same.

Rolland's contribution to the anthology compared the heroism of present-day Belgians to Flemings of centuries past, evoking the image of the stalwart Flemish hero Egmont, who had been immortalized by Goethe and Beethoven.[24] Rolland declared that Belgium's soil, "watered by the blood of millions of warriors," had proven to be fertile for painting and music from the time of the Renaissance to the age of Maeterlinck.[25] He drove his point home by noting that Belgium was the land of Rubens and Till Eulenspiegel, a folk figure whose escapades had been appropriated for the subject of an orchestral tone poem by Germany's most renowned living composer, Strauss.

Fifty-seven years of age when the war broke out, Elgar was disconsolate that he was too old to serve. When the initial invitation to contribute to *King Albert's Book* came in November 1914, Elgar resisted, but his attention was finally drawn to a poem by the Belgian writer Émile Cammaerts, whose wife was the daughter of Marie Brema, creator of the role of the Angel in the Birmingham premiere of *Dream of Gerontius* (1900). Although only the French text, "Chantons, Belges, chantons!," was originally provided with music, Tita Brand Cammaerts quickly translated her husband's poem into an English version, "Sing, Belgians, Sing," which allowed Elgar's work to be performed before both French- and English-speaking audiences. The dual version of Elgar's piece, titled *Carillon,* presented no problems of prosody, as the text is spoken principally at times when the orchestra has fallen silent. The most overt musical symbolism of the piece, which was patently intended for consumption by a popular audience, lies in a stepwise descending tetrachord whose four pitches, projected in triple meter, are clearly calculated to portray the quality of randomness associated with bell ringing.

The popularity of Elgar's *Carillon* might have been predicted, for throughout the ages and in numerous cultures the bell had served to summon people's attention,[26] and nowhere did it enjoy greater historical resonance than in Belgium, where bells were not only a symbol of wartime courage but the heralds of the Armistice. At the premiere of *Carillon* on 7 December a reporter for the *Christian Science Monitor* noted that it was virtually impossible not to succumb to the contagious quality of the music in the current climate. Yet a critic for *The Times* of London the following day was blunt in his assessment: "If this is all that the tragedy of Belgium can bring from a musician, it seems a small tribute." Nonetheless, early in 1915 Elgar took *Carillon* on a successful tour with the London Symphony Orchestra in a program that included Mozart's *Eine kleine Nachtmusik*, Beethoven's overture for *The Creatures of Prometheus*, Dvořák's "New World" Symphony, and Saint-Saëns's Piano Concerto in G Minor. The tacit message in the inclusion of Mozart and Beethoven was clear: all Germans were not to be demonized, and the great masters of the past could not be blamed for the current calamity.

Thomas Hardy's contribution to *King Albert's Book*, "Sonnet on the Belgian Expatriation," reinforced the association between Belgium and the sound of the carillon, and underscored the carillon's potent symbolism. Hardy described his dream of the "people from the Land of Chimes" arriving in England with their bells in tow and hoisting them in local towers, only to face reality.[27]

> Then I awoke: and lo, before me stood
> The visioned ones, but pale and full of fear;
> From Bruges they came, and Antwerp, and Ostend,
>
> No carillons in their train. Vicissitude
> Had left these tinkling to the invaders' ear,
> And ravaged street, and smouldering gable-end.[28]

A country struggling for a historical identity could only have taken pride in the forty-seven-bell carillon at Bruges, whose tower dated from 1280 and whose bells were cast in 1743. The large forty-five-bell carillon of Malines was even more staggering in size, weighing in at thirty-three and one-half tons. These bells were not only repositories of national cultural history, they were tempting targets for the enemy as they could be captured, melted down, and turned into guns, cannons, and other military instruments.[29] This dual wartime symbolism was powerful, and the English poet Siegfried Sassoon spoke directly to the issue in a poem titled "Joy-Bells":

> What means this metal in windy belfries hung
> When guns are all our need? Dissolve these bells
> Whose tones are tuned for peace: with martial tongue
> Let them cry doom and storm the sun with shells.[30]

The symbolism that the carillons carried throughout the war was matched only by their capacity to announce the advent of peace. A post-

Armistice notice in *The Musical Times,* which recalled the popular anxiety over the fate of the bells at Bruges as well as Longfellow's well-known paean, verified that the bells of the carillon were intact, even though the Germans had severed all the connecting wires to the keyboard.[31] A report in the same journal on 1 May 1919 confirmed that the renowned carillon of Malines was also recovered unharmed, and it provided a touching sense of the carillon's role in the war just ended.

> During the German occupation much was done by the citizens of Malines to prevent the Huns from playing their national melodies on the carillon. The essential parts of the connections with the clavier were removed, throwing every bell out of action, and the great bell, Salvator, was lifted out of its bearings, so that it could not be rung. Plaster models were made of the Hemony, Van den Gheyn, and other bells, and both bells and models were safely hidden. All this had been accomplished before the Huns notified their intention of requisitioning the bells. There was a tremendous storm of protest, strongly supported by the great Cardinal Mercier, the intensity of which caused the Huns to abandon their project of stealing the bells. . . .
>
> When the news of the Armistice was received, the devoted friends of the carillon succeeded after great effort in lifting Salvator (eight tons) into its bearings. This took four hours to accomplish, but by three o'clock on the afternoon of November 11 the great bell hurled his enormous voice of triumph over the whole city, while the long file of grey uniforms, creaking wagons, and cannon began the Hun retreat in the direction of Louvain. The Grande Place was filled with an enormous and frenzied crowd, waving their hats and singing the Belgian National Hymn and "God Save the King," while the last of the Huns, with lowered heads, departed.[32]

The powerful imagery of the carillon during wartime was employed by Louis Durey, who composed a work titled *Carillon* in 1916, and in the postwar period Elgar returned to the theme once more in his "Loughborough Memorial Chime," which was written for the opening of the Loughborough War Memorial Carillon on 22 July 1923. In the following decade Francis Poulenc, who served as a young man in World War I, composed a set of piano *Nocturnes* in 1934, of which one, "Les cloches de Malines," unmistakably reflected personal memories of the Great War.

In the spring following the premier of *Carillon* Elgar set another of Cammaert's poems, "Une voix dans le désert," and Cammaert's wife provided the English translation as before. The lyrics portray not only the desolation and widespread starvation of domestic animals along the battle corridor[33] but also one of the most universal symbols in all Europe and northern Asia, that of a crow pecking out the eyes of a dead soldier.[34] The text then shifts to a period in which "Every church will open its door, Antwerp, Ypres, and Nieuport, / The bells will then be ringing." But in addition to the carillon, Elgar further supported Belgium's musical legacy and the historic role of Flemish musicians by inserting an extended citation of a familiar setting of the "Ave Maria" by one of the grand masters of the Renaissance, Jacques Arcadelt.[35] "Une voix dans le désert" was planned not as a concert work but as a stage piece requiring costumes and scenery, and at its first performance at the end of January 1916 it was offered as part of a triple bill that included *Cavalleria Rusticana* and *I Pagliacci*. Elgar's wife recorded that the orator appeared draped in black before a blood-red curtain and that she "looked picturesque—a type as it were of suffering Belgium."[36]

COUNTERING CHARGES FROM HOME AND ABROAD

If England's composers fought the war not only with their music but also with their opinions, the latter were clearly in need of being sorted out. In a 1916 essay, "Music and the War," Sir Charles Villiers Stanford, one of the pioneers of the English musical renaissance and the teacher of Vaughan Williams and Holst, attempted to clarify the reasons behind the prevailing feeling that English composers were inferior to Continental composers. Stanford first reflected on his affection for the German tradition in light of his studies in Leipzig in 1874, where he had met Brahms, a composer for whom he held a lifelong affinity.[37] That registered, he launched an attack on Strauss that was extraordinarily vitriolic, and, unlike Elgar, he showed no hesitation in condemning Germany as a nation. Strauss, with his enormous assemblage of orchestral players and massive sound effects, was labeled a counterpart to General Theodor von Bernhardi and the general staff.[38] Then in a conclusion clearly tinged with envy, Stanford boldly predicted the demise of Germany as a leader in the world of music.[39] Obviously a war-inspired attempt to keep the prospect of rejuvenation in the arts in England alive, Stanford's position explicitly reflected ongoing efforts by both the English and the French to dismantle the importance of recent German music.

The reason for this self-consciousness was clearly identified in a book about England by Oscar Schmitz that was published in Germany in 1914, shortly after the outbreak of the war. Its title was *Das Land ohne Musik* (The Country without Music), and for all its scurrilous tone the volume gave point, as nothing else could have, to the underlying forces behind England's campaign for recognition. A rich history of natively composed music had unfolded on English soil from the Middle Ages through the Baroque era. But recognition of the fallowness that had characterized the period between the death of Purcell and the appearance of Elgar had spawned the desire at the end of the nineteenth century to achieve some sort of parity with Continental composers. This in turn prompted a campaign to herald a genuine English renaissance.

This crusade was launched in 1881 by Sir George Grove's plan to create a Royal College of Music, a national conservatory equal to the finest music conservatories on the Continent. Grove's first edition of *The Dictionary of Music and Musicians* had already begun to appear in 1879 in some measure as a reaction to the Franco-Prussian War at the beginning of that decade. Grove acknowledged the dominance of German musicians and England's current reputation as an unmusical country, emphasized the social and moral value of music as well as its importance in English history, and stressed above all its power for directing the future. Crucial appointments to the Royal College were Stanford and Sir Hubert Parry, professors at Cambridge and Oxford, respectively, who believed in the importance of the Schumann-Brahms tradition for England's musical future. Testimony to this German connection was the fact that Stanford, a successful opera composer before joining the college's faculty, had had his operas performed in Hanover as well as in German at Convent Garden in 1884 with Hans Richter conducting.

Yet, while on the one hand the renewal that Elgar's *Enigma Variations* and *Dream of Gerontius* brought to British music at the turn of the century was welcomed as providential, on the other hand Elgar's success was so potent that the largely self-taught composer, who came from the British working class, increasingly seemed to pose a one-man challenge to the musical renaissance movement in which he had previously taken no part. By trading on Strauss's recent endorsement as "Meister" and an English progressivist and by accepting an appointment at the University of Birmingham, Elgar in effect founded a "Midland School" that was distinct from London and Oxbridge circles.[40]

The resultant insecurity among the academics not surprisingly prompted a series of assaults that included published critiques of Elgar's music by Stanford and others that alluded to Elgar's Catholicism and his lack of a formal education. This mean-spiritedness inevitably inspired a defense by his supporters, and the matter was pursued over the next several years. Like the members of the cults that were being nurtured by Rolland and d'Indy on the Continent at the time, Elgar defenders invoked Beethoven and Goethe, appealing to time-honored classical values that transcended issues of nationalism. In truth, Elgar's infatuation with Beethoven could be dated to 1873, when as a young lad of sixteen he purchased his first Beethoven score, the Sixth Symphony. The attraction was soon confirmed in a lengthy *Credo* of 306 measures that the young composer constructed out of themes extracted from Beethoven symphonies. In the inaugural issue of a new music quarterly, *Music and Letters,* which appeared shortly after the war was over, George Bernard Shaw summed up his personal feelings as well as the hopes of a nation.

> Elgar has not left us any room to hedge. From the beginning, quite naturally and as a matter of course, he has played the great game and professed the Best. He has taken up the work of a great man so spontaneously that it is impossible to believe that he ever gave any consideration to the enormity of the assumption, or was even conscious of it. But there it is, unmistakable. To the north countryman who, on hearing of Wordsworth's death, said "I suppose his son will carry on the business" it would be plain today that Elgar is carrying on Beethoven's business. The names are up on the shop front for everyone to read. ELGAR later BEETHOVEN & CO.[41]

Shaw further complained that, while it was now fashionable to rave about Debussy and Stravinsky as composers of the hour, to claim Elgar's *Cockaigne* overture as the equal of Wagner's overture to *Die Meistersinger* was to risk "a gaffe that will make your grandson blush for you. Personally, I am prepared to take the risk," he concluded. "What do I care about my grandson? Give me *Cockaigne.*"[42]

Once again the Beethoven standard had been applied as a test for canonization. Elgar had recently given Shaw plenty of ammunition with the completion of three classically styled chamber works: the Violin Sonata in E Minor of 1918, a string quartet in the same key from the same year, and the Piano Quintet in A Minor of 1918–1919. Shaw had attended the first private performance of the string quartet in January 1919 in Elgar's home, and when the new violin sonata premiered two months later, all the critics were quick to note its lack of modern tendencies and its directness of expression. One critic said that it was almost as if Elgar were saying, "See what can be done yet with the old forms, the old methods of composing, the old scales."[43] Indeed, the debt to Brahms and Franck is audible from the opening statement of his violin sonata, and in a letter of 6 September 1918 Elgar confessed, "I fear it does not carry us any further but it is full of golden sounds and I like it[:] but you must not expect anything violently chromatic or cubist."[44] The choice of words is telling, since throughout the

Great War a charge of "cubism" had been used to connote boche art, not only among the painters but even in the music of Debussy.[45]

The English taste for Beethoven and Brahms hardly faltered throughout the war, although shortly after the outbreak of hostilities all German music was temporarily banned. A Queen's Hall Promenade concert on 15 August 1914, for example, commenced with the national anthems of the Allied nations and continued with Tchaikovsky's *Capriccio italien* as a substitute for an earlier planned performance of Strauss's *Don Juan*. Later an all-Wagner evening was replaced by a program devoted to French and Russian composers, and Beecham planned a series of programs that were totally devoid of German music. Moreover, musicians of German birth disappeared almost overnight from the rosters of the London orchestras.

By April, however, *The Musical Times* was already carrying advertisements of a Bach-Beethoven-Brahms festival in Queen's Hall, including performances of the B-minor Mass, the *Missa solemnis*, the Ninth Symphony, and *Ein Deutsches Requiem*—a lineup that might have been taken straight from the programs of the Berlin Philharmonic at the time. And in September of 1915 Newman published the first in a series of articles that continued each month through December on "Brahms and Wolf as Lyrists," in which he praised Donald Tovey's musical summary in *German Culture: The Contribution of Germans to Knowledge, Literature, and Life*. For all the preoccupation with respect to a British musical profile and its promise for the future, it was clearly impossible to ignore the importance of the German legacy even in wartime.

The best the British had been able to muster was a resounding attack in August 1915 on the generally accepted notion of Germany's scholarly preeminence in the preparation of editions of Renaissance sacred music.[46] Carl Proske and Franz Xaver Haberl, both of Ratisbon, and virtually all other previous German editors were roundly criticized for their commercial and nonscholarly approaches, while French editions, particularly those of plainchant by the monks of Solesmes, were praised.[47] Such delayed criticism regarding publications stretching back to the 1870s and 1880s had clearly been prompted by the war. Yet in the following month an article pointed out with surprising honesty that contemporary British scholars had failed to publish a corpus of their own music from the period of the early English renaissance, comparable to the German scholars' editions of the Roman, Flemish, and Spanish schools.[48] It concluded with this injunction: "Let us at least learn something from the German enterprise and organizing power, and by setting on foot a scheme for a 'corpus' of our old music, commencing perhaps with the complete works of Tye, Tallis,

Whyte, Byrd, and Gibbons . . . , help to redeem one of our many national reproaches." However suspect in its particulars, Germany's leading role in humanistic scholarship had been recognized even as the germ had been sown for England's own pioneering series, *Tudor Church Music,* which would be published between 1922 and 1929.[49] National musical histories had unambiguously been called to the colors.

3   The Old Lie

Dulce et decorum est pro patria mori.
Horace, *Odes*

Here dead lie we because we did not choose
To live and shame the land from which we sprung.
Life, to be sure, is nothing much to lose;
But young men think it is, and we were young.
A. E. Housman, *More Poems*

Just as the call to arms in 1914 triggered a search for national identity and
increased the pull of patriotism, so it soon became clear that not all the
voices of caution and dissent could be silenced. Bertrand Russell, the English philosopher and mathematician, although forty-two years of age and
beyond conscription age, daringly broadcast his position in a letter that appeared in *Nation* on 16 August 1914: "And all this madness, all this rage,
all this flaming death of our civilization and our hopes, has been brought
about because a set of official gentlemen, living luxurious lives, mostly stupid, and all without imagination or heart, have chosen that it should occur
rather than that any one of them should suffer some infinitesimal rebuff to
his country's pride."[1]

In light of the negative reception given Romain Rolland's much milder
questioning of the motives of those who wage war, it is not surprising that
no major composer in any country undertook to complete and produce an
opera that overtly advertised such a sentiment while the war was under
way. The mixing of high art with contemporary war politics was generally considered inappropriate in the world of opera, and when touched
upon such topics were introduced only obliquely. The most important
Italian opera composer of the day, Puccini, who had recently as well as
touchingly addressed the issue of national identity in *Madama Butterfly*
(1904), remained mute on the topic, as did the composer of *Ein Heldenleben*—his purported plea for peace in *Die Frau ohne Schatten* (1919) notwithstanding.

Philosophers and statesmen have argued from time immemorial that a
lie is sometimes a necessity when made in the public interest,[2] but the view
of war as a noble mission when coupled to sporting adolescent energy has

held an appeal bested by few other fictions. Roundly endorsed in numerous quarters in Great Britain, yet derided in others as the "Old Lie," this accounting of war provided an expedient point of departure for a satirical antiwar opera composed by the self-taught Havergal Brian (1876–1972), an idiosyncratic composer and devotee of Elgar. Called *The Tigers*, the centerpiece of its plot is the announcement of a law requiring every male under seventy-five years old to serve.[3] The opera commences with bank holiday celebrations at the beginning of World War I and proceeds to recount the predicaments experienced by an enlisted regiment during training on the home front.[4] The opera depicts a zeppelin attack on London; the first, in 1915, was followed by forty-one raids, with the worst taking place in October. From the symphonic variations on "Has Anybody Here Seen Kelly?" to overt parodies of Wagner's *Die Walküre, Tristan und Isolde,* and the battle scene from Strauss's *Ein Heldenleben,* Brian's opera traverses a wide cultural and musical landscape. Written principally between 1917 and 1919, the three-hour opera includes appearances by Red Indian, Alexander the Great, and Napoleon in addition to Pantaloon and Columbine, and the final curtain brings echoes of *Götterdämmerung.* Throughout, Brian's attitude toward those who declare and make war is extremely cynical, and the composer, who lived to a ripe old age, never saw a performance of it.[5]

Yet Brian was not the only one to boldly proclaim the view that war was a betrayal of the young by the old, who shook their fists in heavy oratory, declared war, sent their offspring to fight the battle, and stayed home. Indeed, it was a sentiment that was repeated with riveting impact by a small group of disillusioned British war poets that included Siegfried Sassoon, Wilfred Owen, and Robert Graves.

Unlike those who condemned the Old Lie (a term inferable from Horace's ancient axiom, "Dulce et decorum est pro patria mori"), Rupert Brooke rhapsodized in his poem "Peace" that he had reached adulthood in the nick of time: "Now God be thanked Who has matched us with His hour, / And caught our youth, and wakened us from sleeping." Brooke's haunting verses meshed readily with the Pre-Raphaelite view of youth as frozen in time and beauty, a vision that was reflected in the numerous paintings of nobly garbed knights sacrificed in the defense of their country included in *King Albert's Book.* Such imagery paralleled much of the idealized, highly patriotic British music in the same collection, such as Alexander Mackenzie's "One Who Never Turned His Back," a setting for voice and piano of a text from Robert Browning's "Asolando," and Frederic H. Cowen's "Hail!," a hymn to Belgium on a poem by John Galsworthy. All were patently written with the hope of capturing the public imagination in the same way that Brooke's verse had.[6]

The trenchant nature and popularity of another Brooke poem, "The Soldier" (If I should die, think only this of me: / That there's some corner of a foreign field / That is forever England), virtually guaranteed that it would be set to music, and one of the best-known composers to do so was John Ireland, who composed the song in 1917, and whose second piano trio, written in the same year, carried the explicitly announced subtext of "boys going over the top."[7] More surprising, the London music publisher Elkin & Co. announced in *The Musical Times* on 1 April 1918 that it would issue a setting of "The Soldier" by Henry T. Burleigh, Dvořák's well-known African American pupil and a noted composer of songs, arranger of spirituals, and collector of minstrel melodies.[8] Although "The Soldier" makes a reasonable bid at being a simple art song in the piano accompaniment, Burleigh's setting is not far removed from many of his arrangements of Negro spirituals. The marking *"quasi una marcia funebre"* sets the general mood, but the insistent dotted rhythms at the beginning ultimately give way to rhetorical elaborations and a citation from "Rule Brittania" that follows a reference to "some corner of a foreign field / That is forever England." Here colonialism is in full flourish, and Burleigh's bloodline is nowhere in view. Particularly paradoxical is the fact that the text, which speaks of a soldier's glory in laying down his life for his country, was set to music by a black composer whose country had yet to join the fray and whose race was destined to suffer constant humiliation when it finally did so.

Like Ireland and Burleigh, the English war poets were for the most part traditionalists, despite frequent intimations of the avant-garde in their brutal imagery and language. As Paul Fussell has observed of these poets, English composers understood that if their works were to find their mark with the public at large, obscurity could not be the order of the day.[9] Furthermore, virtually all anglophone composers shunned settings of the raw-edged anger expressed by Owen and Sassoon, even as their other music on war themes addressed an extraordinary range of issues: nationalism and patriotism; piety and faith; nostalgia for home, friends, and lovers; martial pride; the historic role of the church in stamping out the infidel; the role of women as keepers of the flame and hearth; the camaraderie and bonding inherent in the soldier's life; and the vulnerability of children, civilization's only hope for the future.

Among the poets, none exposed the Old Lie with more directness than Wilfred Owen in his celebrated "Dulce et decorum est." The poem, which describes a gas attack in grisly detail, concludes with Horace's lines, known to every English schoolboy, that proposes that it is "agreeable and morally proper to die for one's country."

> If you could hear, at every jolt, the blood
> Come gargling from the froth-corrupted lungs,
> Obscene as cancer, bitter as the cud
> Of vile, incurable sores on innocent tongues—
> My friend you would not tell with such high zest
> To children ardent for some desperate glory,
> The old lie: Dulce et decorum est
> Pro patria mori.[10]

Wartime posters warned of the devastating effects of chlorine gas, and the American painter John Singer Sargent, who was born in Italy and spent most of his life in London, momentarily abandoned the flattering portraits of elite society for which he was justly celebrated to paint *Gassed*, one of his most compelling pictures, for the British War Memorials Committee in 1918–1919. The painting adds a ghostly luminosity to the image captured in a photograph at Béthune in April 1918.[11] Sightless soldiers, each with his hands on the shoulder of the man in front of him, convey the impression not merely of wounded men but also of the blind leading the blind—a powerful metaphor for those ugly times. The irony is enhanced by barely visible soldiers playing soccer in the distance.[12]

Owen's poem was later echoed in even more devastating language by Ezra Pound in the fourth poem of his semi-autobiographical *Hugh Selwyn Mauberly*, published in 1920.[13] Decrying an age in which beauty, as defined in the marketplace, had become mechanical, and in which the pianola had replaced Sappho's lyre,[14] Pound recalls those who fought in search of adventure and others who served from fear of censure. Hammering away at the Old Lie by way of conclusion, he reviews that some died "pro patria" but "non 'dulce' non 'et décor'"; that, having fought believing in old men's lies, they returned home, unbelieving, to a lie, to "usury age-old and age thick / and liars in public places."[15] Even Rudyard Kipling, whose sense of empire and glory had been immortalized in his "Recessional," reduced the judgement to a two-line poem, "Common Form": "If any question why we died, / Tell them, because our fathers lied."

The ancient sentiment found in Horace's lines was ripe for exhumation and rebuttal. Yet for the general public the bitter truth of Sassoon's and Owen's poetry, which was prompted by their accumulating sense of frustration with the war, would have been hard to swallow at the time, and when their poems eventually appeared they were received in many quarters as evidence of latent cowardice or were charitably acknowledged as a reflection of neurasthenic collapse. For in fact both poets had served a protracted stay at Craiglockhart War Hospital, a center for the treatment of shell-shocked soldiers, and Owen's poetry first appeared in the hospital's literary journal, *Hydra*.

From another perspective, Charles Villiers Stanford claimed in "Music and the War," an essay from 1916, that during national convulsion and international wars music's most potent role was that of a rallying cry.[16] He went on to caution, however, that "the individual expressions of the greatest composers, when called upon to celebrate the concrete successes of their countries, have generally been on a level of excellence inferior, often far inferior, to that of their best work." He then noted that it was generally in the works without an announced program that the profoundest test of the human spirit shone: not in a work like Beethoven's *Wellington's Sieg* for example, but rather in the "Agnus Dei" from his *Missa solemnis,* where in the concluding "Dona nobis pacem" "the whole tragedy of war finds its most sublime expression called forth by the prayer for peace."[17]

Several English song composers provided telling testimony to the price of war on less grand terrain. One of the most impressive was George Butterworth, who enlisted during the first month of hostilities and was killed in the Battle of the Somme in 1916.[18] Many of Butterworth's song settings are on texts from A. E. Housman's *A Shropshire Lad* (1896) and are given to the pastoral idyll, whereas several others, like "The Lads in Their Hundreds"[19] and especially "On the Idle Hill of Summer," published in 1912, virtually foretell the composer's ultimate fate. The strophic musical response of the latter song, where essentially the same music is used for each stanza, cannot disguise the steady unfolding of the textual drama.

> On the idle hill of summer
> Sleepy with the flow of streams,
> Far I hear the steady drummer
> Drumming like a noise in dreams.
>
> Far and near and low and louder,
> On the roads of earth go by,
> Dear to friends and food for powder,
> Soldiers marching, all to die.
>
> East and west on fields forgotten
> Bleach the bones of comrades slain,
> Lovely lads and dead and rotten;
> None that go return again.

Far the calling bugles hollo,
High the screaming fife replies,
Gay the files of scarlet follow:
Woman bore me, I will rise.[20]

ELGAR'S WOMEN AND FALLEN HEROES

The combination of womanly sacrifice and fallen heroes in *A Shropshire Lad*, plus the folksong-like simplicity of its language, redolent of England's west country, proved to be uncommonly attractive to composers throughout the war as well as in its aftermath, and in time some four hundred musical settings were made.[21] Accompanying the description of the agony attendant to the miseries of war are invocations of the Old Lie, and sometimes Houseman's reference is explicit, as in the lines that serve as an epigraph to this chapter. Indeed, it would have been surprising had all English composers completely resisted addressing the issue—pro or contra.

No better example exists than Elgar's response to a suggestion made early in 1915 that he write a Requiem Mass for the slain, which resulted in a setting for chorus and orchestra of three war poems taken from the collection *The Winnowing Fan* by Laurence Binyon, deputy keeper in charge of oriental prints and drawings at the British Museum. Elgar set Binyon's "To the Fallen," followed by "To Women" and "The Fourth of August," and the three were ultimately gathered together under the title *The Spirit of England*, a piece for soprano, chorus, and orchestra. The appeal of the work was clearly to the choral tradition that had flourished in England from the time of Handel and Mendelssohn. Furthermore, Elgar had had substantial experience with the English choir festival, and he knew its considerable attraction for the lay public.[22]

The first complete performance of Elgar's new work under his baton was given at the Royal Albert Hall on 24 November 1917.[23] "To Women," the second movement, is the most lyrical of the piece, and only its topicality and inflated textual sentiment for peacetime audiences can account for the fact that it has not entered the ranks of Elgar's most esteemed works (CD track 1). The text begins:

Your hearts are lifted up, your hearts
That have foreknown the utter price.
Your hearts burn upward like a flame
Of splendour and of sacrifice.

For you, you too, to battle go,
Not with the marching drums and cheers

But in the watch of solitude
And through the boundless night of fears.

Elgar then introduces a more menacing tone to accompany the next verse:

Swift, swifter than those hawks of war,
Those threatening wings that pulse the air,
Far as the vanward ranks are set,
You are gone before them, you are there! [24]

The composer added the annotation "Aeroplanes" to the opening two lines of this stanza in his score.[25] The instrumental accompaniment is fashioned from timpani rolls and pulsing tremolos in the bassoons and the violas. However tentatively, Elgar had depicted the Londoner's firsthand experience of aerial warfare, which became increasingly common from 1915 on.

The central topic here, the mixture of pride and sorrow felt by women as they encouraged soldiers to march to the front, had become increasingly visible in poetry and poster art as well as popular song lyrics. Phillis Dare's music-hall song, for example, opened with the words "Oh, we don't want to lose you, / But we think you ought to go." In 1916 the *London Morning Post* pushed the sentiment to an extreme when it published a letter from the mother of an only child, who sought to "uphold the honour and traditions not only of our Empire but the whole civilized world." The letter was immediately reprinted in pamphlet form, and 75,000 copies were sold in less than a week. The author tolerated no cries of peace.

We women pass on the human ammunition of "only sons" to fill up the gaps. . . . We gentle-nurtured, timid sex did not want the war. . . . But the bugle call came. . . . We've fetched our laddie from school, we've put his cap away. . . . *We* have risen to our responsibility. . . . *Women are created for the purpose of giving life, and men to take it.* . . . We shall not flinch one iota. . . . [Should we be bereft, we shall] emerge stronger women to carry on the glorious work our men's memories have handed down to us for now and all eternity.[26]

The concluding line of Housman's "On the Idle Hill of Summer" ("Woman bore me, I will rise") had rarely received so startling a reflection, and the Queen Mother was reported to have been "deeply touched." Conversely, such chilling patriotism served up in so pious a tone stunned the poet Robert Graves to such a degree that he was later moved to include the entire text in his *Good-Bye to All That* (1929).[27] One of the earliest rejoinders to this perspective had appeared in an August 1914 diary entry by the German artist Käthe Kollwitz, whose son, Peter, would be killed on the Western Front two months later: "Where do all the women who have watched so carefully over the lives of their beloved ones get the heroism to send them to face the cannon?"[28]

Women, historically exempt from military service, had naturally assumed their traditional role as minders of the home front, but following the introduction of conscription in England in 1916 they found unexpected liberation in new job opportunities. Later, with the cessation of hostilities and a return to the status quo, many were disappointed to find that the suffrage movement had not advanced, and that they were expected to return to their former roles as wives and mothers.[29] The opening lines of Elgar's concluding movement, "For the Fallen," metaphorically reinforces this sentiment: "With proud thanksgiving, a mother for her children, England mourns for her dead across the sea." The ensuing *tempo di Marcia* was inspired, Elgar tells us, "when the dear lads were swinging past so many, many times: as far as I know anything the themes and tunes are my own."[30] Contrary to expectations, however, no tunes accompany the following lines:

> They went with songs to battle,
> They were young,
> Straight of limb, true of eye, steady and aglow.[31]

The chorus sings softly hushed, on a single pitch, in a seeming rejection of the initial line of text. The effect is haunting, forcing the listener to reconcile the overt discrepancy between text and music.

This sense of anomaly is soon mollified, if not erased, through the composer's subtle choice of keys: having raised the key level in the second movement from G to A♭, in the final movement Elgar ascends yet another semitone to the key of A minor—a symbolism that seems contrary to the title, "For the Fallen," yet one that confirms the affirmation contained in the movement's most renowned lines, which follow the *marcia* section:

> They shall not grow old as we that are left grow old.
> Age shall not weary them, nor the years condemn.
> At the going down of the sun and in the morning,
> We shall remember them.[32]

Despite the anger of many British war poets at such pious platitudes, the music is still frequently performed on Remembrance Day in England.[33] And its text, which even Sassoon judged "the finest expression of a certain aspect of the war,"[34] serves as a reminder to countless visitors to the British Museum to this day. In 1921 a memorial to the sixteen men from the museum who "fought and fell" was erected at the front entrance. Commissioned from Eric Gill, the relief is inscribed with those four poignant lines.

Elgar initially balked at one of the stanzas in the last movement, which accuses the enemy of inhumanity and its own brand of falsehood:

> She fights the fraud that feeds desire on Lies
> In a lust to enslave or kill
> The barren creed of blood and iron
> Vampire of Europe's wasted will.[35]

Elgar could not easily forget the support he had received from Hans Richter and Richard Strauss early in his career, and in the final analysis he determined that, rather than setting such lines of accusation anew, he would quote a passage previously composed for the demon's chorus in *The Dream of Gerontius.*[36]

The accumulating months of the war, which soon turned into years, gradually eroded a general critical reticence to speak of national animosity in the arts, and in the lead article for *The Musical Times* of 1 July 1917, titled "Elgar's 'Fourth of August,'" Ernest Newman spoke to this newly developing perspective. For the first time many Englishmen had come to feel a national hatred for Germany, a country now perceived as a totally immoral, malevolent, and not quite human enemy. Newman even claimed that the Germans had only succeeded in "sanctifying the heads of the young who had died for this land of ours." The necessity for such a succession of noble proclamations became clearer with every hour of the war, as musicians, poets, and journalists alike increasingly served as chief functionaries alongside the politicians.

Of the work's premiere performance, the critic of *The Sheffield Daily* wrote on 4 May 1916, "Never since 'Gerontius' has Elgar given us music that carries so unmistakable a ring of sincerity throughout the whole course." Newman took the point a step farther and wrote shamelessly of a nation's capacity for sacrifice. The Old Lie had rarely been so baldly portrayed.

> In no country, one almost dares to say, can the emotion for the dead have quite the same thrill as ours; for the men who have died for England have for the most part given their lives as a voluntary sacrifice. As Mr. Binyon sings:
>
> > They laughed, they sang their melodies of England,
> > They fell open-eyed and unafraid.
>
> It is love and gratitude and pride and sorrow for these children of England and their self-sacrifice,—a sacrifice of which Rupert Brooke, in

the eyes of lovers of art, will be for ever the shining symbol,—that Elgar sings in such noble accents in the third of these new works of his. . . . Here in truth is the very voice of England, moved to the center of her being in this War as she has probably never been moved before in all her history.[37]

OTHER WAR REQUIEMS

Like Elgar during the war years, Frederick Delius explored the traditional forms in a series of chamber works that included the Violin Sonata no.1, completed in 1914, a string quartet and a cello sonata of 1916, and three string concertos of 1915–1916. Delius also turned to matters more explicitly reflective of a period of turmoil, including especially a Requiem for soprano, baritone, double chorus, and orchestra. It was written between 1914 and 1916, but was first performed only in 1922. Dedicated "to the memory of all young artists who lost their lives in the war," the first movement is an affective work for chorus and baritone solo that opens with these words:

Our days here are as one day; for all our days are rounded in a sleep; they die and ne'er come back again. Why then dissemble we with a tale of falsehoods? We are e'en as a day, that's young at morning and old at eventide, and departs and never more returns.[38]

Drawing from Shakespeare, Nietzsche, and the Bible, Delius speaks of weaklings who "drugged themselves with dreams and golden visions, and built themselves a house of lies to live in." For Delius, a proclaimed atheist, the house of lies was that of institutional religion, be it Christian or Muslim. But in his injunction to make the very most of our brief lives and to die fearlessly, he countered the accusations of Owen and Pound and forwarded a proposition that resounded in lyrics from virtually every country that took part in the Great War.[39] Delius's final movement pursues this basic perspective but also strikes a pantheistic note redolent of Brahms's *Ein Deutsches Requiem* and the conclusion of Mahler's *Das Lied von der Erde* (1911): "Everything on earth will return again. Springtime, Summer, Autumn and Winter: And then comes Springtime—and then new Springtime." There is pity and hurt in Delius's music, and only transient gusto and little militance, as resignation sets in with the recognition of nature's eternal cycle. Yet for all its merit and frequent beauty, the work seems to languish in a pervasive inertia. Not surprisingly, it had little immediate impact when it was first performed, and it remained largely unknown until its publication in 1965.

Elgar's contributions notwithstanding, musicians expected some single, universal work for the concert hall to emerge during the war, one that would capture the popular imagination and provide an unmistakable insight into the human condition. This expectation remained largely unfulfilled, not only in England but also elsewhere. Yet Hubert Parry, variously director of the Royal College of Music, professor at Oxford, and president of the Musical Association, preached that there was an equally honorable alternative to the writing of masterpieces. In his role as founder of the Music in Wartime Committee in 1914, one of whose principal missions was to enable professional musicians to give concerts in hospitals and camps, Parry urged his students not to enlist, arguing that they could better serve the nation as musicians at home. Parry himself wrote *From Death to Life* (1914) at the beginning of the conflict, followed by *A Hymn for Aviators* (1915) and his choral song "Jerusalem" (1916). The latter proved to be one of England's most powerful wartime hymns. Set to a text of William Blake that calls for the building of a new Jerusalem on England's grassy shores, it was first performed at a "Fight for Right" meeting on 28 March 1916 at Queen's Hall.[40] Parry's last composition was his *Songs of Farewell* (1916–1918), which served both as an expression of desire for escape from nationalist obsessions and ultimately as a personal farewell to life.[41] He died in 1918, only a month before the Armistice was signed. Elgar paid his respects by attending the funeral.

The pace of Elgar's composition slowed markedly following *The Spirit of England*, although in March 1917 he agreed to set some verses by Kipling. Once again rejecting pleas from Binyon to write a war requiem, Elgar began work instead on his Cello Concerto, which was completed in 1919. From the fractured punctuation and hortatory declamations of the cello in the first movement's introduction to the pages of melancholy that follow, the music has repeatedly been heard as fulfilling the spirit of the original request for a requiem. Whatever the appropriate perspective, and despite the persistent and clichéd use of the adjective "autumnal" to describe the work, there can be little argument that the concerto represents Elgar's farewell to composition and in a personal way reflects an artist's depression over civilization's futile battles.[42]

An age had now passed, and Elgar, who lived until 1934, realized that his music spoke with the tongue of a waning era. Yet in an article, "On Funeral and Other Music," written following the first performances of *The Spirit of England* in 1916, Newman accurately observed that "with the exception of Elgar, none of our composers, so far as I know, has produced music, inspired by the War, that expresses anything of what the nation feels in these dark days. . . . Only out of an old and a proud civilisation could such music as this come in the midst of war. It is a miracle that it should have come at all, for Europe is too shaken just now to sing."[43]

Expressions of England's hopes on the musical front could be periodically spotted in the works of Vaughan Williams and Holst. Vaughan Williams, although over forty, enlisted as a private in August 1914 and served in the field ambulance corps in France and Macedonia.[44] Holst, only two years his junior, had tried to enlist and was rejected. Von Holst (he later dropped the "von") briefly became an object of suspicion when it was rumored that he was a German spy who was using his musical activities as a cover for espionage. The charge was all too typical of a wartime hysteria that scrutinized any and all German connections—a state of affairs that would later infect America in an especially virulent manner. A police enquiry found nothing, however, and in October 1918 Holst was finally accepted for war work and departed for Salonika as a YMCA organizer of music among the troops in the Near East.

Both Vaughan Williams and Holst had set Walt Whitman's *Dirge for Two Veterans* to music in 1911 and 1914, respectively,[45] and "Mars" from Holst's *The Planets*, commenced on the eve of the war's outbreak, was ultimately destined to verify more than the fact that war was imminent. Completed by 14 August 1914, immediately following the outbreak of war, "Mars" conjures up the image of gathering armies and the accumulating frenzy of the populace before bringing the offensive to a halt in a series of grinding dissonances. In this stirring march in quintuple meter Holst ushered in a powerful and dynamic music whose sheer gusto was without parallel in English music to that time. It rivaled the demands of Strauss (under whose baton Holst had performed as trombonist in 1897 and 1903), Schoenberg, and Mahler in the number of performers, which in addition to the normal complement included bass flute, bass oboe, six instead of the normal complement of four horns, two tenor trombones, bass trombone, tenor and bass tubas, extended percussion, celesta, xylophone, organ, and women's chorus.

Tellingly, the second movement of *The Planets*, called "Venus, the Bringer of Peace," offers a quite different perspective. And the main theme of the fourth movement, "Jupiter, the Bringer of Jollity," later reappeared as the hymn "Thaxted," host to one of England's great patriotic texts, written by Cecil Spring-Rice.

> I vow to thee, my country, all earthly things above,
> Entire and whole and perfect, the service of my love;
> The love that asks no question, the love that stands the test,
> That lays upon the altar the dearest and the best;

The love that never falters, the love that pays the price,
The love that makes undaunted the final sacrifice.[46]

Before leaving for France with an ambulance unit in June of 1916 Vaughan Williams had written somewhat optimistically to Holst, "I feel that perhaps after the war England will be a *better* place for music than before—largely because we shan't be able to buy expensive performers etc. like we did." By the following autumn his tone had turned to despair. In a letter to Holst he noted that of the seven members of his group who had enlisted in August 1914 only three were left.[47] Remarkably, it was during this very period, when he was within earshot of the front, that Vaughan Williams commenced his *Pastoral Symphony*. Evidence of his proximity to the clash of arms has been noted in the passage for natural trumpet in the slow movement, which has been held to reflect the composer's memory of a weary bugler's call across the battlefield. For all the work's undertow, its tranquility and title naturally prompted critics to view it as both anomaly and compensation even though Vaughan Williams noted that the idyllic moments depict the French countryside in the stillness following battle, not a Cotswold landscape.

The quiet intensity of Vaughan Williams's view is reflected in a note to Holst written during the Battle of the Somme, "I am 'waggon orderly' and go up the line every night to bring back wounded and sick in a motor ambulance."[48] George Butterworth, who was a close friend of Vaughan Williams and collaborator in the English folksong movement, was killed at this very time. The hushed entrance of a textless solo voice against rolling drums in the finale of the *Pastoral Symphony* is spectral in its effect and confirms the sense of loss. It is understandable that Vaughan Williams's biographer, Michael Kennedy, judged the work, begun in 1916 but completed and premiered in 1921, as Vaughan Williams's war requiem.[49] Walter Benjamin, who later reacted violently against the "pseudo-romantic simulation of pastoral tranquility in cemeteries that were disguised as bucolic landscapes,"[50] might have objected, but he would have misunderstood. Some music historians have contended that the Romantic pastoral died forever with the Great War. Others have argued that the Romantic muse not only survived but also persevered with a renewed and even more urgent sensibility, only to be finally silenced in the killing fields of World War II.[51] As Britten's *War Requiem* of 1961 would eventually testify, however, it could not to be suppressed for long.

If during the period of the conflict performances of earlier war-inspired pieces by Holst or Vaughan Williams failed to achieve either the popularity or the range of Elgar's efforts, both composers left behind an unambiguous record of their commitment to church and nation. Holst's most eloquent testimony came in *The Hymn of Jesus,* where in the prelude a solo trombone sounds the ancient Gregorian melodies and the choir intones the Latin texts of the "Vexilla regis" ("The Royal Banner forward go, / The Cross shines forth in mystic glow") and the "Pange lingua": ("Sing, my tongue, the glorious battle, / Sing the last, the dread affray; / O'er the Cross the Victor's trophy; / Sound the high triumphal lay; / How, the pains of death enduring, / Earth's Redeemer won the day.")

This sacred-secular dramatization of the "passion of man" suggests that Christ had merely prepared the way for an understanding of mankind's dilemma, which transcends religion or creed. Thus, like Delius, Holst grappled less with questions of national identity than with a search for universals. Nonetheless, Holst's "Ode to Death," presented as part of his *Hymn to Jesus* at its premiere in 1920, was specifically dedicated to the memory of the composer's friends who had been killed in the war. It was one of the first in the long parade of post-Armistice pieces of remembrance.

4   The Symphony of the Front

In peace there's nothing so becomes a man
As modest stillness and humility;
But when the blast of war blows in our ears
Then imitate the action of the tiger:
Stiffen the sinews, summon up the blood,
Disguise fair nature with hard-favor'd rage;
Then lend the eye a terrible aspect.
William Shakespeare, *Henry V*

In me the tiger sniffs the rose.
Siegfried Sassoon, *The Heart's Journey*

Peace is marked by an uneasy stillness, war by a tumultuous roar, and in *Henry V* Shakespeare tapped a terrifying reality known to every Tommy, Fritz, and poilu on the front: War is Noise! That the sound of uninterrupted bombardment was the most difficult aspect of life in the trenches to accept was depicted by poets, musicians, and painters of numerous nationalities throughout the conflict.[1] Owen, in his "Anthem for Doomed Youth,"[2] conveyed as few others the incessant accompaniment to a soldier's daily life, one that persisted to his final moments: "What passing-bells for these who die as cattle? / Only the monstrous anger of the guns."

Six months after he had left the Eastern front, the renowned violinist Fritz Kreisler spoke of the "almost hypnotic state while on the firing line which probably prevents the mind from observing and noticing things in a normal way."[3] Robert Graves complained that a soldier's leave was particularly difficult because people at home could not understand life at the front. When asked why he did not attempt to tell them, Graves responded, "You couldn't: you can't communicate noise, noise never stopped for one moment—ever."[4] The deafening volleys of sound could continue, unremitting, for hours and even days at a time. In such an environment disorientation typically culminated in stupor, or shell shock, which was clinically recognized for the first time.

This Symphony of the Front lasted for four years,[5] and in its final season Cecil Barber wrote an article for *The Musical Times* of London called "Battle Music" that dramatized the reality of these observations.

No need even to dredge the Berlioz autobiography for the necessary words, for tautological epithets such as "grandly terrible" come feebly to the mind on meeting a hostile barrage, with its colossal orchestra of men and munitions reinforced by all the material wealth that a nation can cast into a world-wide melting-pot. Here is a combination of all . . . the wildest harmonies—of colour and form and sound, with Night for manuscript! And Murder is the motto-theme—wholesale murder, in fact. . . .

Everything has been peaceful up to now—peaceful that is for the Front. . . . Then, without warning . . . the storm bursts, *ffff*. The pentecostal calamity is at hand, with its mighty rushing wind and tongues of riotous fire, above the strident blast of the batteries. For the guns, with their weary gleams of gold, supply a pedal to the frantic exordium; and superimposed on this, as the textbooks have it, move notes of lighter calibres, all vociferous however and deadly in their utterance. . . . The various timbres stand out clearly—the melancholy passage of great shells, the whizz and bang of smaller ones, the long swishing strides of the gas shells, the almost farcical crack and stentorian echo of the Stokes contingent, and the constant spurt of snipers' fire, *molto staccato*, in stupendous counterpoint.[6]

Cessation of the din from the front, however momentary, brought an understandable thirst for music of a more organized kind. A full-page advertisement placed by the YMCA that appeared in the same English journal only three months later argued for its therapeutic value. It judged that in any group of two thousand men there were at least twenty-five to thirty-five musical souls "to whom a chance of singing or playing once again is like a breath of new life after the horrible sights and sounds of war." Virtually all soldiers enjoyed listening to music, the advertisement said: "Men straight out of the trenches, mud-caked, hungry, and ready to drop with fatigue, will stop on their way back for rest—just to listen to a band." The piece concluded with a plea for £5,000 to be spent entirely for new music and instruments as well as more conductors and music teachers, whose transfer at the front was to be arranged by the YMCA.[7] The message is a poignant and forceful reminder that music was not considered a frill but a virtual necessity for survival. It also lends solid confirmation to the proposition that one of the functions of organized music in society "is to make people emotionally equal for a certain time."[8]

One of Siegfried Sassoon's less familiar war poems, "Secret Music," also corroborates in an extraordinarily explicit way the YMCA's claim regarding the power of music and its healing role for the human psyche during times of stress. Opening with the sentiment "I keep such music in my brain / No din this side of death can quell," the poem ends:

> To the world's end I went, and found
> Death in his carnival of glare;
> But in my torment I was crowned,
> And music dawned above despair.[9]

There were occasions when music was performed right on the battlefield with fife, drum, bugle, and even bagpipe—each of which carried historic military connotations. A particularly startling reminder of its role was played out in the Battle of the Somme—the bloodiest offensive in world history, lasting almost five months and causing more than a million casualties. Among the soldiers who served and fell with the Foreign Legion on 1 July 1916 was the American poet Alan Seeger, who had written his own memorable epitaph only a few months before: "I have a rendezvous with Death, / On some scarred slope of battered hill." During the battle British foot soldiers were heard singing the following lyrics to the tune of "Coming through the Rye" as they moved into position:

> We beat them on the Marne,
> We beat them on the Aisne,
> We gave them hell
> At Neuve Chapelle
> And here we are again! [10]

Shortly after tunneling under the German lines and laying ten gigantic mines, which were blown up shortly before 7:30 a.m., the British began a daylight attack. Sixty-six thousand British troops, heavily weighted with equipment, climbed out of the trenches and advanced in what has been described as a ceremonial step of one yard per second. The Tyneside Scotsmen marched to the sound of the bagpipes; the Eighth East Surrey came out kicking footballs. Fourteen thousand soldiers fell in the first ten minutes. It later became clear that the aircraft-directed artillery barrage intended to provide cover had not been coordinated, and one-third of the British shells were duds. Yet for all the ultimate tragedy of an ill-conceived plan, its ritualistic execution, coupled with the camaraderie of a sporting match, was extraordinary, as though the attack were some sort of apocalyptic soccer game with musicians cheering the players on.[11]

The journalists back home traded heavily on this vision of innate British sportsmanship at the front and even reported that "they tell their battles over in the spirit of a man recounting a fast run with the hounds or a good day's work after big game."[12] The image had in fact been repeatedly promoted in a series of PALS recruitment campaigns that were designed to enlist large groups of local lads with the promise that they could serve together. The campaign enrolled an estimated 500,000 men via football (soccer) organizations by the end of 1914.[13] It is only with this background that we can understand the irony in Sargent's later juxtaposition of gassed soldiers and soccer-playing Tommies in the distance.[14]

If the picture of soldiers marching into battle kicking footballs to the sound of the bagpipes abridges the inherent danger of the situation, endless reminders confirm that there was very little that was glamorous about fighting in the trenches and in no man's land. Although soldiers' songs were heartily or affectionately sung in the pubs prior to shipping out or along the trail and during quiet moments behind the front lines, the idea that "La Marseillaise," "God Save the King," "Roses of Picardy,"[15] and "It's a Long, Long Way to Tipperary" floated above the battlefield more or less continuously is unwarranted. A notice in a 1916 issue of *Le périscope*, a French soldiers' newspaper, unceremoniously exploded the myth of song's invigorating powers at the moment of assault with the following trenchant observation: "[The poilu] eats his bully-beef with caution and mutters when there is a shortage of food. He does not sing as he goes into attack, preferring not to waste his breath."[16] At the same time, there were reports that when time permitted a regimental band might play Chopin's "Funeral March" in a brief service to commemorate a fallen comrade.[17]

Recordings of some of the more popular tunes made their way to the front where they were played on portable gramophones, including one manufactured by Decca that was labeled a "Trench Model." Performed live, many of these songs were confined to billets or sung almost exclusively at rest, but many of the most memorable were marching songs.[18] Their texts ranged from satire targeted at superior officers, mock heroics, and the military system in general to the celebration of drink and sex. The sheer number of variants, a generous sample of which has been preserved along with the locations that initially inspired them, literally defies categorization.[19]

Traditional tunes, including hymn tunes, were inevitably conscripted in the war's darkest hours and outfitted with topical texts. The fundamental question of "The New Army and Its Musical Needs" was recognized early on in an article in *The Musical Times*. It noted the importance of building an *esprit de corps* through squad drills, gymnastics, and the development of camaraderie. Humor was considered indispensable, but it was also pointedly noted that "the fact of the 'Kitchener' trying to make cheerful noises on the march for himself, is the most undeniable indication of a musical need." The anonymous reporter then told of Rudyard Kipling's eloquent speech at the Lord Mayor's recruiting-band meeting at the Guildhall, wherein he related the story of "the magical effect of the regimental march—an old county tune—on the cholera-stricken 'Lincolns.'"

> Have bands, and plenty of them, by all means,—if you can get them. . . . A drum and fife, *and* a bagpiper, at the disposal of every company captain would work wonders. As to recruiting, it is to be questioned whether the bunkum of a more or less theatrical "recruiting march" would attract intelligent men nearly so much as seeing a platoon, like a happy family, swinging along its daily task to the pulsating beat of the drum, the merry chirrup of the fife—spontaneous, like the song of the lark—or the compelling and forceful skirl of the bagpipe. The very soul of true soldiering finds expression therein; and if there is any man who has not yet come under its influence, let him try a march amongst good comrades to the tune of "Green Sleeves," "Joan's Placket," "Rory O'Moore," "Rosin the Beau," "The Buff Coat," "Larry O'Gaff," "Johnnie Cope," or an old English Hornpipe, or Irish Jig or Scots Reel in its own particular idiom, the fife or bagpipe. Love of country, pride of race, historic glory and all things that make for Patriotism speak under these circumstances more clearly than under the influence of the most inspired orator.[20]

In addition to the spotlight placed on the role of music, the report pointedly recognized a fundamental new development in the makeup of the service. Whereas the British Expeditionary Force that first arrived in France in August 1914 was a professional army of working-class citizens who were commanded by officers of the old aristocracy, shortly thereafter they were joined for the first time by a new army commanded by volunteers, known as the "Kitcheners" (in allusion to Secretary for War Lord Kitchener).[21] The majority of the educated junior officers in Kitchener's New Army, who were directing action at the tactical level and experiencing the conflict firsthand, disappeared quickly within the first year or two, and the whole notion of a romantic war died with them. They left behind a handful of memoirs, endless poetry, and some of the most forceful lines about war ever uttered in the English language.[22]

CHRISTMAS 1914

On Christmas Eve 1914, British soldiers posted tiny Christmas trees in their dugouts and quietly began to sing the old Christmas tunes. Countless diary notices and letters—many of them printed in daily newspapers back home—confirmed the mood of celebration that developed at the front.

Lieutenant Sir Edward Hulse of the Scots Guards wrote of his plan to get together a small party and take a position only about eighty yards from the enemy, where "from 10 p.m. onwards we are going to give the enemy every conceivable song in harmony, from carols to Tipperary. . . . My fellows are most amused with the idea, and will make a rare noise when we get at it. Our object will be to drown the now too-familiar strains of *'Deutschland über Alles'* and the *'Wacht am Rhein'* we hear from their trenches every evening."[23]

Other reports spoke of a boche band's improvised performance of their national anthem being answered by Allied mouth-organ experts who "retaliated with snatches of ragtime songs and imitations of the German tune."[24] Clearly, elements of a musical contest were brewing as a sublimation of the struggle on the battlefield. Preparations for such a change in mood at the front had started to appear on the evening of 23 December, when hymn singing among the British, including a fine quartet, was heartily reciprocated by the Germans.[25] By Christmas Eve, as trees began to light up on both sides of the trenches, numerous reports of singing and merry-making were to be heard all along the front, with soldiers from both sides shouting greetings across the cold air of no man's land. The familiar songs of childhood, especially "Silent Night," which was known to English and German troops alike, created an atmosphere of nostalgia and of sorrow for the condition of war.[26]

Other sounds also broke the silence on that Christmas Eve: "Es ist ein' Ros' entsprungen" (Lo, How a Rose E'er Blooming), sung or played on a harmonica or bagpipe; a German soldier playing Handel's familiar "Largo" from *Xerxes* on a violin. The son of the kaiser, Crown Prince Wilhelm of Prussia, who was then commander of the German Fifth Army in the Argonne region, visited the front lines himself and reported that a well-known concert singer attached to headquarters staff as an orderly officer sang Christmas songs. On the following day, he said, "some French soldiers, who had climbed up their parapet, continued to applaud until at last he gave them an encore."[27]

Elsewhere a singer from the Paris Opéra quietly intoned "Minuit, Chrétiens, c'est l'heure solennelle"; French and English soldiers raised their voices, along with their enemies, in German, Latin, and English carols such as "O Tannenbaum" and "Adeste Fidelis"; a German regimental band played the national anthems of Germany and Britain as well as "Home, Sweet Home."[28] A flood of memories of childhood and the folks back home summoned by these tunes gradually spread across the front.

On Christmas Day tales of fraternization beyond the realm of music, especially on the Anglo-German front, were so widely reported that the general scene cannot be doubted: soldiers from both sides meeting in no man's land, conversing, reading from the Bible, exchanging food, tobacco, and haircuts; shooting and sharing the runaway hare or stray pig for Christmas dinner; even engaging in sporting contests—another pattern of sublimation for actual combat.[29] One officer recorded that they spent all Christmas morning fraternizing and singing songs. "I have been within a yard in front of their trenches," he said, "have spoken to and exchanged greetings with a colonel, staff officers and several company officers. All were very nice and friendly." Dramatic proof of such encounters appeared on the front page of the *Daily Sketch* for 5 January 1915, where a photograph of Major Buchanan-Dunlop was accompanied by the headline "Major Who Sang Carols between the Trenches" and a picture of soldiers singing next to a lighted Christmas tree.[30]

One soldier told of a German NCO starting his troops off on a marching tune, to which the Tommies responded with "Boys of Bonnie Scotland, where the heather and the bluebells grow" and continued with everything from "Good King Wenceslas" to "Auld Lang Syne," in which British, Scots, Irish, Prussians, and Württembergers all joined in. He concluded, "It was absolutely astounding, and if I had seen it on a cinematograph film, I should have sworn that it was faked!"[31]

Back home, however, singing the familiar German carols made some people uneasy, as was made clear in the lead article by Edmonstoune Duncan in the 1 December 1914 issue of *The Musical Times*. Devoted to a general review of the history of the Christmas carol, it concluded: "Two things stand clear: a man can no more make a carol than a Christmas tree. Such things only grow in the ages. The other is—How easily we can do without German carols, if we try!"[32] Attempts to inject an anti-German bias into the world of music appeared intermittently throughout the war, but it is noteworthy that the immediately preceding issue of the same British journal had included an arrangement of "Silent Night," whose melody was correctly attributed to the German Franz Gruber (1818). Some music, it was clear, belonged to the ages and to all countries.

CONCERTS AND SOLDIER SONGS

By mid-September 1915 the French commander-in-chief, General Joseph Joffre, had given the command to "entrench," and this led not just to localized "digging in" but to the construction of a system of trenches that extended some 450 miles from the Belgian coast to the Swiss frontier. This image of the Western Front accurately summarized the acute sense of immobility that set in shortly after the first few weeks. Troop movement came to an abrupt standstill, and the front line changed no more than ten miles over the next four years. Barbed wire entanglements lay between the frontline trenches and no man's land, a distance that varied between 25 yards and half a mile, with an average of no more than 250 yards. This consequent sense of stricture and confinement helps to explain not only the need for release on the first Christmas but also the sense of community that developed among the troops as the war progressed.

Many of the tunes born in the trenches have disappeared, but some surviving lyrics tell grim stories. One concerned Ypres, a city with a population of around 20,000 in western Belgium near the French border, which had been a famous cloth-weaving center since medieval times. During the Great War it also became the site of three major battles. The first, between October and November 1914, saw the British successfully stop the Germans, who were said to have "hurled themselves [into battle] with reckless abandon . . . while singing patriotic songs"[33] in their race to the sea. In the second battle of Ypres, which occurred in April and May 1915, both the Germans and the English resorted to the use of chlorine gas for the first time during the war.

In the final battle of Ypres, which was known as Passchendaele and was waged between October and November 1917, the British attack on the Germans brought an advance of only five miles at a cost of 275,000 Allied and 200,000 German lives. The tragedy and futility of these battles were compounded in March, when even those territorial gains were won back by the Germans in only three days.[34] To the Tommy, the town of Ypres (pronounced "ee-pruh" but known as "Wipers" or "Eepray") stood in many ways as an embodiment of the war's hopeless stalemate. Not surprisingly, one of the most haunting and disturbing verses to come out of the entire conflict was inspired by the seemingly endless battles for this village. It was sung to the tune "Sing Me to Sleep," a pre-1914 sentimental ballad.

> Far, far from Wipers
> I long to be,
> Where German snipers
> Can't get at me.
>
> Damp is my dug-out,
> Cold are my feet,

Waiting for a whizz-bang
To put me to sleep.[35]

The sequence of battles for Ypres was ultimately immortalized by the conferring of the British Military Cross and the French Croix de Guerre upon the town.[36]

Another favorite, "Old Soldiers Never Die," sung to the tune "Kind Thoughts Can Never Die," concluded its first stanza with the words "They simply fade away." This song was well remembered, and it was quoted by General Douglas MacArthur many years later when, having been recalled by President Truman during the Korean War, he addressed the United States Congress in a personal soliloquy of elevated sentiment. The general neglected to recall, however, that the second stanza concluded with the words "Old soldiers never die / Young ones wish they would."[37]

Entertainment near the front that relied upon irreverent proclamations concerning age and rank provided a necessary and welcome relief from the confinement and incessant barrage of light and sound in virtually every theater of the war. Soldiers reacted, as they always have, in an exaggerated fashion to any possible note of levity in both the concerts and films that were offered as momentary respites. Developed talent had very little to do with the various variety numbers, and as one soldier put it, "Everybody is ready to laugh at everything and mirth is the predominant feature of the whole performance."[38] Soldiers performing as cross-dressers invariably proved to be a big hit in a world deprived of feminine companionship.[39]

Most popular entertainment near the front was in large measure a mirror of the music hall tradition, and a performance during September 1917 for the British 29th Division, which featured a trick cyclist, a Charlie Chaplin mimic, a "girl" vocalist, and various simpleton parodies of recent events, could almost have been stolen from Jean Cocteau's scenario for Sergey Diaghilev's ballet *Parade*, which had premiered the previous May. The English music hall had historically portrayed the soldier in numerous guises, but beyond the stock characters the ones that attracted special attention were those of the Romeo, the fighting man, and the veteran. Official British army policy that permitted only six soldiers in every hundred to marry and openly discouraged men "from taking any responsibility for liaisons they had entered into" understandably promoted the soldier's reputation as a philanderer. Music hall acts were quick to pick up the stereotype. One particularly blatant song was performed by James Fawn in the revue *Mind the Baby* in 1887. The lyric was an early expression of an outlook that continued right through the period of the Great War:[40]

You all know what a soldier is;
At least the nursemaids do,
He's very fond of making love,
He doesn't care who to.

Another outlet for the soldier's grousing and caricature was frontline journalism, and "trench newspaper fever" was epidemic in virtually all infantry units. It has been estimated that there were some 400 French trench papers and at least 107 British ones. Papers like the British *Wipers Times*, which appeared in various guises between February 1916 and December 1918, boldly advertised fictitious events such as a production "for one week only" during Christmas 1916 of a "Grand Operette" titled "William, Tell!," an obvious reference to Kaiser Wilhelm, not Gioacchino Rossini's opera of 1829.

Further evidence of a sharp talent for high-low punning appeared in the 8 September 1917 issue, which announced a new revue titled "Good-Bye-ee-e, We Mos-cow," which featured selections from "RIGALETGO" (fig. 1). The revue's name was a conflation of the title of the immensely popular song, "Good Bye-ee" ("Wipe the tears, baby dear, from your eye-ee"), and, of course, "Mos-cow" for "must go."[41] And the selections from "Rigaletgo" referred not to Verdi's *Rigoletto* but to the city of Riga, an important Russian seaport that had surrendered to the Germans only five

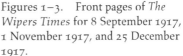

Figures 1–3. Front pages of *The Wipers Times* for 8 September 1917, 1 November 1917, and 25 December 1917.

days before, on 3 September 1917.[42] The production also announced the participation of the entire "BALLY RUSSE," which was not to be confused with Diaghilev's renowned troupe. "Bally" was an English euphemism for "bloody"—and the "bloody Russians," following a series of defeats and a revolution at home, were on the brink of deserting the Allied cause and being removed from the war altogether by the Bolsheviks, who would seize power in November.[43]

The 1 November 1917 issue of *The Wipers Times* announced two new Wagnerian opera productions by Wilhelm and Co. (fig. 2). One, "Götterdammerhaig," compounded *Götterdämmerung* with the name of General Douglas Haig, the commander of British forces and the bullheaded architect of the disastrous Battle of the Somme, who was not only "stubborn, self-righteous, inflexible, intolerant . . . and quite humorless" but also known to be innocent of all artistic culture.[44] Also advertised was a production of "Fritz Ran and I'm Sold" (Fritz was the German G.I.)—an allusion so oblique that it might have given even the most inveterate lover of *Tristan and Isolde* momentary pause. And reference to the familiar English folksong "The Keel Row" at the bottom of the same announcement alluded to the fall of the German chancellor, George Michaelis ("Mike Hayliss"), as result of a "row" following a mutiny on board a German battleship at Kiel.[45]

Further testimony to the sophistication of the writers for *The Wipers Times* appeared in the headlines for Christmas Day 1917: "This Week, and for One Week Only. Maude Allenby in her famous series of Eastern dances, including the Gaza Glide, Beersheba Bunny Hug, and the Jerusalem Jostle" (fig. 3). Maud Allen was a Canadian dancer, noted for her exotic dances, who had commissioned an Egyptian ballet, *Khamma,* from Debussy in 1912. In the spring of 1915, however, Allen had become involved in a notorious scandal known as the "Billing Case." Following a private performance of Wilde's *Salomé,* an independent member of Parliament, Noel Pemberton Billing, had made potentially libelous comments about her in his magazine, *The Vigilante.* Allen sued, and for a period the story competed with news from the front in the newspapers. The clever double-entendre in *The Wipers Times,* however, rested primarily upon the names of a Lieutenant-General Maude and General Allenby, commander of the Egyptian Expeditionary Force,[46] and Beersheba, Gaza, and Jerusalem had only recently been captured by the British in October, November, and December 1917, respectively.[47]

Such allusions in a soldier's trench paper, however limited its distribution, point to a significant level of cultural sophistication, not just on the part of the writers but also on that of a considerable portion of the paper's readership. It has been noted that by 1914 "it was possible for soldiers to be not merely literate but vigorously literary," which was clearly understood to extend to a familiarity with the titles of the some of the most famous operas and performers.[48]

By Christmas of 1915 much of the jollity had disappeared, and warnings had been issued that the fraternization of the previous year was in no way to be repeated. Ominously, one report spoke of having heard a voice singing music from *La traviata* suddenly cut off "mid-aria as though a door had been slammed shut."[49] At home, too, jokes, pantomimes, and other entertainment during the first Christmas had understandably carried wartime references, such as the immensely popular tongue twister "Sister Susie's Sewing Shirts for Soldiers." By the second Christmas the most popular song of the season was "Keep the Home Fires Burning," which was introduced to troops by the composer, Ivor Novello. Few wartime songs captured both the soldier's homesickness and his capacity for endurance so successfully: "There's a silver lining / Through the dark clouds shining, / Turn the dark clouds inside out / Till the Boys come Home."[50] Such songs, like the carols remembered from childhood, evoked nostalgia for home and underscored the widespread hope for a return to peace.

While many of the inescapable class lines of civilian life naturally transferred to the war zone (with the educated classes typically assuming the highest rungs of leadership), the lyrics of many of the most popular songs also nourished a sense of egalitarianism unimaginable in peacetime.[51] Sassoon conveyed something of this mix of nostalgia and camaraderie, as well as his affection for and identification with his own troops, in a poem called "Concert Party" from the collection *The Picture Show*.[52] Conjuring up the surreal quality that hovered over virtually all entertainments near the front, the poem opens in the early twilight as "shoals of low-jargoning men drift inward to the sound." "Drawn by a lamp," like moths to a flame, toward the "jangle and throb of a piano," the soldiers arrive at the show where they ask the "warbling ladies in white" to sing them "the songs of our own land." The troop of pinch-hit entertainers give their all with tunes like "God Send You Home," "A Long, Long Trail," "I Hear You Calling Me," and "Dixieland." The concert ends, silence descends, memories of home fade away, and the soldiers drift back to their base camp and to their private worlds of fear and loneliness.[53]

Years later, in his autobiographical *Memoirs of George Sherston*, Sassoon recalled the concert party and its importance for the war-weary soldier.

> What else do they get, besides this vague gratitude? Company football matches, beer in the canteens, and one mail in three weeks.
> I felt all this very strongly a few evenings ago when a Concert Party gave an entertainment to the troops. It wasn't much; a canvas awning; a few footlights; two blue-chinned actors in soft, felt hats—one of them jangling ragtime tunes on a worn-out upright; three women in short silk skirts singing the old, old soppy popular songs; and all of them doing their best with their little repertoire.
> They were unconscious, it seemed to me, of the intense impact on their audience—that dim brown moonlit mass of men. Row beyond row, I watched those soldiers, listening so quietly, chins propped on hands, to the songs which epitomized their "Blighty hunter," their longing for the gaiety and sentiment of life.[54]

The soldiers' songs and the rag-tag entertainment, which were to be found on the Salonika, Palestine, and Western Fronts alike, became an emblematic antidote to the deafening and unremitting roar of the battlefield. They offered not just organized sound as a counter to the random barrage of explosions, but a moment of mental escape, however brief or of whatever quality. Among the professional entertainers who visited the Western Front, few brought the spirit of the London musical review to the troops with greater success than the kilted Scots vaudeville minstrel Harry

Lauder, who lost his own twenty-two-year-old son on the Somme in January 1917.[55] Even in Gallipoli, where soldiers were largely deprived of songfests or organized music of any kind, the Scotsmen who were pinned down on a narrow strip of shoreline in October 1916 took comfort in the sounds of a band playing Elgar's "Salut d'amour" on the quarterdeck of a British battleship a mile distant in Morto Bay.[56]

There was always an alternative, however, when no entertainment was at hand. As anyone who has ever served knows, the marching soldier is by definition a singing soldier. Robert Service, who was an ambulance driver and reporter in France during the war years, captured the essence of the lusty-voiced Tommies.

> Oh, weren't they the fine boys! You never saw the beat of them,
> Singing all together with their throats bronze-bare;
> Fighting-fit and mirth-mad, music in the feet of them,
> Swinging on to glory and the wrath out there.
> Laughing by and chaffing by, frolic in the smiles of them,
> On the road, the white road, all the afternoon;
> Strangers in a strange land, miles and miles and miles of them,
> Battle-bound and heart-high, and singing this tune,
>
> *"It's a long way to Tipperary . . ."*[57]

There seemed to be a magic about "Tipperary" that surpassed that of all other songs. Curiously enough, it had originally been published in 1912 and was a relatively obscure bit of Irish music-hall balladry that had been largely forgotten until it was revived during the war. Reprinted as sheet music with the marking "Sung by The Soldiers of the King" and a picture of George V, it was now claimed as "The Marching Anthem on the Battlefields of Europe" (fig. 4). The painter Walter Richard Sickert, an Englishman of German birth who stood staunchly against the notion of war, caught the song's appeal in an oblique and evocative way in his painting *Tipperary*, with a scene that shows one of his favorite models playing the piano in a pub from the viewpoint of "a volunteer soldier who has leapt to his feet and joined in the singing with gusto." John Charles Dollmann, who before the war had been mostly concerned with rural landscapes and sporting scenes, also painted a *Tipperary* in 1915 that captured the camaraderie of the singing soldier portrayed by Service.[58]

The Musical Times testified to the song's popularity when it printed a discussion of the piece and a reproduction of the original score in facsimile on 12 December 1914. The singing or whistling of "Tipperary" had quickly

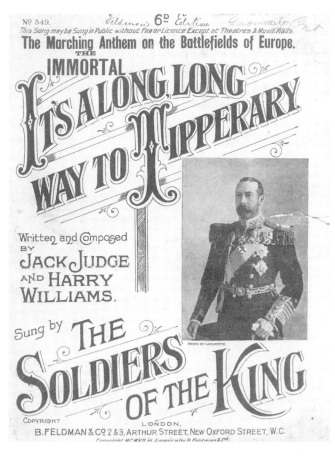

Figure 4. Cover for Jack Judge and Harry Williams's "It's a Long, Long Way to Tipperary," 1912, which was recast as a war marching song. (Music © 1912 B. Feldman & Co., London.)

become one of the most recognizable civilian gestures of patriotism, and before the year was out it was reported that large sections of the army had had such an overdose of it that "attempts to start it were often howled and whistled down."[59] The ability of "Tipperary" to carry a hymnlike aura of openly inspirational quality under the right conditions was matched by numerous other songs that emphasized the distance from the front to home, including "There's a Long, Long Trail" and "Keep the Home Fires Burning."[60] Presciently, Sassoon captured the symbolism of all such songs in a poem called "Song-Books of the War," in which he projected their nostalgic force for a generation fifty years later.[61]

NATIONAL AIRS AND POPULAR AND RETEXTED TUNES

The war was barely a month old when *The Musical Times* carried several articles on the relationship of music to war, including the relative aesthetic stature of various national anthems. One argued that war was "no longer the place for music. Hers the role to refresh and invigorate—to nerve man to fight the real battle of life—to provide him with fresh visions of eternal beauty: things which Bach and Beethoven do better than all the battle-hymns and patriotic songs in the world."[62] It was a familiar argument not only with respect to the perceived limitations of openly nationalistic art but also in its recognition of two German musical titans by an Allied critic.

Newman was of the same opinion, and he pronounced his belief that in time of war the psychology of the crowd dominates, leaving no room for the real artist. Wagner's "Kaisermarsch" was deemed "a poor thing in comparison with Wagner's other music," and the "banging and firing and strutting" of Brahms's "Triumphlied" was judged as "not really allied to his reflective temperament." He further declared that the national anthems of the world were "on the whole, a deplorable lot." The Austrian national anthem was good only because it had been written by Haydn without any thought of the nation. "Die Wacht am Rhein" was a "thoroughly commonplace tune," and the Belgian "La brabançonne" was "a poor thing to the outsider who judges it simply as music." The one national song that was "worth the paper it is written on" was "La Marseillaise."

> There is genius in that, though it is the genius of the amateur. It is weakest at the end, as an amateur's music always is: the final phrase of the song seems to me like a ridiculously small and unimpressive tail attached to a big and fierce tiger. . . . But "La Marseillaise" is for the most part the right kind of thing. . . . We should have reason to congratulate ourselves if, in default of our recognised composers, some Rouget de Lisle were to spring out from the ranks of the people to-day; but one sadly doubts whether the people can produce him, or would recognise him if they saw him. Their taste has been irreparably debauched. It's a long, long way from Tipperary to "La Marseillaise."[63]

Nobility of expression was not, however, the main criterion for most of the tunes and texts sung by the soldiers. Indeed, many songs were too grisly for export from the front, even as they served the soldier's momentary need to look death squarely in the face and ridicule it. "When the Guns are Rolling Yonder" ("You'll be lying in the rain with the shrapnel in your brain and you'll never see your sweetheart any more")[64] was a cruel mockery of the old revival hymn "When the Roll Is Called Up Yonder, I'll

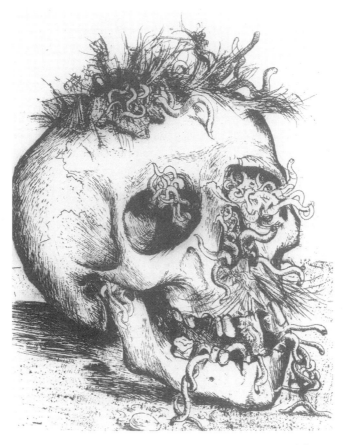

Figure 5. Otto Dix, *Skull*, 1924. (© 2002 ARS New York/VG Bild-Kunst, Bonn.)

Be There," and along with numbers like "The Hearse Song" ("The worms crawl in and the worms crawl out, they'll crawl all over your chin and your mouth") these songs provided a classic example of Grand Guignol that equaled or surpassed any photograph taken during the war. Both of these songs provided unmistakable sonic prototypes for later visual reminders like Otto Dix's *Skull* of 1924 (fig. 5).

There was a small body of English songs that did endure. "Pack Up Your Troubles in Your Old Kit-Bag," written in 1915, was one of them, as were the anthems of nostalgia that carried the soldier's heart and mind homeward. Sassoon emphasized the point in his *Memoirs of a Fox-Hunting Man.* Having fallen "asleep to the roar and rattle of trench warfare four miles away," he related how he awoke the next morning to the sound of a "soldier cook singing 'I want to go to Michigan' at the top of his voice about three yards away. But however much he wanted to go to Michigan, he was lucky not to be in the trenches, and so was I."[65]

Virtually all European countries contributed to the arsenal of war songs, and although most of these songs were soon forgotten, many of the British favorites were destined to find a new audience in America after 1917. As the Great War retreated from view it began to take on an almost surreal quality, owing in no small measure to the tunes that remained in public memory.[66] By the time of the Great Depression, for example, the annual rendition of "Stille Nacht" over the radio on Christmas Eve by the renowned contralto Ernestine Schumann-Heink recalled not only the sounds from the trenches on Christmas 1914 but the singer's personal tragedy. Four of her sons had fought in the Great War, three of whom had worn Allied uniforms and one of whom had perished on a German submarine.[67]

In 1913 Schumann-Heink invested another familiar tune with new popularity when she began to feature Frederick E. Weatherly's "Danny Boy."[68] Weatherly, who had previously provided English librettos for Ruggiero Leoncavallo's *I Pagliacci* and Mascagni's *Iris*, had grafted the poignant farewell of a parent seeing a boy off to an impending Anglo-Irish War onto "Londonderry Air," one of the most time-honored melodies of the British Isles.[69] The new lyrics were completed only a few months before the beginning of World War I and were at the ready during the Easter Rebellion of 1916 as well as the post-Armistice period, which brought civil war to Ireland. Although Weatherly wrote the lyrics shortly after the loss of his father and only son, he said that he wrote it for Ireland with the hope that both the Ulstermen and Sinn Fein might one day sing it. Like "Silent Night," Schumann-Heink's sponsorship imbued this Irish tune with the pitiful spectacle of a man fighting against his own kin.

The melody, of ancient stock but first published in 1855, had been given various texts over the years, including the familiar "Would God I Were a Tender Apple Blossom." But while Sir Hubert Parry was not the only one to judge that the melody was the most beautiful ever written, the addition of Weatherly's text infused the tune with a pathos that was rarely equaled in any wartime song of remembrance.

> Oh, Danny Boy the pipes, the pipes are calling
> From glen to glen, and down the mountain side,
> The summer's gone, and all the roses falling,
> It's you, it's you must go, and I must bide.[70]

In the three stanzas that follow, compensation is sought for a sorrow that would be eternal by projecting the idea that the parent might die and the son, surviving, might return to visit his father's grave. Softly and compassionately, the Old Lie had been addressed and modified once more.

In the postwar era a nostalgia bordering on romance attended many of these songs. By that time, however, listening to "There's a Long, Long Trail" and "Tipperary," it was as though they could still be heard echoing from a group of weary soldiers—this time marching not to the trenches but down the ghost road.

Part 3

FRANCE

5 Mobilization and the Call to History

Dining on the rue Royale on 1 August 1914, the American novelist Edith Wharton watched the crowds thronging the streets of Paris.[1] Notices of mobilization had been posted throughout the city by 4 p.m., the military had commandeered all of the buses, and taxis were also soon appropriated to move troops to the front to fight in the Battle of the Marne.[2] Outside Wharton's restaurant a small red-coated band of Hungarian musicians blared rounds of patriotic music, and the intervals between the courses, prolonged with so few waiters left to serve, were broken by the ever recurring obligation to stand up for "La Marseillaise," to stand up for "God Save the King," to stand up for "God Save the Tsar," the Russian national anthem, to stand up again for "La Marseillaise." Music, too, had been mobilized, as Wharton noted.

> As the evening wore on and the crowd about our window thickened, the loiterers outside began to join in the war-songs. "*Allons, debout!*"—and the loyal round begins again. "La chanson du départ!" is a frequent demand; and the chorus of spectators chimes in roundly. A sort of quiet humour was the note of the street. Down the rue Royale, toward the Madeleine, the bands of other restaurants were attracting other throngs, and martial refrains were strung along the Boulevard like its garlands of arc-lights. It was a night of singing and acclamations, not boisterous, but gallant and determined. It was Paris *badauderie* at its best.[3]

Wharton may have been unaware that *badauderie* in this instance also included the ransacking of the Café Viennois for not having consented to the playing of "La Marseillaise."[4]

The repeated singing of "Le chant du départ" confirmed that all was not idle pleasantry that evening. Other, more ominous ceremonies were taking place. Throughout the night streams of people followed the reservists to the Gare du Nord and the Gare de l'Est, where trains were ready to take them to the front. In a review of the state of music in Paris during the first two years of the war, J. G. Prod'homme later recalled how "the little beer café orchestras, after having sent out to all the corners of the earth the patriotic strains of the *Marseillaise* and the *Chant du départ,* were silenced, their members for the most part mobilised. All theatres and show places had closed their doors, and Paris lived through its dull, gloomy evenings in the silence of death."[5]

"Le chant du départ," born during the French Revolution, was first performed in public on 4 July 1794. The text, by Marie-Joseph Chénier, had been set to music by Etienne-Nicolas Méhul, a composer considered "the greatest French symphonist between Gossec and Berlioz."[6] Although the song failed to catch on during the reign of Napoleon Bonaparte, it was revived at various junctures in the nineteenth century, including the Revolution of 1848 and the Franco-Prussian War. Jules Michelet, one of the first and most important of French nationalist historians, wrote proudly and effusively of its effect upon the citizenry, and a collection of France's most important patriotic tunes compiled during the Great War, *Marches et chansons des soldats de France,* correctly ranked "Le chant du départ" next to "La Marseillaise" in impact and importance (CD track 2).[7] Its opening words read:

La Victoire en chantant	Victory, singing,
Nous ouvre la barrière,	Opens the barriers for us,
La liberté guide nos pas.	Liberty guides our steps.
Et du Nord au Midi la trompette guerrière	And from North to South war trumpets
A sonné l'heure des combats.	Signal that the hour of combat is at hand.
Tremblez ennemis de la France,	Tremble, ye enemies of France,
Rois vires de sang et d'orgeuil.	Kings drunk with blood and pride.
Le peuple souverain s'avance,	The sovereign people go forward,
Tyrans descendez au cerceuil.	Tyrants go ye to the grave.
La République nous appelle,	The republic calls to us,
Sachons vaincre ou sachons périr.	Conquer ye or perish.
Un Français doit vivre pour elle,	Just as a Frenchman must live for her,
Pour elle un Français doit mourir.	So for her a Frenchman must die.[8]

Singing "Le chant du départ," Parisians would inevitably have recalled another familiar and potent bit of imagery: the sculpture by François Rude

pour le triomphe
Souscrivez à l'emprunt national
LES SOUSCRIPTIONS SONT REÇUES A PARIS ET EN PROVINCE
À LA
BANQUE NATIONALE DE CRÉDIT

Figure 6.   Poster for a loan subscription drive.

that adorns the Champs-Elysées face of the Arc de Triomphe. Called "Le départ," it shows a group of idealized figures moving to defend a threatened France.[9] It was an image that was made increasingly familiar by a wartime poster that featured Rude's gathering in tandem with soldiers of the Napoleonic Empire descending in a surging sweep through the Arc de Triomphe to join and inspire the modern-day poilu as he leaves for battle (fig. 6). On 11 November 1920 the intimate association of the Arc de Triomphe with the Great War would be sealed for all time with the placement of the tomb of the Unknown Soldier at its base, which carried the following inscription: "Ici repose un soldat français mort pour la Patrie. 1914–1918."

Other songs of departure soon reinforced a façade of bravura and an al-most surrealist mixture of topics ranging from girlfriends and forthcoming leaves to derision of the ideal military life.[10] Paul Cezano's "Le régiment de Sambre et Meuse," whose lyrics written in the wake of the Franco-Prussian War celebrated the virtue of seeking glory in a patriotic death, was revived and recited at train stations all over France in 1914.[11] It goes with-out saying that the French also had their "Tipperary"—not only in a French adaptation of this very tune ("It's a long way to Tipperary / From Marseille to Calais")[12] but also in the completely irreverent "La Madelon," a song that vied with the sacred national anthem in popularity. Heard in Paris even more frequently than in the trenches, it concerns a young maid who services men on leave from the front, and, when proposed to, responds "Et pourquoi prendrais-je un seul homme / Quand j'aime tout un régi-ment" ("And why should I take only one man, / When I love the whole regiment").[13] Predictably, this and many other tunes were outfitted with textual variants during the course of the war,[14] and, equally predictably, censorship of inappropriate lyrics was regularly applied in the interest of maintaining moral behavior. This was true of songs intended for café-concerts, music halls, theaters, fund-raising benefits, and public concerts—all of which had to be cleared by the prefect of police—as well as the songs performed for the servicemen, which were supposedly subject to scrutiny by military officers.[15] Nothing could prevent the troops from confecting their own versions at the front, however, where the issue of censorship was totally irrelevant.

THE SILENT MUSE AND WAR PAGES

Not all musical sentiments were expressed in national and popular song. Debussy, by any estimate the leading French composer of the time, had strong opinions, and he repeatedly registered them, as in the following no-tice published in March 1915.

> For seven months now, music has been subordinated to the military re-gime. Although strictly confined to barracks or ordered out on chari-table missions, she has in general suffered less from inactivity than from her mobilization. . . . Today, when the virtues of our race are be-ing exalted, the victory should give our artists a sense of purity and re-mind them of the nobility of the French blood. We have a whole intel-lectual province to recapture! That is why, at a time when only Fate can turn the page, Music must bide her time and take stock of herself be-fore breaking that dreadful silence which will remain after the last shell has been fired.[16]

Debussy's language—"virtues of our race," "sense of purity," "nobility of the French blood"—would seem to surpass the patriot's love of country and court the tone of the nationalist zealot.[17] Yet Debussy, an antimonarchist who in the following year would refuse to sign a proclamation that called for a ban on the performance of German music in France, was no doubt evincing, at least in part, his depression over a state of noncreativity triggered by the war. His remark that France had "a whole intellectual province to recapture" and that music had "suffered less from inactivity than from her mobilization" also signaled the fact that the "mobilization of intellect" had also included the conscription of music. The president of France, Raymond Poincaré, had used the phrase in an appeal to the Académie Française for their support in the formation of a *union sacrée*.[18] This effort attempted to bring together a secular, science-oriented, and cosmopolitan vision of French intellectual culture on the one hand, and, on the other, a lettered group of men divorced from university culture, whose anti-Dreyfusard, traditionalist, and Catholic orientation advocated the overthrow of the parliamentary Third Republic.[19]

From a personal perspective Debussy's remark to the effect that "Music must bide her time and take stock of herself" openly signaled that the outbreak of war had left him totally devastated and essentially mute as a composer. As early as 8 August 1914, only five days after Germany had declared war on France, he indicated this to his publisher, Jacques Durand: "I am just a poor little atom crushed in this terrible cataclysm. What I am doing seems so wretchedly small. I've got to the state of envying Satie who, as a corporal, is really going to defend Paris."[20] The next month Debussy wrote to a friend that he felt the Germans' barbarity had surpassed all expectations and added, "I believe that we shall pay dearly for the right not to love the art of Richard Strauss and Schönberg. As for Beethoven, it has happily been discovered that he was Flemish." Debussy's announcement of the latter discovery had to do with the fact, increasingly touted by the French, that Beethoven's grandfather had been born at Malines and did not move to Bonn until around 1731 or 1732.[21]

There was no escape hatch for Wagner, however, and the veneration almost universally accorded him in France during the fin de siècle almost totally disappeared. Debussy, following a considerable personal struggle, now attempted to bypass Wagner, judging that his glory was based solely on the fact that he summarized centuries of musical formulas, which he felt only a German would have attempted. One need do no more than recall the elaborate system of Wagnerian leitmotifs employed by Debussy in *Pélleas et Mélisande* (1902) to understand his conclusion, however: "Our mistake was in trying for too long to march in his steps." Debussy then speculated, "What could be interesting and surprising is what those who have fought in this war—who have been 'on the march' in all senses—will do and think. French art needs to take revenge quite as seriously as the French army does! And its cathedral at Rheims goes back further in time."[22] Once again, it was clear that *revanchisme* had developed a new head of steam through a new and powerful alliance with the arts. Nonetheless, Debussy finished with a wry observation that indicated his sense of humor had not totally deserted him: "I have once more taken up playing the piano a bit, oddly enough on a Bechstein; my only excuse is that it is not paid for! That can be placed under the heading 'Contributions to the War.'"[23]

On 21 September he wrote again to his publisher, saying that for the past two months he had "not written a note nor touched a piano: I realize that it is of no importance in light of current events; but I cannot refrain from reflecting with sadness . . . at my age, time lost is lost forever."[24] If Debussy's personal response to the nation's call for a "truly French" music was complicated by his growing feelings of inertia as a composer, he was not alone. A sense of torpor permeated French high culture in general during the war years. Many publishers suspended publication, for example, and numerous authors were mobilized and sent to the front.[25] Tellingly, the only new pieces written by Debussy between the summer of 1914 and the summer of 1915 were a "Berceuse héroïque" for *King Albert's Book* and a café-concert "Valse" for an organization called "The Blessing of the Wounded."[26]

Like Elgar's "Carillon," Debussy's "Berceuse héroïque" spoke to the plight of "poor little Belgium" and featured a somewhat jolting and banal citation of the Belgian national anthem, "La brabançonne" (CD track 3).[27] Debussy had never drawn upon national anthems before composing the second book of *Préludes* for piano (1910–1913), where he cited "God Save the King" in the "Hommage à S. Pickwick, Esq." and "La Marseillaise" in the concluding prelude, "Feux d'artifice" (Fireworks). In both instances he pressed strongly upon national issues by citing highly recognizable musical material. But while the Belgian national anthem was now understandably receiving a new wave of attention, its recognition quotient was low.[28] In his "Berceuse héroïque" Debussy cited its first two phrases in the key of C major before juxtaposing the opening motif against an accompaniment in D flat (ex. 1). It was a gesture that specifically matched his recent manipulation of "La Marseillaise" in "Feux d'artifice" with respect to method, register, and pitch—a solution entered there in an effort to suggest the tune as heard from a distance (ex. 2). In "Berceuse héroïque," however, the

Example 1. Claude Debussy, "Berceuse héroïque," mm. 37–43. (© 1915 Durand, Paris.)

Example 2. Claude Debussy, "Feux d'artifice," from *Préludes*, book 2, mm. 96–100. (© 1913 Durand, Paris.)

attempt to upgrade the citation through the invocation of such progressivist techniques in the company of patriotic fanfares misfired.

Such manipulations did not go unnoticed at the time, and they were judged either as inappropriately arcane or as a sign of impending decline. Newman, for example, registered a totally damning verdict.

> The truest expression of the country's feelings in a time like this is one to which the simplest soul has the key, in virtue of its simple humanity. That expression I believe Elgar to have found in the four works of his that have been inspired by the war. The utter irrelevance, the too self-conscious egoism of a deliberately super-subtle idiom was shown us

some time ago by the "Berceuse héroïque" that Debussy wrote for King Albert's book.[29]

Debussy's thoughts on the matter had already been recorded in a letter of September 1914. "Never, in any epoch have art and war made for a good marriage," he said. "[Art] must take a stance without even having the right to mourn."[30] His feelings about the "Berceuse" were even more explicitly voiced in a note to his close friend Robert Godet in January 1915. "It was very hard [to write]," he said, "especially as the 'Brabançonne' stirs no heroic thoughts in the breasts of those who weren't brought up with it." Apologetically, he concluded, "It's the best I could do, feeling the continued proximity of hostilities as a physical restraint. Added to which there's my military inferiority—I wouldn't know how to use a gun."[31] Even a year later he was still concerned about the piece, and he apologized for it in a lengthy letter to the music critic Émile Vuillermoz in January 1916, noting "that the music of war is not made during a time of war."[32]

Later that year Debussy's deep concerns about the deteriorating state of his muse appeared in numerous reports to friends. In a letter to Stravinsky in October 1915, for example, he poured his heart out at length. Beginning with a hint of optimism and continuing with the prediction that when the cannons subsided the enemies of false grandeur and organized ugliness would have to be faced, he entreated Stravinsky to be "with all your strength a great Russian artist. It is so wonderful to be of one's country. . . . And when the foreigner treads upon it, how bitter all the nonsense about internationalism seems."

Pace Romain Rolland. Yet the exclusionary voices of Frenchness were beginning to claim a dominant perspective in numerous quarters, and Debussy now turned to his earlier deep-seated premonitions about the Germans.

> In these last years, when I smelled "austro-boches" miasma in art, I wished for more authority to shout my worries, warn of the dangers we so credulously approached. Did no one suspect these people of plotting the destruction of our art as they had prepared the destruction of our countries? And this ancient national hate that will end only with the last German! But will there ever be a "last German?" For I am convinced that German soldiers beget German soldiers.[33]

In closing, Debussy warned of the difficulties the composer faced in helping the national cause: "It must be confessed that music is in a bad situation here. . . . It only serves charitable purposes, and we must not blame it for that. I remained here for more than a year without being able to write any music. . . . Unless one is personally involved in it, war is a state of mind contradictory to thought."[34]

Not all of Debussy's negative feelings were directed toward the Germans, as a surprisingly petulant letter to Godet in January 1916 discloses. Invoking a pointed and purposeful war imagery, he records a blistering, if equivocal, assessment of his renowned younger colleague, Stravinsky. He concludes, however, with an unavoidable acknowledgement: "I have recently seen Stravinsky. . . . He makes a profession of friendship for me, because I have helped him carve out a perch from which heights he now throws grenades which, however, do not explode. But, once again, he is extraordinary."[35] There can be little doubt that whatever Debussy's feelings of envy with respect to Stravinsky's recent successes (the premiere of Debussy's ballet *Jeux*, for example, had been virtually ignored due to the ruckus surrounding the premiere of Stravinsky's *Le sacre du printemps* only a few weeks later), they were exacerbated by the mounting sense that his own creative muse was deserting him, and, perhaps, by his feelings that the Russian had forsaken Paris for a safe haven in neutral Switzerland. It would also have been apparent to Debussy by this time that Stravinsky's explosive entrance onto the world musical scene had taken place in France, and that his enlistment in the promotion of French neoclassical values was already under way. Equally important, however, Debussy now seemed powerless to compose the forceful musical statement that would be commensurate with his reputation. Little could he have known that Stravinsky would suffer a similar problem, for which he would find a different solution.

EN BLANC ET NOIR

In the summer of 1915 Debussy recovered his full composer's voice. One of his first large pieces was a work for two pianos titled *En blanc et noir*, published in December. Each of the movements was dedicated to a friend who had died in battle and also carried an epigraph. The first was drawn from Gounod's *Roméo et Juliette* and was generally understood at the time as a reference to those who avoided military service by falsely claiming medical disability.[36] The second movement is headed by a quotation signed "François Villon, Ballade against the Enemies of France (*envoi*)," which concludes with the words "those are not worthy to possess virtues who would wish ill of the kingdom of France."

The clarion device used in the second movement is similar to one that Debussy had recently employed in "Berceuse héroïque," and it was no

Example 3.   Claude Debussy, *En blanc et noir,* second movement. (© 1915 Durand, Paris.)

doubt intended to be heard as a French call-to-arms. Contrarily, there can be no mistaking the import of Luther's diatonic melody, here strikingly set against menacing, march-like staccato patterns insistently infused with dissonant seconds (CD track 4). Stravinsky, the dedicatee of the set's third piece, was soon to quote a distorted version of "Ein' feste Burg" in *Histoire du soldat,* and his recollection of Debussy's *En blanc et noir* can hardly be doubted. Yet several questions arise in both instances: Why choose a Lutheran chorale to express French stalwartness in a time of war with Germany instead of "La Marseillaise"? Did both composers, with such firm anti-boche biases, intend to signal through such an appropriation not only their shared universal faith but also a retort to the offensive German slogan used throughout the war, "Gott mit uns"? Debussy obviously foresaw the possibility of a misunderstanding and spoke to the issue early on. Realizing that, as he put it, "one might 'take' the hymn by Luther to be imprudently misleading in a 'Caprice' for the French," he noted that "toward the end, a modest carillon sounds a foreshadowing of the Marseillaise" as a prophecy of eventual victory over the Germans.[37] A close perusal of the score reveals that, indeed, the French national anthem is deftly woven into the musical fabric, although it is completely stripped of its characteristic rhythmic profile and therefore is virtually inaudible in performance (ex. 3).[38]

Direct or indirect quotation aside, other musical symbols are readily discernable, and Ned Rorem has gone so far as to identify "rumbling cannons, skewered bugle blasts," and "soft drum rolls beneath marching feet" in Debussy's second tableau.[39] The description is especially apt in light of the reverence Debussy had expressed for the supreme master of the French Renaissance program chanson, Clément Janequin (c. 1485–1558), and he may well have felt that he was offering a modern-day counterpart to this important chapter in French music history. Something of Debussy's admiration for Janequin had appeared earlier in the patterns of his "Quant l'ai ouy le tabourin," one of his *Trois chansons de Charles d'Orléans*, from 1908. And even more recently, in March 1914, Debussy had characterized the famed Renaissance composer's renowned "La guerre" (or "The Battle of Marignon") as a "marvelous masterpiece" that "conveys all the hubbub and the rough way of life at an army camp. It is noted down shout by shout, noise by noise: the sound of the horses' hooves mingles with the fanfares of trumpets in a subtly ordered tumult. Its form is so direct that it would almost seem to be 'popular music,' so accurate and picturesque is the musical representation of these events."[40] It is a description that might have been transferred outright to the second movement of *En blanc et noir.*

Despite the fact that knowledge of Debussy's ill health had circulated widely among those in his musical circle, the flurry of activity signaled by his return to composition did not silence reaction to his new four-hand composition. Saint-Saëns specifically recorded his disaffection for the work in a letter to Fauré: "I advise you to look at the pieces for two pianos, *Noir et Blanc* [sic], which M. Debussy has just published. It is unbelievable, and we must at all costs bar the door of the Institute to a gentleman capable of such atrocities, fit to be placed beside cubist paintings."[41] The charge of "atrocities" sounds strangely like a charge against the wartime enemy, and it is altogether remarkable that Saint-Saëns (reversing the nouns in the title to correspond to a familiar moral judgment, "black and white") would have taken such pointed aim at the most revered living composer of France. His remarks unambiguously imply, however, that he had swallowed the currently pervading notion in the art world that any work smacking of the avant-garde, and Cubism in particular, should be labeled "boche."[42]

What of the charge of avant-gardism in such a straightforward admixture of well-known anthems, snippets, and discordant accompaniment? Saint-Saëns's indictment was simply another chapter in the ongoing demand to denounce modernist tendencies and return to the past in a search for a truly French music—a search that had led to an ongoing series of cultural wars among members of the highly nationalistic Action Française, French socialists, the Schola Cantorum, proponents of the Conservatoire National Supérieur de Musique, journalists, scholars, the salons, and other groups of professionals. Not surprisingly, their several agendas were alternately consistent and contradictory in detail. The right-wing Action Française, for example, was monarchist, anti-Semitic, strongly nationalistic, and widely supported by Roman Catholics. It advocated a return to the past that presupposed the overthrow of the parliamentary Third Republic and the restoration of the king. Debussy, while sympathetic to the Action Française's emphasis upon a national legacy, was neither a practicing Catholic nor a believer.[43]

Among the several alliances were those pledged to d'Indy and the Schola Cantorum on the one hand, and to Debussy on the other, with the critics Louis Laloy and Émile Vuillermoz being the two most notable and influential proponents of the latter.[44] Fauré, who had taken over the leadership of the Conservatoire from Théodore Dubois and who had attempted academic reform that more nearly accorded with the Schola's emphasis on counterpoint, history, and the symphony, was widely known as a mediator when confronted with competing musical agendas. But numerous voices continued to pursue the distinction between *harmonistes* (read Debussy) and *contrapuntistes* (read d'Indy), an attitude that Italian composer Alfredo Casella summarized in an influential article of 1909 titled "Musiques horizontales et musiques verticales."[45]

That was only the beginning of what turned out to be a national *affaire,* a notion underscored in a book by two journalists, C. Francis Caillard and José de Bérys, titled *Le cas Debussy.* The debate entertained any and all arguments, including social, aesthetic and political ones, that implied that Debussy was not truly a "French" composer. Ultimately this led to a secession from the d'Indy-controlled Société Nationale de Musique (SNM) and to the formation of a new society, the Société Musicale Indépendante (SMI), whose founding members included Ravel, Laloy, Vuillermoz, Charles Koechlin, and Jean Marnold. Similar developments in intellectual circles followed and contributed to the ongoing debate regarding the goals of a nation.

Fauré reluctantly agreed to become the newly formed society's president, although neither he nor Debussy was hostile to the old society or even to d'Indy himself. A series of published arguments followed that fueled the "Debussyiste" affair, but from the beginning it was clear that the entire polemic was geared to the difficult question of what constituted a genuine French music. Stimulated by the controversy of the preceding decade, the issue of a national musical identity inevitably assumed a mounting importance with the outbreak of the Great War. Attempts at fusing the mission of SNM and SMI during the war under the rubric of a *union sacrée* led to the creation of Festivals de Musique Française and a Ligue pour la Défense de la Musique Française. By 1916 the renowned pianist Alfred Cortot, who was serving as chief musical propaganda officer in the Ministère des Beaux-Arts, played an important role in promoting the common goals of these two organizations. But as the reactions of composers Maurice Ravel, Charles Koechlin, and music critic Émile Vuillermoz would soon make clear, the factions were to prove irreconcilable.[46]

Saint-Saëns had always been less of a conciliator than Fauré, and his dislike of *En blanc et noir* was no doubt further exacerbated by personal jealousy. Especially in England and America Saint-Saëns was considered by many as the most important living French composer. Nothing could have more clearly advertised Saint-Saëns's awareness of the affection accorded him abroad than his rousing song "Honneur à l'Amérique." Published in 1917, its lyrics, given in both French and English, proclaimed that America and France were now "comrades in arms" and that the grand alliance begun in the days of their respective revolutions was now directed "against the thrice-cursed Hun . . . beneath the flags now so proudly united" (fig. 7). At home the previous fondness that Saint-Saëns and Debussy had shared for early French composers, Rameau in particular, and their promotion of a genuine French style now dissolved in the face of perceived avant-garde qualities in Debussy's newest work.

Charles-Marie Widor, organist, composer, and an important figure in the French musical world, had recently been elected as permanent secretary of the Académie des Beaux-Arts. He was especially concerned that this revered assembly represent the best artistic personalities of the time and not turn into an old boys' club. Hoping to insure its perpetual renewal, and putting aside the swirling controversy as well as his own personal tastes, he invited Debussy and the sculptor Rodin to present themselves as candidates. Saint-Saëns and Fauré succeeded in delaying things until 1918, however, and both Debussy and Rodin died before they could be elected.[47] It is good to remember, however, that throughout his last years Debussy was inspired by the thought that composing was the one contribution he could make to the war effort. "I want to work," he said, "not so much for myself, but to give proof, however small it may be, that even if there were thirty million Boches, French thought will not be destroyed."[48]

NEOCLASSICISM AND NATIONAL IDENTITY

In the aftermath of France's catastrophic defeat in the Franco-Prussian War, a neoclassical aesthetic had once again sprung up, and in the fin-de-siècle period, when both revolutionary and prerevolutionary traditions were aggressively revived in France, a historically based "classicism" was increasingly equated with the notion of French art as the heir of the Greco-Roman legacy. Neoclassicism was thus passionately embraced in French music and

Figure 7.   Cover for Camille Saint-Saëns's "Honneur à l'Amérique,"
1917. (Music © 1917 Durand et fils, Paris; photo courtesy of Sibley Music
Library.)

the arts during the Great War and in the immediate post-Armistice period
as a direct appeal to the historic traditions of the nation.

During the war the modernist Republican notion of classicism was
premised largely upon the idea that Greece had bequeathed to France a
legacy of individual liberty and that from Rome had come a veneration for
the rule of law and republicanism. Combined, they had provided the foundation for the rational social order that stood at the very heart of the French
Revolution, epitomized by the principles of *liberté*, *égalité*, and *fraternité*.

Conversely, the neoroyalists' notion of classicism stemmed naturally from their crusade for a return to the Latin virtues of proportional clarity, seen as the only secure basis for a truly French culture, in place of modernism, cosmopolitanism, and Germanic traditions and institutions in general.[49] It was in response to this neoroyalist perspective—which attributed prewar modernist innovations by the likes of Picasso and Matisse to non-Latin, specifically German, influences—that these very painters executed a *volte-face* and adopted an openly Neoclassicist style.[50] The charge that all modernist art was "boche" had prompted a stunning reversal.

In the fall of 1914 the internationalist Émile Boutroux, only recently home from Berlin, where he had delivered an address to a highly appreciative audience of scholars in the spring of that year on "French and German Thought: The Mutual Advantages Each Can Offer the Other," now insisted that the German cultural tradition was based at an absolutely fundamental level on an "antagonism to Greco-Roman civilization."[51] He stated that nineteenth-century historiography and the philosophical tradition in Germany after Kant had been founded on the unambiguous assertion that "the first duty of [German] truth is to be opposed to that which Greek and Latin thought—classical thought—recognized to be true."[52]

Equally important was the claim that Germany's almost mythical emphasis on cultural autonomy was opposed to the cosmopolitanism of the classical tradition. One Frenchman observed that "the German race wanted to be indebted to no people but itself . . . [and thus] borrowed nothing from outside."[53] To a degree this assertion mirrored a long-standing perspective, from the time of the seventeenth and eighteenth centuries, which acknowledged that although German composers might have relied heavily upon foreign models, they had early on recognized their potentially destructive influence.[54] As a consequence, the German attitude tended to promote insular solutions that in turn served an escalating sense of nationalism. This perspective helps us to understand how in the 1920s Schoenberg could maintain that his approach to the old forms of suite, sonata, and variation was quite distinct from the French Greco-Roman view of Neoclassicism: he argued that his historical base was national and in no wise cosmopolitan.[55]

In the prewar period scholars generally had taken pains to emphasize the international character of classical culture, but in 1915 the French philosopher Victor Basch, while recognizing that both France and Germany had classical antecedents, argued that by that year Germany had completely abandoned this portion of its heritage "in favor of an exclusionary and aggressive nationalism."[56] French musicians and audiences increasingly scrutinized foreign repertoires, German in particular. Although Wagner was clearly "out," consensus was eventually reached that only contemporary German or Austrian works not in the public domain should be prohibited. Saint-Saëns had been an early and ardent supporter of the music of Handel, Bach, Mozart, and Beethoven,[57] and the curriculum at d'Indy's Schola Cantorum was varied and clearly not geared to an exclusively French perspective. There students studied plainsong together with the Renaissance polyphony that was based upon it, French folksong, which held a kindred monophonic position, and Italian opera and monody of the early seventeenth century. The final object of attention at the Schola, seemingly somewhat at odds with the preceding list and France's legendary commitment to the lyric tradition, was the symphony as epitomized by Beethoven and all subsequent composers, especially Franck, who honored his cyclic inclinations.[58]

Rolland concluded his 1908 collection of essays, *Musicians of Today,* with a long, multipart retrospective titled "The Awakening: A Sketch of the Musical Movement in Paris since 1870," which culminated in an appraisal of "The Present Condition of French Music." He noted that Debussy, whom he called the leader of the young school, had been attacking Wagnerian art in his various critical writings in the *Revue Blanche* and *Gil Blas,* and he made the following assessment of Debussy's music:

> His personality is very French—capricious, poetic, and *spirituelle,* full of lively intelligence, heedless, independent, scattering new ideas, giving vent to paradoxical caprice, criticising the opinions of centuries with the teasing impertinence of a little street boy, attacking great heroes of music like Gluck, Wagner, and Beethoven, upholding only Bach, Mozart, and Weber, and loudly professing his preference for the old French masters of the eighteenth century. But in spite of this he is bringing back to French music its true nature and its forgotten ideals—its clearness, its elegant simplicity, its naturalness, and especially its grace and plastic beauty.[59]

This call to clarity and simplicity in the name of the regeneration of French music had already become apparent as early as *Pelléas et Mélisande* (1902), wherein Debussy set out to recapture the principles of French declamation. Debussy's desire to make a historical connection with the French genius became a virtual obsession that crested with the onset of war. Developing perspectives throughout the nation ultimately coalesced along lines of blood and race that were held as prerequisites for a discernible French style, and increasingly, if gradually, these perspectives tended to suppress cultural outreach to formerly acceptable sources.[60]

There were numerous other developments throughout the late nineteenth and early twentieth centuries that put the spotlight on the early musical glories of France. A spate of editions of early French music, for example, began to pour from the presses during World War I, continuing a practice that had begun at the turn of the century.[61] In such a time and climate—which Debussy characterized as one side being "blinded by the last rays of the Wagnerian sunset" and the other "frantically hold[ing] onto the neo-Beethovian formulae bequeathed by Brahms"[62]—it is hardly surprising that many Frenchmen believed German culture to be a threat and that increasing steps were taken toward exclusionary policies. Thanks to his publisher's response to his personal request for "any work that you can give me," Debussy was able to occupy himself after war broke out with the task of making editions of Chopin's waltzes and polonaises to supplant the German ones.[63]

Aside from the pieces that he managed to write in response to the times, his compositions formed two clearly defined units: a set of three sonatas, from an originally planned set of six, including one each for violin and piano (fig. 8), for cello and piano, and for flute, viola, and harp; and two books of six études each for solo piano. The appearance of these instrumental chamber works, the first since his early String Quartet (1893), could only have pleased Romain Rolland, who had previously announced his belief that the best hope for the future of French music lay in chamber music.

Debussy's *Études* from 1915 reveal the composer's continuing search of the grand tradition for the basis of a truly "French" music. The publication of a set of twelve studies in two books of six pieces each signaled his continuing indebtedness to a Baroque organizational model, and his use of technical indicators like "Pour les agréments" and "Pour les notes répétées" as titles at the beginning contrasts sharply with the placement of the literary titles of his *Préludes* (1910–1913) in parentheses at the end. One of the most curious specimens of antiquarianism is the concluding étude of the first book, "Pour les huit doigts," which rigorously exploits patterns capable of being performed with the four fingers of each hand, exclusive of the thumbs, in a manner reminiscent of, but even more rigorous than, Baroque exercises for the clavecin.

A prototype for this kind of keyboard writing can be spotted earlier, of course. The studied diatonicism à la Clementi at the beginning of "Dr. Gradus ad Parnassum," for example, which opens the *Children's Corner* suite (1908), clearly prefigures "Pour les cinq doigts," which opens the first book of *Études*.[64] And the penultimate offering from Debussy's second collection of *Préludes*, labeled "Les tierces alternées," forecasts the later study

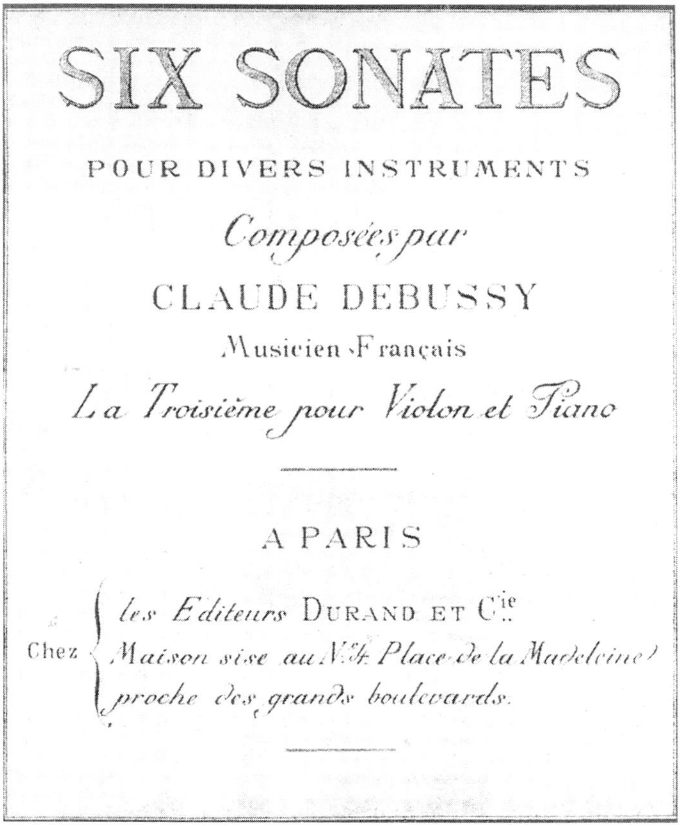
SIX SONATES

POUR DIVERS INSTRUMENTS

Composées par

CLAUDE DEBUSSY

Musicien Français

La Troisième pour Violon et Piano

A PARIS

Chez *les Editeurs* DURAND ET Cie
Maison sise au N° 4 Place de la Madeleine
proche des grands boulevards.

Figure 8. Cover for Claude Debussy's "La troisième pour violon et piano," from *Six sonates pour divers instruments,* 1917. (Music © 1917 Durand, Paris.)

"Pour les tierces." Yet it was also clear that the painstaking pursuit of technical ideals in the *Études* could never be read as an iconoclastic spoof of eighteenth-century manners in the fashion of Erik Satie's contemporaneous *Sonatine bureaucratique* of 1917.[65] For the *Études* were, above all, a consummate articulation of Debussy's personal understanding of the French keyboard tradition.

Debussy was well aware of the sense of departure embodied in his *Études.* "Recently," he wrote Stravinsky in October 1915, "I have written nothing but pure music, twelve piano études and two sonatas for different instruments, in our old form which, very graciously, did not impose any tetralogical auditory efforts."[66] How interesting that Debussy should cite the sonata as one of "our old forms" in light of its strong Germanic associations. His distinctly Gallic approach to the sonata is clarified, however, in the movement titles for the Sonata for Cello (Prologue, Sérénade, Finale) of 1915 and the Sonata for Flute, Viola, and Harp (Pastorale, Interlude, Final) of 1916. Debussy had given notice: the French sonata had a history of its own.[67]

The cello sonata, often considered the strongest of the three late works designated as sonatas, is also the most daring. For while the initial "Prologue" can be read as a motivically clear and reasonably straightforward sonata-allegro design that takes its triplet figure from the opening gesture of the "Prologue-overture" to Rameau's *Les fêtes de Polymnie* (1745), which Debussy had recently edited,[68] the second movement, "Sérénade," is another matter altogether. Here the sustained and legato lines traditionally written for a solo cello are largely ignored, and, as Roger Nichols has noted, the composer "seems to have been bent on turning it into a bass guitar."[69] The effect is no doubt intended: the second movement is titled "Sérénade," and Debussy toyed with the idea of subtitling the piece "Pierrot fâché avec la lune" (Pierrot, Angry with the Moon). The movement is marked by a series of brief, nervous figurations, many of which are infused with sliding *portamenti*—performed *pizzicato*—or are colored by *flautendo* techniques, where the cellist is asked to bow lightly over the end of the fingerboard to produce a flutelike tone. No doubt Saint-Saëns would not have approved. The logical unfolding of events is further compromised by perpetual variations in speed and freely modulating ideas that, in the process of making a fleeting reference to the opening figure of the first movement, finally come to rest on an unstable tritone.

What are we to make of such devices? In the wake of Schoenberg's recently premiered *Pierrot lunaire* (1912) and both Stravinsky's and Ravel's even more recently articulated infatuation with its instrumentation in the *Three Japanese Lyrics* (1912–1913) and the *Trois poèmes de Stéphane Mallarmé* (1913), respectively, Debussy's attitudinizing clearly signals a linguistic update in the pursuit of a genuinely French art. Pierrot belonged to the age of Watteau, and his image had been repeatedly adopted by Debussy and other French composers at the turn of the century.[70] Just two years prior to writing his cello sonata Debussy had decried the shameful neglect of his illustrious French forebears at length,[71] and during the very season that he composed the first of his three sonatas, made this report:

> In fact, since Rameau, we have had no purely French tradition. His death severed the thread, Ariadne's thread, that guided us through the labyrinth of the past. Since then, we have failed to cultivate our garden, but on the other hand we have given a warm welcome to any foreign

salesman who cared to come our way. We listened to their patter and bought their worthless wares, and when they laughed at our ways we became ashamed of them. We begged forgiveness of the muses of good taste for having been so light and clear, and we intoned a hymn to the praise of heaviness. We adopted ways of writing that were quite contrary to our own nature, and excesses of language far from compatible with our own ways of thinking. We tolerated overblown orchestras, tortuous forms, cheap luxury and clashing colors, and we were about to give the seal of approval to even more suspect naturalizations when the sounds of gunfire put a sudden stop to it all.[72]

Once more the point was forwarded that Frenchness in music was best clarified through contrast with German qualities and by emphasizing prerevolutionary roots. By this time it had become fashionable to decry Strauss's orchestral excesses and Schoenberg's tonal waywardness, and the glitter of the Russian wing was also now being subjected to new scrutiny. Debussy had even ventured the opinion that Stravinsky was beginning to veer dangerously toward Schoenberg, and when war broke out the Russians stopped coming to Paris. Some of them, like the Ballets Russes designers Larionov and Goncharova, returned to Russia; Stravinsky moved to Switzerland.

In a letter to composer André Caplet of 10 June 1916 Debussy indicated his pleasure in the news that his cello sonata had virtually made it to the trenches,[73] but a letter to Robert Godet of 7 June 1917 reveals that his final sonata, the one written in 1917 for violin and piano, had been composed during a time when his old doubts had begun to return. He expressed his lack of faith in the work with undue severity and concluded resignedly that "this sonata will be interesting from a documentary point of view and as an example of what an invalid can write in time of war."[74]

The violin sonata is a stronger work than Debussy's remarks suggest, even though its reputation ultimately suffered in part because of the composer's initial estimate.[75] Clearly, as Debussy insisted, it was not a picturesque war sonata in the manner of *En blanc et noir* or his blatantly propagandistic "Noël" for homeless children, but rather a sonata written in time of war.[76] Yet, in another sense, Debussy's embrace of "absolute music" for the first time since his early string quartet was unquestionably born of attitudes that were profoundly inspired by the war itself. Patriot, nationalist zealot, Neoclassicist? Debussy sidestepped all such labels and indicated the overriding force behind each of his last works by signing them simply *musicien français* (see fig. 8).[77]

6   War and the Children

. . . the child's sob curses deeper in the silence
Than the strong man in his wrath!
　　　　　　Elizabeth Barrett Browning,
　　　　　　　　　The Cry of the Children

In wartime Paris the offices of the various charities that registered and distributed tickets for food, clothing, and lodging were frequently manned by writers and artists, whose lists included André Gide, Jacques-Émile Blanche, and the young Darius Milhaud.[1] One of the most important of these charities, the Children of Flanders Rescue Committee, was organized in 1915 by Edith Wharton, who referred to it as "my prettiest and showiest and altogether most appealing charity."[2] It was a particularly odd characterization that unwittingly betrayed the difficulty Wharton experienced in reconciling her New York society manner with a wartime project aimed at the masses.

Her overall commitment and generosity were, nonetheless, hardly to be questioned, and it was in order to sustain these charities through the winter of 1915–1916 that Wharton determined to compile *Le livre des sansfoyer* (The Book of the Homeless).[3] *King Albert's Book* had already vividly demonstrated that an anthology of works by illustrious composers, artists, literary figures, and statesmen could be an ideal method not only of raising funds for a variety of war relief efforts but of enlivening a sense of Allied solidarity. That the propagandistic value of her work was not lost on the French government is indicated by the fact that in 1916 she was made a chevalier of the Légion d'Honneur, a distinction that was only rarely awarded to women or foreigners.[4]

Something of the tone and appeal of the book can be sensed in the opening "Letter from General Joffre," dated 18 August 1915: "The United States of America have never forgotten that the first page of the history of their independence was partly written in French blood. Inexhaustibly generous and profoundly sympathetic, these same United States now bring aid and solace to France in the hour of her struggle for liberty." Theodore

Roosevelt's introduction to the book, which immediately followed Joffre's tribute, censored America's tardiness in joining the conflict with surprising candor: "The part that America has played in this great tragedy is not an exalted part; and there is all the more reason why Americans should hold up the hands of those of their number who, like Mrs. Wharton, are endeavoring to some extent to remedy the national shortcomings."[5]

After outlining the general operations of her charity, Wharton turned to the main theme of her collection, pointedly headed "The Children." Describing the arrival of a procession of refugees at the Villa Béthaine, including crippled old men, Sisters of Charity in white caps, and about ninety small boys, each carrying a small bundle, Wharton recalled, "They took a long look and then, of their own accord, without a hint from their elders, they all broke out together into the Belgian national hymn. The sound of that chorus repaid the friends who were waiting to welcome them for a good deal of worry and hard work."

The overriding theme of the collection was articulated by Thomas Hardy's poem "Cry of the Homeless," dated August 1915,[6] and the American author William Dean Howells offered his own verses on the same theme under the title "The Little Children."

> "Suffer little children to come unto me,"
> Christ said, and answering with infernal glee,
> "Take them!" the arch-fiend scoffed, and from the tottering walls
> Of their wrecked homes, and from the cattle's stalls,
> And the dogs' kennels, and the cold
> Of the waste fields, and from the hapless hold
> Of their dead mothers' arms, famished and bare,
> And maimed by shot and shell,
> The master-spirit of hell
> Caught them up, and through the shuddering air
> Of the hope-forsaken world
> The little ones he hurled,
> Mocking that Pity in his pitiless might—
> The Anti-Christ of Schrecklic[h]keit.[7]

Such appalling imagery was a striking example of the prevailing tendency to cast the German as the ruthless barbarian, the unfeeling Hun. Numerous horrible stories circulated. The "Report of the Committee on Alleged German Atrocities," which was issued by a British committee chaired by James Bryce, former ambassador to the United States, offered a tale, soon picked up in a cartoon (fig. 9), of a two-year-old child who stood in the way of a soldiers' charge in a village: "The man on the left stepped

Figure 9.   Edmund J. Sullivan, "The Gentle German," period cartoon.

aside and drove his bayonet with both hands into the child's stomach, lift-ing the child into the air on his bayonet carrying it away on his bayonet, he and his comrades still singing".[8] Henry James, whose anti-German sentiments were as strong as Wharton's, called Howells's poem "fine and forcible and most feeling" and "really grim and strong and sincere." When upon reflection Howells attempted to withdraw it, James was successful in persuading him to leave it in.[9] Poetry and posters of this kind contrasted dramatically with the popular portrayal of the Allied soldier gently fraternizing with little children. A Paris school diploma for the year 1917–1918, for example, reproduced the scene of a seated Allied soldier assuming the role of the compassionate savior as he receives two young children in the village square.[10]

NOËL OF THE CHILDREN WHO NO LONGER HAVE A HOME

Wharton did not solicit Debussy for a contribution, although she might well have, for at about the same time as she was compiling her anthology the composer, now ravaged with cancer, took up his pen once more to write the text and music of his last completed composition, "Noël des enfants qui n'ont plus de maisons." An extraordinary song, it carries not only the weight of the composer's physical and emotional condition but also that of one of the nation's most agonizing problems: the fate of children who had been made homeless during war.

The song was Debussy's most personal musical proclamation concerning the devastating impact of the lingering conflict. At the same time it moved suspiciously close to being an unabashed piece of heart-tugging propaganda.[11] The extent of Debussy's intended appeal is emphasized by the fact that the Durand publication of 1916 included the English translation by Mme. Swayne St.-René Taillandier cited below—something that was unique for any first edition of a Debussy song (CD track 5).

Nous n'avons plus de maisons!
Les ennemis ont tout pris, tout pris,

Jusqu'à notre petit lit!

Ils ont brûlé l'école et notre maître
aussi.
Ils ont brûlé l'église et monsieur
Jésus-Christ,
Et le vieux pauvre qui n'a pas pu
s'en aller

Nous n'avons plus de maisons!
Les ennemis on tout pris, tout pris,

Jusqu'à notre petit lit!

Bien sûr! Papa est à la guerre,
Pauvre maman est morte!
Avant d'avoir vu tout ça.

We have no *homes!*
The enemy has taken all, has
taken all,
Down to our little *beds!*

They have burned the *school*
and our *schoolmaster* too,
They have burned the *church* and
Mr. *Jesus Christ*,
And the poor old man who
couldn't get away!

We have no *homes!*
The enemy has taken all, has
taken all,
Down to our little *beds!*

Of course! *papa* is away at war,
Poor *mama* is dead!
Before seeing all of that.

Qu'est-ce que l'on va faire?	What shall we do?
Noël, petit Noël, n'allez pas chez eux,	*Christmas!* little Christmas! Don't go to them,
N'allez plus jamais chez eux,	Never go again to them.
Punissez-les!	Punish them!
Vengez les enfants de France!	Avenge the children of France!
Les petits Belges, les petits Serbes,	The little *Belgians*, the little *Serbs*,
Et les petits Polonais aussi!	And the little *Poles* too!
Si nous en oublions, pardonnez-nous Noël	If we forget any, forgive us.
Noël, surtout, pas de joujoux,	Christmas! Christmas! above all no *toys*,
Tâchez de nous redonner le pain quotidien.	Just try to *give us our daily bread*.
Nous n'avons plus de maisons!!	We have no *homes!*
Les ennemis ont tout pris, tout pris,	The enemy has taken all, has taken all,
Jusqu'à notre petit lit!	Down to our little *beds!*
Ils ont brûlé l'école et notre maître aussi.	They have burned the *school* and our *schoolmaster* too,
Ils ont brulé l'église et monsieur Jésus-Christ,	They have burned the *church* and Mr. *Jesus Christ*
Et le vieux pauvre qui n'a pas pu s'en aller	And the poor old man who couldn't get away!
Noël, écoutez-nous	*Christmas!* Hear us,
Nous n'avons plus de petits sabots:	We have *no little shoes:*
Mais donnez la victoire aux enfants de France!	But give the victory to the children of France! [12]

That many had been waiting for a popular song of some sort from Debussy was suggested in a letter of 13 February 1916 from Blanche. Announcing that Ravel had thrown his projected opera "La cloche engloutie," with a text by Gerhart Hauptmann, onto the fire and was soon expected to become a bombardier, Blanche expressed the hope that Debussy was working on an equivalent of "Tipperary." [13] Debussy must have been aware that the text alone of his new song would ensure a kind of popular success unknown to any of his many extraordinary earlier ones. In a letter to Dukas from the first days of April 1917, Debussy noted that he had organized a series of performances of music for a war relief organization, Aide Affectueuse aux Musiciens, for whom he had created his sonata for flute, viola, and harp.

From the financial standpoint, it was very well run. I can also verify how our public remains attached to the same sentimental songs! The real success of these three performances was for *Noël pour les enfants qui n'ont plus de maisons*—words and music by C. Debussy. You can see that from the following: "Mama is dead; Papa is off to war; we have no more little wooden shoes; we would like bread more than toys"; and for a conclusion: "Victory to the children of France." It's no more cunning than that. It is only that it goes straight to the heart of the citizenry.[14]

The appeal of Debussy's song was destined to broaden as the war continued. This was especially true after the summer of 1917, when Germany began returning enslaved French and Belgian factory workers who were no longer effective—40 to 60 percent of them children in poor health.[15] A poster of the time, sponsored by the Fatherless Children of France, Inc., endorsed the heroic work of the American Red Cross and underscored the plight addressed in Debussy's lyrics (fig. 10). Moreover, the music claims a theatricality that is unique in the composer's entire song output. Its gradual drive into the upper registers virtually forces the voice to take on a childlike quality that, together with the menacing triplet figure at the words "Punish them" conjures up memories of Debussy's *Pelléas* at the moment when the child Ynold is being threatened by Golaud.[16] Ultimately, the ominously insistent repeated notes of the piano part recall nothing so much as Schubert's "Erlkönig"—even more to pianists than to listeners unaware of the technical problems inherent in the octave repetitions common to both pieces. The mesmerizing focus on death and the child effectively confirms the link.[17]

The parentless child was one of the most powerful emblems of the war, but the image of a child at Christmas was understood to be especially potent by many songsters, including Debussy. The theme of children was represented even in Paris cabarets, and a set of songs published by Heugel in 1916, *Les chansons de la Woëvre (Verdun 1915)*, with words by André Piédallu and music by Henry Février contains a "Lettre de petit Pierre à Papa Noël."[18] The child, waiting near the fireplace for Santa's arrival, anticipates that he will leave some sweets and toys in his wooden shoe. He then tells Santa that his father is off chasing the boches and has killed more than one of them. "If you like," the child finally concedes, "you may put all of my bonbons in his pocket, over there near Verdun."[19] Debussy may have created a similar symbolism of a child's Christmas in "Noël des enfants" at about the same time, but he had clearly pressed the point even further.

Figure 10. Walter DeMaris, "Have You Room in Your
Heart for Us?," propaganda poster from about 1918.

WAR IN A TOY BOX

Throughout the conflict the effects of the war on children fostered a potent
imagery, and numerous acts of heroism, both real and imagined, prolifer-
ated.[20] In juvenile literature, for example, there were numerous injunctions
for school children to assume the role of the soldier in their hearts as a
reflection of their patriotism.[21] Eventually these various strains coalesced
into a specific war culture that held as its central objective the intellectual
and moral mobilization of youth. Concurrently, the notion of the child-
hero took on palpable dimensions of reality as numerous stories of front-
line bravery began to circulate. Whatever their basis in truth, they were
generously and repeatedly presented as absolutely authentic. Numerous,

and allegedly actual, cases were reported of tortured and wounded boys and girls aged seven to sixteen. One, purportedly gored by a bayonet, died singing "La Marseillaise."[22]

It was an image that had been used earlier in the period of *revanche* following the loss of Alsace-Lorraine in the Franco-Prussian War and that was brought to its ultimate expression in a chanson with refrain titled "Le petit crucifié." The song depicts an Alsatian child who dreams with his mother of returning one day to France and joining an army of liberation. Caught by his father, who had gone over to the Germans, in the act of drawing pictures of valiant French soldiers on a public wall, the boy announces his intention to become a soldier himself when he reaches the age of twenty. The father answers, "I am a German, you know, and you are going to see how I treat anyone who dares to love the French." The child is bound with a rope and sadistically nailed, hands and feet, to the wall. Dying in his mother's arms, he whispers, "Vive la France, I die for you, whom I love to my last breath."[23] The shameless heart tugging of Debussy's song appears tame by comparison.

In a similar vein, an illustration in *King Albert's Book* by the painter William Nicholson titled "The Belgian of To-Morrow" shows a small boy six or seven years of age holding a rifle with bayonet, which he has picked up in an abandoned house.[24] It was a theme that found countless echoes in the following months. The cover of a *Petite bibliothèque de la Grande Guerre* volume titled *1914–15!*, for example, shows a slain child alongside his toy gun.[25] In Charlotte Schaller's two astonishingly graphic works intended for a young audience, *En guerre* and *Histoire d'un brave petit soldat* (1915), and in similar publications, war anecdotes were offered in sometimes surprisingly grisly detail. By frequently portraying these child-heroes not as fictional personalities but as though they had been taken from real life, World War I propaganda differed drastically from that of the 1871–1914 period.[26] As the *Petite bibliothèque de la Grande Guerre* put it, "The war, this time, was one of extermination and without pity. . . . It is for this reason that there were so many child heroes. In one sense, the proposition is justified: the heroic children of 14–18 were the sign of a new stake in total war."[27]

On the political front the idea of a "war made for the children" held a powerful propagandistic potential that was constantly exploited. In the fine arts this pervasive theme assumed a variety of functions for musicians, painters, and poets alike.[28] The notion that the scars of war could be spotted on such seemingly innocent terrain deserves examination as a background to the appearance of Debussy's *La boîte à joujoux* (The Toy Box).

Debussy planned and composed the work in 1913 in collaboration with French illustrator André Hellé, who contributed the elaborate artwork for the 1918 publication.

In 1915 Hellé had executed a volume titled *Alphabet de la Grande Guerre, 1914–1916,* "for the children of our soldiers," which has been described as "one of the most violent alphabets published in France during the war."[29] Its cover figure is clearly dependent upon the French tradition of the *images d'Épinal,* which had been pressed into the service of children's propaganda in virtually all of the nineteenth-century wars, including the Franco-Prussian War (fig. 11). Between 1914 and 1918 some three hundred new plates were created, all on the subject of war.[30] Hellé's alphabet book for children was anything but unique. In Great Britain, for example, *ABC of Our Soldiers,* published in 1916, began with "A for the aviators who fly so high; B for the British, who never despair." Other volumes included *An ABC for Baby Patriots.*[31] In the same year the Austrian ministry of the interior published *Wir spielen Weltkrieg! Ein zeitgemässes Bilderbuch für unsere Kleinen* (Let's Play World War! A Contemporary Picture Book for Our Little Ones) as a mode of official indoctrination.[32] And the French brought out, in addition to Hellé's publication, numerous others such as *ABC des trois couleurs,* which associated *A* with *"aéroplane," "abri"* (shelter), and *"artillerie"; B* with *"baïonnette," "béret"* (worn by the French Alpine regiments), *"bombe," "Boche,"* and *"Belge."*[33] All had the same focus: introducing the letters of the alphabet by means of words and images of war.[34]

Hellé, who was widely known as a cartoonist and an illustrator of children's books, also provided the libretto, the costumes, and the scenery for *La boîte à joujoux.* Debussy suggested that the principal roles should be acted by children and that dance should not be introduced. He also claimed that the work was "Simplicity itself—quite childish. . . . The characters have to retain the angular movements and burlesque appearance of the cardboard originals, without which the play would lose all its significance."[35] Written on the eve of World War I, when general assumptions of inevitable conflict prevailed, the original text was no doubt less politically innocent than it might at first appear. By the time of the work's premiere, which was delayed until December 1918—six months after the composer's death and a month after the Armistice—its message had been sealed.

When the score was finally published Hellé wrote the following explanation as a preface to the work: "Toy-boxes are really towns in which toys live like real people. Or perhaps towns are nothing else but boxes in which people live like toys." The work centers on the world of a cardboard soldier

ANDRÉ HELLÉ

ALPHABET
DE LA GRANDE GUERRE
1914-1916

pour les enfants de nos soldats

Figure 11.   André Hellé, cover for *Alphabet de la Grande Guerre, 1914–1916 (pour les enfants de nos soldats)*, 1915. (Berger-Levrault, Paris, 1915.)

who falls in love with a doll, who finally betrays him for Polichinelle. The similarity to the characters in Stravinsky's recently premiered *Petrushka* (1911) is too obvious not to be noted, but Hellé took the story a step further into a wartime setting. Debussy described it thus in 1914: "The soldier learns of this and terrible things begin to happen: there is a battle between wooden soldiers and *Polichinelles*. In short, the soldier in love with the beautiful doll is gravely wounded in the battle, the doll nurses him

Figure 12. André Hellé, "Le champ de bataille," illustration from *La boîte à joujoux,* 1918. (Music © 1918 Durand, Paris.)

and . . . they all live happily ever after." [36] Debussy no doubt began to doubt the optimistic ending in the years that followed.

The first edition of Debussy's piano score included numerous color illustrations by Hellé, and the second tableau, titled "Le champ de bataille" (The Battlefield) (fig. 12), includes scenes with toy soldiers, cannons exploding with green peas (fig. 13), and the despondent girl—all providing vivid witness to the work's relevance in the real world. Debussy's musical response reflects the toy box's potpourri contents: French folk tunes, Hindu chant, and music-box effects; themes from Mendelssohn's "Wedding March" (from *A Midsummer Night's Dream*); themes from his own ragtime-inspired "Golliwogg's Cakewalk" (from *Children's Corner*), *Jeux,* and an English folk tune, "The Keel Row," previously used in "Gigues" (from his orchestral *Images*). All are served with a subtle irony and projected onto a fantasy scrim of a child's make-believe world, where people from diverse ethnic cultures are obliged to live together. In this tableau, however, a series of battle scenes follows in quick succession: the soldiers "fall in" to battle formation, accompanied by a pulsing march rhythm that makes a pitch-specific reference ($E\flat^7$ / $F\flat$) to "The Dance of the Adolescents" from Stravinsky's *Le sacre du printemps* (ex. 4, m. 3) and the familiar military

Figure 13.   André Hellé, "Les soldats se mettent en rang de bataille," illustration from *La boîte à joujoux*, 1918. (Music © 1918 by Durand, Paris.)

march music from Gounod's *Faust* (mm. 5–7). This in turn leads to a scene, marked "*Animé et féroce*," in which Polichinelle returns with other Polichinelles, artillerymen, and cannons and the *bataille* immediately ensues, at which point the music makes a reference to the scurrying opening of "Feux d'artifice."[37] Thus, for all the toy-box origins of the work, in the context of the time the work must surely have seemed less a reflection of Debussy's interest in the world of children *per se* than in the subtle parallels between the child, the puppet, and the adult, and their shared helplessness to act in an increasingly menacing world.

A preserved curtain for a French marionette theater from the war period, showing a colorful but grim picture of a battlefield with cannons, underscores with rare explicitness the visual and literary material that was being introduced into children's puppet theater.[38] By the time that Debussy's "ballet for marionettes" was premiered in 1918 with Hellé's sets and costumes, an interpretation of this work in light of the war could hardly have been forestalled. In 1919 Hellé's *Le livre des heures héroïques et douloureuses des années 1914, 1915, 1916, 1917, 1918* was published. Appearing shortly after the Armistice, the volume achieved a certain celebrity and, with its somewhat pacifist tone, provided a notable contrast to his much more aggressive wartime alphabet for children.[39]

Confirmation of Debussy's awareness of the relevance of his toy box war to the war that broke out shortly thereafter is confirmed in a work written in December 1914. A "Noël pour 1914," which survives in manuscript, was composed for tenor, chorus, bugles, and piano as a Christmas present for

Example 4.   Claude Debussy, "Les soldats se mettent en rang de bataille," from *La boîte à joujoux*. (© 1918 Durand, Paris.)

his wife Emma, and in it Debussy tellingly cites not only motifs from "La Marseillaise" but also the soldier's motif from *La boîte à joujoux*.[40]

JOAN OF ARC

One of the preoccupations of the Catholic Church in its concerted wartime effort to mobilize children was the organization of children's prayers for national victory. It pursued the theme vigorously in publications like the children's magazine *L'étoile noëliste,* which described the collective prayers of a committee of cadettes and their wartime pilgrimages to the Holy Virgin to pray for victory and peace for France. In August 1918 the magazine stressed that children were at least as numerous as combatants, and recommended taking up the "arms of prayer in order to aid our soldiers in vanquishing the enemy."[41] Children were given various military ranks of soldier, corporal, and sergeant depending upon the frequency of communion, with officer ranks being reserved for daily communicants. Children as young as seven years of age were enlisted in acts of mortification, hours of silence, and other acts of penitence. This ultimately led to a "Children's Crusade" under the protection of the Virgin Mary and Jeanne d'Arc.[42]

During the Great War France may have produced "the first grand moral and intellectual mobilisation of the concept of childhood in the field of European politics,"[43] yet the cult of the boy hero was hardly new. During the American Civil War, for example, boys of sixteen and younger fought on the battlefield.[44] In the Great War the popular notion of youthful combatants was enhanced by the image of the preadolescent child that graced posters and appeared in countless newspaper photographs from the first moment that the refugees began to stream out of Belgium toward Paris. The image reappeared in virtually every conflict of the twentieth century, and Debussy was one of the first composers to tap its theme directly, unapologetically, and with telling effect.

Like "Noël des enfants qui n'ont plus de maisons" before it, Debussy's *Ode à la France*, written in the last months of the composer's life, bore testimony to a children's war culture rooted in both the revolutionary Jacobin tradition and Catholic mythology focused on the figure of Saint Joan.[45] Throughout the Belle Époque, moreover, revanchist songs that called for the recovery of Alsace-Lorraine had been sung in the *café-concerts*, and it has been contended that "the war of 1914 was prepared for as much in the *café-concerts* as by the general staff."[46] Among the flood of such songs, "La marche Lorraine," which portrays Joan of Arc leading the fight for France's "sacred soil," was not atypical.[47]

With his *Ode à la France* Debussy called upon not only Joan of Arc, the adolescent warrior, but also, through her androgyny, the dual characteristics of the boy soldier and the vulnerable young maid. Debussy was not the first musician to make use of Joan of Arc's story.[48] In the nineteenth century it had served as the basis for Verdi's opera *Giovanna d'arco* (1845); for incidental music by Gounod to *Jeanne d'Arc*, a play in five acts by Jules Barbier (published in 1870), and for *Messe à la mémoire de Jeanne d'Arc* (1887), which Gounod "preceded by a prelude with fanfare upon her entrance into the cathedral"; for a *romance dramatique* by Liszt, *Jeanne d'Arc au bûcher* (1846), to words by Alexandre Dumas; and for a *légende mimée* in four tableaux ("Domrémy," "Délivrance d'Orléans," "Le bûcher," and "L'apothéose et chant militaire") (1890) by Widor. The spell Joan cast on Tchaikovsky was already evident in his childhood, as shown by poems and an attempted history of her in 1847 at the tender age of seven, and this fascination culminated in *Jeanne d'Arc* (1881), one of the finest operas of the composer's maturity.[49] The French folklorist Jean-Baptiste Weckerlin, librarian of the Paris Conservatoire, also included several traditional songs on the subject of Joan, with piano accompaniment, in his *La chanson populaire* (1886) and a *Chansons populaires du pays de France* (1903).[50] And throughout the Great War her statue at the Place des Pyramides became a popular site for public gatherings and social protests.

It was no surprise, then, that the 1917–1918 season of the Paris Opéra was inaugurated by a special performance of Raymond Roze's opera *Jeanne d'Arc,* given as a benefit for the French and British Red Cross, and that the production realized £5,000 from tickets and programs sold by the nurses.[51] Throughout the war the rise in popularity of Joan of Arc was meteoric. The year 1916 brought a film on this heroic figure by D. W. Griffiths, released in French and English versions, and on Christmas Day of that year Cecil B. DeMille's *Joan the Woman,* starring the celebrated Geraldine Farrar, opened in New York.[52]

St. Joan's beatification was announced in 1909,[53] but her canonization came only in 1920, when the Catholic Church made her a saint in an attempt to reconnect with the French population, which was abandoning Catholicism in increasing numbers.[54] In light of Joan of Arc's perennial popularity, and especially her escalating role as intercessor during the war, her appearance in Debussy's last project was well prepared. *Ode à la France* sets a text that Debussy had requested from his friend Laloy following the battles of Verdun and the Somme. The published version, for soprano, chorus, and orchestra, was completed after his death by Laloy and Marius-François Gaillard.

When the work was published in 1928 Laloy wrote an article about the *Ode à la France,"*[55] in which he recalled Debussy's attitude toward the war as well as his growing depression over the sufferings of his nation. Laloy concluded that Debussy's

> music nonetheless affirms convictions easily applicable to the world of politics: without hatred against any particular nation, it detests tyranny. It is not his German nationality, rather it is the abuse of force for which he reproaches Wagner—opposing to him the generous integrity of another German, Beethoven—of whom he writes, "his strict and royal mastery was easily the reason for those puffs of hot air so grandly shelled out without any precise warrant." It has been remarked that Wagner counted for nothing in the war of 1914, having already ceased to live in 1883. That is just the evidence. One must always be suspicious of evidence. The music of Wagner is of a conqueror who does not tolerate resistance, who obliges the listener to passive obedience. . . . Debussy, in his time, was the only musician in France who had no fear of Wagner. Without revolt, he freed himself from his obsession.[56]

Even in death the specter of Wagner loomed over Debussy. Furthermore, the assertion of music's intimate connection with the world of politics underscored attitudes that Laloy, an especially influential figure at the time and the chief aesthetic spokesman for Debussy from 1903 on, had previously forwarded at the École des Hautes Études Sociales as early as

1905.[57] Laloy, Rolland's successor as lecturer in music history at the Sorbonne, held as one of his primary concerns the location of Debussy within the grand French tradition.[58]

In an explicit attempt to define his independence from Wagner, Debussy even worked on a libretto between 1909 and 1912 with the thought of re-setting the legend of Tristan and Isolde in a dramatically different fashion. The project, originally promoted by Laloy, was never completed.[59] Claims that Debussy had freed himself from Wagner were especially timely in light of the anti-Debussyiste campaign launched by Jean Cocteau in his *Le coq et l'arlequin: Notes autour de la musique* (1918). There, in the interest of promoting Satie as the leader of a new French School, Cocteau attempted to relocate Debussy outside the French tradition and even to paint him as a successor to Wagner, a charge he similarly leveled against Stravinsky! As Laloy suggests, no allegation could have been more damning in the war climate.

Cocteau further stated that the aim of French music was to free itself not only from the vapors of Debussy and Mallarmé but also from German influences and what he called the "Russian trap." Once more, these aspirations were clearly tethered to wartime perspectives. How paradoxical, then, that the premiere on 18 May 1917 of the Cocteau-Satie-Picasso collaboration, *Parade* (1917)—sponsored by the *crème de la crème* of Parisian high society for the benefit of the *mutilés de guerre* of the eastern Ardennes region—brought protests against Picasso's "cubist" costumes and the ballet's confusing simultaneity of action, and that boos and shouts of boche art were silenced only with the appearance of a wounded and uniformed Apollinaire on stage.[60] How paradoxical, too, that charges against Debussy over his indebtedness to Wagner had been made by this group of young Turks despite Debussy's well-known anti-German bias and his adoption of the title *musicien français* from the summer of 1915 on. Confusion was obviously king in this war of aesthetics,[61] for just as the beginning of the war had brought the curious and unwarranted reassessment of Cubism as boche art, so too was Debussy subjected to a wholesale reevaluation that became increasingly entangled in circular arguments of national identity.[62]

Laloy's written introduction to the *Ode à la France* provides further insight into Debussy's mental state and his genuine involvement in the world crisis, and it is especially valuable as one of the few reports of the composer's final months by an eyewitness.[63] Laloy recalls how Debussy, following the testimony of his feelings toward the war in his "Noël" and "Berceuse," dreamed of writing a more important work and how, despite the composer's deteriorating health, Laloy began work on the libretto for the *Ode à la France* in the beginning of January 1917. Several versions of the libretto followed and were abandoned because of their length. Debussy spoke continually about specific soldiers' songs and the rhythms for an "air de marche" as a model for the libretto-in-progress, but when Debussy died, Laloy was uncertain as to how much, if anything, Debussy had composed. After some months Emma Debussy discovered the *Ode à la France* among the manuscripts that had been laid aside in a compartment of her husband's safe. "It was not a sketch," Laloy said, "but clearly laid out for piano and voice, on fifteen leaves of very fine writing." Although the most characteristic instrumentation was indicated, Laloy did a considerable amount of reconstruction (the facsimile reveals the extent of his contribution), which was needed to provide both coherency and a conclusion.[64]

The orchestration of *Ode à la France,* for soprano solo (the voice of Joan), chorus (by turns the voice of heaven and of earth), and orchestra, was finally entrusted to Marius-François Gaillard, with the consent of the composer's wife. "The last work of Claude Debussy proceeds from the same inspiration as the *Martyrdom of Saint-Sébastien,* in a style as pure and a sentiment even more poignant," Laloy concluded his review. "One will soon be able to judge: the first audition will be given on April 2, at the Salle Pleyel, in a concert that will also include other unpublished works of this great musician, but from an earlier time, and of which the profits are to be reserved for his monument."

Laloy's assessment of the *Ode* fails to note the propagandistic tone of certain lines that vie with the imagery found in the texts Cammaerts wrote for Elgar, in wartime poster art, in the poem that Wharton wrote for her wartime anthology, and in the text that Debussy created for his own "Noël." Joan commences the *Ode* by describing the smoking cities of France that have fallen to the invader and the pervading sense of hopelessness among the women and children.[65] Another familiar image follows: "The day closes without hearing the tolling of the bells. What is that cry? Who weeps? I see the blackened body of France spread out before me." Joan implores the Virgin Mary for help, saying that she is too weak and trembling to wash her own bloody face and to raise her crushed bones once more. Sounds of "Save us," intoned by the sopranos, are followed by "We come from our country to fight the enemy," sung by a soldiers' chorus of tenors and basses who promise to expel the invader without mercy. The scene closes with Joan's benediction as her ashes fall on the unburied dead and the chorus projects visions of celestial fire. Cocteau would later use a similar image in his own "Joan of Arc": "Burn someone like Joan! She is born again from her ashes, flies up and fills the horizon with an *arc-en-ciel*, a rainbow." [66]

If Debussy's music suffers the same impediments of all such completions, the piano score permits a reasonable assessment of the basic musical materials. Laloy's comparison with the *Le martyre de Saint-Sébastien* (1911), one of Debussy's more elusive and mystical scores, which also teeters between the sacred and secular, is not far off the mark. Best viewed more as a final echo of Debussy's desire to leave behind a personal testimony of his feelings about the Great War than as a neglected *opus ultimum*, it attests to the fact that the composer of *Children's Corner* and *La boîte à joujoux* had recognized in the figure of Joan not only her perennial and mythic authority but also the adolescent's power to represent a nation's profoundest historical goals.

In Blanche's notebooks, which cover the war years with the insight of a man who was privy to the taste of *le tout Paris* and the thought of its inner artistic circle, we find vivid testimony to Debussy's unique position to speak at such a time. There on the evening of 24 February 1916 Blanche penned a stark comparison between Debussy and the most prominent living German composer. Having opened a score of Debussy and having found only enchantment, he then turned to *Electra, Salome, Rosenkavalier,* and *Joseph.* Here he finds "nothing but the bellows of the lungs panting with effort. Debussy, Richard Strauss: modern France and modern Germany." He then asks,

> The genius of Debussy? Precisely everything which the enraged Germans do not understand and for which they envy us: the form, under the appearance of indecision; the design hidden by changing nuances like the spray of a watering hose in the sun. The melody rises straight toward the sky like a waterspout and falls back in shattered iridescence. In order to catch this shower of precious gems, these diamonds reduced to droplets, the student of Brahms holds out his hand, closes it, reopens it, dumbfounded: it has evaporated and there is nothing inside. It is an atmospheric art . . . above all, melancholy, alert, joyous.[67]

Although Blanche's critique plays to the most obvious stereotypes of the day, it nonetheless defines the considered essence of a nation as seen through its music in a time of war. Few would deny that "Noël des enfants" and *En blanc et noir*, armed with their explicit and persistent symbolism, met his criteria for a French art that paradoxically courted atmospherics yet prized focus and that decried bombast even as it traversed the range of human sensibilities. There was the secret. There was the French seed.

As the war continued, with no end in sight, Debussy's cancer relentlessly ravaged his body, and rumors of his illness gradually circulated among his friends, including older ones with whom he had lost contact.[68] By early 1918 the situation appeared hopeless, and all knew the end was near. Long-range weapons began their deadly pounding of Paris on March 23, and during the final days of his life Debussy could hear the sound of the shells exploding in the streets outside his apartment. Despite the imminent threat to his personal safety he was considered to be too weak by this time to be removed to the cellar for protection. On Monday, 25 March 1918, at ten o'clock in the evening, Claude Achilles Debussy, *musicien français*, died.

Prod'homme, in an obituary written for the October 1918 issue of *The Musical Quarterly*, observed that Debussy had died "ninety-one years to the day after Beethoven, and at about the same age," and, noting that his fatal illness had been known for many months, condemned the Académie des Beaux-Arts for its tardiness in receiving him into its ranks. Behind the invocation of Beethoven lay a multifaceted story that had been further enriched by the Great War and that also obliquely supported Prod'homme's final prognostication concerning posterity's judgment of his subject:

> Coming in these days through which we are living, this death will arouse emotion in the little world of musicians only, for the general public cares less than ever at the present time for any art but the art of war. This is but another reason for trying to trace the too short career of a composer whom the future will judge more calmly than his contemporaries and who will hold, whether people like it or not, the chief place in our musical history of this quarter of the century.[69]

Although Prod'homme's estimate was to prove unarguable and, given its date, understandably modest, it may still not be commonly understood to what a remarkable degree the Great War provided the clarification of Debussy's essential Frenchness and his final profile as a musician.

7 War Games, 1914–1915

Only he is an artist who can make a riddle out of a solution.

Karl Kraus, *Nachts*

Romain Rolland believed that music could signal profound social changes prior to their appearance, and similarly, when the Great War erupted the composer Alexander Skriabin welcomed it as a manifestation of his own apocalyptic views. Others contended that the explosive language of Stravinsky's *Le sacre du printemps*, originally titled "The Great Sacrifice" and given its premiere little more than a year before the outbreak of World War I, had also virtually prophesied the price of nationhood in the conflict to come. However we may choose to hear *Le sacre* today, numerous chroniclers of the time spoke of its symbolism for the war period. "Often during the scientific, chemical 'cubist' warfare, on nights made terrible by air raids, I have thought of *Le sacre*," Jacques-Émile Blanche recalled,[1] and as early as 1915 Jean Cocteau registered his opinion that in retrospect Stravinsky's *Le sacre* appeared as a "prelude to war."[2]

All of these reactions are comprehensible if only by virtue of the work's astonishing concluding scene, "La danse sacrale," which centers on the spectacle of human sacrifice in the name of the colony or tribe and openly portrays a familiar test of societal values. The critic Jacques Rivière noted that the sacrificial chosen one was "absorbed into a social role, and without giving any indication of comprehension or interpretation, she acts according to the will and under the impact of a being more vast than she."[3] Richard Taruskin has pointed out more recently that this adolescent, of dubious gender, is an "expendable creature" marked "for pitiless forfeiture."[4] It was clearly an awareness of these sociopolitical factors, which transcended the parameters of Primitivism and Russian cultural roots, that accounted for the first series of critical reactions. Recall, too, that the work's initial reception took place not in Russia but in Paris and London and that its cre-

ator was virtually the only internationally recognized composer of the period who spent the entire period of the war far from his native land.

A succession of compensations followed as Stravinsky turned away from
the violent manner and swollen orchestral apparatus of this pathbreaking
score and began to write almost exclusively for chamber ensembles. Of
equal significance is the fact that during the war he began a vigorous program of setting Russian folk texts, which included *Les noces* as a centerpiece and ended abruptly and forever with the completion of *Mavra* in
1920. Concurrent with this self-conscious assertion of national identity by
an artist in exile, Stravinsky paradoxically began to insist upon the structural aspect of his music and to deny any and all programmatic associations
in his purely instrumental pieces. But musical structure, posing as a game
of proportion, has frequently concealed or openly supported a narrative
quotient—a fact amply demonstrated by the genres of symphony, tone
poem, sonata, and string quartet throughout the nineteenth century, and it
should not be surprising to discover that Stravinsky's proclivities in this direction were reasonably acute if frequently unacknowledged.

Stravinsky's denial of any and all programmatic associations began immediately following *Le sacre du printemps* with his *Three Pieces for String
Quartet*, written from March through July 1914. Despite the work's abstract title and the repetitive nature of the music, which throws the spotlight on its formalistic apparatus and Cubist structure, surviving correspondence between Stravinsky and Cocteau confirms that the first piece
was originally intended as an illustration of the battle of David and Goliath
for a ballet that was never produced.[5]

The appeal of this particular biblical story for the times was dramatically
underscored by the Munich-based painter Albert Weisgerber, whose *David
und Goliath* was completed in 1914 just prior to the artist's departure for
the front, where he was killed in May 1915.[6] Similarly, his compatriot,
playwright Georg Kaiser, adopted the title *David und Goliath* for one of his
strongest statements about the war. And in the poem "David and Goliath,"
from a larger collection of the same name, Robert Graves provided a striking contrast between the innocence of youth and the barbarity of the adult
male tyrant by speaking of the selfless sacrifice of two Davids—one the
Old Testament figure, another a friend recently killed in battle.[7]

Stravinsky completed his version of the David and Goliath contest in the
months just before the Black Hand assassinated Francis Ferdinand, archduke of Austria, in Sarajevo in June 1914. A complex of simple ideas are
presented simultaneously but independently of one another in this compo-

sition, and the dysphasia that results from the compulsive reiteration of the limited source materials carries more than a hint of the madness of a runaway machine. The dizzying yet magically controlled reshuffling of ideas is finally resolved when two persistently colliding patterns finally align. This constructive apparatus openly invites an exploration of the work in terms of a game—an obsessive war game between a giant and a shepherd that is based on a Russian competitive type of male dancing that honors Cocteau's meticulously detailed narrative.[8] Cocteau's later dismissal of the projected ballet as being "uselessly complicated by a text from the Bible" does not wash: his awareness of the pertinence and force of the scriptures for contemporary secular action was soon made evident in the title of the journal, *Le mot* (1914–1915), that he co-sponsored with designer Paul Iribe.[9]

Three Pieces for String Quartet was premiered from manuscript by the Flonzaley Quartet in Chicago on 8 November 1915. At the New York debut of the work in Aeolian Hall on 30 November the work was given the title "Grotesques." The performance was introduced by Daniel Gregory Mason, a Columbia professor and a recent pupil of d'Indy's in Paris, who spoke of the pieces as contrasting studies in popular, fantastic, and liturgical moods.[10] These designations accorded with the titles later provided by the composer when they were orchestrated in 1928: "Dance," "Eccentric," and "Canticle," although in both instances David's opening *Totentanz* survived without any hint of his legendary battle.

Following the New York premier of the work, the future Pulitzer Prize winner Amy Lowell wrote a set of poems in which she claimed to have attempted to "reproduce the sound and movement of the music as far as is possible in another medium."[11] Lowell had gone to England in 1913, where she had linked up with the imagists, alienated Ezra Pound, and provoked others with her ostentatious behavior and appearance. Back in New York in 1915 and filled with recent memories of life in wartime England, Lowell implied that all three of Stravinsky's pieces were capable of being read as a commentary on the current European struggle.

In the first of her poems Lowell openly evoked Futurist and Cubist values with the words "Bang! Bump! Tong!"—a sonic concoction that would inescapably have been heard as an anglophonic equivalent of *Zang, Tumb, Tuum* (1914) by Marinetti, one of the most militant of the Italian Futurists. And images like "petticoats," "stockings," "wooden shoes beating the round, grey stones," "delirium," "drunkenness," and "hot flesh," conjure up the rape of Belgium and the flight of refugees. Similarly, Lowell's second poem, which ends with a grave-digging scene that conjures up death in the trenches ("white Pierrot . . . claws a grave for himself in the fresh earth with his finger-nails") recalls Stravinsky's perseverate two-note descending figure. In the third poem an allusion to the groaning of a church organ together with Latin citations from the Mass for the Dead ("Requiem aeternam dona eis, Domine" and "Lacrymosa dies illa") support not only the liturgical references identified by Mason but also the fact that, for Lowell, the music was specifically a solemn, nightmarish farewell to those who had fallen in battle. Her response confirms that she had listened carefully and perceptively to Stravinsky's music which, following the introductory measures, plays conspicuously and repeatedly on the opening four-note motif of the "Dies irae." Notes by Ernest Ansermet, the Swiss conductor, for the 1919 London performance of the string quartet indicate that either he had read Lowell's poem by that time or their commonly shared perspective was virtually unavoidable. "The third [piece]," Ansermet wrote, "represents priests chanting in church, now in plainsong, now with a suggestion of the Dies Irae."[12]

Unlike the dance scenario developed by Cocteau around the subject of David and Goliath in February 1914 prior to the composition of the first piece, Lowell's interpretations following the New York performances of November 1915 were completely new readings of the music, obviously prompted by a war that had already reached a stalemate in the trenches.[13] Indeed, her poems vividly illustrate the power of that war to prompt fresh rereadings in terms of unfolding events. They also clearly mirrored the wartime objectives of the English imagist group, led by Ezra Pound, to bring Modernist works to the masses through an appeal to popular taste.[14]

It may not have been Lowell's attachment of poetic imagery to his *Three Pieces for String Quartet* that deepened Stravinsky's resolve to avoid programmatic compositions, but it seems more than a little coincidental that shortly after their publication he initiated a campaign, through the agency of Ansermet, to suppress all programmatic aspects associated with the work, even those linked to its genesis. In March 1919, only a month after Ansermet had assigned a narrative ingredient to each of the movements, the Swiss conductor offered the view that the string quartet was intended to suggest "neither situations nor emotions" and insisted that the composer "has affixed no programme or titles to his pieces, and wishes them to be listened to abstractly."[15] This revisionist ploy had important implications in the years immediately following, when Stravinsky repeatedly endorsed this perspective for virtually all of his untexted music.[16] Although Stravinsky's escalating interest in Neoclassic formalist arguments—in-

creasingly tuned to France's emphasis upon proportional and textural clarity[17]—heated up in direct response to the war, careful scrutiny reveals that
underlying narratives did not totally disappear.

A MARCH, A DEDICATION, AND A DRAWING

The opening "March" of Stravinsky's *Trois pièces faciles* for piano duet,
written in December 1914, offers a specific opportunity to test the appeal
of miniature musical war games. The set contains a "March" dedicated to
Casella (CD track 6), a "Waltz" to Satie, and a "Polka" to Diaghilev, and all
three are generic types with a rich history. The secondo, the lower part, is
extremely simple in each of them, while the primo, the upper part, is more
complex (a relationship that is reversed in his *Trois pièces faciles* composed
shortly thereafter). This dualism gives rise to an element of game, or contest, which, in the case of the "March," freezes the lower part in an absolutely rigid pattern with respect to rhythm and pitch. Despite the extreme
simplicity of the lower-sounding part, which is confined to three pitches, it
clearly maintains the controlling hand in the argument. The game is anchored in the unvarying duple metrics of the lower part—left-right, left-
right—against which the capricious maneuvering of the upper part can
only be termed evasive.

The metaphor of the game is compounded in a set of signals in the upper part which, after commencing with a fanfare, immediately announces
a motto figure, A1 (ex. 5a), an octave higher, against a silent secondo; this
figure is twice rhythmically extended, A2 and A3 (ex. 5b, ex. 5c), and set
off by the silent secondo part, A2 and A3. A perusal of the score reveals that
these three variants use two of the three pitches of the lower ostinato figure
even as they persistently avoid the lowest pitch, G, until the end of the
piece.[18] When in the last measure the initial rhythmic form of the motto is
finally sounded on the crucial pitch, G, in three different registers, capture
is achieved and the "March" is brought to an immediate and peremptory
conclusion. The alignment of pitch with rhythmic pattern proves to be the
key to the resolution of the contest. Stravinsky's son Soulima later made a
faithful arrangement for solo piano of the "Waltz" and the "Polka," but not
the "March," whose three-tiered complexity virtually precludes adaptation
for a single player.

Ultimately, however, and despite the disclaimers of Ansermet and Stravinsky, we are bound to ask if the "March" is simply a game of pattern and
pitch or, like the first of the *Three Pieces for String Quartet*, a game with a
scenario that is more specific than its generic title would suggest. Here the

Example 5.   Igor Stravinsky, "March," from *Trois pièces faciles*. (© 1919, 1991 for all countries by Chester Music, Ltd. International copyright secured. All rights reserved. Reprinted by permission.)

evidence is more direct. We are obliged to note that the work is provided with a dedication, and we know that the dedicatee, Casella, was on particularly familiar terms with Stravinsky during this period.[19] That same year, 1914, Casella wrote two sets of piano duet music of his own. One, for marionettes, is titled *Pupazzetti,* and its insistent left-right, left-right ostinato in the opening "Marcietta" is clearly related to Stravinsky's "March."[20] The other, *Pagine di guerra* (War Pages), with an appended subtitle "Four Films," was written at about the same time. The opening movement of the latter—whose title, "In Belgium: Procession of Heavy German Artillery,"

Figure 14. Cover for Alfredo Casella's *Pagine di guerra*, 1915. (Music © 1915 G. Ricordi.)

is amply reflected in the drawing that appears on the title page of the collection—has a somewhat more raucous ostinato (fig. 14).[21]

In *Dialogues and a Diary* Stravinsky speaks of the genesis of his own "March" and his relation to Casella at the time.

> I played the Polka [from the *Trois pièces faciles*] to Diaghilev and Alfredo Casella in a hotel room in Milan in 1915, and I remember how amazed both men were that the composer of *Le sacre du printemps* should have produced such a piece of popcorn. For Casella a new path had been indicated, however, and he was not slow to follow it; so-called neoclassicism of a sort was born in that moment. But Casella was so genuinely enthusiastic about the Polka that I promised to write a little piece for him, too. This, the March, was composed immediately on my

return to Morges. A little later I added the ice cream wagon Valse in homage to Erik Satie, a souvenir of a visit with him in Paris.[22]

A piece of popcorn, ice cream wagon music? Despite the attempt to deprecate the music, Stravinsky did not totally disguise the importance he attached to this series of miniatures.[23] Given the clarity of focus and emphasis on elementary quasi-mechanical patterns, the composer's later claim that the piece exhibited a clear relation to a developing French-oriented Neoclassicism ought not to be dismissed. At the same time it is reasonable to question if Stravinsky's little four-hand "March" is sufficiently bellicose to qualify as a war document.

A sketch page of the piece, now in the Sacher Archive in Basel, Switzerland, offers some intriguing clues. At the bottom of this sketch a cannon explodes in a fiery red volley, while at the top a golden burst from another cannon spews the letters "MARRRRCHF" in red and in counterpoint with the angularly displaced letters in black that spell the name of the dedicatee, ALFREDO CASELLA! (fig. 15). The sketch is dated 19 December 1914 and carries more than a passing connection with the aggressive slogan that appeared regularly on the letterhead of Marinetti's personal stationery: "Marciare. Non Marcire." (Advance [march]. Do not stagnate [rot].)[24]

Just prior to World War I Italy was still officially a member of the Triple Alliance with Germany and Austria, but it proclaimed its neutrality when Austria declared war on Serbia at the end of July 1914. Then, as the first months of the war passed, Italy determined to reclaim those districts that had been in Austrian possession since the summer war of 1866 and to rectify the borders that had left Italy open to invasion since that time. Italy now approached the Allies to see what advantages might be gained by joining their coalition, knowing full well that if the war ended before a choice was made Italy would be left with an empty hand. A treaty was ultimately signed in London on 28 April 1915 between Italy, Great Britain, France, and Russia, wherein it was stipulated that in return for intervention Italy was to receive the Trentino and all the Tirol up to the Brenner Pass, Gorizia, Trieste, Istria, and Dalmatia down to Cape Planka.[25] A week later Italy denounced its triple alliance with Germany and Austro-Hungary.

Stravinsky's "March" from *Trois pièces faciles* was thus written some months before Italy had clarified its role in the conflict to come, and its martial theme is clearly related to the virulent public debate between Italian pacifists and interventionists. Moreover, beyond the dedication to Casella, a specific reference to Italy appears in the graphic component that Stravinsky appended to his sketch for the work. For the letters that spew

Figure 15.   Sketch page for Igor Stravinsky, "Marche," from *Trois pièces faciles,* 1914. (Paul Sacher Archive, Basel; photo courtesy of Robert Craft.)

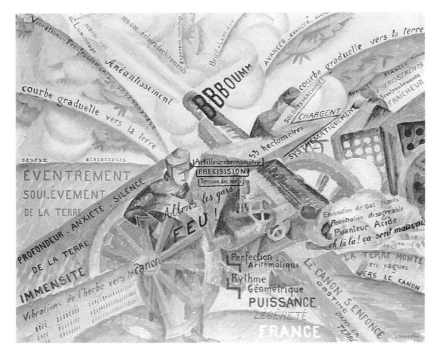

Figure 16. Gino Severini, *Cannon in Action,* 1915. (Photo courtesy of Volker W. Feierabend, Milan; © 2002 ARS New York/ADAGP Paris.)

forth from the cannon openly reflect the Italian Futurists' loudly advertised appetite for war and, especially, their fascination for what their leader Marinetti called *parole in libertà* (words in freedom).

The symbolism of Stravinsky's sketch is similar to that of *Cannon in Action,* a vivid painting from 1915 by the brilliant Italian Futurist Gino Severini, who had been resident in Paris since 1906 and who was well known to Stravinsky (fig. 16). It is an extraordinarily sonic painting. A resonating "BBBoumm" explodes from a cannon at the upper center, dominating the maze of other verbal expressions that litter the canvas.[26] This confirmation of the unrelenting din of daily life at the front is counterbalanced, however, by another message, one that echoed Stravinsky's developing attraction to Neoclassicism. At the lower center of the painting the following words appear: "Perfection Arithmétique / Rhythme Géométrique / Puissance / Légèreté / France" (Arithmetical Perfection / Geometrical Rhythm / Power / Lightness / France). Severini wrote about this time that modern painting was capable of expressing the idea of war through symbols better than any naturalistic description of a battlefield or slaughter. His words offered a virtual summation of aesthetic forces currently developing in France and a call to artists to join forces in articulating the essence of war. Stravinsky's "March" indicates that its author had accepted this invitation. The use of martial motifs, in dry-point miniature, openly advertises Stravinsky's kindred perspective, and the graphic cannons secure the message.

Relative to this argument is the fact that in the first months of the war many Russian artists gave up all avant-garde pretensions and drew freely upon folk-art traditions such as the Russian *lubok,* with its bold colors and blatantly inscribed graffiti. It is a perspective that repeatedly served Mikhail Larionov and the rising Cubo-Futurist-Suprematist painter Kasimir Malevich.[27] In addition to current projects and obligations both artists designed popular woodcuts and postcards as official anti-German propaganda. Folk art was somewhat more subtly invoked by Stravinsky's compatriot Aristarkh Lentulov, who left St. Petersburg in 1911 or 1912 and joined the avant-garde in Paris, where he became known as the "cubiste à la russe." In a picture titled *A Victorious Battle* (1914), however, Lentulov softened his Cubist style by executing a mosaic-like surface and abandoned any hint of the fury of the Italian Futurists in what art historian Richard Cork has described as a "curiously childlike canvas" that seems to come directly from the nursery (fig. 17).

The confusion of fallen soldiers, rearing horses, and bayonets, which recalls Paolo Uccello's *The Battle of San Romano* (mid-1440s), is virtually obscured by the luminous halo that spotlights the central figure.[28] At the same time, this cavalry officer, a sartorially splendid chap who bears a striking resemblance to Tsar Nicholas II, gives the unmistakable appearance of being astride a wooden horse from a carousel. Stravinsky's "March" similarly provides a portrait of the *naïf* world of toy soldiers straight out of a coloring book. Stravinsky's manipulation of rigid march rhythms and restricted pitch content against polytonal and metrical high jinks also mirrors the tendency of Lentulov and numerous other painters to defuse war themes through reductive time-space manipulation.[29]

In addition, Stravinsky reflected his immediate concerns by dedicating his work to a contemporary Italian composer and, even less ambiguously, through references to his native Russia. The implication of such a juxtaposition can be traced to Stravinsky's upbringing in St. Petersburg, the most Italianate of all Russian cities, and it is underscored in an entry Stravinsky made in a sketchbook when he was in Rome in May 1917. "The soul of Latins is closer to us Slavs than the soul of Anglo-Saxons," he wrote, "not to mention the Germans, those human caricatures. The Germans are *wunderkind,* but they were never young. The Germans are *überwunderkind,*

Figure 17. Aristarkh Lentulov, *A Victorious Battle*, 1914. (Moscow, collection of M. A. Lentulova.)

since they will never be old either." Pursuing his Latin bias still further, he added: "This is not true of Spain. She is very moving in her old age. And will France really be deprived of the twilight she deserves, and deserves more than any other country?"[30]

Stravinsky had earlier clarified his political sentiments to Rolland, who recorded them in a journal entry for 26 September 1914, only a few weeks after the outbreak of World War I. There, with disarming clairvoyance, he relayed Stravinsky's sense of the inevitability of a future revolution in his native land.

> Stravinsky declares that Germany is not a barbarian state but rather a decrepit and degenerate one. He claims for Russia the role of a noble and healthy barbarism, full of new seeds that will inseminate the thinking of the world. He thinks that after the war a revolution, which is already well prepared, will overturn the Imperial dynasty and create a Slavonic United States. Furthermore, he attributes the cruelties of the tsarist system in part to German elements which have been incorporated into Russia and now run the principal wheels of the government. The attitude of German intellectuals inspires in him a contempt without limit. Hauptmann and Strauss, he says, have souls of a lackey.

He praises the old Russian civilization, which is unknown in the West, and the artistic and literary monuments of the northern and eastern cities. He also defends the Cossacks against their reputation for brutality.[31]

Rolland's journal also registers Stravinsky's thoughts about *Le sacre*, his contempt for the Wagnerian notion of a *Gesamtkunstwerk* and his disdain for the consecrated masters of the past, including Bach and Beethoven. It seems almost unimaginable that Stravinsky would have mentioned the latter composer in a negative light, knowing full well that in so doing he was taking direct aim at Rolland's solar plexus.[32] The Russian expressed admiration for Mozart, however, whose luster he claimed had not paled, and praised Weber for his Italianism. Among his compatriots, Rolland recalled, Stravinsky admitted only Mussorgsky and Rimsky-Korsakov ("a little bit") because the latter had been good to him. Finally, Stravinsky announced to Rolland that his public was now in France and to a degree in England.

Rolland's journal entry of 25 July 1916 reveals the foundation of Stravinsky's opinions on the war. Having engaged Rolland in a lengthy conversation on a boat at Interlochen, the Russian made it clear that he attached little importance to the French Republic, believing (as did Rolland) that a republic could be a reactionary regime, just as a monarchy could be a liberal one. He added that he considered war as healthy, a moral exercise that eliminated the weak and promoted the strong, and that war was necessary for human progress. Finally, he believed it would serve Russia well in the cause of liberty.[33]

Stravinsky's first "war pages" reveal that his immediate thoughts, like Lentulov's, were as much with his native Russia as with the Western Front.[34] But his fixation on setting Russian texts, with their make-believe world centering on the adult-child (or vice versa), as found in *lubok*, folk verse, and the fairy tale, was made to order for addressing some of the most urgent issues of the war period. Years later, in his *Chroniques*, Stravinsky clarified the issue: "My profound emotion on reading the news of war, which aroused patriotic feelings and a sense of sadness at being so distant from my country, found some alleviation in the delight with which I steeped myself in Russian folk poems."[35]

The sincerity of Stravinsky's orientation notwithstanding, few members of any audience (even Russian-speaking ones) would have been capable of appreciating the origins and complexity of these Russian texts in the way that the composer did. Indeed, Stravinsky's understanding had developed only recently.[36] Yet comprehensibility was not the main issue; many of the texts consist of a jumble of words that emphasize verbal play and in some instances were evidently composed as personal greetings or as family entertainments.[37] All bore a transcendental quality of the Ur-primitive, which many Eurasianists saw as the potential foundation of a new, truly Russian art, free of compromising European qualities. Paradoxically, the ambiguity of these pieces was prized by Russian and Western European poets, painters, and composers alike.

Unmentioned in the conversation summarized by Rolland, but frequently expressed elsewhere, was Stravinsky's abiding love and respect for Tchaikovsky. It may be no coincidence that the well-known "March of the Toys" from *The Nutcracker* (1892) opens with a fanfare motif similar to the one used by Stravinsky in his four-hand "March." An even more telling and relevant scene is the opening of Tchaikovsky's opera *Pikovaya dama* (*The Queen of Spades*, 1890). There a group of boys playing soldier sing "One, two, one, two, left, right, left right! All together, brothers, Don't fall out of step!" Of course, Bizet had already introduced the image of marching children playing soldier in *Carmen*. But the specific connection of Stravinsky's little "March" with the opening of Tchaikovsky's *The Queen of Spades* is dramatized by the fact that Stravinsky's three interrupting motto rhythms (see ex. 5) expand progressively in a fashion identical to the accompanying rhythms in the opening scene of Tchaikovsky's opera.[38]

From yet another perspective the act of viewing such serious matters as life, death, and war through the lens of children's games was an evasion as much as a solution. Just as Robert Graves attempted in "The Shadow of Death" to make sense out of the chaos of war by placing events "into a childhood framework in which he would have control of them,"[39] so Stravinsky sought an accommodation through recourse to a child's world of make believe.

Finally, there is an additional message of national character embedded in the "March" that further serves to compound and complete the puzzle. In *Stravinsky in Pictures and Documents*, a volume published in 1978 by Madame Stravinsky and Robert Craft, we learn that "The source of the *Marche* . . . was a tune (No. 486) from a collection of *Old Irish Folk Music and Songs*."[40] Now why would Stravinsky want to manipulate Irish folk material in the construction of a seemingly simple-minded piano duet dedicated to a prominent Italian composer?

Irish political history is almost as complex as Italian history, and the age-old questions of religious difference and home rule, which have plagued Ireland for centuries, reached a new level of intensity at precisely this time, ultimately exploding in what became known as the Anglo-Irish War. The outbreak of World War I furthered the division of loyalties in Ireland, yet 200,000 Irish volunteers eventually departed for the Continent. Such developments would have been known to everyone from the daily newspapers, and Stravinsky, turning to the composition of his march in December 1914, obviously realized that he had made a serendipitous purchase when he acquired his Irish tune collection in London the year before.[41]

Stravinsky's "March" can thus be heard as a children's game, a piano duet for teacher and pupil, a recognition of his colleague, Casella, and an affectionate allusion to Tchaikovsky's march in *The Queen of Spades* or the formally signifying fanfares in the latter's Fourth Symphony. The contrast between the structure of this simple and seemingly didactic piece for piano duet and the formal details of an opera scene or a grand symphonic sonata form is startling in their seeming incongruity. As we shall see, however, Stravinsky would later force such a comparison in another seemingly trivial wartime march, the "Souvenir d'une marche boche." In sum, the work pronounced specifically on Italian, Irish, and Russian national interests just as the growing momentum of the raging international conflict could no longer be ignored.[42]

GAME THEORY, WAR, AND THE LIVELY ARTS

Game theory, a branch of mathematics that was developed in the 1920s, immediately forwarded analogies between recreational games such as poker and bridge and the more serious business of economics and war. It also transcended the classical theory of probability, in which the analysis of games is restricted to aspects of pure chance, by placing emphasis on aspects of games that are controlled by the participants. The theory arose from studies that examined the circumstances of conflicting interest and incomplete information as well as the interplay of rational decision and chance. Those who worked with the theory in its early years were forced to accept the fact that while most actual games eluded full-scale analysis, many could be profitably analyzed in miniature or simplified form.

One of the theory's most fundamental classifications hinges on the number of players, typically specified as singular, dual, or plural. The players are significant not in terms of how many parties are involved but rather in terms of the number with distinct interests. Stravinsky's musical games frequently adopt what Neumann and Morgenstern were to designate as a two-person, zero-sum variety, in which two parties in diametric opposition introduce the element of conflict. Such a context is clearly observable in Stravinsky's so-called easy pieces for piano duet. They are "so-called" because only one of the parts is easy, the other somewhat difficult. While this has the didactic advantage of allowing a young or inexperienced player to be a partner in a somewhat more complex context than would otherwise be possible, it also provides the ingredients of a contest.

From one perspective, the more complex part of Stravinsky's "March" appears to have the upper hand because of its freedom to maneuver, while the simple part is reduced to a repetitive formula. From another perspective the rigidity of the simple part functions as a control mechanism that forces the complex part to undertake acts of evasion in order to avoid capture. On still another front the parts operate on a level playing field: the loss of autonomy by the first pianist—who, for harmonic reasons, typically defers to the second in the use of the pedal—is side-stepped in a construction that calls for no pedal at all. Finally, it should be recalled that, although the duets that constitute *Five Easy Pieces* were written for Stravinsky's children, *Trois pièces faciles* were written for adults (Casella, Satie, Diaghilev) who possessed varying degrees of keyboard prowess. That collectively these eight *Easy Pieces* were not intended solely for the home parlor is confirmed by the fact that the complete set was performed by José Iturbi and Stravinsky in Lausanne, Zurich, and Geneva in 1919.[43]

Clearly, then, these little pieces are viewable from multiple perspectives.[44] While the element of amateurism, which the historian Johan Huizinga has described in *Homo Ludens* as one of the essential preconditions of all play,[45] is in full view, the formal aspect of Stravinsky's miniature war games invites the assessment of similar but distinct principles that can be found in the work of the war poets. The English poets, in particular, saw war as a game inherited from the previous century, when brief and essentially localized conflicts had more of the quality of a skirmish or "a brief armed version of the Olympic Games," as Osbert Sitwell put it: "You won a round; the enemy won the next. There was no more talk of extermination, or of Fights to a Finish, than would occur in a boxing match."[46] Even in the first autumn and winter of the struggle Rupert Brooke could write, "It's all great fun." It was an established English perspective, which led one noted leader to describe his ideal officers as "country men . . . accustomed to hunting, polo and field sport" who considered war "the greatest game."[47] Long after the fighting took a grimmer turn, the notion of war as a game continued to run far deeper than that of an analogy. As we have seen, it took such explicit forms as kicking a football toward the enemy lines while attacking—initially employed by the 1st Battalion of the 18th London Regiment at Loos in 1915—and was still operating as a ploy to generate *esprit de corps* on the Turkish front as late as November 1917.[48]

But as the months turned into years and the daily grimness and toll of human life mounted, the metaphor of the game gradually accommodated to a new perspective. The aspect of a soldier's existence that came to be most consistently explored by such English poets as Robert Graves and D. H. Lawrence, for example, was not the blood and gore but rather the sense of a prevailing organization lacking in civilian life. As a result it has been argued that many of these poets seemed to be "playing the game of structure,"[49] adopting various types of rhymed metrical verse rather than some of the new experiments in free verse that were already well under way. Similarly, and beyond his patent debt to native Russian sources and customs, Stravinsky's music also began to exhibit an escalating attraction to the mechanics of structure in the mid-1910s, especially to miniature or contained forms.[50]

Yet, as with T. S. Eliot's early verse, Stravinsky's traditional points of reference following *Le sacre* underwent "a metamorphosis into fragments, which (intentionally) [did] not intellectually mediate between the poet and his audience" and, as Erik Svarny has judged, an "abortive Classicism" was the result.[51] Such a perspective was in harmony with the opinion expressed by Severini in 1921 to the effect that Cubism was the most interesting new development with respect to discipline and method and that as such it offered the foundation for a new classicism.[52] Severini's ultimate obsession with the Golden Section and the Fibonacci series bears startling testimony to this new direction and its relation to the Great War.[53] Cubism and Neoclassicism had joined in a paradoxical but symbiotic embrace.

Similarly, in Russia, Velimir Khlebnikov and Vladimir Mayakovsky, the two founders of Russian literary Futurism, had initially taken the aesthetic's zeal for war as an excuse to exercise their own search for a new tempo and "the liberation of the word." With the outbreak of Civil War in 1917, however, their verse became more stylized. With Mayakovsky "the shocking force of warfare is miniaturized, the graphic naturalism of his First-World-War poetry is replaced by the style of folk-song and fairy tale," violence is reduced to symbolic gesture, and "hyperbole is used to comic effect instead of to shock."[54] Stravinsky, living abroad, had taken the bait somewhat earlier, setting aside the violent assaults of *Le sacre* for a more oblique statement that turned on folk symbolism, moral deception, and the game. The collective evidence thus supports the historian George L. Mosse's convincing argument that this widespread reduction of war to the terms of a game was an intentional trivialization that "helped people confront war, just as its glorification did."[55] The aesthetics of structure had taken a momentous turn, and with it the whole course of modernism.

8   Charades and Masquerades

> Lord, what a terrible and at the same time magnificent period we
> are living through. . . . My hatred for the Germans grows not by
> the day but by the hour.
>
> Stravinsky, letter to Léon Bakst, 20 September 1914

> There is something suspicious about music, gentlemen. I insist
> that she is, by her nature, equivocal. I shall not be going too far
> in saying at once that she is politically suspect.
>
> Thomas Mann, *The Magic Mountain*

The conductor Pierre Monteux, who was already at the front and had seen
many of his musicians killed or wounded, wrote to Stravinsky in December 1914 that he would never again negotiate with a German publisher and
expressed the hope that a German conductor would never be engaged for
the Ballets Russes.[1] For his part Stravinsky both envied and was concerned
about his numerous friends and colleagues—Ravel and his pupil Maurice
Delage among them—who had joined up in the first days of the conflict.[2]

Stravinsky's reactions to the war appeared in numerous guises over the
next few years, but he never more clearly registered his abhorrence of
the Germans than in a piece for solo piano titled "Souvenir d'une marche
boche" (CD track 7). It has been almost totally ignored, remained unpublished for decades except for its facsimile appearance in Wharton's anthology, *Book of the Homeless*,[3] and is dismissed by Eric Walter White in his
catalog of Stravinsky's works with the following entry: "Thirty-seven bars
of a brash sort of march in C major are followed by a jaunty trio, sixteen
bars long, in F major. The C major march is then repeated *da capo al fine*.
A work of small importance."[4] Completed only six months after the last of
his *Three Easy Pieces,* the work, it will be noted, is not called a march but
rather the *recollection* of a march, and more specifically a German march
with the derogatory connotations attendant to the word *boche*.

Wharton's invitation to contribute to her anthology had reached Stravinsky in a letter of 12 August 1915.[5] A few days later, in a letter of 17 August, Léon Bakst, the renowned designer for the Ballets Russes, pleaded
with the composer to "please take part in this publication; you will be in
good company."[6] Bakst was not mistaken in his judgment, and Stravinsky

would recognize the names of virtually all its contributors, some of whom were personal acquaintances or friends. Stravinsky's "Souvenir" was set down in Morges two weeks later, on 1 September 1915.

Stravinsky's approach to the idea of the march had obviously shifted radically in the period following *Three Easy Pieces,* and all traces of Neo-classicism's refining hand—if we may hold to Stravinsky's assessment of his earlier march—had momentarily gone out the window. In lieu of the interrupting fanfares and *secco ostinato* positioned against metrically intricate filigrees, which were an appropriate accompaniment to Lentulov's toy soldiers, Stravinsky's new march sported a thumping manner that could only be read as a blatant caricature intended to skewer "barbarian" German taste—a cartoon, if you will, not unlike numerous wartime posters of the kaiser or Malevich's boisterous lithographs.[7] Stravinsky was brandishing a brand of crude anti-Germanism not unknown to other Russian artists, and except for a few metrical niceties this bumptious piece might escape detection as a work by Stravinsky altogether.

BEETHOVEN AND DOGGEREL

Soulima Stravinsky, the composer's son, stated that "Souvenir d'une marche boche" was virtually improvised on the spot in a moment of high energy (ex. 6),[8] but this seems somewhat suspect in light of the artfully sly incorporation of a march figure taken from the finale of Beethoven's Fifth Symphony (ex. 7). Taruskin, who identified the quotation, concluded with good reason that the march is a "heavy mockery of everything Teutonic, it makes a pointed jab at Beethoven's Fifth."[9] The observation poses as many questions as it answers, however, the essential one being "Why a jab at Beethoven?" As we have seen, throughout World War I Beethoven's chameleon-like capacity to serve any and all political as well as aesthetic points of view was virtually without precedent in the history of music, and his Fifth Symphony was one of the most popularly invoked musical emblems by both sides during the war. Its citation, therefore, would not have automatically evoked a negative connotation. It is clearly only Stravinsky's musical language—infested with what might be called untutored diatonic grotesquerie[10]—coupled with the title, that insists upon a hostile reading.

However irrefutable the reference to Beethoven in "Souvenir," its meaning is far from unambiguous. Stravinsky's oblique parody of a snippet from the coda to the last movement of Beethoven's Fifth Symphony, detectable only by the most astute musicological sleuth, contrasts sharply with Charles Ives's undisguised citation of the same work's celebrated open-

Example 6.   Igor Stravinsky, "Souvenir d'une marche boche," mm. 13–15. © 1916 Boosey & Hawkes Music Publishers Ltd. Copyright renewed. Reprinted by permission.

Example 7.   Ludwig van Beethoven, Fifth Symphony, fourth movement, coda.

ing motto in his "Concord" Sonata, written at exactly the same time. Stravinsky's circumspect, if also subtly punning, usage of the tail rather than the head would thus seem to be a retort to the unrelenting and variously angled appropriations of Beethoven and his music throughout the war by the French and the Germans, prowar and pacifist alike.

The parody is both subtle and significant in light of the composer's stature. "Igor Stravinsky directs the course of musical evolution today, and his arrival in our musical life is the most important event since Debussy, an event on the order of a Wagner or a Beethoven," Ansermet had written in April 1914, three months before the beginning of hostilities.[11] The comparison, obviously intended to flatter, would not have been received as a compliment by Stravinsky.[12] Stravinsky's estimation of Beethoven, who had played such a significant role in the musical life of nineteenth-century Russia, was more complex, however, and it changed considerably over time.[13] Tchaikovsky's veneration of Beethoven seems to have approached a fixation, and he even went so far as to claim that his Fourth Symphony was modeled directly on Beethoven's Fifth.[14] That Stravinsky had early exposure to this continuing tradition is confirmed in a letter to his teacher, Rimsky-Korsakov, written from the family summer residence in Ustilug on 23 July 1907: "I am enjoying Beethoven's symphonies, which I play four-hands with Katia in the evening. I have many thoughts about Beethoven, but I will tell them to you this winter."[15]

In his *Autobiography* of 1936 Stravinsky reviewed the Beethoven question at length, recalling his preparation to compose a piano sonata in 1924. Noting that he had wished "to examine more closely the sonatas of the classical masters in order to trace the direction and development of their thought in the solution of problems presented by that form," he reported that he began by replaying a great many of the Beethoven sonatas. Stravinsky then made a crucial confession.

> In our early youth we were surfeited by his works, his famous *Welt-schmerz* being forced upon us at the same time, together with his "tragedy" and all the commonplace utterances voiced for more than a century about this composer who must be recognized as one of the world's greatest musical geniuses. Like many other musicians, I was disgusted by this intellectual and sentimental attitude, which had little to do with serious musical appreciation. This deplorable pedagogy did not fail in its result. It alienated me from Beethoven for many years.[16]

Stravinsky then proceeded to emphasize his veneration for the master and his loathing of the "sociologists who have suddenly become musicographers" and who knew nothing of his music but adopted him as a patron saint of whatever cause.

Thus, in light of the persistence of the Beethoven issue from the time of his youth through the early war years in France, Stravinsky's citation of the Beethoven Fifth in his "Souvenir d'une marche boche" is clearly weighted. It is evident that his reference was less a "pointed jab" at Beethoven's music *per se* than a mocking diatribe against the historic critical response and the indiscriminate uses to which Beethoven's music had been and was then being put. In fact, when Stravinsky later turned to conducting, his admiration for the master became increasingly apparent: "But my great conducting ambitions, I am afraid, will never be realized: the first four symphonies and the eighth of Beethoven, and, in opera, *Fidelio*."[17] He never expressed such feelings for the heavier Fifth Symphony, however, which along with the Ninth Symphony was one of the wartime favorites. Stravinsky's citation of the former in his little "Souvenir" was no doubt obliquely directed at correcting current associations of profundity and weight with value in music.

The personal sentiment behind Stravinsky's march need not be doubted. This is made especially clear in a letter solicited from Stravinsky by Rolland in September 1914.

> *Mon cher confrère!* I hasten to answer your appeal for a protest against the barbarism of the German armies. But is "barbarism" the right

word? What is a barbarian? It seems to me that by definition he is someone belonging to a new or different conception of culture than our own; and though this culture might be radically different or anti-thetical to ours we do not for that reason deny its value, or the possibility that this value might be greater than our own.

But the present Germany cannot be considered as a manifestation of "new culture." Germany, as a country, belongs to the old world, and the culture of the country is as old as that of the other nations of Western Europe. However, a nation which in time of peace erects a series of monuments such as those of the Siegesallee in Berlin and which, in time of war, sends her armies to destroy a city like Louvain and a cathedral like Rheims is not barbarian in the proper sense nor civilized in any sense. If "renewal" is what Germany really seeks, she might better start at home with her Berlin monuments. It is the highest common interest of all those peoples who still feel the need to breathe the air of their ancient culture to put themselves on the sides of the enemies of the present Germany, and to flee forever the unbearable spirit of this colossal, obese, and morally putrefying Germania.[18]

"Souvenir d'une marche boche" might not be a masterpiece for the ages, but neither is it merely a flippant caricature or a paradigmatic rejection of European Primitivism in favor of the cultural roots of Russian music in Eurasian folk culture.[19] Rather it is meant to burlesque the crassness of German militarism, not Germany's rich traditions that served as a constant topic in the culture wars of the day. Cocteau, for example, called for a "French art for Frenchmen" and went so far as to refuse a German brand of toothpaste, but he also acknowledged that to be deprived of the music of Beethoven and Schubert was unthinkable.[20]

By the time of his Piano Sonata of 1924 Stravinsky was also seeking an accommodation, and he later described the ornamental style of the second movement of his own sonata as "Beethoven frisé"—a type of filigree that can be spotted in various late sonatas of the master. Even more pointedly, a comparison of the opening of the final movement of Stravinsky's sonata with the second movement of Beethoven's Piano Sonata op. 54 leaves little doubt that the model was specific. A considerable amount of anti-Beethoven talk still lay ahead, however. In one of the last interviews of his life, a time in which he was increasingly drawn to a study of the late Beethoven string quartets, Stravinsky was still railing against the weaknesses of Beethoven's Fifth Symphony: "After the first movement," he said, "the symphony is a little hard to take." And of the finale of the Ninth Symphony he commented that "some of the music is very banal—the last Prestissimo, for one passage, and, for another, the first full-orchestra version of the theme, which is German-band music of the *Kaisermarsch* class."[21]

The surface slightness, not to be confused with sincerity of purpose, of many of the contributions to Edith Wharton's *Book of the Homeless*— Stravinsky's included—can hardly go unnoticed, and no one better summed up the dilemma of the artist when faced with such a task than William Butler Yeats. His trenchant offering for Wharton's collection began, "I think it better that at times like these / We poets keep our mouths shut." Whatever our temptation to dismiss Stravinsky's little march out of hand, the work not only forces a review of the ambivalence of the composer's ongoing relation to Beethoven—from youth to old age—but also signals the fact that Stravinsky's feelings about *Kultur* had intensified dramatically between December 1914 (the date of the *Three Easy Pieces*) and September 1915.

RENARD AND A SOLDIER'S TALE

In June 1918 the critic Jacques Rivière called Stravinsky a "one-man Russian front . . . forcing Germany to the rear."[22] What could Rivière have meant by this? Substantial or fleeting subtexts reflective of Stravinsky's wartime dislocation from Russia and France beckon in numerous pieces, ranging from the last of the *Quatre chants russes* (1918–1919)—with its "prevailing mood of nostalgia and homesickness"[23]—to a potential generalized invocation of the *coq gaulois*, Chanteclaire, in the struggle between the Cock and the Fox in *Renard* (1915–1916). If the details of Stravinsky's libretto in *Renard* were obscured by a collage of Russian folk conventions unfamiliar to Western Europeans,[24] the basic outline of the story was familiar enough. This fact more than anything else must have encouraged audiences at the time to bypass its Russian pedigree altogether and see in the Cock the emblem of France, repeatedly tricked by the Fox into fatally dropping its guard.

Indeed, Chanticleer was invoked in numerous contexts throughout the war, and nowhere more proudly than in Raoul Dufy's *La fin de la grande guerre*,[25] which made a personal offering in the spirit of the *image d'Epinal* with the quadruple symbols of a German eagle crushed beneath the cock's claws and the figure of Joan of Arc rising from the ashes of Rheims cathedral (fig. 18). Dufy's Chanteclaire intones a hymn of victory to the tune of the "Wandering Jew" (marked "Sur l'air du Juif Errant" in the upper left-hand corner), whose sixteen stanzas are provided complete in the border. The first two stanzas read: "Is there anything more sad and horrendous on

Figure 18.   Raoul Dufy, *La fin de la Grande Guerre,* 1915. Reproduced in *Le mot,* 6 March 1915. (© 2002 ARS New York/ADAGP Paris.)

earth than the terrible misery of France and Belgium? Each day the sun sets in blood. The family fathers, the men twenty years of age, the beautiful young girls, and the small children, each day fodder for the devouring wolves."[26]

A national loan subscription drive in 1915 similarly invoked the *coq d'or* as the symbol of French defense (fig. 19), as did Raymond Duchamp-Villon with his *Rooster (The Gallic Cock)* of 1916. Cocteau perpetuated the tradition in the title of his highly nationalistic *Le coq et l'arlequin* of 1918, as did Pablo Picasso with his line figure of a *coq* that graced its cover.[27] So did Cocteau's broadsheet, *Le coq,* of 1920, which not only denounced late-nineteenth-century German music but also boldly branded French Impressionism as its direct heir.[28]

In light of the fact that the story of Renard had even more numerous and ancient antecedents, dating at least as far back as Chaucer's "Chanticleer and the Fox" in *The Nun's Priest's Tale* and continuing through later adaptations by Goethe, the Grimm brothers, Charles Perrault, and Jean de La Fontaine, the invitation to re-read Stravinsky's entertainment was virtually unavoidable. Speaking of his contemporaneous *Histoire du soldat* in later years, Stravinsky pointedly claimed that "*our* soldier, in 1918, was

Figure 19. Jules Abel Faivre, "For France Pour Out Your Money," poster for a loan subscription drive, about 1915.

very definitely understood to be the victim of the then world conflict, despite the neutrality of the play in other respects." He then went on to assert that "*Histoire du soldat* remains my one stage work with a contemporary reference."[29] Nevertheless, it is important to note that the appeal of Renard for the war period was made clear in numerous sources beyond the French ones, ranging from Russian popular entertainment to British war poetry.

Russian wartime circus entertainments, for example, found acrobats, another prominent feature of *Renard,* joining in the wave of patriotic pronouncements.[30] And Anatolii Durov, one of the most famous Russian clowns of the period, loosed a chaotic menagerie of animals as parallels to the real war in his *War of the Animals* of 1915, which played at Petrograd's Circus Ciniselli. This had been based upon a film that Durov had made in late 1914 called *Napoleon Reversed,* which cast the Kaiser (the new Napoleon) as a monkey, "rats as German soldiers, foxes as European diplomats, and pigs as the German General Staff."[31] In one scene the pigs await news of victory but receive instead a message that the Gallic cockerel has annihilated the German army; in another, an enemy spy cast as a fox sets the city on fire. The invocation of Chanticleer and the notion of the spy masquerading as a fox thus not only parallels Stravinsky's *Renard* but is in tune with the moral judgments made shortly thereafter by Siegfried Sassoon in a poem, "Reynardism Revisited."[32]

The opening lines of Stravinsky's text, which follow an introductory march, reveal a similar mixture of barnyard and deadly humor:

> Chuck, chuck, chuck, chuck, chuck, chuck-a-dah, chuck-a-dah
> I'm the king of my yard, chuck-a-dah
> I with my spurs will cut him.
> I with my knife will cut him.
> Beat him black and blue,
> Then stick a knife in him too.[33]

We can conclude that Stravinsky's brash and highly oblique entertainment, which the composer claimed was "not so much satire as gentle mockery and 'good fun,'"[34] borrows numerous features from popular spectacles current at the time that involved the masquerading enemy.[35]

Even more pertinent is the fact that Switzerland was infested at this time with "German agents working, in agreement with Lenin, to undermine the morale of the Russian colony."[36] The Russians were divided into two camps: the defeatists and Germanophiles on the one hand and the pro-Allies, which included Stravinsky, on the other. The notion of Germans spying on the Russians in Switzerland was a reverse counterpart to a series of sensationalized press reports released in Germany at the beginning of August 1914 stating that "according to absolutely reliable reports, large numbers of Russian officers and agents are travelling through our country."[37]

The result was a genuine "spy scare," which paradoxically enough had been instigated by the German government. People were encouraged to be on the lookout for suspicious individuals and report them to the police, and newspapers were quick to fan the blaze. Among the most alarming stories was one in the Munich press that reported that a worker had heard a rumor that two men disguised as nuns had just been arrested. Noticing that the face of a nun he happened to see on the street was covered and that the nun's gait seemed excessively large for a woman, he began to chase her. The nun began to walk faster while a crowd of children shouted "A spy, a spy!" The nun barely managed to escape, running into a nearby house just as a policeman arrived on the scene. Crowds began to fill the streets shouting, "Get him out! Smash his skull in! Slit his throat!"[38] The opening lines of *Renard* come quickly to mind.

Whether Stravinsky intended any anticlerical references in the initial episode of *Renard*—when the Fox appears in a nun's disguise and offers absolution to lure the Cock (fig. 20)—Stravinsky's awareness of these German "spy scares" can virtually be taken for granted. Stravinsky's "gentle mockery and good fun" could also easily have involved awareness of the routine ambivalence and opportunism of the Church with regard to the war as well as the commonly leveled charge that priests frequently hid behind their clerical collars to avoid conscription. Such a reading would have been further encouraged by the Fox's unctuous and false piety, which is served up in a "monklike chant," redolent of orthodox Church Slavonic, when the fox first encounters the Cock: "Greetings, my little red-head beauty / Put aside your pride and come down, sir. / Tell me all your sins. . . . I can't tell you what I've suffered. / But now, dearest boy, I shall give you absolution."[39]

The main reason behind Stravinsky's failure to mention *Renard* as a work with a wartime reference is undoubtedly traceable to the fact that while it had been composed in 1915–1916 as a commission by the Princesse Edmond de Polignac and had been published as early as 1917, the work's premiere at the Paris Opéra was delayed until 1922, by which time the war was over.[40] Even though *Renard* was one of Stravinsky's most thoroughly Russian compositions, exhibiting scant evidence of an impending turn to Neoclassicism beyond its chamber scoring, it is significant that between the composition of *Renard* and its premiere Stravinsky composed his ballet *Pulcinella* (1919–1920).[41] By turning to commedia dell'arte Stravinsky and Picasso flagrantly heralded their personal subscription to a new Latin-based classicism independent of the German stem. Many years later Stravinsky offered another perspective for his new orientation in a remark concerning his native St. Petersburg: "I have often considered that the fact of my birth and upbringing in a Neo-Italian rather than a purely Slavic, or Oriental city must be partly, and profoundly, responsible for the cultural direction of my later life."[42]

Both *Renard* and the immediately following *Histoire du soldat* are

Figure 20.   Mikhail Larionov, "Fox Disguised as Nun," 1922.
Costume design for Stravinsky's *Renard*. (© 2002 ARS New
York/ADAGP Paris.)

morality tales with a pervasive ambiguity. *Renard*'s debut was delayed, but
Histoire du soldat received a timely premiere in Lausanne on 28 September 1918. Relying upon his experience with masquerade in the former
work,[43] Stravinsky described the figure of the Devil in *Histoire* as "the
diabolus of Christianity, a person, as always in Russian popular literature,
though a person of many disguises." Tellingly, Stravinsky's invocation of
the Lutheran chorale "Ein' feste Burg" near the end of the work introduced
a potentially ambivalent moral symbol related to the conflict with Germany—a factor already recognized by Debussy in the middle movement

of *En blanc et noir,* whose final movement was dedicated to Stravinsky. Indeed, the moral confusion that permeates the conclusion of *Histoire* is not to be resolved, and Stravinsky's distorted version of Luther's hymn reflects nothing so much as the chaotic moral state of affairs throughout the war period.

Morality, however, is never a straightforward issue and can be judged from multiple angles, as Meyerbeer *(Les Huguenots),* Debussy *(En blanc et noir),* and Busoni *(Doktor Faust)* had already or would soon demonstrate in their invocation of "Ein' feste Burg," and as anyone who listened at the time to Romain Rolland or Leon Trotsky sorely realized. To put it another way, in war all parties are convinced that they are on the side of right and are even known to adopt the symbols of the opposition in their campaigns. Stravinsky arguably intended his music to endorse ambiguity at both the symbolic and constructive levels. It was an attitude well known during World War I in the Russian circus, where variant readings of patriotism were purposefully projected in vague and ambiguous terms.[44]

When Stravinsky turned to writing *Histoire du soldat* in 1918 he determined that the march could again serve as an organizing factor. Not only does *Renard* open and close with a march, but in March 1915, Stravinsky had written an arrangement for twelve instruments, never published, of the opening march from *Three Easy Pieces,* in what was clearly a preparation for composing *Histoire du soldat.*[45] Other factors also surfaced as Stravinsky began to shape his new theater piece. In the penultimate scene the King offers his sick daughter's hand in marriage to whomever succeeds in curing her. At this point the Soldier joins the Devil, now disguised as a virtuoso violinist, in a game of cards. The Soldier wins (actually by losing the fortune that the Devil's book had brought him and thus reclaiming his soul), recovers his old fiddle, which he had previously lost to the Devil, and restores the Princess to health in a trio of dances, "Tango," "Waltz," and "Ragtime." Both the contest to control the violin, whose magical powers are clearly implicit, and the introduction of a game of cards to vanquish the Devil are symbolic and rooted in Russian gypsy culture. The tradition of the "magic violin" can be traced to a "distinct tradition of the [Russian] Silver Age," and it encouraged Taruskin to view *Histoire du soldat* "as a parable of the Russian Revolution as viewed from afar and with dismay by a Stravinsky who had greeted the events of February 1917 as a liberation, only to see that brief interlude of freedom dashed by a coup."[46] The card game is also more than passingly akin to Velemir Khlebnikov's concurrent and fatal attraction to numerology and theories of destiny in war,[47] and it resonated in numerous paintings of the war period. This is especially evident in the armor-clad soldiers in Fernand Léger's *The Card Game* of 1917 and the crippled bodies in Otto Dix's *The Skat Players* of 1920, where the horrors of war are refracted through the metaphor of a card game.[48]

Although it is clear that various Russian and European themes found their way into *Histoire du soldat,* some have questioned Stravinsky's later claim that *Histoire* "was influenced by a very important event in my life at that time, the discovery of American jazz."[49] The lead instrument's language, for example, has been argued to be more nearly akin to a gypsy *verbunkos* style of fiddle playing than to a jazz violin, which had not yet been introduced in America. And the whole has been held to be a conflation of the *pasodoble* players (cornet, trombone, bassoon) Stravinsky had heard in Seville during Holy Week of 1916, of Geneva wartime restaurant bands (string instruments plus cimbalom), and of the East European village band of the Jewish variety known as klezmer, whose standard quartet of violin, double bass, clarinet, and drums was frequently expanded to include a trumpet and/or a trombone.[50] Odd assortments of winds, strings, and percussion had been finding their way into Paris music-hall entertainments for some time, however, and even in the stage works of Erik Satie from 1913, like *Le piège de la Méduse* (given a private reading at composer Alexis Roland-Manuel's flat) and *Les pantins dansent* (The Puppets Dance) of the same year.[51] Although Stravinsky specifically denied knowledge of the first of these Satie pieces, it is clear that he had an odd assortment of potential models, and all can fairly be judged to have played a part.

At least as interesting as the clarification of the ensemble's potential pedigree, however, is the question of why Stravinsky would have wanted to make a claim for "jazz" in this piece in the first place. Admittedly, its presence may be limited to the little dance labeled "Ragtime," yet even here the essential duple metric ostinato is challenged early on by the insertion of a 3/8 bar, which, according to Taruskin, "effectively derails [jazz's] all-important downbeat pattern."[52] Stravinsky had created a similar and intentional confusion, however, by departing from the duple metrics expected of a march with the introduction of a single 3/4 measure in the opening "Soldier's March."[53] Despite this metric tampering, the perception of the piece as a march is in no danger of being overturned. While the dogged persistence of both melodic figure and ostinato makes priority of one over the other difficult to claim, the ambivalence as well as the periodic "coming together" led Taruskin to tag such manipulations as a "game"[54] (a category we have already explored). But jazz, too, is capable of exploiting the bar line from various angles, and it traditionally looked to multiple ethnic sources, high and low, as a jumping-off point. Finally,

Stravinsky suggested that the source for the trumpet-trombone tune at the beginning of the "Soldier's March" was probably the French song "Marietta."[55] So much for ethnic purity.

The background for the "Tango" also includes a recent proclamation by the pope, and subsequently the archbishop of Paris, that the tango was lascivious and was to be avoided. Perhaps even more pertinent for *Histoire* was the appearance of a "Tango perpétuel" in Satie's *Sports et divertissements* (1914), where the composer included a notice that "the Devil dances the tango when he wants to cool off."[56] The tactic of cultural interplay, therefore, can be correctly linked to a consortium of sponsoring agencies, not least of which was the intercultural Cubist game with which Stravinsky was thoroughly familiar.[57]

However slight the jazz component in *Histoire du soldat* may be, Stravinsky's recognition of the recent American presence in the war—and this no doubt was the primary factor behind the use of a "Ragtime" as the final curative dance for the ailing Princess—is further alluded to in another work written around the same time, his *Ragtime for Eleven Instruments*. It is dated 10 November 1918, the morning of the German surrender, and it carries the inscription "Jour de la délivrance. Messieurs les Allemands ont capitulé." The piece is marked throughout by a rigorous observance of ragtime's regularized ostinato. A third related piece, called "Piano Rag," from 1919, underscores Stravinsky's preoccupation with the new American style and its relation to unfolding world events. Dated "Morges, 1919, 28 juin à midi," it carries the telling penciled commentary: "The bells of the church tolled at noon; at 3 o'clock I heard the cannons at the front which thunderingly announced the signing of the peace at Versailles."[58] Here the organizing properties of a ragtime ostinato are largely abandoned in a search for an imagined improvisatory style that frequently forsakes all metric barring whatsoever.

Clearly none of these pieces are to be judged against the standards of any kind of rag, but their original sponsorship—regardless of liberties, distortions, or faded points of departure—cannot be in question. Stravinsky had shown his alertness to American popular musical trends as early as 1904 when at a gathering of Rimsky-Korsakov's pupils he purportedly scandalized Rimsky's wife by demonstrating the steps of the cakewalk.[59] Then, in the period from 1917 through 1919, a time during which he was invested in testing his Russianness as never before, Stravinsky thrice acknowledged the crucial assistance of the United States in achieving final victory by writing a joyous, improvisatory, free-wheeling, totally imaginary caper *à l'américaine*. Yet, as with Ravel's later adaptations of American jazz in what he called a "French manner," so here the Russian element prevailed.

Understandably, the Western Front engaged only part of Stravinsky's psyche during the war years. For in 1917 a revolution broke out in the composer's native Russia, a revolution for which he originally held high hopes. At the same time, it also signaled the collapse of Russia's intervention in the war in Western Europe, a turn of events that caused widespread alarm among the Allied powers. Although Stravinsky's euphoria later dissipated in the wake of the second, Bolshevik, revolution, his initial enthusiasm was evident in his response to an invitation by Diaghilev to compose a new national anthem for an upcoming concert. Understanding that "Long Live the Tsar" was no longer a possibility, Diaghilev's request for a suggestion of a preferred tune brought a telegram from the Russian legislator Rodzianko, who specified "The Song of the Volga Boatmen."[60] On 8 April Stravinsky composed a harmonization for the piece, whose orchestration he dictated to Ansermet, after which Picasso daubed a red banner at the head of the manuscript.

The work was premiered in Rome on 12 April alongside a Futurist presentation of Stravinsky's early *Fireworks* as a ballet of colored lights. The stage set by the Futurist Giacomo Balla, which betrayed distinct affinities with *Patriotic Hymn,* one of his recent paintings, updated Stravinsky's composition and turned it into a contemporary celebration of nationalist fervor.[61] On 11 May 1917 at the Théâtre Châtelet in Paris Stravinsky's new anthem and "La Marseillaise" introduced a performance of *Firebird.* For the first time in France a large red flag hung in full view, and murmurs spread through the auditorium along with admonitions that Stravinsky's offering would never be accepted in St. Petersburg.[62]

Stravinsky's harmonization of "The Song of the Volga Boatmen" has been traced in part to a setting that Balakirev first published in 1866,[63] but the new setting must also have been influenced by Stravinsky's memory of Glazunov's earlier elaboration of it in his symphonic poem *Stenka Razin* (1885), a work that had been performed in Paris as early as the International Exhibition of 1889.[64] Despite the familiarity of the melody and the official sponsorship, the decidedly leaden "Hymn to the New Russia," as Stravinsky titled it, was understandably deemed inappropriate not only because of the tune's association with an era of serfdom in the Old Russia but also because of its decidedly pessimistic sound.[65] On a personal level the

Russian Revolution was also a disaster for Stravinsky. As Robert Craft stated, "It separated him from relatives and friends—forever, in some instances—as well as from his entire formative world. He lost home, citizenship, property, sources of income, manuscripts, libraries, personal possessions, and even the copyright protection for his works. Moreover, it was no longer feasible for him to compose music using his native language."[66]

The Great War came to an end almost simultaneously with the completion of *Histoire du soldat*, although the Russian Revolution was to drag on until 1920. One more war page remained to be written by Stravinsky, however, and once again it was less trivial and more telling than its brevity might suggest. On New Year's Day 1919, seven weeks following the signing of the Armistice, Stravinsky arranged "La Marseillaise" for solo violin. The work has been somewhat loosely described as a patriotic reflection of the Franco-Russian Alliance. Never published, it was relegated to a forgotten footnote in the history of pieces for violin written by Stravinsky at this time for the violinist Paul Kochanski, an association that foreshadowed his later collaboration with Samuel Dushkin.

Why, however, would Stravinsky have set "La Marseillaise" for solo violin—surely not the most obvious choice for a national anthem? There is no chorus to recite the text, no brass choir to invoke solemnity of purpose. Yet, in light of Stravinsky's most recently completed opus, *Histoire du soldat*, there can be little misunderstanding of the instrumental choice. In *Histoire* the Soldier uses the violin as a means of curing the Princess, and the Devil, once he regains it, uses its magic to conquer the soldier. In the closing pages of the score, captioned "Triumphant March of the Devil," the symbolism takes another turn: the music offers a graphic portrayal of the victory of the Devil over the Soldier, with the percussion representing the Devil and the violin the Soldier's soul. As Robert Craft has aptly described it, "the wind instruments and double bass gradually drop out and, after a few final splutters, the violin as well, leaving the percussion to conclude the drama alone."[67]

Thus, in *Histoire* the violin was employed as a vacillating symbol in the soldier's losing struggle with the Devil. In his new setting of "La Marseillaise" Stravinsky restored the violin's lost magic power and used it to celebrate the Allied victory over the forces of evil. The simplicity of the setting, which left the tune's melodic, metric, and rhythmic dimensions largely unaltered, displayed nothing so much as unaffected gratitude for the end of the conflict and sentiment for the country that had played host to and sponsored the composer's rise to international fame. By this time Stravinsky's hopes for the Russian Revolution had been completely dashed, and his setting of the French national anthem confirmed, among other things, that he had found a new spiritual home, however temporary. As composer Arthur Lourié later suggested, at this juncture Stravinsky had become a composer of "universal" significance precisely because he had been able to free himself of the European component in his seemingly national style. "For the first time," said Lourié, "Russian music lost its 'provincial,' 'exotic' quality." It had become "a thing of capital significance, at the very helm of world music."[68] Yet, in the immediate years ahead some critics began to charge that Stravinsky's developing language, increasingly branded as Neoclassicist, was arbitrary, superficial, and incapable of serving a virile French music of the future.[69]

9 Church, State, and Schola

Upon the last page of his great work, Rolland relates the well-known legend of St. Christopher. The ferryman was roused at night by a little boy who wished to be carried across the stream. With a smile the good-natured giant shouldered the light burden. But as he strode through the water the weight he was carrying grew heavy and heavier, until he felt he was about to sink in the river. Mustering all his strength, he continued on his way. When he reached the other shore, gasping for breath, the man recognized that he had been carrying the entire meaning of the world. Hence his name, Christophorus.

Stefan Zweig, *Romain Rolland*

Christopher, bearer of Christ, who had borne the symbolic weight of Rolland's *Jean-Christophe*, surfaced once again in Wharton's *Book of the Homeless* with a single-page excerpt from d'Indy's recently completed *La légende de Saint-Christophe* for chorus and orchestra. The score had been finished by the end of 1913, but the orchestration took the better part of another two years, and the work was not performed at the Opéra until 1921.

D'Indy was one of the most prominent pedagogical and philosophical forces in musical France and the only composer besides Stravinsky to be represented in Wharton's collection. D'Indy's inclusion in the volume is hardly a mystery. From the beginning of 1915 Wharton, at the instigation of d'Indy, arranged concerts with the express purpose of aiding musicians who were out of work because of wartime curtailments. The series was inaugurated with a vocal recital that was held in Wharton's apartment on 31 December 1914; d'Indy was the accompanist.

Wharton's second thoughts on the whole matter were relayed to Mary Berenson, wife of the art connoisseur, in a letter of 12 January 1915: "I vaguely thought one had only to 'throw open one's doors,' as aristocratic hostesses do in fiction. Oh, my! I'd rather write a three-volume novel than do it again. . . . However, it's the only chance of hearing any really good music this winter, and we *are* hearing it."[1]

Wharton had every reason to express her delight in the music, especially in light of the suspension of virtually all musical activity in Paris during the Battle of the Marne. This first and most serious threat to Paris of the entire war began on 5 September 1914 and lasted four days. When it was over the Germans had retreated the some sixty miles they had gained and had been pushed back across the Marne. In time, Paris attempted to reestablish some semblance of normal life with the implementation of a war charity tax and a series of *matinées nationales* inaugurated on 29 November. It featured an ensemble made up of members from the Colonne and Lamoureux orchestras—a "holy alliance" prompted by the war—and singing of the national anthems of the Allied nations. Fauré and d'Indy appeared with mezzo-soprano Claire Croiza in performances chiefly of excerpts from works by Franck, Massenet, Bizet, Saint-Saëns, and Fauré. Gradually the musicians performing in the *matinées* undertook more extended pieces, including the *Symphonie française* by Dubois, Berlioz's *Symphonie fantastique*, Rimsky-Korsakov's *Sheherazade*, and Stravinsky's *Petrushka*. Music by German composers was understandably absent.[2]

Claire Croiza, who had debuted in 1908 as Delilah in Saint-Saëns's opera and who by 1915 had established herself as one of the most successful champions of the *mélodies* of Debussy, Fauré, and Duparc, also appeared at Wharton's afternoon concerts, as did Lucien Capet, the teacher of many successful musicians, including Arthur Honegger. Capet, a violinist, was a renowned soloist and the leader of a succession of quartets who frequently played the Beethoven cycle. In 1911 he had played at the Beethoven Festival at Bonn with a group that included Henri and Marcel Casadesus. Marcel, the cellist and an antiquarian, had been killed in action on 31 October 1914,[3] and Capet was thus obliged to play without his colleagues. The cachet of the performing artists notwithstanding, Wharton began to tire of managing the details for the concerts, which included printing the programs and arranging for the refreshments. After a half-dozen well-attended *matinées* she handed the project over to friends, whom she encouraged to promote concerts for the refugee hostels at the elegant Ritz Hotel, where larger audiences could be accommodated and more money taken in.[4]

VETERAN, MONARCHIST, CLASSICIST

Born in 1851, d'Indy was barely of age for the Franco-Prussian War of 1870–1871. Yet he had served gallantly in the defense of Paris as a member of the 105th Battalion of the National Guard, whose history of the war years he wrote and published in 1872.[5] D'Indy also wrote the "Marche du 76ème régiment d'infanterie" for military band in 1903, whose title recalled his personal experiences in the conflict, and even earlier he had alluded to his youthful military encounter in the final movement of his most popular work, the *Symphonie sur un chant montagnard français* (Symphony on a French Mountain Air), completed in 1886. Its central folk tune gradually settles in over a march ostinato and accompanying fanfares, and in this combination of native folk repertoires and ominous march rhythms d'Indy conveyed not so much the threat of potential invasion as his intense feelings for his native France and the necessity of vigilance and preparedness.

D'Indy's concerns accorded with the French view, still prevalent in 1914, that the war was by definition motivated less by hawkish nationalism than by defensive patriotism. The absence of the former was something that had been noted early on by the government, which recognized the need for official and unofficial propaganda to rouse the spirit of citizenry and soldiers alike.[6] D'Indy's monarchist opposition to the Third Republic, which escalated during the Dreyfus Affair, was grounded in his sense of loyalty to the nation and its army and not to the political state. Henceforth, d'Indy considered his own political and professional goals as one and the same.[7]

Early evidence of d'Indy's classicist bent had been manifested in a book published in 1899 titled *De Bach à Beethoven*. Here he reflected an attitude that had been struck in 1896 with the founding of the Schola Cantorum, where folksong and plainchant were paired with Beethoven's symphonies as the foundation of a musical education.[8] An emphasis that transcended the practical training of the musician, typical of the state-run Conservatoire National Supérieur de Musique, reflected d'Indy's belief in a thorough study of the history of music. The prominence accorded plainchant and Renaissance polyphony was given a prestigious boost with the issuance of the famous *Motu proprio* of 1903, in which Pope Pius X laid down principles concerning music that corresponded almost exactly to those already operative at the Schola. The introduction of public education in France and the elimination of religious training in the schools at precisely this time had so sorely tried Catholics that d'Indy obviously took private pleasure in noting this agreement.

D'Indy's beliefs were set out in a number of publications, including his *Cours de composition musicale* (published 1903–1950), and were reinforced in biographies of Franck (1906) and Beethoven (1911–1913) that paralleled Rolland's devotion to these two figures even as they were in part intended to be a refutation of them. D'Indy's antiquarian interests were similarly reflected not only in his editions of operas by Monteverdi (*Orfeo, Poppea,* and *Ulisse,* all in 1904) and Rameau (*Hippolyte et Aricie,* 1902;

Dardanus, 1905; and *Zaïs*, 1911) but also in his revival performances of these works. It is not too much to insist that the continuing twentieth-century infatuation with Monteverdi's operas and the periodic interest in Rameau's stage works began with d'Indy.

D'Indy's antiquarianism was also matched by a pronounced antipathy to modernism in any guise, and in his role as sometime critic for the *Revue musicale* he pointedly pronounced Stravinsky's recently premiered *Le sacre du printemps* as "the delight of the esthetes, a masterpiece according to the rites of the little modernist school." He did allow that it was a "work of great rhythmic, if not musical, interest" and that it signaled "a true artistic temperament." But a little later he wrote to one of his friends, "I would hope it [*La légende de Saint-Christophe*] to be a good, solid ensemble, not like Stravinsky's, which I find decidedly poorly orchestrated."[9] Thus, d'Indy's conservative values in politics and religion, which became increasingly chauvinistic in the period immediately before World War I, were matched by an equally conservative view in music. His battle against the "moderns" of the period extended beyond Stravinsky to disapproval even of Ravel and eventually of the group of young composers known as Les Six, with the exception of Honegger, who had studied conducting with him.

THE LEGEND OF ST. CHRISTOPHER

The higher ranks in the French army and navy were typically held by Catholics, and the Republicans linked militarism with clericism for this reason. D'Indy's fervent Catholicism and his faith in the army served as the basis for his nationalistic and social views, and *La légende de Saint-Christophe*, which was premiered in the period immediately following the Armistice, mirrored not only d'Indy's personal wartime loyalties and prejudices but also those of a significant portion of conservative, neo-royalist, Catholic society as well.

D'Indy's *Saint-Christophe* gave concrete evidence of the ongoing interaction between the forces of French national politics and the world of music. The work begins as the young Christopher goes into the world in search of the strongest master so that he can serve him. His first adventure takes him to Babylon and the Queen of Love, who plays the perfect Herodias in enlisting his service; the second meeting is with the King of Gold, who believes only in the power of money—a stereotypical reference to Jews. The second scene shows Christopher in the service of the King of Gold, who continues to preach the power of money as the strongest force in the universe, creating envy, inciting crime, and preaching injustice in the name of justice. The Prince of Evil, whom the King of Gold fears above all others and to whom he has sworn an oath of loyalty, arrives. The latter offers Christopher all his gold if he will protect him, and Christopher in turn announces his loyalty to him.

Act 1, scene 3, which contains the excerpt d'Indy offered to Wharton's wartime anthology, concludes with a warning from the deceived people, who shout "War, war to our superiors, to our master; hatred to the powerful, to kings, to priests. Destroy them all!" A crowd of soldiers in the Army of Evil cries "Hatred, hatred to Christ, to Charity. May the partisans of Love die on the cross like Christ their master! To the cross, to the cross." The voice of a child is heard in the distance: "O Holy Cross, our only hope." It has been noted that throughout the scene, "stylistic features of Debussy and Stravinsky are ruthlessly parodied," and later Christopher's baptism and the conversion of the Queen of Pleasure are awash in the magic fire music of *Die Walkure*.[10]

For *The Book of the Homeless* d'Indy offered an autograph of a choral excerpt from this scene, not yet published at the time, which begins with the following words of the Historian:

> And during the long years, Christopher served the Spirit of Darkness, and, little by little, evil seized his heart. He used its force to oppress the weak and to wage war against divine works. But he was chosen by God, a miracle saved him from eternal damnation, and the Cross revealed to him the power of Love.[11]

The Historian is immediately answered by a *choeur récitant*, and it is the opening of this passage that d'Indy offered to Wharton.

> O Holy Cross, which carries the greetings of the World; Your immortal strength stops the fisherman on the route of evil. And your spell of enchantment reveals to him the Heavens, his future home.[12]

It is hard to imagine two more contrasting pieces than Stravinsky's caricature march and d'Indy's solemn chorus, which stand juxtaposed in Wharton's anthology. Yet while the subtext of d'Indy's larger work may be somewhat more subtle than Stravinsky's, it is far from ambivalent: the Holy Cross—a powerful force—is characterized as possessing an "immortal strength" well suited for stopping evil and promising eternal life. The appropriateness of such sentiments in a war anthology could hardly be argued, especially in light of the fact that the war of the Allied Nations was seen in many quarters as a war of the church: loyalty to the principles of the church, whether Protestant or Catholic, and patriotism were held to be the same. This perspective was reiterated in pulpits throughout the Continent, in England, and later in the United States in sometimes startling fashion.

Nonetheless, the role of the Catholic Church in France during the war is more complex than such a summary judgement would suggest.[13] That d'Indy's *Saint-Christophe* is also anti-republican and anti-Semitic may not be obvious in the excerpts quoted here, but its message is clear from details of the score and a prefatory booklet. "Understand that I'm not making any actual allusions," d'Indy protested, "and that the characters are not called Dreyfus, Reinach, nor even Combes . . . that would do them too much honour." The aim, instead, was to trace the corrupting influence of the Judeo-Dreyfusard clique: "'Pride'—'pleasure'—'money'—in conflict with *les fleurs du bien* = 'faith'—'hope'—'charity'."[14] D'Indy's stance need have surprised no one, for as early as 1900 he had recorded his sentiments with startling candor.

> My dear friends, do not mistake that which we ought to seek in our works of art. It is not profit. Leave this trade to the too numerous semites who encumber music, since it is susceptible to becoming a business. It is not even for personal glory, an ephemeral and unimportant result. No, we ought to aim higher, we ought to see farther. The true goal of art is to teach, to elevate gradually the spirit of humanity, and, in a word, to "serve," in its sublime sense: "dienen"—that which Wagner put into the mouth of the repentant Kundry in Act 3 of Parsifal.[15]

To serve, in this instance, meant to serve France and especially the Catholic hope of a restored Church at the center of the nation's government. How odd, though, that d'Indy would call upon a moral dictum of Wagner, a composer who in the eyes of many at the time symbolized German triumphalism.

D'Indy candidly called his work a *"drame anti-juif"* in a letter of 1903, at the time he first conceived La légende de Saint-Christophe,[16] and his Catholic orientation was compellingly signaled by the adoption of the idea of a medieval mystery play instead of an opera. Building upon the experience gained in writing L'étranger, an opera devoted to themes of Christian benevolence, which had premiered in Brussels in 1903 and was much admired by Debussy,[17] he now hoped to contrast the "nauseous" influence of the "Judeo-Dreyfusard" values of lust and avarice presented in the first act with ensuing demonstrations of Catholic faith, hope, and charity. To support this argument, d'Indy unified his drama structurally through the adoption of a system of Wagnerian leitmotifs, about a third of which are drawn from Gregorian chant.[18]

D'Indy was quick to point out the work's historical predecessors: "As in the ancient mystery plays or in the early oratorios of Animuccia and Carissimi, a historian recounts for the listener everything that would be unnecessary to present scenically but which is indispensable for the comprehension of the drama."[19] The work's division reflects the laws of the Trinity, with three acts and three scenes in each of them, and the music of the choruses betrays the composer's familiarity with Beethoven's *Missa solemnis* and even Debussy's recently premiered *Le martyre de Saint-Sébastien*—notwithstanding the fact that d'Indy had dubbed Debussy's oratorio "abominable music, as old-fashioned as it is pretentious."[20]

The work's indebtedness to Bach, specifically to the contrapuntal wonders of his Passions and the B minor Mass, which d'Indy revered, is also clear. For d'Indy this was the canonic German repertoire that had to be preserved in light of the recent inroads made by the Austro-German Expressionists. From 1905 on the Schola Cantorum had come under the relentless criticism of Émile Vuillermoz, who had appointed himself as the defender of the art of Fauré, Debussy, Ravel, and Casella. The attacks centered not only on the perceived doctrinaire and formalistic teaching of the Schola but especially on the emphasis it placed upon counterpoint. The latter was clearly a matter of record and had been highlighted by d'Indy's refusal to teach harmony at the Schola as a separate subject, as they did at the Conservatoire. There, it was charged, counterpoint was taught largely in terms of chord progression. But in the eyes of the Conservatoire the study of harmony could claim a national and scientific basis grounded in the Enlightenment and the figure of Rameau, whereas counterpoint held religious associations that were suspect for the curriculum of a republican institution.[21]

These opposing views sparked a war of harmony versus counterpoint that Vuillermoz launched in the *Mercure musical* with a further castigation of the Schola as a "hotbed of bigoted Catholicism, anti-Semitism, and extreme nationalism."[22] In addition to the sermonizing inherent in its subject matter, therefore, the highly contrapuntal excerpt that d'Indy chose for inclusion in Wharton's *Book of the Homeless* was a pointed reminder of his belief in the art of counterpoint as the basis of composition and its capacity to help define the essence of French values (ex. 8).

Immediately following the outbreak of hostilities d'Indy began the task of orchestrating *La légende de Saint-Christophe,* which he finished in the spring of 1915. He prepared numerous concerts, including the first of a

Example 8.   Vincent d'Indy, "O Sainte Croix," act 1, scene 3 of *La légende de Saint-Christophe*. (From Edith Wharton, *Book of the Homeless* [London: MacMillan & Co., 1916].)

series of *soirées musicales* for the benefit of war relief, for which occasion he formed an entirely female orchestra. He also directed programs for refugees at the Schola in November 1915, largely of French music but also of Bach's *St. John Passion,* and he made arrangements for a number of those who came from the destroyed music school at Rheims to be lodged at his school.[23]

PROBLEMS WITH BEETHOVEN, PROTESTANTS, AND JEWS

In 1915 d'Indy became involved in plans for an Édition nationale, published by Sénart, to replace the classic German editions of Griepenkerl, Tausig, and Bülow, which were now considered to be a "contradictory textual mess." The reigning French pianist, Alfred Cortot, was to investigate the keyboard works of Chopin and Schumann, the violinist Capet took charge of the string repertoire, and d'Indy reserved Beethoven for himself. Mozart's works, edited by Guy Ropartz, were judged by d'Indy to be sufficiently represented by two or three sonatas for violin and four sonatas for piano, "all the others being boring and without musical interest." *Pace* Ravel and Stravinsky! D'Indy laid out the principles that would govern the Édition nationale, placing special emphasis on the suppression of the too numerous and fanciful expression markings of the German editions, on practical prefaces, and on loyalty to the text of the original manuscripts. D'Indy also took part in another, similar edition, the Édition de musique classique, released by Rouart-Lerolle. He did not, however, participate in the Durand Édition classique, as one might have expected, because a controversy provoked by the publication of a booklet intended to explain the significance of *La légende de Saint-Christophe* obliged him to leave the prestigious publisher, who had issued the majority of his works composed before that time.[24]

D'Indy's devotion to Beethoven was evident in matters well beyond the preparation of editions or the programming of his music on the concerts that he conducted. Beethoven had been a pillar of d'Indy's instruction at the Schola and a model for young composers in his *Cours de composition.* During the period immediately leading up to the Great War, however, the movement spearheaded by Rolland that had turned Beethoven into something of a god and an apostle of the Revolution for the French now met with resistance from an unexpected source. The reaction came from the Schola itself, a stronghold of Catholic France, where a quite different view of Beethoven was being created. In 1913 d'Indy published a biography of Beethoven in which any summons to a personal religion inspired by

Beethoven was firmly resisted and countered by d'Indy's personal Catholic credo, to which, he held, Beethoven had firmly subscribed.[25] Edith Wharton was incensed, noting that d'Indy "demolishes practically the whole of the Beethoven legend, including the identity of the *Unsterbliche Geliebte*, and describes his life as a series of artistic and financial triumphs! True to French principles of book-making, he gives no authority whatever for these statements."[26]

D'Indy's love of Beethoven, which was genuine, found no greater expression than his reverence for the *Missa solemnis*, and he considered the attempts by musicologists such as Romain Rolland, J.-G. Prod'homme, Jean Chantavoine,[27] and even his old friend Julien Tiersot to turn it into a nondenominational Mass based upon Beethoven's ideals for humanity to be sheer impudence.[28] The symbolic power of this work for d'Indy, especially in wartime, was dramatized in a letter of 29 March 1918. A performance of the *Missa solemnis* at the Schola was interrupted by the sounding of a bombardment alert, forcing completion of the work a few days later. "How poignant it was," he reminisced, "to direct the *Dona nobis pacem*, this extraordinary masterpiece, in full battle! And during this very time they buried poor Debussy, whose career has been cut short."[29]

During the war d'Indy arranged conferences for the purpose of comparing French and German music,[30] and he wrote an article for the 27 April 1916 issue of the American journal *Musical Courier* that argued the need for Americans to liberate themselves from German domination. At the same time d'Indy opposed Saint-Saëns's search for an injunction against the performance of Wagner's music in France, an argument in which he was joined by Ravel and numerous others. On the political front, however, French President Poincaré's summons at the beginning of the conflict for a "sacred union" of all French peoples in the fight against the Germans had proven to be a fiction almost from the beginning of the conflict. It is true that Protestants and Catholics alike were capable of accord in their disavowal of Germany's religious institutions, even of the same denomination. André Spire even argued in his *Les Juifs et la guerre* of 1917 that, as anti-Semitism was essentially a German concept, all Jews should side with France. But many Catholics regarded Catholicism as the backbone of French patriotism, as Monseigneur Marbeau pointedly demonstrated in a 1915 memorial service for the fallen in Saint-Denis.[31]

Ultimately, the notion that France was a historic nation with an overriding singular identity could not be made to square, on the one hand, with the growing perception by Republican anticlericals that the loyalty of French Catholics to Rome superseded their loyalty to France, and, on the other, with the brand of Catholic nationalism that believed the country to be ruled "by a nefarious coalition of Jews, Protestants, and Freemasons."[32] Indeed, French Catholic ideals, as expressed in the daily *Echo de Paris*, emphasized France's role as the "eldest daughter of the Church" and the historic links between church and state. They also argued for the rebuilding of France into a Catholic community of old, in which Joan of Arc would be the national symbol, not Marianne, the female incarnation of the French nation dating from the Revolution.[33] This explains the zealous campaign for the canonization of the Maid of Orleans, which began in the fin de siècle and led to her beatification in 1909 and her canonization in 1920. It was in this environment, too, that Fernand de la Tombelle, one of the professors at the Schola, had written a *Cantate à Jeanne d'Arc*, which d'Indy conducted in 1909. Catholics had infused the notion of patriotism with their own private vision of a *union sacrée*.[34]

Signs of trouble had begun to appear, however, from the time that formal diplomatic relations between France and the Holy See were severed in July 1904, just prior to passage of the French law that separated church and state in 1905. With the death of Pope Pius X on 20 August 1914, shortly after the outbreak of the war, and the succession of Benedict XV, a career diplomat, hopes began to soar that better relations between France and the Church might follow. Despite a comprehensive moral and humanitarian stand, Benedict's pacifist agenda soon led to larger problems, including several independent bids for a negotiated compromise peace with Germany, the first of which saw him attempting to persuade American president Woodrow Wilson to act as mediator.[35] When reports began to spread that Pope Benedict's agenda included settling all disputed territories like Alsace-Lorraine and the Trentino by negotiation, the wrath of the Allies fell upon him.[36] In such a climate there is little wonder that rumors concerning the biased agenda of d'Indy's *Saint-Christophe*, many of which had a basis in fact, were destined to grow.

Rolland's Jean-Christophe describes d'Indy's Schola Cantorum as pious but intolerant and headed by "a very pure man, very cold, willful, and a little childish."[37] Rolland had earlier included essentially the same traits in a largely positive portrait of d'Indy written in 1903, which was reproduced in his *Musiciens d'aujourd'hui* of 1908.[38] There, however, Rolland spoke presciently and at length of d'Indy's suspicions regarding Jewish and Protestant musicians alike.

> If Goudimel is mentioned, it is because he was Palestrina's master, and his achievement of "turning the Calvinist psalms into chorales" is dismissed as being of little importance. Handel's oratorios are spoken of as

"chilling, and frankly speaking, tedious." Bach escapes with this quali-
fication: "If he is great, it is not because of, but in spite of the dogmatic
and parching spirit of the Reformation." . . .

M. d'Indy hails from the Middle Ages, and not from antiquity,
or from the Renaissance, which he confounds with the Reformation
(though the two sisters are enemies) in order to crush it better. "Let us
take for models," he says, "the fine workers in art of the Middle Ages."
In this return to the Gothic spirit . . . there is a name—a modern one
this time—that they are fond of quoting at the *Schola;* it is that of
César Franck.[39]

D'Indy's attack on Protestantism had taken numerous forms over the
years, including encouraging Ropartz to accept the directorship of the
Strasbourg Conservatoire in 1907. D'Indy urged extension of French
influence in this culturally disputed region and warned especially against
the evils of the Alsatian Albert Schweitzer, whose recent book on J. S. Bach
had, he felt, reduced Bach's influence to a set of Protestant ideals.[40]

Through his pedagogy—not through his sermons on the moral value of
art but in his emphasis upon the national history of his art and through
the example of his own craftsmanship—d'Indy had helped to clarify the
foundations of French music. More important, through his directorship at
the Schola he had also assisted in identifying a musical canon that took notice of the historic contribution not only of France but of Italy and Austro-
Germany as well. For d'Indy the beacons of truth were clear: France, the
Catholic Church and plainsong, Monteverdi and Rameau, Beethoven and
Franck. In the curriculum of the Schola the symphony was viewed as the
quintessential locus for moral debate capable of edifying the listener—a
perspective completely at odds with the state Conservatoire, where the
symphony took second place to French lyric forms.[41]

Although d'Indy's veneration of Beethoven was unmistakable, his curricular embrace of the symphony was also clearly tethered to the thought
that the French might "better the Germans on their own ground."[42] Between 1916 and 1918, realizing, no doubt, that a performance of his great
war document, *La légende de Saint-Christophe,* was destined to be delayed
because of production considerations, d'Indy undertook to write a blatantly
propagandistic third symphony, his *Sinfonia brevis de bello gallico.* He laid
out the intentions behind his "short symphony of a French war" in a letter to Ropartz on 4 January 1918, which described the several movements
thus: "*First movement,* mobilization, the Marne; *Scherzo,* gaiety at the
front; *Andante,* Latin art and German Art ('l'art latin et l'art boche')"—
which bears clear testimony to the colliding forces behind a resurgent Neo-

classicism—and "*Finale,* victory, with the hymn of St. Michael as peroration." He concluded with an unexpected remark that reveals an extraordinary self-consciousness regarding his position with respect to the avant-garde: "The symphony has nothing of Stravinsky in it . . . but too bad!"[43]

This, as it turned out, was to be the least of d'Indy's worries. The work, whose sketches were finished on St. Christopher's Day 1917, was replete with picturesque details: a German military march that interrupts the first movement in an evocation of the battle of the Marne, the sounds of bugles and the barracks in the Scherzo, a crude allusion to contemporary German music in the Adagio, and the booming of the bass drum in imitation of the cannon as victory is hailed in the finale's concluding hymn. Nevertheless, the symphony was judged a noble failure. Not only was it not well received, it failed to ease the way for the presentation of d'Indy's views in *La légende de Saint-Christophe.* The "Queste de Dieu" from the second act of *Saint-Christophe* was performed by the Concerts Colonne Lamoureux on 1 April 1917, but the première of the whole, which was presented at the Paris Opéra, was delayed until July 1921. With allusions on virtually every page to music of diverse epochs—from the middles ages to the twentieth century—it was one of the composer's most remarkable scores.[44] Its implicit stance on a host of musical, social, religious, and racial issues was, however, so politically charged that the work had virtually no chance of survival, although few would have challenged d'Indy's loyalty to his country, his devotion to his Church, or his capacity to see beyond national distinctions in his veneration of Beethoven.

10 Neoclassicism, Aviation, and the Great War

> The century of aeroplanes has a right to a music of its own.
> Claude Debussy, *S.I.M.*, 1 November 1913

> A tennis player or a watchmaker or an airplane pilot is
> an automatism, but he is also criticism and wisdom.
> Bernard De Voto, *Across the Wide Missouri*

Debussy and d'Indy were not the only French composers to confront the prospect of war in highly personal terms. Two days following the declaration of war Ravel wrote to his favorite pupil, Maurice Delage, that he had become completely preoccupied with defining his personal role in the struggle that lay ahead. "I'm working," he wrote. "Yes, I'm working, and with an insane certainty and lucidity. But, during this time, the blues are at work too, and suddenly I find myself sobbing over my sharps and flats!"[1] It was at this time that Ravel began work on the Piano Trio.

Four days later he wrote to his brother: "As I felt I was going to go crazy, I took the wisest course: I'm going to enlist."[2] Ravel, who was thirty-nine at the time, confessed to his Polish friend Cipa Godebski that despite the irrationality of it all he was going to sign up, completely out of an act of conscience. The letter concluded with, "And now, if you wish: Vive la France! but, above all, down with Germany and Austria! or at least what those two nations represent at the present time. And with all my heart: long live the Internationale[3] and Peace! That's why I'm signing up," to which he added a postscript, "and why not: long live Poland."[4]

Ravel worked at a furious pace, accomplishing in five weeks, according to his own estimate, the work of five months. His objective was to finish the Piano Trio before he enlisted, and he was heartsick when he was found ineligible for service because he was slightly underweight. "I'm going to begin a suite of pieces for the piano," he announced, "as I was obliged to interrupt two important works, which, however, were not very timely: *La cloche engloutie*, in collaboration with Gerhart Hauptmann, and a symphonic poem: *Wien!!!*"[5] To Mme. Casella he confided that he had to set aside the last of these because "there is no way that the work can be called *Petrograd*."[6] Only five days earlier Ravel had written a letter to Roland-Manuel that left no doubt that he had come down with a war fever: "Oh God! When I think that they just destroyed Rheims cathedral! . . . And that my physical condition will prevent me from experiencing the splendid moments of this holy war, and taking part in the most grandiose, the noblest action which has ever been seen in the history of humanity (even including the French revolution)!"[7]

Ravel's announcement that he had abandoned a work based upon Gerhart Hauptmann's *The Sunken Bell* of 1897 was hardly a surprise. Although Hauptmann was the most prominent name in German letters and had won the Nobel Prize for literature as recently as 1912, the war had made Ravel's collaboration with him an impossibility. Furthermore, if "La cloche engloutie" immediately brought to mind Debussy's renowned prelude, "La cathédrale engloutie," the latter title had a different resonance for the French people, following the bombardment of Rheims. Moreover, the bell, as Elgar, Cammaerts, Hardy, and others had demonstrated, had become a symbol of Belgium and more generally of eventual Allied victory. The notion of a "sunken" bell was now as untimely as a German title, "Wien" (Vienna), a work that was later to become *La valse*.

During this period Ravel began some of the most brilliant works of his entire career, including the Piano Trio (1914), *Le tombeau de Couperin* (1917), and *La valse*, providing vivid testimony that the war had stirred the creative impetus in Ravel. His productivity was a startling contrast to the "dreadful silence" then being experienced by Debussy. On 29 August 1914 Ravel wrote to his publisher, Jacques Durand, that he had completed his trio,[8] but in a letter of 1 October to Roland-Manuel, one of the composer's closest confidants at the time, he argued that he was tired of being told that he was in effect "working for the fatherland by writing music."[9] There was also a note of sadness in his confirmation that he had at last finished his trio, "like poor Magnard."[10] Albéric Magnard, a pupil of d'Indy and a devotee of classical forms, had written a piano trio in 1904 and had been killed by the Germans on 3 September 1914 at his country villa in Baron.[11]

If Ravel's Piano Trio is taken to represent a genuine turn from the style of *Gaspard de la nuit* and *Daphnis et Chloë* and a recall of the formalisms of the early String Quartet and slightly later piano *Sonatine*, it must be considered only a hesitant step in the pursuit of neoclassical texture and controlled expression. The trio was, above all, the composer's first response to the war, as acutely felt as Debussy's initial contributions and couched in far more personal terms. The Basque rhythms of the opening movement recall his mother's family roots, and the modal Passacaglia is as plaintive and soulful as a folk spiritual. But the trio as a whole is too emotional, too surging, too filled with climaxes and bravura writing to be written off as a sudden capitulation to the French call to the classics. In light of the times and Ravel's state of mind, the trumpetlike fanfare in the piano during the development section of the closing movement can with reason be heard as a distant call from the battlefield and the piano triplet flourishes in the concluding pages as a projection of eventual triumph. The latter, however, are set against incessant trills in the violin and cello parts, which are fused into a single line of alternating measures of quintuple and septuple meter that push the music to the brink of hysteria. It is a vision of victory bathed in the inescapable delirium of the preceding battle, one that vividly certifies Ravel's claim that he was working with "an insane certainty and lucidity."[12]

"TROIS BEAUX OISEAUX DU PARADIS"

Not all of Ravel's commentaries on the war were so oblique. Between December 1914 and February 1915, Ravel composed *Three Songs for Unaccompanied Mixed Chorus*. A setting of his own poetry, it is his only unaccompanied choral work. Here Ravel's call is undisguisedly to a French musical legacy that preceded the masters of the seventeenth and eighteenth centuries. "Nicolette," which opens the set, mimics the programmatic chanson style of the renowned "Le chant des oiseaux" by Clément Janequin, particularly in its use of onomatopoetic patter-speech. The narrow range pattern repetition and the "la-la" refrains in the concluding "Ronde" similarly reach back to Renaissance prototypes, and the musical texture was similar to that invoked by Janequin in his "La guerre." That the latter was familiar to composers and audiences of Ravel's generation through the editions of the musicologist Henri Expert had already been made clear by Debussy in an article of March 1914.[13] And d'Indy, who had busied himself with the revival of France's illustrious musical past over the preceding decade, had also made a practical edition of the same and similar pieces and performed them to enormous popular acclaim at the Schola Cantorum.[14]

But it is in the central "Trois beaux oiseaux du Paradis" that Ravel made his most unambiguous reference to the conflict. Dedicated to Paul Painlevé, a renowned Sorbonne professor of mathematics who in 1910 had obtained the first parliamentary grant for aviation and who would later become minister of war, prime minister, and finally minister of aviation,[15] the piece paints a loving textual picture that is clearly geared to a nation newly thrust into a world conflagration (CD track 8). The text begins with the soprano announcing that "Trois beaux oiseaux du Paradis" (Three lovely birds from Paradise) have flown by, but she is immediately interrupted with a line that becomes a refrain: "Mon ami z'il est à la guerre" (My belov'd is to the fighting gone). The three birds are then identified: "Le premier était plus bleu que ciel" (The first was bluer than Heaven's blue); "Le second était couleur de neige" (The second white as the fallen snow); "Le troisième rouge vermeil" (The third was wrapt in bright red glow). The first (sung by a tenor), brings "a glance of azure," and the second (sung by a contralto) leaves a kiss on the beloved's white brow. The third bird (a bass), when asked what it brings, offers "Un joli coeur tout cramoisi" (A faithful heart all crimson red). The refrain of the beloved who has gone off to war appears once more. The soprano then concludes, "Ah! Je sens mon coeur qui froidit. . . . Emportez-le aussi" (Ah! I feel my heart growing cold. . . . Take it also with thee).

The English translation by Mme Swayne St.-René Taillandier was provided along with the French in the original 1916 edition published by Durand, who that year also published Debussy's "Noël des enfants qui n'ont plus de maisons" with an English translation by the same translator. In both compositions the symbolism was intentionally easy to read. In Ravel's work the colors of the three birds are a metaphor for the French flag as well as heaven or paradise (blue), purity (white), and sacrifice (red), and the poem's parenthetical refrain ("My belov'd is to the fighting gone") refers insistently to the price of war.

Birds, especially swallows and nightingales, had long been symbols of hope, but never more so than in the period between the Franco-Prussian conflict and World War I, during which few songs were more popular than "L'oiseau qui vient de France."[16] When a German dirigible made a forced landing at Lunéville in 1913, a parody version, "Voilà l'Zepp'lin qui vient en France," made its appearance.[17] The imagery of flight and wings introduced by Ravel in the first stanza also invites recall of the common interest of both composer and dedicatee in the new aerial dimension of war. Painlevé had been the first Frenchman to fly with Wilbur Wright in 1908, and the next year he had created the first course in aeronautical mechanics at the École Aéronautique. Then, in the first weeks of the war, Ravel approached him as a reference in an attempt to find appointment as a pilot in the French air corps.

The simplicity of the text and the repetitious quality of the music, both of which court a conspicuous naïveté, establish a mood that is at once chaste and melancholy and stoke the nationalist fires in a sure but quiet manner. The closing stanza of Ravel's song brings a sudden *frisson* with the soprano's

"Ah" backed by a chorus that enters *fpp (bouche fermée)* as the mounting implication of the allegory's refrain is brought to a soft but chilling end. If Ravel's voice is somewhat quieter than that of many other composers in their early war pieces, the fact that Ravel wrote his own texts, as Debussy did for his "Noël," openly advertises the composer's personal involvement.

THE WOUNDED MUSE

Ravel's *Tombeau de Couperin* was initially conceived when he began to compose the Piano Trio.[18] He described the as yet unnamed new set as "a French suite—no, it isn't what you think: *La Marseillaise* will not be in it, but it will have a forlane and a gigue; no tango, however."[19] Ravel's allusion to the tango reflected not only the current fashion of "tango-teas" but also the recent proclamations by the Catholic Church banning tangos as inherently lascivious. That very year, 1914, the pope himself had reportedly proposed that the forlana, a dance of Italian origin, be introduced as a substitute. By way of response, Ravel wrote Cipa Godebski that he was transcribing a "Forlane" by François Couperin, which, he maliciously reported, he would like to have "danced at the Vatican by Mistinguett and Colette Willy in drag."[20] Ravel's own "Forlane" is, in effect, a disguised (if not transgendered) version of Couperin's "Forlane," which had appeared in the April issue of *La revue musicale de SIM* shortly before Ravel's letter to Godebski. Together with the "Rigaudon," which has been convincingly traced to the "Premier tambourin" of Rameau's *Troisième concert* (available in an edition by Saint-Saëns), these two movements offer the most conspicuous evidence of specific modeling.[21] Considered as a whole, however, Ravel's ultimate embrace of prelude, fugue, forlane, rigaudon, and minuet (although no "gigue," despite his initial projection) signaled a wholesale reclamation of the *style ancien* that had been endorsed in France in the decades following the Franco-Prussian War and previously savored by Ravel himself in the *Menuet antique* of 1895, as well as more recently in the "Menuet" of his *Sonatine*.

To assert that "there is nothing specifically warlike in any of these short movements written in forms of the Baroque suite,"[22] however, is to miss the thrust of Ravel's set. The early dismissal of avant-garde movements such as Cubism as boche-inspired had quickly brought compensatory signs of realignment toward Neoclassicism in Paris, especially among the painters.[23] First conceived in July 1914, the month in which the war broke out, and completed only between June and November 1917, *Tombeau de*

Couperin had a lengthy gestation. Following a decline in the composer's health and the death of his mother on 5 January of that year, he was promised a temporary discharge from military service. A month later, however, he was still writing to Madame Fernand Dreyfus that "My captain keeps telling me that 'I've got to snap out of it.' He's putting me second in command on a vehicle, and is going to take me for a ride near the front. I know very well that it won't be enough."[24]

Ravel was not alone in his feelings of despair, for by this time the war had reached a stalemate not only in geographical terms but on the psychological front as well. From June to August 1917 some 40,000 French troops became involved in a series of so-called mutinies, which included the carrying of the red flag through the streets and the firing of revolvers, the refusal of troops in some instances "to return to the trenches" or to take part in fresh attacks even as they reluctantly agreed to hold the line, cries for peace, and charges of butchery laid directly at the doorstep of the French high command.[25] One of the songs of protest was apparently so effective and widespread that an official offer of exemption from further military duty was offered to anyone who would identify its author. Beginning with the words "It's finished, we've had enough," the song bid farewell to life, love, and women and concluded with an unambiguous sentiment: "We're finished forever with this filthy war."[26] By this time not only the troops but also the French people were totally disillusioned with the protracted struggle. It was during this period that Ravel brought *Tombeau* to its completion, and once finished he dedicated each of the suite's six pieces to the memory of a friend who had died in the war.

Beginning with the precisely etched ornamentation of the opening "Prélude," the aesthetic stance is calculated and overt. The equally proper "Fugue" is appropriately rigorous in its application of inversion and stretto, and it constitutes a possible salute to Louis Couperin, one of whose thirty-two fugues employed these techniques in an identical fashion. Ravel's inclusion of a fugue could also have been intended as a kind of manifesto directed at the *contrapuntistes* of the Schola Cantorum, where Ravel's music was literally reviled. But it could equally have been intended as a rejoinder to the judges of the Prix de Rome, who had rejected at least seven different fugues submitted between 1899 and 1905.[27]

Sandwiched between the opening "Prelude and Fugue" and the concluding "Toccata," the "Forlane," "Rigaudon," and "Menuet" recall France's celebrated school of clavecinists in the seventeenth and eighteenth centuries in their techniques, textures, and titles.[28] They virtually an-

nounce, in the spirit of Neoclassicism, a "call to order" for a troubled society as well as the plausibility of achieving it through an appraisal of
France's national history, which had always emphasized rationality and
a devotion to clarity of form. This endorsement, visible in the work of
painters like Picasso and Severini as well as composers like Debussy and
Stravinsky,[29] had momentarily called a halt to the idea of modernism as
perpetual progress and had endorsed the idea that a review was not necessarily a retreat.[30]

THE "TOCCATA" AND THE WAR IN THE AIR

All pianists who have played Ravel's *Tombeau de Couperin* know that from
a performer's perspective the concluding "Toccata" makes the greatest
technical demands of the entire suite.[31] It is dedicated to the memory of
Captain Joseph de Marliave, who was killed in the first days of the war, on
24 August 1914, after leading his men under ferocious enemy fire and,
grievously wounded, refusing to be carried by his men to safety.[32] De Marliave was the husband of the pianist Marguerite Long, who promoted
Ravel's music and who gave the first performance not only of *Tombeau* but
also of the Piano Concerto in G Major.[33] Yet Ravel's "Toccata" is far from
being merely a protracted, virtuoso *moto perpetuo* for one of the legendary interpreters of his music. First of all, François Couperin never wrote a
piece so designated, and unlike the classically ordered dances that precede
it, the obsessive drive of Ravel's dazzling finale forces us to ask how it asserts the essence of the French national spirit. If during the war the whole
issue of nationalism was, as Kenneth Silver has persuasively detailed, "less
a subject for art than a style,"[34] what is the referent of the "Toccata," which
clearly leaves the age of Couperin behind?

Given the explicit war perspective provided by the composer, the repeated notes that open the "Toccata" and that persist throughout the piece
at various elevations immediately invoke the world of the *mécanique*—
one might even argue that they represent the sonic arsenals of war, the forward grinding of armored cars and tanks, and the rat-a-tat-tat of machine
guns. Particularly relevant in this context is the knowledge that Ravel inherited a love of aviation from his father, and his continuing fascination
with airplanes led him to express a preference for the air force above all
other branches of the service.

We know that the Germans first hit Paris with small bombs on 30 August 1914, and Ravel's expressed interest in joining the air force may even

have been triggered by these events. Throughout the war years Ravel's letters repeatedly attest to his ongoing fascination with the air corps.[35] One from April 1915, addressed to Ralph Vaughan Williams, asks after the composer and concludes, "As for me I am very busy doing nothing. It took me eight months to manage to get into the Thirteenth Artillery Regiment. Now I am awaiting my nomination as a bombardier in the Air Force for which I have asked and it can't be much longer in coming through."[36] Another, written on 9 March 1916 to his mother after he had been on duty for many months, speaks not only of the sense of danger as he neared the front but also of his orientation to the skies.

> Everything reminds you of it. The airplanes going there, the convoys filled with soldiers, and at every turn in the road, you see the same sign: V . . . [for Verdun] and an arrow. Almost every night, zeppelins are reported by the sirens at the factory and the train station. When the region is seriously threatened, they sound the "attention" in town. Then all the inhabitants go out in the street with their noses up, just like in Paris.[37]

Less than three weeks later Ravel wrote to the singer Jane Bathori about his daily life as a soldier and his fading aerial fantasies: "I'm far away from Paris and far away from music; I'm a poilu, dressed in goatskin, with helmet and gas mask, who drives on forbidding roads, even into the midst of the 'gigantic struggle.' The service is beginning to get interesting, to the point that I'll end up forgetting about my lovely dreams of aviation."[38] The dreams would not go away, however, and on 29 May 1916 Ravel lamented to Mme. Fernand Dreyfus that he was momentarily obliged to put aside all thoughts of aviation in order to keep his truck in repair.[39] But on 2 June 1916 he finally conveyed to Mme. Casella in Rome that it appeared as though his dreams had come to an end: "I feel increasingly weak and tired out. Just as I was about to be allowed to transfer into aviation, the major dissuaded me: enlargement of the heart, nothing terribly serious, but after all!"[40]

Ravel's fantasies of joining the air corps were not unique. Even before the war a general awareness of the potential for human flight had been growing exponentially on both sides of the Atlantic. On 17 December 1903 the Wright brothers had made the first controlled, sustained flights in a power-driven airplane at Kitty Hawk, North Carolina. Just six years later, in 1909, the first international air races, sponsored by the *New York Herald*, were held at Rheims in France, with an American, Glenn Hammond

Curtiss, winning with a craft of his own design. And in July of the same year the French aviator and inventor Louis Blériot made the first crossing of the English Channel in a heavier-than-air machine, flying from Calais to Dover in thirty-seven minutes.

Only a month before the Académie Française had sponsored a poetic competition on the theme "the conquest of the air" that forecast not only an avalanche of air poetry during the war but also a heady interest in the subject by painters, poster makers, and writers of novels and literary manifestos alike. And in Paris the popularity of Wilbur Wright threatened to transcend that of Buffalo Bill and Nick Carter.[41]

Beginning in 1915 the Germans gained a clear advantage in the air with Fokker planes equipped with a novel synchronization system that allowed pilots to fire their machine guns through their revolving propellers without hitting the blades (fig. 21).[42] In 1916, however, the French began to take command of the air with newly introduced British De Havillands and Farman Experimentals, and the most advanced of the French single-seat fighters, the Nieuport 17 biplane (nicknamed "Bébé"), also had a machine gun with a synchronized firing mechanism mounted in front of the pilot.

In the concluding "Toccata" of *Tombeau de Couperin* (CD track 9), the hail of sixteenth notes that virtually never falter throughout the piece invites an alternating set of images: the steep ascent of aircraft followed by the plummeting dive; a series of swooping spirals; the hypnotic regularity of the engine and propeller, and, when deployed in a series of repeated staccato notes in various ranges, a rain of meticulously coordinated and deadly machine gun fire at both high and low altitudes.

Ravel completed the "Toccata" in September 1917, shortly before the death of the French ace Georges Guynemer, whose memory the French chamber of deputies voted to perpetuate by having his name inscribed in the Panthéon.[43] Lucien Hector-Jonas carried the public mood for immortalization of airmen a step further in a painting of October 1918 titled *Les héros de l'air ne meurent pas* (Heroes of the Air Do Not Die). The painting depicts Guynemer, who has been snatched from his falling aircraft by a figure who may be taken for Winged Victory or Winged Fame,[44] being placed astride the winged horse Pegasus, who will carry him to eternal life (fig. 22). By this time people had become aware of not only the sheer technological marvel of flight but also its human component. A new kind of modern-day hero had been born. Poets and artists alike now identified the aviator with a list of familiar flying personalities, including Arabian princes on flying carpets, Perseus and his winged sandals, Wagner's flying Valkyries, Icarus, and countless angels and archangels.[45]

Figure 21. Fokker airplane poster, about 1914–1917.

Several French writers had predicted aerial warfare in the last decades of the nineteenth century,[46] and H. G. Wells had foretold the bombing of New York in his *The War in the Air*, published in 1908 with horrifyingly realistic illustrations. In May 1911, during the preliminaries to the Paris-Madrid air race, aviation's dangers were strikingly brought home when one contestant's aircraft went out of control, killing the French minister of war and

Figure 22.   Lucien Hector-Jonas, *Les héros de l'air ne meurent pas*,
1918. (Photo courtesy of Musée des Deux Guerres Mondiales, Paris.)

severely injuring the prime minister and the oil magnate Henry Deutsch
de la Meurthe, the leading patron of French aviation and sponsor of numerous previous air shows.[47]

Deutsch had been an important contact for the Wright brothers when
they first attempted to sell their early machines to the French. He also established a prize of 100,000 francs to be awarded to the first person who
flew in a lighter-than-air craft from the Parisian suburb of Saint-Cloud to
the Eiffel Tower, circumnavigated it, and returned in thirty minutes or less.

Alberto Santos-Dumont, a Brazilian living in France, won the prize in 1901 with a petrol-fueled dirigible, delighting Deutsch because it vindicated his belief, stated as early as 1889, that "in the petrol engine lies the solution to the problem of aerial navigation."[48]

By the time that Deutsch established L'Institut Aérotechnique on 6 July 1911 at the University of Paris with a handsome endowment, one of the principal areas of concern was air traffic control.[49] In the opening address by the vice-rector at the inauguration of the institute, however, the point was clearly made that its establishment on the parade grounds of the École Militaire de Saint-Cyr was symbolic, and that dirigibles and airplanes were seen not only as potential agents of national defense but inescapably as instruments of war.[50] It was a point that Deutsch himself acknowledged in his own address on this occasion, even as he spoke of the peaceful dreams of a nation and the human race.[51]

This background proved essential to developments on the musical front. Deutsch had previously given evidence of a talent for composition in numerous songs, one of which, "Vers les cieux" (1909), carried the subtitle "À la conquête de l'air."[52] In addition, among his instrumental pieces are a "Ballade aérienne" for violin and piano (1902) and *Morceaux divers pour pianos* (1900–1908), which include "En automobile" (1902), "En métro" (1903), and "En dirigeable" (1908) (fig. 23).[53] Tellingly, in 1914 he also wrote a *mélodie* to his own text titled "La mort d'Icare."[54] Then, during the very season in which the aeronautical institute was inaugurated, Deutsch composed a "lyric epic in three scenes" to a poem of Henri Cain titled *Icare*. The work was orchestrated by Camille Erlanger, a winner of the Prix de Rome, and was published before the year was out by Gabriel Astruc. It was premiered in 1912 at the Paris Opéra.[55] Astruc had been Diaghilev's French manager and producer since 1907, and his newly conceived and constructed Thèâtre des Champs-Élysèes opened on 2 April 1912, only a little over a year before it hosted the memorable premiere of Stravinsky's *Le sacre du printemps*.[56] Such lofty sponsorship can only be explained by the fact that in addition to his patronage of French aviation Deutsch de la Meurthe had helped bankroll the Ballets Russes.[57]

The story fashioned by Cain for Deutsch's project was based on the familiar one of Daedelus's son Icarus, who longed to take to the skies. Ignoring his father's warnings of danger, he escapes from Crete with artificial wings made for him by his father and falls to his death in the Aegean when he soars too close to the sun, melting the wax with which his wings are attached. Here, however, Cain introduces a twist to the story: Icarus refuses the Sirens' invitation to remain with them on earth and instead accepts an

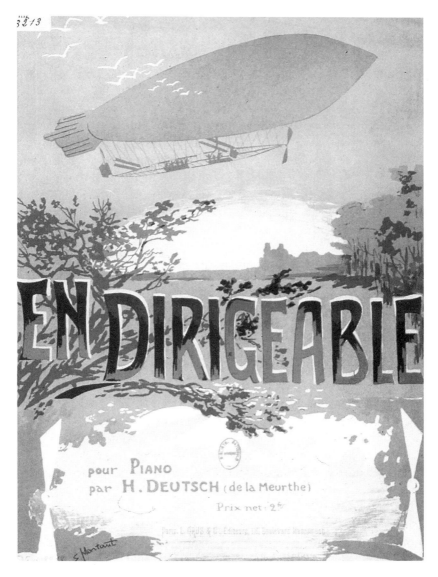

Figure 23.   Cover page for Henry Deutsch de la Meurthe's "En dirigeable," 1908.
(Photo courtesy Bibliothèque Nationale, Paris.)

offer from "Le Génie de la Science" to witness a vision of the future before his final ascent into heaven. The horizon, clearing to a radiant glow, reveals an apparition of contemporary humanity, including "the rugged and noble army of workmen now in ecstasy before the exploits of the aerial navigators, who glide in the starry sky."[58]

Icarus's proclamation of an unprecedented miracle ("O miracle inouï!") sparks a shower of ascending arpeggios. The Génie then brings the modern note to its conclusion by stating that though Icarus is now dead, his dream is destined to live on. The music undertakes a series of harmonic maneuvers by thirds and one telling tritone at the mention of "death" (ex. 9). The chorus concludes the text, followed by a brief orchestral coda that offers a shower of cascading arpeggios that rise, fall, and cadence on E major (anticipating the ending of Ravel's "Toccata") (CD track 10).

LE GÉNIE DE LA SCIENCE

O toi qui le premier osas quitter la terre	O you, who are the first to dare to leave the earth
Et sonder le mystère	And probe the mystery
Du gran ciel ignorè!	Of the vast, unknown heavens!
Tu ne dois pas mourir désespéré!	You must not die devoid of all hope!
Regarde—L'avenir s'éclaire!	Behold—the future shines forth!

ICARE

O miracle inouï!	O wondrous miracle!

Le Génie then concludes that even though Icarus may die, he is destined to return, perhaps centuries later, as a radiant star from the darkness, and that other mortals will follow his path and become the masters of space. The world, acclaiming Icarus, will then break the old laws handed down by the gods and will soar the boundless sky in majestic flight.[59]

The invocation of a French *Génie de la Science* is telling. Throughout the war the faculty of sciences at the University of Paris insisted that French pure science exhibited greater originality and rigor than the Germans' applied science. Even Painlevé, who as minister of public instruction in 1915 clearly recognized the importance of industrial applications of science and supervised the creation of the *Direction des inventions intéressant la défense nationale*, spoke in 1918 in opposition to German science, characterizing it as a "gigantic enterprise in which an entire people applied themselves relentlessly to creating the most formidable killing-machine ever produced." Conversely, he argued, French science was dedicated to the

Example 9. Deutsch de la Meurthe, "O toi qui le premier osas quitter la terre," from *Icare*. (© 1911 G. Astruc, Paris.)

"distinterested search for truth."[60] Throughout the war years it became increasingly obvious to many that the secret of Germany's economic power rested in its effective merger of science and industry, and the benefits that French science had reaped from the Germans remained a controversial issue well into the decade of the 1920s.[61] *Icare* may not have been for the ages, but it provided unmistakable evidence that Deutsch was a trained musician whose compositional style was clearly at home with the chromatic harmonies and lyric clichés of the day. One's admiration is further enhanced, however, if one contemplates a similar accomplishment by the likes of the Standard Oil baron John D. Rockefeller or Henry Ford, his nearest equivalents in the United States.

Given Deutsch's reputation as one of France's most important patrons of aviation and Ravel's personal acquaintance with Painlevé, who served on the board of Deutsch's new institute, Ravel could hardly have been unaware of these developments and of the import of Deutsch's musical sojourns.[62] The extent to which aviation was increasingly garnering the attention of people in the arts had been dramatized even by the Russian designer for the Ballets Russes, Natalia Goncharova. In 1913 she had painted a vibrant *Aeroplane over Train*, and in a series of lithographs created in 1914 she updated her subject for a world now aflame. One, *Angels and Aeroplanes*, dramatized the angels' beneficent patronage and assistance in a new aerial war (fig. 24).[63] Another in the series shows the angels acting as airborne machines, dropping deadly boulders on a city below.

In the same year H. G. Wells carried the metaphor a step further in *The World Set Free* by emphasizing the pilot's mortality: "So it was that war in the air began. Men rode upon the whirlwind that night and slew and fell like archangels. The sky rained heroes upon the astonished earth."[64] The French aviator Blériot also invoked mythology, proclaiming that "the most beautiful dream that has haunted the heart of men since Icarus is today a reality."[65] Erik Satie's drawings of uncertain date confirm that the fascination for dirigibles and other improbable *machines volantes* was virtually epidemic (fig. 25).[66] And Cocteau, who was a personal friend of the French air ace Roland Garros, about whom he wrote a poem that compared him to Christopher Columbus, Jules Verne, Tristan, and the Valkyries,[67] would soon announce his intention to include not only the sounds of dynamos and typewriters but also the roar of sirens and airplanes in his score for the ballet *Parade* (1916).[68]

Deutsch, who was one of the first to use gasoline-propelled motors to power dirigibles and, later, airplanes, had already suggested that a series of repeated notes could stand as metaphor for the purr of a running motor in

Figure 24.   Natalia Goncharova, *Angels and Aeroplanes,*
1914. (© 2002 ARS New York/ADAGP Paris.)

his "En dirigeable." [69] Carrying a succession of specific markings throughout, the work begins with a slow preludial "Dans le hangar," followed by a
"Sortie" in the same tempo, and a section labeled "Mise en marche du moteur" (starting the engine) in a livelier Allegro Moderato (ex. 10a). The insistent chain of repeated notes that is introduced here continues over the
next ninety-five measures, marked by a series of labels that includes
"Changement de direction" (change of direction), "Vers les hauteurs" (toward the heights), and "Fluctuat nec mergitur" (moving in a wave-like motion without dropping precipitously). The pace shifts momentarily with a
cascade of arpeggiated triplets at "Planant dans le libre espace" (gliding
in free space) (ex. 10b). Following a "Descente" the music returns to the
motor's incessant beat in "Vers le hangar" (toward the hangar) (ex. 10c) be-

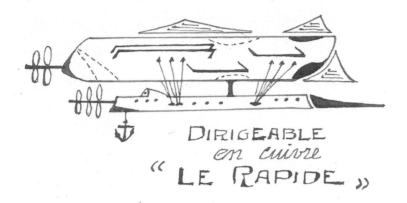

Figure 25. Erik Satie, "Dirigeable en cuivre 'Le rapide,'" undated. (By permission of the Houghton Library, Harvard University; collection of Mrs. Robert Woods-Bliss, MS MUS 193 [101].)

fore it relaxes once again at "Arrêt.– Lancement des guide-ropes" (halt – securing of the guide-ropes), "Atterrissement" (landing), and "Rentrée au hangar" (return to the hangar). Nothing could more clearly dramatize the prevailing notion that music was capable of sketching the complete course of an aerial flight.[70]

In Ravel's "Toccata" the tempo marking, "Vif," at 144 to the quarter note (ex. 11a), is the same throughout, except for one brief passage marked "Un peu moins vif," where the music—much like Deutsch's sections marked "Planant dans le libre espace" and "Descente"—seems to glide momentarily in a gradual descent over a period of ten measures before rising again. In a more generalized discussion of *Tombeau* that nowhere touches on the issue of aviation, Carolyn Abbate has tellingly addressed this very issue: "Ravel is a machine, and happily so," she observes, but *"Ralentir,* like improvisation, is a musical sign betraying human presence in the performance machine."[71] Reclaiming the original tempo, Ravel's music then hurtles itself into a series of spirals and loops, settling three times in increasingly lower regions,[72] where the register and the repeated, single-pitch staccato figure contrasts with its elevated appearance as the opening salvo of the piece (ex. 11b).[73] It also offers a convincing portrayal of machine-gun fire directed from the ground against low-flying aircraft.[74] Ravel had, of course, invoked rapid repeated notes in previous works for the pi-

Example 10. Deutsch de la Meurthe, "Mise en marche du moteur," "Planant dans le libre espace," and "Descente," from "En Dirigeable." (© 1908 L. Grus & Co., Paris.)

ano, but here their persistent and increasingly ominous appearance in variable registers is markedly different from their brief introductory role in "Scarbo" *(Gaspard de la nuit)*, for example, or their triplet-figure imitation of a Spanish guitar in "Alborada del gracioso" *(Miroirs)*. One could also argue that the repeated notes of Prokofiev's "Toccata" (1912) were of recent memory, and that Debussy's designation of a "Toccata" to close his *Pour le piano* (1901) could be viewed as a formal precursor. Yet despite their collective potential as generic models of the keyboard toccata, neither of these works could claim the explicit wartime context that Ravel openly advertised for his *Tombeau de Couperin*.[75]

In the "Toccata" Ravel's stealthy celestial navigation, which includes a series of acrobatic loops and spirals, continues until the penultimate page, where for the first and only time in the piece a notated thirty-second-note rest appears in all parts marked by a fermata—a choking catch breath, pos-

Example 11.   Maurice Ravel, "Toccata," from *Tombeau de Couperin*. (© 1918 Durand, Paris. Joint ownership Redfield and Nordice. Exclusive representation by Éditions Durand, Paris. Reproduced by permission of Éditions Durand.)

sibly signaling the deathly silence of an enemy aircraft's motor following a strike or, perhaps even more plausibly, the momentary but deliberate killing of the engine—a familiar maneuver known as a stall (ex. 11c).[76] The appeal of the latter image stems from the fact that the Nieuport biplane was "powered by a nine-cylinder rotary engine. . . . This engine ran at only one speed—full tilt. . . . The only possible speed control was the ignition switch, by which the pilot could 'blip' the engine off and on as he maneuvered."[77] Ravel's solitary fermata, therefore, appears less as a metaphor for a mechanical breakdown than as a symbol of the pilot's control over the machine.[78] The music immediately responds with a dramatic and abrupt free fall of four octaves, after which the pilot navigates his final climb from the lowest regions of the keyboard. At the very end patterns that may have originated in the splashing fountains of Ravel's *Jeux d'eau* (1901) are restricted to a simple, unadorned E-major triad, and the work concludes with what might be heard as a final and victorious "hurrah" if one is also prepared to see in the downward catapulting slur of the final measure an enemy aircraft plummeting to earth.

Obviously there is no need to insist upon the specific details of the preceding interpretation: a "Forlane" may be heard simply as a "Forlane" and a "Toccata" just as a "Toccata." But with a title page announcing a *tombeau* with historic implications and displaying a funerary urn drawn by the composer, and with the several movements each dedicated to a soldier who had fallen in battle, Ravel left listeners with little doubt about the work's specific subtext (fig. 26).[79] It is also important to underscore once again the degree of France's passion for aviation at the time. For despite the fact that "powered flight" was first achieved in the United States, Paris was the indisputable capital of aviation before the First World War: "No other Western city prized aviators more highly, nor responded to their exploits with more intense enthusiasm."[80]

Ravel's conclusion of *Tombeau de Couperin* by way of a "Toccata" rather than another Baroque dance invites speculation as to the composer's intentions. Of all the pieces that make up the suite, it is the "Toccata" that is most clearly written for a virtuoso solo performer, and it is no small coincidence that the aviation ace was routinely referred to at the time as a "virtuoso."[81] Such a collection of fanciful ideas, however, begs for more specific evidence that the composer explicitly believed in music's capacity to undertake a portrayal of aerial flight.

FLIGHTS OF FANCY

Ravel was not alone in his fixation on the airplane during the Great War. In the visual arts Fernand Léger's *The Crashed Aeroplane* (1916),[82] George Grosz's *Air Attack* (1915) (an urban scene with figures fleeing in panic),[83] and Robert Delaunay's *L'hommage à Blériot*,[84] all bespoke the contempo-

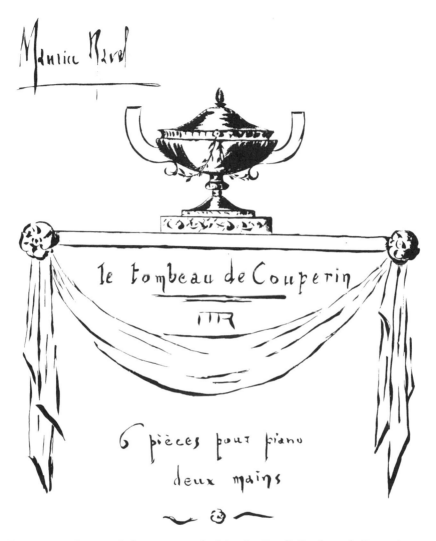

Figure 26. Cover with funerary urn for Maurice Ravel's *Tombeau de Couperin,* 1918. (Music © 1918 Durand, Paris.)

rary fascination with flight, as did the paintings of Mario Sironi, Gino Severini,[85] and Natalia Goncharova. Among the poets, novelists, and science fictionists who succumbed to its spell, Filippo Marinetti, Gabriele D'Annunzio, and H. G. Wells might have been expected to speak of its electrifying authority, given their taste for violence or fantasy in envisioning a brave new world. But even the pacifist-idealist Romain Rolland could not refrain from recognizing in the concluding installment of *Jean-Christophe* that with the advent of the airplane a new day had dawned.

Like many of his contemporaries, Rolland seemed to put aside the notion that the future of aviation would inevitably involve an encounter with death. Enthralled by the appearance of a new kind of hero, his contemplation of the dark side of man's conquest of the air was counterbalanced by a new sense of adventure. So it was, too, for Ravel. Despite his personal confrontation with the horrors of the front, where he felt the tear of shrapnel, knew the scent of enemy gunpowder, experienced exposure with a broken-down truck near enemy lines for ten days, and suffered what he called "exhausting, insane, and perilous service," the exhilarating fascination of flight rendered danger in the skies largely invisible, regardless of the pilot's short life expectancy.[86] Indeed, Ravel's "Toccata" offers freewheeling acrobatics tuned as much to an emblematic conquest of time and space as to a specific dogfight.[87] Especially as a result of the disorientation brought on by prolonged confinement in the trenches, soldiers frequently developed the need for a coherent vision, and the flier and his aerial perspective were ideally suited to fill this need.

It is interesting to recall in this regard François Couperin's habit of introducing highly programmatic pieces with extravagant titles in his dance suites. Allusions vary from musical portraits of friends and patrons to descriptions of natural phenomena and events. Even here, though, things are not always what they seemed. The whirring motion of his "Les petits moulins à vent," Couperin confided, was really about chatterboxes rather than windmills, and "Les papillons" alluded to fashionable ladies' hairstyles rather than butterflies.[88] In the preface to his 1713 collection of keyboard pieces, Couperin even went so far as to beg indulgence. "The titles reflect my ideas," he said. "I may, [however], be forgiven for not explaining them all." Similarly, Ravel did not "explain" each of the pieces of his *Tombeau* even though he did provide potent clues to the meaning of the work. Like the commemorative cemeteries that imposed a serene formality through neatly placed crosses, the suite's opening prelude, fugue, forlane, rigaudon, and menuet reviewed and celebrated the classical heritage of his native country. Then, by way of conclusion, Ravel offered what may be inferred to be a homily regarding a new technology that transcended the war itself and pointed to a new and brilliant future for the human spirit.

But that is not all. Ravel's fascination with the airplane continued long after the war, and he was not alone. The American George Antheil composed an *Airplane Sonata* in 1922, and a performance of it at the Théâtre des Champs-Élysées on 4 October 1923 caused a riot that brought the composer immediate notoriety. In 1926 the Ballets Russes de Monte Carlo mounted a production of Constant Lambert's *Romeo and Juliet,* choreographed by Bronislawa Nijinska, in which Serge Lifar, as the ill-fated Romeo, was costumed as an aviator who, instead of dying with his beloved Juliet, danced by Tamara Karsavina, elopes with her in an airplane.[89] The movie *Wings,* released in 1927, was the first of a series of almost two dozen aviation films produced by Hollywood over the next decade.[90] And in 1928 Paul Hindemith and Kurt Weill initiated collaboration on a project with Bertolt Brecht, *Lindberghflug,*[91] which was sparked by the new American hero's traversal of the Atlantic the year before.

In 1930, in an interview devoted to his *Boléro,* Ravel spoke of plans for a tour of North and South America and concluded, "The date depends on when I finish the two works I have pending: a symphonic work, a description of a flight, and a piano concerto which I will perform myself."[92] Only a few months later, in a letter to Manuel de Falla, Ravel referred to a new project titled "*Dédale 39,* which you can guess is an airplane—and an airplane in C." An autobiographical note is suggested by the fact that Ravel was thirty-nine when he first attempted to enlist in the air corps. The same or a related project was referred to once more in an unpublished letter to French composer and conductor Manuel Rosenthal, in which Ravel referred to plans for a symphonic poem inspired by aviation to be called "Icare."[93] The choice of title in both instances would have virtually demanded comparison with the *épopée lyrique* of Deutsch, who had died in 1919. By 1930 Ravel's old friend Paul Painlevé had finished his term as premier of France and, more recently, as minister of war, had given the welcoming speech at a dinner in Lindbergh's honor following his celebrated trans-Atlantic flight in 1927. It seems likely that it was these events that precipitated Ravel's projection of a new work in praise of aviation.[94]

Ravel's final testimony to his continuing interest in the conquest of the air came in the late summer of 1933, by which time Painlevé had become France's minister of aviation. Reflecting on the possibility of noise serving as a source of inspiration as well as prospects for a music of machines, Ravel turned directly to the idea of writing what he now called "An Airplane Symphony."

> The airplane, which has done so much to bring greater convenience, faster travel, and to facilitate discovery in these times—what a theme for a symphony it would make! Great flights showing the epic courage of our aviators, the perils of earth, sea, and sky, could all be interpreted into music which would be a *monument to our heroes of the air.*[95]

None of these projected plans came to fruition, but Ravel's repeated testimony confirms his belief in music's ability to address such topics and suggests that some of the details had been clearly sketched in his mind. It also encourages a "close reading" of a work like the *Tombeau de Couperin* fashioned not solely from an abstract analysis of pitch, rhythm, texture, and register but also in conjunction with an appraisal of evidence provided by its title page, multiple dedications, and the events that served as a backdrop to its creation.

Although he never wrote such a piece himself, Debussy also registered his awareness of the symbolic force of the airplane for his time, its natural affinity with the world of the musician, and his specific familiarity with the performance of Deutsch's *Icare*. In a letter to his publisher, Durand, on 27 September 1913 he wrote, "I don't know why they don't make M. Deutsch director of the Opéra. He certainly likes music because he's not afraid to put it on; even though he can't have got much pleasure out of it so far!"[96] Then, in a review of November 1913, only two months later, Debussy protested the artificiality of those "symphonic painters" who tried to depict the various seasons of the years and judged that Music was the art closest to Nature.[97] He then offered a surprising conclusion that could almost have been uttered by Marinetti or Russolo.

> Is it not our duty, on the contrary, to try and find the symphonic formulae best suited to the audacious discoveries of our modern time, so committed to progress? The century of aeroplanes has a right to a music of its own. Let those who support our art not be left to waste away in the lowest ranks of our army of inventors, let them not be outdone by the genius of engineers![98]

In light of its chronological proximity it is inviting to view Ravel's "Toccata," a virtuosic but stylistically disjunct finial to his Neoclassicist homage to Couperin, as a specific, if unwitting, response to Debussy's charge. Before the war both Debussy and Ravel had betrayed their personal appetite for aviation with frequent visits to the airdrome at Issy-les-Moulineaux, the site of some of the most important early French air shows and accidents. Others flocked there too. On 4 June 1913, following a performance of *Le sacre du printemps* conducted by the composer, the famous aviation photographer Jacques Lartigue confided to his diary what he had liked most about Stravinsky's ballet. "*Vroum, vroum, vroum . . .* the orchestra made a deafening noise," he rejoiced. It reminded him, he said, of the roaring airplane engines as they took off at Issy-les-Moulineaux.[99]

Debussy and Ravel were not the only composers to summon Apollo to a new technological age, but in light of Ravel's testimony regarding his dreams for an "Airplane Symphony" and a symphonic poem variously referred to as "Icare" and "Dédale 39," it seems reasonable that he might have been tempted to undertake a related portrait during the period of his active service: a salute to French air aces like Guynemer, Blériot, and Garros and to personal associates like Painlevé and Deutsch, whose fascination with the conquest of the air and the dawn of a new age Ravel shared.

Part 4

ITALY

11 The World of the Future, the Future of the World

> We want to glorify war—the only hygiene of the world—
> militarism, patriotism, the anarchist's destructive gesture,
> the fine Ideas that kill, and the scorn of woman. . . . We want
> to demolish museums, libraries, fight against moralism,
> feminism, and all opportunistic and utilitarian cowardices. . . .
> It is in Italy that we launch this manifesto of tumbling and
> incendiary violence, this manifesto through which today we
> set up Futurism, because we want to deliver Italy from its
> gangrene of professors, of archaeologists, of guides, and of
> antiquarians.
>
> E. F. T. Marinetti, *Manifesto of Futurism*

> I love Italian opera—it's so reckless. Damn Wagner, and his
> bellowings at Fate and death. Damn Debussy, and his averted
> face. I like the Italians who run all on impulse, and don't
> care about their *immortal* souls, and don't worry about the
> ultimate.
>
> D. H. Lawrence, letter of 1 April 1911

Lawrence was only partly right, of course. The Italians may have been running largely on impulse, but, as citizens of a predominantly Catholic nation, many of them diligently practiced the Care of the Soul, at least at confession and communion. He was correct, however, if he was thinking about the Futurists: for they were by definition anti-Church and less concerned about ultimate questions than with planning a glorious tomorrow and making it come true if necessary through war. Unlike Lawrence, however, they were against Verdi, Puccini, and Italian opera in general, which they held to be representative of a hopelessly incrusted tradition.[1]

Despite the richness and antiquity of its culture, Italy was a fledgling nation. A united Kingdom of Italy had been proclaimed by parliament only on 17 March 1861, an act that joined Lombardy, Piedmont, Parma, Modena, Lucca, Romagna, Tuscany, and the two Sicilies under the reign of Victor Emmanuel II of the Piedmont House of Savoy.[2] Even though a new nation was in the process of being born, signs that Italy was growing old and weary had been sensed by Rolland's hero Jean-Christophe at the time that he began to test the third country that was to form a part of his envisioned European synthesis. He felt that the southern world was absolutely essential to the northern and that, as Stefan Zweig put it, "only in the trio of Germany, France, and Italy does the full meaning of each voice become clear."[3]

Artists as well as politicians always seem to be talking about and predicting the future. Paradoxically, the charted paths to their iridescent kingdoms are typically strewn with calls for sacrifice, as though the stated willingness to pay such a high personal price is proof of the worthiness of the cause. For Ambrose Bierce, the archetypic American cynic, the "Future" as defined in his *Devil's Dictionary* (1881–1906) was "that period of time in which our affairs prosper, our friends are true, and our happiness is assured."[4] Others, like H. G. Wells, shared something of the gusto exhibited by the Italian Futurists. "It is possible," he proclaimed, "to believe that all the past is but the beginning of a beginning, and that all that is and has been is but the twilight of the dawn. It is possible to believe that all the human mind has ever accomplished is but the dream before the awakening."[5] For Filippo Marinetti, whose manifestos began to issue with ever-increasing frequency beginning in 1909, the future offered not only promise but also a way to the promised land. A new dynamic era had been announced with the dawn of the machine age, and many of these machines were potential instruments of destruction. For Marinetti, war was not only possible but also necessary. The old stagnant society would have to be rooted out.[6]

Gabriele D'Annunzio, poet, novelist, dramatist, and soldier, had foreshadowed Marinetti's stance on a number of these points, a fact that did not endear him to the latter.[7] D'Annunzio not only shared Marinetti's passion for aviation, but his inflamed oratory was a decisive factor in bringing Italy into the war on the side of the Allies and in sustaining enthusiasm for it. "Never before has the Latin genius fallen so low; it has totally lost the sense of its proud energies and heroic virtues; it drags itself in the mud, it revels in humiliation," D'Annunzio declared to the French ambassador to Saint Petersburg in June 1914. "War, a great national war, is its last chance of salvation."[8]

In 1911, only three years before the unleashing of the Great War, D'Annunzio had provided Debussy with a French libretto for the mystery play *Le martyre de Saint-Sébastien*. Here the confusion of Christian and pagan virtues was played out through the identification of Christ with Adonis, and it is little wonder that the work was placed on the Papal Index two weeks before its premiere and that the archbishop of Paris warned Catholics not to attend under threat of excommunication. D'Annunzio and Debussy issued a statement for the press, however, in which they described the work as "the lyrical glorification not only of the splendid Christian athlete but of all Christian heroism."[9] D'Annunzio's belief in a privileged class of men who were responsible for human progress through personal sacrifice and war, if need be, was expressed in lines like "the handsome youth lying bathed in purple blood" and "the world is red with my torture."[10] The finale incorporates the author's profoundest dreams of the aviator-warrior, with Sebastian's soul exclaiming, "I come, I ascend. I have wings. All is white. My blood is the manna which whitens the desert of Sin." Indeed, the poet insisted that, for him, the main appeal of the early Christian martyr derived from a conviction that "the common people have a built-in capacity for redemption through suffering."[11]

Nonetheless, D'Annunzio's introduction of a chamber of Chaldean fortunetellers gazing at the planets alongside Christian miracles that convert Erigone, the virgin daughter of Icarus, suggests something of the confusion that characterizes his ambivalent text. Performance problems plagued the four-hour work at its premiere, problems that a team of artists, which included choreographer Michel Fokine, set designer Léon Bakst, and dancer Ida Rubinstein (D'Annunzio's paramour of the moment), could not overcome. The premiere was chastised in certain quarters not only because D'Annunzio was a Wagnerian but also, and especially, because Rubinstein, who had commissioned the work, was a woman and a Jew. It was a factor noted by members of the Action Française as well as the archbishop of Paris, who called the work "offensive to Christian consciousness."[12] Later assessments tended to blame D'Annunzio's libretto for whatever problems beset the work, and Debussy ultimately provided an abbreviated version that lasts but an hour and reveals some of his most iridescent music.[13]

D'Annunzio's vision of a youthful Italy that would supplant an aging and corrupt ruling class was a seductive corollary to the interventionist's rage over Italy's lack of national power. Spurred by Benedetto Croce's historically supported idealism, which was now widely misread to conform with the Futurists' agenda, Italy entered the war.[14] Incited by the strong-arm tactics of D'Annunzio and the young Benito Mussolini, Italian nationalists took to widespread demonstrations and mob violence, setting the stage for the signing on 26 April 1915 of the Treaty of London, which specified the territorial spoils that were to accrue to Italy. The provisions contained in the agreement were to haunt deliberations at the Versailles Peace

Conference in 1919, a fact satirically noted in a song of that year by E. A. Mario called "Tarantella di Versaglia."[15]

FUTURISM AND MUSIC

Marinetti's *Manifesto of Futurist Poetry* appeared in 1909. Similar manifestos, all reverencing urban dynamism, speed, and the polyphony of noises inspired by the machine age, appeared over the next three years for painting, sculpture, and music.[16] The finished musical scores that emerged directly from the Italian Futurist movement were of little consequence in terms of their durability as concert pieces. Francesco Pratella, the only trained composer of the group, was the author of the principal manifestos on music.[17] He also wrote a *Musica futurista* (1912) for orchestra, which had a cover page drawn by Umberto Boccioni, but for all its claims the conservative score failed to reflect the rhetoric of the Futurist movement. More promising perhaps, from a Futurist perspective, was "Gioia, saggio di orchestra mista," from Pratella's opera *L'aviatore Dro* (1920). The score calls for *scoppiatori* (exploders) and *ronzatori* (buzzers) and in the choral part only the rhythm is indicated, with "pitch and duration being arbitrary and independent."[18] Following an initial manifesto on music in 1910, Pratella's "Technical Manifesto" of 1912 got down to cases and explicitly recommended employment of rhythmic irregularities, atonality, and microtones. In retrospect, Pratella's vision seems little more than a mirror of Ferruccio Busoni's *Entwurf einer neuen Ästhetik der Tonkunst* (Sketch of a New Aesthetic of Music, 1907), which projected the use of microtones and electronic music in the future.

It was Luigi Russolo, a painter by training, who brought the Futurist movement in music to a head. He opened his Futurist manifesto, "The Art of Noises" (1913), with the declaration that ancient life was all silence, but that with the invention of the machine in the nineteenth century noise was born: "Today, Noise triumphs and reigns supreme over the sensibilities of men." Admitting that he was not a musician and therefore held no acoustical predilections, but rather was a painter determined to renew everything, he concluded, "And so, bolder than a professional musician could be, unconcerned by my apparent incompetence, and convinced that all rights and all possibilities open up to daring, I have been able to initiate the great renewal of music by means of the Art of Noises."[19]

The Futurist arsenal has been repeatedly and tediously if also necessarily described. For while the immediate results were slim, the implications of Futurism for an increasingly mechanized society were not. Russolo's noise machines, which he labeled *intonarumori* (noise intoners), were designed to produce the sounds detailed in his theories.[20] A single "exploder" *(scoppiatore)*, whose name and product vividly mirrored the Futurists' call for war, was demonstrated in Modena in 1913, but the first public concert incorporating them was not given until 21 April 1914 in Milan,[21] when three of Russolo's pieces for noise intoners—*The Awakening of a City, Luncheon on the Kursaal Terrace,* and *Meeting of Automobiles and Aeroplanes*—were performed.[22] In the last of these, which Russolo referred to as a "Network of Noise," the two most recent advances in transport received one of their earliest acknowledgements in the world of music.[23] The Futurists' proclivity for public ruckus-making also extended to the concerts of other musicians, a fact that was mentioned by Busoni in a letter from Milan of 13 May 1913 to the Dutch pianist Egon Petri: "Remarkable evening yesterday; after the second Sonatina something like an uproar arose at the back of the hall, Condottiere Marinetti engaged in fisticuffs with some of the rebels, from the artists' room I heard squabbling voices and one very loud one which repeatedly bellowed *'Fuori'* [Get out]!"[24]

These happenings seemed but a prelude to the event of 15 September 1914, shortly after the outbreak of war, when Marinetti, Boccioni, Russolo and others interrupted a festive evening of Puccini at the Teatro dal Verme in Milan by ceremonially burning an Austrian flag while Marinetti flourished an Italian one. Eleven Futurists were arrested the next day following a similar demonstration in the Milan Galleria.[25] The realization of the Futurists' interventionist agenda was just around the corner.

VISIONARY CLASSICIST

Busoni was not only a highly respected composer but a virtuoso pianist, and like more than one artist with that particular combination of talents, he was obliged to rely upon his performing abilities to support his creative career. Busoni's Romantic base continued to vie with various impulses from the cutting edge, but the forces of Neoclassicism, which he dubbed *Die junge Klassizität* in 1921, proved to be the most important influence. It was an aesthetic that he defined as an organic flowering based upon the clarity of earlier models rather than a sterile revival of the past, one that promoted Bach and Mozart as the quintessential models for the modern composer.[26] The keyword in the term, however, was *junge,* a generational qualifier that identified Busoni's predisposition not toward a *new* classicism, which he felt sounded like a return, but rather toward a vision propelled by *youth*— a concept that was to take on "powerful and irrational overtones" in Weimar Germany.[27]

Regardless of the modifying adjectives, Busoni, like Thomas Mann, saw Goethe as the most probable basis for a new classicism that was akin to Bach.[28] Although Busoni's piano arrangements of Bach in particular ultimately signaled his return to the past and assumed the status of signature pieces,[29] in a letter to the musicologist Hugo Leichtentritt in November 1915 Busoni emphasized his "boundless admiration for Mozart." He also declared his "initially instinctive, later rationalized rejection of Wagner, whose influence has afflicted me, of all my contemporaries, the least."[30]

In January 1916 Busoni played Beethoven's "Emperor" Concerto in a program that included his own *Indianische Fantasie*, which was based on Amerindian melodies, and Franz Liszt's *Totentanz*—all of which were capable of being deconstructed as scores with nationalist messages or a subtext concerning war. The following March, however, a performance of Wotan's "Abschied" provoked an outburst in a letter to Petri, wherein he spoke of "gods and heroes on stilts, the nightmare of my fifty year's life— heroes, as Heine says, who had the courage of a hundred lions and the brains of two donkeys!" The direction in which Busoni was headed as a composer was clear. He contrasted Wagner's heroic bombast with the puppet *Teatro dei Piccoli*, which he had recently seen at Rome in a performance of a Rossini comic opera.[31] Then, in concerts that followed in Zurich, he programmed Mendelssohn's "Italian" Symphony, his own *Rondò arlecchinesco*, and Beethoven's "Eroica" Symphony, although he was clearly beginning to have problems with the latter. "The Latin attitude to art with its cool serenity and its insistence on outward form, is what refreshes me," he confided to Petri. "It was only through Beethoven that music acquired that growling and frowning expression which was natural enough to him, but which perhaps ought to have remained his lonely path alone. Why are you in such a bad temper, one would often like to ask, especially in the second period."[32]

Busoni knew the puppet *teatro meccanico* from his childhood days in Trieste, and the idea of tapping the commedia dell'arte had been renewed in June 1913 when Schoenberg gave a private performance of *Pierrot lunaire* (1912) in Busoni's home. The first draft of his libretto for *Arlecchino*, an opera in one act, was sketched shortly thereafter, with the protagonist cast as a spoken role, and the text was completed in October 1914, two months after the outbreak of World War I. Busoni started to work on the score in November, but it was dropped when he and his family left for the

United States in January 1915, although there was some talk of it being performed at the Metropolitan Opera in New York. Unhappy in the United States, where he felt increasingly isolated, he returned to Europe, taking up residence in Zurich. The opera was completed in Zurich in August 1916 and received its first performance there on 11 May 1917.

Ferruccio Dante Michelangelo Benvenuto Busoni's *Arlecchino* begins with a reading from Dante's *The Divine Comedy*, followed by the judgment "Incontinence, thou art for all mankind the tempter, and leadest us down to Hell." The opera is choked with symbols, a fact that is openly announced at the beginning of the work: " 'Tis not for children, nor for gods, this play; for understanding people 'tis design'd. The sense of what the characters may say, may well escape an all too literal mind." Allusion piles on top of allusion, and at the close of a reading from Dante, Arlecchino arrives and announces, "While you are setting Dante to music, the barbarian is at the town gate, soon he'll be here." Such words recalled not only Kipling's *For All We Have and Are* of 1914[33] but also Cocteau's joyous invocation of Dante (accompanied by the caption "Dante on Our Side") on the cover of his magazine *Le mot* for 15 June 1915, which was prompted by Italy's declaration of war on Austro-Hungary (fig. 27).[34] An original allusion to Turks was changed to barbarians, once again reinforcing the reference to the Germans: "Horns instead of ears, hair and beard unshaven. . . . Men for battles and for slaughter, drunkards, heretics, hellgate porters come to rape our wives and daughters!" Later Arlecchino, posing as a recruitment officer, arrives to tell the cuckolded Matteo that he has three minutes to pack up his belongings and be off. To the question "Will you allow me to take my Dante with me?" comes this reply: "No one shall ever say that in a war our culture went to ruin!" This is set to a music marked *in modo di marcia funebre.*

All of this may strike one as curious in light of the fact that the opera is written in German. But this is commedia dell'arte at its most ferocious, and no authority is spared: the Church (Busoni was never able to accept his mother's devout Catholicism), conventional opera, and human nature are all pilloried in a fashion that could only have pleased the Futurists even as its indictment of war would have displeased them. Busoni's *Arlecchino* appears to commence as a kind of prank, but "the joke turns sour," as Stefan Zweig wrote in his report of the first performance. "Arlecchino . . . finally becomes the philosophic mocker and raisonneur of the World War. The whole is a caprice, a play of moods, but of a humour which tries to conceal deathly earnest."[35]

Busoni, who was hoping to establish a *nuova* commedia dell'arte with

Figure 27.   Jean Cocteau, *Dante on Our Side*, cover for *Le mot*, 15 June 1915. (© 2002 ARS New York/ADAGP Paris.)

Arlecchino—he called it a *Marionetten-Tragödie*—intended to register his protest against Wagner's solution for music-drama in the process of affirming that his own Latin origins were as important as his German training and intellectual character. Mozart comes to mind as Matteo reads Dante; as he prepares for war a *marcia bergamesca* by Gaetano Donizetti (so identified in the score)[36] is sounded; Wagner is summoned at moments of impending doom, of course; and a *bel canto* love duet is sung, only to be denounced by the heroine as an operatic sham. Busoni's voice is never in doubt, and in many places it seems to prefigure the musical language of Hindemith's slightly later *Das Nusch-Nuschi* (1920), another opera for marionettes. The tradition of the commedia dell'arte, puppet theater, and the mask, recently revisited in *Petrushka* and *Pierrot lunaire*, had taken a new turn and now forecast a cultural climate that would sponsor Stravinsky's *Renard, Pulcinella,* and *Oedipus Rex,* Falla's *El retablo de maese Pe-dro,* and Ravel's *L'enfant et les sortilèges.*[37]

Equally important in Busoni's turn to puppet theater as the basis for opera—a notion to which he was to return in his last opera, *Doktor Faust*—were the examples of Gordon Craig, whose *The Art of Theatre* Busoni owned, and Rainer Maria Rilke, whose influential article on puppets had been written only a month before he met Busoni in March 1914.[38] The puppet has carried potent and magical powers from antiquity in virtually all cultures, but its use in the immediate postwar period may well have been promoted less by the symbol of man being manipulated by higher forces than the sheer absence of the human. An inanimate object that nonetheless moves, the puppet carried the potential of creating anxiety—the apparition of the dead in motion. The analogy between puppets and powerless citizens may have seemed less valid than the specter of "mummies and corpses made to dance."[39]

It is noteworthy that just when Busoni was completing *Arlecchino* some members of the Futurist assembly had begun to adjust their sights. In 1913, well before his departure for America in 1915, Busoni had met any number of the Futurists, including Marinetti and Boccioni. After his return to Italy Busoni again met Boccioni, one of the most gifted of the Futurist painters and sculptors, while both were guests of a mutual friend at San Remigio in June 1916. During the three weeks they spent there they developed a strong sympathy for each other's work. Boccioni, who was on leave, painted a portrait of Busoni (fig. 28). In this painting, executed virtually on the eve of his own death in the war, Boccioni turned away from the aggressiveness of his Futurist style, denounced Cubism, abstraction, and the use of polymaterials (which he had only recently proposed in his own book, *Futurist Painting and Sculpture*), and embraced Cézanne.[40]

Boccioni had just turned thirty-three, and war still seemed "a wonderful, marvelous, terrible thing." He was called back to active service in early June, and from there he wrote to Busoni, for the last time, in August.

> I can only thank you for giving me the courage to endure this appalling life. . . . I shall leave this existence with a contempt for all that is not art. There is nothing more terrible than art. Everything that I am now facing is child's play compared to a good brushstroke, a harmonious line of verse or a properly placed chord. By comparison everything else is a matter of mechanics, habit, patience of memory. Only art exists.[41]

Later that month Busoni wrote a letter to Petri in which he makes clear the impact of Boccioni's death on 17 August and expresses his anger at the

Figure 28.   Umberto Boccioni, *Maestro Busoni*, 1916.
(Photo courtesy of Galleria Nazionale d'Arte Moderna,
Rome.)

jingoistic obituaries in Italian newspapers, which glossed over Boccioni's
importance as an artist.[42] Busoni also noted, no doubt somewhat ironically,
that Boccioni had been killed not by a machine gun or a tank, or in an airplane, but by falling from a horse.[43] Marinetti or D'Annunzio would no
doubt have demanded a replay, but they were quick to claim that thirteen
Futurists—including Boccioni—were killed during the war, by whatever
means, and that another forty-one were injured, including Russolo and
Marinetti himself.[44]

In a letter of 19 September 1916 Busoni announced the completion of
Arlecchino and said that he found himself incapable of subduing his feel-

ings about Boccioni. "Apart from the fact that I loved him, he was at last, after a lengthy interval, an Italian painter of historical significance. And he felt he was only at the outset!"[45] Once again a theme so dear to the English war poets had been resurrected, that of doomed youth struck down in its prime.[46] Equally important, however, was the fact that Boccioni's reconsideration of figure and perspective came at precisely the same time as Picasso's turn toward an *Ingriste* mode, the Cocteau-Satie-Stravinsky move toward Neoclassicism, and Busoni's own completion of a reductive *Sonatina ad usum infantis* (1917), which he cited in his marionette opera about war. A broad range of the prewar avant-garde was now in the process of rediscovering history.

As he approached *Arlecchino* Busoni was acutely aware of the compositional means upon which he was depending. This is evident in his editions and transcriptions of numerous works of J. S. Bach, which he had begun in the last decade of the nineteenth century and now took up again with renewed interest.[47] Although Bach and Mozart increasingly served Busoni as points of orientation, his earlier piano concerto with choral finale (1904) had betrayed a decided bias toward Beethoven. While he found it difficult to escape Beethoven's influence altogether, by February 1919 Busoni had managed to make the final break, as he announced in a letter to a friend.

> It is—I believe—a matter of historical fact which one can already formulate 'at this juncture,' that music from the death of Wagner until at least 1923 will simply be described as *post-Wagnerian* or *neo-Wagnerian*, Stravinsky and Schoenberg not excepted, just as Tintoretto and Tiepolo still belong to the world of Titian. . . . I am making no post-war proclamation when I sincerely believe that the moment has arrived to shake off nineteenth-century Germany. And do not be shocked if I mention—in this sense only—Beethoven in the same breath as Wagner.[48]

Other aesthetic opportunities now beckoned, although as it turned out Busoni's earlier and enthusiastic projection of a future for microtones and electronic music ultimately proved to be a momentary Futuristic vision, one that dissolved in the face of an unresolved conflict between Futurism and Neoclassicism. As Busoni put it, his path would now take off from the successors of the "school" of Mozart—from Cherubini, Rossini, and Mendelssohn. He felt that the "fatal popularization" of Beethoven's Ninth Symphony had led only to confusion and had borne no fruit and that the followers of Wagner signified "an unbroken regression." As to where music would go from here, he answered, "To Young Classicality, but not 'back'"—rather onward to his dreams in *Doktor Faust.* Nuanced versions of Busoni's vision for a new music were also promoted by other composers. Postwar editions emphasizing Italy's classical heritage—of Gesualdo by Pizzetti and of Monteverdi by Malipiero, for example—were complemented by Casella's editions of not only Scarlatti but also Beethoven. Significantly, the latter of these also gave a clear indication that Italy's review of its classical heritage would not be confined to Mediterranean composers.[49]

Part 5

GERMANY-AUSTRIA

12 "Dance of Death"

> All is lost! . . . Contrition remains; but it explains nothing,
> for it does not say what led to it.
>
> Schoenberg, *Totentanz der Prinzipien*

The German empire of 1914, an unequal federation of twenty-five con-
stituent states of which Prussia was the strongest, had been forged in the
Franco-Prussian War of 1871 During the ensuing *Kulturkampf*, which
sought to bring unity out of a conglomerate of multiple ethnicities and re-
ligions, Protestant Germany pushed to enlist the loyalty of Catholics to the
nation much as France did in its calls for a *union sacrée*. Yet despite its lack
of political and social unity or a colonial base equal to that of Britain or
France, Germany had cause to be proud for reasons other than its growing
industrial and military might. Its cultural achievements were the envy of
the world; its exceptional public schools and universities were considered
models; and in the fields of medicine, natural and social sciences as well as
humanistic disciplines, Germany was viewed as preeminent.

For those who most identified with the arts, the term *Kultur* defined the
very essence of the Great War, and its meaning was symbolized by historical figures such as Goethe, Kant, and Beethoven. Claims to cultural excellence in other parts of the German-speaking world posed as many problems as they solved, however. Despite the presence of a distinct Viennese
School in the world of music from the eighteenth century on, at the outset of the Great War the concept of an independent Austrian state—or,
more particularly, a Vienna-centered culture—was difficult to identify in
light of the multiple nationalities within the Hapsburg monarchy and Austria's cultural and linguistic ties with Germany. Indeed, it has been noted
that "state patriotism" in Austria—clearly visible in August 1914 both in
officialdom and the populace alike—was "not coterminous with national
identity as it was in either France or Germany."[1] It was an issue that plagued
all Austrian citizens and one with which the Austrian poet Hugo von

Hofmannsthal struggled in an attempt to create what he called "an organic synthesis between German and Slavic 'being,' which could overcome national difference."[2]

The problem was not easily resolved, however. When the Hapsburg Empire collapsed in 1918, Hofmannsthal was still promoting the dream of a new Austrian identity in a Salzburg Festival, of which he, along with Richard Strauss, stage designer Alfred Roller, and director Max Reinhardt, was a spiritual founder. Yet, his claims of cosmopolitanism could not disguise the fact that the historic culture of Salzburg and, consequently, its festival ideals, were both German and Roman Catholic to the core.[3]

The specific role of music in promoting a sense of a German national feeling had been of central importance throughout the nineteenth century, and some argued that it was "quite possibly of more importance than German literature."[4] Yet the esteem, even overriding superiority, that could not be denied Austro-Germany in the world of music ran counter to a developing sense that German national identity could only be asserted through a war, a view increasingly regarded as preordained.[5] Friedrich von Bernhardi's book *Deutschland und der nächste Krieg* (Germany and the Next War, 1911), which was quickly translated into English and widely diffused in inexpensive editions, spoke openly of war as a "life-giving principle," as an expression of a superior culture, and indeed, as a contemporary piece put it, "the price one must pay for culture."[6]

As the war progressed the adjective "Austrian" meant little beyond its simple identification with entente-oriented notions of national self-determination. The most momentous turn in Austrian identity came in the autumn of 1916, when it became apparent that Austria-Hungary was incapable of containing the Russians, the Italians, or the Romanians. As a consequence the Austro-Hungarians were obliged to accept a subservient role in a Joint High Command with the Germans. For the Viennese, proud of their musical heritage, the idea of assimilation into a pan-Germanic tradition was difficult to swallow. Indeed, the delayed performances of both Strauss's *Salome* (1905) and Janáček's *Jenufa* (1904) by a decade and more after their respective premieres only confirmed that official Austrian culture was slow to open up to other nationalities. However, an early ban on Viennese performances by French, British, Russian, and Belgian artists early on in the war ultimately proved impossible to implement, and while premieres were limited to German or Austrian composers such as Alexander von Zemlinsky and Richard Strauss, standard Italian works by Verdi and Puccini continued to be performed regularly along with Bizet's *Carmen*, Tchaikovsky's *Eugene Onegin*, and Rossini's *Guillaume Tell*.[7]

THE LOST BRIGADE

In the prewar years Expressionist poets and musicians, many of whom became furious pacifists once the conflict exploded, set about inventing a new syntax,[8] and the poets recorded their spectral visions of the impending war in numerous verses.[9] Expressionism by definition emphasized an inner spiritual and psychological vision as opposed to a record of external events. As a consequence, distortion counted. In the world of music this had led to toying not only with phraseology and paragraphing but also with tonality, which now seemed on the brink of disappearing altogether.

This condition was most readily perceivable in the music of Arnold Schoenberg. In 1907, little more than a decade after Mahler had penned his own soldier songs in *Des Knaben Wunderhorn*, Schoenberg set a text by Viktor Klemperer, "Der verlorene Haufen" (The Lost Brigade), as part of a contest sponsored by the Berlin periodical *Die Woche* (CD track 11).[10] Like Schoenberg, Klemperer was a Jew baptized as a Protestant, and in his meditation on Klemperer's verses Schoenberg later claimed to have made "a decisive step forward."[11] Although neither music nor text completely crossed the border into the visionary inner world of Expressionism, both now teetered on the edge.

More important than the contest was the import of Klemperer's verses, which were as prescient of the struggle to come as they were a backward glance.

Trinkt aus, ihr zechtet zum letzten
    Mal,
Nun gilt es Sturm zu laufen;
Wir stehen zuvörderst aus freier
    Wahl,
Wir sind der verlorene Haufen.

Wer länger nicht mehr wandern
    mag,
Wer Füsse schwer geworden,
Wem zu grell das Licht, wem zu
    laut der Tag,
Der tritt in unsern Orden,

Trinkt aus, schon färbt sich der
    Osten fahl,
Gleich werden die Büschen singen,
Und blinkt der erste Morgenstrahl,

Drink up, you've caroused for the
    last time,
Now the assault is to begin;
We stand at the front out of free
    choice,
We are the lost brigade.

Those who no longer want to
    roam,
Who have become weary of foot,
For whom the light is too bright
    and the day too loud,
They join our ranks.

Drink up, the east is already turn-
    ing pale,
Presently the rifles will be singing,
And when the first ray of morning
    gleams,

So will ich mein Fähnlein schwingen.	I will be waving the banner.
Un Wenn die Sonne im Mittag steht,	And when the sun stands at midday,
So wird die Bresche gelegt sein;	The breach will have been made;
Und wenn die Sonne zur Rüste geht,	And when the sun sinks,
Wir die Mauer vom Boden gefegt sein.	The wall will be swept to the ground.
Und wenn die Nacht sich niedersenkt,	And when night falls,
Sie raffe den Scheier zusammen,	Let her draw the veil together,
Dass sich kein Funke drin verfängt	So that no spark is caught in it
Von den londernden Siegesflammen!	By the glowing flames of victory!
Nun vollendet der Mond den stillen Lauf,	Now the moon completes her silent course,
Wir sehn ihn nicht verbleichen.	Yet we do not watch her fade.
Kühl zieht ein neuer Morgen herauf—	A fresh new morning approaches—
Dann sammeln sie unsere Leichen.	And they are coming to collect our corpses.[12]

At first glance, "Der verlorene Haufen" might seem to glorify war, but Walter Flex, a popular German poet of World War I, more clearly signaled the heart of Klemperer's verses in preaching the need for courage to face a certain, if also pointless, death. This, he argued, was possible through a moral stance that rested on "faith in God, an understanding of the nation's need to progress through the historical continuum, and belief in the lasting bonds of comradeship. . . . Facing death in the proper frame of mind, rather than defeating the enemy, or even confronting him, has become the infantryman's prime concern."[13] It was a point of view shared by Richard Dehmel, the poet who inspired Schoenberg's *Verklärte Nacht*.

This was not an exclusive Austro-German perspective, however, for it could be found in the war literature of many countries—in the verses, for example, of Rupert Brooke ("Now, God be thanked Who has matched us with His hour") and Alan Seeger ("I have a rendezvous with Death"). Seeger was even more explicit in a letter he wrote home. "It is by far the noblest form in which death can come," he said. "It is in a sense almost a privilege to be allowed to meet it in this way." It was a sentiment also endorsed by Adolf Hitler upon hearing of German mobilization in Munich on

1 August 1914: "[I] sank down upon my knees and thanked Heaven out of the fullness of my heart for the favour of having been permitted to live in such times." [14]

The church worked mightily to promote this belief, and the German clergy made an especially prominent use of the themes of death and resurrection, suffering and redemption, as a means of advocating war. The theology of war had found a new equation: faithfulness to family and *Vaterland* were seen as tantamount to serving God and Christ.[15] The vision of the fallen soldier as a rejuvenating societal force was a potent image that was plumbed repeatedly in many countries, but none more so than Germany, where its early promotion by the political right was eventually endorsed by the Weimar Republic.

Such a mythic attitude of service was further supported by one of the most forceful developments of the Great War, namely, a renewed attention to camaraderie, which held promises for a powerful sense of nationhood in a post-Armistice world. The German *Volk* was envisioned as nothing less than a *Männerbund*, a group of comrades "reinvigorated by the 'new men' who had come back from the front" and mindful of those who had given their lives for their country.[16] It is little less than extraordinary that historian Ernst von Salomon would later identify these "new men" as "*verlorene Haufen*," conservative radicals and discontents drawn largely from the ranks of ex-soldiers and the unemployed, who after the war composed the Freikorps, the predecessor of the Storm Troopers in the Nazi era and Klemperer's personal nemesis.[17]

Pronounced in Schoenberg's "Der verlorene Haufen" is the progression from the first light of sunrise to the sun at midday, followed by the glowing sunset at evening, the appearance of the moon, and the completion of the cycle with the approach of a new morning when the corpses are carried away. This emphasis upon the circularity of life and the intractableness of fate was a theme that resonated throughout the Great War and was implicit in popular German soldier songs such as "Morgenrot"[18] as well as in the text and structural detail of Berg's opera *Wozzeck*. In the same year that Schoenberg wrote "Der verlorene Haufen" he penned an extraordinarily moving a cappella chorus, *Friede auf Erden* (Peace on Earth), a prayer that seemed to ask for a stay of what many saw as an inevitable war.

Not only did Schoenberg's two pupils, Berg and Webern, follow him into the world of Expressionist song, but his brother-in-law Alexander Zemlinsky also probed new harmonic, if still tonal, terrain with uncommon security. One of Zemlinsky's few songs written during the war, "Harmonie des Abends" of 1916 (a setting of Baudelaire's "Harmonie du soir"), brought a new meaning to the French poet's verses. As the poem opens evening draws in with a somber silence; as it closes, the curtain falls on a glorious Viennese past:

Ein Herz, dem es bangt, wenn der Tag sich verhüllt	A heart that's afraid when the day becomes veiled
Sucht Strahlen, die aus der Vergangenheit steigen.	Seeks rays that arise from the past.
Die Sonne, sie scheint sich verblutend zu neigen.	The sun seems to decline, bleeding to death.
Gleich einer Monstranz in mir leuchtet dein Bild.	Like a monstrance your image glows in me.
O schmerzlicher Walzer, o schmachtender Reigen!	O sorrowful waltz, o yearning roundelay! [19]

The image of the "sorrowful waltz," incorporated as a thrice-repeated refrain in Baudelaire's original ("Valse mélancholique et langoureux vertige!"), would soon be addressed in different ways by Ravel in his apocalyptic *La valse* and by Schoenberg in the proto-serial "Waltz" finale of his *Five Pieces* for piano (1923). The original French image is completed in a slightly different fashion in the German translation ("O schmerzlicher Walzer, o schmachtender Reigen"). Tellingly, Arthur Schnitzler had addressed the theme of the "yearning roundelay" in his play *Reigen*, of 1900, which was not produced until 1921 and then closed down as obscene. An exposé of Vienna's highly stratified society, the play argued the Freudian notion that "the image and the beloved are not the same." [20] The "round game" in question was the perpetual and necessarily unsuccessful search for the satisfaction of (sexual) desire, which in turn was capable of being read as an indictment of nations in their never-ending quest for fulfillment and identity. It was a metaphor that Berg had likewise invoked in the Ländler- and waltz-laden idiom of "Reigen," the last of the *Three Pieces* for orchestra, completed in July 1915. [21]

Numerous German composers and institutions were quick to recognize the price of war yet buckle under the weight of practical obligations. Max Bruch, who had experienced the Franco-Prussian War, presciently wrote in a letter to his daughter that "streams of blood will be the price for justifying our cause, for the shocks and horrors of this war will be greater than any other hitherto." [22] With his son at the front, Bruch hurriedly renounced his honorary doctorate from Cambridge University even as he complained that no German university had offered him one by way of replacement. He also expressed amazement that his membership in the Société des Auteurs Compositeurs had been terminated and professed not to understand why he, together with Engelbert Humperdinck and Siegfried Wagner, had been thrown out of the Paris Académie. Deprived, like Richard Strauss, of his foreign royalties, Bruch was compelled to write several works with broad appeal for a wartime public—works like the homophonic *Heldenfeier* for six-part chorus and organ from January 1915, which immediately became popular with church choirs, and *Die Stimme der Mutter Erde* for mixed chorus, organ and orchestra from October 1916, which emphasized a patriotism based upon the natural yearning for the motherland.[23]

The Berlin Philharmonic was also quick to raise the flag. Hundreds of concerts featuring Beethoven's works were given, and sixty-six performances by the orchestra during this period consisted of works by Beethoven alone.[24] The trend to program Beethoven's works even led to a debate concerning whether his music was being too frequently performed.[25] Wagner-Abende, Bach-Beethoven-Brahms festivals, and a healthy dose of Mozart, Strauss, Schubert, Weber, Gluck, and Mendelssohn dominated the concert landscape, enlivened with only an occasional work by Liszt or Tchaikovsky. Rarest of all was a performance on 8 October 1914 of the American composer Edward MacDowell's Second Piano Concerto in the company of Beethoven's Third Piano Concerto and Busoni's arrangement of Liszt's *Rhapsody espagnole,* with Busoni conducting.[26] At the time, of course, the United States had not yet entered the war.

French composers were ostracized, too, except for the occasional piece by Berlioz or a short number on a dance program by Bizet—both allowed by a Berlin policy that permitted the performance of compositions by composers of enemy nations if they had died before 1914.[27] Debussy's *La mer* (1905) was performed by the Berlin Philharmonic for the first time on 9 November 1918, eight months after the composer's death,[28] and no Ravel was heard until his *Daphnis and Chloë* was presented on 20 December 1920, followed by a performance of *La valse* on 16 May 1922. Stravinsky did not appear on a Berlin Philharmonic program until his *L'oiseau de feu* belatedly joined the roster on 2 November 1922, followed by the city's first hearing of *Le sacre du printemps* on 20 November. The music of Elgar, whose *Dream of Gerontius* had been performed there as early as November 1902, whose *Enigma* variations (1899) had been introduced in February 1908, and whose overture to *Cockaigne* (1901) appeared in October 1913, was not only dropped during the war years but had failed to make a reappearance as late as the hundredth anniversary of the Berlin Philharmonic in 1982. Nor had a single work by Holst or Vaughan Williams ever been programmed by the latter date. Indicative of Germany's prevailing musical conservatism, Schoenberg's *Five Pieces for Orchestra,* op. 16, of 1909 was not performed in Berlin until 11 December 1922. Clearly, Paris and especially London had been receptive to new musical developments to a degree matched by neither Berlin nor Vienna during the twentieth century's first two decades.

JACOB'S LADDER

Schoenberg, who had already celebrated his fortieth birthday, was obliged to report for an army medical examination on 20 May 1915. Found in sufficiently good physical health to serve, he enrolled as a one-year volunteer on 15 December and was stationed in Vienna. The menial duties, the authoritarian atmosphere, and the impossibility of continuing with his creative work left the composer distraught.[29] Whatever his renown as a musician, Schoenberg's talents were never put to use in the service, although the Germans typically kept a full complement of musicians near the front.[30] Following minimal duty, and repeated attempts to obtain release on grounds of poor health, Schoenberg was discharged in October 1916.

He immediately set to work on an oratorio, *Die Jakobsleiter,* but was again called up in September 1917, this time for lighter military duties before being discharged on medical grounds only a month later. In the interim Schoenberg wrote to Busoni, having heard of the latter's article, "Der Kriegsfall Boccioni" (The War Case of Boccioni), which was published in the *Neue Zürcher Zeitung* on 31 August 1916. Schoenberg's concern for Boccioni mirrored not only the composer's own interest in painting at this time but also his belief that whether one was a musician or a painter the meaning of life was to be found only in the use of one's talents to their fullest. Writing from Vienna the following November, a decidedly chastened and dispirited Schoenberg declared:

> I hear that you are in Zurich, that you have written an article about peace, that the war is thus afflicting you—hence I must write to you immediately. I am suffering terribly from this war. How many close relationships with the finest people it has severed: how it has corroded half my mind away and shown me that I can no better survive with the remainder than with the corroded portion.
>
> Please send me your article about peace and let me have other news of yourself. If only we *two* and the *likes of us in every country* could sit down and deliberate on a peace settlement. Within a week we could pass it on to the world and with it a thousand ideas which would suffice for half eternity, for a half-eternal peace. . . .
>
> I was a soldier for ten months; now I have been exempted, because

in the end I was unfit for service at the front. Of course, I have been through a good deal! Consider: an apprentice soldier at forty-two years of age; when one has, after all, made the greatest sacrifices all one's life to maintain one's independence, suddenly to become a trainee and to have to take orders from idiots![31]

Busoni replied ten days later, noting that his essay on Boccioni was "not a pacifist publication but one in which art—in a brief innuendo—was weighed up against war." He encouraged Schoenberg "to remain optimistic and work towards peace": "That will be our proudest victory, when we can hold up the products of our creativity against the destruction of the other! Durability versus decay."[32]

Woodrow Wilson had sent a note to all the warring countries in Europe on 18 December 1916 that proposed conditions for an end to the hostilities. Schoenberg, aware of these developments, had at first delayed responding to Busoni, but on 30 January 1917 he wrote from Vienna that he had been moved to a direct act of emulation. Inspired by President Wilson, he had written a paper on the subject of peace, and he asked Busoni for help in publishing it, if possible, in a neutral paper under a pen name.[33] Schoenberg asked Busoni's opinion of a fifteen-point plan, which sought to establish a broadly deployed international peacekeeping force whose principal objective would be to prevent the manufacture of arms and the training of troops.[34] Responding to Busoni's inquiry concerning his composing, he continued:

My work in progress; you ask after it; it is scarcely worth mentioning. During the war, before I was called up, I started work on a major project. A symphony. In four movements. The first two on poems by Dehmel, the other two on my own texts. The first movement: "Freudenruf," the second "Der bürgerliche Gott," the third "Totentanz der Prinzipien," the fourth "Der Himmelsleiter." I have finished the text of the third, that of the fourth is two-thirds completed. As long as there was any prospect of peace, I was able to work. Then my courage left me. In the army it was, of course, impossible to work. And now: it isn't much.[35]

Although Schoenberg was supposed to conduct his *Gurrelieder* (1900–1911) in New York, he informed Busoni that he was not going to be able to go "because the English are letting nobody through."[36] The English attitude should have come as no surprise. After war broke out an avalanche of patriotic doggerel aimed at England appeared in the German popular press, perhaps best epitomized by Ernst Lissauer's "Hassgesang gegen England" (Song of Hate against England). Published in a Munich newspaper in September 1914, it was taught to schoolchildren, recited in the trenches, and proclaimed from the vaudeville, theater, and opera stages to rousing applause. Professing that the German nation loved and hated as one, the song's repeating refrain proclaimed that England alone was their foe ("Wir haben alle nur einen Fein: *England!*").[37] German musical films endorsed this sentiment in a welter of clichéd lyrics, many of which paradoxically also suggested that the British Empire ought to have joined Germany against their common historic enemy, France.[38]

The symphony that Schoenberg described to Busoni had been inaugurated in the period of 1912–1914, but it was never completed. The scherzo of the original symphony used a theme composed of all twelve tones of the chromatic scale, although the composer later cautioned that "this was only one of the themes. I was still far away from the idea of using such a basic theme as a unifying means for a whole work."[39] Schoenberg's concern for such technical questions must be viewed in light of the attending subject matter. On 15 January 1915 he completed a monologue, "Totentanz der Prinzipien" (Dance of Death of the Principles), that served as the basis of this scherzo, and three days later he commenced the text for *Die Jakobsleiter,* which he envisaged as the fourth movement of the projected symphony.[40]

In the nineteenth century the "Dance of Death" had been exploited as a theme by composers such as Liszt and Saint-Saëns. More recently it had appeared in Strindberg's social morality play, *The Dance of Death* (1901), and Hugo Ball, a German émigré in Zurich who had founded the Dada movement, penned a satiric "Totentanz" in 1916, which was sung by Richard Huelsenbeck at the Cabaret Voltaire.[41] The painter Otto Dix also adopted the theme in his retrospective *Dance of Death 1917 (the dead man's mound)* of 1924, and, as we shall see, so did Alban Berg in his opera *Wozzeck.*[42]

Schoenberg's notes confirm that he had originally intended his "Totentanz" to be staged, and he described it as follows: "Orchestral prelude, brief sketch of an event, in a hard, dry tone; then a funeral, speech at the graveside, all very short; brief pause, followed by heavy bells behind the scenes. During the ensuing scene these become ever louder and more frequent, and the sound gradually turns into a furious pealing." As the speaker commences the bells continue to peal in the background, and when they cease he delivers "a passionate and combative address, seeking to trace the fundamentals of human existence" throughout the whole range of human emotions. The commandment "Thou shalt" demands a reply "I must" from the hero, who is not yet prepared to offer it.[43] In Schoenberg's sketch the competition between personal and social goals, the sacred and profane, loom against the background of a war in progress. Alexander Ringer sums up the situation vividly.

> For, as millions rallied around their respective flags, blessed ceremoni-
> ously in the name of the Prince of Peace but unfurled in an open spirit
> of hatred, Schoenberg had begun wondering with Rilke whether the
> world-wide "death-dance of principles" did not also spell the death of a
> god fashioned in the image of man. Only the artist of genius, ordained
> by the divine lawgiver and supreme force of history, seemed left to
> carry the torch of truth into an unfathomable future.[44]

Jakobsleiter, which ultimately became a separate composition, begins with the following words spoken by the Archangel Gabriel: "Whether to right or to left, forward or backward, uphill or downhill—you must go on, without asking what lies before or behind you." Schoenberg's use of a twelve-note theme, which is subject to manipulation through inver-sion and retrograde devices, is the direct graphic response to this injunc-tion. If the work as a whole is so dense and symbol-laden that it is difficult to follow as narrative, the sense of personal spiritual mission is never in doubt. Worshippers of idols are denounced, the need for prayer is recog-nized, and Jacob wrestles with the Angel. The idea of the Chosen One (clearly identified with Schoenberg and his increasing sense of Jewish iden-tity) is then introduced in a passage concerning the dissolution of the ego that, given Schoenberg's impending military service, has patently autobio-graphical overtones. Schoenberg's induction was an event of such ominous personal importance that his pupil Winfried Zillig has hypothesized that it virtually accounts for the fact that Schoenberg did not complete his planned symphony.[45]

Finally readied for performance only in the 1970s, *Jakobsleiter* remains Schoenberg's central document from the period of the Great War. There is no need to parse its philosophy or its technical construction further in or-der to sense the personal and spiritual crisis it represented for the com-poser. The pursuit of a method of composing with twelve tones, which fol-lowed, confirms that in this work Schoenberg had been confronted with a vision and the most important challenge of his life.

A VISION FOR THE FUTURE

For all of Schoenberg's predisposition toward the composition of serenades, suites, septets, quartets, and concertos in the decade immediately following the war, he denied any relation whatsoever to the Neoclassicist infatuations that were preoccupying other composers, while for Stravinsky and those who rallied around him the reduction of forces, the clarification of textures, and the reclamation of the older forms increasingly began to serve as a lifeline to a cultural past as well as the lifeblood of a new age.[46] Schoenberg wrote a pair of marches to frame his *Serenade* of 1923, but here war was as much out of view as a resuscitated classicism. And the fractured waltz that closes his *Five Pieces* for piano, from the same year, bore little resemblance to either the café-concert atmosphere of Debussy's triple-metered "La plus que lente" or "Page d'album," the stylized simplicity of Stravinsky's "Waltz" from *Three Easy Pieces,* or the anxious commentary of Ravel's *La valse.* Similarly, the "Minuet" that appeared in Schoenberg's *Suite* for solo piano (1921) shared little affinity with the central movement of Ravel's earlier *Sonatine,* which carried the same designation. Here, in a pair of dance types with strong Viennese ties, Schoenberg made two of his earliest attempts at introducing a new method of composing with twelve tones. Pitch had finally surrendered to a newly structured order in a nontonal world, and equally disturbing, if not more, the expected triple meter, which lies at the very heart of both dance forms, had virtually disappeared. Nothing could have made clearer Schoenberg's rejection of the entire notion of Neoclassicism as a retro, Latin-based affair.[47]

At the same time Schoenberg's intermittent recomposition and arrangement of eighteenth-century works during the 1920s and 1930s—Bach's chorale preludes (1922), his great Prelude and Fugue ("St. Anne") in E♭ for organ (1928), the Georg Monn cello concerto (1932–1933), and the concerto for string quartet and orchestra after Handel (1933)—disclosed a decided ambivalence. The conservative revolutionary continued to emphasize that he believed in a transitional evolution, yet he had clearly come to feel a need to underscore a connection with the past. This he accomplished not only with refurbishings of early compositions but also in newly composed works that espoused a tonal base.[48]

What is the significance of these multiple strands of evidence with respect to the national psyche in wartime? From the beginning Schoenberg not only foresaw the war as a figurative national Dance of Death but also feared the ultimate defeat of Germany and Austria as an assault upon his own creative identity. As a consequence he struggled to reconcile his personal views with the apocalyptic scene drawn by Karl Kraus in *Die letzten Tage der Menschheit* (The Last Days of Mankind). Schoenberg eventually leaves us with little doubt concerning the question of nationality and his relation to it. His remark as late as the 1920s, for example, regarding his discovery of a new method of twelve-tone composition that would ensure the supremacy of German music for the next hundred years was only a be-lated reflection of Germany's wartime notion of *Kultur*. Far from being a reaction to Germany's defeat, Schoenberg's pronouncement reflected a longstanding cultural argument, one made several decades before in Wag-ner's *Art and Politics*, regarding the historic destiny of German culture and its dependence on music.[49] With the rise of the Third Reich, however, Schoenberg understandably began to vacillate and ultimately to recognize that he was more a Jew than a German.[50]

The choice was difficult, and it led to a delicate balancing act between the new music and the received German tradition. Later, in 1931, Schoenberg wrote a two-part essay titled "National Music" that explicitly clarified the role of the arts in politics and provided an alternative for a nation that was plainly suffering from a deep-seated, lingering sense of inferiority follow-ing its military defeat. "Any people can acquire hegemony in art," Schoen-berg argued. "It seems not even to depend on dominant power in the eco-nomic or military field." Rather, there seemed "to be only *one* power that regulates international success: the power of genius, the power of the idea, the art of representation."[51]

In this essay Schoenberg observed that two centuries of preparation had been required for Germany to assume leadership in music—a period dur-ing which the music of the Netherlands, France, and Italy, by turns both contrapuntal and homophonic, was ascendant. The contrapuntal art of Bach had changed everything, Schoenberg argued, and the simultaneous ap-pearance of "the art of development through motivic variation" signaled that German music had now transcended its sources. He then quickly noted a contemporary parallel with the change from an art of harmonic rela-tionships to an art of composing with "twelve tones related only to each other."[52]

In the second part of "National Music" Schoenberg further advanced the claims for his own historic role in this tale of German ascendancy through a direct comparison with a Latin-based art.

> Here is a remarkable fact, as yet unnoticed: Debussy's summons to the Latin and Slav peoples, to do battle against Wagner, was indeed success-ful; but to free *himself* from Wagner—that was beyond him. His most interesting discoveries can still only be used within the form and the way of giving shape to music that Wagner created. Here it must not be overlooked that much of his harmony was also discovered indepen-dently of him, in Germany. No wonder; after all, these were logical consequences of Wagner's harmony, further steps along the path the latter had pointed out.

After offering his opinion of Debussy's music,[53] Schoenberg zeroed in on his main point.

> It is a remarkable thing, as yet unnoticed by anyone—although a thousand facts point to it, and although the battle against German music during the war was primarily a battle against my own music, and although (as somebody said recently on the radio, not realizing or understanding what he was saying) nowadays my art has no line of succession abroad . . . ; remarkably, nobody has yet appreciated that my music, produced on German soil, without foreign influences, is a living example of an art able most effectively to oppose Latin and Slav hopes of hegemony and derived through and through from the traditions of German music.[54]

In reiterating Germany's obsessive denial of outside influences, Schoenberg endorsed the essence of the lingering Nietzschean dream, spelled out in *The Birth of Tragedy* (1872), that Wagner's great promise was a culture created by and for Germans that would parallel that of the classical Greek world.[55] It is also one of the supreme ironies of twentieth-century music history that these views were expressed by an Austrian composer who within two years would renounce his citizenship and his adopted Lutheran ties, reaffirm his Jewish heritage, and depart permanently to a new life in America. Despite the seeming certitude regarding the path of his own music as tethered to nationalist perspectives recently clarified during the Great War, the chilling similarity of his own rhetoric to that of the Nazis must have already begun to dawn on him.[56]

13 "The Last Days of Mankind"

> A fire, running from the earth to the sky, and a crashing
> noise coming down, like trumpets! . . . Still, everything
> still, as though the world were dead.
>
> Georg Büchner, *Woyzeck*

In a letter to Gerty von Hofmannsthal on 22 August 1914, Richard Strauss registered pride in Germany's initial battlefield successes. "These are great and glorious times," he wrote, "one feels exalted, knowing that this land, this people . . . must and will assume the leadership of Europe." Shortly thereafter, however, on 12 September, it was reported that Strauss had refused to sign a manifesto of German artists and intellectuals, explaining that "declarations about things concerning war and politics are not fitting for an artist, who must give his attention to his creations and to his work." [1] How an artist's thoughts and actions might come together was soon evidenced in the 19 October 1914 premier in Vienna of Strauss's *Festliche Praeludium*, for large orchestra with quintuple woodwinds and organ. Then, on 6 November, Strauss's *Ein Heldenleben* (1899) was performed in Berlin.

Strauss's *Josephs-Legende*, the ballet written expressly for Diaghilev's ballet in 1914, had premiered literally on the eve of war as Strauss was being awarded an honorary doctorate from Oxford University. Strauss expressed only annoyance with the Serbs when Francis Ferdinand was assassinated and reaffirmed his conviction that there would be no world war. Shortly afterward, when he was proved wrong, he was faced with the fact that a large part of his savings, acquired over thirty years and deposited in London, had been confiscated. Strauss's reaction was practical: he would simply have to work even harder and start saving all over again.

Strauss's central essay during the first year of the war, however, was *Eine Alpensinfonie*, which he had commenced in 1911 under the title "The Antichrist Symphony." The work's ultimate title, which underscores the pantheistic note that hovers over the whole, is clearly reminiscent of Mahler, and in fact news of Mahler's death in 1911 came just as Strauss was becoming absorbed in his symphony. In telling his story, which covers twenty-four hours in the mountains in twenty-one related sections, Strauss called for more than 150 players, including 20 horns and quadruple woodwinds, an assemblage whose size the composer was never to surpass, and whose scoring took one hundred days to complete.

Strauss's mountain journey commences and ends in the night, traversing the arch of light of a single day. Beginning with a tranquil ascent through woods and Alpine pastures, the climbers take the wrong path into the thicket and undergrowth, emerge onto a glacier, and, following a stormy struggle for the mountain top, achieve the summit in a moment of blinding radiance. Visions, mists, fading sunlight, and calm before the storm precede nature's final outburst in a scene of terrifying fury replete with the wind machines used in *Don Quixote* (1898). The descent commences, clouds dissolve, sunset arrives, the mountain is left behind, and night covers nature's panorama once more.

This is surely more than another Mahlerian nature symphony (although Mahlerites would protest that his third and sixth symphonies are more than that, too).[2] Given the years of its composition, 1911 through 1915, and its premiere under the composer's direction in Berlin on 25 October 1915, the symphony invites a reading as an allegory of humankind perpetually in search of some glorious and transcendental destination, stumbling down the wrong path to perilous encounters, followed by moments of calm before beginning the next, circular journey toward a calamitous rendezvous. By the time Strauss had completed the work, metaphor had hardened into reality: the Alpenkorps, an elite mountain division drawn from Bavarian guard and German light infantry, had been formed and was destined to play a notable role in the Battle of Verdun of 1916.[3]

Whatever the complete subtext of the work, Strauss's *Alpensinfonie* is the closest that Strauss ever came to defining man's natural proclivity for apocalyptic action—as if to say that the human urge to flex, to extend, and to conquer is in large part a response to nature's challenge. More specific to the period, however, is the fact that, as the historian George Mosse has detailed, in German culture the mountain had long symbolized national, as well as human, willpower, simplicity, and innocence, and, during the war it had come to stand "above all for the revitalization of the moral fiber of the *Volk* and its members."[4] Although Strauss's opera *Die Frau ohne Schatten*, completed in 1917 and premiered in Vienna in 1919, spoke not only of social trauma relatable to the collapse of Hapsburg Austria of World War I but also of social regeneration linked to the promise of childbirth,[5] during the war it was Strauss's *Alpensinfonie* that provided the most vivid backdrop to a nation's aspirations.

Among the members of the Viennese School it was Anton Webern who retained the closest spiritual link with this nature world of Mahler and Strauss, a paradoxical development considering that he ultimately endorsed the most rarefied implications of Schoenberg's compositional method. Indeed, the most consequential of Webern's predilections—spirituality and nature motifs delivered with concision and clarity—were in evidence well before any turn toward Schoenbergian Serialism.[6] During the war years Webern, like many composers, suffered the severe anxiety brought on by conflict between his sense of patriotism and his awareness of the ugliness of war. A letter to Schoenberg in late August 1914 captured the full force of the moment for the thirty-one-year-old Webern, and probably for most Austrians.

> I can hardly wait any longer to be called up. Day and night the wish haunts me: to be able to fight for this great, sublime cause. Do you not agree that this war really has no political motivations? It is the struggle of the angels with the devils. . . . Nothing but infractions of international laws: the apparently long accomplished mobilization of the Russians, the deceitful negotiations, the bribes among each other, the dum dum bullets, etc.—what nauseating filth! By contrast, the open, honourable position of our nations. Lord, grant that these devils will perish. God indeed ordains it already. This victory march of the Germans toward Paris. Hail, hail to this people! A thousand times already I have apologized in thought for having sometimes been a little suspicious especially of Protestantism. But I must say that I have come closer to it during these times. Catholic France! They have raged against Germans and Austrians like cannibals. Those left behind are interned somewhere in southern France—hard labour, bread and water their lot. And the most ridiculous of all—these Englishmen! They who up to now have only intrigued and who, once they were in battle, ran away so fast that the cavalry could not keep up. Perhaps, as I am writing to you, the Germans are already in Paris, and the Russians, too, will soon be chased away. . . . Oh, everything will end well. . . . The courage of our soldiers in the face of death and their daredevil fighting spirit are said to be without example. If only I could soon take part. How gladly.[7]

Webern's compulsive turn toward the setting of texts at this time can to some degree be read as mirroring the composite forces facing him. In the folk piety and nature study that inform the first and last songs of opus 12 from 1915, for example, we discover a composer whose themes, it appears, have not changed. Not only is he attracted to a Goethe nature study of the flower and the bee in "Gleich und gleich," he is also drawn to the folkish simplicity of "Der Tag ist vergangen" (The Day Has Ended) (CD track 12). The latter, specifically labeled a "Volkslied," plays on the irony, uncertainty, and brevity of life, as do many of the poems in Arnim and Brentano's edition of *Des Knaben Wunderhorn*, which Webern admired and periodically set.[8]

Composed on 13 January 1915, the song invites a reading as a soldier's prayer. The foursquare antecedent-consequent structure and the clear tonal orientation of the melody contrast notably with the piano accompaniment, which has crossed the boundary into the world of atonality.[9]

Der Tag ist vergangen	Day has ended,
die Nacht ist schon hier,	night is finally here,
gute Nacht, o Maria,	goodnight, O Maria,
bleib ewig bei mir.	remain always with me.
Der Tag is vergangen,	Day has ended,
die Nacht kommt herzu,	night draws nigh,
gib auch den verstorbnen	give also to the dead
die ewige Ruh.	Eternal Peace.

Only a few weeks later Webern's desire to serve was fulfilled. Having repeatedly failed the physical exam, he was finally passed in February 1915, following which he joined a reserve infantry regiment. Not surprisingly Webern was quickly disillusioned about army life, and his nationalistic bravado began to fade, as a letter to Schoenberg in March reveals: "I lie on the floor on a straw mattress, in dust and dirt crowded together with other '*Einjährige.*'" *Einjährige* were recruits with high education, who only had to serve one year. "This is really terrible and truly not necessary," he continued, a little naively, "for how much more efficient one would be if one could live privately in cleanliness."[10] Webern was repeatedly transferred, and eventually he was assigned—some might argue providentially as well as symbolically—to a crack battalion of Carinthian mountain troops. But when the string quartet that he had organized departed for the front, he found himself again longing "for a type of duty in which I can, in quietude, direct my thoughts again to that which is really my calling. And thus I could perhaps await the end [of the war] more patiently."[11]

During his time in and out of the army, from February 1915 to December 1916, Webern completed one of his most substantial and developed songs, "Wiese im Park" (Lawn in the Park),[12] which begins:

All time has vanished. With a backward view,
pausing, I stand with green on ev'ry side

and see the mirror'd swans that calmly glide.
This was my country too.

And concludes with this couplet:

A day that's dead opens its blue eyes.
And ev'ry thing is old[13]

Karl Kraus, who wrote these lines, was a Jewish convert to Catholicism who brooked ambiguity along with apocalyptic visions in his powerful five-act play, *Die letzten Tage der Menschheit* (1915–1922).[14] Here the familiar diatribe against the cult of wartime heroics is mixed with an unmistakable loyalty to his homeland. This is evident not only in "Wiese im Park" but also in "Ein Winterabend" (A Winter Evening), which Webern set as the conclusion to his opus 13. Here the poet speaks metaphorically of the homeward return of the weary traveler and concludes with a communion setting of bread and wine on the table.

Kraus was not the only contemporary poet to whom Webern turned. In the same month that he completed "Der Tag ist vergangen," Webern sketched but never finished settings for two poems by Georg Trakl, who had died two months earlier. Preoccupied with alcohol and drugs and haunted by visions of incest and suicide, Trakl addressed the despair of many poets and artists before and during World War I. He had served as an army pharmacist in Galicia in 1914, where he lacked sufficient drugs to ease the pain of the ninety severely wounded men in his charge, and where he had seen a man shoot himself in the barn where they were lying. Recoiling from this desperate act, he staggered outside only to witness a row of local peasants, suspected as "traitors," who had just hanged themselves.[15] Suffering a total mental breakdown in the wake of these traumatic experiences, the poet then took his own life.[16]

Webern set six of Trakl's poems in his opus 14, and the final poem, "Song of a Captured Blackbird," opens with a phantasmagoric vision of abandoned battlefields and forgotten warriors in a postwar period struggling in vain to find peace. Sketched in nine distinct drafts between 1917 and 1919,[17] Webern reduced his ensemble to a spare chamber group of clarinet, bass clarinet, violin, and cello, whose instrumental rotation from song to song is in direct emulation of Schoenberg's *Pierrot lunaire*. Webern also intensified the crux of Trakl's lyrics through the freeing abstraction of atonality, a rest-infused vocal style, and a fascination with large intervals.

Lines such as "Dying beneath the olive tree" and "Dew, dripping slowly from the flowering thorn" also support an interpretation of the text proposed by Ludwig von Ficker, the poem's dedicatee, as a religious drama with specific references to the Mount of Olives, the Crucifixion, and the crown of thorns.[18] As such it was in direct conformity with the German perspective that viewed the nation as a custodian of Christ's blood and the fallen soldier as predestined in his resurrection to lead a people.[19]

Trakl had argued in an earlier poem, "Crucifixus" (1909), that God's love had become manifest in Christ, who as a free person could choose to lay down his life. Now, in "Dunkler Odem," Christ's Passion has been transformed from historical theme to wartime homily.[20] The work closes with the words "brech-endes Herz" (broken heart), offered as madrigal-esque gasp.[21] No funeral march here, only the solitary crucifixion of a nation presented in tandem with a symbolic hope for the future.[22]

A MARCH AND A SOLDIER'S TALE

The "March" that concludes Alban Berg's *Three Pieces* for orchestra, op. 6, written in 1914, immediately following the assassination at Sarajevo, has been linked to the composer's affection for the music of Mahler and has been called the quintessential preparation for an understanding of *Wozzeck*, which followed immediately.[23] George Perle has proposed that the "March" was

> in its feeling of doom and catastrophe, an ideal, if unintentional, musi-
> cal expression of the ominous implications of that event [the assassina-
> tion]. Fragmentary rhythmic and melodic figures typical of an ortho-
> dox military march repeatedly coalesce into polyphonic episodes of
> incredible density that surge to frenzied climaxes, then fall apart. It is
> not a march, but music *about* a march, or rather about *the* march, just
> as Ravel's *La valse* is music in which *the* waltz is similarly reduced to
> its minimum characteristic elements. In spite of the fundamental dif-
> ferences in their respective musical idioms, the emotional climate of
> Berg's "marche macabre" is very similar to that of Ravel's postwar
> "valse macabre." [24]

As in "Reigen," which preceded it, the composer is reacting to the specter of national catastrophe and the impending death of the Austro-Hungarian empire.[25]

The first Viennese performance of Georg Büchner's play *Woyzeck*, at which Berg was present, took place almost simultaneously, on 5 May 1914. Fair copies of the opening "Präludium" and concluding "Marsch" from the *Three Pieces* were sent to Schoenberg on 8 September,[26] by which time Berg was already actively engaged in the writing of *Wozzeck*.[27] But although Berg had clarified his intention to write an opera based upon Büchner's play in the months just prior to the outbreak of war, after completing some preliminary sketches he did not take up the project again until 1918 and completed it only in 1922.[28]

Berg's preparation for taking on such a large project was related not only to his exposure to Georg Büchner's play, however, but also to his Viennese contemporary Karl Kraus, whose satires Berg admired and read regularly in the journal *Die Fackel*.[29] Berg had been aware of Kraus's writings as early as 1908, and early drafts of his play *Die letzten Tage der Menschheit* began to appear in *Die Fackel* in May 1916. Then, in September 1919, the fourth and fifth acts of Kraus's drama were published separately as a book. Berg, who was reading it, wrote to his wife, "Nobody must talk to me now for the next two or three days."[30] Although originally resistant to Kraus's virulent pacifism, Berg had shown signs of coming around to his views as early as August 1914,[31] and his opera *Wozzeck* gradually began to take the shape of a critique of the Great War.

Kraus's play was one of the most stinging indictments of the Central Powers to come out of the war. Comprising 220 scenes and more than 500 characters and relying heavily upon newspaper clippings, collages, and quotations, it takes the form of a documentary that attacks the authorities, the jingoistic crowds, and especially the press. The war is seen as a "tragic carnival" in which society had been turned topsy-turvy and all social order destroyed. The center of Kraus's attack was not primarily on Austria, however, but on its more efficient and commanding ally, Germany. Modernity, encapsulated in the German technological war machine and cultural materialism, is depicted as the logical heir of the Jewish notion of a chosen people who worship money above all. Kraus's anti-Semitism was anything but uncommon during the war, and as the war continued Jews were increasingly cast as the "enemy within."[32]

The German authorities charged with manipulating public opinion also waged open warfare against popular amusements and entertainment that played to "moral laxity, flagrant self-indulgence [and] wasteful dissipation of material and spiritual resources."[33] Albeit for different reasons, Kraus also proclaimed a passionate distaste for mass popular culture, including the press, film, and especially operetta. Although he felt a strong kinship for Jacques Offenbach, he viewed most contemporary operetta as shallow, morally corrosive, and a form of escapism. Particularly offensive to Kraus was the composer Franz Lehár, who pointedly joined tours to the Western Front and whose operettas Kraus found not only frivolous but "a narcotic to transmute the ugliness of war into agreeable fantasy."[34]

Berg agreed. The futility of the war was gradually beginning to dawn on him, and on New Year's Eve 1914, the first time that he had been deprived of spending this annual celebration with his wife, Berg was doubly reflective. The truce of Christmas 1914 had just taken place in the trenches, and the young composer wrote to his wife that his thoughts understandably had turned again to the war. One paragraph in particular endorses Kraus's indictment of operetta as beneath contempt.[35]

> Our corrupt condition—by which I mean the aggregation of stupidity, avarice, journalism, business spirit, laziness, selfishness, capriciousness, deceit, hypocrisy and all the rest—hasn't changed at all. Sometimes there are things which look or sound like an improvement, but they turn out to be merely a set of clichés that would go well into cheap lyrics for singing, howling, or spitting by our society of operetta enthusiasts. In fact I offer this as a suggestion to Herr Leo Fall—to produce a patrol march based on the tune "In the Park," Herr Lehár to fart a waltz "Shoulder to Shoulder," Herr Eysler to sick up a sentimental number "Our Poor Soldiers in the Trenches." Herr Oscar Straus should have first option of a "Gavotte for Cripples."[36] A public that did not shudder at these gentlemen's peacetime output is still ripe for such masterpieces.
>   Yes, the war has to continue. The muckheap has been growing for decades, and in its midst there is still no trace of cleanness to be found. Believe me, if the war ended today, we should be back in the same old sordid squalor within a fortnight.[37]

The German government was actually in accord with Berg on some of these matters. From the first months of the war censorship had been broadly applied to a range of popular entertainment, including operettas, musical comedies, vaudeville acts, and other forms, such as ragtime music, that were deemed entirely too "frivolous" in light of the "gravity of the times."[38] Although Kraus and Berg were obviously making a point regarding Viennese modernist high culture as opposed to mass popular culture, they obviously knew that a counterargument could readily be made. In addition to its escapist potential, operetta contributed to the war effort with thoroughly propagandistic themes,[39] and rather than serving merely as a symbol of Austria's moral degeneration and a flight from reality, it endorsed the social possibility of a "happy ending."

At about the same time it became apparent that the war had begun to affect Berg's aesthetic judgement. The Belgian poet and dramatist Maurice Maeterlinck, previously one of Berg's favorites, was suddenly blacklisted because he had protested the German occupation of his country. The same was true of Debussy, whose "hazy harmonies" Berg now compared unfavorably with Schoenberg.[40] The realities of the war came ever closer to the young composer, however, and on 8 November he recorded a scene that had obviously shaken him: "Today I saw a long column of wounded soldiers—horrible. And soon afterwards a company of soldiers shouting and singing, on their way to the front. These are memories that won't be wiped out in a hurry. I sometimes feel here as if I were living outside this world." [41]

Berg, an asthmatic, was finally called up on 14 August 1915. He immediately undertook infantry basic training and, not unexpectedly, suffered a total breakdown in health in November.[42] He was then assigned to the war ministry office in Vienna.[43] A meeting with Schoenberg on 27 August 1916 found the two composers talking "almost entirely about the war, and then about what should happen to Europe after it. [Schoenberg] thought there was only one solution, the *Republic of Europe,* just like the United States of America." [44] In a letter written in June 1918 Berg spoke of "the filthy war" and his dismay that it had resulted in "three years stolen from the best years of my life, totally, irretrievably lost." [45] In a second written in August he sealed the link between his wartime experience and his new opera, *Wozzeck,* which he had recommenced writing in July of the year before: "There is a bit of me in this character, since I have been spending these war years just as dependent on people I hate, have been in chains, sick, captive, resigned, in fact humiliated." [46]

Berg's compositional solution for *Wozzeck* reveals a combination of the familiar and the unsettling—the contrasting qualities of realistic verismo and hallucinatory Expressionism—by layering its scenes in such a way as to create a fusion between the two. Berg's designation of the second scene of the first act as a "Rhapsody," for example, actually conceals an alternating structure between the rhapsody proper and the accumulating strophes of a hunting song. The former is associated with Wozzeck's delirium and is identified by a three-chord progression, while the latter is wedded to melodies that Berg said were fashioned from folklike intervals of the fourth and the audible regularity of compound duple meter. The hunting song may be read as a metaphor of the inability of the huntsman (Wozzeck-soldier) to shoot the hare (Drum Major–prey or enemy) which eats off the "greeny grass" (Marie-homeland) "right down to the roots."

The "Rhapsody" proper serves as a ritornello in which the phrase "This place is accursed!" recurs. It ends with a series of fearful utterances, leading Wozzeck's companion to shout, "Hey! Are you mad?" Wozzeck, ignoring him, continues, "This weird quietness. It's sultry. Makes you want to hold your breath. . . . A fire, running from the earth to the sky, and a crashing noise coming down, like trumpets!" The sun sets, the drum

Example 12. Alban Berg, *Wozzeck,* act 1, scene 2, mm. 1–4. (© 1926 Universal
Edition A. G., Vienna.)

sounds, and Wozzeck says, "Still, everything still, as though the world
were dead." "Night!," his companion barks. "We've got to get back." Curtain. The offstage military band is heard approaching.

This scene is as vivid a projection of impending world doom as any to
come out of the Great War, a vision that is in tune with the ruminations of
Kraus's contemporaneous *Die letzten Tage der Menschheit.* It is also a mirror of the unseen forces at work in our daily lives, a message that Olivier
Messiaen obviously understood and later recalled when he adopted the
identical three-chord sequence of Berg's "Rhapsody" (ex. 12) as the basis
for his "Offertoire: Les choses visibles et invisibles" (Things Visible and
Invisible) in his *Messe de la Pentecôte* for solo organ of 1950 (ex. 13).[47]

Berg encouraged the listener to forget about his formal constructions,
however, and any attempt to relate the pavane of act 1, scene 1, to its expected meter (2/2 with upbeat) ultimately proves as unrewarding as the
search for a compound meter in the gigue.[48] Yet, despite the fact that the
chosen dance designations are mirrored only by the loosest analogy in
the music itself, the use of baroque titles, ritornello structures, and self-
contained numbers suggests the forces of an impending revival of Neoclassicism.[49] Finally, it is of more than passing interest that Berg's score for
act 1 was already complete by 1919, well before Schoenberg's use of baroque dance designations in his *Suite* for piano (1921–1923).

The use of dance types was potentially anything but neutral, however.
In 1913 Kraus had written a satirical poem, "Tod und Tango," about a
dancer who murders his wife, is acquitted, and actually advances in his position at the bank. The symbolism of the "dance of death" is made explicit
in the night scene of Kraus's *Die letzten Tage der Menschheit,* which takes
place in a ballroom filled with society's elite. Written in the same period as
Wozzeck, between 1915 and 1922, it includes the following grisly vision:

Example 13.   Olivier Messiaen, "Offertoire: Les choses visibles et invisibles," from *Messe de la Pentecôte*, mm. 1–2. (© 1950 Alphonse Leduc, Paris; reproduced by permission of Alphonse Leduc.)

"The sound swells into terrible music. . . . A high pile of rotting unburied corpses. A flock of ravens swarms over the carrion, croaking." The birds show special preference for picking over the remains of the most honored men, and before the final scene of destruction, a group of hyenas dances a tango around the corpses.[50]

Berg similarly invokes a dance of death in *Wozzeck* during the inn scene of act 3, scene 3, where Wozzeck predicts that the end is near: "Dance, all you, dance away! Leap, sweat, and reek! For some day soon, he'll fetch you . . . The Devil!" In this scene, which follows the death of Marie, Wozzeck discovers blood on his elbow and is overpowered by its smell. Not only does the language parallel act 3, scene 2, of Kraus's *Die letzten Tage*, but Marie's murder takes place in exactly the same act and scene of *Wozzeck*. Similarly, the polka that ensues in Berg's inn scene serves as a direct counterpart to Kraus's tango.[51] The opening of the rhythmic motif that permeates the entire scene (_ _ . _) (and which would later be used as the Fate motif in his opera *Lulu*) is also, coincidentally, the retrograde of a basic tango pattern. Berg's attendant musical symbolism is unmistakable: the pattern is based on a compulsive death rhythm that owes its genesis to Mahler's Sixth Symphony.[52] Subject to subtle transformations that led the composer to label the entire scene as an "invention on a rhythm," the basic pattern is much more than an abstract construction and validates the polka as an obsessive dance of death that announces the demise of the protagonist.[53]

In the closing scenes of the opera many of the themes of war are brought to a horrendous domestic conclusion. Having killed his wife, Wozzeck throws the murder weapon into a pond, and when he attempts to retrieve it he drowns to the chilling cry "Das Wasser ist Blut" (The water is blood), a harrowingly familiar scene on the pockmarked, rain-drenched, corpse-strewn battlefields of the Great War. It is interesting to note that Wozzeck's inadvertent drowning while searching for the murder weapon and washing Marie's blood from his body was a textual change made by Berg that was in no way suggested by Büchner. The composer seemed to imply that in his unsuccessful attempt to retrieve the murder instrument, Wozzeck had lost control even over the terms of his own death and that, like his native country, his dreams and visions had disappeared in a sea of blood.[54]

In the final scene Wozzeck and Marie's child rides his hobbyhorse. A game of ring-around-the-rosy by children playing nearby is interrupted by news that everyone has gone to the pond. Rushing to join the crowd, one of the children taunts Wozzeck's progeny with the hurtful "Du! Dein Mutter ist tot" (You! Your mother is dead), italicizing the wartime plight of the parentless child readily familiar to German-speaking countries in the soldier song "Annemarie."[55]

Mein Regiment, mein Heimatland, meine Mutter hab ich nie gekannt. Mein Vater starb schon früh im Feld, ich steh allein, allein auf dieser Welt. Ich heisse Annemarie, einjeder kennt mich schon, ich bin ja die Tochter von ganzen Bataillon!	My regiment, my homeland, My Mother have I never known. My Father died prematurely on the battlefield, I remain alone, alone in this world. I am called Annemarie, everyone knows me already, I am the daughter of the whole battalion!

In the opera Wozzeck's child, guileless and unfathoming, continues to ride as the curtain falls—"Hop, hop. Hop, hop." The emptiness of the stage at the end is palpable and accentuates the sense of void that inevitably follows all cataclysmic action. In this instance it also underscores Wozzeck's incapacity to redeem his manhood even in an act of fatal violence.[56]

Büchner's *Woyzeck*, which was written over a century before Berg turned to reshuffling its pages, dealt openly with the plight of humankind through the image of the downtrodden soldier, but it was not set in wartime, and its locus was not the battlefield. The source of Wozzeck's personality disorder goes far beyond a surface diminution of masculinity as a result of submission to military authority and reveals a total inability to cope with "reality." By the time of the premiere of Berg's opera, its principal topic now clearly pointed to the pervasive alienation that had come to settle over the whole of Europe because of the war. Furthermore, while Berg may have denied that the instrumental formalisms that he injected into his opera reflected an attraction to the tidying forces of Neoclassicism as articulated by the French, *Wozzeck* unambiguously signaled a search for structure and a call to order in a society that both Berg and Kraus agreed had run amuck.

Berg's postwar despondence, nationalist pride, and indebtedness to Kraus are all conveyed in a letter to the pianist-composer Erwin Schulhoff on 27 November 1919.

> You are wrong if you imagine me to be an imperialist or a militarist.
> . . . I asked myself in August 1914 whether a people that treats its
> own greatest men . . . in the way that the German people did and does,
> doesn't actually deserve to be defeated. . . . Only Karl Kraus, my stron-
> gest support at that time and in the days to come, dared speak the truth
> about it. . . . In spite of all that, I still believe in the German people. Not
> in the people of today, or in the Viennese or the Berliners, but perhaps
> in the Thuringians, in the Alpine peoples. In the people who have pro-
> duced Beethoven, and all the absolutely great ones through Mahler
> and Schoenberg (names such as France—despite Debussy, Ravel, and
> Satie—and other Entente nations cannot produce). . . . Believe me,
> though I was never in the fighting, nor ever wounded, I suffered no
> less in my military service. . . . All these years I suffered as a corporal,
> humiliated, not a single note composed—oh, it was dreadful.[57]

The score of *Wozzeck* provides telling evidence of Berg's need to temper the agonies of a runaway Expressionism as epitomized by Schoenberg's *Erwartung* of 1909. Yet the solution Berg offers in *Wozzeck* was not so much a response to the hallucinations of Schoenberg's disoriented Woman stumbling over the dead body of her lover, or to its tonally unsettling music as it was a measured stocktaking and an orderly reappraisal of its inner vision for a postwar world. The unveiling of Berg's opera in Berlin in 1925, only a year after the delayed premiere of *Erwartung* on 6 June 1924, guaranteed the inevitable and necessary comparisons.[58]

In a way that virtually no other piece of the musical theater had attempted, *Wozzeck* placed the spotlight on the returning soldier who could no longer function and who struggled helplessly for an identity in a postwar world. This crisis of masculinity—triggered in World War I by the prolonged display of manly courage to no military effect—had resulted in a new male disorder: shell shock, "a male appropriation of what psychiatry had previously construed as the singularly female condition of hysteria."[59] The congruence had already been recognized by Captain Charles S. Myers of the British army's medical corps as early as 1916.[60] Rather than being a peculiarly female affliction, Elaine Showalter observes, hysteria must be seen as a "culturally permissible language of distress" for all who have been muted or silenced,[61] and, as Jay Winter has suggested, the term "shell shock" was obviously devised as a means of bypassing stigma and providing a vehicle "of consolation and legitimation."[62] More paradoxical, however, was the fact that the suppression of women's freedom to choose in a patriarchal society had become increasingly equated with the loss of power by male youth subject to conscription in wartime. It was an argument that Virginia Woolf, among others, made repeatedly from 1915 on. In many ways, then, *Wozzeck* and *Erwartung* may be correctly read, and were originally offered to the public, as an unexpected but complementary pair.[63]

In a letter of July 1915 that reflected his personal despair over the war, Rainer Maria Rilke mentioned that he had been busy reading Strindberg's *Spöksonaten* (Ghost Sonata), which he called "the most important thing in the theater besides Georg Büchner's *Wozzeck*." Recalling its power during its recent revival at the Hoftheater, he took special note of

> how even around the recruit Wozzeck all the greatness of existence stands, how he cannot prevent, now here, now there, before, behind, beside his dull soul, horizons being torn open onto violence, immensity, the infinite; an incomparable play, the way this misused person in his stable-jacket stands in universal space, *malgré lui*, in the infinite relationship of the stars. That is theater, that is what theater could be like.[64]

Little could Rilke have known that Berg had just commenced a work that would show what a modern opera could be like. In 1925, seven years after the Armistice had been signed, Berg's *Wozzeck* premiered in Berlin, and its continuing success was matched by few operas written after it in the twentieth century.

MOMENTARY *FRATERNITÉ*

The Society for Private Musical Performances, which Schoenberg organized with the help of Webern, Berg, pianist Edward Steuermann, and others in the immediate post-Armistice period, provided a showcase not only for the most avant-garde Viennese musical language of the day but, surprisingly, for musical scores from former enemy countries as well. In the opening season of 1918–1919, twenty-six concerts with forty-five compositions were presented. In light of the keenly felt legacy of Gustav Mahler, it was not surprising that the very first concert was devoted to a piano-duet arrangement of Mahler's Seventh Symphony performed by Bachrich and Steuermann, who had been coached by Schoenberg in a relentless series of rehearsals. On the same concert, however, Steuermann also played the Fourth and Seventh Piano Sonatas of Skriabin. On 30 May 1919 Berg's early Piano Sonata and a group of Josef Hauer's piano pieces were played alongside Busoni's *Six Elegies*, Debussy's *Proses lyriques*, and Ravel's *Gaspard de la nuit*. A week later a piano-duet arrangement of "Reigen" from Berg's *Three Pieces* and Webern's *Passacaglia* shared the program with Bartók's *Bagatelles* for piano and Stravinsky's *Berceuses du chat* and *Pribaoutki*, the latter prompting an ecstatic response from Webern.[65]

By April 1921, when a repertoire summary was published, it was clear that the music of the three Viennese composers had been less frequently performed than that of others. Of the 226 compositions performed to that date, musicologist Hans Moldenhauer calculated that "thirty-four were by Reger (still hardly known at that time), twenty-six by Debussy, twelve each by Bartók and Ravel, eleven by Skriabin, ten by Mahler (mostly in transcriptions), nine by Stravinsky, seven each by Busoni and Richard Strauss, six each by Hauer and Szymanowski, and five each by Suk and Zemlinsky."[66] Perhaps most remarkable of all were the series of four concerts given in the week of 7–14 March 1920 at the Mozarteum Hall in Prague, in which Steuermann and Rudolf Serkin performed Schoenberg's *Three Piano Pieces*, op. 11, in the company of Debussy's *En blanc et noir!*[67] Programming the Debussy in light of its clear anti-German origins was an extraordinary act of rapprochement. Such ecumenical harmony was not to last for long, however. In the 1920s Parisian Neoclassicism squared off against Viennese Serialism in one of the ugliest and most protracted aesthetic battles of the twentieth century.

Part 6

THE UNITED STATES OF AMERICA

14 "The Yanks Are Coming"

> We intend to begin unrestricted submarine warfare. We shall endeavor to keep the United States neutral. In the event of this not succeeding we make Mexico a proposal of alliance on the following basis: Make war together, make peace together, generous financial support, and an understanding on our part that Mexico is to recover the lost territory in Texas, New Mexico, and Arizona.
>
> Arthur Zimmermann, telegram to the German minister in Mexico City, 19 January 1917

American entertainers and politicians alike maintained an uneasy neutrality following the outbreak of the war in August 1914. Al Jolson was already showcasing the popular English wartime song "Sister Susie's Sewing Shirts for Soldiers" in *Dancing Around* when it opened on 10 October 1914 at the Winter Garden Theater in New York. Another of the rousing songs from the same season was Blanche Merrill's "We Take Our Hats Off to You, Mr. Wilson." Popularized by both Nora Bayes and Fanny Brice, it took on a new meaning as Wilson campaigned for reelection in 1916 on the slogan that he had kept the nation out of war. Other songs were more equivocal. "Go Right Along, Mr. Wilson," A. Seymour Brown's early campaign hit of 1915, for example, endorsed Wilson's peace efforts even as it openly asked the country to ready itself for whatever sacrifices might eventually be called for.

Germany's policy of unrestricted submarine warfare finally turned the tide. In April 1915 the Cunard liner *Lusitania*, which had become one of the wonders of the twentieth century by crossing the Atlantic in four and a half days in 1908, sailed from New York. As it departed the ship's band played "Tipperary" and a Welsh male chorus sang "The Star-Spangled Banner" in a hearty bicultural send-off. On 7 May, however, the *Lusitania* was torpedoed by a German U-boat and sank just off the coast of Ireland. Among the 1,198 people who perished were 63 children and 128 Americans. Theodore Roosevelt called it piracy and murder and demanded immediate action, and *The New York Times* described the Germans as "savages drunk with blood."[1] President Wilson's protest was measured, although it was still too strong for Secretary of State William Jennings Bryan, who resigned in the belief that Wilson's posture was destined to lead the country straight to war.[2]

Opinion in the United States turned irrevocably against the Central Powers. Songs like "When the *Lusitania* Went Down" and the "Lusitania Memorial Hymn" immediately captured the public outrage in a way that recalled the "Remember the Maine" fever that had triggered the Spanish-American War.[3] "You provide the pictures and I'll provide the war," the newspaper tycoon William Randolph Hearst had told one of his illustrators in 1898, and now American music publishers launched what seemed to be a campaign to prepare the populace for inevitable intervention in the European conflict. The first of the *Lusitania* songs was published by Leo Feist in 1915 and recorded at once.

Warnings against America's involvement continued to come from various quarters. On 11 April 1915, only a few weeks before the sinking of the *Lusitania*, Henry Ford, a leading pacifist and a virtual icon of American self-reliance, vision, and industry, had told *The New York Times* that the war would not have come had the money spent on armaments in Europe been used for building tractors. The moneylenders and munitions makers were the real perpetrators of the war, Ford charged, with obvious reference to the German industrialist Gustav Krupp. If America entered the war, he said, he would refuse to build military vehicles. (It was a pledge Ford would ultimately fail to keep when he later turned to the manufacture of tanks for the American Expeditionary Force.)[4]

Joining Jane Addams of Chicago's Hull House, Ford undertook a worldwide campaign for universal peace in August 1915 with a pledge to get the boys out of the trenches by Christmas, a project that momentarily had the support of numerous European heads-of-state including Pope Benedict XV. The plan was doomed to failure, however, and Ford's personal mission aboard a Peace Ship to Europe proved to be a fiasco, although he captured the headlines by recommending that soldiers in the trenches go on strike to force a peaceful settlement. Irving Caesar, pacifist and the lyricist for Vincent Youmans's "Tea for Two," was aboard as Ford's personal secretary. The next year his "When the Armies Disband" was set to music by the young George Gershwin, launching a collaboration that would last into the early 1920s and include the wildly popular "Swanee."[5] No more than three weeks after the ship docked in Norway on 19 December, however, Ford headed for home, leaving his peace commissioners behind. *The New York Times* quoted reporter Elmer Davis, who accompanied Ford, as saying that the group aboard the Peace Ship was "the largest and most heterogeneous collection of rainbow chasers that ever found a pot of gold and dipped into it for six weeks."[6]

The faction favoring war, however, included some of America's most prominent men of letters, including college presidents and older established publishers and editors, who continued to view war in a highly romantic way, even suggesting that "war was a severe but necessary lesson in moral idealism."[7] Oliver Wendell Holmes may have told Harvard's graduating class of 1895 that war's message was "divine," but in 1915 it was especially chilling to hear talk of "the chastening and purifying effect of armed conflict" issuing from the office of Princeton's president, John Grier Hibben.[8]

American propaganda and U.S. Army enlistment posters left no doubt about the direction in which the nation was headed. In H. R. Hopps's *Destroy This Mad Brute*, for example, which appeared in 1916, a year prior to America's entrance into the war, an enormous gorilla held a terrified damsel in a pose that for a later generation would automatically recall King Kong and Fay Wray (fig. 29). In this instance, however, the monster wears a German spiked helmet with "Militarism" inscribed across the front and carries a club provocatively labeled *Kultur*.[9] As if to forestall any possible misunderstanding of its message, the poster displays the following words beneath the crumbling ruins of a village on the other side of the pond: "If this War is not fought to a finish in Europe, it will be on the soil of the United States." Advertisements for numerous films served the same purpose, including especially *The Kaiser, the Beast of Berlin*, which was filled with scenes of endless atrocities taken straight out of the British Bryce Report. The billboard announcing its arrival at the Broadway Theatre in New York, which featured a stern likeness of the helmet-clad Kaiser, even carried an open invitation to a mock brawl: "Warning! Any Person Throwing Mud at This Poster Will *Not* Be Prosecuted."

Around 1915 some openly pacifist songs had held an almost unrebuttable appeal when wedded to the voice of motherhood. "I Didn't Raise My Boy To Be a Soldier" (subtitled "A Mother's Plea for Peace, respectfully dedicated to every Mother—everywhere"), for example, predicted that as many as ten million young soldiers would march needlessly off to war and argued that if mothers around the world stood up, they could put an end to the fighting.[10] Its rousing chorus no doubt appealed to a great segment of the American population when it was first released.

> I didn't raise my boy to be a soldier,
> I brought him up to be my pride and joy.

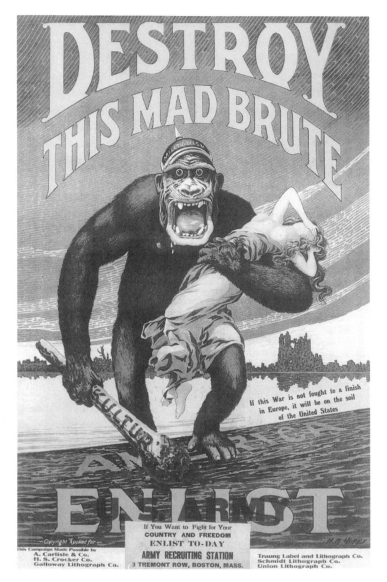

Figure 29.   H. R. Hopps, "Destroy This Mad Brute," propaganda poster, 1916.

Who dares to place a musket on his shoulder,
To shoot some other mother's darling boy?

Let nations arbitrate their future trouble,
It's time to lay the sword and gun away.
There'd be no war today
If mothers all would say,
"I didn't raise my boy to be a soldier." [11]

Aided by the fact that it lent itself to ragtime interpretations by popular pianists, the song achieved an enormous vogue, and its publisher Leo Feist
boasted that more than 700,000 copies were sold in the first eight weeks. A
recording of it, coupled with the equally pacifist "Stay Down Here Where
You Belong," by Irving Berlin, was quickly made by Morton Harvey and
released in March 1915. [12] Pro-war sentiment was now gaining momentum,
but "I Didn't Raise My Boy To Be a Soldier" continued to sell well until
April 1917, the month the United States entered the war, when the Victor Talking Machine Company understandably withdrew the recording. [13]
Notwithstanding songs like "My Country, Right or Wrong," "Wake Up,
Uncle Sam," and "Fight for the American Flag," the vast majority of the
tunes clearly favored non-participation prior to America's involvement. [14]

Before America's entrance into the war, the young Cole Porter also
wrote his first professional musical, "See America First," which opened for
a short run in March 1916. Despite the title, the composer himself left
for Paris the following year. Claims that he had joined the French Foreign
Legion proved false, however, and when the conflict ended he remained in
France, married a southern belle of means, and became the toast of the
Riviera. [15]

When America finally joined the Allies in April 1917, Theodore Roosevelt belligerently told an audience at Oyster Bay, Long Island, that Germany had become a menace to the whole world. "The man who does not
think it was America's duty to fight for her own sake in view of the infamous conduct of Germany toward us stands on a level with a man who
wouldn't think it necessary to fight in a private quarrel because his wife's
face was slapped," he proclaimed. Roosevelt's remarks were prompted by
President Wilson's declaration of war on 6 April, which came in the face
of evidence that was too potent to ignore. General John Joseph "Black
Jack" Pershing had pursued the Mexican revolutionary Pancho Villa into
Chihuahua after he launched a raid on Columbus, New Mexico. [16] Then
on 19 January 1917, the German foreign secretary, Arthur Zimmermann,
sent the German minister in Mexico City a telegram that promised the

Mexican government the return of its former territories in the United States if it joined the war on the side of the Central Powers.

On 23 January the German ambassador in Washington wired Berlin and proposed that, in addition to the promises made to Mexico, $50,000 be spent to influence members of the U.S. Congress to keep America out of the war. The ambassador's telegram was intercepted by British cryptographers in London and decoded two days before its arrival in Berlin. Informed of its contents and faced with news that an American cargo ship, the *Housatonic,* had been sunk by a German submarine on 3 February, President Wilson broke off all diplomatic relations with Germany.[17] Nothing could have better clarified the fact that America's occupation of Haiti and the Dominican Republic from 1915 to 1916, the purchase of the Virgin Islands the next year, and current involvement in Mexican politics were not isolated episodes but were rather "part of a regional strategy to pre-empt German influence."[18]

Further submarine attacks in March and the threat of invasion from the south suddenly brought the legend on the gorilla poster home with a new and threatening immediacy. But it took two months of open submarine warfare before the U.S. Senate voted in favor of war on 4 April. That was followed two days later by endorsement in the House of Representatives and President Wilson's declaration of war. Pershing was immediately recalled from Mexico and named to head an American Expeditionary Force, which was to be sent to France.

Pershing's "police action" in Mexico evoked few lyrics in the United States, although it did stir up a few in Mexico.[19] In songs written by Americans prior to the United States's entrance into the war, most references to farewells and departed loved ones pointed to Britain and rarely to Pershing's cavalry, which was positioned south of the American border. Between 1914 and 1917, however, American tunesmiths showed that they could address the competing claims of isolationism and preparedness in a persuasive and forceful manner.[20] The prospect of heartbreak should America enter the war in Europe was the theme of three songs published in New York in 1915: "Bring Back My Soldier Boy to Me," "Daddy, Please Don't Let Them Shoot You," and "Don't Take My Darling Boy Away" ("Don't send him off to war / You took his father and brothers three / Now you come back for more").

Once America entered the war, newly minted tunes such as "If They Want to Fight, All Right, but Neutral Is My Middle Name" quickly became unfashionable. The mood had changed. Official persecution of conscientious objectors began.[21] And in Edith Wharton's new novel, *The Marne*

(1918), one of her characters even extolled the Old Lie: "Dulce et decorum est pro patria mori."

WAR SONG AS INTERVENTIONIST PROPAGANDA

Once war was declared it was imperative that public opinion be mobilized simultaneously with the conscription of troops. Predictably enough, in 1917 and 1918 a flurry of counterresponses appeared to the earlier pacifist songs, including "I Didn't Raise My Boy To Be a Coward," at least five different versions of "I Didn't Raise My Boy To Be a Slacker," "I'm Going To Raise My Boy To Be a Soldier and a Credit to the U.S.A.," and the rambling flag-waver "I'm Sure I Wasn't Raised To Be a Soldier (But I'll Fight for Dear Old Red, White and Blue)." Another song from 1917, "America, Here's My Boy," reflected the totally different perspective of a mother who declared that, having only one son, she had raised him for America, but that if she had another he too would march proudly alongside his brother. It was outmatched only by the ultimate patriotic offering, "If I Had a Son for Each Star in Old Glory," which its publisher Leo Feist claimed was "doing its bit by helping recruit regiments for Uncle Sam."

A trickle of songs written before April 1917, such as "My Country, I Hear You Calling Me," reflected the steady movement toward military and industrial preparedness that followed the passage of the National Defense Act in mid-1916. Almost simultaneously with Wilson's declaration of war, Irving Berlin, Edgar Leslie, and George W. Meyer summed up the new mood with a song, "Let's All Be Americans Now," that was immediately recorded by the American Quartet. Such war tunes served to remind the country of its ethnic diversity. Whereas prewar songs such as Irving Berlin's "Hey Wop" (1914) and "Angelo" (1915) had humorously caricatured Italian, Irish, and other ethnic populations, creating a lucrative business for Tin Pan Alley,[22] any question regarding immigrants' loyalty to their native land could now lead to suspicion and alarm. As a consequence, Roosevelt's challenge of "100% Americanism" became a rallying cry addressed to all U.S. citizens and pointedly so to immigrant populations. The issue was specifically introduced in posters like the one devised for the Third Liberty Loan drive that carried the caption "Are you 100% American? Prove it! Buy U.S. Government Bonds." Here potentially demeaning ethnic stereotyping had given way to a direct challenge to serve and support the country in visible ways.

Failure to buy war bonds, slowness to respond, and even silence were frequently taken as signs of disloyalty, giving zealots an excuse to display their patriotism. Cases are documented in which German immigrants were forced to kiss the flag, tarred and feathered for resistance or refusal to buy war bonds, and, in extreme instances, beaten and even lynched.[23] "Let's All Be Americans Now" (1917) called on citizens to set aside loyalty to a previous homeland (including England, France, and Italy as well as Germany) and "fall in line / You swore that you would, / So be true to your vow, / Let's all be Americans now!"[24]

Instruction in German, one of the most popularly studied modern foreign languages in American high schools, was widely outlawed. The California State Board of Education condemned German as "a language that disseminates the ideals of autocracy, brutality and hatred,"[25] and the study of French was elevated to a new prominence alongside Latin even in such inland states as Kansas.[26] How different America's solution was from that of France! In a surprising recognition of the classical foundation of eighteenth-century German literature as well as the practical fact that most citizens of Alsace—whom France hoped to welcome home following the war—were German-speaking, the Sorbonne indefinitely renewed the contract of its main professor of German literature and language in 1915.[27]

In America any citizen of German descent came to be considered a potential saboteur. Attacks on German-Americans, or "hyphenated Americans" as Theodore Roosevelt labeled them, and on all things German were not only vicious but also frequently absurd. The first word in familiar terms such as "hamburger steak," "dachshund pup," and "German measles" were routinely replaced with the word "liberty." War hysteria even led to the lynching in April 1918 of a law-abiding citizen whose only crime was the possession of a German family name and to the acquittal of its perpetrators by a St. Louis jury on grounds that they had been motivated by patriotic concerns.[28] In the world of popular song a few pro-German items were copyrighted and published in America in 1914–1915 by the Leipzig-based publisher Breitkopf & Härtel. They soon gave way, however, to songs of the virulent "Beat the Hun" variety.[29]

Something of this change of musical manners can be followed in the programs given by the U.S. Marine Band from 1914 through 1918. The performance of a rich parade of German marches under the direction of its German-born leader, William Santelmann, could hardly have failed to raise eyebrows as the war progressed. On 13 January 1914, for example, Franz von Blon's "Durch Kampf zum Sieg" (Through Battle to Victory), H. L. Blankenburg's "Germanentreue" (Fidelity to Germany), and Heinrich Warnken's "Treu zu Kaiser und Reich" (Fidelity to the Kaiser and Empire) all appeared with their German titles on a program performed at the White House following the playing of John Philip Sousa's "Hands Across the Sea."[30] The Marine Band recorded the last two of these German marches for Victor only a few weeks later, along with Wilhelm Wacek's "Krupp March" and Carl Friedemann's "Grand Duke of Baden."[31]

Even after the outbreak of war, on 14 September 1914 and 18 January 1915, Warnken's march, now listed as "True to the Empire," appeared on Marine Band programs. "Durch Kampf zum Sieg" (still in German) also made a reappearance in a concert on 28 December 1914 and then again on 12 April and 27 December 1915 with the English title "Through Battle to Victory," while Blankenburg's march was played as "German Fidelity" on 17 January 1916. By 15 July 1918, however, Santelmann was showcasing Von Unschuld's march "America First" in the company of Puccini, Meyerbeer, and "The Halls of Montezuma." Santelmann's pro-German bias notwithstanding, all concerts throughout the period from 1914 through 1918 conspicuously concluded with a playing of "The Star-Spangled Banner."

Immediately following announcements of the departure of American troops for France a new theme appeared, and on 26 April the opening of the *Passing Show of 1917* included the smash hit "Good-Bye Broadway, Hello France!" Filled with references to Miss Liberty, sweethearts, wives, and mothers, it went on to hail Pershing's arrival in France as America's way of repaying its debt to that country for Lafayette's role in the American Revolution (fig. 30).[32] The propaganda value of the famous statesman's name had been tapped earlier in the war by the Lafayette Escadrille, a group of adventurous young pilots who attached themselves to the French military air service toward the end of 1916 and who continued to fly under French colors for a year after America's entry into the war.[33] Living the high life, they ate, drank, gambled, and made merry to a steady stream of rags, fox trots, and opera arias issuing from their gramophones.[34] This hard-drinking fraternity acquired a pair of lion cubs and named them Whiskey and Soda. As the life expectancy of Allied pilots who faced German air aces ranged from eleven days to three weeks, it is no wonder that these pilots created a song for themselves that was not only packed with bravado but also undisguisedly directed at a roster of familiar themes.[35]

> So stand by your glasses steady,
> This world is a world of lies.
> Here's a toast to the dead already;
> Hurrah for the next man who dies.

Figure 30.   Cover for "Good-Bye Broadway, Hello France,"
1917. (Music © 1917 Leo Feist, Inc., New York.)

> Cut off from the land that bore us,
> Betrayed by the land that we find,
> The good men had gone before us,
> And only the dull left behind.

Such words were for private consumption, of course, and not meant for the
folks back home. Yet this unbridled cynicism found further justification
when, with America's entry into the war, the black pilot Eugene Jacques
Bullard was denied transfer from the Lafayette Flying Corps to the U.S.
Army Air Service.[36]

The reference to Lafayette in "Good-Bye, Broadway, Hello, France!" was
not the only thing remembered about the song. After the Armistice Jean
Cocteau parodied its title in France with "Adieu New York, Bonjour Paris,"
a title that was in turn borrowed in 1919 by the French composer Georges

Auric as the title of a foxtrot with a somewhat different message. As Auric explained in an article of 1920, grateful as most French composers were for the rejuvenating effects of American popular styles, he felt that it was now time to put them aside and search for pre-Debussyiste French values.[37] As it turned out, only the first part of this injunction was to prove hollow.

When the United States entered the war American musical theater suddenly seemed to come of age, prompted in large measure by the need to develop an alternative to Viennese operetta. Ingredients from operetta, musical comedy, and revue—all of European origin—were now amalgamated into an identifiably more American form that relied heavily upon the spirit of ragtime. Tunes indebted to European music-hall balladry continued to issue from Broadway in 1917 in profusion, however; they included "Till the Clouds Roll By" from *Oh, Boy!* by Jerome Kern; a patriotic finale by Victor Herbert in *The Ziegfeld Follies*, which opened in June and starred W. C. Fields, Will Rogers, and Fanny Brice; and "Will You Remember (Sweetheart)" from Sigmund Romberg's *Maytime*, which opened in July and ran for 492 performances.

Other revues that opened in New York in 1917 included *Over the Top*, which showcased the popular comedian Joe Laurie, Fred and Adele Astaire (originally Austerlitz), and the music of Romberg. *Going Up*, based on the 1910 play *The Aviator*, opened at the Bijou in November and featured "The Further It Is from Tipperary" ("The closer it is to Berlin").[38] The *Cohan Revue of 1918* opened on 31 December 1917, featuring Nora Bayes singing "The Man Who Put the Germ in Germany," in which the chorus begins and ends with the following series of irresistible patriotic puns:[39]

> We're proud of the WILL we found in Wilson
> The man who put the US in USA . . .
> But the world is now aflame
> At the HELL in Wilhelm's name,
> The man who put the GERM in Germany.

This play on words was soon invoked in the title of a film short, *Kicking the Germ Out of Germany*, released by Rolin-Pathé in 1918, which featured Harold Lloyd taking raucous pleasure in mistreating the Kaiser.[40] In March 1918, however, the pun acquired a sinister new meaning when the globe was caught in the grips of an influenza epidemic that took many more lives in six months than the fighting did in an entire four years.[41] Songwriters and lyricists were not to be stilled, and songs such as "Spanish Flu Blues" and a ragtime number, "Oh, You Flu!," were offered in an attempt to alleviate the suffering.[42]

Theodore Morse adapted a melody from Gilbert and Sullivan's *The Pirates of Penzance*, using the lyrics "Hail, Hail the Gang's All Here." The result was one of the popular hits of 1917, along with "You're in the Army Now."[43] Civil War songs such as "Just Before the Battle, Mother" and "Tramp, Tramp, Tramp" were also revived, as were Carrie Jacobs Bond's "I Love You Truly" (1901) and Herbert's "Ah! Sweet Mystery of Life" from *Naughty Marietta* (1910). Nostalgic reminders of things left behind appeared in songs like "Back Home in Indiana" and "For Me and My Gal."

In 1918 songwriters traded on this early momentum and offered a cornucopia of melodies and lyrics: the sentimental "Till We Meet Again" by Richard A. Whiting and Richard Egan, the stuttering "K-K-K-Katy" by the Canadian-American Geoffrey O'Hara,[44] and the uncomfortably probable "Somebody Stole My Gal" by Leo Wood. *Oh, Look!* opened in March, featuring an adaptation by Harry Carroll of the central section of Chopin's *Fantaisie Impromptu* in the song "I'm Always Chasing Rainbows," that would later be revived during the American Depression. And the vaudeville trooper Mae West, then twenty-six, also did her bit for her country by appearing in *Sometime*, which opened in October, singing Rudolf Friml's "Any Kind of Man."

As the war edged toward its conclusion the music industry was kept busy with songs like "We're Going through to Berlin," "We Are Going to Whip the Kaiser," and "We Shall Never Surrender Old Glory." With "Just Like Washington Crossed the Delaware, General Pershing Will Cross the Rhine" (fig. 31), America once again found itself "Looking backward through the ages" at "hist'ry's pages" and the "Deeds that famous men have done" before settling on a chorus that drew a direct parallel between the American Revolution and the struggle in Europe.

> Just like Washington crossed the Delaware,
> So will Pershing cross the Rhine;
> As they followed after George
> At dear old Valley Forge,
> Our boys will break that line.
>
> It's for your land and my land
> And the sake of Auld Lang Syne;
> Just like Washington crossed the Delaware,
> Gen'ral Pershing will cross the Rhine.[45]

Pershing's stock was so high that the first official American war picture made under the auspices of the U.S. Signal Corps and Navy Photographers was *Pershing's Crusaders* (1918).[46] A poster released in conjunction with

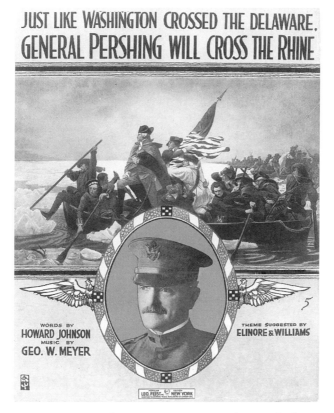

Figure 31.   Cover for George W. Meyer and Howard John-son's "Just Like Washington Crossed the Delaware, General Pershing Will Cross the Rhine," 1918. (Music © 1918 Leo Feist, Inc., New York.)

the film openly implied that his cavalry missions were considered to be so noble as to be likened directly to the Crusades of the Middle Ages (fig. 32).

More than one composer, including Sousa, aspired to write the ultimate American war song, but in terms of a rousing national chant none succeeded like George M. Cohan did with "Over There." Following Woodrow Wilson's declaration of war against Germany on Friday, 6 April 1917, Cohan pondered its meaning on a train into New York and then holed up at home all the next day. His daughter, Mary, recalled that on Sunday her father announced that he had just finished a new song that he wanted to sing for the family. He then placed a tin pan from the kitchen on his head and, using a broom for a gun, began to mark time as he sang:

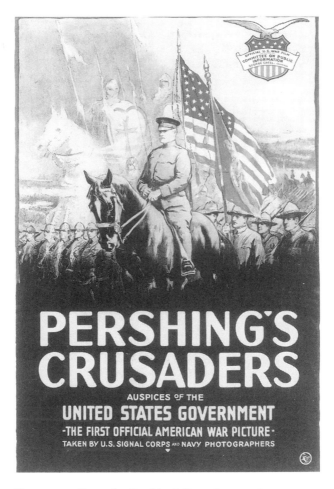

Figure 32.   Poster for *Pershing's Crusaders*, 1918.

Johnnie, get your gun, get your gun, get your gun,
Take it on the run, on the run, on the run;
Hear them calling you and me,
Every son of liberty.
Hurry right away, no delay, go today.
Make your daddy glad
To have had such a lad.
Tell your sweetheart not to pine,
To be proud her boy's in line.

Cohan then began to march back and forth, arms swinging, as he embarked
on the chorus:

Over there, over there,
Send the word, send the word over there,
That the Yanks are coming, the Yanks are coming,
The drums rum-tumming everywhere.
So prepare, say a prayer,
Send the word, send the word to beware,
We'll be over, we're coming over,
And we won't come back till
It's over over there.

"We kids had heard, of course, that the United States was at war," his daughter concluded, "and now here was Dad acting just like a soldier. So I began to sob, and I threw myself down, hanging for dear life to his legs as he marched, begging him, pleading with him not to go away to the war. I kept clinging to him until he stopped."[47]

Cohan had created a classic. And while he later said that all he did was dramatize a bugle call, he had captured something of the American spirit of the moment and had summed up the euphoria and confidence that Americans would need to sustain themselves for the remainder of the war. By donating his royalties from the song to war charities, he provided a further model for Americans—a factor that no doubt later played a role in his being awarded a special congressional medal. No other American World War I song, including Whiting's "Till We Meet Again," could ever match it; none would be remembered longer. Immediately following its first public performance at a Red Cross benefit at the Hippodrome in New York City in the fall of 1917, its opening three-note motif took on a symbolism for future American composers as powerful as the opening notes of "Taps."

Norman Rockwell created a memorable sheet music cover for "Over There," and the song became so popular that Enrico Caruso, the most renowned singer in the world at the time—popular or classical—recorded it in both French and a richly accented English laced with extra vowels (fig. 33). "This Great World Wide Song Hit Now Has Both French and English Lyrics," Leo Feist's edition advertised on its cover. Drums imitated machine-gun fire in Caruso's recording, anticipating James Reese Europe's sonic arsenal in "On Patrol in No Man's Land." And Caruso substituted the word "boys" for "Yanks" in the fifth and sixth lines out of deference, no doubt, to other national sensibilities.

Throughout the war various maneuvers were employed to inflame the minds of people at home with stories of enemy atrocities. Some were true, some were false. The attempt to capitalize upon the power of such potent imagery was nowhere more manifest than in the British "Report of the

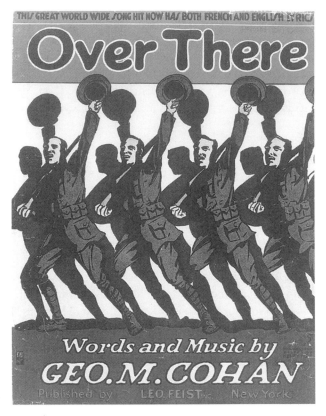

Figure 33.   Cover for George M. Cohan's "Over There,"
1917. (Music © 1917 William Jerome Publishing Corp.,
New York.)

Committee on Alleged German Atrocities." In an attempt to influence
opinion at home it included stories about the mutilation of children with
singing soldiers used as a backdrop.[48] "War Babies" (1916), which pledged
that Americans would care for orphaned Belgian children, makes Debussy's
lyrics for "Noël des enfants" seem tepid. In the opening verse two children
are held in the embrace of their dead mother amid the rubble and thunder
of war, and the song concludes with the following chorus:

> Little war babies, our hearts ache for you,
> Where will you go to, and what will you do?
> Into a world full of sorrow you came,
> Homeless and helpless, no one knows your name.
> Gone is the mother love tender and true,
> Gone is your dead daddy, too;

But you'll share in the joys
Of our own girls and boys,
War babies, we'll take care of you.[49]

The fact that Al Jolson could turn such a song into a hit tune in 1916, which he did, indicates the degree to which American sympathies for the European crisis had already been fine-tuned before Wilson declared war. To further challenge America's neutrality, the cover of the sheet music bore a photograph of a row of Belgian orphans.[50]

Purportedly conscious of the patriotic need to reduce paper consumption, some publishers issued so-called War Editions, a format that was 10 inches by 7 inches instead of the typical 13$\frac{1}{2}$ inches by 10$\frac{1}{2}$ inches. "To Co-operate with the Government and to conserve paper during the War, this song is issued in a smaller size than usual," the front cover of one of Leo Feist's editions conspicuously proclaimed. "Save! Save! Save is the watchword to-day. This is the spirit in which we are working and your co-operation will be very much appreciated." Feist's patriotic claims were, however, to be taken with a grain of salt, as "publishers printed only small numbers of this special issue, while simultaneously producing normal-sized originals of the same songs," suggesting "that the war edition may have been more a matter of patriotic publicity than enforced necessity."[51]

WOMEN AND THE WAR

"The Bravest Heart of All," a tribute to the International Red Cross by Arthur J. Lamb and F. Henry Clique, eulogized the English nurse Edith Cavell, who had been executed by the Germans only a few weeks earlier, in October 1915, for helping prisoners escape.[52] While the sheet music dramatically depicts a stoic nurse standing before a firing squad, tales of her martyrdom typically failed to mention that the French had shot two nurses that year for the same offense. The mobilization of public hatred through such images—contrasted in this case with a British poster that cast a German nurse callously emptying water from a canteen onto the ground in front of a group of soldiers dying of thirst—contributed powerfully to quieting periodic talk of a compromise peace.

Once America declared war the American Red Cross became the ultimate symbol of compassion. Will Mahoney's "The Girl Who Wears a Red Cross on Her Sleeve" portrays a young nurse who "works with the heart of an angel, / 'Mid the sound of the cannon's roar" and advertises the pride of a mother who states that although she had no boy, "It just filled me with joy / To give my darling girl when war began." Other popular tunes that praise the organization's work are "Angel of No Man's Land," "My Angel of the Flaming Cross," "That Red Cross Girl of Mine," and "I Don't Want to Get Well (I'm in Love with a Beautiful Nurse)."[53]

Several popular American lyrics of 1918, including "Joan of Arc, They Are Calling You" and "Girls of France," invoke Joan of Arc, as though she were an adopted patron saint.[54] The former calls upon her to "Come lead your France to victory" and notes that France's sons "at Verdun, bearing the burden, Pray for your coming anew." The latter, however, opens its first verse with the reminder that the "Girls of France" had formerly been thought of as "Something to fondle and then to forget." The chorus concludes:

> Girls of France, girls of France,
> We're mighty proud of you;
> When shadows fell and all was dark
> You led your sons like Joan of Arc.

No figure had been more popular in forging the mythology of the sacred union of the French people than Joan of Arc, and Debussy was busy composing *Ode to France,* which invoked her vision and spirit at the very time when her image was becoming increasingly popular in America in song, poster, and hymn. A more fully secular American society had no historic counterpart to her, no figure that so clearly coupled the highest aspirations of church and state in a holy war, and it is hardly surprising that the myth surrounding "The Maid of France" was widely adopted. Her name also completely fascinated American soldiers, Protestant as well as Catholic: in the immediate postwar months prior to repatriation visits to her birthplace in Domrémy proved to be almost as popular as trips to Paris.[55]

Throughout the war one of the most potent and enduring symbols of womanhood was understandably that of the home-front Mother, whose name was invariably capitalized and a famous song from 1915 spelled it out: "M-O-T-H-E-R, a Word That Means the World to Me."[56] Of all the "mother" songs, few could match the picture of "Mother Machree" (in Irish parlance "machree" means "my dear"), with silver shining in her hair and a brow "all furrowed and wrinkled with care." Written in 1910 by a trio of young Americans for an Irish show, *Barry of Ballymore,* it was destined to do wartime service when John McCormack embraced it as a signature song.[57] With America's entrance into the war, a former partiality for themes relating to the suffragette movement now gave way not only to the image of motherhood and the personal sacrifice of her sons ("America, Here's My Boy") but also to a mother's patience ("The Little Grey Mother

Who Waits All Alone") and especially her value as a recruitment ploy in songs like "America Needs You Like a Mother, Would You Turn Your Mother Down?"

Another song written before the outbreak of war that subsequently acquired a new meaning was "Peg O' My Heart." It took its name from a theatrical sensation of 1912 starring Laurette Taylor and was prompted by a competition for a song with the same name as the play. The music was composed by German-born Fred Fischer and the lyrics by Canadian Alfred Bryan, both established songwriters. Introduced in the Ziegfeld Follies of 1913, its sentiment was ready for adoption by every soldier who had left a girl behind ("Altho' her heart is far away, / I hope to make her mine some day"). The single woman who waited loyally for her sweetheart ("She Wore A Yellow Ribbon") figured prominently along with her prophecy regarding both the outcome of the battle ("If He Can Fight Like He Can Love, Good Night Germany!")[58] and promises for a postwar world ("Yankee Doodle Wedding" and "Little Regiment of Your Own").

Women increasingly played a crucial role in various volunteer efforts, and the U.S. Army and Navy nurse corps, newly activated, sent 25,000 women abroad as ambulance drivers, telephone operators, and hospital staff and relief workers.[59] Although the role played by women in such vital jobs was uncontestable, their presence near the battlefields of France offered other possibilities that were impossible to ignore. "I'm Going to Follow the Boys"[60] promoted an exaggerated naïveté in the opening verse with the declaration "I don't know a thing about the war / I don't see what they're having it for / But when it comes to things like osculation / That's where I'd be missed." The comforts offered by female companionship are underscored again at the end of the chorus with the words, "If one little kiss or more can help them win the war, / Why I'm going to follow the boys!" The image of the female camp follower, or *vivandière,* is sanitized with a patriotic message but not entirely effaced. The musical elements invoked to accompany these sentiments attest to the standardization of an arsenal of figures and motifs in countless songs written throughout the war years. The opening of the refrain echoes bugle calls and cites an instantly recognizable patriotic favorite (George M. Cohan's sensation of the hour, "Over There"), but the syncopation is ragtime and the lyrics are mock heroic: "There's a feeling down in my heart, / That I'm a Joan of Arc, / So I'm going to follow the boys!"

Women had increasingly begun to link their acts of loyal wartime service to goals of racial and gender equality. At the same time, the traditional male view that women "signified the things for which men fight;

they are not the comrades with whom men fight,"[61] still held powerful sway. "I Loved an Amazon," a poem published in the *Stars and Stripes* in 1918, openly expressed the dismay of a soldier, home on leave, upon seeing the unfeminine spectacle of his wife participating in a women's defense and drill group. The opening of the twenty-four-line poem sums up his chagrin.

> I hastened home to find my child
> Alone, unfed, provoked and riled.
> My wife I found—my search was long—
> The center of a female throng.
> That voice, with love once soft and low,
> Was shouting, "Right by section—HO!"[62]

By 1917 full voting rights for women had been achieved in thirteen states, and between 1916 and 1921 some 500,000 black women from the South took steps to combat social and economic disfranchisement by relocating to the North and Midwest.[63] Woman's suffrage was just around the corner. First proposed in the United States in 1848 and advanced by Susan B. Anthony's National Woman Suffrage Association from 1869 on, women's right to vote would be fully realized throughout the country only in 1920 with the passage of the Nineteenth Amendment to the Constitution. Clearly, the Great War helped to bring unsuspected resolution to more than one issue at home.[64]

Numerous songs of the period put the spotlight on women's wartime efforts, including their role in jobs formerly considered male occupations. Warning that the roles of chauffeur, police officer, executive, traffic cop, and house painter might in future no longer be the exclusive province of men, the lyrics of "You'd Better Be Nice to Them Now" suggested that women were becoming "more independent each day." It was an issue that increasingly came to the fore as servicemen returned home with a certain anxiety about the relationship of the sexes and their respective roles in a postwar economy.[65]

Such exaggerated fears about the home front were matched by an ignorance of life at the front by the people back home. Nostalgia, patriotism, blatant propaganda, and concerns regarding disease, race, and gender flooded the songs and posters of the day, and critics seldom attempted to judge their individual merit. A writer for the *New York Evening Post* in August 1918 did broach the subject of the barrage of "New Songs of War," however: "Vulgar and Cheap? No doubt, they are often so. Yet the cheapest song may often seem transfigured for singers to whose deepest sentiments it somehow makes an appeal. . . . We can afford to have the people singing many shabby, faulty songs, along with better ones, but we could never afford to have them singing none at all."[66] Vulgar and cheap they may have been, yet numerous concert artists sang them not only at bond rallies but in their more formal concert programs. Realizing the public's desire for "good melody ballads," Leonard Liebling noted in the *Musical Courier* for August 1918 that such well-known artists as Enrico Caruso, Alma Gluck, John McCormack, and Ernestine Schumann-Heink were now placing such songs on their programs. "Our nation is being stirred fundamentally at this moment," he said, "and the primitive and elemental rather than the subtle and cultured emotions and impulses [are] ready to react to the reductions of sentiment, written, spoken, or sung—especially sung."[67]

Between mid-1914 and mid-1919 a torrent of American patriotic songs were composed, of which 35,600 were copyrighted and some 7,300 were published.[68] Frederick Vogel, in a careful assessment of what he calls the "Song Deluge," concludes that although

> a few Great War songs were as catchy as the opening production
> number in a Broadway musical . . . , as the months passed the market-
> place for songs quickly resembled an insatiable maw, ever eager for
> more songs to digest. The hundreds that were published simply over-
> whelmed the public; the result was that even many respectable songs
> were neglected by potential buyers unable to keep up with publishers'
> offerings.[69]

TROOP ENTERTAINMENTS ABROAD

The variety of entertainment for American troops abroad did not vary much in kind from those offered other Allied troops prior to the entry of the United States into the conflict. The YMCA had some 35,000 volunteers in the field who set up shows, lectures, movies, and performances by stock companies in areas occupied by the American Expeditionary Force. The first to arrive were a mixed lot, including the pianist and singer C. E. Clifford Walker, a French musician, named Maletsky, with a troupe of performing rabbits, and Cobbina Johnson, described as a grand opera contralto. Later groups that made their way to the front appeared with names like the "Y Minstrels," "Just Girls," and the "Scrap Iron Jazz Band"—the latter encouraging the inference that their instruments were *objets trouvés* from the battlefield. Song leaders also made their appearance accompanied by a healthy supply of songbooks, and they encouraged soldiers to sing Civil War favorites such as "John Brown's Body," "Dixie," "When Johnny

Comes Marching Home," "Marching through Georgia," and "The Battle Hymn of the Republic," the latter sometimes updated with words such as "Down with the Kaiser."[70]

Songs sung not by the entertainers but by the soldiers themselves in the long tedious hours of waiting for the next round of action were frequently of a totally different cast. "I Don't Want to Be a Soldier," familiar to the British Army from the time of the Napoleonic Wars, flew in the face of prevailing national sentiment by ridiculing military valor. Dozens of similar songs circulated in World War I, illustrating the disparity between the nobly expressed perspectives at home and frontline cynicism. One of the recurring figures in Anglo-American war songs was the "reluctant warrior," who is the narrator in the following partial set of lyrics, which were applied to the tune of "The Darktown Strutters' Ball":[71]

> Machine gun bullets whizzing all around me.
> Old tin hat feels mighty small,
> Inside it I want to crawl
> And hug the ground, just like a porous plaster.
> . . . .
> And when the shells are dropping near,
> I'm afraid I'm stopping here,
> In No Man's Land where they play
> That shell-hole rag, Whizz-bang!

Many entertainers forced such cynicism into the background, however, or parodied it with such comic skill that the bitter edge disappeared. Similar sentiments were also frequently served up in burlesque fashion along with more serious, nostalgic matter in *The Stars and Stripes*, the paper for American G.I.s and the equivalent of the British *Wipers Times*. The best-known example of mock mayhem and irreverence was concocted by Irving Berlin for an all-soldier show, *Yip, Yip, Yaphank*, created to raise money for a service center. Opening at New York's Century Theater in August 1918 with a cast of 350 recruits from Camp Upton at Yaphank, Long Island, the show featured in addition to "Mandy" and "Soldier Boy" one of the most popular lyrics of the entire war, "Oh, How I Hate to Get Up in the Morning," which captured the essence of one of the soldier's most familiar complaints. Snuffing out a life was an understandable, if rhetorical, retaliation for the daily morning dose of psychological torture.

> Someday I'm going to murder the bugler,
> Someday they're going to find him dead;
> I'll amputate his reveille, and step upon it heavily,
> And spend the rest of my life in bed.

The song was revived with equal success in 1942 for Berlin's Broadway musical *This Is the Army*, which toured until 1945. Another song originally intended for *Yip, Yip, Yaphank,* "God Bless America," became America's most popular patriotic song following an Armistice Day broadcast in 1938 by Kate Smith.

A grab bag of soldiers' songs like "Hinky-Dinky, Parley-Voo?" "She Is a Lulu," "Hail! Hail! The Gang's All Here," "Good Morning, Mr. Zip-Zip-Zip," "I Want to Go Home," and "Après la guerre fine [sic]" flourished at and near the front.[72] Most feigned a happy-go-lucky attitude, but "When the Guns Are Rolling Yonder," borrowed from the British and sung to the old revival hymn "When the Roll is Called Up Yonder," took a grim view.

> You'll be marching up to battle
> Where those damned machine-guns rattle,
> But you'll never see your sweetheart any more.
> When you're hanging on the wire
> Under heavy hostile fire
> Oh, you'll never see your sweetheart any more.
>
> When your lungs are filled with gas,
> You'll be thinking of a lass,
> But you'll never see your sweetheart any more.
> Lying in the mud and rain,
> With a shrapnel in your brain,
> Oh, you'll never see your sweetheart any more.
>
> *Chorus:* When the guns are rolling yonder,
> When the guns are rolling yonder, etc.,
> I'll be there.[73]

The soldier's capacity to change his sentiments on a dime is apparent from items included in army songbooks such as "The Tail of the Lonesome Swine" (parodying "The Trail of the Lonesome Pine") and "Underwear, Underwear" (sending up "Over There").[74] Many of the songs sung in camp—such as "Old Black Joe," "My Old Kentucky Home," "Silver Threads among the Gold," "Indiana," "I Want to Go Back to Michigan," "Missouri Waltz," and "For Me and My Gal"—had virtually nothing to do with the war per se. They simply recalled home.

One month after Wilson declared war John Philip Sousa, then sixty-two, was recruited by fellow composer John Alden Carpenter to train young bandsmen at the Great Lakes Naval Training Center. Directing Liberty Loan rallies and Red Cross relief drives until his discharge in January 1919, Sousa also composed numerous songs on war themes, including a setting of "In Flanders Fields" at the express invitation of John McCrae.[75]

But even if the best of his wartime marches, "Sabre and Spurs" and "Solid Men to the Front," never achieved the popularity of the British "Colonel Bogey,"[76] Sousa could proudly claim that his arrangement of the "U.S. Field Artillery March" became one of the most familiar and enduring musical emblems of the war. He might have failed to write the great war song that many predicted he would, but his very presence contributed mightily to the national *esprit de corps*.

The sheer volume of American popular songs that issued from the presses during the Great War is vivid testimony to the power of music to speak to the widest imaginable range of topics and social issues. Sheet music had been selling in the millions by the turn of the century, a fact that reflected the popularity of the piano in the American home. In 1900 New York boasted 130 piano factories with 200 retail outlets,[77] and the advent of sound recordings further increased the dissemination of the most popular numbers. Any attempt to control or censor such an avalanche of tunes, as the French attempted to do, would have been futile.

In addition, with the advent of war the daily newspaper not only furnished continuous material for a thriving industry but in its Sunday supplements also offered samples of these newly published songs, emphasizing topicality, concise lyrics, and simple melodies.[78] English songs that had found favor early in the war, like "Keep the Home Fires Burning" and "Pack Up Your Troubles in Your Old Kit Bag," were also borrowed and quickly became favorites in America, and sheet music sales were aided by their typically striking covers. More somber covers, such as the one for "After the War Is Over" ("Will there be any 'Home Sweet Home'"), tried to prepare people for eventual personal tragedy. When the war did end, songs that aimed at striking a comic note, like "How Ya Gonna Keep 'Em Down on the Farm," spoke not just of the youth who had come from the agricultural heartland of America but of a generation with new perspectives, hopes, and expectations.

If many of the war's tunes and lyrics composed near the field of action were never set down and disappeared forever, a host of the more popular ones flooded the parlors of America not only throughout the war but also for years afterward. Although many ended up packed away in boxes or relegated to the bottom of the piano bench, the favorites, both rousing and sentimental varieties, were reclaimed and introduced to the children of the Depression by their parents as they gathered round the piano on the long winter evenings following Sunday supper.[79] Little could this younger generation have suspected that the backward glance implicit in these nostalgic songfests with their parents was but the prelude to a war just out of view—a war in which some of their fathers would serve once more, this time alongside their sons.

15 "Onward Christian Soldiers"

> Lord our God, help us to tear their soldiers to bloody shreds
> with our shells; help us to cover their smiling fields with
> the pale forms of their patriot dead; help us to drown the
> thunder of the guns with the shrieks of their wounded,
> writhing in pain; help us to lay waste their humble homes
> with a hurricane of fire; help us to wring the hearts of their
> unoffending widows with unavailing grief. . . . For our sakes
> who adore Thee, Lord, blast their hopes, blight their lives,
> protract their bitter pilgrimage, make heavy their steps, water
> their way with their tears, stain the white snow with the blood
> of their wounded feet! We ask it, in the spirit of love, of Him
> Who is the Source of Love, and Who is the ever-faithful
> refuge and friend of all that are sore beset and seek His aid
> with humble and contrite hearts. Amen.
>
> Mark Twain, "The War Prayer"

Randolph Bourne, a youthful intellectual who was bitterly opposed to America's intervention in the European conflict, would have been in total sympathy with Twain's mocking piety.[1] Embittered at those who cloaked the call to arms under the guise of promoting a struggle that would make the world safe for democracy, Bourne died at the age of thirty-two in the flu epidemic that swept the country shortly after the Armistice, and in the 1920s he became something of a hero for the "Lost Generation."[2] Countering the pragmatist approach to war mouthed in the pages of the *New Republic* by the philosopher and educator John Dewey, his former professor, Bourne recalled "the virtuous horror and stupefaction which filled our college professors when they read the famous manifesto of their ninety-three German colleagues in defense of their war" in 1914. Bourne also noted that within two years these same professors, encouraged by the war-mongering of the likes of Dewey and Teddy Roosevelt, had joined the chorus of those willing to conscript American troops by the hundreds of thousands and to send them to die on the battlefields of France.

Bourne charged that the richer and older classes on the Atlantic seaboard, especially those with French or English business and social connections, were behind this swelling war fever. From America's East Coast, he alleged, it spread like wildfire, "touching everywhere those upper-class elements in each section who identified themselves with this Eastern ruling group." For America's ultimate capitulation to the warmongers Bourne blamed the intelligentsia, who "identified themselves with the least democratic forces in American life," forgetting "that the real enemy is War rather than imperial Germany." The farmers, small business people, and workingmen were apathetic, he argued, and it was they who had reelected President Wilson because he had promised to keep America neutral. "There is work to be done to prevent this war of ours from passing into popular mythology as a holy crusade," Bourne concluded.[3] His warning tellingly mirrored the 1912 injunction of Karl Kraus: "When a culture feels that its end has come, it sends for a priest."[4] For a country whose culture was just forming, the chronology would have to be adjusted.

CHURCH, STATE, AND MORAL RECIPROCITY

Bourne had good reason to be concerned, for even President Wilson, despite his seeming pacifist inclinations, had made it clear that he staunchly believed that it was impossible to divorce progress from religion, that Americans were custodians of the spirit of righteousness, that power in such hands was by definition good, and that all who would challenge such power were by definition unwitting agents of Satan.[5] American intellectuals and politicians were not the only ones who subscribed to the notion that the current struggle was a holy crusade. In Austria, Anton Webern called the war a "struggle of the angels with the devils," and in France, Maurice Ravel feared that he might be prevented from participating in the "splendid moments of this holy war." Nonetheless, it was clear that the fervor behind America's entrance into the conflict had unmistakable religious overtones, with a majority of American clergymen resolutely defending the preservation of democracy as a noble enterprise that justified the taking up of arms.

Many of the issues that had been debated by Romain Rolland, French intellectuals, and the Catholic Church had found a new nesting ground. In America a good deal of the Christian perspective on the war had been inherited directly from England,[6] and endless tracts and monographs in their common language appeared on both sides of the Atlantic throughout the struggle—works with titles like *The Call of the Sword, The Twentieth-Century Crusade, The Christian Witness in War, Christ's Challenge to Man's Spirit in This World's Crisis, Christian Ethics in the World War, The*

Church and the War, and E. Hershey Sneath's collection of essays, *Religion and the War.* "The entry of the United States into the world-war has been in a degree unexampled in the history of this country a response to the appeal of righteousness," Williston Walker of Yale University's school of religion proclaimed in the last of these. "No action in which the nation has ever engaged has been so unselfish. We have taken our part in the struggle without hate, and with full consciousness of the prospective cost in life and treasure, that certain principles of justice may prevail."[7] America looked for "no indemnities, no annexations, and no pecuniary rewards," he noted, and its stance was consonant with the primary teachings of religion.

Most of the Christian ministers writing at the time strained to preach brotherhood and the concept of "love thine enemy" before settling down to rationalize a war that pitted Good against Evil. That the political and economic needs of developing nations everywhere had gradually but surely come to dictate the very basis of morality was being made abundantly clear. More than a decade after the Armistice had been signed the American Ray Abrams noted that "the rise of modern Nationalism has become a religion with its sacred scriptures, dogmas, ritual, propaganda, priests and devotees. It has in the absence of a national church in this country become a great unifying religious force for all the peoples of the nation."[8] The idea was not new, of course, but rather the echo of an ancient and familiar dictum that had been recently revived by the French writer and critic Jacques Rivière. Having converted to Catholicism just prior to the outbreak of World War I, he concluded in 1915 that "All war is a war of religion."[9] The war as an article of faith had been endorsed in virtually every country in Europe from the beginning of the conflict. But nowhere was piety linked more conspicuously with the war than in France, where the call for a *union sacrée* challenged Catholics and secularists alike to support the nation's involvement in the war.[10]

Resounding throughout most of the American tracts on morality in relation to the current struggle was the belief that the issues at stake were universal[11] and that the war had touched people everywhere and had dissolved forever all possible claims of isolationism. Paradoxically, the dissolution of isolationism was now joined to the concepts of patriotism and national identity, and it became increasingly clear that the concept of a world war had not only changed the meaning and scope of human mores but also had propelled America into the international arena of political and economic power.[12]

Preachers on both sides of the Atlantic frequently shunned the blessing of the peacemakers as delivered by Christ in his Sermon on the Mount and spoke bluntly regarding the role of music in the Church Militant's call to battle. "Onward Christian Soldiers" was a predictable and perennial favorite on both sides of the Atlantic. "The Christian Church ever loves to represent Our Lord's service under military figures of speech," the dean of Durham Cathedral accurately noted, and Reverend Archibald Alexander assured his London congregation in 1918 that while hymns like "Gentle Jesus Meek and Mild" were just fine for little children, what departing soldiers needed to hear was "The Son of God Goes Forth to War."[13] Canon Basil Wilberforce also offered the following updated lyrics for the hymn "Stand Up, Stand Up for Jesus, Ye Soldiers of the Cross" in his homily delivered on 9 August 1914, shortly after the declaration of war.

> O Rank and File of England, bold privates of her line,
> Whose battle deeds outnumbered, in deathless glory shine.
> Sharp spurs have we to honour, but ye without their aid,
> Rush on the deadly breeches and storm the barricade.[14]

Randolph McKim struck a similar note in a sermon delivered in Washington, D.C., in 1918: "It is God who has summoned us to this war. It is His war we are fighting. . . . This conflict is indeed a crusade. The greatest in history — the holiest. It is in the profoundest and truest sense a Holy War."[15]

Many popular American songs of the day played to the power of prayer and, especially after the series of bombings of Rheims Cathedral, addressed the destruction that had visited sanctuaries large and small. The cover of the 1918 song "The Tale the Church Bell Told," for example, vividly transfers the message of Rheims to a ravaged country village. Like the lyrics of this song, literary portrayals of bombed villages frequently began with a description of a church spire from a distance — not only because it was a feature that typically dominated the horizon but also because narrative attempts to connote the real world were always in search of a satisfactory code that could represent the most elevated aspirations of the human spirit.[16] It was a perspective endorsed in the opening of Sassoon's personal *Memoirs of an Infantry Officer* and in the beginning of the second scene of Stravinsky's *Histoire du soldat*, which carried the description, "A crossroads in the open country, showing a frontier post and the village belfry in the distance."

Some clergymen were capable of astonishing nuances when it came to the Christian injunction to "Love Thine Enemy." Edward Bosworth, a Congregational minister and dean of Oberlin College, fashioned this embarrassment: "To take life in hate is a dreadful deed. The Christian soldier in friendship wounds the enemy. In friendship he kills the enemy. He never hates."[17] A similar statement had no doubt prompted Mark Twain to pen "The War Prayer." It was an argument that had been perpetuated in America from the time of the Revolutionary War. But as chaplains fed such homilies to the soldiers at the front, the American doughboy had no trouble recognizing the inherent hypocrisy and parodied the sermons of a 63rd Division chaplain in devastating fashion with stanzas sung once again to the hymn "Stand Up, Stand Up for Jesus, Ye Soldiers of the Cross":

> I do not wish to hurt you
> But (Bang!) I feel I must.
> It is a Christian virtue
> To lay you in the dust.
>
> You—(Zip! That bullet got you)
> You're really better dead.
> I'm sorry that I shot you—
> Pray, let me hold your head.[18]

George W. Down, speaking at Asbury Methodist Episcopal Church in Pittsburgh, countered Bosworth's sentiments, however: "I would have driven my bayonet into the throat or the eye or the stomach of the Huns without the slightest hesitation, and my conscience would not have bothered me in the least."[19] American sentiments were clearly a match for the outbursts of hate that came from all sides from the first days of the war.[20] Strangest of all, perhaps, was the proclamation by Charles A. Eaton of Madison Avenue Baptist Church, New York. "We fight because we are Christians, and we will win because we are Christians," he asserted, ignoring, of course, the fact that Germany was not only a Christian country but also the very heartland of the Reformation.[21]

BILLY SUNDAY

For Quakers, Mennonites, Amish, Russian Molokans, and members of the Church of the Brethren, nonresistance to evil was a matter of faith, and few of the patriotic Great War chants so familiar to other denominations are found in the hymnals of these pacifist congregations. Government policy in the United States also held that members of these denominations were to be excused from combat assignment. When the Santa Fe Railroad brought German-speaking Mennonites to Kansas from Russia's Crimea in 1874 to plant their drought-resistant and high-yielding Turkey red wheat, railway officials, recognizing their beliefs, helped to obtain the passage of a state law that exempted from military service all those who opposed war on religious grounds.[22] This is not to say that these groups were untouched by the Great War. Mennonites of German ancestry, for example, had left Pennsylvania and settled in southern Ontario in 1806 in a town they called Berlin, but they changed the name to Kitchener in 1916. The pacifist beliefs of these groups were incomprehensible to evangelical war lovers, and when conscientious objectors began to identify themselves, public policy and popular sentiment conflicted head-on. Not unexpectedly, condemnation and persecution followed.[23] "If you turn Hell upside down, you will find 'Made In Germany' stamped on the bottom," raged evangelist Billy Sunday. "The man who breaks all the rules, but at last dies fighting in the trenches is better than you God-forsaken mutts who won't enlist."[24]

Before the war Sunday had played an especially prominent role in the Prohibition movement, which was strongly rooted in the heartland of America. There the prevailing sentiment was rural, Protestant, anti-alien, anti-Catholic, and, as time passed, increasingly evangelistic.[25] In 1895 the Anti-Saloon League was formed, and it became the driving force behind the campaigns for prohibition in a number of states between 1906 and 1913. German beer-drinking communities were especially hard hit, and when the war mania began to snowball in 1915–1916, the transfer of Prohibition energies to the War against the Hun was readily accomplished under the slogan that alcohol, and especially beer, was a direct agent of the kaiser in America. During the war a number of states passed Prohibition laws, so that by the time national Prohibition was enacted in 1919 by the Eighteenth Amendment to the Constitution, twenty-six states had already voted themselves dry. Nonetheless, during the campaign for Prohibition numerous songs that did not support the cause of the temperance leagues flourished, including "Prohibition Blues,"[26] written by the singer Nora Bayes in 1919, and "How Are You Goin' to Wet Your Whistle When the Whole World Darn Goes Dry?"

Prior to 1917 Billy Sunday had not hesitated to say that "the war in Europe was a sideshow compared to the damnable effects of the saloons."[27] With the United States's declaration of war, Sunday found a new message, and the following day three thousand ardent supporters jammed Pennsylvania Station to welcome him to New York for a revival that was to last ten weeks. The day after his campaign was launched *The New York Times* ran this headline:

16,000 CHEER FOR WAR AND RELIGION
MIXED BY SUNDAY

*Sermons Brought Up to Date to Sink the Kaiser
with the Devil as an Enemy Alien*

Sunday's opening sermon, which was reported by *The New York Herald* of 9 April 1917, revealed that he had finally and decisively changed his tune: "In these days, one is either a patriot or a traitor, in the cause of Jesus Christ, in the cause of the country."[28] And *The New York Times* for 19 February 1918 reported him as saying, "I tell you it is Bill against Woodrow, Germany against America, Hell against Heaven. . . . Either you are loyal or you are not, you are either a patriot or a black-hearted traitor. . . . All this talk about not fighting the German people is a lot of bunk. They say that we are fighting for an ideal. Well, if we are, we will have to knock down the German people to get it over."

Although Billy Sunday lived on until 1935, it was with his New York City revival of 1917 that he achieved the peak of his fame,[29] and his tale merits special consideration with respect to the role of music in galvanizing public opinion during the war. A former professional baseball player who had become an ordained Presbyterian minister in 1903, Sunday had become famous well before the war as a flamboyant speaker in more than three hundred transcontinental revival meetings, which brought in an audience estimated at between eighty and one hundred million people. Preaching a fiery and fundamentalist theology, he addressed a country that was in the throes of a grand transition from an agrarian to an industrial society.

Heywood Broun, the *New York Tribune*'s drama critic, noted Sunday's dramatic talents in September 1915 when he reviewed George M. Cohan's new comedy *Hit the Trail Holliday*, in which Cohan was cast as Billy Holliday, a parody of Billy Sunday. According to Broun, Cohan had

> forced a comparison between himself and his greatest rival in the use of dramatic slang, and strange as it may seem, it is George and not Billy who cracks under the strain. . . . George Cohan has neither the punch nor the pace of Billy Sunday. . . . It is true that Cohan waved the flag first, but Billy Sunday has waved it harder. . . . It is in language that the superiority of Sunday is most evident. . . . All in all we believe that Sunday has more of the dramatic instinct than Cohan.[30]

Billy Sunday's initial equivocation about the war can be attributed at least partially to the fact that he was of German extraction—the family name was originally Sontag—but it also mirrored a prevailing American sentiment that favored neutrality prior to 1917.

Sunday's other biases were equally easy to spot: he not only campaigned passionately for the prohibition of alcohol, which he believed was at the root of most societal ills, he also flirted with the Ku Klux Klan and displayed openly racist views that were especially evident in the segregation of whites and blacks in his revival meetings in the south. In a crusade that took him to Atlanta in the autumn of 1917, however, he tried a new tack: preaching to a white congregation of over twelve thousand, backed by an all-black choir.[31] A prominent black preacher thought that Sunday "might have found the key to bringing the races together,"[32] but Sunday vacillated: "I am not going to plead for the social equality of the white man and the black man. I don't believe there is an intelligent white man who believes in social equality or an intelligent and reasonable colored man who believes in social equality. But before God and men every man stands equal whether he is white or whether he is black."[33]

Congregational singing understandably played a crucial role in Billy Sunday's revival meetings, just as it would in the crusades of Aimee Semple McPherson.[34] As sensational and highly admired as Sunday's sermons were, it was when the singing started that the entire congregation felt the glow that came with personal and collective participation.[35] Sunday's choir director, Homer A. Rodeheaver, was one of his most effective allies. Rodeheaver, who served with Sunday for over twenty years, had established his own music publishing company in Winona Lake, Indiana, prior to the war, and in 1915 he issued his *Songs for Service,* his third anthology of the most favored and successful revival hymns.[36] Among other rousing wartime tunes in the collection were "In the Service of the King," "A Rainbow On the Cloud," "Stand Up, Stand Up for Jesus, Ye Soldiers of the Cross," and, especially, "The Fight is On."

On the afternoon that opened Sunday's New York crusade a capacity crowd filled the tabernacle well before the scheduled time of 2:00 p.m. Rodeheaver, who was both choir leader and master of ceremonies, sang and played a trombone solo, and after telling a few entertaining stories led the two-thousand-voice choir in a rendition of "Onward, Christian Soldiers," accompanied by two grand pianos that were played with increasing fury.[37] Sunday, whose arrival caused a gasp, then launched into the sermon with which he commenced every campaign, "Have Ye Received the Holy Spirit?" Gradually fueling a steamroller of enthusiasm, he ended his sermon by inviting his cheering spectators to join in the "Battle Hymn of the Republic."

In the evening service the same formula was infused with a more generous amount of American patriotism. "Look at the millions of poor, tortured Belgium as she turns her weeping eyes over three thousand miles of ocean, her bleeding hands outstretched toward the Stars and Stripes for help," he implored his congregation. "Our flag has never been unfurled for conquest, and we're not unfurling it for conquest now. We don't want an acre of German land or a cent of German money. We're unfurling the flag for the liberty of the world!"[38] Sunday projected taking his crusade personally to Europe and the trenches, but President Wilson diplomatically persuaded him that he could be of greater service to the country by remaining at home.[39]

The climax to Sunday's services was always the call for converts, and this he delayed until the twelfth night of his New York campaign. When the moment came he climbed on a chair and proclaimed, "Do you want God's blessing on you, your home, your church, your nation, on New York? If you do, raise your hands." Hands went up all over the auditorium. He then clinched the invitation. "How many of you men and women will jump to your feet and come down and say, 'Bill, here's my hand for God, for home, for my native land, to live and conquer for Christ?' " A pause was followed by the invitation, "Come on; come on!" This was the signal for Rodeheaver's choir to launch into "Onward, Christian Soldiers." As streams of men and women wound their way toward the pulpit the choir shifted to "Just as I Am, without One Plea." Throughout the call the choir sang continuously, repeating the familiar tunes that stressed personal humility and perseverance in America's just cause. Rodeheaver adhered to the philosophy that "it was never wise to change the invitation song as long as people were coming forward, even though we had to use it over and over." He also believed that the music should match the tenor of the sermon, so that "if the preacher closes his sermon with a challenge to men, literally daring them to come and take their stand for Christ, then we certainly do not want to pick out something like 'Softly and Tenderly Jesus is Calling' or 'Just as I Am,' but a song like 'Stand Up for Jesus,' 'Onward, Christian Soldiers,' 'I Am Resolved No Longer to Linger.' "[40]

Many of these songs were already well known as the tide of war began to swell. When Methodist bishop Luther B. Wilson urged Christian men and women to fall in line and march forward singing "As He died to make men holy, let us die to make men free!"[41] he knew that his words would be recognized as the concluding line of the final stanza of Julia Ward Howe's "Battle Hymn of the Republic" (1862). Set to music composed by William Steffe in 1852, it had become one of the most familiar tunes in America during the Civil War, and it was ready for conscription in the Great War.[42] American churches received ample encouragement for the promotion of such texts from the English clergy, who had launched a campaign to vilify Germany's devotion to Nietzsche and his renunciation of Christianity as the basis for moral action. And they were especially interested in countering the German slogan that galled them most, "Gott mit uns," which suggested that the Germans were God's chosen people.[43] Ironically, an identical claim was now being made for all Allied Christians.

HYMNS, SENTIMENTAL AND MILITANT

Among the Americans who were natural heirs to the Anglican hymn tradition was Horatio Parker. Appointed head of the music department at Yale in 1894, Parker wrote numerous occasional works, including compositions for Yale's bicentennial in 1901, Theodore Roosevelt's inauguration, the dedication of the Albright Art Gallery in Buffalo in 1905, and the dedication of the John Wanamaker department store in Philadelphia in 1912. Such assignments established Parker as the nearest American equivalent to Elgar as composer laureate in matters of church, state, and community.

In 1915 Parker penned a three-page patriotic hymn, "Gloriosa Patria," and in 1916 he composed a full-fledged war piece titled *An Allegory of War and Peace* for mixed chorus and band, described in the *Boston Herald* as "one of the most dramatic scenes . . . depicting . . . mothers who have given their sons for both war and peace." A more utilitarian, and briefer, piece on a familiar theme was Parker's "The Red Cross Spirit Speaks" of 1918, which appeared in several choral arrangements. A solo version was sung by Louise Homer in a Carnegie Hall concert conducted by Walter Damrosch, in which Homer performed in "a red satin gown, arms outstretched, making a Red Cross."[44] Parker's desire to confirm, even advertise, his loyalty was linked to the impulse, common at the time, to suppress any hint of former Germanophilia.

Karl Muck, the German conductor of the Boston Symphony Orchestra, was a friend of Parker's. When Muck became the object of intense vilification after America's entrance into the war, Parker found it difficult to completely break off the friendship, as did many other musicians nurtured by German culture.[45] In 1917 Parker notified Novello, his music publisher in London, that he was allotting some of his royalties to the music section of the Professional Classes War Relief Council. In return he received a warm letter of thanks from the English composer Sir Hubert H. Parry, who headed the "Music in Wartime" Committee, in which he outlined the scope of some 770 concerts that had been given in the previous year at camps, hospitals, and for the Red Cross. "I hope on the whole you will think us worthy recipients," Parry concluded. "And I wonder how you like coming in together with us. I think Wilson was eminently right to stand out as long as he could. I admired his management of a very difficult situation throughout, immensely. I should have liked the States to have kept out of it if it had been possible, but it has proved not to be."[46]

At the time of the Great War Parker was acknowledged by prominent musicians as "the most representative church composer in America."[47] Indeed, he had begun his professional career as organist and choir director at Trinity Church, Boston, and during his lifetime he served repeatedly as consultant for the hymnal selection committee of the Protestant Episcopal Church and as the principal editor for the edition that appeared in 1903. That edition of *The Hymnal* included twenty-six of his own hymns, with eight of them printed twice to different texts. With America's entrance into the war, a new edition was published, in which the following words appeared in the preface:

> The hymns added find a place either because they are great religious verse, or because they express the experience and aspiration of our time. These are hymns intended to voice our yearning for larger social service, for deeper patriotism, for a more eager obligation to the winning and maintaining of a free world, for a higher enthusiasm towards the unity and extension of Christianity. This Hymnal of 1918 cannot escape the marks of the Great War,—its tragedy, its sympathy, its loving sacrifice, its gratitude because God has given us the victory for the right and the true.[48]

Hymns were sung by the soldiers on both sides of the Atlantic largely because of their familiarity, their lack of melodic or rhythmic complexities, and their adaptability as marching songs.[49] Even some of the more popular British tunes of the day could be sung at different tempos by the marching soldier, allowing them to "take on an almost hymnlike, inspirational quality." One song in particular, Ivor Novello's "Keep the Home-Fires Burning," popularized by the tenor John McCormack among others, attests to this near devotional quality: "Keep the home-fires burning / While your hearts are yearning. / Though your lads are far away, / They dream of home. / There's a silver lining / Through the dark cloud shining; / Turn the dark cloud inside out, / 'Till the boys come home."

There can be no question that the faith of the soldiers and the people back home sustained them mightily throughout the war, and that hymnody as an expression of that faith was a readily transportable and effective antidote for the human dilemma in moments of impending danger as well as in times of bereavement. Despite the voices of conscientious objectors, which were drowned out in a sea of vilification, or the peacemakers, whose loyalty was also often held suspect, the Christian churches in Europe as well as in America accommodated handily to the ancient argument of a "justified war."

Protestant hymns were not, however, the sole appeal to the "highest principles" in the United States. The national anthem proved to be as potent as any hymn that Martin Luther or Julia Ward Howe had ever imagined, and it inspired debates and controversies as heated as any that ever surrounded "La Marseillaise."[50] With the country's entrance into the war, America felt itself coming of age as a nation, self-consciously but surely. Understandably, "The Star-Spangled Banner" served as a prominent agent in this act of self-identification. The most popular sanctuaries in which it was performed were the concert hall and the public meeting space, which, as it turned out, were entirely capable of masquerading as houses of worship.

16   The 100% American

"Patriotism": Combustible rubbish ready to the torch of any one
ambitious to illuminate his name.

Ambrose Bierce, *The Devil's Dictionary*

There can be no fifty-fifty Americanism in this country. There is
room here for only 100% Americanism, only for those who are
Americans and nothing else.

Theodore Roosevelt, speech to the State
Republican Party Convention, 19 July 1918

Despite Roosevelt's ringing oratory near the end of the war, just what constituted "100% Americanism" was far from clear, and its meaning with respect to America's involvement in a foreign conflict was even less so. The
term's implicit connotation of freedom from foreign influences held a paradoxical appeal for a country composed principally of immigrant stock. A
doctrine of Manifest Destiny, based upon principles inherent in the Declaration of Independence, had been published as early as 1839 by John
O'Sullivan, editor of the *Democratic Review*. Promoting a philosophy of
expansionism, O'Sullivan preached that the Declaration of Independence
demonstrated "at once our disconnected position as regards any other nation; that we have, in reality, but little connection with the past history of
any of them, and still less with all antiquity, its glories, or its crimes. On
the contrary, our national birth was the beginning of a new history."[1]

Following the social and political fracture of the Civil War, debates over
the nation's identity as a Union addressed whether it was appropriate that
Confederate soldiers should be memorialized as patriots, whether the
Union's perspective on the Civil War and Reconstruction would be accepted
as official history, and what role the symbols and rituals of the Confeder-
acy might play in the life of the nation.[2] During the period of the Great War
the issue was partially answered when many of the Civil War tunes from
the South, "Dixie" preeminent among them, refused to fade and continued
to serve the nation at large. Such competing allegiances within America's
own brief history only highlighted the uneasiness surrounding the notion
of "100% Americanism." Any such concept had to stem from an imagined
idea of nationhood, one supported by patriotic traditions that had devel-

oped in the course of an ongoing social dialogue.[3] Following the Civil War a series of Indian Wars, which undertook to annihilate the Plains Amerindians who resisted being moved onto reservations, prepared the way for territorial expansion westward. This popularly received imperialism strengthened the American concept of nationhood, a concept that was endorsed again in the Spanish-American War of 1898, when troops from North and South mixed for the first time since before the Civil War.[4]

When America finally entered the Great War some songs like "The Dixie Volunteers" of 1917 openly attempted to preserve the identity of the "Dixie boys" as "Southern laddies . . . from the land of Old Black Joe," who "behind their regimental band" looked forward to "playing tunes from Dixieland" as they gave "the Kaiser a chase."[5] But others, like "Dixie Doodle" of 1918, whose very title conflated ideas of Confederate and Yankee, proclaimed that "there are no boys in blue or gray": "It's just one country" beneath the "Stars and Stripes of Dixie Doodle and the good ole U.S.A."[6]

However grand the hope for a new and binding federation at home that was no longer indebted to foreign influences, the struggle for a singular and independent voice in the concert hall had been largely unsuccessful. With America's entry into the war, Daniel Gregory Mason, composer and professor at Columbia University, announced his concern over a new set of values that seemed to challenge the current state of musical affairs.

> In the discussions of "American music" that go on perennially in our newspapers and journals, now waxing in a wave of patriotic enthusiasm, now waning as popular attention is turned to something else, in war time much stimulated by an enhanced consciousness of nationality . . . , a sharp cleavage will usually be observed between those whose interest is primarily in the music for itself, where it comes from, and those in whom artistic considerations give way before patriotic ardor, and propaganda usurps the place of discrimination.[7]

Notwithstanding attempts to encourage a national style based upon local repertoires, most American "classical" composers and performing musicians continued to journey to Europe in search of a finishing school. With the dawn of the twentieth century, however, the issue of Americanism had gained increasing momentum, and in January 1915, immediately following the outbreak of war in Europe, a new music journal, the *Musical Quarterly*, was launched in New York. Following the lead article by Waldo S. Pratt, "On Behalf of Musicology," which identified a fledgling discipline that was not to come of age in America for several more decades, was a feature on America's most important composer of art music to that date,

Edward MacDowell. No composer had wrestled more with the issue of an "American music" than the German-trained MacDowell had; no composer had resented more the advice of Dvořák on how to achieve it; and no living American composer was more internationally recognized.[8] This was followed by a report on "The Measurement of Musical Talent" from Iowa City by Carl Seashore, one of the most prominent music educators in America, who implied, however obliquely, that the identification of those with the highest musical aptitude in the country might serve some higher national goal.

Despite the prevailing isolationist mood, it was apparent that music scholars were anything but oblivious to, if also deficiently informed about and sorely puzzled by, contemporary developments in Europe. In "Some Aspects of Modern Music," which appeared in the same issue of the *Musical Quarterly*, W. H. Hadow described Arnold Schoenberg's piano pieces as giving "the impression that they mean something to which I have not yet the clue. They start on a different hypothesis from other music, like Lobatchevski's geometry which started on the supposition that the triangle contained less than two right angles." If Schoenberg was not a totally unknown quantity to American musicians, many of his path-breaking scores, such as *Five Pieces for Orchestra* and *Pierrot lunaire*, had rarely been heard in America.[9] Yet recognition of Schoenberg's stature was to become almost obligatory for American periodicals in the years immediately ahead, and *Modern Music*, an important journal that began publication in 1924, devoted an extraordinarily prominent position to him in its inaugural issue.

Hadow also reviewed with dismay the Italian Futurists' belligerent assault on anything and everything smacking of tradition—the academy, the opera house, and the Church. Yet the fact that a war was raging in Europe and that the Futurists had been on the front line, fanning the flames, was nowhere acknowledged. Nor did Hadow mention America's own Futurist composer, pianist Leo Ornstein, who lived in New York City when not concertizing abroad.[10]

In the second issue of the *Musical Quarterly* another European specter loomed in Henry Gilbert's eloquent plea regarding the plight of American composers, whose works were rarely programmed by American orchestras because they were typically, and unfairly, judged by European standards. He charged that "many works which are not in the least significant, nor important to the development of an American school of composition, are given the high honor of a finished performance and a wide-spread publicity."[11]

In the same issue the prominent English composer Charles Villiers Stanford contributed an essay on "Some Thoughts Concerning Folk-Song and Nationality," but it contained not even the slightest hint of any relevance of his chosen topic to the current conflict in Europe. Edward Burlinghame Hill, a Harvard professor who had studied with John Knowles Paine as well as with Charles-Marie Widor in Paris, offered a lengthy study of Vincent d'Indy in which he argued the strengths and weaknesses of the French composer's music, but offered no discussion of the composer's position in French cultural life, his relation to church and state, or the relation of either to the war.

D'Indy was no stranger to musical audiences in America during the early years of the war, however, and even though *The Musical Quarterly* may have failed to remind its readers of the cultural consequences of the European conflict in its initial issues, by April 1916 another journal, the *Musical Courier*, carried an article by d'Indy that went straight to the point. Written in the form of an open letter to the correspondent of the *Musical Courier* at Columbia, South Carolina, and dated ten months earlier, it was printed with the headline "D'Indy Calls on America to Free Itself from German Musical Domination."

> Boffres, 20th of July, 1915
> *Dear Mr. Bellamann:*
>
> You ask me about musical matters in the United States; I do not feel any embarrassment in replying to you, for in the last ten years my opinion has not changed.
>
> In 1906 I was asked by a review in New York to give my opinion upon precisely the same subject. In the article which I sent in response I expressed my opinion very frankly—that is a habit that has done me a great deal of harm during my life, but from which I do not know how to depart. I said then that it was in all ways disastrous for the United States to submit, as I had verified during my visit in 1905, to the musical tutelage and domination of the Germans. Why do Americans, who seem to have it very much at heart to show themselves original in all other things, not seek to be themselves in music?
>
> Why support at great expense German orchestras? Why imitate in their compositions the German works? Why not stand upon their feet without the aid of an everlasting German cane ("Deutsch Stock")? That is what I said in 1906.[12]

The expression "Deutsch Stock" was a double-entendre, referring to Frederick Stock, who had been the conductor of the Chicago Symphony Orchestra since 1905 and who was of German birth.

D'Indy concluded his letter with an announcement of the work of French publishers, particularly the firm of Rouart, Lerolle & Co., in preparing "an exact and honest edition of all the classic works," which had been necessitated by the "cheap German editions" with their "shameless falsifications of the original texts." Not surprisingly, he not only recommended that Americans use the French editions but also advised that they ought to investigate French methods of instruction—even as he warned against rushing "toward French music after having submitted so long to the domination of German music." D'Indy's formula for promoting a musical culture independent of Germany could not escape the need for a model, however, and with little reluctance France was offered as the best at hand. "Above all," d'Indy concluded,

> let America provide her own orchestra players and singers so as to be able to send back to their homes all the Germans who encumber the American orchestras and all the exotic singers who proclaim bad traditions. . . . Let America cause to be studied in the universities and conservatories (according to the French technical systems, which I believe to be the best) all music and works of beauty.[13]

Throughout the early years of the conflict and prior to its own engagement in it, America received periodic appraisals of the avant-garde in wartorn Europe. Of special interest was the perceived relevance of Europe's historic tradition for the contemporary scene there. It was an issue discussed at length by the German musicologist Hugo Leichtentritt, who had come to the United States when he was fifteen and had studied composition with Paine at Harvard before returning to Europe. He completed his doctorate in 1901 and remained in Europe until 1933, when he joined the faculty of Harvard. Leichtentritt was thoroughly conversant with Continental musical traditions. In "The Renaissance Attitude towards Music," published in the fourth issue of the newly founded *Musical Quarterly*, he made special note of the six books by the Late Renaissance Italian madrigalist Carlo Gesualdo,

> whose harmony is so unusual, even eccentric, that it could not be appreciated before the 20th century, because it surpassed in strangeness anything that had been produced up to our own age. Only at present, in the age of Richard Strauss, Debussy, Scriabine, Busoni, can one see that this great impressionist Gesualdo is akin to these modern masters, their brother. He is three centuries ahead of his time in his novel and extremely daring use of tonality or rather lack of tonality, his bewildering manner of modulation, his fine sense of colour in harmony.[14]

Fascination with the Late Italian Renaissance madrigal was again endorsed in the *Musical Quarterly*'s first issue for 1916 in an article by Egon Wellesz titled "Schoenberg and Beyond."[15] Here the authority of the past and its relevance for the avant-garde was protested by one of the most informed Germanic composer-historians of the day, and in specifically summoning the Renaissance tradition Wellesz pointedly contradicted the Italian Futurist credo "Down with the Past" with an example from their own culture. Wellesz, an Austrian, was a composer himself as well as a musicologist and a pupil of Schoenberg, and like the remarks of Leichtentritt, his are extraordinary in their recognition of the contemporary force of Italian Renaissance musical culture. Betraying no hint of bias against the traditions of the enemy, Wellesz's observations force us to recall that the revival of interest in and retrieval of the Renaissance Italian madrigal in the early twentieth century was due in large measure to the efforts of German musicologists. It was a movement that flew in the face of the perception that Germany had rejected all outside influences, and it eventually culminated in Alfred Einstein's path-breaking three-volume *The Italian Madrigal* of 1949—a testimony to forty years of archival study and transcription.[16] Wellesz's remarks read in part:

> Whether the paths which Schönberg treads are destined to become the highways of the music of the future, or whether they are just the last spurs of the old romantic music, here grotesquely distorted to its extreme limits, is an entirely different question, for which we may at present find a psychological but not an aesthetic answer. We have a similar phenomenon in the history of the music of the sixteenth century, in the person of the Italian composer, Gesualdo, Prince of Venosa . . . which we cannot observe again until we reach the later works of Richard Wagner. The age which succeeded Gesualdo was interested in other problems and did not follow in the path pointed out by him. . . . The same fate may be in store for Schönberg.[17]

Further dramatic endorsement of the continuing relevance of this issue to the developing contemporary musical scene in America would appear a decade later. On 30 December 1927, in a League of Composers concert given at Town Hall in New York, two adventurous and highly chromatic madrigals, by Gesualdo ("Tu m'uccidi, oh crudele") and Luca Marenzio ("Solo e pensoso"), were performed.[18] Unspoken but unmistakably implied was the power of the European Grand Tradition, the absence of a counterpart to it in America, and the benefits that could accrue from an awareness of the former.[19]

One of the few essays in the early issues of the *Musical Quarterly* to refer even obliquely to the fact that a war was going on in Europe—a remarkable omission in light of the fact that so many of the contributors were Europeans themselves—was an article in the same issue by T. Carl Whitmer of Pittsburgh. Here the question of political power vis-à-vis aesthetic power was raised, and the argument was put forward that history testified to the fact that smaller or economically less developed countries need not despair.[20]

> I have always been interested . . . in the difference in size between a country and its great men. As has been said, "When Germany was small it produced Bach, Beethoven, Goethe, Schiller, Schubert. When England was small—the size of Belgium—it had its greatest literature." A country does not need full development to create a genius. That is a theoretical mistake we are making in America: looking for our great Expressor only when everything is where you imagine the end of the Melting Pot period ought to be![21]

"THE STAR-SPANGLED BANNER"

As America waited for the appearance of its "great Expressor," another repertoire was ready and waiting to serve the needs of the moment. The power attendant to war tunes, hymns, and national anthems was reviewed in the very first issue of *The Musical Times* published in London following the declaration of war.[22] The near obsession with the topic was dramatized by the appearance of an article by H. C. Colles, "National Anthems: Their Birth and Parentage," which was occasioned by the fact that the conductor Sir Henry Wood had brought together the national anthems of the four principal Allies in a Promenade Concert at Queen's Hall on 1 September.[23] An article on the Russian national anthem also appeared in the February 1915 issue, along with the observation that the Russian hymn, virtually unknown three months previously, was now heard more frequently than "La Marseillaise."[24] In none of these articles, however, is "The Star-Spangled Banner" mentioned even in passing. America had yet to enter the war and had yet to proclaim an official national anthem.

These were only the first in the months and years to come of numerous articles in the English-language journals of London and New York that were devoted to the history and evaluation of national hymns. In the June 1915 issue of *The Musical Times*, for example, an article appeared under the *nom de plume* "Scrutineer" that was titled "Germany's Claim to 'La Marseillaise,'" which argued the thesis, previously reported and now judged to be bogus, that the French national anthem was actually based on the "Credo" of a manuscript mass from 1776 that had been housed in a church in Meersburg on the Bodensee.[25] The issue of pedigree was also picked up in the opening of Frank Kidson's "The 'Star-Spangled Banner': An Exhaustive Official Inquiry" in the March issue of *The Musical Times*. Written as a review of Oscar Sonneck's 1914 revision of a 1909 study of America's increasingly popular national tune, Kidson adopted a war image that was becoming more and more familiar: "The writer who essays the apparently innocent task of conscientiously writing the history of a national song or tune, generally finds himself in a position of an unfortunate soldier fast amid a barbed wire entanglement and subjected to a hail of bullets from the enemy's firing line."[26]

The business of national tunes was becoming a serious business, but the British as well as Oscar Sonneck, the head librarian of the music division of the Library of Congress, were sensible enough to center their arguments on questions of lineage rather than the issue that most concerned a large number of Americans at the time—namely, the tune's suitability as a national anthem. Sonneck had issued his thorough and revised report on "The Star-Spangled Banner"[27] exactly one hundred years after Francis Scott Key, a Washington, D.C., lawyer, jotted down its words as he witnessed the bombardment of Fort McHenry by the British. Although the poem had been written in September 1814 to match a British tune (not an Irish one as held in some quarters) called "To Anacreon in Heaven," and although it had long been popular in the United States (and had been recognized by Puccini as early as 1904 to be the ideal leitmotif for the American naval lieutenant in *Madama Butterfly*),[28] "The Star-Spangled Banner" had yet to be designated as the official national anthem.[29]

Following the Spanish-American War an association of some of the most prominent lyricists and composers in America had been formed to consider the composition of a new and "more appropriate" national anthem. Some maintained that Key's words were no longer apt; others judged that the melody was too difficult for the public to sing. A third contingent even asserted that the music's triple meter made it difficult, if not impossible, to march to without doubling the tempo.[30]

Realizing that an appropriate substitute could never be composed by committee, the ten thousand members of the National Song Society endorsed "A New National Anthem," originally published in 1909 but now slightly amended. Support for the song was loudly proclaimed until 1915 when, recognizing the failure of the campaign, the society began looking for a more favorable candidate. It finally settled on "My Own United

States," by Stanislaus Stangé and Julian Edwards, but this failed as well. And in 1916, a year that witnessed an explosion of patriotic songs in America, "The Star-Spangled Banner" was finally designated as the national air for all official military use by President Wilson under executive order. Even then the choice continued to be roundly debated under the Harding and Hoover administrations, and it was officially confirmed by the Congress only in 1931.[31]

One of the most vocal critics of "The Star-Spangled Banner" was a certain Kitty Cheatham, whose pocket-size booklet *Words and Music of "The Star-spangled Banner" Oppose the Spirit of Democracy Which the Declaration of Independence Embodies* was excerpted for an article that appeared in *The New York Times* on 10 February 1918 and reprinted in its entirety in *Musical America* on 2 March. Privately published, the pamphlet included an appendix of over fifty pages of correspondence that had resulted from its circulation. The article argued that "The Star-Spangled Banner" was an inappropriate hymn in the present crisis because it had been written at a time "when disruption threatened to separate nations and in which sentiments are opposed to the oneness we must finally attain, viz., the inseparable unity of Great Britain and America."[32] Moreover, it had originally been a drinking-song, she observed—a forceful objection in light of the rising tide of Prohibition: "The loyal Americans of this hour, who retain and defend the spirit of 1776, the spirit of the Pilgrim Fathers, who planted on this soil the standard of liberty and 'freedom to worship God,' indignantly protest, rebel, against the perpetuation of 'The Star-Spangled Banner,' because it is *not* American, because it is of Bacchanalian origin."

Cheatham also railed against the song because its lyrics spoke of death and destruction in lines like "bombs bursting in air" and "rockets' red glare." This in turn led to lengthy invocations of the Bible and calls for charity in the name of Christ, even as she protested her loyalty to America and reviewed her family's prerevolutionary pedigree at every turn. Her entire argument was summarized by a single statement: "This country will not be free until she expresses herself in her own anthem, which will be born of American high ideals."[33] Yet, despite the various campaigns to depose "The Star-Spangled Banner," it enjoyed increasing favor throughout the war.

The anthem was featured at numerous recruitment rallies and bond tours along with popular film stars like Mary Pickford, Douglas Fairbanks, Charlie Chaplin, and Lillian Gish, all of whom frequently appeared in person prior to the showing of highly propagandistic Liberty Loan films. When the fourth loan drive was launched in September 1918 in Washington, D.C., at the National Press Club, Metropolitan Opera star Geraldine Farrar sang "The Star-Spangled Banner" on the steps of the treasury building and sold the first bond to William G. McAdoo, the secretary of the treasury.[34] The emphasis placed upon financing the war through the voluntary purchase of war bonds was initially made in the interest of keeping income taxes down—a policy distinctly geared to the advantage of the wealthy and promoted by means of posters, rallies, and flag-waving songs.[35]

THE FOUR-MINUTE MEN AND THE MOVIES

One of the most famous images of World War I is the American recruitment poster showing Uncle Sam over the legend "I Want You for U.S. Army." Designed in 1917 by James Montgomery Flagg, it was a clear imitation of a 1914 British image by Alfred Leete showing Lord Kitchener, the British secretary of state for war, declaring, "Your Country Needs You." The power of the steady gaze and the pointed finger coupled with the slogan's use of the second person singular was neatly summarized by the British recruitment film commissioned in 1916 that carried the simple title *YOU!*[36] The technique was not unknown to composers and wordsmiths of endless wartime propaganda pieces, and its use was explicit in numerous titles such as "America Needs You" and "America Needs You Like a Mother (Would You Turn Your Mother Down?)," both from 1917, and even more than a little accusatory in a Third Liberty Loan poster, which asked, "Are You 100% American? Prove It! Buy U.S. Government Bonds."

President Wilson formed a new agency dubbed the Committee on Public Information (CPI) and placed it under the direction of George Creel, whose purpose was to foster the concept of "100% Americanism" and all the sacrifices this might entail in the effort to win victory in Europe. It was the first ministry of propaganda ever formed in the United States. Creel proved to be an effective agent, although his initial intentions, which seemed to be good, quickly escalated into a strident patriotism that brooked no hint of disloyalty. The extent of the evangelistic zeal that marked his every action was strikingly caught in the title of his memoirs, which were printed shortly after the war: *How We Advertised America; the First Telling of the Amazing Story of the Committee on Public Information That Carried the Gospel of Americanism to Every Corner of the Globe.*[37] The title advertised a concept that Wilson was the first president to promote—namely, that American principles were ripe for export.[38]

Parades, posters, slogans, and news releases organized by the CPI exhorted every American citizen to be on the alert for internal spies, especially people of German birth. Creel then announced the formation of the "Division of Work with the Foreign-Born." It organized "Loyalty Leagues" in numerous ethnic communities throughout America, sponsored rallies and pageants, and achieved one of its grandest triumphs in a "pilgrimage" to Mount Vernon on the Fourth of July 1918, where Americans of foreign birth gathered to "manifest their loyalty to the United States and their devotion to free institutions." There, in the presence of President Wilson, the Irish-born tenor John McCormack sang the "Battle Hymn of the Republic" as the representatives of thirty-three ethnic groups respectfully processed past Washington's tomb.[39]

A group of volunteers called the Four-Minute Men—named for the minutemen, who pledged to be ready to fight on a minute's notice both before and during the Revolutionary War—gave four-minute speeches at all manner of public gatherings. They proved to be especially effective. Predictably, as war momentum gathered, numerous patriotic groups vied for equal time, and the CPI attempted to maintain some control over the situation. This it did in part by enlisting the endorsement of the National Association of the Motion Picture Industry, "which named the Four-Minute Men as the official and authorized representatives of the United States Government in the movie theaters of America."[40] One of their most popular themes centered on the various atrocities that the Germans had committed in Belgium, a theme that was repeatedly mined in CPI films.[41]

The biggest success of all CPI propaganda films was *Pershing's Crusaders*, which opened in New York in May 1918 before an assemblage of military and social celebrities, with a concert by a seventy-voice choir of "Four-Minute Song Men" featured during reel changes. Preparedness was preached as shots of American doughboys in the front-line trenches were shown, and the distinguished audience hissed on cue at a prewar picture of the Kaiser reviewing his troops.[42] Between June and September some 30,000 Four-Minute Men reportedly gave rousing speeches in theaters and public venues across the nation, and over 13,000,000 men registered for the draft.

Periodic attempts were made to contain the oratory of the Four-Minute Men, which with some regularity showed an inclination toward bombast. One of the most effective additions to their performances, however, proved to be the introduction of "Four-Minute Singing." The announcement that appeared in the CPI *Bulletin 38* for September 1918 carried the slogan "Let us get it going with a swing" and advised that if the official Four-Minute Man was incapable of leading the music, he should recruit a qualified substitute. "The Singing Army, whether it be a fighting army or a working army, cannot be beaten," the *Bulletin* suggested in its effort to keep the industrial army at "white heat" through a program of patriotic song. Slides of music and lyrics were prepared that could be projected on the screen, including such favorites as "America," "The Star-Spangled Banner," "Columbia the Gem of the Ocean," "Battle Hymn of the Republic," "Dixie," "When Johnny Comes Marching Home," "There's a Long, Long Trail," "Keep the Home Fires Burning," "Pack Up Your Troubles," "When You Come Back," "Tramp, Tramp, Tramp," and "America the Beautiful."[43] Understandably, the music publishers were ecstatic in light of the prospect for increased sales, and the number of these tunes that are vividly remembered even today is impressive.

The CPI had originally formed its own film division for the purpose of creating short documentaries, but it quickly moved toward the production of feature-length stories that relied upon a heady mixture of fact and fiction with an eye to their propaganda value. "Viewed as a drama, the war is somewhat disappointing," the producer-director D. W. Griffiths remarked,[44] but this was no doubt in part because of the cumbersome quality of the kinetoscope, which made filming the war no easy proposition. Nonetheless, by 1916 England had also begun to realize that the motion picture was a valuable propaganda tool, and a Committee on War Films was organized to record scenes from the Battle of the Somme, which was then in progress. Despite the logistical restrictions cameras managed to film artillery batteries in action, marching infantrymen, soldiers in the trenches moving into attack position, and the returning wounded. The resulting footage, including some faked scenes, was filmed over a period of two weeks in early July and was then edited and released as the *Battle of the Somme*. It was the most widely viewed film of the war, opening in thirty-four London cinemas on 21 August and booked in more than a thousand provincial theaters by early September. Endorsed by the prime minister, David Lloyd George, and shown at Windsor Castle to King George V and Queen Mary, who responded enthusiastically, it brought a new level of realism to the folks back home.[45]

Obviously, none of this prevented the fledgling movie industry from devising patently nationalistic commercial studio films. Hollywood launched a series of "anti-Wilhelm" movies, for example, that reached its apogee with *The Kaiser, the Beast of Berlin,* which concluded with the Kaiser being placed in the custody of King Albert of Belgium.[46] Although all of the films made at this time were silent, in the sense that there was no sound track and the dialogue was printed on the screen, many had scores composed specially for them that were intended for live performance. Holly-wood's fascination with opera and opera stars led to the advertisement of Thomas Dixon's *The Fall of a Nation* as the first grand opera cinema and "The First Original Score to a Great Picture Ever Made by an Eminent Composer."[47] A story of America conquered by foreign invaders with the aid of immigrant citizens, it opened in June 1916 with an accompanying score by Victor Herbert. Preaching a low tolerance for pacifists, it carica-tured William Jennings Bryan and Henry Ford as ambassadors who "carry flowers to the enemy, only to be captured and forced to peel potatoes." Al-though it prompted only a modest reception, plans had initially been made to send the ten-reel film to the nation's largest cities, complete with tour-ing orchestras.[48]

The same month brought the release of Thomas Ince's *Civilization*, a film *Motion Picture News* characterized as "a sermon based on the use-lessness of war" and the failure of humanity throughout nineteen centu-ries to accept the teachings of Jesus Christ.[49] The three-hour film, which employed numerous scenes involving artillery, submarines, and aerial bombardments, was an enormous success. In October it was shown at the White House, but whether the music for the film—composed by Victor L. Schertzinger, arranged by Lee Orean Smith, and published by Leo Feist in the same year—was used for this event is not certain.[50]

The most famous of all films to appear at this time, and by common as-sent one of the greatest ever produced in America, was D. W. Griffith's *In-tolerance*, which opened in September 1916. A direct response to charges of pacifism and bigotry in his earlier film *The Birth of a Nation*,[51] the film was intended primarily as a testimony to the destructive force of intoler-ance throughout human history. Four stories—the fall of Babylon, the crucifixion of Christ, the St. Bartholomew's Day massacre, and the misery in a strike-ridden mill town and the urban tenements of contemporary America—were accompanied by the music of Joseph Carl Breil. The score for full symphony orchestra, which was characterized by pastiche, allusion, and an operatic leitmotif convention, was closely synchronized with the ac-tion, and the production was destined to be remembered as a watershed in the history of music and film.[52]

On Christmas Day 1916, four months before America's entry into the fray, Cecil B. DeMille's *Joan the Woman* opened in New York, starring Farrar.[53] DeMille spoke of Joan of Arc as one "who single-handed awoke a nation from an unpatriotic sleep into such activity and valor that France for all time has continued a free nation."[54] She had been reintroduced to America in 1915 with Frank Sturgis's song "Joan of Arc, They're Calling

Figure 34. Geraldine Farrar in a Liberty Loan Drive Pageant.

You," written for the stage production *This Way Out,* and was soon to be invoked in War Savings Stamps campaigns. Despite the appearance of Farrar, Hollywood's operatic aspirations were not advanced in this movie, although a keyboard score by William Furst was published by G. Schirmer in 1917.[55]

Farrar's previous films for DeMille had been banned in Canada because of her alleged pro-German sentiments. Farrar had enjoyed a considerable success in Germany prior to her rise to fame in America, and she had maintained friendly relationships with many of her German colleagues throughout the war. Her attractiveness to men, including a totally enamored and frustrated Arturo Toscanini, was legendary. But the fact that she was a personal acquaintance of both the Kaiser and the crown prince and was known to have displayed an inscribed picture of the former on her piano seemed to confirm rumors of a romantic liaison with the enemy. In addition, a pattern of speech and behavior led many observers to conclude that she had crossed the line. By the following March the opera star was virtually obliged to give assurances that she had always been 100 percent pro-American. When at the first film presentations of *Joan the Woman* in Boston she tied an American flag around her body—instead of posing against the shadow of the French fleur-de-lis as she had done in the movie—and sang "The Star-Spangled Banner," all was forgiven. A recruiting station was set up in the lobby of the theater, and censors everywhere dropped their objections (fig. 34).[56]

With Hollywood's cooperation the objectives of George Creel's CPI propaganda machine were quickly coming to fruition, and the ubiquity of the anthem that Farrar so freely sang was now reflected in another film advertised at government recruiting offices. Attended by a Marine Corps representative in many theaters, it was called simply *The Star-Spangled Banner,* and it concerned a young Englishman who developed a love for the U.S. Marine Corps and the American flag.[57] The gathering potency of "The Star-Spangled Banner" for a nation whose schools did not yet fly flags and whose citizenry rarely removed their hats or sang at the playing of the national anthem before the 1890s [58] was now beyond dispute and would soon have powerful ramifications in the concert hall, well beyond anything that could have been anticipated.

17 "Proof through the Night"

> No man has any business to be engaged in anything that
> is not subordinate to patriotism. If the Boston Symphony
> Orchestra will not play "The Star-Spangled Banner," it ought
> to be made to shut up. If Dr. Muck will not play it, he ought
> not to be at large in this country.
>> Theodore Roosevelt, 3 November 1917

> [I leave America with] no regrets as the country is being
> controlled by sentiments which closely border on mob rule.
>> Karl Muck, 21 August 1919

Of all the modes of public participation following the declaration of war by the United States, it was the singing of the national anthem at civic events and in the concert hall that provided the most potent rallying point and gave proof of America's resolve in the dark hours of the Great War. It was a factor that was quickly understood by American orchestra managers, who early on realized the need to neutralize the heavy dose of music by German and Austrian composers that had long dominated American orchestral programs. But just as boycotting this repertoire in favor of works by little-known American composers was unthinkable, so some sort of recognition that the country was at war quickly came to be felt mandatory. National policy and enemy alien laws now directly began to affect conductors and performers of German ancestry alike, many of whom applied for citizenship.

The degree of negative sentiment directed toward "hyphenate citizens" during the period of World War I, especially the largest of such groups, the German-Americans, was inordinate. In 1916 the American theologian and social moralist Reinhold Niebuhr wrote candidly about Christianity's refusal to confront social problems in an article in the *Atlantic Monthly* titled "The Failure of German-Americanism." He spoke openly of the deficiency of this group in responding to the civic and moral responsibilities in their new country.[1] Noting how the country now found itself broken into racial groups "whose old-world loyalties seem more powerful than their new allegiance," he proclaimed that "America is facing the problem of the 'hyphen.' . . . With this problem on our hands, it is natural that larger alien groups should engage our particular attention, and that their doubt-ful loyalty, or divided allegiance, should especially arouse our indignation." Niebuhr had no doubt been encouraged in the bluntness of his indictment by President Wilson's State of the Union message delivered on 7 December 1915. Wilson spoke at length on the "infinitely malignant" hyphenates: "There are citizens of the United States . . . born under other flags but wel-come under our generous naturalization laws to the full freedom and op-portunity of America, who have poured the poison of disloyalty into the very arteries of our national life." [2] The German-American press in partic-ular resented Wilson's stinging attack, while American papers like the *Chi-cago Daily News* ran cartoons that openly warned of spies, conspiracies, and bomb plots. Predictably, when America finally entered the war in 1917, a virulent debate arose as to whether enemy aliens resident in the United States ought to be subject to the draft.[3]

THE CHICAGO SYMPHONY ORCHESTRA

The German issue also had to be squarely faced in the question of mu-sic programming, which amongst American orchestras had traditionally been heavily weighted toward the German repertoire. The first concert of the Chicago Symphony Orchestra after the outbreak of war in Europe had been a typical all-German program of Weber, Beethoven, Strauss, and Wagner,[4] and the opening concert on New Year's Day 1915, which was ded-icated to the memory of the orchestra's first conductor, Theodore Thomas, was devoted solely to Beethoven and included the "Eroica" Symphony and the Fourth Piano Concerto, performed by Harold Bauer. Fritz Kreisler played Beethoven's Violin Concerto on 9 and 10 April, although he would later be barred from giving concerts in Jersey City and Pittsburgh, not only because he was Austrian but because he had actually donned an army uni-form in the early months of the conflict. Kreisler soon decided that it would be wise to postpone further concerts in America for the duration of the struggle, except for a few concerts on behalf of war charities that had al-ready been announced. While the symphony orchestra in Pittsburgh took the prize for patriotic zeal by banning German music completely from its programs, the Chicago Symphony continued to show a preference for the German repertoire through the 1916–1917 season, which ended with a program of Beethoven, Brahms, Strauss, and Wagner, followed by the first performance in Chicago of Mahler's Eighth Symphony on 24 April, shortly after America's declaration of war.[5]

Changes were in the wind, however, and the first concert of the orchestra's 1917–1918 season, given on 12 October, opened with a performance of "The Star-Spangled Banner" before launching into Wagner's overture to *Rienzi* and Beethoven's Sixth Symphony. What a curious juxtaposition it was: America's new national anthem alongside the very composition that not too many years later would be heralded by Adolf Hitler as the embodiment of Nazi aspirations.[6] After intermission the Chicago program settled on music of the Allies: *Ballade: "Tam O'Shanter"* by America's George Whitefield Chadwick, *Prélude à l'après-midi d'un faune* by France's Claude Debussy; and orchestral rhapsodies by England's Frederick Delius and Italy's Alfredo Casella. The second program, given on the 12 and 13 October, also began with a performance of the national anthem and featured the newly finished First Symphony of Chicago's own John Alden Carpenter. Many later programs that season also included works by Americans, native or naturalized. Then, in response to a series of newspaper charges that some members of the orchestra were openly pro-German, Charles H. Hamill, a vice-president of the Orchestral Association, decided that it was necessary to address the audience and provide assurances. No mention was made of the citizenship of the orchestra's membership, nor were pledges made regarding repertoire.

The conductor, Frederick Stock, like his predecessor Theodore Thomas and many members of the orchestra, was of German birth, and it is more than a little startling to learn that because of the makeup of the orchestra itself, before World War I rehearsals were typically conducted in German. Stock's loyalty was never in question, but appearances meant everything in the climate of growing anti-Germanism, and the Chicago Symphony adopted a collective resolution in which its members declared their "unswerving loyalty to the Government . . . in the great cause for which it has taken up arms against the rulers of the German people."[7]

Stock had promoted the playing of patriotic works with his own *Festival March* of 1910 (a work that incorporated a grab bag of American tunes, from "The Star-Spangled Banner" and "The Old Folks at Home" to "Yankee Doodle" and "Dixie") as well as a *Festival March and Hymn to Liberty* of 1913.[8] Such programming paved the way for the practice, beginning on 21 December 1917, of starting each program with a performance of either "America" or "The Star-Spangled Banner." Stock, trained in Cologne, had been resident in America since 1895 and had been the conductor of the Chicago Symphony Orchestra since 1905. But owing to negligence his first papers in the process of applying for citizenship had expired, and he was obliged to apply again in 1916. Because of the escalating wartime hysteria surrounding German-Americans who were not citizens, Stock determined that it would be best for him to resign temporarily. Although from the beginning Stock had made clear his intention to become an American citizen, his request was accepted by the Chicago Symphony Orchestra's board of trustees with regret on 17 August 1918 until such time as he attained citizenship. This he did only on 22 May 1919, by which time the war was over.[9]

THE BOSTON SYMPHONY ORCHESTRA
AND "L'AFFAIRE MUCK"

In Boston the situation was handled less amicably. The extent to which German culture had come to dominate American orchestral societies was acknowledged with dismay some years later by Philip Hale, critic and program annotator for the Boston Symphony Orchestra, in an article in the *Boston Home Journal*.

> German is spoken at rehearsals of orchestras composed of men of various nationalities, and supported by Americans. And when the chief supporter and patron of the Boston Symphony Orchestra wished the other day to express to the orchestra his personal gratification at the work of the past year, it is said that he composed with care a letter in the German language which was read aloud in German by an imported German.[10]

Karl Muck had been the conductor of the Boston Symphony Orchestra since 1906, when the Kaiser had released him from his appointment as principal conductor of the Royal Opera House in Berlin. He performed intermittently in both cities until 1912, after which he settled more or less permanently in Boston. Despite growing anti-German sentiment, Muck's high standards won him many admirers, and by 1916 the critics were beginning to express their feeling that it would be difficult to think of the orchestra without him.[11] Henry Higginson, founder and sustainer of the Boston Symphony, who had turned eighty in 1914, managed for three years to find an artful balance between his admiration for the German-Austrian roots of most of the players and all the conductors to that time and the personal loyalty he felt for his native country as a Civil War veteran.

The tide turned, however, on 30 October 1917. That morning's edition of the *Providence Journal* contained an editorial demanding the performance of "The Star-Spangled Banner" during the symphony's concert that evening in Providence. "It is as good a time as any to put Professor Muck to the test," concluded the *Journal*'s editor (later discredited as a zealot and spy-chaser). On the afternoon of the same day Higginson received tele-grams containing a similar demand from the Rhode Island Council of Defense, the Liberty Loan Committee, and the secretaries of several exclusive women's music societies, including especially the Providence Chaminade Club. Charles Ellis, the orchestra manager, ignored all of these requests, particularly in light of the fact that none of the patriotic ladies who signed the telegram were regular subscribers. His decision was supported by Higginson. Treating these events more or less as a series of nuisance communications, Ellis nonetheless halted further ticket sales to avoid an onrush of rabble-rousers at the evening concert.

Even though Muck remained totally innocent of all these developments, reports began to circulate in the papers the next day that he had refused to play "The Star-Spangled Banner." Higginson publicly defended his actions and exonerated Muck of any complicity, but despite his protests the onus of the affair naturally fell upon the conductor because of his alien status. All arguments regarding the appropriateness of performing patriotic airs at public concerts or their inherent musical worth meant little in light of the temper of the times, and Muck's few words did not help matters. "Why will people be so silly!" he asked. "Art is a thing by itself and not related to a particular nation or group. It would be a gross mistake, in violation of artistic taste and principles, for an organization such as ours to play patriotic airs." [12] All the hubbub over "The Star-Spangled Banner" had been brought to a head, of course, by the controversy attendant on the search for a new national anthem in the immediately preceding years and more particularly by President Wilson's recent designation of the work as the national anthem for the armed services. Zealots everywhere were quick to recognize the opportunity and press the cause further.

In Baltimore, where the Boston Symphony was scheduled to perform in the fall season, the former governor of Maryland, Edwin Warfield, joined the fracas and announced that Muck would not be permitted to lead the orchestra there. "I told the Police Bureau," he said, "that this man would not be allowed to insult the people of the birthplace of 'The Star-Spangled Banner.'" [13] Warfield then judged "The Star-Spangled Banner" to be "a symphony incomparable, at a time like this, greater than anything ever composed in Germany, more glorious and befitting the hearing of true Americans than the work of any composer, living or dead." [14] He then upped the ante by gladly offering to lead a mob to prevent the Boston Symphony from performing it in Baltimore. [15]

The controversy had now become a national issue, and on 2 and 3 November *The New York Times* published two vitriolic statements by the distinguished conductor of the New York Philharmonic, Walter Damrosch, who was himself German-born and -trained. Noting Muck's reluctance to perform the national anthem, Damrosch concluded that he "should not enjoy hearing him do so. Considering his citizenship and his feelings toward our war, this would be an act of hypocrisy."[16] Theodore Roosevelt then followed with a true-to-type salvo, stating that he was "shocked, simply shocked, to learn that anybody can apologize for Dr. Muck on the ground that the music [of "The Star-Spangled Banner"] is not artistic, but only patriotic." Roosevelt went on to proclaim his own commitment to "100% Americanism."[17]

The story spread like wildfire to the international press, and two months later the *Musical Times* of London was still reporting that "Dr. Karl Muck (Prussia), who refused to conduct the 'Star-Spangled Banner' at a concert given by the Boston Symphony Orchestra, later altered his mind and condescended to guide the players through its mazes."[18] The account did accurately acknowledge a fact that frequently seemed to have been forgotten, namely, that prior to the second Damrosch attack, which appeared together with Roosevelt's remarks, Muck had amicably agreed to conduct the national anthem in an arrangement taken from Victor Herbert's *American Fantasy* at a regular Friday afternoon concert in Boston and again in a Carnegie Hall concert on 9 November.[19] This seems to have been offered as a decoy, suggesting that Herbert's arrangement satisfied artistic criteria not met by the standard versions and that it was this issue which formed the basis of Muck's original objection. But Muck also offered his resignation to Higginson, who refused it even as he announced that the national anthem would be performed at every concert in the future, with Muck conducting.

Matters seemed to have subsided almost completely before Mrs. William Jay, a vociferous attacker of German music in New York City during the war, once more took up the cause. The Boston orchestra was scheduled to give a performance in Carnegie Hall on 14 March 1918, and Mrs. Jay, backed by the Daughters of the American Revolution, Dr. Will T. Manning, the rector of Trinity Church, Mr. George L. Ingraham, former justice of the appellate division of the New York State Supreme Court, and others campaigned to prevent them from playing. She proposed a series of tests before Muck should be allowed to conduct in New York, including proof that he had never served in the German army and that he currently held Swiss citizenship.

Finally, in light of a series of provocative headlines in *The New York Times,* such as "City is Confident Ban Will Be Put on Dr. Muck" and "Kaiser's Direktor and Band Reach City," hundreds of policemen had to be detailed to patrol Carnegie Hall, and door checks were conducted to insure that only subscribers were admitted.[20] Muck began with a performance of the national anthem before launching into what was reviewed as an exceptionally vigorous performance of Brahms's Third Symphony.[21] Higginson then appeared before the audience and presented Muck's Swiss credentials, answered the questions that had been proposed by Mrs. Jay, and retired to thunderous applause—all of which was dutifully reported in the press the next day.

But the issue would not die, and the affair culminated in the arrest of Muck by Boston police and Department of Justice agents upon his return to his residence on the evening of 26 March 1918. The following evening Muck had been scheduled to conduct a long-awaited performance of Bach's *St. Matthew Passion,* a work for which he had prepared a new edition based on early source materials. Without making specific charges, the authorities placed him indefinitely in the East Cambridge jail pending a search of his personal effects and formal indictment. It wasn't until the following year that the *Boston Post* reported that his incarceration had been based upon the fact that he had had an affair with a twenty-two-year-old girl in the Back Bay and that letters had been intercepted by federal agents disclosing his continuing loyalty to the Kaiser and his deep distaste for Boston society.[22] Muck remained in the Cambridge jail until 6 April 1918, when he was sent to Fort Oglethorpe, Georgia, and imprisoned as a "dangerous enemy alien" for the remainder of the war. He was joined by Ernst Kunwald, conductor of the Cincinnati Symphony, who was also charged with espionage.

The coup de grace was delivered by the newspaper headlines asserting that Muck was a German spy. After more than a year at Fort Oglethorpe, Muck was finally released, and when he sailed for Europe on 21 August 1919, *The New York Times* and the *Boston Globe* both reported that he was leaving the United States with no regrets and with a bitter feeling toward the newspapers and a country that in his opinion had conducted a witch hunt.[23] He also reiterated his denial that he had refused to play "The Star-Spangled Banner," and concluded with a simple statement that may have disguised his cultural identity but that also underscored the confusion in the matter: "I am not a German though they said I was. I considered myself an American."[24] Subsequently, from 1922 to 1933, he enjoyed a highly successful tenure as director of the Hamburg Philharmonic Orchestra.

Muck was replaced by Pierre Monteux while Boston awaited the decision on a permanent choice. American conductors were among those considered for the post for the first time in the history of the orchestra; also mentioned as possible candidates were Ernest Bloch, Ossip Gabrilowitsch,

Vincent d'Indy, Sergey Rachmaninoff, Leopold Stokowski, and Sir Henry J. Wood. Henri Rabaud, who satisfied the desire to avoid a German at the helm, was eventually chosen.[25] The percentage of German works programmed by major American symphony orchestras did diminish notably between 1917 and 1919, even as the number of French works predictably increased.[26] With Rabaud now at the helm, compositions by Saint-Saëns, d'Indy, Jean Roger-Ducasse, and other French composers began to appear.

With Damrosch firmly in charge at the New York Philharmonic, the French repertoire was understandably less in evidence there, but statistics reveal that both Boston and New York struggled to find useable items by American composers, including new works by Rubin Goldmark, George Whitefield Chadwick, and Edgar Stillman Kelley.[27] In his final interview before returning to Europe, Karl Muck had reported that twenty-nine German-born members of the Boston Symphony had been interned. Some observed that the single salutary result of the tempest over "The Star-Spangled Banner" had been an improvement in the position of American orchestral musicians, and in September 1918 Boston chose Frederic Fradken to become the first American-born violinist to assume the position of concertmaster of a major orchestra.

One further perspective surrounding *l'affaire Muck* is worth recounting. In his memoirs, published in 1926, Damrosch reexamined the Muck story at considerable length—after apologizing that it would be impossible to review all the details. On balance it was clear that while he admired Muck as one of the noble conductors of his day, he was not about to give him a clean bill of health. Damrosch repeated stories that Muck had taken a cottage at Seal Harbor, Maine, during the summer of 1917, where he purportedly had a wireless that allowed him to communicate with a fleet of German submarines cruising off Mount Desert Island. The mission of these subs, it was rumored, was eventually to capture and hold for ransom all of the millionaires of Bar Harbor. A neighbor was also reported to have heard Muck in a telephone conversation plotting the bombing of Faneuil Hall in Boston and the birthplace of Henry Wadsworth Longfellow in Portland, Maine.

Damrosch discounted such stories in the main, but he censured what he called Muck's supercilious attitude and his denigration of the artistic merit of "The Star-Spangled Banner." He concluded that Muck should have resigned in light of the conflict of interest between his nationality and his host country.[28] Damrosch also twice recounted his meeting with a Swiss ambassador who denied Muck's claims to Swiss citizenship—this despite the proof offered by Higginson. Damrosch conceded that Muck's father had been a Swiss citizen and that Muck himself had been born there. But he noted that because Muck had departed at an early age for Germany, where he had received all his education and several important professional appointments before coming to America, he was a German in the eyes of the Swiss.[29] Damrosch was quick to agree with this assessment, having himself arrived in America from Germany at the age of nine.

The Secret Service had followed every rumor and clue regarding reports of Muck's spying activities and found them to be without foundation. Nevertheless, Damrosch concluded with the unspecific, although apparently damning, innuendo that the agency had, indeed,

> discovered other disagreeable things in regard to him which had no connection with the war but which made him liable under the laws of our country. An incriminating package of letters was shown to him, and on his acknowledgment that he had written them he was given the choice of internment as a prisoner of war at Fort Oglethorpe or of being arrested on another charge and brought before the civil courts for trial. He naturally threw up his hands and accepted the former as the lesser evil. As he was released after the war on condition that he return to his own country, I cannot see that he has cause for anything but gratitude toward this country and its lenient treatment of him.[30]

Damrosch's judgments seemed clearly driven as much by his need to prove himself a loyal American citizen of German descent as to set the record straight about Muck—although their attention to the Beethoven symphonies during the war period, for example, was remarkably similar.[31] Yet the degree to which Damrosch threw himself into a war relief project, called the "American Friends of Musicians in France," and the fact that he later undertook a trip to Europe while the war was still on corroborated his well-intentioned, if somewhat zealous, commitment to playing a prominent and unmistakable role as a 100 percent American ambassador of music.

GOOD CITIZENSHIP

Sergey Rachmaninoff arrived in America at the very moment that hostilities ceased in Europe. Although he had displayed gifts as a pianist at an early age, leading to concert tours of France, England, and America, Rachmaninoff had increasingly occupied himself with composition and conducting following his graduation from the Moscow Conservatory in 1892. With the outbreak of the Russian Revolution, Rachmaninoff made up his mind to quit Russia for good, and he left for Scandinavia with his family on 23 December 1917 under the pretext of giving a series of concerts. He never returned. Continuing on to America, he arrived on 10 November 1918, the day before the Armistice was signed.

At the age of forty-five, and with a wife and daughter to support, Rachmaninoff decided that his best course was to launch an all-out career as a concert pianist. In April 1919 he was approached by Thomas Alva Edison with a contract to make a series of gramophone recordings, but a falling out with the inventor led him to sign a contract with the Victor company, which he honored until his death.[32] At about the same time Ampico, a rival of Duo-Art in recording on perforated piano rolls, was looking for a universally recognized artist and invited Rachmaninoff to make some test recordings. The results pleased both the company and the composer and resulted in the production of thirty-four music-roll recordings over a period of the next ten years. Among the pieces that were captured by Ampico were a group of transcriptions that Rachmaninoff had made of pieces by Schubert, Kreisler, and others. Most timely of all, however, was an unpublished transcription of "The Star-Spangled Banner" that Rachmaninoff had performed in December 1918 at the opening recital of his first tour following the arrival of his family in America. Even if it was not a dazzling patriotic display—compared, for example, to Vladimir Horowitz's later paraphrase of Sousa's "The Stars and Stripes Forever"—Rachmaninoff had obviously made his arrangement and performed it publicly as a signal of loyalty to his newly adopted land. This was apparent in light of not only the brouhaha that had recently occurred in Boston but also the fact that at that time Rachmaninoff was still considering offers to conduct 110 concerts in thirty weeks with the Boston Symphony Orchestra and to assume the post of conductor for the Cincinnati Symphony. Rachmaninoff eventually refused their invitations on account of the heavy burden that such a commitment would impose.

Offers to Rachmaninoff of this kind were more than understandable in light of his undeniable virtuosity as a pianist and the strong appeal of his music to the populace, yet less so with respect to his status as a newly arrived immigrant whose loyalties to the United States had yet to be tested. Rachmaninoff was at the height of his creative powers during the war period, having recently composed the Third Piano Concerto (1909), *The Bells* (1913), the Second Piano Sonata (1913), and the two sets of *Études-tableaux* (1911, 1916), but only the spiritual beauty of his *Vespers* (All-night vigil, 1915) for unaccompanied chorus invited interpretation as an oblique response to the sacrifices of the war years. Now, in a quite different vein, the composer offered his transcription of "The Star-Spangled Banner" to mark his adoption of a new home and a new career.[33]

Concerts performed by the U.S. Marine Band and conducted by their German-born conductor, William F. Santelmann, at the Marine Barracks, the Capitol, and the White House, for example, uniformly concluded with "The Star-Spangled Banner" throughout the period from 1914 through 1918. But it was on 3 July 1916 that this notice first appeared at the bottom of the program: "The entire audience is required to stand to attention, men with their hats removed, while the National Anthem is being played."[34] In October 1917 a War Information Series prepared by the War Department and published by the Committee on Public Information appeared with the title *Home Reading Course for Citizen-Soldiers.* The series consisted of thirty lessons with titles such as "Your Post of Honor," "Nine Soldierly Qualities," "Getting Ready for Camp," "Your Equipment and Arms," and "Playing the Game." Lesson No. 25 was devoted to "Saluting the Colors" and "The National Anthem." A mandatory etiquette prescribed for soldiers not in formation was followed by one for civilians that included standing at attention, hat removed, and right hand placed opposite the left shoulder. The "common habit of rising slowly, standing in a slouching attitude, and sometimes even carrying on conversation" during the playing of the national anthem was decried as inappropriate behavior for the cultivation of feelings of pride and patriotism for one's country. The proclamation then concluded with a stern warning: "It goes without saying that disrespect to the American flag can not be tolerated. If any such instances come to your attention, you should report them at once to the proper authorities in order that they may be dealt with in accordance with the law."[35]

It was not long before this new litmus test for loyalty found its first victim. At a Victory Loan pageant held on 6 May 1919 in Washington, D.C., a man was shot in the back three times for refusing to rise for the playing of America's newly proclaimed national anthem. The next day the *Washington Post* reported that as the victim fell to the ground "the crowd burst into cheering and handclapping."[36] Frontier justice, invoked in the name of preserving the federation, had announced its survival even in the nation's capitol. Yet it was also clear that the recent christening of a national musical emblem had failed to resolve America's continuing struggle for national identity. Indeed, nothing could have more unmistakably ratified the warning that "when flags and the fictions they stand in for are protected but people are destroyed, something is wrong."[37]

Not surprisingly, in the period just ahead "The Star-Spangled Banner"

continued to beckon numerous musicians and composers of radically different orientations. The tradition of making arrangements of the national
air, begun by John Philip Sousa,[38] Victor Herbert, and John Knowles Paine,
was continued not only by Rachmaninoff, Stravinsky, Damrosch, and Toscanini, but in time also enriched through settings by popular personalities such as Louis Armstrong, Duke Ellington, Jimi Hendrix, and Whitney
Houston.[39] A deconstruction of the full testimony behind each of them
would provide a valuable lesson in the variant meanings of patriotism.

OPERA AND BALLET IN NEW YORK

Goyescas, o Las Majas enamoradas, a new opera by Enrique Granados,
was premiered at the Metropolitan Opera in New York in January 1916. It
was the first Spanish opera ever performed at the Met, and Granados's visit
to the United States was noted on the diplomatic front (Spain, like the
United States at the time, was neutral). On 7 March 1916 Granados performed at the White House for President Wilson and his guests, playing
his own "Danza valenciana," excerpted from his opera, and a sonata by
Domenico Scarlatti.[40] *Goyescas* did not enjoy a spectacular success,[41] but
there was understandable shock when news arrived that on the return voyage Granados's ship, the *Sussex,* had been torpedoed by a German submarine, and that the composer and his wife had perished. Coming in the wake
of the sinking of the *Lusitania* the previous year, this tragedy heightened
America's concerns over freedom of the high seas and led President Wilson
to issue an additional ultimatum to the Germans.[42]

Nonetheless, performances at the White House by the U.S. Marine
Band in the following months continued to include German staples such as
Wagner's "Entrance of the Gods into Walhall" from *Das Rheingold* on
10 July 1915 and 1 July 1916, as well as "War Fanfare, and King's Prayer"
from *Lohengrin* on 26 August 1916. And, just as America was entering the
war on 2 April 1917, the same band played Wagner's prelude to *Parsifal*
alongside Beethoven's overture to *Fidelio* and Bruch's First Violin Concerto.[43] Only the month before, however, on 2 March 1917, the rising pro-
war sentiment had been unmistakably evident in a performance of Umberto Giordano's opera, *Madame Sans-Gêne,* which had received its world
premiere at the Metropolitan Opera under Toscanini's baton only two years
before. Neither star of the 1917 production, Geraldine Farrar or Pasquale
Amato, could compete with the waving of the French flag while the chorus
sang "La Marseillaise" (a trick Giordano had previously used in *Andrea*

Chenier, set during the French Revolution), which reportedly brought the audience to its feet.[44]

News of America's declaration of war came midway through a performance of *Parsifal* on Good Friday, 6 April, and it clearly cast a pall over the German wing of the opera house. Two German productions planned for the concluding week of the season, *Die Meistersinger* and *Tristan und Isolde,* were performed according to schedule. At the final performance of the season, on 13 April, Johanna Gadski, one of the reigning Wagnerian singers of her time, was granted permission to announce her "retirement" rather than be officially dismissed. Not only was she married to Captain Hans Tauscher, a reserve officer in the German army and a representative of the Krupp munitions firm in America, her husband had been accused, although acquitted, of plotting in 1916 to blow up the twenty-seven-mile-long Welland Canal.[45] Gadski had also garnered an unsavory reputation in the press because she had hosted a jubilant party following the sinking of the *Lusitania* in 1915, and few of those who read the remarks of the New York critics were deceived by the report that her engagement was terminated because of "the deterioration of Mme. Gadski's voice and art."[46] Gadski would not return to North America again until 1929.

Following America's entrance into the war, the entire German repertoire of the Metropolitan Opera was dumped, despite the objections of the general manager, Giulio Gatti-Casazza, who faced the daunting prospect of replacing between forty and forty-five performances of German works with little more than a week's notice. Many German singers were dismissed, and a few sued. Olive Fremstad, who had sung her first Isolde in Mahler's debut at the Metropolitan Opera in 1908, and who was reported as reengaged in November 1917, failed to return and, indeed, never appeared there again. Tellingly, during this same period in England, Beecham continued to conduct the operas of Mozart as well as Wagner in English translation even though London had become the target of repeated zeppelin raids.

The Metropolitan Opera's 1918 season was scheduled to open on 11 November, and little could Gatti have predicted what that date would bring. The opera chosen for opening night was Saint-Saëns's *Samson and Dalila,* and the coincidental signing of the Armistice on that date brought acclamations of prophecy on the part of the management. Monteux's direction of the ballet sequences highlighted the Frenchness of the production and brought special cheers from the audience.[47] Soprano Louise Homer, an American product, and Caruso, a citizen of an Allied nation and the most beloved singer of his time, provided the necessary and ideal balance for the occasion.[48] Following the final curtain, Caruso reappeared and led the audience in "The Star-Spangled Banner," the "Inno di Garibaldi," "La Marseillaise," and "God Save the King."[49] In March Caruso would be hurriedly recalled from a concert in Ann Arbor to sing the national anthem once again at the Met on the occasion of President Wilson's address to the League of Nations.[50]

After the Armistice, musical institutions across America were faced with the dilemma of maintaining or adjusting their policies regarding returning German artists and the repertoires with which they were associated. Although Pittsburgh had initiated an all-out ban of German music and the California state schools had removed German folksongs from children's music books, operas like *Die Zauberflöte* (1791) and *Tristan*, which had been suppressed over the past year at the Metropolitan, ultimately proved too powerful to resist once the war was over. The road back would be a gradual one. On 28 December Carl Maria von Weber's *Oberon* (1826), starring the young Rosa Ponselle, was allowed under the pretext that it had originally been written in English, a rationale mirrored in numerous lieder recitals in translation throughout the period. But an attempt a year later, on 19 October 1919, to bring back selections from German opera sung by former Metropolitan singers at New York's Lexington Theater was met with a storm of protest by American Legionnaires, and the *Sun* concluded, "The fact is, that people who have fought Germans do not at present like the sound of the German tongue."[51] It would take time, but over the next few years German opera, initially in English translation and then in the original language, together with ideal casting regardless of nationality, would gradually be welcomed home to the Met. However, some of the opera's former stars, such as Maria Ivogün, Claire Dux, Lotte Lehmann, and Alexander Kipnis, had left for the friendlier climate of Chicago.[52]

An entirely different affair caused an equal stir at the Metropolitan Opera during this period. Although Vaslav Nijinsky, the virtuoso star of Diaghilev's Ballets Russes, had refused an invitation by Richard Strauss to dance in his new ballet, *Josephs-Legende*, he did attend its premier in Paris on 17 May 1914, a performance that featured Diaghilev's new discovery, Léonide Massine. It was a gala affair at which the French government accorded Strauss the cross of the Légion d'Honneur. Having broken with the great Russian impresario following his marriage, Nijinsky and his wife, Romola, traveled to Hungary just as war broke out. Nijinsky was a pacifist and a Russian, but his wife was the granddaughter of Francis de Pulszky, the founder of Hungarian democracy and friend of Lajos Kossuth, a legendary hero of the Hungarian revolution of 1848. Nonetheless, both of the

Nijinskys had been detained as prisoners of war, and they were ultimately released only after the American ambassador in Vienna intervened in response to a plea from Diaghilev. The Russian impresario was in New York for performances at the Metropolitan Opera, and his most famous dancer was to be released "on parole" only for the length of the engagement, with the specific stipulation that he not return to Russia.[53]

In the meantime Nijinsky had again met with Richard Strauss and had now agreed to choreograph *Till Eulenspiegel,* a production that was planned for New York. Nijinsky's American debut took place on 12 April 1916 in a program that consisted of *Prince Igor, Le spectre de la rose, Sheherazade,* and *Petrushka.* It was followed by the premiere of *Till* on 25 October of that year. Diaghilev took no interest in the Strauss production and never even saw it, claiming that times had changed because of the war and that, in any case, he now considered Strauss's familiar score as pure *cabotinage* (showing off).[54] Monteux, who was to have conducted *Till Eulenspiegel,* also joined the boycott, announcing that although he had recently performed Schumann's *Carnaval,* Strauss was a living boche. The contract was broken and another conductor engaged. A tour followed, however, under Nijinsky's directorship, including three performances in Washington at the end of November in the presence of President Wilson, whom Nijinsky thanked for help in securing his release from Austria.[55] When the season was over Nijinsky spent time in Spain and then South America, but his mental disintegration had begun. Although he would live until 1950, his career had effectively crumbled in the midst of the Great War.

18 "On Patrol in No Man's Land"

> There can be no disagreement over the proposition that the
> lot of colored soldiers in the armies of the United States—
> in the past, and at the present, is much different than that
> accorded to white soldiers; very little to be really proud of;
> very, very much to be ashamed of—much that is humiliating
> and depressing.
>
> R. S. Abbott, editor of the *Chicago Defender*,
> November 1915

All-black units served in the historically segregated armed forces of the United States as late as the Korean War.[1] No fewer than 3,000 black soldiers, freed from slavery, had fought in the army of the American Revolution.[2] Others figured in the War of 1812 and the Battle of New Orleans of 1814, and as many as 200,000 served in the Union army and navy during the Civil War.[3] During the Great War there were four black regiments in the regular army: the 24th Infantry, which had served on the Mexican border since 1916; the 25th Infantry, stationed in Hawaii throughout the war; the 9th Cavalry, stationed in the Philippines since 1916; and the 10th Cavalry Regiment, which had patrolled the Mexican border and had served elsewhere in the West from 1917 on.[4]

For a moment following the performance of the 10th Cavalry Regiment in the first skirmish of the Spanish-American War, at Las Guasimas, Cuba, on 24 June 1898, one might have thought on the evidence of one popular lyric that the conflict in Cuba had been a watershed in U.S. Armed Forces race relations as well as a marker of America's aspirations as a world power.[5]

> We used to think the Negro
> Didn't count for very much,
> Light-fingered in the melon patch
> And chicken yards and such.
>
> But we've got to reconstruct our view
> On color more or less,
> Now we know about the sentry
> At Las Guasimas.[6]

Subsequent degradation and humiliation continued nonetheless, although on one frontier during World War I the African American soldier captured the attention of all who came in contact with him. The role of black service musicians in maintaining high levels of morale was soon a matter of record among the Allies and Central Powers alike, and their musical contributions were destined to reverberate long after the Armistice.

THE "HELLFIGHTERS" OF THE 369TH REGIMENT

John Philip Sousa, who with the encouragement of John Alden Carpenter played an important wartime role in the U.S. Navy on the home front, wrote numerous marches (mostly forgotten) during this period, and above all made a classic arrangement in 1918 of "Over Hill, Over Dale" that became known as "The U.S. Artillery March." He was not the only American bandsman to play a crucial role during the Great War, however, and in many ways the black musician James Reese Europe was equally consequential.[7] Europe was born in Mobile, Alabama, in 1880, and when he was nine years old his family moved to Washington, D.C., where they lived just a few doors from the Sousa residence. Sousa and the Marine Band claimed a long-standing relationship with the black community in Washington, where the band regularly played for commencement exercises at Howard University. Members of the band also taught promising black children. Among them was young James Reese Europe, who received instruction in piano and violin.

In 1904 Europe went to New York where he directed shows and, in 1910, organized a black musicians' union. Performances with his own symphony orchestra at Carnegie Hall followed, and almost overnight Europe achieved professional notice as both composer and conductor. In 1913 he joined the dancing couple Vernon and Irene Castle, who had discovered the infectious quality of his syncopated rag rhythms at a white high-society party. In his engagements with the Castles, Europe increasingly began to incorporate wind instruments into the traditional string-based dance ensemble, and soon his dance orchestras came to be known as bands.[8]

In the summer of 1916, almost a year before America entered the war, a new all-black regiment of the New York National Guard was formed, and that September Europe enlisted as a private and was immediately assigned to a machine gun company. By this time Jim Europe had developed important associations with musicians like James Herber (Eubie) Blake and Noble Sissle, and Europe explained to the latter that, having lived in New York for sixteen years, he felt the need for an organization of Negro men that could "bring together all classes of men for a common good."[9] Sissle enlisted shortly after Europe, and their commanding officer, recognizing the importance of music and parades in establishing morale, asked Europe to organize and develop the finest band in the U.S. Army. Initially Europe was reluctant, but when his requests for an expansion of the standard complement of twenty-eight musicians to forty-four and a handsomely increased budget were met, largely thanks to a director of the U.S. Steel Corporation, he relented.[10] John D. Rockefeller Jr. was also an admirer and sent several checks in support.[11]

Jim Europe's growing sense of patriotism was especially remarkable in light of the persistent discrimination that he and all African American soldiers encountered. Following America's entrance into the war, for example, a request by the 15th Regiment for inclusion in the farewell parade down Fifth Avenue was rejected. This insult was compounded by a remark made to Europe as they marched off to join the Rainbow Division in France, to the effect that "black was not one of the colors of the rainbow."[12] Shortly thereafter the announcement that the 15th Regiment would take up training at Spartanburg, South Carolina, brought a warning from the town's mayor, dutifully reported in *The New York Times*, that "with their northern ideas about race equality, they will probably expect to be treated like white men."[13]

A series of racist incidents followed. Although the band's concerts were warmly appreciated by many Spartanburg residents, it was ultimately deemed best that the all-black regiment be transferred. Rather than indicate retreat by shipping them to another location in the United States, it was determined that the group should be sent to France to complete their training. Ultimately the regiment joined a convoy to France, arriving on New Year's Day 1918. They were the first African American combat group to set foot on French soil, and their band immediately struck up the "Marseillaise" in a rhythmically spirited rendition that French soldiers initially failed to recognize as their own national anthem. Orders came from General Pershing to proceed to a center where an engineering detachment was busy building facilities to support a multi-million-man force, and musical instruments were exchanged for pick and shovel. Assignments were made even more difficult by the traditional injunction against black soldiers serving with white ones.

Eventually American entertainment organizers got word that Europe's band was in France, and when they heard the group in person they were completely won over. Orders followed from General Pershing to have them transferred to a location where they could entertain soldiers who were on a week's leave. In the period that followed Europe and his band played in numerous places, and programs that featured Sousa's "Stars and Stripes Forever" and "plantation" melodies and finished with "Memphis Blues" invariably brought down the house. "Jazz spasms" and "ragtime-itis," to use Sissle's words, worked the crowds into a frenzy. France, which had previously "gone ragtime wild" over performances by John Philip Sousa in 1900,[14] now came down with a high fever.

Repeated attempts to have the 15th Regiment reassigned to combat duty fell on deaf ears because of America's Jim Crow policies. The unit was given two choices: return to the United States and await assignment to a proposed black division, or accept immediate transfer to the French Army, which had already integrated French colonial troops into its ranks and was now in desperate need of reinforcements. The regiment's commanding officer accepted the latter proposal at once, and at the end of March Europe's regiment, carrying the colors of New York state, marched to the front and became the first American unit to join a French combat force. The 15th Infantry Regiment vanished and the 369th Infantry Regiment, U.S. Army, was born.

The soldiers of the new Trois Cents Soixante-Neuvième, as they were dubbed, soon impressed the French as well as the enemy with their adeptness at throwing grenades and in hand-to-hand bayonet combat. Although the signs of bigotry typically encountered with American troops remained largely out of sight, numerous cartoons of the period emphasized that the *poilu* was French and white, and portrayed black soldiers "as stupid and even savage."[15] The Germans also bristled and charged that the Allies had "brought black troops to subdue European soldiers."[16] It was an issue that would resurface at the end of the war when Germans became angered because men of the *Tirailleurs Sénégalais* from French West Africa participated in the Allied occupation of the Rhineland.

Nonetheless, genuine friendships developed between the French and black American soldiers, and the level of cooperation between the two forces seemed nothing short of miraculous in light of recent experiences in the U.S. Army. Here both sides needed each other. They were soon ordered to move closer to the front, and Lieutenant Europe turned over his responsibilities with the band and took charge of instructing his troops in the use of the French machine guns and protection from gas attacks. Europe was the first African American officer to lead his troops into combat during the Great War, and of that he was understandably very proud. During this period Europe gained firsthand experience with raids into no man's land, and in time so did his troops. Sissle remained behind with the regimental band, which continued to perform.

Just how important the role of music had become was vividly described by the well-known journalist Irvin S. Cobb, who visited groups near the front. Formerly a Southern humorist who relied heavily upon the ridicule of black speech, Cobb expressed a change of heart in an article for the *Saturday Evening Post* of August 1918.

> If I live to be 101 I shall never forget the second night, which was a night of a splendid, flawless full moon. We stood with the regimental staff on the terraced lawn of the chief house in a half-deserted town five miles back from the trenches, and down below us in the main street the band played plantation airs and hundreds of negro soldiers joined in and sang the words. . . .
>
> And when the band got to "Way Down Upon the Suwannee River" I wanted to cry, and when the drum major, who likewise had a splendid barytone voice, sang, as an interpolated number, "Joan of Arc," first in English and then in excellent French, the villagers openly cried.[17]

Cobb and a group of reporters had arrived following an attack by a German patrol of two dozen men earlier that morning, and, seeing the wounded firsthand, Cobb took pains to describe the men of Europe's regiment not just as a group of musicians but as heroic fighters.

FROM THE TUILERIES TO THE RECORDING STUDIO

Europe and his machine gunners came under heavy German artillery fire during the third week in June 1918, and Europe, the victim of a gas attack, was transferred to a field hospital. When Sissle arrived at the gas ward to check on him, Europe was propped up in bed with a notebook in his hands. As Sissle approached, Europe announced that he had just completed the chorus of "On Patrol in No Man's Land," based on the bombardment the night before. It was to become one of the band's most popular hits after the group's return to the United States.[18]

Jim Europe was sent to Paris for a few weeks to recover from the gas attack, and then, in August, his band was ordered back to Paris to give a concert at the Théâtre des Champs-Élysées. The program, dominated by national airs, was ecstatically received. In the fading months of the war Europe's group played countless concerts that held Allied audiences spellbound. Even when his band played alongside some of the elite bands of Europe (including the British Grenadiers Band, the French Garde Républicain, and the Royal Italian Band) in a concert given in the Tuileries Gardens, Europe could report that although his band "could not compare with any of these, yet the crowd, and it was such a crowd as I never saw anywhere else in the world, deserted them for us. We played to 50,000 people, at least, and, had we wished it, we might be playing yet."[19] The leader of the Garde Républicain approached Europe and asked him for a score of one of the jazz compositions, but he returned the next day saying that his group couldn't seem to get the same effects.

"Jazz" as a loosely defined term suddenly came in for a great deal of attention, and Charles Welton of the New York *World* wrote an article in the spring of 1919 that focused on Jim Europe and his band.[20] All the writers took pains to point out that the essence of jazz was not in the score but in the manner in which it was played, and that virtually any piece of music could be "jazzed." The various articulations, types of mutes, and embouchure manipulation that produced blue notes and other smears and slurs were described in detail.

At first the performance style of ragtime seemed to be beyond the reach of white musicians altogether. Of one thing there could be no doubt: the style was born among African Americans, and they had every right to proprietary claims regarding any and all issues of "authenticity." The question of this syncopated music's appeal to French nonblack audiences has been the subject of considerable investigation; it has been charged to its unarguable visceral attraction, to the prevailing Primitivist aesthetic amongst the practitioners of "high" art in Paris, especially in painting and music,[21] and finally to the idea that this group of men, who had exchanged machine guns for trumpets and trombones, offered their music as a kind of "welcome compensation . . . to war-torn France."[22]

A few weeks after the Armistice the "Hellfighters" of the 369th Infantry Regiment were awarded the Croix de Guerre. And when the final tally was made, it was discovered that the 191 days the regiment had spent in action was the longest stretch served by any group of American soldiers, black or white, during the Great War. Yet they had always fought attached to a foreign service and had never been attached to an American brigade or division (fig. 35).

The regiment arrived back in the United States on the *S.S. La France* on 12 February 1919, and five days later they held a joyous victory parade up Fifth Avenue and home to Harlem. The less pleasant memories of the regiment's departure in the fall of 1917 were momentarily erased, and the denial of permission to black troops to join in the victory parade down Pennsylvania Avenue in Washington, D.C., following the Civil War was all but forgotten.[23] A report in the New York *World* on 18 February 1919 noted that during the parade and the reception the previous day "the Negro troops practically owned the city." In an extraordinarily lengthy write-up

Figure 35. 369th Regiment "Hellfighters" with damaged
instruments, 1919.

of the events and their significance, of which the following is only a sample,
the reporter caught the boisterous nature of the occasion.

> The town that's always ready to take off its hat and give a whoop for a
> man who's done something—"no matter who or what he was before,"
> as the old Tommy Atkins song has it—turned itself loose yesterday in
> welcoming home a regiment of its own fighting sons that not only did
> something, but did a whole lot in winning democracy's war.
>
> In official records, and in the histories that youngsters will study in
> generations to come, this regiment will probably always be known as
> the 369th Infantry, U.S.A. . . .
>
> The Police band was at the front of the line of march, but it was a
> more famous band that provided the music to which the Black Buddies
> stepped northward and under the Arch of Victory—the wonderful jazz
> organization of Lieut. Jimmie Europe, the one colored commissioned
> officer of the regiment. But it wasn't jazz that started them off. It was
> the historic *Marche du Régiment de Sambre et Meuse*, which has been
> France's most popular parade piece since Napoleon's day. As rendered
> now it had all the crash of bugle fanfares which is its dominant feature,
> but an additional undercurrent of saxophones and basses that put a new
> and more peppery tang into it.
>
> One hundred strong, and the proudest band of blowers and pound-
> ers that ever reeled off marching melody—Lieut. Jimmie's boys lived

fully up to their reputation. Their music was as sparkling as the sun that tempered the chilly day.

Four of their drums were instruments which they had captured from the enemy in Alsace, and ma-an, what a beating was imposed upon those sheepskins! "I'd very much admire to have them bush Germans a-watchin' me today!" said the drummer before the march started. The Old 15th doesn't say "Boche" when it refers to the foe it beat. "Bush" is the word it uses, and it throws in "German" for good measure. . . .

The noise drowned the melody of Lieut. Europe's band. Flowers fell in showers from above. Men, women and children from the sidewalks overran the police and threw their arms about the paraders. There was a swirling maelstrom of dark humanity in the avenue. In the midst of all the racket there could be caught the personal salutations: "Oh, honey!" "Oh, Jim!" "Oh, you Charlie!" "There's my boy!" "There's daddie!" "How soon you coming home, son?"[24]

Jim Europe was discharged from active duty on 25 February 1919, and he immediately set about making plans for a national tour with his 369th Hellfighters. It was launched on March 16 with a performance in New York that included "Sambre et Meuse," the nostalgic "Plantation Echoes," and a group of jazz tunes including "St. Louis Blues." Ecstatically received concerts followed in Philadelphia, Boston, Cleveland, Pittsburgh, Indianapolis, St. Louis, and Chicago.

Four recording sessions were held during this period, and one of the most impressive takes, on 14 March, was of Europe's own "On Patrol in No Man's Land," sung by Noble Sissle (CD track 13).

What's the time? Nine?
Fall in line.
Alright, boys, now take it slow.
Are you ready? Steady!
Very good, Eddie.
Over the top, let's go.
Quiet, lie it, else you'll start a riot,
Keep your proper distance, follow 'long.
Cover, brother, and when you see me hover,
Obey my orders and you won't go wrong.
There's a Minenwerfer [German mortar] coming—
Look out [bang!].
Hear that roar [bang!], there's one more [bang!],
Stand fast, there's a Very light [flare].
Don't gasp or they'll find you all right.
Don't start to bombing with those hand grenades (rat-a-tat-tat-tat).

There's a machine gun, holy spades!
Alert, gas! [sirens] Put on your mask,
Adjust it correctly and hurry up fast.
Drop! There's a rocket from the Boche barrage.
Down, hug the ground, close as you can, don't stand,
Creep and crawl, follow me, that's all.
What do you hear? Nothing near,
Don't fear, all is clear.
That's the life of a stroll,
When you take a patrol
Out in No Man's Land.
Ain't it grand?
Out in No Man's Land.
(Come on, boys, go to it!)[25]

Readers today may detect a proto-rap cadence to the lyrics, but whatever its legacy, there had never been a popular song quite like it, one in which the musicians attempted to recreate the noise and confusion experienced in battle. Indeed, the "bangs," "rat-a-tat-tats," and "sirens" can all be heard on the recording, and one can only wonder if there might not also have been an occasional visual element on the word "flare" in live performance.[26] The Pathé company, who recorded the pieces, promoted them as "jazz," but it must be understood that the word was new, that its meaning was imprecise, and that the syncopation and jazz effects offered by Europe's group contrasted vividly with the music of most typical military bands of the time.[27]

Other songs that were recorded by Europe's band, such as "All of No Man's Land Is Ours," in which a soldier phones home from dockside, put the spotlight on the new technology of the telephone, familiar to audiences from "Hello, Central. Give Me No Man's Land." The latter was a song that Al Jolson had interpolated in Sigmund Romberg's *Sinbad* of February 1918 and that he recorded in March.[28] Another tune by Europe's group, "My Choc'late Soldier Sammy Boy," recalled the victory parade in which Reese's troops had taken part only the month before the recording. Here a happy mother watches proudly as her "choc'late soldier Sammy boy" marches by and "throw[s] out his chest" with "medals pinn'd on his breast."

The word "choc'late" is obviously employed with a note of racial pride and in a manner that recalls Noble Sissle's and Eubie Blake's "Mammy's Little Choc'late Cullud Chile," published and recorded in 1917 and later revived for the revue *The Chocolate Dandies* of 1924. The "Sammy" in the final line should also not be misread as a diminutive of (Little Black)

Sambo; it simply meant one of Uncle Sam's soldiers. Nora Bayes substituted "Sammys" for "Yanks" in her recording of "Over There," and John Alden Carpenter wrote a song titled "Khaki Sammy," one of many "Sammy," "Sammie," and "Sammee" songs composed between 1917 and 1919. Only one of these, "Sambo Sammies," by Hartley and Hall, published in 1918, conflated the term with the racial stereotype.[29]

"How Ya Gonna Keep 'Em Down on the Farm" ("After they've seen Paree?"), another of the songs recorded in March 1919, was typically understood to refer to young American soldiers from rural areas. Although it had only recently been introduced, many singers were quick to record it, including Nora Bayes and Arthur Fields. When sung by Sissle and backed by Europe's ensemble, however, the lyrics could easily be heard as a reference to black soldiers who might now find it difficult to accept the old prejudices having had their first taste of racial equality while serving in France.[30]

Pieces recorded by Europe's Hellfighters for Pathé included "That Moaning Trombone," "Memphis Blues" (one of the earliest recordings of the W. C. Handy classic), "Plantation Echoes," "Dixie Is Dixie Once More," "St. Louis Blues," and "The Darktown Strutters' Ball." One of the most fascinating was a piece called "Russian Rag," written by George L. Cobb in 1918 and based on a work known to aspiring young pianists everywhere, Rachmaninoff's "Prelude in C-sharp Minor." Widely recorded at the time, "Russian Rag" reflected interest not only in Russia as a wartime ally and as a country that was now fighting a revolution at home but also in Rachmaninoff, who had recently immigrated to America. The early African-American jazz musicians' interest in appropriating the European classics — whether a prelude by Rachmaninoff, a wedding march by Mendelssohn, or a Debussy chord progression — was already being demonstrated elsewhere by numerous performing groups. Hearing Will Marion Cook's Southern Syncopated Orchestra perform pieces based on all three composers later that year, the conductor Ernest Ansermet confirmed what was becoming increasingly apparent to all who listened to this newly evolving music when he remarked, "Thus, all, or nearly all, the music of the Southern Syncopated Orchestra is, in origin, foreign to these Negroes. How is this possible? Because it is not the material that makes Negro music, it is the spirit."[31]

After so recently escaping death at the front, Europe was fatally stabbed in New York only two days after the fourth recording session, on 7 May 1919, by his drummer, Herbert Wright, following a professional reprimand. James Reese Europe's promise had been prematurely stilled, but his dream was pursued by numerous other black musicians. Europe may not have been the first to introduce "jazz" to the Continent, but he was an immensely important figure, not only for disseminating African American musical culture on the Continent but also for introducing Paris to one of jazz's characteristic ensembles.[32]

Above all, Europe was instrumental in garnering recognition and respect everywhere for black performers, composers, and conductors alike. Throughout the 1920s developments among classical composers as well as jazz artists on the Continent built solidly upon the legacy of musicians such as Europe, Sissle, and Blake; Sissle and Blake were specifically cited by Milhaud as major influences during that period, when the whole issue of Primitivism as a chic high-cultural phenomenon suddenly came face-to-face with the issue of racism.[33] For a weary postwar world, the basic question of humankind's potential for inhumanity seemed to resonate in the spirited art of a beleaguered people. At Europe's funeral on 13 May 1919 the choir sang "Abide with Me" and "Lead, Kindly Light," a quartet sang "Dear Old Pal of Mine," and Henry T. Burleigh, a longtime friend, sang "Now Take Thy Rest." And at the very end the bugler of the "Old 15th" played "Taps."

THE "DAMNABLE DILEMMA"

Europe's Hellfighters had not only helped to introduce "jazz" to the Europeans but also proven to be model soldiers and courageous fighters as well. This was especially important in light of the numerous stereotypical judgments of cowardice and disloyalty leveled against American blacks and of the periodic lynchings early in the war. A. Philip Randolph, one of the editors of the *Messenger*, founded in 1915, was prominent among those who spoke pointedly to the issue of racism and the war: "Lynching, Jim Crow, segregation, and discrimination in the armed forces and out, disfranchisement of millions of black souls in the South—all these things make your cry of making the world safe for democracy a sham, a mockery, a rape of decency, and travesty of common justice."[34]

W. E. B. Du Bois, who founded the NAACP in 1910 and spoke dynamically about the shortcomings of American democracy, termed the situation a "damnable dilemma."[35] The black press had understandably argued the appropriateness of enlistment in a war fought by a country that so badly mistreated its people and even weighed in with the fact that Germany had never wronged blacks personally. Others thought that the cause of civil rights might be advanced by a loyal showing at such a moment of national emergency, and in his controversial editorial "Close Ranks," even Du Bois concluded that the fight for racial equality ought to be temporarily suspended in light of the need for a total subscription of America's citizenry to the war effort. Whatever the effect of his homily, when the final tally was made, over 200,000 African American men had served in the armed forces overseas during the Great War.[36]

One of the anomalies of the period was the continuous production of "coon songs," some written by black musicians themselves, that propagated stereotypical minstrel portrayals of the jovial, shiftless "darky." The continuation of this tradition during wartime prompted such ludicrous titles as "When the Boys from Dixie Eat the Melon on the Rhine." At the same time, many of the war-inspired lyrics understandably cast African Americans as highly popular entertainers, as the *Ziegfeld Follies of 1918* hit sung by Eddie Cantor attests.

> When Uncle Joe Steps into France
> With his ragtime band from Dixie-land
> See the Soldiers swaying
> When Uncle Joe starts playing a ragtime ditty,
> So sweet and pretty.
>
> When they play the Memphis blues,
> They will use a lot of shoes,
> And fill them full of darky gin,
> They'll rag their way right to Berlin.[37]

Even here, however, amid the racist stereotyping is an underlying current that recognizes and pays tribute to the contributions of groups like the Hellfighters. In numerous other songs, however, undiluted prejudice abounds; one example is "Jefferson Brown," in which the purported cowardice of an African American man working in a munitions factory is scandalously caricatured.[38] In a few songs, such as "When the Good Lord Makes a Record of a Hero's Deeds He Draws No Color Line" by Harry De Costa, the composer of "Goodbye My Chocolate Soldier Boy," such distinctions are denied, although specific acts of valor are curiously restricted to the Civil and Spanish-American Wars. One of the most mean-spirited songs of the war, Martin and LeBlanc's "Nigger War Bride Blues" (1917), openly ridiculed the plight of husbandless black wives. But in general the tunes and texts inspired by world conflict were less given to caricature and insult than other novelties of the time and especially of the prewar period, which had produced such unconscionable titles as "Every Race Has a Flag but the Coon."[39] African Americans were not the only soldiers subjected to derogatory ethnic references in wartime song lyrics. Italian Americans, for example, were confronted with "Hey, Wop, Go Over the Top!" and "When Tony Goes Over the Top," which included lyrics like "With a rope of spagett / And a big-a stilette, / He'll make-a the Germans sweat."[40]

John Jacob Niles, who arrived in France as an aviator with the American Expeditionary Force in December 1917, set down a totally unknown repertoire that addressed the personal role of the black soldier in the Great War. Taking note of a volume of French war songs titled *Les chants du bivouac*, Niles decided to keep a notebook of similar tunes that he heard sung by American soldiers. He soon concluded that "the imagination of the white boys did not, as a rule, express itself in song. They went to Broadway for their music, contenting themselves with the ready-made rhymes and tunes of the professional song-writers."

In time Niles began to encounter African-American troops who, while they were familiar with music-hall numbers, were more inclined to sing "the legend of the black man to tunes and harmonies they made up as they went along."[41] It was a new kind of folk music, based upon familiar traditions that had been adapted to the situation at hand. Niles notated a number of these pieces, including the "Whale Song" and the "Going Home Song." The latter protested the desire to go home, away from top sergeants and the powdered "wild women" of France.[42] Whether or not this particular song originated among black soldiers, it was remembered and sung spontaneously by soldiers of all races at Remembrance Day ceremonies at the Royal Albert Hall in London as late as 1927.[43]

Some songs, such as "Don't Close Dose Gates," were never printed or recorded in any way except by Niles, but here the expressed hope that things might be better on Judgment Day is especially touching.

> Jesus said he wouldn't mind if I was a little late,
> When he pardoned me my sins . . .
> Good Book says it doesn't matter 'bout de color ob your face,
> So I'm sure comin' in.[44]

Others, like "Lordy, Turn Your Face," understandably relied upon the tradition of the spiritual and reflected, in a startling anticipation of Jerome Kern's "Ol' Man River," the fact that many of the Negro ranks were detailed to tasks with little potential for glory.

> Black man fights wid de shovel and de pick—
> Lordy, turn your face on me—
> He never gits no rest 'cause he never gits sick . . .
> Lordy, turn your face on me.[45]

If the contribution of African Americans in the Great War "was both obscured and depreciated in song,"[46] it must be added that the impact of their music making during that period was also disproportionately high in relation to their numbers—a fact that was in no small measure responsible for ushering in a new sensibility of the talent and humanity of a people. A more positive assessment of the World War I black musician's stature, as measured by his contribution to American and world culture, was registered in the 10 June 1918 issue of the *St. Louis Post-Dispatch,* wherein Noble Sissle described the band's first presentation of jazz to a French audience. Its conclusion is a nice piece of prognostication.

> French officers began to pat their feet, along with the American General, who, temporarily, had lost his style and grace. . . . [Europe] turned to the trombone players who sat impatiently waiting for their cue to have a "jazz spasm" and they drew their slides out to the extremity and jerked them back with that characteristic crack. The audience could stand it no longer, the "jazz germ" hit them and it seemed to find the vital spot. . . . Among the crowd listening was an old woman about sixty years of age. To everyone's surprise, all of a sudden she started doing a dance that resembled "Walking the Dog." Then I was cured, and satisfied that American music would some day be the world's music.[47]

Whatever changes in perspective may have been wrought for the good on the musical front, it is sobering to recall that only two decades later, with the unleashing of yet another world war, black soldiers once again served in American armed forces that were totally segregated.

BANDMASTERS AND THE BIRTH OF AN AMERICAN CONSERVATORY IN FONTAINEBLEAU

Toward the end of the war Walter Damrosch accepted the invitation of the French to conduct the Pasdeloup Orchestra of fifty players on a tour of recreation centers, camps, and hospitals. He had received, among the three endorsements required by the sponsoring YMCA, one from Theodore Roosevelt, who wrote, "Mr. Walter Damrosch is one of the very best Americans and citizens in this entire land. In character, ability, loyalty, and fervid Americanism he, and his, stand second to none in the land. I have known him thirty years; I vouch for him as if he were my brother."[48]

With such a clean bill of health from America's superpatriot, Damrosch was on his way. In June 1918 he arrived in Paris, which a million and a half people had deserted in the face of the continuing German bombardments.

Although he was officially sponsored by the YMCA, Damrosch had been inspired to undertake the tour by the American Friends of Musicians in France, a war relief project to which he had become passionately committed. In the ceremony that followed his Paris concerts Damrosch presented a substantial check intended for the families of orchestral musicians now serving at the front. The conductor's enthusiasm was momentarily checked, however, when he was informed ever so amicably that, having been born in Germany, he could not be issued a *carte rouge*, which would permit him to travel outside Paris.

It was during the summer of 1918 that Damrosch first met Nadia Boulanger and learned of the compositions of her recently deceased sister, Lili. Lili Boulanger had been the first woman to receive the Prix de Rome, in 1913. When all the male winners of the prize had returned home at the first call for mobilization, Lili Boulanger had returned as well, and in 1915 she and her sister Nadia formed a Paris Conservatoire branch of the Comité Franco-Américain.[49] They attended to the needs of former conservatory students who were now in the service, corresponding with them, sending packages, and even correcting the harmony exercises sent back to them from the front. The sisters kept in contact with the soldiers principally through a gazette that they typed, mimeographed, and sent out each month. One of the questions they asked was "Should German composers like Brahms and Wagner be played at our concerts during the war?" Of the fifty-eight responses they received, accompanied in several cases by lengthy essays on art and nationality, forty-seven somewhat unexpectedly answered "Yes" for Wagner and Brahms. Only three supported the inclusion of Beethoven and the classic composers, two remained undecided, and six voted a blanket "No."[50]

Damrosch was so impressed with the music of Lili Boulanger that he organized and conducted a concert of her works in Paris, and upon his return to New York in December he programmed her *Pour les funérailles d'un soldat* (1913) for mixed choir, baritone solo, and orchestra (fig. 36).[51] During the final months of the war there were other important matters to attend to, however. All concerns about Damrosch's German birth were ultimately smoothed out, and Damrosch was called to General Pershing's quarters to discuss the specific possibilities of improving the army bands. General Pershing proved to be sympathetic to the role of music in raising the spirits of his soldiers, but he had also been struck by the inferiority of American bands when compared to some of the crack French and English ensembles. His plan was to improve the general standard of the American army bands by providing a headquarters band as a kind of model. "When peace is de-

Figure 36.   Cover for Lili Boulanger's *Pour les funérailles d'un soldat.* (Music © 1919 by Société Anonyme des Éditions Ricordi, Paris.)

clared and our bands march up Fifth Avenue, I should like them to play so well that it will be another proof of the advantage of military training," Pershing said.[52]

There were over two hundred U.S. military bandmasters in France at the time, and Damrosch agreed to examine them all in batches of fifty each week. A band was then put at his disposal to test their conducting skills. Eventually Damrosch proposed that a music school be formed at which groups of fifty bandmasters would undergo a course of eight weeks, and at which some forty instrumentalists could receive a period of twelve weeks' training on their individual instruments from first prize graduates of the Paris Conservatoire who were serving in the French army.[53] Pershing gave his enthusiastic stamp of approval, and Damrosch in return promised to have the school up and running by October if a proper building could be found.

The first school was opened at Chaumont, with Francis Casadesus, conductor, composer, and pupil of César Franck, serving as director, and André Caplet placed in charge of classes in conducting, harmony, and orchestration. Philip James, who later enjoyed a remarkable career as composer, conductor, organist, critic, and educator on the music faculty of New York University, was one of those who took the conducting test. Even at this time he was a published composer, whose songs were being sung by the likes of Amelita Galli-Curci and Alma Gluck. James was affiliated with the American Expeditionary Force Bandmaster and Musicians School at Chaumont from late November 1918, and he attested that the band there was remarkable, "the nearest approach to a symphony orchestra I have ever heard."[54] In April 1919 James received his commission and returned to the United States as conductor and commanding officer of the Allied Expeditionary Forces General Headquarters Band, now known as "General Pershing's Band."[55] He led the band on a nineteen-city Victory Loan tour, and, like Europe's tour with the Hellfighters at about the same time, James's concerts were wildly received as emblematic of America's contribution to final victory in the Great War.

On his last visit to Chaumont, Damrosch had made a toast and asked for a pledge from the authorities there that for the remainder of the war the bandmasters' school would continue to run at its high standard, which it did from October 1918 until June 1919, when the last members of the Expeditionary Force departed for the United States. Casadesus spoke to Damrosch of the earnestness with which the students tackled their studies, and Damrosch in turn urged him to find some way to continue the work that had been launched by founding a school somewhere near Paris for American men and women to undertake advanced study each summer for a period of three months.

These talks eventually led to the formation of the Conservatoire Américain in Fontainebleau, whose program was inaugurated with a performance on 4 June 1919 by Damrosch's New York Symphony Society, then on tour in Europe.[56] The whole town participated in the festival, and the tradition, one that lasts to this day, of training young American musicians in Fontainebleau was born. Charles-Marie Widor played an organ recital of his own and Saint-Saëns's works before a lobster and champagne lunch. Then military bands and 150 choristers performed for the guests on the palace grounds. The Harvard Glee Club under the direction of Dr. Archibald T.

Davison sang works by Saint-Saëns, Duparc, Chadwick, and Liszt, and at intermission the French 103rd Infantry Regimental Band performed works of Saint-Saëns and Widor. When night fell, colored lanterns surrounding the carp pool and a large float flying the Tricolor and the Stars and Stripes were suddenly illuminated.[57] A display of fireworks, which continued until midnight, expressed France's appreciation to America for having helped turn the tide of the war.

The next month, on the Fourth of July, a Franco-American celebration in Paris culminated in a parade from the Arc de Triomphe down the Champs-Élysées to the Place de la Concorde, with French airmen swooping and maneuvering to the delight of the crowd. On 13 and 14 July, the French national holiday, Damrosch conducted two concerts, the first exclusively for American soldiers and Red Cross nurses and the second for the benefit of the French Red Cross. The first was performed at the Théâtre des Champs-Élysées and the second at the Salle du Conservatoire, a hall never before offered to a foreign conductor. The decrepit state of the orchestra necessitated the last-minute commandeering of an oboist here, a trumpeter there—some brought in by taxi from assignment in the Garde Republicain and other organizations—but the concerts were thunderously received.

At the concert for American soldiers Damrosch played Victor Herbert's medley of American airs, which brought the audience's most tumultuous approval when the orchestra cited the familiar and rousing "Dixie." The following day the program included Debussy's *Prélude à l'après-midi d'un faune*, Franck's *Variations symphoniques,* with Alfred Cortot as pianist, and Saint-Saëns's Third Symphony, with the organ part played by Boulanger. The entrance of the organ, supported by drum rolls and trumpet fanfares, could only have been heard as a suitably triumphant note for all Allied parties.

From this occasion a historic alliance was forged. During the next few weeks Damrosch toured some of the sites that had been most severely damaged in the war. With Boulanger as his guide he visited Rheims, where they saw not only the cathedral but also the ruined school of music (fig. 37). Thus the establishment of a school in Fontainebleau for Americans was momentous, not so much as an affirmation of the superiority of the European tradition of musical training as a symbol of France's reclamation of its musical tradition, which it now chose to share with its transatlantic ally. Attempts to establish a federally supported American national conservatory in the United States had been floated in Congress during 1917–1918 and periodically in the postwar period in no small part because Americans

Figure 37. Nadia Boulanger and Walter Damrosch viewing the ruins at Rheims, 1919. (Photo courtesy of Annette Dieudonné.)

felt that it should not be necessary for their musicians to train abroad. The emergence of an "American School" in Fontainebleau paradoxically made such efforts obsolete.[58]

Fontainebleau may not have been the haven for musicians that the writers of the "Lost Generation" found in Paris during the 1920s, but this relocation of a group of highly gifted American composers to France was instrumental in the development of an American tradition of composition. At Fontainebleau the American students were able to test their identity as well as their talents against a European standard—a standard, it must be added, that had for decades defined the proper training of the complete musician. Their journey abroad also tacitly acknowledged the need to remedy their collective ignorance of the most recent European developments in musical composition. At the time that Damrosch went to Paris, Stravinsky's *Le sacre du printemps* had yet to be performed in the United States—indeed would not be until 1922—and the European avant-garde was poorly represented at American recitals and concerts.

The postwar exodus of American composers to France contrasted sharply with the obligatory travels of musicians to Germany in the prewar period. If the Great War now seemed to focus attention on Paris as the citadel of culture, it also reinforced its image as an emblem of Allied victory after a long and difficult siege. But Paris's legendary interest in music had also taken a new turn as a result of exposure to American soldiers. The American composer George Antheil later confirmed in a pinpoint assessment his appreciation of the power of this new offering in the post-Armistice period and especially his sense that it provided an American alternative to the prewar European avant-garde.

> The first Negro jazz band arriving in Paris during the last year of the great war was as prophetic of the after-war period immediately to come as the *Sacre* was prophetic of this selfsame war, declared only a year after the stormy scenes at the Champs Élysées Théâtre in 1913. . . .
> [Negro music] absorbed this period so naturally that in 1919 we find the greatest Slavic composer living [Igor Stravinsky] writing "Piano-rag-music" and "Ragtime" almost without knowing it, and a whole school of young composers springing up in Paris deeply influenced by American Negro musics.[59]

Antheil's nomination of Jim Europe's band as a prophetic successor to Stravinsky's ballet was nothing less than astounding. Capturing the wave of the moment, he also laid out a path for American influence in the future.

Beyond jazz, which seemed to be recognized everywhere, appreciation for the American band tradition, long a mainstay of American culture and known to Europeans from Sousa's numerous tours at the turn of the century, continued to grow. Sousa's role at home in the musical education of young bandsmen was crucial to a future standard of excellence. But with Jim Europe's example and the military band training programs in the Pershing-Damrosch school at Chaumont, western Europe had been alerted to a new generation of musicians and to new frontiers for the exploration of musical excellence.

The story of Nadia Boulanger's importance for the musical training of young Americans is a legend in itself, but it is essential to point out that her success as a teacher was linked to the relationship that had developed during the war between the Americans and the French. America's new French orientation and Boulanger's rising reputation were evident when in 1928 Ravel, acting as an intermediary, asked if she would be willing to take Gershwin as a pupil.[60] The foundation of Boulanger's pedagogy was not jazz or other popular fare, of course, but she had demonstrated a sensitivity to their vitalizing potential in, for example, the work of the young Aaron Copland. This is clear enough from a letter written by Copland to Boulanger in anticipation of her arrival in New York on 31 December 1924 for the premiere of his new *Organ Symphony*, which said in part: "Already I have seen one concert announced that you must not miss—at the Met-

ropolitan Opera House, Paul Whiteman is to give a concert of jazz music—
nous y serons. I won't go on to tell you all the other events you must
not miss, you will know of them soon enough." [61] Copland's enthusiasm is
readily explained by the fact that Whiteman had conducted the premiere
of Gershwin's *Rhapsody in Blue* on 12 February 1924 at New York's Aeolian Hall.

Whatever the ingredients in the mix, the idea of a readily identifiable
"American Music" took new root beyond the shores of the United States
during and immediately following the period of the Great War. Earlier, of
course, Edward MacDowell's music had become increasingly well known in
Europe, and the Jubilee Singers of Fisk University had brought the power
of the Negro spiritual to audiences in England and Germany between 1873
and 1875.[62] Performances by John Philip Sousa's band had also caused
newspaper headlines to report that Europe had "Gone Ragtime Wild" as
early as 1900. Irving Berlin, George Gershwin, and other Tin Pan Alley
composers were another factor. Yet none achieved a postwar acclaim that
surpassed that of America's black jazz musicians.

Beginning with the transportation of American musicians, many of
color, to European shores from 1917 through 1919, and followed in the
1920s by a host of new lights like Copland, Roy Harris, Gershwin, and Cole
Porter, Europeans began to take a new measure of American music. Responding to the attention, the Americans began to showcase their musical wares with a new confidence and to join the nation's bid for global
recognition.

19 Coming of Age in America

> How much longer are we going to think it necessary to be
> "American" before (or in contradistinction to) being cultivated,
> being enlightened, being humane, & having the same intellectual
> discipline as other civilized countries? It is really too easy a
> disguise for our shortcomings to dress them up as a form of
> patriotism!
>
> Edith Wharton, letter of 19 July 1919

Although the first three years of World War I took place without the
physical presence of U.S. troops on the battlefield, numerous issues coincidental to the struggle were of necessity addressed in America well before
its direct involvement. Nation-states are initially forged from ideas promoted by a small group of people. Territory may be seized and revolutions
may be won, but the business of creating a collective sense of loyalty to the
nation must be built slowly, usually after mustering the citizenry in a
defining battle. Triumph over others brings a sense of self.[1] The wars
fought by the United States after the Revolutionary War were not self-
defining. The Civil War did not draw the nation together—indeed, it
proved to be a divisive event for a very long time after its completion, and
although the Indian wars and the Spanish-American War promoted national aspirations, neither really clinched the matter. It was only with
World War I that America finally put her fledgling nationhood to a truly
global test.

While America prized the political independence it had wrested from
Europe in a revolution, its status as a colony in artistic matters was more
difficult to alter. Attempts to forge a national musical identity were unsuccessful because the new nation was too busy with the resolution of more
pressing problems, too young to have spawned an adequate concert repertoire in the post-Revolutionary period, and, later, too dependent upon Europeans to supply the composers or the artists in sufficient number to sat-
isfy the demands of the concert hall. By way of compensation, America
began to develop repertoires and performers that would appeal more directly to the general populace.[2]

With respect to the issue of musical training, the aspirations for an
emerging national style, and the direction that both ought to take, Ameri-

can composers had been receiving a considerable amount of free advice from the Europeans for some time. Vincent d'Indy made recommendations, and during a three-year stay in America during the 1890s Antonín Dvořák advanced the idea that the cause of a national music could best be served through attention to the kind of music that would speak to the citizenry at large.[3] If his own study of the music of black and native Americans was Dvořák's attempt to discover the basis for such a national style, the idea that such repertoires might be accepted as representative was disquieting to many middle-class Americans and openly rejected by others.[4]

Dvořák's injunction was nonetheless pursued by a number of composers, including his pupils Will Marian Cook, Henry T. Burleigh, and Rubin Goldmark, as well as others such as Arthur Shepherd, Henry Gilbert, and Arthur Farwell. On the other hand, the professors primarily responsible for the education of young composers at Yale, Columbia, Harvard, and the New England Conservatory—the most important schools before World War I to offer such training—were Horatio Parker, Edward MacDowell, John Knowles Paine, and George Chadwick, all of whom had studied in Leipzig or Berlin.[5]

With America's entrance into the war in April 1917, the role of art and music in society understandably took on a new urgency, so that an assessment at the beginning of 1918 by Walter Spalding, called "The War in its Relation to American Music," was timely as well as predictable. Spalding, a professor of music theory at Harvard, bravely launched his argument with a consideration of music's potential role in securing this coveted sense of national identity.

> This present war has certainly made us face such questions as what we are as a people, whether there is such a thing as American national spirit, what valuable contributions we are making to the fine art of living, and what role we are to play in the broad scheme of human destiny. In the first place, we are certainly a derived nation as far as the material and tangible aspects of our make-up are concerned; that is, we are of mixed blood; we speak the English language, not that of the aboriginal inhabitants of the country; our social customs and governmental policies are founded upon those of England, of France, and of other countries. . . . In literature, painting, sculpture and architecture we have already attained a high degree of independence,—this statement being corroborated by the spontaneous approval of foreign critics given to the creative work of our artists in these fields—but in music, the most elemental of the arts, we are still in our infancy. It is quite easy to eulogize American music, and to insist upon the existence of a national

American idiom, but if any comparative estimate is desired between our music and that of the Italians, the French, the Germans and the Russians, we have only to listen to a representative composition of the European nations to be aware of greater warmth and vitality of imagination than are to be found in any work which has come from America.[6]

Given the implied limitations of repertoire, the opinion could have been refuted only with the utmost caution—although it is telling that Spalding made no mention of America's flourishing role in the popular realm. America's insecurity was further compounded by the recognition of Germany, its archenemy on the battlefield, as the leading power in terms of composers, whom Spalding unabashedly ranked in the following fashion: first rank, Wagner, Brahms, Richard Strauss; second rank, Franck, Debussy, Tchaikovsky; third rank, Grieg, Dvořák, Puccini. From such a base it was a short distance to Spalding's conclusion that "America has not yet produced an original composer who could win a place higher than the third rank." He drew special attention, however, to the fact that Russia had for many generations been entirely under the influence of Italian music, and that prior to the Franco-Prussian War France had, save for opera, been almost totally reliant upon German imports for its symphonies, chamber music, pianoforte literature, and art songs. "Liberated and stimulated by the shock of war, thrown upon their own resources," he concluded, "the French in the few decades since 1870 have created a genuinely national school. The application to our own situation is too obvious for special emphasis. For many years we have depended almost entirely upon Germany for musical literature, for instruction, and for executive artists."

Then, as if by way of replying to d'Indy's recent injunction that America should seek to expel the dominating German influence in search of a national voice, Spalding concluded:

> Let history record that, this very year 1917, free America resolved that she would rely as little as possible on those who are paid to come and make music for her. Our country has vitality, imagination, and freedom. A living American music will grow to full manhood only if fostered by national sentiments, and what Russia, France, and Germany have done, the world will certainly expect of us once we really and earnestly try.[7]

Such brave words were no doubt welcome in most quarters. Even if many felt that they had been made belatedly, it was now apparent to all that the war was serving as a potent agent in the campaign for a new era in

American music. Just what that music might be in a "melting-pot" society was another question.[8]

JOHN ALDEN CARPENTER

No composer not resident on the eastern seaboard was held in higher esteem during the years of the Great War than John Alden Carpenter. The son of a wealthy Chicago industrialist, Carpenter had studied with Paine at Harvard, and in 1906 he had taken some lessons in Rome with Elgar. His *Adventures in a Perambulator* of 1914 was one of the first scores to bring him attention, and a developing interest in ragtime and jazz was first audible in his Piano Concertino, which was premiered by the Chicago Symphony Orchestra on 3 March 1916. When America declared war on Germany Carpenter importuned his friend John Philip Sousa to undertake the training of young bandsmen at the Great Lakes Training Center. Shortly thereafter, in September 1917, Carpenter himself was appointed to a five-member National Committee on Army and Navy Camp Music, whose task it was to standardize the songbooks used in army and navy training camps. Carpenter seems to have taken unexpected delight in this assignment, telling a reporter,

> The work that we are doing in various army and navy training camps has given me one of the biggest musical thrills that you could possibly imagine. What we are working on is simply the idea of mass singing among the soldiers and sailors as a stimulus to military efficiency. We are not interested in the question of music as an art or music as a recreation—these two elements will take care of themselves in due time. What we are trying to do is to help create a spirit and maintain a spirit that will help win the war.[9]

Carpenter expressed his belief in the power of song to "fuse together the many diverse racial elements" of the army, but he went even further in predicting the role of war as a determinant in the ultimate discovery of an American voice.

> Through the war is to be found that national conscientious basis of the American school of music. The school will be absolutely American, neither Negro nor Indian, but fully American. Americans of the day are only those who lived through a war—the Civil War, for instance. The others, who have since that time immigrated to America, are Americans, but their hearts may or may not be American. Through this war everyone here will become truly American, and the music in the camp will stimulate the development of our national music.[10]

The campaign for "100% Americanism" had received a boost, and Theodore Roosevelt as well as Wilson's propaganda czar, George Creel, would have applauded.[11]

In addition to the task of finding suitable bandmasters to implement their lofty goals, a task he shared with Sousa, Carpenter served on the Committee on Army and Navy Camp Music, which in 1918 became enmeshed in an attempt to establish a standardized musical text for "The Star-Spangled Banner." Rejecting an earlier Sonneck-Sousa-Damrosch version that made claims to historical authenticity, they offered a new version based upon original variants. Carpenter later explained that his committee, which included Walter Spalding, had ruled out "historic authenticity, for the simple reason that the American people have no interest whatever in 'authenticity' and will proceed to sing the song the way they are used to singing it regardless of every document that can be produced to the contrary."[12]

A "Service Version" of "The Star-Spangled Banner" was published by the Oliver Ditson Co. with a notice that a summary of the committee's deliberations could be obtained from the chairman, Peter Dykema, at the University of Wisconsin.[13] Permission to perform and reproduce this version was freely granted to all, "provided it be printed without change of melody, harmony or rhythm." No mention was made about prohibiting transposition. This was an option that would no doubt have been exercised in practice, given the fact that the anthem was written in the key of C instead of the traditional B-flat, and, as a consequence, its highest note was pushed to G, a pitch even further beyond the range of the typical audience. The back page of this new issue contained a comparative essay on "The Origin of 'The Star-Spangled Banner'" by William Arms Fisher, a pupil of Dvořák and later author of the lyrics to "Going Home." The brief article also reprinted the earliest popular version of the tune "To Anacreon in Heaven," which was known in America as "Adams and Liberty." There, the numerous changes that had occurred in this familiar music over the years were clear for all to see, including not only the melody and rhythm of the opening figure but also the lack of a raised fourth scale-degree, added later, on the words "dawn's *early* light."

Carpenter had recently established a fine reputation as a composer of song cycles with *Gitanjali*, on texts of Rabindranath Tagore, of 1914, and *Watercolors: Four Chinese Tone Poems*, of the next year. Carpenter also set another of Tagore's texts from the *Gitanjali*, "The Day is No More," in September 1914, which had implications for a world newly at war: "The shadow is upon the earth. . . . In the lonely lane / There is no passer-by . . .

I know not, if I shall come back home." In the summer months of 1917 he composed two more songs of significance on war subjects. One, "The Home Road," was inspired when he witnessed a group of inductees, suitcases in hand, follow a seven-piece band; Carpenter, ruminating on what the future might hold for them, wrote both words and music (CD track 14). It is a patriotic anthem in a simple two-part form that makes reference to "Tipperary" in both lyrics and rhythm without directly quoting the music. Here, however, the road to Tipperary is clearly the road to Carpenter's native Midwest.

> Sing a Hymn of Freedom, Fling the banner high!
> Sing the songs of Liberty, Songs that shall not die.
> For the long, long road to Tipperary, Is the road that leads me home.
> O'er hills and plains, By lakes and lanes,
> My Woodlands! My Cornfields! My Country! My Home! [14]

The accelerating popularity enjoyed by "The Home Road" in early postwar America soon earned for it a place somewhere between Elgar's *Pomp and Circumstance* and Irving Berlin's "God Bless America." One critic of the time stated "that amid the welter of patriotic songs which have been called into being of the present crisis one has caught the spirit of the hour. If one may hazard a guess as to the future, it is that 'The Home Road' of John Alden Carpenter will become a part of our folklore." Although this did not happen, conductor Frederick Stock regularly programmed the song for the Chicago Symphony Orchestra's children's concerts, and the renowned German-American contralto Ernestine Schumann-Heink, who in the postwar years sang untiringly for American veterans of World War I, recorded it for RCA Victor.[15]

On 20 August 1917 Carpenter completed his second popular song of that summer, "Khaki Sammy," a high spirited oom-pah march with words and music by the composer. Once more, the composer's midwestern roots are advertised in the opening lines.

> All the way from Illinois,
> To a little old town in France,
> All the way from Illinois,
> To make those Deutschers dance.[16]

The song was dedicated to and made popular by the vaudevillian Nora Bayes. Known at the beginning of the war for pacifist songs like "I Didn't Raise My Boy to Be a Soldier," Bayes changed her tune dramatically once America joined the conflict, with a series of patriotic performances that included Cohan's "Over There."

Carpenter's two other war songs were more introspective and were cast in the time-honored format of the lullaby: "The Lawd is Smilin' through the Do'" and "Berceuse de guerre." The latter, completed in August 1918 just before the Armistice, set a French text by Cammaerts, the Belgian poet who had provided Elgar with the lyrics for *Carillon* and *Une voix dans le désert*. Carpenter emphasized its French orientation not only in the title but also in the citation of the folk lullaby "Dodo, l'enfant do" as a recurrent refrain. It was a familiar tune that Debussy had incorporated in his piano piece "Jardins sous la pluie" from *Estampes* as well as in the "Rondes de printemps" movement of the orchestral *Images*. In Carpenter's song a mother comforts her child as she thinks of her husband who is away at the front. The fire dwindles, and as the rain lashes the windowpanes, she wonders if it is raining and thundering where he is, if he is well and warm, and if he has received her last letter.

At the song's conclusion the composer tightens the impact of Cammaerts's lyrics by omitting the final stanza and ending with the following mesmerizing vision—a vision that is reinforced by a dramatic vocal ascension over the last six lines before falling to a hushed recitative on "et les yeux clos" (and with closed eyes).

> The lamp burns low, the fire dwindles.
> We shall have to go to bed.
> The child is clasping its wee fists.
> Is my big child sleeping, too?
> Sleeping peacefully before the battle?
> Is he running madly
> Through the shells?
> Or is he lying in some hole,
> With open mouth and with closed eyes?
>
> *Sleep, sleep, baby, sleep.*[17]

Although the concluding refrain—"Dodo, l'enfant do, / L'enfant dormi, / Dodo, l'enfant do"—may bring to mind Carpenter's earlier and highly popular song "The Sleep That Flits on Baby's Eyes" (from *Gitanjali*), the focus placed here upon the most grisly portion of the text provides a vivid and explicit imagery that seldom found its way into the art songs of any nation. The alternation between the lullaby proper and the mother's interior monologue is clearly distinguished through the invocation of a restrained modality with a single flat in the key signature for the former and a more chromatic and restless manner in five flats for the latter. Several singers took it up in the years immediately after the war, and in 1940 Carpenter made an English instrumental arrangement that he called "War Lullaby."[18]

"Berceuse de guerre" gave clear evidence of what a wartime art song might be.[19] Yet, despite a sure craft and an unarguable musicality, despite the gung-ho qualities, the temporary popularity of some of his war songs and the beauty of many others, Carpenter's early exposure to German models in his study with Paine at Harvard, alongside his ongoing attraction to French and English repertoires, made it difficult for him to develop a resolutely American voice for the concert hall. His desire to help was evident not only in the syncopated rhythms of his *Concertino* for piano and orchestra of 1915 but also in his later *Krazy Kats,* a jazz ballet of 1921. *Skyscrapers* (1923–1924), originally intended for Diaghilev, exhibits an infectious vitality associated with the American urban scene. But its incorporation of tenor banjo, six saxophones, traffic lights, minstrel tunes, and the inflections of jazz as a condiment rather than as essence spelled a manner that became almost obligatory in the postwar period.

COMING TO TERMS WITH THE EUROPEAN AVANT-GARDE

In his 1918 article Spalding corroborated the largely held opinion that because of its diverse ethnic base America was at a disadvantage in the absence of a single folksong and dance tradition, even as he endorsed Dvořák's prescription for looking inward, regardless of an inherent diversity. How striking that through the period of the Great War hardly any American critic argued that a composer might look outward to the recent and invigorating models of the European avant-garde.

A few composers such as Charles Griffes showed a tepid interest in the current musical tumult in Europe. Something of this awareness can be spotted in Griffes's Piano Sonata written in December and January of 1917–1918. But it was hardly a call to the avant-garde. While the aesthetic perspective of Griffes's abstract wartime works patently refused American source materials and patriotic texts, three sets of children's pieces for piano, published in 1918 under the nom de plume "Arthur Tomlinson" and containing titles like "Yankee Doodle," "Marching through Georgia," "The Star-Spangled Banner," and "Dixie," unabashedly reflected the composer's awareness that America had sent its young men from the North and the South to Europe. Griffes's wartime *De profundis* of 1915, however, is something of an anomaly. Casually referred to by the composer as "a tribute to Wagner"—an odd characterization for the times—it contains generous patches of Skriabin and Debussy combined with what would later be heard as a cocktail-lounge blues.

From the beginning of the century to the conclusion of World War I the Chicago Symphony Orchestra gave only limited attention to the contemporary scene in Europe as well as America.[20] Debussy's *Prélude à l'après-midi d'un faune* had been performed in Chicago's Orchestra Hall as early as 23 November 1906, followed by performances of his *La mer* in the 1908, 1909, and 1918 seasons as well as the complete *Trois nocturnes* in 1916. Not a single score by Ravel was performed by the Chicago Symphony Orchestra throughout the period of the Great War.[21] After the war the first of his works to be performed was heard on 7 November 1919 in an unusual version of the *Introduction et allegro,* originally scored for harp, flute, clarinet, and string quartet and now amplified for the full string section. The second suite from *Daphnis et Chloé* (1912) was not programmed until 1923, a season that also saw the orchestra's first performance of *La valse.*

The first work of Stravinsky to be played by the Chicago Symphony Orchestra was the early and unadventurous *Feu d'artifice* in the 1914 season,[22] but the *Firebird Suite* would have to wait until 1920, *Le sacre du printemps* until 1924, and *Petrushka* until 1930. Surprisingly, the Chicago premiere of Schoenberg's *Five Pieces for Orchestra,* op. 16, had taken place just before the war, in 1913, but it was not performed again until the 1925 and 1933 seasons. Even the Romantic *Verklärte Nacht* was performed there for the first time only in 1921. Richard Strauss, who was a favorite with the orchestra from the 1890s on, was represented by *Don Juan* in every season between 1914 and 1917, although *Ein Heldenleben* was understandably dropped between 1911 and 1921. Holst's *The Planets* similarly made its debut in the final season concert for 1921 in the company of Beethoven, Brahms, and Wagner.

Three weeks after the Armistice, Prokofiev, whose *Love for Three Oranges* had been commissioned and would be premiered by the Chicago Opera in 1921, appeared in Chicago playing his First Piano Concerto (1912) and conducting his recent *Scythian Suite* (1915). Of the latter, the critics could speak only of its "din and noise." Calling it "hyper-modern," one of them wondered, "Will this be 'the music of the future'?"[23] Chicago would soon have another opportunity to answer this question when Prokofiev's new Third Piano Concerto received its world premiere there in the 1921 season.

The Boston Symphony Orchestra did well with the French repertoire throughout the period,[24] and it was a tradition that continued in the immediate post-Armistice era when two Frenchmen directed the orchestra. Muck had offered only Stravinsky's *Firebird* and ventured a single performance in 1914 of Schoenberg's *Five Pieces,* which won him no kudos and, according to Virgil Thomson, "scandalized the hell out of [Archibald Davison]," Harvard professor and conductor of the Glee Club.[25] New York did not hear Schoenberg's orchestral set until Stokowski took the Philadelphia Orchestra there in 1922. New York also played host to the Ballets Russes's production of *Firebird* and *Petrushka* prior to a transcontinental tour in 1916, but America would have to wait until 1922, well after the end of the war, before Stokowski offered an isolated performance of *Le Sacre du printemps* in Philadelphia. And Pierre Monteux's introduction of the work came in his last season with the Boston Symphony Orchestra, on 23 January 1924, when it was belatedly received as a masterpiece.[26] The Boston Symphony also performed Bartók's music for the first time in 1926 when it introduced his *Dance Suite* of 1923.

It is hardly surprising that there were no members of the modernist or avant-garde camps mentioned in Spalding's 1917 international ranking of composers. The fact that neither Stravinsky nor Schoenberg nor any of the Americans such as Ives, Ornstein, or Cowell made the cut is indicative not so much of a conservative taste as of an acute lack of exposure to their works in the concert hall—a condition that, with the exception of Stravinsky, was to be rectified only rarely in the immediately ensuing decades. Indeed, parallels to the excitement triggered by the Armory Show of European avant-garde painting that had stunned New York when it opened on 17 February 1913 were hard to find in the world of music. Even later performances of these composers' works were largely limited to concerts sponsored by the various composer leagues.

The movement was handsomely assisted, however, by the arrival from France in 1915 of Edgard Varèse, who two years later was clever enough to put aside his avant-garde agenda in order to organize and conduct a performance of Berlioz's *Requiem* on 1 April 1917. Billed as a memorial in honor of all the soldiers who had been killed in the war, the concert was perfectly timed. The following day President Wilson carried his war message to Congress, and four days later he declared war against Germany.[27]

Such a gesture by a French composer on American soil served more than the cause of Allied solidarity, and ultimately the Great War did encourage a loosely organized American avant-garde that received notice from a small segment of professionals. And even as late as 1931–1932 Nicolas Slonimsky was still attempting to prove a point with a series of landmark concerts in Paris, Berlin, and Budapest that were devoted to some of the trailblazing scores from the northeastern United States and Mexico, including works by Carlos Chávez, Henry Cowell, Ruth Crawford, Roy Harris, Charles Ives, Amadeo Roldán, Carl Ruggles, Adolph Weiss, and Edgard Varèse. Despite good intentions, the concerts were variably and often negatively received, and throughout the 1920s the music of America's East Coast avant-garde had minimal impact upon the concert-going public at large.[28]

The decidedly modest acceptance by leading performing artists and institutions of art music written by American composers led many to view the campaign for approval on the concert stage as a losing battle. A prevalent opinion, expressed both in and out of print throughout the nineteenth century and up to the time of World War I, continued to hold that American composers had yet to come of age and that the best of them could not withstand comparison with Europe's leading figures.[29] The only answer to such a charge was, obviously, "Stop comparing." Americans were beginning to learn, and, as the critic Edward Rothstein so trenchantly put it, "Identity is not just a declaration of belonging; it is a declaration of opposition. Identity is a dissent from the universal; it declares an exception."[30]

LEO ORNSTEIN: AMERICA'S FUTURIST

Leo Ornstein was one of America's most daring composers during the war. He may have appeared to be declaring an exception with respect to American manners, but his orientation was clearly tied to the Futurists, one of the noisiest factions of the European avant-garde. If it was not completely clear how the pursuit of their aesthetic might promote the development of a native American expression, at least a potent argument was within view: Futurism's fundamental fascination with the contemporary urban community was increasingly focused on taking the accelerating pulse of America's industrial society.

Music publishers were understandably not averse to the advertising potential of such movements, and among the new works listed at the end of the *Musical Quarterly*'s final issue for 1916 was Ornstein's "Ultra Modern Compositions," published by the Carl Fischer Music House. The advertisement described Ornstein as the "Futurist of Futurists" and a "composer whose works are exciting the most intense controversy among the world's great music critics." That the Futurist issue in the world of music was considered a lively one is evident not only from the brief article in the April 1916 issue of the same journal by the London critic Nicholas C. Gatty, titled "Futurism: A Series of Negatives," but especially from the full-blown and respectful, if cautiously suspicious, article by Charles Buchanan,

"Ornstein and Modern Music" that appeared in the April 1918 issue of *Musical Quarterly.*

The only problem was that Leo Ornstein was an émigré, a child prodigy who had studied at the Petrograd Conservatory before he fled with his family in 1905, during a period of intensified Jewish persecution that followed the Russian Revolution. Suddenly transported to New York's Lower East Side, he continued his studies and gave his first piano recital in 1911. His first attempts at composing music with a modern cast came with his "Danse sauvage" (Wild Men's Dance) and "Suicide in an Airplane." The scores for both exhibit thick clusters of notes and betray Primitivist and Futurist leanings in their titles. By 1913 he had returned to Europe, where he had played the first of these compositions in Vienna for Theodor Leschetizky, the great piano pedagogue, and in Paris for M. D. Calvocoressi. In addition he had appeared in the salon of the Princess de Polignac and had met Busoni in Berlin and Roger Quilter in Oxford. His London recital of 27 March 1914, which included "Danse sauvage," a sonata and some preludes of his own, Busoni's transcription of three Bach chorale preludes, and a group of Schoenberg's piano pieces, was openly advertised as a "Pianoforte Recital of Futurist Music." The critics concluded that Ornstein's music was "equal to the sum of Schoenberg and Skriabin squared."[31] A second Futurist recital was given in London on 7 April, and the critics bolted.

Although Ornstein protested his independence from the Italian Futurist movement and held no truck with its politics, his music and titles betrayed an undeniable aesthetic allegiance. Even if Ornstein's music failed to enter the mainstream of American musical life in part because of performance difficulties, he must be judged a visionary who tried to point to an alternative that found few advocates at the time. Even though a work like "Suicide in an Airplane" may have mirrored the contemporary fascination for flight and the machine's ability to act as an instrument of human destruction, the musical score did not live up to its title. For despite the predictable dissonant clusters, the generous infusions of ragtime, and a mildly pervading sense of peripeteia, the net result failed to hint at an impending reality, namely that membership in the soon-to-be-formed Lafayette Escadrille would be tantamount to suicide.

In late 1914 or early 1915, with the war already showing signs of stalemate, Ornstein wrote "Two Impressions of Notre-Dame," whose luminescent parallel chord streams recall the technique employed by Debussy in "La cathédrale engloutie" of 1910. But in their additional accumulation of dissonant clusters and the occasional violent outbursts that recall the rapidly changing, buzzing dissonances in Debussy's "Feux d'artifice," Ornstein reflected less the luminescent washes of Monet's Rouen Cathedral series or Debussy's engulfing waters than Edith Wharton's memorably vivid description in *Fighting France* of the decaying façade of Notre-Dame at Rheims.[32]

When America became involved in the war two years later, Ornstein wrote a set of ten compositions for solo piano, *Poems of 1917,* which he dedicated to the piano virtuoso Leopold Godowsky. The original titles appended to each of the ten pieces were "No Man's Land," "The Sower of Despair," "The Orient in Flanders," "The Wrath of the Despoiled," "Night Brooding Over the Battlefield," "A Dirge of the Trenches," "Song Behind the Lines," "The Battle," "Army at Prayer," and "Dance of the Dead."[33] Although in light of the dedicatee the set is predictably virtuosic, there are elements that transcend all performance possibilities. The fourth of these pieces, for example, "The Wrath of the Despoiled," begins with four staves marked r.h., l.h. / r.h., l.h. (four hands) and continues with the following combinations: r.h., r.h., l.h. (three hands); r.h., l.h. (two hands); r.h , l.h. / r.h., l.h. / r.h., l.h. (six hands). The effect is that of hands appearing (four), disappearing (three, then two), and multiplying (six). The spectral appearance and disappearance of hands in a set of pieces that are designated for solo piano on the title page takes the disturbed imagery of Ravel's later *Frontispice* and Concerto for the Left Hand to a new level. Waldo Frank's lengthy textual *Prelude to "Poems of 1917,"* which speaks of a world spinning hopelessly out of control in a total confusion of love and hate, leaves little doubt as to the intended effect of the set.

The Futurist years proved to be Ornstein's moment, but it remained unclear just how he might contribute to the discovery of a lasting American musical language. Many of Ornstein's later works, such as the Quintet for Piano and Strings, commissioned by Elizabeth Sprague Coolidge in 1927, retained some of the urgency of his early works, now tempered by a more controlled structure. Varèse and Cowell, of course, were contemporary soul mates, and Ornstein's flights of fancy were to hold a special postwar appeal for the young George Antheil. Throughout the period of the European conflict, however, and despite some fitful attempts at avant-gardism in the teens and early twenties, the American musical signature seemed to resist congealing on Futurist air.

CHARLES IVES: PRIVATE WITNESS TO THE GREAT WAR

Of all those who were composing at this time, no figure provided more vivid testimony to the possibility of a truly American avant-garde than

Charles Ives. If the evidence has inevitably encouraged a certain amount of mythologizing and controversy about the wellsprings of his style, the formative influence of his father, his childhood musical encounters, and the possible retrodating of certain works in the interest of establishing a chronological priority over potential European models, the music still inspires awe and invites the search for an explanation of the war's role as a catalyst in the eventual codification of American musical values.

Ives went to Yale, where he studied with Horatio Parker and was repeatedly led by his teacher through the favored assignment of composing settings of German texts that previously had been set by the Romantic masters. In contrast to Griffes's songs, which were the product of a four-year residency in Germany, Ives's settings reflect an exposure to German repertoires through his teacher in New Haven. Ives's settings are no less interesting, and many would argue they are more compelling than Griffes's. Indeed, Ives's settings are so striking and so sure that in some instances they challenge the originals in their impact.[34] Chadwick, who had been Parker's former teacher, proclaimed that Ives's setting of "Feldeinsamkeit" of 1897 was not only "almost as good as Brahms" but also "as good a song as [Parker] could write."[35] The modern listener may be inclined to agree.[36]

In light of the fact that Ives was a highly successful insurance underwriter and composed only in his spare time, the sheer quantity of his output is astonishing. Although he is often remembered primarily as a writer of symphonies and chamber music, Ives wrote an extraordinary group of songs, 114 of which he published at his own expense in 1922.[37] By the time America became involved in the war, Ives had already developed a range of compositional approaches that not so much commandeered hymn tunes, American popular idioms, and the principles of the classic European tradition, alongside a more brazen contemporary experimental perspective, as they demonstrated a capacity to amalgamate and transcend their sources in extremely personal and unpredictable ways.[38]

The first signal we have of Ives's reaction to the European conflict came with his composition of "From Hanover Square North at the End of a Tragic Day the People Again Arose." The work was triggered by news of the sinking of the *Lusitania* on 7 May 1915 and a subsequent event that made an extraordinary impression on Ives. He later related the circumstances at length.

> Everybody who came into the office, whether they spoke about the disaster or not, showed a realization of seriously experiencing something. (That it meant war is what the faces said, if the tongues didn't.) Leaving

the office and going uptown about six o'clock, I took the Third Avenue "L" at Hanover Square Station. As I came on the platform, there was quite a crowd waiting for the trains, which had been blocked lower down, and while waiting there, a hand-organ or hurdy-gurdy was playing in the street below. Some workmen sitting on the side of the tracks began to whistle the tune, and others began to sing or hum the refrain. . . . The hand-organ man wheeled the organ nearer to the platform and kept it up fortissimo (and the chorus sounded out as though every man in New York must be joining in it). Then the first train came in and everybody crowded in, and the song gradually died out, but the effect on the crowd still showed. Almost nobody talked—the people acted as though they might be coming out of a church service. In going uptown, occasionally little groups would start singing or humming the tune.

Now what was the tune? It wasn't a Broadway hit, it wasn't a musical comedy air, it wasn't a waltz tune or a dance tune or an opera tune or a classical tune, or a tune that all of them probably knew. It was (only) the refrain of an old Gospel Hymn that had stirred many people of past generations. It was nothing but—*In the Sweet Bye and Bye*. It wasn't a tune written to be sold, or written by a professor of music— but by a man who was but giving out an experience.[39]

Ives's response to this scene begins with a unison chorus, joined by various instruments, heard in the distance singing the opening text of the "Te Deum" in English on a Gregorian psalm tone. Later the principal orchestra enters with intimations of "In the Sweet Bye and Bye," followed by a series of variants and the citation of a host of popular fragments. The piece climaxes in a mélange of Ivesian polyrhythms, dissonances, and textural confusion, followed by a coda whose serenity mirrors the aftereffect of the experience upon the crowd.[40] "In the Sweet Bye and Bye" carried potent implications for Ives's story, for it is a gospel funeral hymn whose text promises that "the Father waits over the way, to prepare us a dwelling place there" and concludes with the refrain, "In the sweet bye and bye, / We shall meet on that beautiful shore." Textually, it offered the musical equivalent of a funerary oration, the time-honored means of capturing the pathos and sacrilege of war from the time of the Greeks to Lincoln's Gettysburg Address.[41] As a gospel hymn it emphasized the collective national memory of the nineteenth-century American camp meeting, which had a keen personal resonance for Ives.[42] As the title of the work clarifies, however, the locus of the hymn shifted to a present-day railway station—a symbolic point of departure in Europe from the opening hours of the war. An American counterpart had replaced "Le chant du départ."

Had Ives speedily completed "Hanover Square," which was begun in

1915, it might have served as a propaganda tool by those who were intent on promoting America's intervention in the war. But as the work was not finished until 1919 and was fully scored only in the 1920s, it was not ready to join Edward Hopper's poster *Smash the Hun* of 1918 or to serve as an orchestral touring piece while the war was still on, as several of Elgar's compositions did. Admirers of the work, which included Ives himself, would probably have realized, however, that even if the composition had been completed earlier its progressive language would have precluded such use.

The texts of numerous of Ives's songs from the period, many of which he wrote himself, reveal that the issues of the day remained very much in the forefront of his thoughts. At the turn of the twentieth century an openly Romantic but anti-European approach sought to establish "Americanness by quotation" by making musical references to familiar songs, which could evoke a time, or a place, or even a set of values.[43] This method is dramatically manifest in Ives's patchwork song "The Things Our Father Loved" ("and the greatest of these was Liberty") of 1917. Peter Burkholder, in a lucid parsing of this song, has called attention to the fact that beyond the specific citation of particular tunes—in this instance "In the Sweet Bye and Bye" and "The Battle Cry of Freedom," along with "My Old Kentucky Home" and "On the Banks of the Wabash"—lies a cumulative emotional resonance for a society.[44]

America's impending role in the European conflict is treated even more explicitly in the first of a group of three war songs, "Sneak Thief," which Ives sketched around 1914 but left incomplete. A hodge-podge of quotations, from "Marching Through Georgia" and "The Star-Spangled Banner" to "Reveille" (incorporated at the words "get up"), it is one of Ives's most aggressive and dissonant songs and a candid protest against Germany's invasion of Belgium. Ives also wrote three war songs shortly after America entered the war. The first is a setting of "In Flanders Fields," a poem by John McCrae, a Canadian who had formerly been a medical consultant for Ives's law firm and who had been killed in action in 1915. The text became a favorite during the war, and Ives's setting was the first of many.[45] Ives's business partner, Julian Myrick, had suggested he use the poem, and the result was first performed at a luncheon for the managers of their insurance firm, held at the Waldorf-Astoria Hotel around 15 April 1917.

Ives created a tour de force of melodic collage for "In Flanders Fields," and his use of borrowed materials is so clear that even a group of businessmen might have been expected to understand the song's general thrust at first hearing. McCall Lanham, the singer at the first performance, later acknowledged, however, that neither he nor his accompanist could make "head or tail of it."[46] "Columbia, the Gem of the Ocean," "America," "The Battle Cry of Freedom," and "Reveille" all join in a vigorous romp that celebrates the history of the federation. Even more telling, however, is the juxtaposition of a fragment ("Aux armes, citoyens") from "La Marseillaise" against another ("My country 'tis of Thee") from "America" at the text "Take up our quarrel with the foe!" The collective "our" obviously refers to France, the United States, and England (whose "God Save the King" provided the melody for "America").

Less obvious, however, is the reference to Debussy, who had placed "God Save the King" in octaves in the bass of his "Hommage à S. Pickwick Esq. P.P.M.P.C." and the identical interior snippet from "La Marseillaise" in the soprano of his "Feux d'artifice," both from the second book of *Préludes*, which had been published only a few years before, in 1913.[47] Given Ives's equivocal opinion of Debussy, the reference must be seen as a rare example of fraternity, particularly regarding the Frenchman's affinity for quotation. At the same time, Ives's musical response, which in this instance is far removed from the Impressionist language he was entirely capable of using, implies a critique of the fundamental aesthetic distance between the two composers even as it italicizes the common cause of France and America.[48]

The various levels of ambivalence in Ives's other war songs have been persuasively argued, but in "In Flanders Fields" the overriding sentiment seems clear enough.[49] The song carries no hint of the Christmastide fraternization of 1914, no citation of "Deutschland, Deutschland" or "Die Wacht am Rhein" to complement the appearance of "La Marseillaise," "Columbia, the Gem of the Ocean," and "God Save the King." Christmas 1914 was best forgotten, for Flanders Fields had since become the symbol of death, now graphically conjured up in McCrae's opening stanza (CD track 15).[50]

> In Flanders fields the poppies blow
> Between the crosses, row on row,
> That mark our place, and in the sky
> The larks still bravely singing fly,
> Scarce heard amidst the guns below.
>
> We are the dead. Short days ago
> We lived, felt dawn, saw sunset glow,
> Loved and were loved, and now we lie
> In Flanders fields.

In the final stanza the mood changes and Ives's music with it.

Take up our quarrel with the foe!
To you from falling hands we throw
The torch. Be yours to hold it high.
If ye break faith with us who die
We shall not sleep though poppies grow
In Flanders Fields.[51]

The bravura citation of national tunes, discussed above, suddenly dominates the musical landscape, only to fall away at the final couplet over the
sound of fading march rhythms in the piano and a brief lowering of the
head on the final words "in Flanders Fields." Ives was essentially a pacifist,
and his ambivalence about the very idea of war was understood. Here the
swagger resists any hint of parody, and his commitment to the struggle
now that America had entered the war is never in doubt.

Another, even more robust, war song, dated 30 May 1917 by Ives although not printed until 1922, is "He Is There!" Considered by Ives spe-
cialists as a later version of "Sneak Thief," its raucous music constitutes a
near parody of every patriotic song ever written in wartime and is a blatant
sonic poster that George Creel's Committee on Public Information ought
to have been glad to promote. The musical citations include "Tenting Tonight," "Battle Cry of Freedom," and "Marching through Georgia," and
Ives explicitly identified the New England pedigree of each of them in a
note appended to the edition that appeared in 1922.[52] The generous grab
bag of tunes also includes a veritable arsenal of Americana that recalls the
country's history, from the Revolutionary War ("Yankee Doodle") to the
firing on Fort McHenry in 1814 ("The Star-Spangled Banner") and the
Civil War ("Dixie"). The opening two verses, which tell of a "little Yankee
with a German name" who "marched beside his granddaddy" in the Dec-
oration Day parade commemorating the Civil War, evoke the keen memory that Americans still had of that war, the last and in some ways the most
telling conflict in the country's history. The text also reflects Ives's abhorrence of the anti-German contagion that had swept the country and, as a
composer's note confirms, underscores his understanding of the "added
strain that American soldiers of German descent are under."[53]

Ives's belief in a world "where all may have a 'say'" and where there is
"Liberty for all" is summed up in the third verse of "He Is There," which
concludes with a "Hip Hip Hooray" for the little boy, now grown, who
"marches to the Flanders front." The chorus then brings the tale into the
present by openly inserting references to well-known wartime tunes —
although Ives parries the obvious invitation to incorporate Cohan's "Over
There" by referring only to its rhythmic pattern. The text ("He'll be there,

he'll be there") also recalls the concluding phrase, "I'll be there," in the old-time hymn "When the Roll Is Called Up Yonder." In 1942 Ives changed the words, updated the message, effected an orchestration with the help of Lou Harrison, called it "They Are There!," a "War Song March," and atypically promoted its performance in the hope that it might serve as a morale booster.[54]

The most affective of Ives's war songs, "Tom Sails Away," composed in 1917 and published in 1922, uses a text that he wrote himself (CD track 16). While the British infantryman was familiarly referred to as "Tommy" (Tommy Atkins) in the Great War, the complete text reveals that Ives's perspective is universal.

> Scenes from my childhood are with me.
> I'm in the lot behind our house up on the hill,
> A spring day's sun is setting,
> Mother with Tom in her arms is coming
> Towards the garden; the lettuce rows are showing green
>
> Thinner grows the smoke o'er the town,
> Stronger comes the breeze from the ridge,
> 'Tis after six, the whistles have blown.
> The milk train's gone down the valley.
> Daddy is coming up the hill from the mill,
> We run down the lane to meet him.
>
> But today, in freedom's cause Tom sailed away
> For over there, over there, over there!
> Scenes from my childhood are floating before my eyes.[55]

H. Wiley Hitchcock has noted that in the edition of *Fifty Songs* of 1923 Ives omitted the "3 Songs of the War" altogether and that when he reintroduced "Tom Sails Away" in his *Nineteen Songs* of 1935, he dropped "the enthusiastic World War I sentiment of 'in freedom's cause.'"[56]

Yet, in either version, few American songs before "Tom Sails Away" captured so poignantly and with such restraint the sense of home and the personal sacrifice attendant to all wars. Even the virtually unavoidable citation of "Over There" in the penultimate line is entered with a caution that miraculously escapes both sentimentality and nationalistic bravado. And the unresolved chords, built on fifths and fourths that are left hanging at the song's conclusion, endorse not only a sense of memory but also the ambivalence of personal values versus duty to one's country.[57]

Despite Ives's initial pacifism, once war was declared his commitment was complete. Rejected as an ambulance driver, he worked tirelessly for the Liberty Loan drives in the manner of numerous public personalities. The extent of his emotional involvement is reflected in the diary of his wife, Harmony, who noted that Ives suffered a heart attack shortly after a meeting with a representative of a Liberty Bond committee chaired by Franklin Roosevelt, during which the composer had argued unsuccessfully for the sale of smaller fifty-dollar denomination bonds.[58] Ives's deep cynicism about the political process had already been demonstrated as early as 1912 with a song fragment whose text ran: "Vote for Names! All nice men, three nice men: Teddy, Woodrow and Bill. After trying hard to think what's the best way to vote I say: Just walk right in and grab a ballot with the eyes shut and walk right out again."

In the post-Armistice period Ives poured out his discontent over a mounting nationalistic tone and the repudiation of the League of Nations that Harding's election implied in a bitter song, "Nov. 2, 1920." It carried the following subtitle: "Soliloquy of an old man whose son lies in 'Flanders Fields.' It is the day after election; he is sitting by the roadside, looking down the valley towards the station." Tom had sailed away but had not returned home, and his father now speaks.

> It strikes me that
> Some men and women got tired of a big job;
> But, over there our men did not quit.
> They fought and died that better things might be!
> Perhaps some who stayed at home
> Are beginning to forget and to quit.[59]

Ives's postwar song series essentially brought down the curtain on his creative career.[60] *Serenity*, a "unison chant" of 1919, pictures Christ kneeling in prayer on the hills of Galilee and concludes with "Take from our souls the strain and stress, and let our ordered lives confess, the beauty of thy peace." The mood of the epigraph written and initialed by Ives that precedes his setting of Edwin Markham's "Lincoln, the Great Commoner" (1921) is more defiant. Insisting that, faced with the stress of life, the curse of war, and man's vindictiveness, "What needed to be borne—he bore! What needed to be fought—he fought! But in his soul, he stood them up as—naught!"[61]

The heart attack Ives suffered in September 1918 led him to revise and set in order many of his larger works, including the monumental "Concord" *Sonata* (1910–1915) for solo piano, which was published in 1920. Ives's repeated citation of the opening motif of Beethoven's Fifth Symphony in this work prompted an observation in his "Essays before a Sonata" (1920) that recalls the efforts of Stravinsky, Ravel, and others to come to terms with the Beethoven myth and a venerable German culture during the war years.

> And there sits the little old spinet piano Sophia Thoreau gave to the Alcott children, on which Beth played the old Scotch airs, and played at the *Fifth Symphony*. . . . All around you, under the Concord sky, there still floats the influence of that human-faith melody—transcendent and sentimental enough for the enthusiast or the cynic, respectively—reflecting an innate hope, a common interest in common things and common men—a tune the Concord bards are ever playing while they pound away at the immensities with a Beethoven-like sublimity, and with, may we say, a vehemence and perseverance, for that part of greatness is not so difficult to emulate.[62]

Elsewhere Ives further clarified his opinion about the great master: "I remember feeling towards Beethoven [that he's] a great man—but Oh for just one big strong chord not tied to any key."[63]

Only a few shorter pieces and a scattering of songs followed. One of the latter, titled "1, 2, 3," contains the epigrammatic line—"Why doesn't one, two, three seem to appeal to a Yankee as much as one, two!"—with potentially anti-Viennese overtones. Explicitly denigrating the potentially effeminizing poison of the waltz, it also reflects a cantankerous, decidedly macho spirit that values the steady beat of the march as well as the American two-step. Other late songs reveal Ives's disaffection for national politics; still others, such as "Like a Sick Eagle" and "Premonitions," reflect his own illness and presentiment of death. But while such thoughts were premature—Ives would live until 1954—his creative career for all intents and purposes had come to a halt, and he lived the remainder of his days in virtual retirement from both the insurance business and music. In a memo of 1931 Ives made clear that the war period had been a dramatic turning point.

> In 1917 the War came on, and I did but little in music. I didn't seem to feel like it. We were busy at the office at this time with the extra Red Cross and Liberty Loan drives and all the problems that the War brought on. As I look back, I find that I did almost no composing after the beginning of 1918. The only music composed in 1918 were two songs or choruses for male voices—but later turned into brass choruses.
>
> In October 1918, I had a serious illness that kept me away from the office for six months, and I have not since been in my former good (very good) state of health, nor have I seemed to get going "good" in music since then. (I'd start things, but they didn't seem to work out . . .) I don't know how to account for it except that what strength

I had was used up during the day in what I had to do at the office, and it seemed impossible to do any work in the evenings, as I used to do.

During the last years or so, I've completed nothing.[64]

Champions like Henry Cowell, Aaron Copland, John Kirkpatrick, and Elliot Carter eventually arranged for the performance and publication of Ives's works, and recognition came slowly but surely, including a belated Pulitzer Prize in 1947 for his Third Symphony (1904–1911). "His music was not so much ignored as it was totally unknown," Charles Hamm has observed of Ives's composing years. "As a result, the music of Charles Ives played no role in the struggle for a national identity which occupied most American composers in the decades when his compositions were written."[65]

Had the bulk of Ives's compositions been brought before the public nearer the moment of their creation, such music would surely have baffled the American public—a public that was, for the most part, almost totally ignorant of avant-garde developments in Europe. At the same time, an orchestral piece like "The Housatonic at Stockbridge" might well have been recognized as a powerful and attractive score of quasi-Impressionist Americana, one spiritually in harmony with, if also more progressive than, contemporary works by Griffes and Carpenter. And, had a song such as "Tom Sails Away," first performed in New York on 11 May 1963, become known, it might have been recognized for the extraordinarily communicative song it is—a rare example, indeed, of a first-class American art song prompted by and written during the war. All we know is that it is a story that never happened, one that we seem destined to reconstruct over and over again and ask, "What if?"

Part 7

POST-ARMISTICE

20 "Goin' Home"

My devotion to my own land is well known. I have many
friends in France, Belgium, England, and Russia. How could
I change my feeling towards them? How could any personal
enmity enter in? To bridge over the abysses of hatred that
this war will leave behind it—that must be the mission of
the artist.

Fritz Kreisler, 1 January 1915

For me the open world was the only possible one, I knew no
other: what did I not owe Russia—it made me what I am, from
there the inner me went forth, all my instinct's homeland, all
my inner origin is *there!* What do I not owe Paris, and will
never cease to be grateful to it for. And the other countries!
I can, I could take nothing back, not an instant, in no direction
reject or hate or despise.

Rainer Maria Rilke, letter to Leopold
von Schlözer, 21 January 1920

The Armistice came and then the peace, but no new order fell automatically into place. The violinist Fritz Kreisler, who had been forced to withdraw from the American concert stage following a campaign of personal
vilification because he had served in the Austrian army, returned safely to
an admiring public. Yet, on the political front, Wilson's Fourteen Points
were rejected by the Allies, the U.S. Senate refused to ratify the Treaty of
Versailles—the document was ultimately endorsed by the European signatories in the Hall of Mirrors, but created as many problems as it solved—
and the League of Nations soon proved to be a hollow concept with little
promise for the future.

Despite these disappointments and the widespread social disorder that
followed the war, many of the aesthetic debates of the preceding years were
now soberly revived and reviewed. Whatever urgency was apparent in such
deliberations seemed to center on the possibility of societal renewal through
the arts. Although such questions must have seemed decidedly marginal to
many citizens, in July 1919 George Bernard Shaw wrote a challenging article, "The Future of British Music," that was aimed directly at the issue.[1]

There he argued the importance of music in identifying a nation's soul, and he warned the public that it must encourage its composers and performers if music was to prosper in the postwar period. His faith in the importance of Elgar for this task led six months later to a remarkable claim.

> Certain things one can say without hesitation. For example, that Elgar could turn out Debussy and Stravinsky music by the thousand bars for fun in his spare time. That to him such standbys as the whole-tone-scale of Debussy, the Helmholtzian chords of Scriabin . . . are what farthings are to a millionaire.[2]

Such a bizarre claim only underscored England's postwar sense of inferiority in matters musical. Shaw further claimed for Elgar a Handelian universality and a sure hand capable of turning out a symphonic adagio "such as has not been given since Beethoven died," but he also wisely acknowledged that "though [Elgar] has a most active and curious mind, he does not appear in music as an experimenter and explorer, like Scriabin and Schönberg. He took music where Beethoven left it, and where Schumann and Brahms found it."[3]

England's relation to the avant-garde in the postwar period—particularly with respect to music—was an issue of special concern. Understandably, Elgar's importance was repeatedly underscored even as his noble and telling backward glance at a faded Edwardian era did little to clarify the country's musical future. Vaughan Williams's star was just beginning to rise, and the iconoclastic snap of the young William Walton that would soon appear in *Façade* (1922) was just out of view. In sum, Shaw's proclamation read less as an attempt to align Britain with the rising fashion of Neoclassicism than as an extraordinary unwillingness to face up to the challenge of prewar developments on the Continent.

By 1918 Siegfried Sassoon had come to the conclusion that all soldiers at the front were victims, Germans as well as British, and, returning home in the late summer and autumn that year after having spent two tours at the front, he found that only through classical music could he distance himself from the war. In the following months he adopted music as a potent symbol for a modern age, hailed music's purity as well as its power to heal, and in five "musical" poems contrasted the ageless qualities of a work like Bach's B minor Mass with the Philistinism of the middle class and their taste for ephemeral fashion. In "Evensong in Westminster Abbey," which evokes Handel, and "Hommage à Mendelssohn," through reference to the composer's Prelude in A-flat Major, which he defended against contemporary snobbishness, Sassoon joined Shaw and offered an escape to the past and a welcome contrast to the hard, analytical edge of modern times.[4] In "Concert Interpretation (*Le sacre du printemps*)," however, he pushed his argument in a different direction with a vicious attack not so much on the contemporary musical scene as on those audiences who blindly followed the critics. Directing his attention to the public who had rejected Stravinsky's *Le sacre* "with hisses—hoots—guffaws" because he had "jumped their Wagner palisade / With modes that seemed cacophonous and queer," [5] the poet scathingly observes that once the work was accepted by the critics, the public unthinkingly followed suit. Sassoon's language then becomes dynamic-, texture-, and instrument-specific (although the opening word "bassoons" should have been in the singular rather than the plural form).

> Bassoons begin . . . Sonority envelops
> Our auditory innocence; and brings
> To me, I must admit, some drift of things
> Omnific, seminal, and adolescent.

> Polyphony through dissonance develops
> A serpent-conscious Eden, crude but pleasant;
> While vibro-atmosphere copulations
> With mezzo-forte mysteries of noise
> Prelude Stravinsky's statement of the joys
> That unify the monkeydom of nations.[6]

More than a sonic mirror of the introduction to Stravinsky's ballet, the last of these lines makes pointed reference to the recently ended conflict. Sassoon then considers an audience's docile and polite reaction to a live performance of *Le sacre*. No signs of riot this time in the Grand Circle, and the audience is listening to "this not-quite-new audacity / As though it were by someone dead,—like Brahms."

Sassoon will have none of it, however, and invites the audience to "Lynch the conductor! Jugulate the drums! Butcher the brass! Ensanguinate the strings! Throttle the flutes!" Before anything can happen "the music blazes and expires; and the delighted Audience is clapping."[7] For Sassoon, who had served at the front and thrown his military medals into the sea, the sheeplike audience who now responded favorably to the appraisal of a critical elite who had changed its tune and declared *Le sacre* a masterwork was the same uncomprehending but malleable collective who had stayed at home during the war, callously applauded news of each victory, and blindly accepted reports of treachery. Art had once again mimicked life, and Sassoon had delivered himself of a sermon.

ARMISTICE AND CELEBRATION

With the signing of the Armistice at eleven o'clock in the morning on 11 November 1918, Germany was brought to its knees, and both the Austro-Hungarian and Ottoman empires disappeared from the map. Imperial Russia had expired the year before, and Europe would never again be the same. Between nine and ten million people had been killed in the war, and twice that number had been wounded. What had it all been for?

One of the most welcome benefits of the new era of peace was that, to borrow the earlier words of Oliver Wendell Holmes Sr., it brought "silence, like a poultice . . . to heal the blows of sound."[8] A series of varied reactions followed: joyous celebration, a sort of dazed realization that the insanity had ended, and the hope that a new beginning—however ill defined—lay just ahead. Looking back at the effects of war on the musical world, one American critic offered an optimistic appraisal. Attacking all those who professed that the Great War had brought the death of art everywhere and an indifference to concerts in the world of music in particular, he judged that instead the war had given "an impetus to music and the other arts which crowded into a few months the equivalent of years of effort. To put the matter bluntly, it seems as though the war was the best thing which ever happened to music."[9] Such post-Armistice euphoria was destined to abate in the months ahead. Whatever the fraternal feelings of a renowned violinist, the dark musings of a German philosopher poet, the bitter assessment of a British war poet, or the optimism of an American music critic, certain unassailable realities followed the signing of the Armistice.

The task of commemorating the war necessarily began even before it was over. July 14 had been consecrated by the French parliament in 1880 as a symbol of the irreversible victory of republicans over the monarchy, and on that day in 1915—the first Bastille Day after the outbreak of hostilities—the ashes of Rouget de Lisle, author of "La Marseillaise," were symbolically moved to Napoleon's grandiose mausoleum at Les Invalides. At the ceremony President Poincaré reviewed the original circumstances surrounding the defense of the Alsatian city of Strasbourg, the city that gave birth to the national hymn, and placed in perspective its relevance for 1915.[10]

The first Bastille Day following the Armistice, in 1919, saw a celebration commonly remembered as the grandest in French history. Even a group of anarchists who brandished a red flag before the church of the Trinité could not mar the proceedings. When the parade started filing down the avenue of the Elysian Fields and the music of the 28th Infantry heralded the cortege of a thousand *mutilés,* hearts sank before giving thanks that the end had finally come.[11]

Perhaps the most touching scene of all took place in Strasbourg—a city lost by the French in the Franco-Prussian War of 1870 and the stage for a defeated musical France in an "Olympic Contest" of May 1905. Now, on 14 July 1919, Alsace and Lorraine had been restored to France and delirium reigned in Strasbourg. After the review of troops in the morning at the Place de la République, twenty-five thousand children from the area, little tricolor flags in hand, cheered and sang "La Marseillaise"—a hymn born in Strasbourg. "La *Marseillaise* ought to be called *l'Alsacienne,*" one contemporary exclaimed.[12]

It had been decided in 1916 that British war dead would be buried where they had fallen in battle, and by the end of the war there were more than twelve hundred British grave sites in France. These were eventually consolidated. Two English architects were placed in charge of making recommendations for suitable monuments,[13] and a series of guides to the battlefields was inaugurated.[14] Few visitors came in the early months following the war, but by the late 1920s the manicured cemeteries had become virtual gardens and lured numerous tourists. Monuments to the dead also sprang up in villages and cities not only in England but also throughout the United States and in profusion all over Europe.[15]

The Basilica of Sacré-Coeur on the crest of Paris's most prominent hill, the butte Montmartre, had been begun in 1874 as a monument to the dead of the Franco-Prussian War. Shortly thereafter, in 1877, Gounod wrote a *Messe du Sacré Coeur de Jésus* for mixed chorus and orchestra. The structure was completed in 1914, just as the Great War was commencing, and its long-deferred consecration in 1919 was inevitably a victory celebration.[16]

In Milan, La Scala hosted an evening in honor of Franco-British troops on 20 November 1918. Admission was free, the house was packed, and many were turned away. One commentator reported that "Maestro Tullio Serafin—himself a soldier and just recovering from the effect of a severe motor accident—gave a slashing presentation of the Royal Italian March, following which came the British National Anthem, and the boys in khaki joined in lustily singing the Brabançonne, and the American Hymn." Then came "La Marseillaise," sung by Emma Vecla and a chorus of French soldiers, followed by the Garibaldi Hymn, which brought the theater to its feet. "Va pensiero" from Verdi's *Nabucco* and "Guerra, guerra!" from Bellini's *Norma* met with a storm of applause. The high points of the evening were renderings of "Tipperary" by British Tommies and "Le chant du combat" by French poilus.[17] Trench songs followed, and the evening threatened never to come to an end. Indeed, the event was encored at the same location two weeks later. Both were a last "hurrah" before returning home to face the realities of a new life.

"GOIN' HOME"

The celebrations notwithstanding, it was the private ceremonies of home-coming for ordinary soldiers that proved to be the most emotional in the lives of countless families. Tellingly, in 1922 the lyrics of "Goin' Home" were added by William Arms Fisher to the most memorable melody from Dvořák's "New World" Symphony of 1893. A pupil of Paine at Harvard as well as of Dvořák in New York, Fisher turned the Czech composer's plaintive English horn solo from the symphony's slow movement into a pseudo-spiritual with words that virtually all ensuing generations of Americans were to associate with the tune.[18]

The melody was infused, Dvořák said, not only with his own personal memories of home and a "sense of the tragedy of the black man as it rings in his 'spirituals,'" but with "something of the loneliness of far-off prairie horizons, the faint memory of the red man's bygone days."[19] Fisher's text transcended all these connotations, however, and became an emblem of the nostalgia that accompanied the troops who had begun to be mustered out in 1919 and 1920.

As it happened, the descendants of Dvořák's "redman" were accorded automatic admiration as noble, "instinctive" warriors—a recognition that had been denied to most African Americans.[20] Relying upon their historic reputation as fleet and fearless combatants, Amerindians were frequently given assignments as scouts and admired for their "blood-curdling" war whoops, which purportedly scared the daylights out of Germans long familiar with the tales of Karl May and James Fenimore Cooper.[21]

Traditional Amerindian cultural values, which had long been the object of eradication by U.S. federal policies, had been strengthened during the war through the joint participation of tribesmen from many different Amerindian nations in their native dances, songs of victory and death, and burial rituals.[22] The YMCA even helped in this matter by organizing group meetings for Amerindians to "sing their own songs and hear and speak their own languages."[23] One Lakota victory song ran:

> The Germans who were charging, now they are crying
> The Germans who were charging, now they are crying
> They are crying.[24]

The repetitive and epigrammatic nature of such texts was typical of traditional war and victory songs of the Plains Indians, and the metaphor of making the enemy cry was shared by many of them.[25]

The old songs of victory over other tribes or against Custer and his cavalry were updated with a new enemy. When Amerindian veterans returned home in 1918 and thereafter, they were frequently met at train depots by their families. Victory dances were performed on the spot, and these celebrations were essential to the preservation of the new lyrics that the soldiers had added to their traditional songs.[26] Navajo songs reflected the fact that theirs is a world filled with ghosts, especially the ghosts of the enemy that one has killed in war, and unless the Navajo warrior engaged in an "Enemy Way" ceremony after returning from battle, it was understood that those ghosts were capable of haunting him forever. Such rituals took on a renewed importance in the post-Armistice period, and not surprisingly the lyrics for most of the songs in this ceremony were less epigrammatic and more poetic than the typical war song.[27]

Upon their return, however, twelve thousand Amerindians, many of whose fathers had fought the U.S. Army, found that their experience in the U.S. military did not accord readily with their isolated native cultures, and most were suddenly caught in a new no man's land: they were "too 'Indian' to be fully accepted as equals in white society, but too 'assimilated' to easily reenter Indian society." [28] Furthermore, federal policy did little to alleviate the problems of their return, settling instead on the awarding of certificates of appreciation and American flags rather than offering aid for faltering farms or chronic unemployment on reservations. Yet, as Ben Black Bear acknowledged in both narrative and song, there was one compensation. Because of the Lakota's contribution to the war, the practice of ritualistic dancing, which had been denied prior to 1918, was returned to them "along with the feathers which they had asked for." [29]

During the Great War any male Amerindian who was a citizen or who had announced his intention to become one was subject to the draft. Those of the latter group who served were automatically awarded citizenship, something that was not conferred upon Amerindians at large until 1924. Although returning to the United States was a mixed blessing for many veterans, many of those who had served in the war understandably claimed with pride that the role they had played in defeating Germany was absolutely crucial to, and in some way perhaps even responsible for, this blanket conferral of citizenship on a people.[30] At the same time, there was no doubt a sorrow at the inescapable realization of the Native American's loss of hope for collective sovereignty.

"Going Home" was also the title of an African American trench song,[31] and there is evidence that Dvořák modeled a number of the tunes in his "New World" Symphony after spirituals sung to him by his pupil, Henry T. Burleigh.[32] Burleigh published several arrangements of spirituals during the war, including "Nobody Knows De Trouble I've Seen," "I Don't Feel No-Ways Tired" ("For I hope to shout glory when dis worl' is on fire"), and "You May Bury Me in De Eas'" ("You may bury me in de Wes', / But I'll hear de trumpet soun' in dat mornin'"), all from 1917. Other spirituals published in the early post-Armistice period spoke of the collective sorrow of the nation regardless of race; the most obvious were songs like "Balm in Gilead" ("There is a Balm in Gilead to make the wounded whole") and "Don't You Weep When I'm Gone" ("O mother, don't you weep when I'm gone. / For I'm goin' to Heavn' above") of 1919 as well as "Ain't Goin' to Study War No Mo'" of 1922. In light of their enormous communicative power to all people, there need be little wonder that singers like Roland Hayes and Marian Anderson had an enormous success when they began to include spirituals on their recital programs in the 1920s and 1930s.

In his newly composed words to Dvořák's English horn melody, Fisher, a collector and arranger of spirituals himself, traded on this tradition by coupling a longing for home with an awareness of an experience now left behind.

> Goin' home, goin' home,
> I'm agoin' home;
> Quiet-like, some still day,
> I'm jes' goin' home.
> It's not far, jes' close by,
> Through an open door,
> Work all done, care laid by,
> Gwine to fear no more.
>
> Mother's there 'spectin' me,
> Father's waitin', too,
> Lots of folks gathered there,
> All the friends I knew.
>
> Home, home,
> I'm goin' home.[33]

Fisher's arrangement noted that "when desired the text may be sung without dialect," thus inviting its use by singers of different ethnic backgrounds. The renowned bass Paul Robeson emphasized its relationship not only to the spiritual tradition but also to other songs of pain and suffering by placing it in recital alongside "Balm in Gilead," the "Volga Boat Song," and Bach's "Christ lag in Todesbanden." He also suppressed the dialect version by clearly pronouncing, at least on a preserved recording, "going" for "goin'" or "gwine," "just" for "jes," and "expecting" for "'spectin'."[34] He also emphasized its potential as a postwar signature song by substituting "Going to kill no more" for "Going to fear no more" and "Brother" for "Father" in the third stanza.

"MY BUDDY"

Remembrance and commemoration found expression in ways ranging from the official, the patriotic, and the religious, to the informally ribald, affectionate, and sentimental. Heitor Villa-Lobos recapitulated the progression from war to victory to peace in a triptych of symphonies, which were titled "A guerra" (1919), "A vittoria" (1919), and "A paz" (1920). An outpouring of songs celebrated victory and expressed hopes for peace, beginning with William H. Gardner and Caro Roma's popular chant "Ring Out! Sweet Bells of Peace" and continuing with the high note of optimism expressed in Seitz and Lockhart's "The World Is Waiting for the Sunrise," which was introduced in London in January 1919. Denigration of the enemy was now set aside for the joy of homecoming parades and family reunions in a deluge of popular songs, of which some 3,300 were copyrighted during the first seven months of 1919.[35]

Eubie Blake and Noble Sissle, now home, also offered timely songs of romance and reunion with "Love Will Find a Way" and "I'm Just Wild about Harry" in an all-black revue, *Shuffle Along*, which opened on 23 May 1921 at New York's 63rd Street Music Hall. It starred a teenage Josephine Baker and ran for 504 performances. Other songs endured into the post-Armistice period for a quite different reason. "The Old Grey Mare," a popular song from 1917, for example, was proudly included in a collection of *American War Songs* published by the National Society of the Colonial Dames of America in 1925 along with the notice that it was "one of the important songs of the World War."[36] One textual parody of this song that had been particularly popular during the war was "The poor old Kaiser ain't what he used to be, / Many long years ago."[37] But the 1925 collection claimed that "The Old Grey Mare" was now used as the official marching song by numerous posts of the American Legion, a veterans' organization that had been founded in Paris in March 1919 by members of the American Expeditionary Force.[38] The relationship between a man and his horse during wartime was summed up by the expression "Quarante hommes et huit chevaux" (forty men and eight horses)—a reference to the capacity of a train transport car—and its English equivalent was borrowed by the "40 and 8" clubs for veterans that arose in America in the postwar period. The title of the American Legion song placed less emphasis on the noble wartime role played by the horse—poignantly reflected in the poetry of George Patton and the correspondence of Elgar[39]—than on nostalgia for the good old days. At the same time, it hinted at the search for lost camaraderie, which was soon to become indispensable in the formation of American Legion posts throughout the country.

Remembering wartime associations and joining veterans' groups were identical propositions to many in the postwar period, but when soldiers reconvened, the "crisis of masculinity" was also inevitably revisited as veterans searched for the meaning of their collective experience. Analyses of veterans' groups at the time, even in France, have shown that they were anything but aggressively militarist organizations. They disavowed the chauvinistic patriotism, which they argued had led only to war, and they called for a pacifism that would embrace the highest ideals of a supranational organization and rational patriotism or love of country in equal measure.[40]

During the requisite review to adopt such a platform, a crisis was triggered by memories of the soldier's obligatory obedience to orders and his prolonged observation of or participation in maiming or killing without discernible military purpose.[41] Memories of the price paid prompted a need to perpetuate the memory not only of fallen comrades but also of times spent together under such horrendous conditions. As a result, a number of postwar songs spoke with surprising directness of the soldiers' strong emotional interdependence.

An anonymous article in the *Musical Times* on 1 March 1915 had included a vivid report on the development of bonding among new recruits before it turned to discussing music as an agent in the establishment of a cohesive spirit among the group. Pointing out the necessity of turning inductees into soldiers in the shortest possible time, the writer noted that squad drill and gymnastics were necessary before

> ésprit de corps becomes comprehensible, and the glory of the soldier's life begins to dawn. Incidentally it may be added, the "chum" now emerges. There is no accounting for the attractive force which brings and keeps "chums" together; they "jus' growed," like Topsy—but the

fact remains, and their devoted constancy is "lovely and pleasant" as that of Saul and Jonathan.[42]

This act of male bonding, which had been evidenced in wars from time immemorial, produced a comradeship that surpassed simple friendship. Noel Coward characterized it as "a sort of splendid carelessness . . . holding us together" that went "beyond even what love you have, something intangible and desolately beautiful."[43] The sentiment was something that the British novelist Virginia Woolf had a difficult time comprehending. In *Three Guineas* she concluded testily, "If you insist upon fighting to protect me, or 'our' country, let it be understood soberly and rationally between us that you are fighting to gratify a sex instinct which I cannot share; to procure benefits which I have not shared and probably will not share."[44] Woolf, who like other feminists, Bloomsbury aesthetes, and a few Cambridge dons such as Bertrand Russell, was an ardent pacifist,[45] may not have read the issue quite correctly. Yet she properly sensed that apart from the aggression required of the warrior was a factor of life in the trenches that was completely beyond her ken: a potentially emasculating submission to authority, wedded to a protective acceptance of male bonding.[46] In another sense, however, Woolf's rage against patriarchy, which was understandably joined to her hatred of war, was paradoxically anchored in what she perceived as a tyranny against not only women as a class but also a generation of young men sent off to war.[47]

Paul Fussell has contended that erotic feelings on the front—what he cautiously called "a sublimated (i.e., 'chaste') form of temporary homosexuality"[48]—and their later and affectionate recall in literature and poetry was virtually predictable.[49] Joanna Bourke argues conversely that although traditional forms of male bonding known from English public schools, sports clubs, and the like were no doubt "transferred into the war zones," once there, "instead of being strengthened, the bonds snapped."[50] Indeed, the idea of soldierly bonding was most explicitly evident in the texts of numerous songs that appeared following the cessation of hostilities. Whatever the perspective on the issue, there can be little quarrel with the observation that war explored the "ambiguity of building political authority out of affectionate bonds between men—or of making art out of feelings for another person."[51]

As early as 1890, during a period of relative calm, Felix McGlennon composed a striking song entitled "Comrades," performed by Tom Costello, that depicted the emotional attraction among soldiers. It retained its popularity in England well into the 1930s. The piece recalls a martial air in its opening three verses, but its prevailing sentiment can be gathered from the words of the lilting chorus and the final verse, where the mood suddenly changes to a dramatic *agitato*, in accord with the concluding description of personal sacrifice.

> Comrades, comrades
> Ever since we were boys,
> Sharing each other's sorrows,
> Sharing each other's joys.
> Comrades when manhood was dawning,
> Faithful what-e'er might be-tide
> When danger threatened, my darling comrade
> Was there by my side.
>
> In the night the savage foe-man,
> Crept around us as we lay,
> To our arms we leap'd and faced them,
> Back to back we stood at bay.
> As I fought, a savage at me
> Aim'd his spear like lightning's dart,
> But my comrade sprang to save me,
> And received it in his heart.[52]

Stéphane Audoin-Rouzeau has warned that on a purely social level this "fraternity of the trenches was largely illusory." It was a legend that was born during the war among soldiers of middle-class origin and was then transferred to become "the heart of the veterans' movement," in which these soldiers "occupied most of the leading places."[53] Thus, such postwar activities were patently born of a desire to preserve in civilian life the sense of freedom from the constraints of class and social behavior that they had experienced during the war.[54]

In 1922, the same year that the lyrics of "Goin' Home" were added to Dvořák's familiar melody, one of the most popular hits of the post-Armistice period was published by Leo Feist. "My Buddy" had lyrics by Gus Kahn (author of "Memories" and "I'll See You in My Dreams") and music by Walter Donaldson (composer of "How Ya Gonna Keep 'Em Down on the Farm" and Kahn's collaborator in "Makin' Whoopee").

> Nights are long since you went away
> I think about you all thru the day
> My Buddy, my Buddy
> No Buddy quite so true.
>
> Miss your voice, the touch of your hand
> Just long to know that you understand

My Buddy, my Buddy
Your Buddy misses you.[55]

The piece was dedicated to Donaldson's fiancée, who had recently died, but the gender of *buddy*, which is defined in informal usage in the United States as a "comrade or chum," would not have been in doubt for the returning veterans.[56] During the war the term was also adopted as a synonym for *beau*,[57] and the first edition cover for "My Buddy" displayed a picture of a girl looking into space and holding a picture of a soldier in her left hand. Yet appearing as it first did, some four years after the Armistice, when soldiers had long since returned to their sweethearts, the song's refrain was no doubt heard by many veterans as an affectionate song of remembrance for former army buddies.[58]

Indeed, the notion of "buddies," an American expression, had been extremely popular from the very beginning of the war when the "Pals," or "Chums," battalions were formed in England as an enlistment device. Originally announced in Liverpool by Lord Derby in late August 1914, the idea was to raise a cadre of local lads who could be persuaded to join the army with the promise that they would serve alongside their friends. Eventually the idea spread throughout the whole of northern England and Scotland, where over a hundred such battalions were formed by the end of the year. Because of their lack of experience and because of overt miscalculations on the part of their commander, however, the ranks of the 16th Highland Light Infantry Battalion (Glasgow Boys Brigade) were diminished by half in the Battle of the Somme, a fate shared by the majority of the "Pals" battalions.[59]

During the course of the war isolation from home and the need for understanding and affection in the face of death had fueled an emotional dependency that ran deeper than anything most men had ever experienced as civilians. As a consequence, and regardless of their sense of relief at the conclusion of hostilities, not all soldiers were eager to leave the battlefield and immediately return home.[60] "How can one enjoy life without this highly spiced sauce of danger?" the American aviator Eddie Rickenbacker asked. "What else is left to living now that the zest and excitement of fighting airplanes is gone?" The Armistice, he noted, also meant "the end of that intimate relationship that since the beginning of the war had cemented together brothers-in-arms into a closer fraternity than is known to any other friendship in the world."[61]

The argument has been repeatedly and protectively forwarded that this intimacy was a virile, manly contact known in the civilian world chiefly in the field of sports. In the latter, however, the sense of personal danger is narrowly limited and hence devoid of one of the strongest factors in the bonds of war. Surviving a life-threatening situation ultimately depended on teamwork and an unwavering sense of loyalty to fellow soldiers, and among the troops this kind of loyalty quickly became more personal than national. For the sense of devotion premised upon the issue of one's very survival—daily, hourly, and protracted over a long period of time—understandably promoted a kind of mutual protectiveness more fundamental than one developed in the common cause of winning a football match. Whatever the original intentions of its authors, "My Buddy" encapsulated this very sentiment accurately and poignantly.

Another song about the special fraternity born in the trenches was "I Wonder Where My Buddies Are Tonight," published in 1926 by Leo Feist, with words by Billy Rose and Raymond B. Egan and music by Richard A. Whiting.[62] The title is an obvious parody of "I Wonder Where My Baby Is Tonight,"[63] published the year before by Walter Donaldson.

> I wonder where my buddies are tonight,
> I wonder how
> They're doing now?
> I wonder if they're being treated right,
> My doughboy pals
> And Red Cross gals?
> You'll find a cross where Goldberg and O'Leary
> Fought side by side and died at Château Thierry.
> The world forgets, perhaps,
> But when day has sounded "Taps,"
> I wonder where my buddies are tonight?[64]

The contrasting citation of Jewish and Irish surnames in the battlefield cemetery reflects not so much the blurring of ethnic differences in search of a fitting line for a rhyming couplet as the recognition that all had served together and found themselves equally vulnerable in battle. And while the use of "Red Cross gals" to rhyme with "doughboy pals" also recognizes the comradeship that was felt across gender lines, a sentiment in tune with the growing suffragette movement, among enlisted men the American term *buddy* and the English expression *mate* were primarily directed at their male comrades in arms.

The penultimate line of the Rose-Egan-Whiting song pointed to another postwar reality in its citation of the familiar bugle call "Taps." Sounded at night as a signal to put out the lights ("Day is done") but also after 1868 at military funerals and Memorial Day ceremonies, it would henceforth resound on Armistice Day as well. Inevitably, in the years ahead, many of the tunes recalled from the war or newly fashioned in the post-Armistice period were destined to tug at the heart of veterans who knew that the former days of their unmatchable and bittersweet camaraderie were gone forever.

21　Ceremonials and the War of Nerves

Memory is not an instrument for exploring the past but its theatre. It is the medium of past experience, as the ground is the medium in which dead cities lie interred.

Walter Benjamin, *A Berlin Chronicle*

Remembering is never just about the past, it's always about the present.

John Bodnar, *Remaking America*

Ceremonies centering on the remembrance of soldiers who had fallen in battle proved crucial to the consolidation of a post-Great War psyche, and the various shrines of the Unknown Soldier that appeared in virtually every country attested to the purgative value of such commemorative sites. In 1917 Charles Villiers Stanford wrote an organ sonata with a Great War motif, subtitled "Eroica," of which a version for full orchestra was performed in London's Royal Albert Hall in 1918; the first movement was titled "Rheims" and the concluding one labeled "Verdun, 1916." Then, when the Armistice finally came, Stanford followed with *At the Abbey Gate,* a work for baritone, chorus, and orchestra that was first performed in March 1921. It took for its subject the Unknown Warrior of World War I, whose bones, together with some earth from the fields where the British fought, had been interred in Westminster Abbey on 11 November 1920 (fig. 38). The inscription on the headstone, in uniform capital letters, begins "Beneath this stone rests the body / of a British warrior, unknown by name or rank, brought from France to lie among / the most illustrious of the land," and it concludes "They buried him among the Kings because he had done good toward God and toward his House."[1] The Gramophone Company, which had earlier captured the roar of the big guns on the frontline at Lille, recorded the burial service and claimed that it was "the first ever sound recording of a major public event."[2]

Focusing on the same locale in his postwar "Evensong in Westminster Abbey," Siegfried Sassoon described a casual observer who wanders into the abbey to collect his thoughts but is impeded by an overpowering

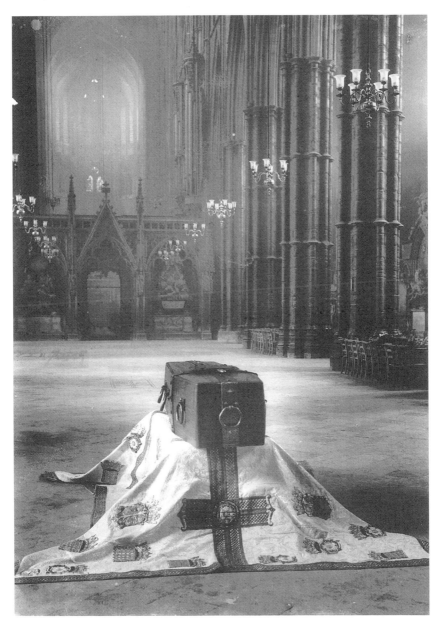

Figure 38. The coffin of the Unknown Warrior, lying in state in Westminster Abbey during the Armistice Day service of 11 November 1920. (© Imperial War Museum, London; photo Horace Nicholls.)

awareness of England's illustrious dead: Milton, Purcell, Shakespeare, Wesley.[3] The stultifying drone of the sermon that follows only serves to emphasize the hollowness of Anglican dogma. When the choir finally enters, singing "Out on the organ's fugue-triumphal tone, / When hosannatic Handel liberates us at last," the music, by the most famous Anglo-German composer of all time, is a redeeming spiritual call from centuries past.[4] Much to Stanford's sorrow, his music never captivated English congregations like Handel's did or attained the success of Elgar's. All too predictably, at its premiere *At the Abbey Gate* served merely as an introduction to the annual performance of Elgar's *Dream of Gerontius*, a work that deals somewhat more universally with the topics of Death and Change.

In Armistice Day celebrations between 1921 and 1925 from Cornwall and Llandudno to Birmingham and Sheffield, ceremonies typically began with a singing of the hymn "O God, Our Help in Ages Past," followed by a prayer, two minutes of silence, placement of wreaths on the local memorial by relatives of those who had fallen in battle, and another hymn (Welsh, Scottish, or Irish depending upon the locale). The observance concluded with the first verse of the national anthem.[5] Armistice Day celebrations continued in Great Britain over the coming decades, but none surpassed the grandeur of the first Empire Festival of Remembrance in the Royal Albert Hall on 11 November 1927. As the *Daily Express* reported on its front page the next day, the climax was reached when "10,000 men and women who served overseas gathered to sing the old Army songs and hear the Prince of Wales." Audiences not only in Great Britain but all over the British Empire participated. "For the first time," the newspaper continued, "the miracle of an Empire broadcast was accomplished. For the first time one man spoke to the whole world. For the first time the Empire thought and felt and sang in unison."[6]

In the same issue of the *Daily Express* the popular inspirational writer H. V. Morton attempted to set down the inexpressible.

> We did not realise until last night that the songs we sang in the Army were bits of history. In them is embalmed the comic fatalism which carried us through four years of hell. How easily we slipped back into it! Cynicism was blown clean out of us. We were young once more as we can never be again and we went deeper into our memories. . . . Thirteen years fell from us. We ceased to see the Albert Hall and the thousands of faces white in the arc lights; we looked into an abyss of memories where long columns passed and repassed over the dusty roads of France, where grotesque, unthinkable, things happened day and night—the brief joys, the sharp sorrows of those days, the insane in-

justices of fate, and above it all the memory of the men we knew so well. . . . It seemed to me that we had caught the only decent thing in the war—the spirit of comradeship. We had come to the hall as individuals; we were now once more an army marching in our imagination to the old music. We laughed because tears were in our heart. We shouted for old songs not on the programme. We encored ourselves. We stamped and shouted our delight.[7]

The singing was marked by a jolly beginning—"Pack Up Your Troubles"—and a solemn ending—"Abide With Me." In between came the sentimental songs like "The Long, Long Trail," "A Perfect Day," and "Keep the Home Fires Burning," as well as such popular bits of humor as "K-K-K-Katy" and "Sister Susie." Some tunes carried a clear note of cynicism; other decidedly unheroic ones, triggered sobering flashbacks to times when only the camaraderie of singing such tunes kept a soldier going.

The cathartic effect of these celebrations, topped only by the even more raucous carnival atmosphere of the "Poppy Day Rags" held by Cambridge University students, was clear enough, although some began to question the appropriateness of boisterous behavior on these solemn days of reflection. Broadcasts of the Festival of Remembrance continued every year after 1927, but by 1936 officials at the BBC had begun to refer to the Albert Hall festivities as a "British Legion sing-song" and to suggest that a more elegiac type of music ought to be performed following such celebrations, along with suitable readings from the Bible. This, it was argued, would serve to "wash out the taste of the super-sentimental orgy from the Albert Hall and reset the frame for these readings."[8]

The Church of England had recognized the power of these annual rituals and the need for local religious services of commemoration in the early 1920s. This in turn led to the designation of the Sunday nearest to 11 November as Remembrance Day, when services were to include an appropriate selection of hymns and canticles.[9] On Armistice Day of 1927, for example, the BBC broadcast a Cenotaph service, as well as a memorial concert in the evening. All of the music was by British composers, except for works by Chopin and Handel, and the old question of national loyalty in the arts was addressed once again by an observer who noted that "Handel was as good as British and Chopin as good as French, although actually a Pole."[10]

In France Armistice Day was similarly observed, although political overtones sometimes erupted. In Étain, a cantonal seat east of Verdun, a band refused to play, charging that the local veterans' association was turning the celebration into a religious, thus political, demonstration. Many of the performing musicians were veterans themselves, however, and pro-

Figure 39. The U.S. Marine Band performing at the burial of the World War I Unknown Soldier at Arlington National Cemetery, 11 November 1921.

tested that "we musicians wanted to make of November 11th a celebration of victory and not a festival of sadness and mourning."[11]

On 11 November 1921, a year to the day following the observances at Westminster Abbey, dedication services for the Unknown Soldier took place in the United States, presided over by the secretary of war. An unidentified American soldier who had been killed in France was interred in a temporary crypt in Arlington National Cemetery.[12] At 11:15 a.m. the casket bearing the remains arrived at the west entrance of the amphitheater and was borne around the right colonnade to the apse and placed on the catafalque. This was followed by the playing of the national anthem by the Marine Band, an invocation, the trumpet call "Attention," thrice sounded, and two minutes of silence. "America" was then played by the band and sung by the audience, followed by an address by the president of the United States, Warren G. Harding (fig. 39).

Next came "The Supreme Sacrifice," a hymn sung by a quartet from the Metropolitan Opera Company: Rosa Ponselle, Jeanne Gordon, Morgan

Kingston, and William Gustafson. The Unknown Soldier was then decorated by the president with the Congressional Medal of Honor and Distinguished Service Cross, followed by the Belgian Croix de Guerre, the English Victoria Cross, the French Médaille Militaire and Croix de Guerre, and comparable medals from Italy, Romania, Czechoslovakia, and Poland. The quartet led the audience in the singing of "O God, Our Help in Ages Past," a psalm and scripture lessons were read, and Rosa Ponselle sang "I Know that My Redeemer Liveth."

The preliminary ceremony concluded with the quartet leading the audience in the singing of "Nearer, My God, to Thee" accompanied by the Marine Band. The remains, followed by the president, vice president, members of the cabinet, and General Pershing, were then borne to the sarcophagus as the band played "Our Honored Dead." The audience left the amphitheater for positions near the sarcophagus as the band played "Lead, Kindly Light." The committal followed. Three wreaths were then placed on the tomb by a representative from New York on behalf of American War Mothers and British War Mothers. The final gesture was made by Plenty Coups, chief of the Crow Nation and the representative of Amerindians, who symbolically laid his war bonnet and coup stick on the tomb of the Unknown Soldier.[13] Nothing could have more tellingly recapitulated America's struggle for territorial and political identity in a series of savage wars with the country's native population. Nothing could have more clearly articulated a nation's dreams for the future. Three salvos of artillery, "Taps," and the "National Salute" brought the ceremony to its conclusion.

It would be another six years before a permanent and more elaborate tomb was constructed above the original marble slab and dedicated on Armistice Day as the Tomb of the Unknown Soldier. It bears the inscription "Here Rests in Honored Glory an American Soldier Known but to God." The erection of the tomb continued the tradition of honoring the unknown dead at Arlington, where a granite sarcophagus on a hill overlooking Washington marks the remains of over 2,000 unidentified soldiers, both Union and Confederate, who had died in the battles around Bull Run.[14]

Less sanguine than the messages of these memorials was a poem composed in 1926 by Billy Rose. Co-author of the lyrics to "I Wonder Where My Buddies Are Tonight," Rose was inspired to write new lyrics, "The Unknown Soldier," to go with the original tune. Its sixth and seventh stanzas reflect on the total emptiness of all the former military pomp, the gold star symbolism, and the popular song ditties that had consumed America during the war and left a country to ponder if the price of the war had been worth it.

Does the gold star in the window
Now mean anything at all?
I wonder how my old gal feels
When she hears the bugle call?
And that baby that sang
"Hello Central, give me No Man's Land,"
Can they replace her daddy
With a military band? [15]

Clearly, remembrance was also capable of harboring bitterness and of serving as a sobriety test for a postwar society.

That the nostalgia carried by many of the tunes of the period preserved their power for later generations was made evident in a ceremony of 14 May 1998 at Arlington National Cemetery. At the exhumation of the remains of the Unknown Soldier from the Vietnam War in the interest of possible identification through newly developed methods of DNA testing, Handel's "Marche solennelle" was followed by the hymns "O Sacred Head, Now Wounded" and "Amazing Grace." The honor guard carried the coffin from the nation's most sacred monument to the hearse, and the national anthem was performed. Describing a scene choked with symbolism for those who held memories of the post-Armistice period of the Great War, *The New York Times* reported that as the hearse drove away "the band played the haunting Largo from Dvořák's 'New World' Symphony, the melody called 'Goin' Home.'" [16]

Yet, for all the power these tunes had to recapture personal pain mixed with national pride, they could not resolve the conflict between Theodore Roosevelt's previous call for untainted Americanism and the suspect glory that many felt to be attendant on the grave of the Unknown Soldier, as John Dos Passos had earlier noted: "How can you tell a guy's a hundred percent," he asked in *USA: 1919*, "when all you've got's a gunnysack full of bones, bronze buttons stamped with the screaming eagle and a pair of roll puttees?" [17]

NERVES, JAZZ, AND THE "LOST GENERATION"

Among the multiple characterizations of the post-Armistice period, the one cited most frequently was neurasthenic exhaustion. Not only had the idea of the soldier's frayed nerves been medically acknowledged in the expression "shell shock," but society at large had also become increasingly aware that it was no simple matter to pick up where they had left off at the outset of the war.

The theme appears in the work of virtually every major writer of the postwar period, including Erich Maria Remarque's *All Quiet on the Western Front*, Robert Sherriff's *Journey's End*, Virginia Woolf's *Mrs. Dalloway*, and Ernest Hemingway's *A Farewell to Arms*. T. S. Eliot played directly upon it in his "nerves monologue" in *The Waste Land*, written at a time when the author himself was under the care of neurologists in Britain and Switzerland.[18] Hardly an invention of the postwar period, neurasthenia had been heralded as a developing correlative to the modern age, especially by the Symbolist Decadence movement in France, from the 1890s on. In the immediate post-Armistice decade "nerves" was increasingly promoted as a cultural by-product, even as the societal touchstone of a historical moment. Yet war was a masculine affair, and nerves belonged to a feminine world—a jolting paradox.

That societal neurasthenia became increasingly associated with America, as opposed, say, to Freud's Vienna, was traceable to the fact that a fast pace and frenetic behavior were increasingly linked to contemporary urban life in the New World, a place now somewhat glamorously charged with courting emotional instability. This perspective could be traced back to an American, George M. Beard, who had introduced the diagnostic category of neurasthenia, or nervous exhaustion, in his *American Nervousness* in 1881.[19] World War I recontextualized the disorder, updating fin-de-siècle themes of nervous disease and sexual terror in the wake of a world cataclysm.

In the eyes of some during the 1920s, signs of frayed "nerves" were evident not only in the migration to France of the so-called "Lost Generation"[20] of American writers but also in most of the American dances that were finding their way to Europe. Despite its seemingly carefree attitude, "jazz," which often found expression in an insouciant, compulsive beat and runaway energy, reflected the societal distress that many were experiencing. The Jazz Age, a fabled era marked by exuberance and mounting prosperity in America, barely concealed the extreme mood swings of the postwar society's collective neurosis.[21] Jazz, originally the product of a victimized segment of American society, was now introduced to upper-crust white Americans and Europeans as the hottest musical fad of the moment. For many in America, however, it was recognized less as a newly triumphant expression of a minority people struggling for political, social, and musical recognition than as an aphrodisiac for a postwar society hell-bent on flaunting a free spirit and advertising its new role as a world power.

Arriving in Paris in the late teens and early twenties, black and white Americans alike were surprised to discover the reigning chic of *art nègre*.

Its popularity, clearly rooted in French colonialism, was quickly exploited.[22] When the French heard principally black American soldiers playing in a distinct and irresistible new dialect they embraced them as emblems of a vital new society that seemed to be beckoning from across the Atlantic. When jazz musicians returned to America with a foreign imprimatur, the status of the music they played escalated precipitously.

From another perspective, even in America where freedom of personal expression purportedly reigned supreme, the unmistakable lack of social equality and economic opportunity for these musicians back home would soon demand attention. Not all societal ills had been solved by the Great War, and no one was more conscious of this state of affairs than black American soldiers. A Statue of Liberty with its head blown off, the former stuff of Liberty Loan posters warning against a potential enemy invasion of America, now began to take on a new meaning.[23] America, which had escaped the disfigurement of shell-pocked landscapes and ruined cathedrals, now offered an invitation to a psychological terrain of manic "highs" and depressive "lows" through the first music that had ever been offered and widely accepted abroad as truly "American." Although originally anchored in the expression of a persecuted black minority, it had now come to define the escape route from the Gay Nineties to the Roaring Twenties for both European and American whites.

American ragtime had made its way to the troops through live performances and recordings. Later Siegfried Sassoon would tellingly write *Dead Musicians III*.

> For when my brain is on their track,
> In slangy speech I call them back.
> With fox-trot tunes their ghosts I charm.
> *"Another little drink won't do us any harm."*
>
> *I think of rag-time; a bit of rag-time;*
> *And see their faces crowding round*
> *To the sound of the syncopated beat.*
> *They've got such jolly things to tell,*
> *Home from hell with a Blighty wound so neat . . .*[24]
> . . . .
> And so the song breaks off; and I'm alone.
> They're dead . . . For God's sake stop that gramophone.[25]

As Sassoon protested, the phonograph was capable of momentarily recapturing or, more properly, of forever "freezing" the memories of former good times spent singing or listening to the latest musical hits with army buddies. But when the recording came to its conclusion, breaking off with the swooshing sound of a needle tracking an empty groove, reality set in: a time gone by was lost forever, and so were the friends. Nostalgia, and even ragtime, could go only so far.

ANTHEIL AND THE SUPPRESSION OF SENTIMENT

The heroic exploits of the air ace had been avidly followed by many Americans, but among the composers of the postwar period none tracked these stories more religiously than George Antheil did. In his autobiography Antheil claimed that as a teenager he had "joined the United States aviation to become a fighting flier in World War I."

> The war stopped before I got over, but it had been my original intention to shoot down as many Germans as possible and, given the opportunity, to capture Kaiser Wilhelm and Crown Prince Wilhelm during some spectacular feat in the last days of the war. . . . Now [1922] I was about to go over into former enemy country and, what was worse, to concertize in it. In all of my publicity from that time onward I carefully omitted the fact that I had at one time been accepted for combat duty in the budding United States aviation (then attached to the Signal Corps), and it still does not appear in any encyclopedia of music or musical dictionary.[26]

Despite the hyperbole that infects his memoirs, there is no reason to doubt that Antheil was sincerely touched by the price, both physical and psychological, that Europe had paid during the Great War. This he made clear in a letter from London to his sponsor Mary Louise Curtis Bok in June 1922.

> "Our only hope is America. . . . Musically—creatively—Europe is exhausted. . . . The War—cataclysmal horror—has changed everything, all fundamentals. . . . This is a new world!"[27]

Although the impact upon Antheil of the period of catastrophe that had just ended was clear,[28] he was more interested in the challenges of the dawning new world than in reviewing the cataclysmic horror of the war. He had been watching the musical trade papers when in mid-February 1922 he saw a notice that the New York impresario Martin H. Hanson was leaving in late May for Europe. The same issue also contained an announcement that the provocative young Futurist pianist Leo Ornstein was leaving Hanson's management. Antheil put the two pieces of information together, realized that Hanson was undoubtedly looking for a replacement for Ornstein, and contacted him.

Antheil set out on a concert tour of Europe with the idea of making a name for himself, and with his *Airplane Sonata,* written just prior to his departure, he paid homage not only to the machine but to a daring new breed of warrior, with which he no doubt identified. W. H. R. Rivers, the British psychiatrist and expert on war neurosis who had treated Owen and Sassoon, had noted that among the soldiers he had observed, pilots had the fewest mental breakdowns. Moreover, unlike trench-bound troops, aviator warriors had a sense of bravado and control over their fate that preserved them from the sexual impotence associated with imposed passivity.[29]

Through the metaphor of the aviator and his craft Antheil looked forward to a future world that he felt would lie "in the vibration of its people. The environment of the machine has already become a spiritual thing. . . . For the great mass of us the war has killed illusion and sentimentality. Hence the birth of the Musico-Mechanists."[30] Like the Dadaists and the Futurists, Antheil announced that his musical domain would henceforth be limited to the banal, where former sentimentality would be replaced by the distortion of popular tunes or styles, and to the mechanistic, which he likened to a music unwinding in time. The *Airplane Sonata* actually incorporated elements of both, although Antheil understandably took pains to spotlight the mechanistic and to emphasize its firm edge. The tempo marking for the first movement, "To be played as fast as possible," underscored his intention to "begin with hard musical objects, perhaps simple banalities, so fast and unalterable that they are born hard as stone, indestructible fragments for all ages." Behind the obviously self-serving metaphors that implied the potential durability of his own creation stood a conviction that was clear enough: sentimentality was out.[31]

Antheil included an airplane propeller, visibly placed alongside a battery of pianos and percussion instruments, in his *Ballet mécanique* of 1924. He later claimed that he had not intended audiences to regard it as a perpetuation of his fascination with the airplane. Avowing that he wanted only the sound, not the sight, of the propeller, he admitted that it was a mistake to include it. He even went so far as to insist that, despite the work's title, he "had no idea of *copying* a machine directly down into music" and only wanted to celebrate the machine in a general aesthetic sense. But he also made the remarkable and revealing claim that the original title for his ballet had been "Message to Mars," which he rejected because he felt that it would have implied "all kinds of moralistic and mystic things."

Antheil decried what he called the misunderstanding of Arthur Honegger (who composed *Pacific 231* in 1923, which depicts the acceleration of a departing train and its return)[32] and Alexander Mosolov (*The Steel*

Foundry, from 1927), who thought that his ballet had been intended as a description of machinery and factories.

> Had they considered it purely as music (as, being musicians, they should have), they might have found it rather a "mechanistic" dance of life, or even a signal of these troubled and war-potential 1924 times placed in a rocket and shot to Mars. The words "Ballet Mécanique" were brutal, contemporary, hard-boiled, symbolic of the spiritual exhaustion, the superathletic, non-sentimental period commencing "The Long Armistice."[33]

Attempts by Ezra Pound to ally Antheil with the painter Wyndham Lewis's Vorticist movement and to separate him from the rudimentary practices of the Italian Futurists led Pound to announce that a "New Vorticist music would come from a new computation of the mathematics of harmony, not from the mimetic representation of dead cats in a fog horn (alias noise tuners)."[34] For all the hoopla, the projections and dreams came to naught, and both Europe and America soon tired of Antheil's shenanigans, of which there were plenty both in the concert hall and in his private life. A performance of *Ballet mécanique* in New York some years after its premiere was greeted almost with mock resistance: one member of the audience raised his cane, to which he had tied a white handkerchief, and the audience broke into laughter. American composer and critic Deems Taylor noted, "I don't know how *Ballet mécanique* ends. I am not even prepared to discuss its possible musical value; but I do know that as a comedy hit it was one of the biggest successes that ever played Carnegie Hall."

Comedy, of course, "was not what Antheil had in mind," as critic Joseph Fennimore has observed.[35] His audacious attempt to forge an avant-garde for America had fizzled. Indeed, the snickers and antics of the audience were virtually a predictable reaction to a jangling mechanism that suppressed sentiment and launched an assault on the nervous system for almost half an hour. Although performances of his "ballet" music in Paris and New York in 1926 and 1927 achieved a certain notoriety, his hoped-for "big success" as a composer never came, either in this mechanistic American reflection on Stravinsky's *Les noces* (which had premiered in 1923), or in those works with a potentially broader appeal like his "Jazz" Symphony of 1924 or his opera, *Transatlantic,* a cynical satire completed in 1928.[36] It was not long before his desperation for public acclaim led him to succumb to the lure of Neoclassicism in a piano concerto. In his attempt to capture the postwar period's sense of emotional exhaustion, he had, in the opinion of many, merely traded the faceless poundings of heavy machinery for the equally impersonal, if more refined, constructions of a music box.

Despite his failure to write a repertoire of pieces that would continue to be performed, Antheil caught the pulse of the post-Armistice era and left behind some remarkable signposts for the age. His awareness of the European avant-garde was complete, and he struggled diligently to be a part of it. Beyond the futuro-mechanistic stance that had been primed by the machines of war, however, he was also aware of the cachet he had as an American and of the special power that African American music exercised over the trend-setters of that period. A few years later, in Nancy Cunard's anthology *Negro* (1934), for which Antheil served as music editor, he confirmed his appreciation of the power of jazz in the post-Armistice period and his sense that it offered an American alternative to the prewar European avant-garde—a terrain where few American composers were prepared to compete. Antheil noted how even Stravinsky, described as "the greatest Slavic composer living" and prophet of the Great War in *Le Sacre du printemps,* had almost unwittingly capitulated to the lure of "American Negro musics" in a series of ragtime pieces of his own.[37]

Antheil's recognition of musicians like James Reese Europe and of music's unique capacity for prophecy in both a pre- and postwar society had been registered by others, but his specific comparison of jazz with Stravinsky's compositions was especially pointed. It was patently designed to promote a postwar realignment of power in the world of music and the special role that America was destined to play in it. America was riding high and with a new confidence; yet, for all the self-assurance that American popular music gave many American musicians, most composers knew that something was missing.

Had the Romantic Age finally expired with the war? Was Expressionism's haunting, if atonal, vision now destined to be tamed by a serial straitjacket? Were the new options to be limited principally to Futurist mechanics, Brechtian social engagement, and Neoclassicist pattern making? Americans seemed to suggest otherwise. Owing in some significant measure to the forces of its popular music, America exercised a kind of musical leadership in Europe in the 1920s and 1930s that was previously unimaginable. The American soldier had come home, but the American composer was soon to return to Europe in increasing numbers, especially to the American Academy in Rome, which offered its first prizes in 1921, and to the American School at Fontainebleau, which opened the next year. But like the young British literary group of the 1920s—W. H. Auden, Christopher Isherwood, and Stephen Spender—who were far more curious about a defeated Germany than a victorious France,[38] many American composers—including Copland, Cowell, and Sessions—also traveled to Berlin and Vienna. They made the journey not so much to face a long-delayed challenge head-on or to take up where the European prewar avant-garde had left off as to learn about their options and, subsequently, to map out a new alternative for the road that lay ahead.[39]

22 The Persistence of Memory

Memory is the enemy of ephemeral politicians and the natural ally of historians and artists . . . but collective amnesia is always the creature of trauma.

> David Drew, notes for *Testimonies of War*

In memory everything seems to happen to music.

> Tennessee Williams, *The Glass Menagerie*

In October 1916 Ravel wrote a friend that he had just read Alain-Fournier's novel *Le grand Meaulnes* (1913), and later he spoke of composing a concerto either for piano or cello based upon it.[1] Although nothing ever came of the idea, Ravel had once again confirmed his belief in the capacity of textless instrumental structures to support a narrative. Further evidence of his attraction to writing seemingly abstract music to a literary subtext soon emerged with the commission in 1918 by the Italian poet Ricciotto Canudo of a preface to his *S.P. 503, Le poème du Vardar*. Ultimately published together with Canudo's *Sonate à Salonique* in 1923,[2] Ravel's piece appeared initially in 1919 in a journal, *Les feuillets d'art*, with an excerpt from *S.P. 503*.[3]

Ravel had known Canudo in Paris at least from 1905, where in the prewar years the Italian poet had been editor of the avant-garde literary journal *Montjoie!* Canudo was renowned for his views on numerous subjects including war, poetry, and the philosophical role of music. Poetry and music were one to Canudo because both used a notation that was not the essence of the work but was rather a mechanism for what he called the ultimate rhythmicization of the air for the duration of a single performance.[4] His insistence upon the intrinsic connection between words and music remained fundamental throughout his life, and his first book, *An Exegetic Vision of the Ninth Symphony of Beethoven*, reflects not only the power of the Beethoven cult at the time but his contention that a comprehensive worldview could be laid out according to the structure of a four-movement symphony. In *Music as a Religion of the Future* (1913) he had also explored the promise of a Cult of Music for the whole world.[5]

TWILIGHT IN BELGRADE: RAVEL'S *FRONTISPICE*

Ravel's response to Canudo's commission was an extraordinary piece for piano that incorporates obvious number symbolism based on the numerals 5 and 3, which Ravel drew from the title of Canudo's poem. *Frontispice*, Ravel's first post-Armistice composition, is a work for five hands, three players. It is composed on five staves and in fifteen measures (5×3), using a 15/8 time signature (which is beamed as five groups of three eighth notes but is actually composed of three statements of a five-note pattern)[6] and a five-measure coda (in which both parts share a common quintuple metric designation).[7]

What is the import of 5 and 3? Notwithstanding the fact that Johannes Kepler had been wise enough to assert that there was a problem inherent in all numerology because it was *ad hoc,* mystics have always been on the lookout for the hidden message of numbers. It has also been noted that in times of chaos the interest in numerology escalates.[8] Canudo's *S.P. 503, Le poème du Vardar* was essentially a philosophical rumination on experiences during the Great War, and the poem's affinity with number is openly heralded in its title—S.P. 503 is the postal sector for Canudo's combat division in the Vardar region of southern Serbia (Macedonia). A decisive battle against the Bulgarian army took place in this very area in September 1918, and the Allied victory there was pivotal for the ultimate conquest of Belgrade, which led to the signing of the Armistice of Salonika and the end of the war in the Balkans. Canudo was engaged in this campaign from 1915 to mid-1918, although he missed its successful conclusion, by which time he was convalescing in Paris. There Picasso painted Canudo in a *zouave* soldier's uniform (fig. 40), capturing him in a role that the poet had already proudly advertised by using "Capitaine Ricciotto Canudo" on the title page of his book *Combats d'Orient* (1915–1916).[9]

Beyond the factual chronology and the title, Canudo's poem imparts other information that is essential for an understanding of Ravel's contribution. When Ravel's *Frontispice* first appeared in *Les feuillets d'art* in 1919 it appeared with "Sonate pour un jet d'eau," the excerpt from *S.P. 503,* and it was preceded by a fanciful lithograph of spraying fountains. Canudo, who claimed a formal association with music for the poem, divided it into four movements.[10] He made this orientation toward musical analogies explicit in 1919.

> Concerning my *Poème du Vardar, S. P. 503,* I would say that I apply the
> most important of the purely musical forms to the construction of cer-

Figure 40.   Pablo Picasso, *Portrait of Ricciotto Canudo in Uniform*, 1918. (Photo courtesy of The Museum of Modern Art, New York; acquired through the Lillie P. Bliss Bequest. © 2002 Estate of Pablo Picasso/ARS New York.)

tain poems (see the "Sonata for a Water Jet" IN THE MANNER OF A FUGUE, already published in *Les feuillets d'art*). And the "Preface" of the poem is a musical frontispiece, an unpublished page of music by Maurice Ravel. Only music has the right to set the atmosphere of a Poem.[11]

Ravel's piece is not a fugue, but its layering is crystal clear, with each of the five highly independent voices entering one by one, and it is explicitly symbolic. Each exposes a pattern that either repeats or is strictly limited with respect to pitch, range, and rhythm (ex. 14).[12] The fifth and last voice

Example 14.   Maurice Ravel, *Frontispice*, page 8. (© 1975 Salabert; reproduced by permission.)

to enter (appearing on the top staff) sounds like a bird trapped in a repetitive song, chirping obsessively but quietly above an undulating firmament. It is a wounded cousin of *oiseaux tristes* that Ravel had evoked more than a decade before in *Miroirs* and more recently and serenely in the "Trois beaux oiseaux du Paradis" for chorus.[13] At the conclusion of *Frontispice* the tonally directionless lower ostinati of Ravel's Infernal Machine are abandoned, the perseverant bird on the top staff is silenced, and the four principal hands coalesce briefly in an unexpected chordal hymn that rises and gradually swells before dissolving in a distant echo (CD track 17).

In "Sonate pour un jet d'eau" Canudo speaks of water spouts, but contrary to expectations promoted by the accompanying lithograph, they are far removed from the world of Ravel's "Jeux d'eau." Rather, the poet tells us, they recall Moses striking the rock whence gushes forth a flow of water, which now turns into blood. In *Combats d'Orient* Canudo had written of the river Vardar at the moment when his troops were in retreat, especially of the strange, luminous beauty of its banks, whose "broad line of liquid light led us, as if we were walking along a road of mirages."[14] For Canudo the moment was characterized by the aimless, repetitive wandering of armed forces in total disorientation. With the portrayal of Moses striking the rock, Canudo cast the scene as a metaphor for the Children of Israel who aimlessly wandered the desert for forty years. The locus is likened to a Macedonian furnace, and the soldiers, digging in, toil desperately at the soil: "We pushed aside its flesh to make trenches in it for us, sex and womb, for this place swallows our virility."[15] All of the imagery of the poem is that of the battlefield. Water is powerless to quench the roaring fires of war; the Vardar, turning red, becomes the symbol of the senseless flow of blood from slaughtered youth.

In Ravel's composition the implacability of nature is mirrored in the numbing circularity of Ravel's five repetitive figures, whose collective impotence matches the soldiers' existence in the trenches, where life is devoid of all hope, all passion. Just as Debussy's *Berceuse héroïque* served as the proving ground for *En blanc et noir,* and just as Stravinsky's keyboard march in *Three Easy Pieces* prepared the way for *Histoire du soldat,* so Ravel's five-hand *Frontispice* served as something more than a symbolic introduction to a war poem by Canudo. A work whose place of publication signals that it was never intended for performance and whose mechanically intransigent ostinati may best be realized on a pianola,[16] as Rex Lawson has suggested, *Frontispice* was a clandestine probe prior to a final series of postwar assessments. In 1919, the year in which *Frontispice* appeared in an out-of-the-way journal where few musicians would ever see it, Ravel not only began composing *La valse*—the bittersweet memory of an empire that had collapsed—but also made a personal journey to Vienna.

TWILIGHT IN VIENNA: *LA VALSE*

In 1916 a National League for the Defense of French Music was formed with the purpose of banning the performance of all music by German and Austrian composers that was not yet in the public domain. Numerous senior colleagues, including d'Indy and Saint-Saëns, had signed the league's notice, but Ravel balked, stating his objections in a closely considered reply to the committee dated 7 June 1916. He lauded the league's "obsession with the triumph of our fatherland," adding that his own feeling of a "need for action" had prompted him to give up civilian life, although nothing had compelled him to do so. Following a protracted argument against the league's position that asserted that "the role of the art of music is economic and social," he announced that he felt there was no need for France to prohibit the public performance of contemporary German and Austrian works: "It would even be dangerous for French composers to ignore systematically the productions of their foreign colleagues, and thus form themselves into a sort of national coterie: our musical art, which is so rich at the present time, would soon degenerate, becoming isolated in banal formulas."

Ravel went on to stress the importance of Schoenberg and the unmistakable Hungarian qualities of Bela Bartók and Zoltán Kodály.[17] He considered Strauss to be the only composer of the first rank in Germany, but he also allowed that some young artists of interest might soon be discovered. "I do not believe it necessary to have all French music, of whatever value, predominate in France and [be] propagated abroad," he concluded. "You will observe, Gentlemen, that our views are frequently so disparate, that it is impossible for me to join your organization. I hope nevertheless to continue to 'act as a Frenchman,' and to 'count myself among those who wish to remember.'"[18]

Writing to Jean Marnold on 24 June 1916, Ravel relayed the curt reply that he had received from the president of the league:

> "I am delighted to learn just how much you appreciate the 'important value' of the musician Schoenberg, and the 'savor' of Messieurs Bartók, Kodály, and their disciples. The National League will be there, at the opportune moment, to warn of your admiration in exchange for an eventual sacrifice, which would be most painful for the public, of your own music."[19]

Ravel momentarily worried that his own letter might be extracted and used as negative publicity by the organization, but he ultimately concluded that even if published it would probably be ignored altogether. Ravel's latter suspicion proved correct, for in spite of the numerous luminaries who lent their name to the cause, the National League floundered and ultimately failed in its campaign.[20] During the first season following the Armistice Ravel pointedly applauded the music of Wagner in a concert performed in Paris at the Tuileries in June 1919.[21]

That was not the end of the German question, however. In March 1918 Cocteau had announced that he was dedicating his *Le coq et l'arlequin* to the composer Georges Auric (only, he said, because he had already dedicated *Le cap de Bonne-Espérance* to his aviator friend Roland Garros). He also called Schoenberg a master but a "blackboard musician," praised Satie, equivocated on Debussy and Stravinsky, and warned against Wagner and the "Russian trap."

> When I speak of the "Russian trap" or "Russian influence," I do not mean by that that I despise Russian music. Russian music is admirable because it is Russian music. Russian-French music or German-French music is necessarily bastard, even if it be inspired by a Moussorgsky, a Stravinsky, a Wagner, or a Schoenberg. The music I want must be French, of France.[22]

Such exclusionary perspectives provide essential background for an understanding of Ravel's postwar posture, for at the end of the war Ravel, in a telling retort, turned directly to that portion of the German-Austrian culture that he had always admired by composing *La valse* (1919–1920). Some years before, in 1911, he had disclosed his affection for Viennese culture, and specifically for the music of Franz Schubert, in his *Valses nobles et sentimentales*. Elegant and stylized, they convey not a hint of anxiety. But in *La valse* a different perspective is announced right from the opening measures. It is an orchestral tour-de-force that not only invites but also virtually demands an interpretation in accord with the political and moral climate of the times.

Here Ravel portrays the ultimate collapse of Vienna's dance signature in a whirlwind of motion that carries an enormous psychological impact. Although "atonality," the apparent keystone to any definition of Viennese Expressionism, is missing, the original model of the waltz and Ravel's attendant harmonic, coloristic, and phraseological distortion nonetheless exhibit overtly Expressionist overtones.[23] Ravel's murky beginning leads, in the composer's own words, to a "fantastic and fatal whirling." This is particularly audible in the closing measures of the composition, where the music attains a kind of vertigo that approaches hysteria and that, for all its tonal base, seems to signal the collapse of a national psyche. The basic sentiment of *La valse* is not anti-German. It speaks, rather, of the disorientation that flourished in the aftermath of the war and in a poignant way testifies to the sorrow over the final dissolution of the Austro-Hungarian Empire.

Ravel's hope that the collapse of empire did not necessarily signal the final disappearance of its musical culture was soon made abundantly clear. In 1920 he went to Vienna on a concert tour, sponsored by the French embassy, that comprised two concerts of his music on October 22 and 25 as well as a third concert on October 23, which was additionally sponsored by Schoenberg's Verein für musikalische Privataufführungen in Wien.[24] The last program, in which Ravel's works were interlaced with compositions by Schoenberg, Berg, and Webern, included a performance of *La valse* in a four-hand transcription played by Alfredo Casella and the composer.[25]

In later concerts of the Verein, Ravel's *Gaspard de la nuit* was repeatedly programmed by Edward Steuermann, who also added the aesthetically and symbolically different, although equally demanding, *Le tombeau de Couperin*. Ravel, in kind, sponsored the performance of Berg's pieces for clarinet and piano, opus 5, on his return to Paris. Then, in 1928, Ravel stated with rare candor that "I am quite conscious of the fact that my *Chansons madécasses* are in no way Schoenbergian, but I do not know whether I ever should have been able to write them had Schoenberg never written."[26] Although he was not blind to what he saw as Schoenberg's fear of charm—which, Ravel noted, "he avoids to the point of asceticism and martyrdom"[27]—the Frenchman openly acknowledged the catalytic presence of a master.

No doubt Ravel's welcome reception in Vienna further dissipated whatever residual bias against Austro-Germany that he may have harbored and could only have buoyed his sentiments regarding the separation of art from politics. Even before his departure for Vienna, Ravel had surprisingly refused a nomination as chevalier of the Légion d'Honneur out of these mounting concerns. This was the same honor that had been accorded to Edith Wharton in 1916 for her contribution to the war effort, and the tendering of it to Ravel in 1920 was obviously meant to express the nation's gratitude for his numerous contributions, both musical and personal, during the nation's darkest hours. Ravel's name had been submitted by the minister of education after having been assured by a friend that it would be accepted. Ravel learned of his nomination only through the press on 15 January 1920, however, and he was stunned.

Perhaps still harboring resentment against an officialdom that had refused him the Prix de Rome on five occasions as a student, Ravel now declined to be honored for his wartime contributions,[28] but was dismayed when the press began to take sides. Many supported Ravel's position, but not everyone in France was sympathetic to what some regarded as an ungrateful refusal. Satie, whose *Trois valses distinguées du précieux dégoûté* (1914) has been seen as a gentle parody of Ravel's *Valses nobles et sentimentales*[29] and whose feelings toward his more illustrious compatriot had become increasingly fickle, now offered the unambiguously caustic remark that "Ravel rejects the Legion of Honor, but his music accepts it."

This most recent *affaire Ravel* may account in some degree for Diaghilev's curious dismissal of *La valse* when he heard the new score in Misia Sert's home in Paris in the spring of 1920, prior to Ravel's journey to Vienna. It occurred in the presence of Massine, Poulenc, and Stravinsky. According to Poulenc's eyewitness account, when Marcelle Meyer and Ravel began to perform the ballet in a two-piano version Diaghilev immediately began to fidget and to show signs of perplexity. When Ravel and Meyer finished, Diaghilev spoke: "Ravel, it is a masterpiece . . . but it is not a ballet. . . . It is the portrait of a ballet." Remarkably, Stravinsky remained silent. Poulenc, only twenty-two at the time, was flabbergasted, but he then witnessed what he claimed served as a model of modesty for the rest of his life.

Ravel picked up his music, tucked it under his arm, and without giving any indication of his thoughts calmly departed.[30]

What could account for this reaction to *La valse*? Remembering that Ravel had initially envisioned calling the work "Wien," could it have been that its Viennese connotations were the source of his audience's anxiety? Had news of Ravel's upcoming concerts in Vienna, which could only have been interpreted as a further attempt at rapprochement between the musical cultures of France and the Austro-German Empire, started to circulate? Had his snub of the Légion d'Honneur underscored this impression? Or, in light of the glut of waltzes composed in a caricature or dry-point *enfantine* style by Satie and Stravinsky during the war years,[31] had Ravel's grand, even grandiloquent, *La valse* brought a burgeoning aesthetic issue to a surprising showdown? Ravel's claim in 1922 that placing the story of his ballet in 1855 precluded the assignment of symbolic meaning to *La valse* in the present was clear enough as a tactic, but in light of the evidence, it does not wash.[32] In any event, it was not the composer's last statement on the tragedy of the Great War, for at the end of the 1920s Ravel's reflections on the issue would be further clarified in the most dramatic and politically charged work he ever penned, the Piano Concerto for the Left Hand.[33]

RE-EVALUATING NATIONAL HISTORIES

Between the premiere of *La valse* in December 1920 and the composer's two piano concertos, which were written at the end of the decade, the search for a new set of options in a postwar world increasingly claimed attention. Already, in the very month that Ravel unveiled his Viennese portrait, Julien Tiersot, librarian of the Paris Conservatoire and renowned historian of the French Revolution and France's folk music, addressed an issue that was on the minds of many of his compatriots: "French Music after the War."[34]

It was foreseeable that Tiersot would review the Wagner question at length, for during the war more than one critic had argued that it was Wagner's music more than any other that had virtually defined the meaning of the word *boche* for the French. When after the Armistice Wagner was once more acknowledged by the Parisian public, it was not because the French people had forgotten the war, Tiersot argued, but because they took sensual pleasure in listening to beautiful music. Escaping Wagner's influence was one thing, he said, but what was needed was a postwar art that signaled the definable genius of a nation, one that could be distinguished from what many saw as the variegated anomalies of the prewar period. In Tiersot's view the anxious search for an exclusively French diction had led many to concoct an art that existed only in the imagination, and he judged the struggle to fix parallels between France's historic past and the present day, as between Rameau and Debussy, to be patently idealistic. He even went so far as to suggest that Debussy, far from having escaped the influence of Wagner, was probably destined to be considered as the last stage of that influence—a notion that coincidentally meshed with some of the recent pronouncements of Cocteau and company.

Although Cocteau argued that he was not against Debussy, only Debussyisme, on a recording accompanied by the Dan Parrish jazz orchestra made as late as 1929 Cocteau could be heard reciting his own text which asserted the necessity of reclaiming the past through an imaginary return to the age of the Golden Fleece ("Toison d'or").[35] Whether his reference was to Jason and the Argonauts or to the order established by Philip the Good of Burgundy in 1430, it would have been difficult for a connoisseur to ignore the implication, however sly, that Debussy, the composer of "Poissons d'or" (Goldfish, 1907), had failed to provide a suitable foundation for the musical future of France.[36]

What such a basis might be was not clear, but in the quest for its identification the impresario-performer Jean Wiéner had begun to explore the possibilities of interface between high and low as well as domestic and foreign musical idioms in a series of concerts from 1921 to 1925. Hoping to succeed where the Dadaists had failed, Wiéner showcased the jazz orchestra of Billy Arnold alongside a player-piano rendition of *Le sacre* and standard performances of works by Milhaud, Satie, Schoenberg, Webern, and the Czech composer Alois Hába in a series of concerts during the 1921–1922 season.[37] Setting aside all notions of "authenticity," he even embraced the idea that American jazz "could be performed by the French as French expression."[38] It was a perspective to which the originators of jazz had already subscribed in reverse with their borrowings from an international repertoire. Furthermore, it was a viewpoint Milhaud had sanctioned when he wrote his jazz ballet *La création du monde* in 1923—a work that, beyond its Parisian Primitivist trappings, carried contemporary and unmistakable American implications for the restructuring of a postwar world.[39]

While Milhaud's younger generation of composers, who had rallied under the banner of Les Six, was somewhat raucously advertising France's role in a new world order, the slightly older generation was left to contemplate the gravity and meaning of the Great War for the future. Ravel, recently turned forty-five, had seen it all. Although he was to wait another decade before setting down his deepest reflections on the matter, he would in essence agree with the notion that it was not only possible to mix the muses and thoroughly permissible for American jazz to be given a French inflection, but that such mutations need not result in a diluted or frivolous account. Indeed, more than one French composer came to argue that such hybrids were capable of carrying an unmistakable accent with an individuality and authenticity all their own.

Another part of the paradoxical mix was provided by historical models, including German ones. Just as Stravinsky set about resurrecting Bach and Beethoven, Ravel moved toward Mozart and increasingly away from Couperin, Janequin, and other early French composers with an almost intoxicating compulsion. In his devotion to Mozart Ravel was joined in the first postwar decade by Stravinsky, Poulenc, and numerous other Allied musicians, for whom the Salzburg musician was the quintessential Italo-German. Here was historical proof of the possibility of a marriage of cultures at the highest level, dreamed of by so many critics and composers in recent years.

Not all German and Viennese music was embraced, however. Like Stravinsky, Ravel had been schooled on an overdose of Beethoven, but unlike him he was not about to reevaluate.[40] In a tone that was overtly mean-spirited he even referred to Beethoven as "le grand sourd" (the great deaf one), and when writing to Mme. Casella following a performance by her husband of the *Sonatine* in Rome, Ravel spoke caustically of an anticipated success for a planned opus 111 of his own—he said he would write the earlier opus numbers later![41] Ravel's most overt feelings about Beethoven's gravitas, however, were imperiously inserted in *La valse*, where the opening motto (_. _) from the Scherzo to Beethoven's Ninth Symphony is repeatedly and pitch specifically recalled.[42]

Ravel was obviously mindful of the complex and sometimes competing subtleties that had accumulated around the concepts of *patrie* and classicism. Uncompromisingly proud of his French legacy, he nonetheless became increasingly offended by the nationalist polemic that pitted French against German art during the dark war years. With his "Piano Concerto for the Left Hand," written more than a decade after the cessation of hostilities, Ravel finally addressed the issue directly and confirmed a judgment made by Jung in 1926 that "the war, which in the outer world had taken place some years before, was not yet over, but was continuing to be fought within the psyche."[43]

A CONCERTO FOR THE LEFT HAND

Writing to Vaughan Williams in September 1919, Ravel reported that he was due to travel to England during the next season but concluded, "I think that it is preferable that I work, if I am still capable of it."[44] Although establishing something resembling a prewar schedule was a high priority for most people, daily life was filled with constant reminders that things were not the same. The war had ended, but the specter of the mutilated soldier was to haunt France for decades, first in the victory parade down the Champs-Élysées on Bastille Day 1919, when armless, legless, eyeless, and heavily bandaged soldiers limped on crutches or were carried in carts before the French populace, then as these men attempted to fit into the postwar society and later through continuing reminders of their presence in daily life, in war fiction, and in film.

Perhaps no composer was more stunned by these reminders than Maurice Ravel. He regularly resisted blindly nationalist perspectives when it came to musical judgments, however, a conviction evidenced by his positive assessment of American symphony orchestras made during a tour of the United States in early 1928. "Your brass have the depth and richness of color which we lack, not only because the instruments are of superior quality but because the first desk players are of German origin," he was quoted as having told *The New York Times* on 26 February. "They therefore obtain a nobility of sound of which the musicians of other countries are only rarely capable. And when we hear a trumpet, it is not a *cornet à piston*. On the other hand your woodwinds are for the most part French, which are the best in the world!"[45] Two days previously he had spoken to a reporter for the same newspaper about America's concern over the development of a national musical identity—an issue he himself had had to face as a composer. Stating that he felt an artist had to be cosmopolitan in his judgments but irreducibly national when it came to the creative act, he said,

> I think that you know that I admire your jazz enormously and hold it in the highest respect—no doubt even more than the majority of American composers. But (even when using this American style in my *Sonata for Violin*) my music manner remains clearly French, even for the least informed listeners. I anticipate that more Americans will become engrossed with their popular sources.[46]

It was a perspective that Ravel was to develop in greater detail on 7 April, some weeks later, in a lecture delivered at a conference at Rice Institute in Houston.

The sum of these observations seemed to indicate that musicians were now addressing more general postwar issues of national identity and cultural interface, and that the pain of the war years had been completely put aside. Ravel's "Piano Concerto for the Left Hand" protests otherwise, however, and it provides poignant testimony to the power of art to function as a repository of cultural memory.[47] Begun in 1929 and completed the next year, Ravel's concerto was written for the Austrian pianist Paul Wittgenstein, brother of the philosopher Ludwig Wittgenstein and pupil of Theodor Leschetizky, who had lost his right arm at the Russian front at the age of thirty. The symbolism was consequently even more powerful than it would have been had Ravel dedicated the concerto to a French or an Allied soldier wounded in the Battle of the Somme. From the time of its world premiere in Vienna on 27 November 1931 and its Parisian debut a year later on 17 January 1933, with the composer conducting,[48] the concerto made an unforgettable visual and aural imprint upon audiences. Even though its first performances were more than a decade removed from the Armistice, the concerto was an unmistakable tribute to all the *mutilés de guerre*.[49]

It seems almost irrelevant to recount that musical etudes for the left hand by Saint-Saëns, Godowsky, Skriabin, Carl Czerny, and Charles-Valentin Alkan were sought out by Ravel as he prepared to write the concerto, for, despite its formidable technical challenges, the concerto clearly transcended the construction of an exercise.[50] Beyond whatever diverse musical sources may have been brought to bear to portray the trauma of a postwar society, the solo protagonist was a poignant visual reminder.

Ravel claimed a pluralistic inspiration for the concerto and wrote on one of the autograph scores that it had been composed under the influence of *"musae mixtatiae,"* or mixed muses, and the thematic use of blue notes and syncopation in the solemn introduction and later in the scherzo are unmistakably derived from American jazz. Ravel, like many of his countrymen, had by the 1920s totally capitulated to the charms of American popular music.[51] Once again Ravel had shown the way to a new, even revolutionary, classicism through a daring synthesis.[52]

Fueled by the ragtime syncopations of James Reese Europe's uniformed Hellfighters and the black jazz ensembles that played the nightclubs in the postwar period, western Europe's recognition of American jazz following the Armistice led to its coronation not only as a vital force in its own right but also as a potential influence in the concert hall. Gershwin and Ravel had become personal friends in the late 1920s, and signs of Ravel's attraction to Gershwin's music are especially obvious in the contemporaneously written

Piano Concerto in G Major, where numerous passages could almost have been written by the American.

A totally different perspective dominates the Concerto for the Left Hand, however. In its eerie beginning a spectral vision unfolds in the lower registers of brass and the contra-bassoon in the manner of *La valse*. The gradual dispersion of the murky atmosphere, the escalating flashes of color in the brass, and the steady ascension from the deepest registers of the orchestra finally lead to an explosive entry by the piano, which then embarks on an extended solo cadenza that asserts the power and authority of the maimed protagonist. The drama of the opening accrues not from the entrance of the piano after an orchestral exposition, in the manner of a classic concerto, but from the calculated and psychologically potent delay of the soloist's entrance, a technique Ravel had used in the *Tzigane* (1924) for violin and piano and the second of the *Trois poèmes de Stéphane Mallarmé* (1913). It is one of the most spectacular openings in the entire concerto literature and surely the most dramatic to come from the pen of Ravel. Henry Prunières, speaking of the first performance in Paris, noted this fact immediately: "From the opening measures," he said, "we are plunged into a world to which Ravel has but rarely introduced us."[53]

For friends of the cinema at the time, the protracted gloom of the introduction followed by the sudden appearance of the left hand in a rising burst of self-acclamation could readily have suggested the slain soldiers in Abel Gance's film *J'accuse* of 1918–1919, who gradually rise from the grave and with gathering momentum march to the village square in a protest against all future wars.[54] Although Ravel never spoke of a specific program behind this concerto, the fact that he wrote it expressly for an enemy pianist who had lost his right arm in battle made further explanation on the part of the composer unnecessary.

Adapting the traditional multimovement concerto to a first-movement sonata design, Ravel took the initial material of his exposition from the opening cadenza. With the arrival of the development section shortly thereafter, virulent and obsessive march rhythms force their way to the fore and dominate the proceedings for the next fifty printed pages of a ninety-seven-page score. It is precisely in these harrowing pages that Ravel compromises his French identity with the injection—alongside potentially triumphant march rhythms—of a profusion of "smeared" blue notes clearly borrowed from American vernacular sources. In this juxtaposition the composer compellingly emphasizes the manic-depressive character of his concerto and its dual national sponsorship.

The recapitulation, prepared by a few measures of accelerando that are abruptly cut off and announced by the first tempo change since the onset of the march, occurs precisely at Ravel's orchestral rehearsal number forty-six.[55] This may or may not relate to Berg's obsessive fixation on the prime number twenty-three, of which it is a multiple, but it does suggest that the perennial specter of numerology may have been significant in the concerto's composition.[56] Berg's reaction had been a response to the mysterious properties of such numbers, recently detailed by the Viennese psychiatrist Wilhelm Fliess, and Ravel may well have encountered this number cult on his trip to Vienna in 1920. Above all, the conspicuous numerology of Ravel's previous *Frontispice* suggests that the composer would have been susceptible to it, especially in light of the concerto's Viennese dedicatee.

Whether or not the location had occult significance, the reprise leads to another solo cadenza equal in length and virtuosity to the opening one, and the work is brought to a conclusion with a dazzling coda. In these closing pages Ravel's heady mixture coalesces in a triumphant blaze that suggests the film footage of the victory march down the Champs-Élysées on 14 July 1919, which appeared in Gance's *J'accuse*. There the wounded lead the parade as the army of the dead march above, *au dessus de la mêlée*.[57] Tellingly, the film had been produced with the assistance of Swiss writer Blaise Cendrars, who was Gance's friend and who had lost his right arm in the conflict.[58]

Like so many novelists, poets, and painters, Ravel had registered a delayed reaction to the ravages of war, and the work's dedication to an Austrian soldier who had lost his right arm in combat removed any doubt as to its message. Unlike the lonely fifth hand of his *Frontispice*, however, the single hand of the concerto was no longer a *"oiseau triste du Paradis"* consigned to a barren landscape, but a powerful symbol of human despair and survival that transcended national identity. It was a symbol that resurfaced in a series of works commissioned by Wittgenstein for the left hand throughout the 1920s and 1930s from Prokofiev, Britten, Strauss, Hindemith, Erich Korngold, Franz Schmidt, and others.[59]

What a bitter irony it is that the last images that we have of Ravel are drawings made following the brain surgery that led to his death in 1937. Although they were executed many years after his near disastrous forays in a military truck at the front, they eerily resemble, and symbolically stand alongside, Picasso's portrait of a wounded and trepanned Guillaume Apollinaire, who died of influenza two days after the Armistice was signed.[60]

Erich Maria Remarque saw front-line action in Flanders in June 1917, and it was from this experience that flowed the most renowned of post-war novels, *All Quiet on the Western Front*. Published in January 1929, co-incidentally just as Ravel was about to commence his "Concerto for the Left Hand," it was a similarly delayed reaction that followed a period of malaise and contemplated suicide. Realizing that memories of the war were the source of his ills, Remarque wrote the novel as a cathartic experience, a fact that he made clear in the preface: "This book is to be neither an accusation nor a confession, and least of all an adventure. . . . It will try simply to tell of a generation of men who, even though they may have escaped its shells, were destroyed by the war."[61] These words could easily have been appended to Ravel's new concerto were it not for the work's triumphant finale.

In March 1931, with the concerto now completed, Ravel was asked by an interviewer what his plans were for the future. He responded that he had been thinking about doing an opera based on *Jeanne d'Arc*, the popular novel by Joseph Delteil (which had also served as the initial inspiration for Carl Dreyer's silent film masterpiece, *La passion de Jeanne d'Arc*, 1928).[62] The following July Ravel confirmed for Calvocoressi his plans for the lyric drama, noting that for the moment he had put it aside in order to complete his Piano Concerto in G Major, which he was obliged to finish by November.[63] In October of that year he was even more explicit about the project, admitting that nothing had yet been written but that he was trying to establish an outline since he had it in mind to write his own libretto. According to his violinist friend Hélène Jourdan-Morhange, Ravel planned to introduce both "Tipperary," "Madelon," and "La Marseillaise" during the battle of Orléans—anachronisms "à la Bernard Shaw," whose *Joan of Arc* had captivated Ravel. The work would include scenes revolving around Joan and her sheep, the court, her meeting with the king, the siege and capture of Orléans, and Joan at the stake. Ravel noted that the completed work would be an opera à la Meyerbeer,[64] but his description pointed instead to the battlefields of Debussy's *La boîte à joujoux*.[65]

The fact that both Debussy and Ravel died amid plans for a work based upon the life and example of Joan of Arc summarizes with remarkable clarity the importance of France's prerevolutionary history for the period of the Great War. Following her canonization in 1920 Joan's continuing appeal was manifested in works by Honegger, Shaw, Brecht, and Claudel. In a way that the familiar national figure of Marianne could not, the Maid of Orleans, as both Schiller and Tchaikovsky had previously realized, cut across social, political, and religious lines and, perhaps more than any other figure, symbolized the historical ideal of moral stalwartness at a moment of both personal and national crisis. If by the end of the century many such interwar forms of commemoration had lost their resonance and had become "the stuff of history,"[66] a review of the dynamic attendant to their creation offers retrospective confirmation of the range of music's sources during the Great War.

23   Prophecies and Alarms

Ancestral voices prophesying war!
Samuel Taylor Coleridge,
Kubla Khan

Paul Hindemith's father had been killed in action in 1915, and his son, conscripted in August 1917 at twenty-two years of age, now determined that the only way to deal with the personal catastrophe brought on by war was to immerse himself in composition. Although at one point Hindemith was within a mile and a half of the front, he continued to compose regularly and was fortunate enough to form a string quartet—an action that allowed him to continue developing his skills as a violinist as well as his knowledge of the chamber repertoire (fig. 41).[1]

Serendipitously, Hindemith's immediate superior was both a great music lover and an admirer of French culture, and he made known his desire to hear a performance of Debussy's string quartet.[2] In due course Hindemith's ensemble arranged a private reading that was uncannily interrupted at the end of the slow movement by an officer who informed them that he had just heard an announcement on the radio that Debussy had died. The effect of this message was profound, as Hindemith later revealed.

> We did not play on to the end. It was as though our performance had been robbed of the breath of life. We felt here for the first time that music is more than style, technique, and the expression of personal feelings. Music reached out beyond all political boundaries, beyond national hatred and the horrors of war, and it became clearer than ever to me in what direction music had to develop.[3]

Following discharge from the army early in 1919 and a period of economic collapse and political crisis in Germany, Hindemith flirted with the alternatives in a trio of operas.[4] One of them, *Das Nusch-Nuschi*, mixed the traditions of Burmese marionette theater with Expressionism as a means of wrestling with the question of war.[5] Then, in the first of a series

Figure 41.   Paul Hindemith, far left, playing first violin in an army
string quartet.

of works labeled *Kammermusik* (1921) Hindemith lampooned the very category of chamber music and the audience alike. Performance directions in-
struct the performers to remain out of sight; the instrumentation, which includes accordion, trumpet, and percussion, flirts with jazz and the cabaret,
and in the finale, which includes a foxtrot, Hindemith advertised his awareness not only of American popular styles but also of the Futurists by ending the work with a siren (thus beating Antheil and Varèse to the punch).
More important, this new "chamber music" was preparation for an eventual turn to the clarifications prescribed by the *Neue Sachlichkeit*, or New
Objectivity, an aesthetic rooted in the rejection of Expressionism and championed by such artists as Max Beckmann, Otto Dix, and George Grosz.[6]

TRIPTYCHS: GRÜNEWALD, DIX, AND HINDEMITH

In retrospect it is clear that the 1920s was the crucial decade for Hindemith's development, with the sonatas, concertos, variations, and fugues
that he wrote in profusion during this period increasingly serving as his
own private "call to order." At the same time, Hindemith could not completely sidestep the search for identification with his native Germany. He
had lived through the war and served in the army, and the immediate postwar Dadaist escape could go only so far. As with Ravel, his most important
testimony to the role of the artist in time of political turmoil did not come
until the beginning of the next decade, when he wrote his opera *Mathis der
Maler* (1934). The opera focuses on the story of Matthias Grünewald, a Re-

naissance painter and reluctant participant in the Peasants' Revolt at the end of the first quarter of the sixteenth century, who ultimately renounces politics for his art, yet can find no exit from his despair. The ultimate message of the opera is that an artist's betrayal of his gifts in the name of political activism is socially irresponsible, and it consequently points to Hindemith's repudiation of his previous engagement with Brechtian themes in a series of sociopolitical *Zeitopern* and virtually forecasts his flight to America in 1940.

Known today primarily as a three-movement symphony that was in the main extracted from his opera of the same name, Hindemith's *Mathis der Maler* makes direct reference to one of Germany's greatest national treasures, Grünewald's altarpiece for the Antonite monastery at Isenheim in southern Alsace (fig. 42).[7] The Isenheim altarpiece, painted in 1515, had miraculously escaped destruction during the Reformation, but the rampant vandalism of the French Revolution had led to its being put in storage in the library at Colmar, France, in 1794. It was returned to public display in the same city in 1853,[8] and improved transportation, journalism, and photography, plus the interest shown by painter Arnold Böcklin, brought escalating attention to Grünewald's masterpiece.

At the outbreak of World War I Max Beckmann, now serving in the German army, was sufficiently concerned for this national treasure that he contacted authorities about the possibility of storing the altarpiece in the Kaiser-Friedrich-Museum in Berlin. With the entrance of the United States into the war in 1917 and the increasing focus of conflict on the Western Front, including the regions of Alsace and Lorraine, the Isenheim altarpiece was relocated for the second time in its history to the Alte Pinakothek in Munich. During this period further renown accrued to the altarpiece through the interest shown by such German literary figures as Rainer Maria Rilke and Thomas Mann. As a consequence, a growing number of viewers anxiously rehearsed their feelings of national identity by expressing their fear that this German treasure would be restored to the French in the event of defeat.[9] Indeed, this came to pass in the fall of 1919, when Alsace and Lorraine were reclaimed by France and the altarpiece was returned to Colmar. The cultural contest between Germany and France was nowhere more clearly epitomized than in the claims to Grünewald's masterpiece.

In 1932, as memories of the horrors of the Great War tangled with the visions of the imminent rise of a Third Reich, Dix called upon the power of the repatriated altarpiece in his *War Triptych* (fig. 43). Projected as early as 1920, but not executed until 1932, the *Triptych* respects not only the form of Grünewald's altarpiece but also telling portions of its imagery in a

Figure 42. Matthias Grünewald, Crucifixion section of the Isenheim Altarpiece, 1515. (© Musée d'Unterlinden Colmar; photo O. Zimmermann.)

Figure 43. Otto Dix, *War Triptych*, 1932. (Gemäldegalerie Neue Meister, Dresden; photo courtesy of Sächsische Landesbibliothek, Deutsche Fotothek. © 2002 ARS New York/ VG Bild-Kunst Bonn.)

conflation of raw subject matter and refined technique. In Dix's central panel the horrendous punctured legs that jut upward on the right recall Grünewald's Christ figure. Even more ghastly is the soldier whose body has been impaled on the stripped remains of a tree trunk—it is a modern-day Crucifixion accompanied only by dead bodies and a lonely survivor who wears a gas mask as protection against the stench of decaying human flesh. Like Grünewald's Christ, the crucified figure looks downward with his one surviving arm raised above his head, but his cross is bent at such an angle that his index finger points not to heaven but to hell.

In Dix's left-hand panel numbed soldiers march automatically off to the front through a misty haze reminiscent of the residue of a recent gas attack, a portent-laden sky before them. The atmosphere not only neutralizes any sense of impending triumph but also virtually announces the inevitable martyrdom of these troops in a manner that is analogous to Grünewald's depiction of St. Sebastian.[10] The journey is completed in the right-hand panel, which shows wounded soldiers, including a self-portrait of Dix as the rescuer, returning from the battlefield. In the predella three "sleeping" soldiers, in the tradition of Resurrection imagery, replace the dead Christ of Grünewald's altarpiece.

Sometime during September 1932 Hindemith revisited Grünewald's Isenheim altarpiece at Colmar, and in early 1933 he commenced the composition of his opera, *Mathis der Maler*. Grünewald's altarpiece is actually a polyptych (although when any one full face is opened, it is a triptych). Unlike Dix's work, the two outer movements of Hindemith's tripartite symphony do not draw on the closed position of the altarpiece, which gives prominence to the central Crucifixion, but rather on the scenes to be found in the middle position of a set of unfolding panels. The "Angelic Consort," which appears on the left panel, is celebrated at the opening of Hindemith's symphony with a folktune, "Es sungen drei Engel ein süsser Gesang" (Three Angels Sang a Sweet Song). The tune is a reference to Renaissance views of the curative powers of music as well as the specific healing mission of the Antonites.[11] It also underscores Hindemith's lifelong belief in the power and relevance of early German folksong—a conviction mirrored in the fact that he always kept Franz Böhme's *Altdeutsches Liederbuch* of 1877 near his worktable. However, unlike Grünewald's angels, who play gambas, Hindemith introduces his memorable melody with trombones, and it has been properly noted that "angels with trombones or trumpets are the enforcers of the last judgment—powerful creatures who pronounce their verdicts over human conduct."[12]

The title of the sorrowful second movement, "Entombment," recalls the predellas of Dix and Grünewald alike. Nonetheless, the framing tonality of the movement, which rises almost imperceptibly from C to D♭, subtly emphasizes the promise of resurrection more than the descent into the grave. While Dix's triptych offers no hope,[13] Grünewald tenders the possibility of "a resurrection of hallucinatory power," which Hindemith affirms with a radiant proclamation drawn from the plainsong "Lauda Sion Salvatorem" in the work's concluding movement, "The Temptation of St. Anthony."

Dix had been the first to provide tangible evidence of the power of the historical Grünewald for modern Germany,[14] and he was widely recognized as the most perceptive chronicler of the Weimar Republic and one of the most ardent voices against the evils of war.[15] As Jay Winter has noted, Dix's three panels and predella offer an unmistakable transference of a religious iconography to the battlefield: "from the road to Calvary, to Crucifixion, to Descent from the Cross, to Entombment."[16] But while, like many of Dix's previous disturbing canvases, the work is still arrowed to the subject of war, in the piling up of detail and attention to tradition the *War Triptych* not only abandons Dada but tames Expressionism's hallucinating fury with a new "fidelity to tangible reality."[17] In this turn to *Neue Sachlichkeit*[18] Dix shares a path with Hindemith, who assumed a new sense of control by introducing earlier techniques for use with a contemporary subject matter.[19]

Not surprisingly, the reception history of the two works is also remarkably similar. Shortly after the *War Triptych* was completed, Dix's initial study for the work, *The Trench*, was sold to the Wallraf-Richartz Museum in Cologne. Reaction was swift: in 1925 the painting was hung behind a curtain, and Konrad Adenauer, the mayor of Cologne (and later West Germany's first chancellor), "revoked the museum's acquisition and dismissed the director from his post."[20] A new era in Germany had begun. Although the painting was repurchased by a different state collection in 1930, it would be only another three years before the Nazis would include it in one of their first attempts to discredit Dix and other artists in an exhibition titled *Images of the Decadence in Art*.[21] In 1938 Dix's powerful canvas became the centerpiece in the renowned *Entartete Kunst* (Decadent Art) exhibition staged in Munich. The painting toured throughout Germany as an example of art that attempted to undermine the will of the German people.[22]

The Nazi regime was consolidating its power in Germany when Hindemith began to write *Mathis der Maler* in 1933. In March 1934 Wilhelm

Furtwängler conducted the first performance of the symphonic adaptation with spectacular success, but in November the *Kulturgemeinde,* an organization devoted to the spiritual education of the Nazi party, announced a boycott of Hindemith's music. Furtwängler courageously came to his defense in the press, but to no avail, and a year later the conductor made his own peace with the German government.[23] By the autumn of 1937 the official music division of the Nazi Party had joined the boycott. Occasional performances of Hindemith's music did take place between 1934 and 1937, but with increasing regularity the composer's scores were to be found amongst the lists of *Entartetemusik.*

Hindemith's drama, whose first full-scale performance took place in Zurich on 28 May 1938, has been judged in some respects to be the opposite of political. Yet both Hindemith and Dix were veterans of the Great War, and their escalating fears of a second world war were based upon personal memories of the first one. In a program note for the Zurich premiere, Hindemith reviewed how Grünewald had been "shaken by the wildly shifting current of his age with all its suffering, disease and wars."[24] In so doing he left the reader with little doubt as to the relevance of the opera's topic for modern times or the direct parallel between himself and the painter.[25]

Numerous church and cathedral monuments to the Great War in Germany took their inspiration directly from the high Gothic imagery of Grünewald's *Crucifixion* or Hans Holbein's *Christ in the Tomb.*[26] And while Hindemith never spoke of the widespread appeal of Grünewald's iconography during the postwar period or registered any awareness of a relationship between his own *Mathis der Maler* and Dix's recent *War Triptych,* for any astute observer of the arts at the time it must have appeared as though the two artists were offering their respective, if quite different, glosses on a common national treasure.[27] Dix said that he painted his triptych because numerous books in the Weimar Republic were "once again peddling the notions of the hero and heroism, which had long been rendered absurd in the trenches of the First World War. People were already beginning to forget what horrible suffering the war had brought them. I did not want to cause fear and panic, but to let people know how dreadful war is and so to stimulate people's powers of resistance."[28]

The borrowing of the triptych form, with its spiritual connotations, to deal with such a horrendous world calamity might at first glance seem inappropriate. But the gradual secularization of the triptych idea—from its original religious and sacramental uses to a secular art that carried unmistakable connotations of societal pathos—can be observed in the work of

many artists over the centuries, ranging from Albrecht Dürer, Hierony-
mus Bosch, and Cranach the Elder to Edvard Munch, August Macke, Otto
Dix, and Max Beckmann.[29]

As another world war dawned, Dix was once again called into service and
was held prisoner in France in 1945–1946, while Hindemith escaped to
America. Despite the difference of their fates, their common attention to
Grünewald's altarpiece had underscored their relation to their country as
well as to each other.[30]

GERSHWIN'S *STRIKE UP THE BAND!*

Many of the films and songs of the 1920s mirrored the wartime mix of
slapstick and propagandistic melodrama, now distilled into a new blend
of high comedy, serious reflection, and sentimental love song. This mixture has been observed in many of Vincent Youmans's songs from this
period, which have been judged to possess a "forced gaiety and pseudo-
evangelism."[31] It was a factor noted at the time by Zelda Fitzgerald, who
remarked in her novel, *Save Me the Waltz*, that "Vincent Youmans wrote
the music for the twilights just after the war."[32]

In 1927 George Gershwin wrote a sly but sharply stinging rebuke of
war in a musical comedy, *Strike Up the Band!* In that same year Dix began
his only other triptych, *Großstadt* (Metropolis), which he completed in
1928 (fig. 44).[33] Here jazz is employed as a societal critique in Dix's painting, reflecting in part the growing anxiety of Weimar culture over the
influx of American popular music. Indeed, while jazz was all the rage in
Paris, its status was considerably more ambivalent in Germany, where an
earlier fascination with America's cowboys and Indians had melded with a
new attraction: the "primitive" in the guise of the African American jazz
musician.

Earlier, in 1922, Dix had incorporated this national perspective as well
as his own personal relationship to jazz in a painting titled *An die Schönheit* (To Beauty) (fig. 45). There the face of a Native American in full head-
dress graces the head of a black musician's drum, updating Karl May's
nineteenth-century view of America's Wild, Wild West by incorporating
the image of the American "primitive." The American Concrete and As-
phalt Jungle—the cityscape—had become the locus of all modern society's
ills, and Dix even portrayed himself as a totally Americanized entrepreneur
and profiteer at the center of the picture. The shadow of Kraus's satirical poem, "Tod und Tango," or perhaps the final dance scene of his just

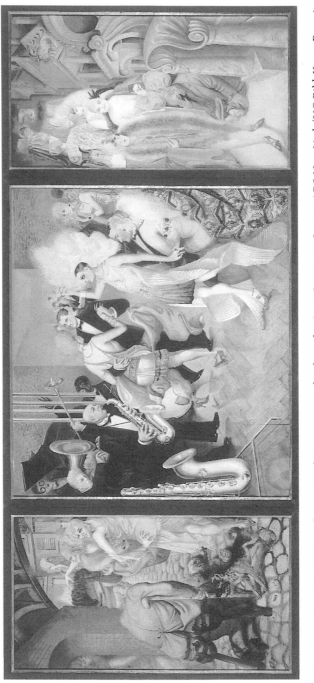

Figure 44. Otto Dix, *Metropolis*, 1928. (Photo courtesy of Galerie der Staat Stuttgart. © 2002 ARS New York/VG Bild-Kunst Bonn.)

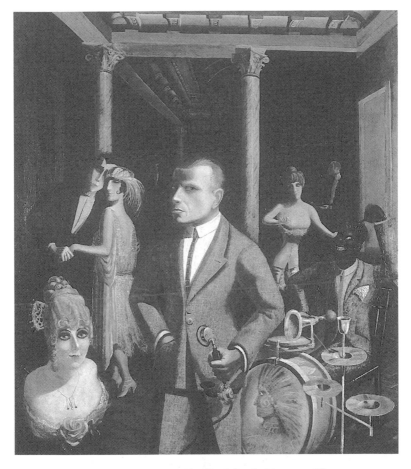

Figure 45.   Otto Dix, *To Beauty (An die Schönheit)*, 1922. (Photo courtesy of Von der Heydt-Museum Wuppertal. © 2002 ARS New York/VG Bild-Kunst Bonn.)

completed *Die letzten Tage der Menschheit,* had clearly fallen across Dix's canvas.[34]

Yet for all the visceral attraction of the black American musician and his natural association with "primitive modernism," there was an uneasiness bordering on anxiety in some German quarters over American-style mass culture and its potential to eclipse European high culture. Despite the embrace of American jazz and its related dances by composers like Hindemith, Ernst Krenek, Kurt Weill, and Hanns Eisler, and despite Gottfried Benn's proclamation of the triumph of "primitivity" or the Bauhaus's endorsement of jazz as a symbol of the modernist vanguard, among conservatives in particular the image of the frenetic Negro jazz improviser could not be made to square with Germany's post-Armistice cultural and racial agendas.[35]

By the time of Dix's *Metropolis* the saxophone had begun to compete with the drum as the central icon of American jazz, and the black musician is now a lonely figure in the background.[36] The placement accurately reflects the state of affairs in Berlin at the time where, despite a prewar familiarity with ragtime and more recent encounters with Josephine Baker and Sam Wooding, the music scene was dominated by largely white, frequently second-rate jazz ensembles. Dix's central panel of *Metropolis* showcases the Americanized New Woman of Berlin caught in the lure of the jazz band. It simultaneously serves as a personification of the city, of mass culture, and of sexual fascination in a postwar world gone amuck.[37] A double amputee on the left side panel negotiates the world of the demimonde on his crutches; on the right sits a counterpart who has not yet been outfitted with prostheses. Unlike the triumphant protagonist in Ravel's Concerto for the Left Hand, both of these *mutilés* have been reduced to the discarded residue of society. Juxtaposed against the carefree atmosphere of the central jazz scene, the framing panels offer a disturbing commentary on the aftermath of a ruinous war.

In the world of music the idea of treating the most disturbing social issues of the day against a jazz or popular background was anything but novel at the time, not only in the works of Tin Pan Alley composers but also in Hindemith's *Hin und zurück*, Krenek's *Jonny spielt auf*, and Weill's *Der Zar lässt sich photographieren* (The Tsar Has His Photograph Taken), all from 1927. All three composers were busy in the second half of the 1920s introducing *Zeitoper*,[38] a new genre of musical theater that regularly availed itself of the condiments of American jazz to make a social point.

In a real sense *Zeitoper* could be seen as a kindred spirit of the efforts of George S. Kaufman and the Gershwin brothers to speak of serious contemporary problems with a stylishly light but conspicuously cynical touch. For in the same year as the trio of German operas just listed, George Gershwin composed a musical comedy, *Strike Up the Band!*[39] In this anticapitalist spoof, the United States goes to war with Switzerland over the price of cheese, and a mythic dairy tycoon, Horace J. Fletcher, offers to finance the operation if the war is named after him. Ira Gershwin was candid when he characterized his lyrics as "satirically pacifistic,"[40] and the power of the original book can be surmised by the fact that it was "defanged" by Morrie Ryskind prior to its opening on Broadway in 1930.[41]

The unbridled profiteering of the war industrialists was a persistent theme among 1920s commentators. Yet the mindless flag-waving and exaggerated bravado that accompanied the quest for victory and survived into the immediate post-Armistice period were endorsed by a vast majority of the American citizenry, who found the hoopla surrounding America's arrival as a new world power virtually impossible to resist.[42] In the period that followed, the rhetoric of war repeatedly demonstrated its capacity to flourish and to ignite an idealized and noisy sense of patriotism.[43] *Strike Up the Band!* like so many other novels and films of the 1920s, took a retrospective but direct aim at this very proposition.

> We fought in nineteen-seventeen,
> Rum-ta-ta tum-tum-tum!
> And drove the tyrant from the scene,
> Rum-ta-ta tum-tum-tum!
> We're in a bigger, better war
> For your patriotic pastime.
> We don't know what we're fighting for—
> But we didn't know the last time.

Gershwin's score contains two of his most popular songs, "Strike Up the Band" and "The Man I Love."[44] More topical numbers included "Oh, This is Such a Lovely War," a number whose title is practically the same as that of a British tune that was known to many American soldiers, "Oh, It's a Lovely War!"[45] and whose text recalls the earlier wartime favorite, "Sister Susie's Sewing Shirts for Soldiers."[46] Gershwin's soldiers, however, coaxed by Swiss girls to forget about their girls at home, camp it up. Other numbers with a war theme include "Come-Look-At-The-War Choral Society" and the "Military Dancing Drill."

Nostalgia for home, which had been mined for literally thousands of popular songs of the preceding period, was affectingly tapped at the end of the show with "Homeward Bound" and a recap of the most memorable melody of the show, now retexted and transgendered for its Broadway run as "The Girl I Love."[47]

"The War That Ended War" that follows finds the girls in the ballroom back home chattering about the imminent return of their boyfriends as the military band plays snippets from "Dixie," "Yankee Doodle," "Auld Lang Syne," and Sousa's "Stars and Stripes Forever." The crowd joins in with an incisive lampoon of every slogan of the age: "Civilization is improving. / Higher and higher we are moving. / This war ends all war." Then comes the grand finale: "Let the drums roll out! / Let the trumpet call! / While the people shout! / Strike up the band!" By now, however, the price of cheese has been forgotten, and the prospect of going to war with Russia over the price of caviar is entered as an impending probability.

By the end of the 1920s World War I was a decade away, and so many failures had transpired on the diplomatic front that the satire in *Strike Up the Band!* must have seemed heavy-handed indeed. Hardly anti-American, the show nonetheless took a hearty swing at America's muscle-flexing, which showed no signs of abating, given the nation's steadily developing industrial might in the postwar world. Few could have foreseen that a stock market crash and the Great Depression were just around the corner. The notion of going to war over the price of Swiss cheese or Russian caviar, however satirically portrayed, would soon no longer seem funny, and, despite the mixture of spirited tunes and at least one heart-melting song in Gershwin's score that was to remain a classic, the topic would soon no longer be seen as appropriate for a Broadway show.

In 1929 a young American infidel, John Becker, wrote his Third Symphony, whose second movement was titled "Memories of War—Sorrow-Struggle—A Protest!" On the title page of this fifteen-minute symphony Becker indicated that the work was a protest against the so-called civilized nations who starve their citizens in times of peace and murder them in times of war. If in another corner of the American musical landscape Gershwin's *Strike Up the Band!* seemed to refuse the pathos and horror of the front and to emphasize the light and the satiric touch, it was also clear that it invited a nation to take a look in the mirror and sounded a not-so-subtle warning that the carefree Roaring Twenties might not last forever. In fact, the "roar" had now begun to sound like a frenetic attempt to drown out reality.

The first sobriety test was not long in coming. Having set down his philosophy in *Mein Kampf* between 1925 and 1927, Adolf Hitler launched his first successful political bid in 1929. Then, in October of that year, the New York stock market collapsed, and a sum nearly equivalent to America's total expenditure in the Great War disappeared overnight. By August 1939 the world situation had become so desperate that, after seeing the newspaper headlines, Nijinsky was moved to pronounce in a rare moment of lucidity, "Act II begins."[48] In hindsight, it was clear that the overture had been playing over the past two decades.

Part 8

EPILOGUE

24 Unfinished Business

> I pondered all these things, and how men fight and lose the
> battle, and the thing that they fought for comes about in spite
> of their defeat, and when it comes turns out not to be what they
> meant, and other men have to fight for what they meant under
> another name.
>
> William Morris, *A Dream of John Ball*

At the end of the Great War the balance of political power in Europe had
been altered but not settled, and most of the old issues of ethnic and national identity were still filed away under the heading "Unfinished Business." Even a decade later, in December 1929, Albert Einstein indicated that
he clearly understood the ongoing nature of this cultural impasse when he
stated in an address at the Sorbonne, "If my theory of relativity is proven
correct, Germany will claim me as a German and France will declare that I
am a citizen of the world. Should my theory prove untrue, France will say
that I am a German and Germany will declare that I am a Jew."[1]

In the world of music there was a similar ambivalence and a great
deal of unfinished business, too. Despite Ernest Newman's judgment that
Strauss was a decadent has-been and Schoenberg a misguided visionary,
the thought that Germany might wait for just the right moment to reassert
its dominant turn-of-the-century position was widely if circumspectly
held. In the eyes of some, the prospect of postwar leadership from Austro-
Germany was tied to the memory of its central role in prewar modernism.

Hans Joachim Moser, one of the most knowledgeable and astute German critics of the state of affairs in the world of music after World War I,
sounded a warning from the other side, saying that German *Kultur* had
suffered a deadly blow from the forces of capitalism, technology, and, especially, the Americanization of German musical life. In Moser's opinion
the disappearance of Germany's folk culture in the wake of rampant ur-
banization had been exacerbated by the infiltration of African American
dialect into popular song and dance during the postwar period—a turn of
events that he felt had been promoted by Jewish-American businessmen.

Moser, like so many other of his countrymen, agreed that music provided not only an "accurate measure of German culture" but offered the

best possible way for a defeated Germany to reassert its influence in the world.[2] Prizing not only folk sources but amateur participation, Moser was little concerned with picking up where the prewar avant-garde had left off. And those Germans who were interested in resuscitating the true modernist movement, which had been halted by the outbreak of hostilities on the battlefield, viewed all the newer trends such as Dada, *Neue Sachlichkeit,* and Neoclassicism as stalling tactics, not a strategy for the main business that lay ahead.

"Modern war takes place within a context of cultural 'modernism' and indeed is one of its causes," Paul Fussell has argued.[3] Others have maintained that, rather than being a product of the war proper, the initial modernist impulse had been sounded in the prewar period and that the arts had taken a pronounced detour once war was declared. For just as the French avant-garde had reembraced traditional subjects and classical forms in the visual arts during World War I, so it had done in the world of music. In most quarters, in fact, modernism was no longer solely equated with extensions of prewar avant-gardism, even though there can be no argument that the latter's vitalizing force continued to flourish beneath the surface of what was seen and heard in the galleries and concert halls in the postwar decades. But, *pace* Schoenberg, many now felt that the "idea of modernism as perpetual progress and invention [had come] to a halt."[4]

Among the numerous possible ancillary observations to this premise, two are especially intriguing: first, the "retro" façade of European Neoclassicism was accompanied by the invigorating, forward-looking forces of *mécanique* and American jazz in a new and liberated postwar industrial world; second, with all the prewar "isms" (Impressionism, Expressionism, Cubism, Primitivism) either abandoned or subjected to new tidying forces, American composers were placed in something of an advantageous position. No longer obliged to "catch up" with the European prewar avant-garde, they were now free to pick and choose strands from various options—many of which they had previously been only dimly aware of—to construct an American music.

Despite the initial impact of the New York Armory Show in 1913 and the appearance of Dada in that city two years later, the first formal New York session of the Société Anonyme, "the first organization devoted to the display and promotion of modern art in America," was not held until 1 April 1921.[5] By that time a number of "modernist" composers living in the eastern United States were already becoming aware of one another. Like Marcel Duchamp, the French-born composers Edgard Varèse and Dane Rudhyar had viewed American culture as a promising alternative to a decaying western Europe and had immigrated to New York. Then, with the increasing visibility of Americans like Henry Cowell, Carl Ruggles, Ruth Crawford Seeger, Aaron Copland, Roy Harris, and Virgil Thomson, America's answer to modernism emerged full force in the 1920s. Predictably, their mission was refueled by repeated returns to Europe for a reassessment.

Gradually American composers began to organize platforms at home to showcase their wares, sometimes in harmony with one another, sometimes with a factious sense of exclusion. Initially they operated through organizations that emphasized foreign cooperation, like the Franco-American Musical Society (later called Pro Musica) and the International Composers' Guild, both founded in 1920–1921, and shortly thereafter through such groups as the League of Composers, established in 1923. A more distinctly American bias was subsequently provided by the American Music Guild, the Copland-Sessions Concerts, and the Pan-American Association—although all of them took pains to avoid provincialism and to promote their works abroad as well as at home.[6]

Encouraged by acclaim for an American musical expression abroad, concert-hall composers like Copland and Antheil "crossed over" with the jazz-inspired Piano Concerto (1926) and the "Jazz" Symphony (1925), respectively, while Gershwin "crossed back" with his *Rhapsody in Blue* (1934), Piano Concerto in F Major, and opera, *Porgy and Bess* (1935). Together they launched a campaign for national recognition that was not to cease for the remainder of the century. Yet the new forces of American jazz, potent and attractive as they were, were rarely applauded by classical composers at the time for what was viewed as their staying power—indeed, their perceived ephemeral nature led composers both French (Milhaud) and American (Copland) to announce the demise of its influence before the 1920s were over. Both composers were concerned with finding an alternative to the prewar avant-garde that could assist in the definition of national values. Both believed that although jazz could offer inflection to a national musical language, it could not provide its essence. Ravel's endorsement carried a similar caveat.

Copland in particular journeyed widely over the next two decades in his quest for an American voice, tapping folk and popular sources both at home and in Latin America. Unwaveringly suspicious of the shortcomings and limitations of a music based principally on popular materials—which he nonetheless incorporated—Copland maintained a vigilant concern for the well-made score that was anchored in the instruction he had received from his French teacher, Nadia Boulanger. For the rest of his career he would grapple with his suspicion of the complexities of the European tradition and his belief in the power of local vernaculars to energize and define a national perspective.[7] Most composers of Copland's generation confronted these issues, flirted with the options, and steadfastly pursued the elusive dream of a distinctly American music.

One of the most pressing concerns was whether Neoclassicism was eligible for membership in the avant-garde or could even be considered as an adjunct to modernism. In other quarters it was hoped that such a perspective might put a check on the fracturing impulses of both Expressionism and Cubism (sonic as well as visual) and compel artists to look for forces that could reemphasize balance and structure, promote cohesion and continuity, and mask the signs of a societal breakdown.[8] Even the elemental power of prewar Expressionism, which had forwarded the possibility of a musical universe freed from a tonal center, had suddenly been reined in by the emergency tidying solution of a "method of composing with twelve-tones."

Perhaps it *was* possible to sidestep the issue of the prewar avant-garde and go on to something else. The idea of composing a grand and stately requiem had occurred periodically throughout the war, not necessarily to settle the future direction of music but in search of an appropriate ritual of commemoration worthy of the sacrifice the war had exacted. Vaughan Williams's *Pastoral Symphony* (1921) and Elgar's Cello Concerto had been designated by some critics as war requiems in all but name, yet in the absence of a text they did not suffice. The best to come of the impulse for texted works was a requiem by Delius (1914–1916), which was virtually unknown at the time, Elgar's popular but nonliturgical *The Spirit of England,* and a *Requiem for the Fallen Heroes of the Allied Armies* by the Russian Alexander Dmitrievich Kastalsky, a pupil of Tchaikovsky and Taneiev, which was premiered in Moscow in the spring of 1916 and performed in Birmingham, England, in November 1917.[9]

The idea also occurred to John Foulds, a well-known British composer of theater music, just as the conflict ended. The premiere of *A World Requiem,* which he composed between 1918 and 1921, was given in the Royal Albert Hall during the Armistice Night Celebrations in 1923 under the sponsorship of the British Legion, and the committee of the British Music Society that championed its first performance included Arnold Bax, Arthur Bliss, Edward J. Dent, Eugene Goossens, Hamilton Harty, and Adrian Boult. The two-hour colossus draws on multiple literary sources such as the Bible, *Pilgrim's Progress,* Hindu poetry, and contemporary free verse and calls for forces (1,200 singers and instrumentalists) equal to Mahler's

Eighth Symphony. The score carried the citation, "A tribute to the memory of the Dead—a message of consolation to the bereaved of all countries." Figures like Roger Quilter, Sybil Thorndike (Shaw's first Saint Joan), and George Bernard Shaw (for whose production of *Saint Joan* Foulds was to provide incidental music the next year) found the *Requiem* a crowning achievement in the history of English music. The public also received it ecstatically, and Donald Tovey, the pro-German English critic and scholar, was highly optimistic about its long-range durability and its potential for replacing the "Armistice Jazz" celebrations that had dominated the first few anniversaries after the war. The work was almost a total failure with the journalists, however. It was judged to be too big, too boring, and, as Ernest Newman put it, "unpleasantly pretentious," although he admitted that there was "considerable skill in the handling of the large masses of tone, and some personality in the harmonic writing."[10] The work also failed to live up to the hope of its composer that it would become an Armistice Night tradition, and when the British Legion withdrew its support after 1926, the disgruntled composer left the country.[11]

The range of musical expression explored between the two world wars by those who held clear memories of the first global conflict was impressive. It exemplified, whether always admitted or not, an ongoing state of inquiry with respect to the possible role that music might assume in the portrayal of world sorrow, the pursuit of national aspirations, the dream of world peace, or the insouciant quest for the good life. Collectively, the various aesthetic options of the twenties and thirties seemed to address the central dilemma of the postwar era and the source of its trauma—namely, the Lost Generation's sense of an idealism betrayed.[12]

Cynicism reigned for a moment between 1915 and 1919 in Dada, although its musical component, being largely confined to cabaret skits, left little trace when the short-lived movement expired. Spreading from Zurich to Paris, Cologne, Berlin, and New York and building on the manifestoes of the Futurists, Dada registered its contempt for bourgeois society, high culture, and the prewar avant garde, and proclaimed that the modern urban scene "was as violent as any battlefield."[13] When Duchamp left his home country in 1915 he protested, "I do not go to New York, I leave Paris." It was clear in the Dadaists' compulsive embrace of caprice and laughter that they were not only challenging the lines of demarcation between high and low culture but also offering an escape route from the fanaticism and horror of the European suicide machine.[14]

In Dada's aftermath Erik Satie endorsed its spirit, and with his final "ballets," *Mercure* and *Relâche* (both from 1924), his career glowed, sputtered, and faded into extinction as an only slightly delayed coda to Dada's brief heyday and rapid demise. It was a zany, nonsensical, anti-art movement whose negativism stemmed directly from a wartime view that the world had spun out of control. Anything was possible, the more absurd the better, and the found object was elevated to the status of a work of art with the insouciant question "Why not?" Laughter was king, but inside the heart was breaking.[15]

Surrealism, Dada's successor, spawned a more memorable, if slight, catalog of pieces from Les Six, including Milhaud's *Le boeuf sur le toit* (1920), the collaborative *Les mariés de la Tour Eiffel* (1921), and Poulenc's *Le bal masqué* (1932) and, belatedly, his take on Apollinaire's *Les mamelles de Tirésias* (1947).[16] It is telling that André Breton insisted on the fact that Surrealism was defined by its relation to the two wars—"both the war it left behind and the one to which it returned."[17] Daniel Albright has also noted that Poulenc's Surrealism "has a strong tendency to mutilation,"[18] from the crippled repairman in *Le bal masqué* to the amputated Thérèse and her castrated husband in *Les mamelles de Tirésias*. By the end of the 1920s, however, Cocteau's saucy, naughty boys had in the main begun the search for a more unambiguous message, and none more so than Poulenc, whose immediate postwar subscription to Neoclassicism was soon complemented by the rediscovery of his Catholic faith. This brought a turn to mass and motet beginning in 1936 and continuing to the end of his life.[19]

The choral *Figure humaine* of 1943 aside, the work that best summed up Poulenc's experience was a setting of a single lyric, "C," of the same year. Composed to a poem by the former Surrealist Louis Aragon, it called on the imagery "of times past" and spoke sadly of the Old Lie ("the long poem of false glories") as it was enacted throughout French history, from the Gallic wars of Julius Caesar to the Great War of the composer's youth. Surrealism's origins in the madness of war is clearly on view, with the overturned cars and the unprimed weapons as reminders, and the whole is infused with history and heartbreak at the final couplet: "O ma France ô ma délaissée / J'ai traversé les ponts de Cé" (O my France, O my forsaken one / I have crossed the bridges of C). The sentiments of *Rapsodie nègre,* the Dada spoof that Poulenc had dedicated to Satie and recited while still in uniform in 1917, were now totally out of view.[20]

The "call to order" that followed the end of World War II was remarkably pointed and clearly analogous to the post-Armistice period of the Great War. Yet consider for a moment the meteoric ascent and ultimate canonization of the Viennese composer Anton Webern. His influence began in the early 1950s—a time when the musical world was in need of revitalization and a fresh start. But how was it that an Austrian veteran of World War I—and a composer from a twice-defeated Axis power, whose musical world was so structured and introspective—could have achieved such immediate postwar acceptance as the new godhead among composers of the Allied nations? And especially by a young Frenchman like Pierre Boulez or an American such as Milton Babbitt, not to mention the Russian-French-American Igor Stravinsky? In light of the latter's physical-psychological displacement in two world conflicts, how does one explain Stravinsky's willingness to accede to Webern the throne of modernity?

Stravinsky was the only one of these composers who belonged to Webern's generation, but Webern's music had meant little or nothing to him before the 1950s. Was it simply super-Serialism's implied "call to order" that held the appeal, much as Neoclassicism had in the 1920s? Was it Webern's martyrdom in an accidental shooting by an American G.I. in 1945 that helped to propel his sainthood? Or did the lingering memory of Germany's pre–World War I leadership once again taunt Allied composers into wondering if they were unwisely bypassing a Viennese discovery of universal potential? It was as though a collective sense of an idealism betrayed had once again sent a postwar generation in search of a Holy Grail, to an art so immaculate that it seemed almost beyond criticism despite its strong invitation to analytical scrutiny. The choice of such a subtle, rare, and elusive expression to serve as the emblematic music for Allied composers of a postwar age was strange enough. But to have it come from the pen of an Axis composer suggests that all these factors must have prevailed to some degree—a perspective that brings to mind Ravel's ecumenical infatuation with Vienna at the close of World War I.

Yet, just as Webern's stock began to hit an all-time high, Benjamin Britten's *War Requiem* of 1961 signaled that a compelling tonal aesthetic had been waiting in the wings and was about to be reclaimed wholesale. The thundering cannonade and unbridled rhetoric of its "Dies irae," in particular, had not been attempted in a choral requiem since Berlioz and Verdi. The initial impact of Britten's masterwork was remarkably powerful upon most audiences, although few composers initially took the cue that such an affective, at times openly histrionic, language might serve a postwar age.[21]

The Requiem brandished a text whose message was almost magically, if also calculatedly, more powerful than the sum of its parts—a textual trope of the Latin Requiem Mass with the World War I poetry of Wilfred Owen. The import of this textual assemblage was unmistakably pacifist, a view that Britten shared with the poet. It was a conviction that had been forming throughout the period between 1939 and 1942, and it had been reflected not only in the composer's momentary flight to America and eventual return to England, where he declared himself a conscientious objector, but also in works like his *Sinfonia da Requiem* (1940) and even his *Serenade for tenor, horn, and strings* (1943). Although seldom viewed as a war document, the latter had already traced the personal convulsions and war-weariness of the country at large with a rare blend of lyric beauty, brio, and world sorrow. In retrospect its texts seem to offer a prescient forecast of colonialism's eclipse, in particular Charles Cotton's opening "Pastoral" ("The day's grown old; the fainting sun / Has but a little way to run") and Alfred Tennyson's "Nocturne" ("Blow, bugle blow, set the wild echoes flying; / And answer, echoes, dying, dying, dying.").[22]

Wilfred Owen had stated that, for all his pacifist inclinations, he felt an obligation to "get some reputation for gallantry" so that his message would find public credibility. Britten saw it otherwise, and with the support of Owen's texts, he left behind one of the few unmistakable testimonies to the power of their common conviction. Britten's *War Requiem* offers a secure and telling review of numerous legacies and symbols, ranging from a reprise of the flying bugles of his own *Serenade* to specific figures, textures, and sonorities from Verdi's *Requiem*.[23] To this he added the ancient authority of liturgical recitation, the tertian harmonies of the English choral tradition from the time of John Dunstable and his Renaissance contemporaries, and the ageless and persistent thorn of the tritone.[24] Britten's tenacious use of this interval (c–f♯) in the opening "Requiem aeternum" finds resolution in "Kyrie eleison" (Lord have mercy) and in the process forces a sober review of the difficult tonal terrain that had been traversed in the decades between the two wars.[25]

In the pages that immediately precede these final sonorities, the sorrow of war's colossal human waste in the shadow of high hopes now stilled is explored in a concluding duet between two enemy soldiers. Here the retrospective cast of Britten's music is dramatically reinforced not only by the juxtaposition of an ancient liturgical text and a World War I poem but also by its gaze at another country in one of its darkest hours. The text of the duet, Owen's "Strange Meeting," reads almost like a paraphrase of Walt Whitman's familiar lines of "Reconciliation" ("For my enemy is dead, a man divine as myself is dead"), which was written during America's Civil War. Owen offers the following counterpart:

> I am the enemy you killed, my friend.
> I knew you in this dark; for so you frowned
> Yesterday through me as you jabbed and killed.

I parried; but my hands were loath and cold.
Let us sleep now . . .[26]

The repeated final line of text is sung against words from the Burial Service, "In paradisum deducant te Angeli: in tuo adventu suscipiant te Martyres" (Into Paradise may the Angels lead thee: at thy coming may the Martyrs receive thee), intoned by a choir of boys that is gradually joined by full mixed chorus and soprano soloist. The soldiers' fading voices are finally silenced, and the chorus offers a musical recapitulation of the Kyrie's opening tritone together with its resolution in the valedictory "Requiescant in pace" (May they rest in peace) and concluding "Amen." In the process a frame is offered for the work as a whole.

If here the closing text of the two enemy soldiers "absorbs homoerotic passion into technique and tempers intimate excitement until it becomes an ally of English literary [here also *liturgical*] tradition"—as Fussell described some of the most forceful English World War I poetry[27]—Britten's music also clarifies the underlying sentiment of Owen's lines from a private and highly personal perspective. Indeed, it is remarkable how this final scene—a self-contained rite in itself—throws into bold relief the fact that the war conferred on its fighting men the authority to cross the boundary of gender in the expression of affection. The issue has less to do with sexual orientation—although this might seem clear enough as a subtext in light of the fact that both poet and composer were homosexual—than with some deeper affinity that the war had permitted the two soldiers to discover.[28] This crossing—this recognition of the oneness of humanity, which is gained only in the face of ultimate personal sacrifice and which paradoxically restores peace and tranquility—prepares the listener for the final resolution of the Requiem.[29]

In some measure Britten's work spoke as much to musical as to moral issues. For beyond the roaring and the resolution, it openly offered hope for the future to those who chose to remember and rededicate. For many, the memories of the two world wars would not fade, and the unkept promises were still there waiting to be kept. Somehow through all the carnage, two of the most difficult of all sermons were being preached once again: that humankind is capable of love, even of a former enemy, both in art and in war,[30] and that the dictation of musical fashion had its limits.

One of the most gripping factors about Britten's work was the fact that this most potent musical testimony to World War I was forged some forty-three years after the signing of the Armistice. For although it was an ostensibly delayed reaction to the holocaust of World War II, Britten's 1961

War Requiem was in fact a retrospective recognition of the global impact of the Great War for the entire century. The unsettling ambivalence inherent in Britten's juxtaposition of sacred and secular had troubled many of the immediate survivors of the Great War, and Hemingway had bluntly recorded his views in *A Farewell to Arms.*

> I was always embarrassed by the words *sacred, glorious* and *sacrifice* and the expression *in vain.* We had heard them, sometimes standing in the rain almost out of earshot, so that only the shouted words came through, and had read them, on proclamations that were slapped up by billposters over other proclamations, now for a long time, and I had seen nothing sacred, and the things that were glorious had no glory and the sacrifices were like the stockyards at Chicago if nothing was done with the meat except to bury it.[31]

One appreciates Hemingway's anger as well as his frustration with words that prefigure with amazing accuracy the later contention that the Great War rendered distinctions between "high" and "low" and "sacred" and "profane" almost impossible to make.[32] At the same time, his perspective suggests that the resolution of such matters was something that could only be offered by ritual that was long delayed and unconnected to liturgical use. "I Wonder Where My Buddy Is Tonight," poppy-day rituals, and annual Armistice Day ceremonies were one thing, but the traditions of communion and Requiem Mass elevated gestures of remembrance to a different level. The struggle to valorize the everyday expressions of the populace offered abundant opportunities, but they could go only so far.

If only for reasons of language, Britten's *War Requiem* understandably spoke to America as to no other nation beside England itself. After hearing the American premiere at Tanglewood, Copland openly expressed his admiration for Britten's achievement, stating that while he felt that he would have been capable of writing such a piece, he doubted that he could have conceived of it. It was a telling confession for an American; it intimated that, for all of the United States's sacrifice in both wars, the nation's collective conscience could not summon up expressions equivalent to that of the British World War I poets nor call upon memories of trench warfare or aerial attacks on American soil.

Yet, in choosing the poetry of Wilfred Owen as a *contrapposto* to the solemn text of the Requiem Mass and the Burial Service, Britten's *War Requiem* was anything but parochial. World War I had joined the image of manliness to nationalism as never before, and Owen's search for personal freedom forced him to rationalize the aesthetic of masculinity with an artistic sensibility as no other poet of the war had.[33] Owen punctuated his awareness of The Old Lie with an alarming reversal of the biblical image of Abraham and Isaac. As laid down in Genesis 22, the father's acquiescence to a command from God to offer up his son as a sacrifice is countered at the last moment by an angel of the Lord, who orders him not to lay a hand on the lad but to offer instead a ram caught in a thicket nearby. In Owen's retelling of the story, which Britten incorporated as a gloss to the liturgical "Offertorium," heavenly intervention is ignored, and the precedent of violence is established.

> But the old man would not so,
> but slew his son, and half the seed of Europe one by one.[34]

Just as Dix and Hindemith had created secular interpretations of Grünewald's altarpiece thirty years before, so now Britten offered a musical commentary on selected and complementary sacred and profane texts. Just as the brave warriors of Walter Flex's novels celebrated the community of men bathing together in clear streams as an antidote to the darkness and grimness of war,[35] and just as the Tommies found a magical and unexpected fraternity with the enemy in no man's land on Christmas Eve 1914, the haunting echoes of distant bugles, the thudding cannons, and the death struggle of hand-to-hand combat are finally exchanged in the *War Requiem* for the calm of paradise by two enemy soldiers who could with justification claim a resting place together in the predella of Dix's triptych.[36]

Owen did not totally sidestep the euphemistic rhetoric prevalent in much war poetry—a "high" diction that was soon to disappear—although in the texts chosen for the *War Requiem* "sleep" appears instead of "slumber" and "dead" stands in place of "fallen."[37] Yet to this poetic cadence Britten now brought a new sobriety and reflection that offered far more than a pacifist document. Pointedly evading the terrifying spectacle of the atomic bomb, which the previous year had lured Krzysztof Penderecki to compose his *Threnody for the Victims of Hiroshima,* Britten's *War Requiem* was essentially a reflection on the empty shell of the old Coventry Cathedral. In the process of fashioning a "ritual that never was" for an edifice that stood only as a ghostly, skeletal reminder, the meaning as well as the meaninglessness of the Great War had found a new and resonant echo.

Notes

INTRODUCTION

1. Discussion and debate over the term "modernism" is vast and ongoing. One of the most helpful primers is the review provided by Peter Child's *Modernism* (London, 2000) as part of *The New Critical Idiom* series. See especially "Words, Words, Words: Modern, Modernism, Modernity," 12–17, and "Identity and War," 161–185.

2. Charles Baudelaire, "The Painter of Modern Life," in *L'art romantique* (Paris, 1869), section 4; reprinted in *Selected Writings on Art and Artists*, trans. P. E. Charvet (Harmondsworth, 1972).

3. Daniel Albright, *Untwisting the Serpent: Modernism in Music, Literature, and Other Arts* (Chicago, 2000), 29–30.

4. Edward Grey, "Viscount of Falloden," in *Twenty-five Years, 1892–1916* (New York, 1925), vol. 2, chap. 18.

5. See Charles S. Maier, "Slaughterhouse Jive," review of Niall Ferguson's *The Pity of War*, *The New Republic*, 28 June 1999, p. 51.

6. David Slater, "Locating the American Century: Themes for a Post-Colonial Perspective," in *The American Century: Consensus and Coercion in the Projection of American Power*, ed. David Slater and Peter J. Taylor (Oxford, 1999), 21. See also Cecilia Elizabeth O'Leary, *To Die For: The Paradox of American Patriotism* (Princeton, 1999).

7. Robert Wohl, *The Generation of 1914* (Cambridge, Mass., 1979), 203.

8. See David Hackett Fischer, *Historians' Fallacies: Toward a Logic of Historical Thought* (New York, 1970), 203.

9. Simon Schama, "Afterword," in *Dead Certainties: Unwarranted Speculations* (New York, 1991). For a similar view of the historian's dilemma in recounting the war from modernist and postmodernist perspectives, see Leonard V. Smith, "Narrative and Identity at the Front: 'Theory and the Poor Bloody Infantry,'" in *The Great War and the Twentieth Century*, ed. Jay Winter, Geoffrey Parker, and Mary R. Habeck (New Haven, 2000), 159–161.

10. The Kansas City Union Station was built in 1914, and after New York's Grand Central Terminal it is the largest in the nation.

11. The next year, on 4 July 1927, General John J. Pershing also led a parade of citizens in Indianapolis to the dedication of an Indiana World War Memorial, which rose two hundred feet high. See John Bodnar, *Remaking America: Public Memory, Commemoration, and Patriotism in the Twentieth Century* (Princeton, N.J., 1992), 82, 87.

12. Regarding the Kansas City restoration, see Shirley Christian's "World War I Museum's New Drive on the Home Front," *The New York Times*, 31 March 1998, p. B2, and her "In Kansas City, Few Trains, but New Life in the Station," *The New York Times*, 15 November 1999, p. B1.

CHAPTER 1. IN SEARCH OF *KULTUR*

1. Romain Rolland, *Journal des années de guerre, 1914–1919* (Paris, 1952), 31.

2. Ibid., 32–33.

3. Thomas Bailey Aldrich, "Leaves from a Notebook," in *Ponkapog Papers* (New York, 1903).

4. See Sarah O'Brien-Twohig, "Imminent Explosion," in *The Great War and the Shaping of the Twentieth Century* (www.pitt.edu/~novsel/ww1 .html).

5. Friedrich Nietzsche, *The Wanderer and His Shadow* (1880), aphorism 278; and Jay Winter and Blaine Baggett, *The Great War and the Shaping of the Twentieth Century* (New York, 1996), 24–25.

6. See especially Niall Ferguson, *The Pity of War* (New York, 1999).

7. John Keegan, *The First World War* (New York, 1999), 10ff.

8. Romain Rolland, *Le voyage intérieur;* English translation by Frank Field in his *British and French Writers of the First World War: Comparative Studies in Cultural History* (Cambridge, 1991), 190.

9. See especially Jane Fulcher, *French Cultural Politics and Music: From the Dreyfus Affair to the First World War* (New York, 1999).

10. David Sices, *Music and the Musician in "Jean-Christophe": The Harmony of Contrasts* (New Haven, 1968), 6–7.

11. The first doctoral thesis on a musical subject was by Jules Combarieu in 1893, followed by Rolland in 1895, Maurice Emmanuel in 1896, and Louis Laloy in 1904.

12. Due to the Ecole's growing prestige, composers of differing perspectives and beliefs ultimately spoke there, including Debussy, Ravel, and even d'Indy. For further discussion see Fulcher, *French Cultural Politics*, 60–63.

13. Henri Bergson, French philosopher, was professor at the Collège de France from 1900 and received the Nobel laureate in literature for 1927.

14. For a useful overview of the Wagner question see Scott Messing, *Neo-*

classicism in Music: From the Genesis of the Concept through the Schoen-berg/Stravinsky Polemic (Ann Arbor, 1988), 3–17.

15. See Romain Rolland, *Mémoires, et fragments du journal* (Paris, 1956), 163–164; and also Martha Hanna, *The Mobilization of Intellect: French Scholars and Writers during the Great War* (Cambridge, Mass., 1996), chap. 5, "The Classicist Revival."

16. Sices, *Music and the Musician*, 128–130. In turn, Berlioz's unique position in the nineteenth century was seen as having cleared the path for the twentieth-century pursuit of French values.

17. Fulcher, *French Cultural Politics*, 107–108. With respect to the implicit larger question see Herman Lebovics, *True France: The Wars over Cultural Identity* (Ithaca, N.Y., 1992), 138ff.

18. Beethoven's grandfather was born in Malines.

19. See Rolland's "Réponse à l'enquête de Paul Landormy: L'état actuel de la musique française," *Revue bleue*, 2 April 1904, p. 424; and Sices, *Music and the Musician*, 132.

20. See Richard Strauss and Romain Rolland, *Correspondence*, ed. Rollo Myers (Berkeley, 1968), 29–79.

21. Romain Rolland, *Musiciens d'aujourd'hui* (Paris, 1908), and the English translation, *Musicians of To-Day*, trans. Mary Blaiklock (New York, 1914), 208.

22. See Friedrich Nietzsche, *Götzendämmerung* (Munich, 1988), and the English translation, *Twilight of the Idols*, trans. R. J. Hollingdale (London, 1990), aphorism 4.

23. Rolland, *Musiciens d'aujourd'hui*, 209.

24. Ibid., 212. The charge regarding cuts seems especially lame in light of the fact that Franck's *Béatitudes* is a longish work that can make little claim to a place among Franck's best. The work takes a tedious two hours and a quarter on a modern recording. Hänssler Classic, CD 98.964 (2 discs).

25. Rolland, *Musiciens d'aujourd'hui*, 213–214.

26. Stravinsky may have initially been introduced to Dukas's work when d'Indy brought it to Russia on a tour in 1904. See Leon Vallas, *Vincent d'Indy*, 2 vols. (Paris, 1946–1950), 2: 59.

27. Magnard was residing and composing at his country estate in Baron when the war began in the summer of 1914; he sent his wife and daughters to safety. While he was at work in his study on 3 September 1914, troops from the German cavalry entered his property and Magnard, firing from an upstairs window, killed two soldiers. The Germans in turn set his house on fire, and he was burned alive with all of his manuscripts, including a recently completed set of twelve songs and the only surviving full score of two acts of an opera, *Guercoeur*. For more on the complex story of Magnard's aesthetic position see Fulcher, *French Cultural Politics*, 74–77.

28. Sices, *Music and the Musician*, 145–146.

29. See Leo Schrade, *Beethoven in France* (New Haven, 1942), 16.

30. See Otto Erich Deutsch, "Dichterische Freiheiten in Rollands Beethoven: Ein kritisches Nachwort," *Zeitschrift für Musik* 9 (1926): 490; and David B. Dennis, *Beethoven in German Politics, 1870–1989* (New Haven, 1996), 116–117.

31. See Schrade, *Beethoven in France;* William Newman, "The Beethoven Mystique in Romantic Art, Literature, and Music," *The Musical Quarterly* 69, no. 3 (1983): 354–387; Alessandra Comini, *The Changing Image of Beethoven: A Study in Mythmaking* (New York, 1987); and Dennis, *Beethoven in German Politics.*

32. Hermann Hesse, "O Freunde, nicht diese Töne," *Neue Zürcher Nachrichten,* September 1914; cited in Hermann Hesse, *If the War Goes On: Reflections on War and Politics,* trans. Ralph Manheim (New York, 1971), 9–14; original German in Hemann Hesse, *Innenansicht eines Krieg,* ed. Ernst Johan (Frankfurt, 1968), 44–45. To this day year-end performances of Beethoven's Ninth Symphony are traditional on New Year's Eve in Leipzig, where Schiller wrote his "Ode to Joy." The legendary conductor Arthur Nikisch set the precedent on 31 December 1918, with a concert in the name of peace and freedom.

33. Hermann Hesse, "To a Cabinet Minister," August 1917; cited in Hesse, *If the War Goes On,* 15–19. See the excellent discussion of the whole Beethoven question during the war in Dennis, *Beethoven in German Politics,* 66–85.

34. Mme. Edgar Quinet, *Ce que dit la musique* (Paris, 1894), 403.

35. Schrade, *Beethoven in France,* 136.

36. Edgar Quinet, *Allemagne au-dessus de tout!* (Paris, 1917). This edition of Quinet's articles on Germany has a commentary by Paul Gautier.

37. Stravinsky's "Souvenir d'une marche boche" and Ives's "Concord" Sonata, both of 1915, argue the symbolic power of the same symphony (pro et contra). See chapters 8 and 19.

38. Republished in the collection of wartime articles under the title *Above the Battle,* trans. C. K. Ogden (Chicago and London, 1916), 56ff.

39. Rolland, *Above the Battle,* 58–59.

40. See Schrade, *Beethoven in France,* chapters 5 and 6.

41. Strauss and Rolland, *Correspondence,* 209.

42. Ibid., 195.

43. Ibid., 82.

44. Ibid., 85.

45. Ibid., 1068.

46. Rolland, *Journal,* 1067.

47. Cited by Stefan Zweig in *Romain Rolland, the Man and His Work,* trans. Eden and Cedar Paul (New York, 1921), 198.

48. Martha Hanna, *The Mobilization of Intellect,* chapter 3, "The *Kultur* War," 78–105, provides an extensive discussion of the argument surrounding the Manifesto of '93.

49. See Jean-Jacques Becker, *The Great War and the French People,* trans. Arnold Pomerans (New York, 1986), 172. The musicologist Leo Schrade was repeating the charge as late as 1942: "Lambert was a soldier of the World War.

He went to the front, as Péguy did, as Rolland refused to do." Schrade, *Beethoven in France*, 16.

50. Numerous personal experiences are recorded in Rolland's *Journal* during this period that reflect his need to transcend national aspirations and to alleviate suffering.

51. Rolland, "Au-dessus de la mêlée," in *Au-dessus de la mêlée* (Paris, 1915), 16.

52. See Igor Stravinsky and Robert Craft, *Memories and Commentaries* (Garden City, N.Y., 1960), 75. Although the war thesis is not prominently pursued, Richard Taruskin's monumental *Stravinsky and the Russian Traditions* (Berkeley, 1996) is virtual testimony to this assertion.

53. Rolland, *Above the Battle*, 19. For Hauptmann's response of 10 September see Ernst Johan, *Innenansicht eines Krieges* (Frankfurt, 1968), 41–43.

54. "Pro Aris," written on October 1914 and originally published in *Cahiers Vaudois* 10 (1914), follows the "Letter to Hauptmann," in Rolland, *Above the Battle*, 24–25.

55. Edith Wharton, *Fighting France, from Dunkerque to Belfort* (Toronto, 1915), 184–186.

56. See Nicole and Alain Lacombe, *Les chants de bataille: La chanson patriotique de 1900 à 1918* (Paris, 1992), 317–318, for the chanson "La prière des ruines," of Roland Gaël and Renéde Buxeuil. Regarding concerts given at Rheims during 1917 see Paul Hess, *La vie à Reims pendant la guerre de 1914–1918: Notes et impressions d'un bombardé* (Paris, 1998), 471–472.

57. See Lacombe, *Chants de bataille*, 177.

58. These pieces in turn recall Georges Rouault's series of lithographs begun during the war years but completed many years later, one of which carries the title "Même les ruines sont détruites"—even the ruins have been destroyed—and another which carries the word "Guerre" above a glowing face of Christ over a similar caption: "Les ruines elle-mêmes ont péri." Leo Ornstein's "Impressions de Notre Dame," op. 16, nos. 1 & 2, of 1914, recorded on Hat Art CD 6144 by Steffen Schleiermacher together with "Danse Sauvage" and "Suicide in an Airplane," also belong to the same period.

59. Rolland, *Journal*, 65.

60. Cited in Jay Winter, *Sites of Memory, Sites of Mourning: The Great War in European Cultural History* (Cambridge, U.K., 1995), 187. See also Frank Field, "Karl Kraus, Bernard Shaw and Romain Rolland as Opponents of the First World War," in *Karl Kraus in neuer Sicht*, ed. Sigurd Paul Scheichl and Edward Timms (Munich, 1986), 158–173.

61. "Above the Battle," in *Above the Battle*, 43.

62. Hess, *Vie à Reims*, 58–59.

63. See Yvan Goll, *Für den Gefallenen von Europa* (Zurich, 1917), 25ff; for an extensive excerpt see Rainer Rother, ed., *Die letzten Tage der Menschheit: Bilder des Ersten Weltkrieges* (Berlin, 1994), 76–77. For a discussion see Margaret A. Parmée, *Ivan Goll: The Development of His Poetic Themes and Their Imagery* (Bonn, 1981), 147–150.

64. For opinions expressed by Henri Massis and Julien Benda see Martha Hanna, *The Mobilization of Intellect*, 98–99. See also Becker, *The Great War*, chap. 4, "The Anti-War Current."

CHAPTER 2. POMP AND CIRCUMSTANCE

1. J. Davidson Ketchum, *Ruhleben: A Prison Camp Society* (Toronto, 1965), 244.

2. Lewis Foreman, "In Ruhleben Camp," an illustrated radio talk, BBC Radio 3, broadcast 24 December 1995.

3. Ernest Newman, "The War and the Future of Music," *The Musical Times* 55 (1 September 1914), 571.

4. Ernest Newman, "The Artist and the People," *The Musical Times* 55 (1 October 1914), 605.

5. See particularly Stuart Wallace, *War and the Image of Germany: British Academics, 1914–1918* (Edinburgh, 1988).

6. Newman, "The War and the Future of Music," 571–572.

7. Ibid.

8. Ibid.

9. Ibid.

10. Michael Short, *Gustav Holst* (Oxford, 1990), 132–133.

11. See Timothy Materer, ed., *Pound/Lewis: The Letters of Ezra Pound and Wyndham Lewis* (London, 1985), 39; and Samuel Hynes, *A War Imagined: The First World War and English Culture* (London, 1990), 101–102.

12. Paul Peppis, *Literature, Politics, and the English Avant-garde: Nation and Empire, 1901–1918* (Cambridge, 2000), preface.

13. The latter sold over 3,000 copies by 1950. See P. Dickinson, "Lord Berners, 1883–1950: A British Avant-Gardist at the Time of World War I," *Musical Times* 24 (1983): 669–672.

14. See Ernest Newman, "Mr. Ernest Newman on French and English Music," *The Musical Times* 59 (1 October 1918), 417.

15. For an especially rich discussion of this issue see Pamela Potter, *Most German of the Arts* (New Haven, 1998), chap. 7, "Attempts to Define 'Germanness' in Music."

16. For some French opinions about English music see Romain Rolland, "L'opéra en Angleterre," in *Les origines du théâtre lyrique moderne* (Paris, 1895); and Joseph de Marliave, "Musiciens anglais" (1906), in *Études musicales* (Paris, 1917), 99–118.

17. For a confirmation of this perspective, see Newman's article, "The New French Recipe," *The Musical Times* 58 (1 October 1917), 441.

18. See Marian Drozdowski, *Ignacy Jan Paderewski: A Political Biography* (Warsaw, 1981), 68; Norman Davies, *God's Playground: A History of Poland*, vol. 2 (Crakow, 1981), 378; and Harold B. Segel, "Culture in Poland during World War I," in *European Culture in the Great War: The Arts, Entertain-*

ment, and Propaganda, 1914–1918, ed. Aviel Roshwald and Richard Stites (Cambridge, U.K., 1999), 58–88.

19. Regarding Elgar's "Polonia" and its background see Joseph Herter, "*Polonia*, op. 76, by Edward Elgar," *Journal of the Elgar Society* 2, no. 2 (1999): 97–109. Completed on 1 July 1915 and premiered five days later, "Polonia" borrowed from numerous sources including the Polish national anthem, a nocturne of Chopin, and Paderewski's "Fantasie Polonaise." *Elgar: War Music*, Pearl SHE CD 9602, contains recordings of "Carillon," "Le drapeau belge," "Fringes of the Fleet," "Une voix dans le désert," and "Polonia."

20. One of the highlights among the various benefit concerts was "A Night in Poland," arranged by Ernest Schelling for a Paderewski Polish Victims' Relief Fund concert in New York on 8 April 1915 that featured the Polish coloratura soprano Marcella Sembrich-Kochanska.

21. Regarding escalating notions of the "barbarous Hun" see Sophie de Schaepdrijver, "Occupation, Propaganda and the Idea of Belgium," in *European Culture in the Great War: The Arts, Entertainment, and Propaganda, 1914–1918*, ed. Aviel Roshwald and Richard Stites (Cambridge, U.K., 1999), 268.

22. See de Schaepdrijver, "Occupation," 282ff., 292–294.

23. See Jay Winter, "Popular Culture in Wartime Britain," in *European Culture in the Great War: The Arts, Entertainment, and Propaganda, 1914–1918*, ed. Aviel Roshwald and Richard Stites (Cambridge, U.K., 1999), 331.

24. Egmont, although a Catholic, had opposed the persecution of the Protestants, and his execution caused a revolution against Spanish rule that was to last for decades.

25. Maeterlinck's name carried a considerable resonance, not only because he had been named the Nobel laureate for literature in 1911, but also because he was admired by artists from the Allied and Central powers alike. His *Pelléas et Mélisande* of 1892 had inspired not only Claude Debussy to write an opera which premiered in 1903 but also Gabriel Fauré, Arnold Schoenberg, and Jean Sibelius to write symphonic poems in 1898, 1903, and 1905 respectively.

Numerous letters by the young Alban Berg also attest to his ongoing fascination with Maeterlinck prior to the war's outbreak. Later Maeterlinck published a collection of wartime essays, *The Wrack of the Storm*, trans. Alexander Teixeira de Mattos (New York, 1919).

26. The power of the carillon for the conquered populace of Alsace-Lorraine in particular during the period following the return of the area to the Germans after the Franco-Prussian War had been clearly summarized in a popular chanson, "Les cloches françaises." Its central message was contained in the refrain, "Sur les têtes des Allemands, / Nous, nous chantons des Marseillaise; / Nous sommmes des cloches françaises." (Above the heads of the Germans, We sing the Marseillaise; We are the bells of France.) See Madeleine Schmidt, ed., *Chansons de la revanche et la Grande Guerre* (Paris, 1985), 111.

27. Despite his renown as a novelist, Hardy thought of himself primarily as a poet.

28. Thomas Hardy, "Sonnet on the Belgian Expatriation," in *King Albert's Book: A Tribute to the Belgian King and People from Representative Men and Women throughout the World* (London, 1914).

29. A similar fate befell many of the instruments in Belgium's village brass bands, whose trumpets and trombones were appropriated by the Germans in their quest for copper. See de Schaepdrijver, "Occupation," 277.

30. Siegfried Sassoon, *Collected Poems, 1908–1956* (London, 1961), 91. It is of interest that "during World War II, 46 of the 213 carillons in Europe were destroyed or the bells requisitioned." See www.grovemusic.com, "Carillon-History."

31. See "The Carillon of Bruges," *The Musical Times* 59 (1 December 1918), 560.

32. Report by W. W. Startmer, *The Musical Times* 60 (1 May 1919), 225.

33. The text includes the phrase "Not a dog, not a cat, Only a flight of crows." Among domestic animals, the horse in particular served gallantly in the war and its slaughter by humans and disappearance in the mud—"an octopus of sucking clay" as the poet Wilfred Owen put it—struck Elgar's psyche to the core. See Jerrold N. Moore, *Edward Elgar: A Creative Life* (Oxford, 1984), 670; and *Edward Elgar: Letters of a Lifetime*, selected by Jerrold N. Moore (Oxford, 1990), 276–277.

34. See Donald Rayfield, "The Soldier's Lament: World War One Folk Poetry in the Russian Empire," *The Slavonic and East European Review* 66, no. 1 (1988): 75. The association is corroborated by Ricciotto Canudo in his *Combats d'Orient* (Paris, 1917), which includes a section labeled "La messe des morts et le choeur des corbeaux" (Mass of the dead and the chorus of crows).

35. Originally composed as a three-voice French-texted chanson that carried the opening text, "Nous voyons que les hommes font tous vertu d'aimer," the work was first published with its Latin contrafactum only in 1845, and was further popularized by Franz Liszt in versions for both piano and organ in 1862. However, the symbolism of the Latin text—not the original French—and the nationality of the composer were sufficiently well known to village church choirs of the time that they served Elgar's purpose admirably.

36. *The Pall Mall Gazette* of 31 January 1916 was less than enthusiastic, however, noting the novelty of combining music, speech, and song, but faulting Elgar for his "excessive restraint."

37. The second movement of Stanford's piano concerto is an ideal place to test the relationship.

38. Charles Villiers Stanford, "Music and the War" (rev. 1916), in *Interludes, Records and Reflections* (London, 1922), 102–124. Interestingly, Holst's *The Planets* had already been composed but not yet premiered when these words were written, and one can only wonder what Stanford might have said about one of his own compatriots had he heard its frenzied first movement, "Mars: God of War."

39. Charles Villiers Stanford, *Interludes, Records and Reflections* (London, 1922), 106–107.

40. See R. A. Stradling and Meirion Hughes, *The English Musical Renaissance 1860–1940: Construction and Deconstruction* (London, 1993), 19ff, 26, 31, 41–53ff. See also Peter J. Pirie, *The English Musical Renaissance* (London, 1979); and Michael Trend, *The Music Makers: Heirs and Rebels of the English Musical Renaissance, Edward Elgar to Benjamin Britten* (London, 1985).

41. George Bernard Shaw, "The Future of British Music," *Music and Letters* 1, no. 1 (1920): 7–11.

42. Ibid.

43. L. Dunton Green, "Music of the Week," *The Arts Gazette*, 29 March 1919.

44. Elgar, *Letters of a Lifetime*, 316. See also Brian Trowell, "The Road to Brinkwells: The Last Chamber Music," in *Oh, My Horses! Elgar and the Great War*, ed. Lewis Foreman (Rickmansworth, Herts, 2001), 371.

45. See chapter 5.

46. Richard R. Terry, "Sidelights on German Art," *The Musical Times* 56 (1 August 1915): 457–461.

47. At the New York international congress on Gregorian chant in 1920 Mocquereau referred to the Gradual *Iustus ut palma* volumes as a "war machine" ("engin de guerre") in the struggle against the German publication privilege, "a kind of scientific 'tank,' strong, invulnerable, and capable of obliterating all of the arguments of the enemy." See David Hiley, *Western Plainchant: A Handbook* (Oxford, 1993), 626.

48. Anonymous article, *The Musical Times* 56 (1 September 1915): 537–538.

49. Richard Turbet, "A Monument of Enthusiastic Industry: Further Light on 'Tudor Church Music,'" *Music and Letters* 81, no. 3 (2000): 433–436, claims that *Tudor Church Music* was envisioned by W. H. Hadow as early as 1916.

CHAPTER 3. THE OLD LIE

1. The letter was written 12 August 1914. Reprinted in *The Autobiography of Bertrand Russell* (London, 1968), vol. 2, chap. 1. See also Peter Parker, *The Old Lie: The Great War and the Public School Ethos* (London, 1987); and Michel Roucoux, ed., *English Literature of the Great War Revisited: Proceedings of the Symposium on the British Literature of the First World War: University of Picardy* (Amiens, 1989).

2. See Edward Rothstein, "Must People Lie? Yes, Absolutely. Or Is That a Lie?" *The New York Times*, 18 August 2001, "Arts and Ideas."

3. For a scene-by-scene plot synopsis see Granville Bantock's "Havergal Brian and *The Tigers*," originally written in 1944 and reprinted in *HB: Aspects of Havergal Brian*, ed. Jürgen Schaarwächter (Aldershot, 1997), 318–333. See also Matthew Richardson's history of the Leicestershire Regiment, *The Tigers* (London, 2000).

4. See Malcolm MacDonald, "Havergal Brian," www.grovemusic.org.

5. Brian's opera, composed from 1916 to 1919 and orchestrated between 1928 and 1929, was posthumously premiered only in 1983. See also Malcolm MacDonald, "Let the Roar of the *Tigers* Be Heard in the Land . . ." and Martyn Becker, "Brian's Impatient *Tigers*," in *HB: Aspects of Havergal Brian*, ed. Jürgen Schaarwächter (Aldershot, 1997), 333–338 and 339–342.

6. In addition to pieces by Elgar, Mackenzie, and Cowen, *King Albert's Book* included Charles Villiers Stanford's setting for unison voices and organ of Bishop Walsham How's hymn "But lo! There breaks a yet more glorious Day" and Edward German's textless "Hymn [Homage to Belgium, 1914]." The music by non-English composers included: André Messager's "Pour la patrie" on a text by Victor Hugo; Claude Debussy's "Berceuse héroïque" for piano solo; P. E. Lange-Müller's "Lamentation" for solo piano; and Pietro Mascagni's "Sunt Lacrymae Rerum!" for piano.

7. Published in 1917, Ireland's "The Soldier" was followed the next year by two additional settings from the collection *1914 and Other Poems:* "Blow out, You Bugles" and "Spring Sorrow." Ireland frequently wrote songs with a highly developed accompaniment, yet he accords all of Brooke's verses a solemn, essentially hymn-like setting in the best tradition of Stanford, his teacher.

8. *Musical Times* 59 (1 April 1918). The music had originally been published in 1916 by G. Ricordi, with whom Burleigh had maintained an intimate connection as editor for many years. Other settings of Brooke's poetry were made by Charles Ives and Sydney H. Nicholson.

9. See Paul Fussell, ed., *The Norton Book of Modern War* (New York, 1991), 35.

10. Wilfred Owen, "Dulce et Decorum Est," in *The War Poems*, ed. Jon Silkin (London, 1994).

11. See Martin Gilbert, *The First World War: A Complete History* (New York, 1994), photo no. 73, following p. 456. The still photograph included there is actually taken from preserved motion film footage. Sargent spent four months at the front in 1918, sketching under a camouflaged white umbrella, and contracted influenza, which placed him in an army hospital with wounded soldiers.

12. See Winter, "Popular Culture in Wartime Britain," 340, who notes that such seeming lightheartedness points to "a defiance of circumstances, as well as adhesion to a collective code of sportsmanlike behavior."

13. Ezra Pound, *Personae: The Collected Poems of Ezra Pound* (New York: Boni and Liveright, 1926), and *Personae: The Shorter Poems*, rev. ed., ed. Lea Baechler and A. Walton Litz (New York, 1990), 4.

14. Hugh Witemeyer, "Early Poetry, 1908–1920," in *The Cambridge Companion to Ezra Pound*, ed. Ira B. Nadel (Cambridge, U.K., 1999), 55.

15. Pound, *Personae: The Shorter Poems*, 4, lines 10–17.

16. See Stanford, *Interludes, Records and Reflections*, 102–103, which includes the essay "Music and the War" that had originally appeared in the

Quarterly Review in 1916. For a more negative soldier's view of the Old Men who had stayed at home see Hynes, *A War Imagined*, 17–18.

17. In the *Berliner Tageblatt*, less than three weeks after the outbreak of war, the critic Leopold Hirschberg proposed the mass distribution of Beethoven's music in specific response to conflict. He was more charitable than Stanford about some of Beethoven's minor war pieces, however, and specifically included *Wellingtons Sieg*, the *Chor auf die verbündeten Fürsten*, and *Der glorreiche Augenblick*. He also claimed that in the "Funeral March" of Beethoven's Third Symphony he sensed Horace's dictum "Dulce et decorum est pro patria mori." See Dennis, *Beethoven in German Politics*, 69.

18. Another was Ivor Gurney, who was gassed at Passchendaele and eventually certified insane in 1922.

19. Recorded by Bryn Terfel and Malcolm Martineau on DGG CD 445 946–2. A number of Housman's poems were set to music, including one of his most popular from *A Shropshire Lad*, composed by George Butterworth: "They carry back bright to the coiner the mintage of man, / The lads that will die in their glory and never be old." See Malcolm Brown, *The Imperial War Museum Book of the Somme* (London, 1996), 298.

20. A. E. Housman, "On the Idle Hill of Summer," in *A Shropshire Lad* (London, 1896).

21. See Bryan N. S. Gooch and David S. Thatcher, *Musical Settings of Late Victorian and Modern British Literature: A Catalogue* (New York, 1976).

22. For more on the war and the English choral tradition see Herbert Antcliffe, "The Effect of the War on English Choral Music," *The Musical Quarterly* 6 no. 3 (1920): 342–353.

23. The first complete performance was given in Birmingham Town Hall on 4 October 1917, with Appleby Matthews conducting. See John Norris, "The Spirit of Elgar," in *Oh, My Horses! Elgar and the Great War*, ed. Lewis Foreman (Rickmansworth, Herts, 2001), 250.

24. Edward Elgar, *The Spirit of England* (London, 1917).

25. Robert Anderson, *Elgar* (London, 1993), 202.

26. Reprinted in Jean Bethke Elshtain, *Women and War* (New York, 1987), 192–193.

27. It also prodded Sassoon to one of his bitterest responses, "Glory of Women." See Siegfried Sassoon, *Siegfried Sassoon's Long Journey*, ed. Paul Fussell (New York, 1983), xii–xiii.

28. Käthe Kollwitz, diary entry for 27 August 1914, in *The Diaries and Letters*, ed. Hans Kollwitz, trans. Richard and Clara Winston (Chicago, 1955).

29. See Susan R. Grayzel, *Women's Identities at War: Gender, Motherhood, and Politics in Britain and France during the First World War* (Chapel Hill, 1999); and Deborah Thom, *Nice Girls and Rude Girls: Women Workers in World War I* (London, 1998).

30. Moore, *Edward Elgar*, 680.

31. Elgar, *The Spirit of England*.

32. Ibid.

33. Basil Maine, *Elgar: His Life and Works* (Portway, 1933), 241.

34. John Hatcher, *Laurence Binyon: Poet, Scholar of East and West* (Oxford, 1995), 198.

35. Elgar, *The Spirit of England*.

36. See Elgar, *Letters of a Lifetime*, 307.

37. Ernest Newman, "'The Spirit of England': Edward Elgar's New Choral Work," *The Musical Times* 57 (1 May 1916): 235, 239.

38. Frederick Delius, *Requiem*, 1914–1916.

39. The list would include verses by Rupert Brooke, Alan Seeger, Richard Dehmel, and Walter Flex, as well as the resurrected lines of Paul Cezano in his celebrated chanson from the Franco-Prussian war, "Le régiment de sambre et meuse."

40. "Jerusalem" is still sung annually by the audience at the conclusion of the London Prom Concerts. Stanford's offering for *King Albert's Book* was also a strophic hymn for unison voices and organ, richly harmonized in the finest Anglican tradition. It carries the inescapable inference that only in a piece capable of being sung by a large congregation could the composer hope to promote national goals.

41. Parry's *Songs of Farewell* and "Jerusalem" are included on Hyperion CDA 662W73, "Cathedral Music by Parry," sung by St. George's Chapel choir.

42. Elgar, of course, wrote other pieces including an incomplete Third Symphony, which was ultimately edited and made ready for performance in 1998.

43. Percy Scholes confirmed the general opinion concerning Elgar's importance for the nation in *The Music Student* (August 1916): 358: "If this country had a 'Musician Laureat' it would be to Elgar that the laurel would be offered. For he, of all our musicians, is the one to whom we turn in times of national feeling to provide us with the musical expression for which our spirits crave."

44. Returning to England for training in the Officer's Cadet School, Vaughan Williams then saw service in France as a second lieutenant in a heavy artillery battery and was demobilized only in 1919.

45. The former drew upon Walt Whitman's visions of the American Civil War as well as lines of 1855 by the British orator John Bright, "The Angel of Death has been abroad throughout the land." Not published at the time, it was reworked only in 1936 when it became part of his larger choral work *Dona nobis pacem*.

46. Cecil Spring-Rice, "Thaxted," in *New Catholic Hymnal* (London, 1971), no. 110. It was sung at the wedding of Diana, Princess of Wales, as well as at her funeral in 1997. For more on the background of the hymn's title see Reg Groves, *Conrad Noel and the Thaxted Movement: An Adventure in Christian Socialism* (London, 1967), 142–143, 163–164, 171–172, 185–186.

47. Ralph Vaughan Williams and Gustav Holst, *Heirs and Rebels: Letters Written to Each Other* (New York, 1974), 45–46. One of the deceased was Cecil Coles, a young composer of promise and a friend of Holst.

48. See *The Royal College of Music (R.C.M.) Magazine*, 40, no. 1 (1959): 22.

49. Michael Kennedy, *The Works of Ralph Vaughan Williams* (Oxford, 1980), 155.

50. See Martin Jay, "Against Consolation: Walter Benjamin and the Refusal to Mourn," in *War and Remembrance in the Twentieth Century*, ed. Jay Winter and Emmanuel Sivan (Cambridge, U.K., 1999), 227.

51. See Sandra M. Gilbert, "'Unreal City': The Place of the Great War in the History of Modernity"; and Douglas Mackaman and Michael Mays, "The Quickening of Modernity, 1914–1918," in *World War I and the Cultures of Modernity*, ed. Douglas Mackaman and Michael Mays (Jackson, Mississippi, 2000), xii and xviii, respectively.

CHAPTER 4. THE SYMPHONY OF THE FRONT

1. For a sample of the literature and poetry see Fussell, ed., *Norton Book of Modern War;* and Anne Powell, ed., *A Deep Cry: First World War Soldier-Poets Killed in France and Flanders* (Stroud, 1998). For painting see Richard Cork, *A Bitter Truth* (New Haven, 1994); and Kenneth Silver, *Esprit de Corps* (Princeton, 1989)

2. See Dominic Hibberd, *Wilfred Owen: The Last Year, 1917–1918* (London, 1992); and Wilfred Owen, *The War Poems*, ed. Jon Silkin (London, 1994), for the complete text.

3. Fritz Kreisler, *Four Weeks in the Trenches: The War Story of a Violinist* (Boston, 1915), 2, 12.

4. "The Great Years of Their Lives" and interview with Leslie Smith in *Listener* 86, no. 2207 (1971): 74. See also Eric J. Leed, *No Man's Land: Combat and Identity in World War I* (Cambridge, U.K., 1979), 126, 131.

5. Karl Kraus, the Austrian satirist, introduced a similar metaphor in a speech, "In These Great Times," on 19 November 1914; published in *Die Fackel* (December 1914); reprinted in *In These Great Times: A Karl Kraus Reader*, ed. Harry Zohn ([Montreal,] 1976): 70: "In these loud times which boom with the horrible symphony of actions."

6. Cecil Barber, "Battle Music," *The Musical Times* 59 (1 January 1918): 25–26. "Stokes contingent" refers to Stoke-on-Trent, a central English county.

7. *The Musical Times* 59 (1 April 1918): 149. For interesting backgrounds on the military band and its historic role in wartime see Robert Giddings, "Delusive Seduction: Pride, Pomp, Circumstance and Military Music," in *Popular Imperialism and the Military, 1850–1950* (Manchester and New York, 1992), 25–49.

8. Ernst Fischer, *The Necessity of Art* (Harmondsworth, 1963), 75. Regarding the power of music in moments of national crisis see Giddings, "Delusive Seduction," 34ff.

9. Siegfried Sassoon, *The Old Huntsman and Other Poems* (New York, 1918).

10. Cited in John Brophy and Eric Partridge, eds., *The Long Trail: What the*

British Soldier Sang and Said in the Great War of 1914–18, rev. ed. (London, 1965), 39; and Gilbert, *First World War*, 258.

11. Regarding the important role of footballs among the English troops see Martin Middlebrook, *The First Day on the Somme* (London, 1971), 124; Paul Fussell, *The Great War and Modern Memory* (London, 1975), 27; John Keegan, *The Illustrated Face of Battle* (New York, 1989), 219; Brown, *Imperial War Museum*, 86–87; Gilbert, *First World War*, 259; and J. G. Fuller, *Troop Morale and Popular Culture in the British and Dominion Armies, 1914–1918* (Oxford, 1990), 85–94.

12. The editor's gloss to *The Great Advance: Tales from the Somme Battlefield Told by Wounded Officers and Men on their Arrival at Southampton from the Front, and Published by Permission* (London, [1916]), 24.

13. For a poster used in the campaign, see Cate Haste, *Keep the Home Fires Burning: Propaganda in the First World War* (London, 1977), 60.

14. For another perspective on the symbol of the football in the trenches see Myles Dungan, *Irish Soldiers and the Great War* (Dublin, 1997), 132.

15. Regarding "Roses of Picardy" see Winter, "Popular Culture in Wartime Britain," 334.

16. Cited in Stéphane Audoin-Rouzeau, *Men at War, 1914–1918: National Sentiment and Trench Journalism in France during the First World War*, trans. Helen McPhail (Providence, 1992), 156.

17. John H. Roper, ed., *Paul Green's War Songs: A Southern Poet's History of the Great War, 1917–1920* (Rocky Mount, N.C., 1993), 133. For more on the symbolism of Chopin's "Funeral March" see Lawrence Kramer, "Chopin at the Funeral: Episodes in the History of Modern Death," *Journal of the American Musicological Society* 54, no. 1 (2001): 97–125.

18. See Brophy and Partridge, eds., *The Long Trail.*

19. See also Patrick MacGill, "Soldier Songs," in his *The Great Push; an Episode of the Great War* (New York, 1916).

20. *The Musical Times* 56 (1 March 1915): 147.

21. "Kitchener's Army" ceased to exist at the beginning of 1916 when conscription replaced voluntary enlistment.

22. See Samuel Hynes, *The Soldier's Tale: Bearing Witness to Modern War* (New York, 1997), 31–34.

23. Hulse's letters were printed in 1916. See Malcolm Brown and Shirley Seaton, *Christmas Truce* (New York, 1984), 56.

24. Ibid., 69.

25. Karl Aldag in Dr. Philipp Witkop, ed., *Kriegsbriefe gefallener Studenten* (Munich, 1928); translated into English as *German Students' War Letters*, trans. A. F. Wedd (Methuen, 1929).

26. See Albert Moren, "2/The Queen's (Royal West Surrey)," interview for *Peace in No Man's Land*, BBC-TV, 1981. Quoted in Brown and Seaton, *Christmas Truce*, 66.

27. Brown and Seaton, *Christmas Truce*, 83.

28. Modris Eksteins, *Rites of Spring: The Great War and the Birth of the Modern Age* (Boston, 1989), 110. Rifleman Graham Williams's testimony in *Saturday Afternoon Soldiers* (unpublished memoir); interview for *Peace in No Man's Land*, BBC TV, 1981, quoted in Malcolm Brown, *Tommy Goes to War* (London, 1978), 66–68.

29. Brown and Seaton, *Christmas Truce*, 116.

30. Ibid., 184–185.

31. Ibid., 117. The violinist Fritz Kreisler corroborated these sentiments on the Eastern front in his *Four Weeks in the Trenches*, 69: "The Russians would laughingly call over to us, and the Austrians would answer. The salient feature of these three days' fighting was the extraordinary lack of hatred. In fact, it is astonishing how little actual hatred exists between fighting men. One fights fiercely and passionately, mass against mass, but as soon as the mass crystallizes itself into human individuals whose features one actually can recognize, hatred almost ceases."

32. *The Musical Times* 55 (1 December 1914): 687–691.

33. Michael Lyons, *World War I: A Short History* (Englewood Cliffs, N.J., 1994), 103.

34. See Robin Prior, *Passchendaele* (Chicago, 1996).

35. Brophy and Partridge, eds., *The Long Trail*, 58.

36. Brown, *Tommy Goes to War*, 60.

37. For these and many other texts see Brophy and Partridge, eds., *The Long Trail*.

38. 2nd Lieutenant E. W. Jacot of the 14th Battalion, Royal Warwicks. See Brown, *Tommy Goes to War*, 132.

39. Ibid., 133. For more on female impersonators in troop concert parties, see Fuller, *Troop Morale*, 106–107. See Marjorie Garber, *Vested Interests: Cross-dressing and Cultural Anxiety* (New York, 1992), for a broader consideration of the issue.

40. See Dave Russell, "'We Carved Our Way to Glory': The British Soldier in Music Hall Song and Sketch, c. 1880–1914," in *Popular Imperialism and the Military, 1850–1950*, ed. John M. MacKenzie (Manchester, 1992), 61. See Roy Palmer, ed., *The Rambling Soldier: Life in the Lower Ranks, 1750–1900, through Soldiers' Songs and Writings* (Gloucester, 1985), for an assessment of the varying attitudes toward the army expressed in broadside ballads.

41. The song "Good Bye-ee" reflected the attitude of the first weeks of the war when numerous young men expressed their desire to get a piece of the action before the war came to what they feared would be an abrupt end. The work was recorded in 1918 on HMV B 902. It is included on *The Great War: An Evocation in Music and Drama Through Recordings Made at the Time* (Pearl GEMM CD 9355).

42. Regarding the importance of the German capture of Riga see Keegan, *First World War*, 339.

43. *The Wipers Times; a Complete Facsimile of the Famous World War*

One Trench Newspaper, Incorporating The "New Church" Times, The Kemmel Times, The Somme Times, The B.E.F. Times, and The "Better Times," with an introduction, notes, and glossary by Patrick Beaver (London, 1973), 217.

44. Fussell, The Great War, 12. For Haig's belief in his destiny as a soldier see Gerard de Groot, Douglas Haig, 1861–1928 (London, 1988), 44, 117–118; and Keegan, First World War, 289.

45. The Wipers Times, 233, 351.

46. For more on General Allenby see Matthew Hughes, Allenby and British Strategy in the Middle East, 1917–1919 (London, 1999).

47. The Wipers Times, 249, 352.

48. Fussell, The Great War, 157. See also Hynes, A War Imagined, 28ff. Audoin-Rouzeau, http://www.pbs.org/greatwar/interviews/audoin4.html, emphasizes that trench newspapers were written mainly by educated soldiers and most of the time were circulated in printing runs ranging from 50 to 300 copies.

49. Lyn Macdonald, 1915, the Death of Innocence (London, 1993), 592.

50. The War Emergency Entertainments sponsored some 1,200 concerts for soldiers, and the Music in Wartime Committee another 5,000 concerts between September 1914 and August 1919. Other concert parties were sponsored by the YMCA, including a series of Concerts at the Front, which brought Ivor Novello to sing for the soldiers. See Claire Hirshfield, "Musical Performance in Wartime: 1914–1918," The Music Review 53, no. 4 (1992): 294–298. See also Gramophone Company, Gramophone Records of the First World War: An HMV Catalogue, 1914–1918, intro. Brian Rust (Newton Abbot, 1975).

51. Audoin-Rouzeau, Men at War, 49–50.

52. For a poem titled "Concert Party: Busseboom," by Edmund Blunden, see Fussell, Norton Book of Modern War, 138–139.

53. See Sassoon, Collected Poems, 100; and Patrick J. Quinn, The Great War and the Missing Muse: The Early Writings of Robert Graves and Siegfried Sassoon (London, 1994), 203.

54. Siegfried Sassoon, Sherston's Progress, in The Memoirs of George Sherston (New York, 1937), 156–157.

55. See Winter, "Popular Culture in Wartime Britain," 340–341.

56. The Musical Times 577 (1 October 1916): 458, 464. Elgar composed "Salut d'amour" as a piano piece in 1888 and orchestrated it the next year.

57. Robert Service, Rhymes of a Red Cross Man (New York, 1916).

58. For a reproduction of Sickert's Tipperary see Cork, A Bitter Truth, plate 49; for Dollman's Tipperary see Rother, ed., Die letzten Tage, 283.

59. Brophy and Partridge, eds., The Long Trail, 213.

60. "Keep the Home Fires Burning" is performed by John McCormack on Mark Best's WWI Songs collection on cassette tape.

61. Sassoon, Collected Poems, 86–87.

62. Edmonstoune Duncan, "Music and War," The Musical Times 55 (1 September 1914): 571–574.

63. Newman, "The Artist and the People." H. C. Colles's "National Anthems: Their Birth and Parentage" immediately follows Newman's article.

64. The song had endless verses as adopted by U.S. troops. See Edward Arthur Dolph, *Sound Off! Soldier Songs from Yankee Doodle to Parley Voo* (New York, 1929), 131–133.

65. Siegfried Sassoon, *Memoirs of a Fox-Hunting Man* (New York, 1929), 351.

66. The literature on popular war songs is rich in all countries.

For Australia see Paul Depasquale, *The Courage Corporate: Adelaide Songs of World War One* (Oakland Park, 1983).

For England see Brophy and Partridge, eds., *The Long Trail;* Roy Palmer, *What a Lovely War: British Soldiers' Songs from the Boer War to the Present Day* (London, 1990); Brian Murdoch, *Fighting Songs and Warring Words: Popular Lyrics of Two World Wars* (London, 1990); and Fuller, *Troop Morale.*

For France see Dominique Bonnaud, *Chants de Bataille* (Paris, 1914); Théodore Botrel, *Les chants du bivouac* (Paris, 1915); Nicole Lucien Boyer, *La chanson des poilus: Recueil des chansons et poèmes dits par l'auteur en France et en Macedoine aux armées de la République* (Paris, 1918); René Brancour, *La Marseillaise et Le chant du départ* (Paris, 1916); Schmidt, ed., *Chansons de la revanche;* Lacombe, *Les chants de bataille;* and Regina M. Sweeney, *Singing Our Way to Victory: French Cultural Politics and Music during the Great War* (Middletown, Conn., 2001).

For Germany see C. Fink, ed., *Neue Kriegslieder* (Shanghai, 1915); A. Angenetter and E. K. Blumml, eds., *Lieder der Einerschutzen* (Vienna, 1924); Wilhelm Schuhmacher, *Leben und Seele unseres Soldatenlieds im Weltkrieg* (Frankfurt am Main, 1928), with an appendix of tunes, 233–245; Bernhard Schwertfeger and Erich Otto Volkmann, eds., *Der deutsche Soldatenkunde* (Leipzig, 1937); Fritz Kredel, *Wer will unter die Soldaten: Deutsche Soldatenlieder mit farbigen Bildern* (Leipzig, 1934); Ernst Johann, *Innenansicht eines Krieges; Bilder, Briefe, Dokumente 1914–1918* (Frankfurt am Main, 1968); Reinhard Olt, *Krieg und Sprache: Untersuchungen zu deutschen Soldatenliedern des Ersten Weltkriegs* (Giessen, 1980–1981); and Heinz Lemmerman, *Kriegeserziehung im Kaiserreich: Studien zur politischen Funktion von Schule und Schulmusik, 1890–1918* (Lilienthal, 1984).

For Italy see A. V. Savona and M. L. Straniero, eds., *Canti della Grande Guerra,* 2 vols. (Milan, 1981).

For the United States see Dolph, *Sound Off!;* and Frederick Vogel, *World War I Songs: A History and Dictionary of Popular American Patriotic Tunes, with Over 300 Complete Lyrics* (Jefferson, N.C., 1995). See also Les Cleveland, *Dark Laughter: War in Song and Popular Culture* (Westport, Conn., 1994). For an assessment of the American popular song repertoire during the war see chapter 14.

67. Brother fighting against brother was not all that uncommon in World War I. See Jennifer Keene, *Doughboys, the Great War, and the Remaking of America* (Baltimore, 2001), 109.

68. Percy Grainger, Australian composer and pianist who moved to New York in 1914, made an arrangement of "Londonderry Air" that appeared in versions for solo piano and wind ensemble in 1915. Grainger spent the years 1917–1919 as a bandsman in the U.S. Army, during which time he became an American citizen.

69. For more on the backgrounds of the song see "Danny Boy: In Sunshine or in Shadow," PBS Home Video DBSS 901 (NBD Television, 1997). See also Myles Dungan, *They Shall Grow Not Old: Irish Soldiers and the Great War* (Dublin, 1997).

70. Frederick Weatherly, "Danny Boy" (London, 1913). Weatherly was also the author of "Roses of Picardy," one of the most commercially successful songs of World War I.

CHAPTER 5. MOBILIZATION AND THE CALL TO HISTORY

1. Wharton, *Fighting France.* See also *C'est l'amour* by Maurice Chevalier, who recorded how the citizenry crowded around the notices announcing general mobilization and how they laughed, cried, and sang patriotic songs. Chevalier was soon to be wounded and taken as a prisoner of war. See also Lacombe, *Les chants de bataille,* 186; and Maurice Chevalier, *Ma route et mes chansons* (Paris, 1950).

2. A scene tellingly recalled by Irving S. Cobb in his essay "To War in a Taxicab," in *Paths of Glory: Impressions of War Written At and Near the Front* (New York, 1915).

3. Wharton, *Fighting France,* 10–11. "*Badauderie:* silliness, idle behavior, lounging about; in contemporary parlance, 'hanging out.'"

4. Jacques-Émile Blanche, letter to Félicien Cacan, Offranville, 6 August 1914, *Cahiers d'un artiste,* 1st ser., June 1914–November 1914 (Paris, 1915), 118.

5. J. G. Prod'homme, "Music and Musicians in Paris During the First Two Seasons of the War," *The Musical Quarterly* 4, no. 1 (1918): 135–136; the translation is by Otto Kinkeldey.

6. David Charlton, "Etienne-Nicolas Méhul," in *The New Grove Dictionary of Music and Musicians,* 20 vols. (London, 1980), 12: 62.

7. Georges J. D. Jouvin and Joseph Vidal, eds. *Marches et chansons des soldats de France* (Paris, 1919). The volume was compiled by a Colonel Jouvin and his regimental music director in 1916 and published in 1919. See also Sweeney, *Singing Our Way to Victory,* 46–53, for a discussion and reproduction of the sheet music; and http://www.defense.gouv.fr/histoire/musique_militaire/sonotheque/marche.htm for sonic versions of the most important French military marches.

8. Étienne-Nicolas Méhul, "Chant du départ," 1794.

9. See Henri Malorey, *L'Arc de Triomphe de l'Étoile* (Toulouse, 1942), 70;

also Louis de Fourcaud, *François Rude, sculpteur: Ses oeuvres et son temps (1784–1855)* (Paris, 1904).

10. For a discussion of German songs of departure see Olt Reinhard, "Kriegslieder und ihre Motive: Abschied," in his *Krieg und Sprache: Untersuchungen zu deutschen Soldatenliedern des Ersten Weltkriegs*, Teil 1 (Giessen, 1981), 99–101; and Ernst Johan, *Innenansicht eines Krieges*, 19–21, for an elaborate "Inschriften aus den Transportwaggons zur Front." For examples of Italian songs on the theme see Savona and Straniero, eds., *Canti della Grande Guerra*, vol. 1, e.g., "Addio mia bella addio," 73–77, and "Addio padre e madre addio," 113–118. Another, "Siamo partiti da Trento bello / e poi sul tren siamo montati, / per andare in Russia a guerreggiar," 292–293, which speaks of Italian soldiers leaving the Trentino by train for Russia, was obviously written prior to the Russian-German armistice of Brest-Litovsk, 15 December 1917.

11. See Sweeney, *Singing Our Way to Victory*, 258–259, for a reproduction of the music. Concerning departure for the front from the train stations, see Lacombe, *Les chants de bataille*, 190–191. Regarding French popular songs and soldier tunes see also Boyer, *La chanson des poilus;* and especially Sweeney, *Singing Our Way to Victory*.

12. See Sweeney, *Singing Our Way to Victory*, 176.

13. Lacombe, *Les chants de bataille*, 268-274, makes a detailed comparison between two of France's most popular songs of World War I, "La Marseillaise" and "La Madelon," in the section "Deux emblèmes, un art et une manière." For the complete text and music see also Schmidt, ed., *Chansons de la revanche*, 134–135, 170–171; for the music to two other French songs from the Great War, "Verdun, on ne passe pas," and "La Madelon de la victoire," see 171–173. See also Ribouillot Calude, *La musique au fusil avec les poilus dans la grande guerre* (Paris, 1996).

14. Regarding "La Madelon" ("Quand Madelon vient nous servir à boire") see Sweeney, *Singing Our Way to Victory*, 130–131, 226–227; and Charles Rearick, "Madelon and the Men—in War and Memory," *French Historical Studies* 17 (1992): 1008. For an English version published in America in 1918 see Vogel, *World War I Songs*, 340.

15. For a rich discussion regarding "The Censorship of Singing from Music Hall to Trench," see Sweeney, *Singing Our Way to Victory*, chapter 3. A notable object of censorship was the song "Réveil nocturne," whose lyrics "told the story of a married couple who had decided to stay in bed instead of going down to the shelter during a zeppelin warning, and the lyrics hinted at sexual antics." See also Regina Sweeney, "*La Pudique Anastasie:* Wartime Censorship and Bourgeois Morality," in *World War I and the Cultures of Modernity*, ed. Douglas Mackaman and Michael Mays Jackson (Mississippi, 2000).

16. Claude Debussy, *Debussy on Music: The Critical Writings of the Great French Composer Claude Debussy*, select. François Lesure, ed. and trans. Richard Longham Smith (New York, 1977), 322–333.

17. See Carlo Caballero, "Patriotism or Nationalism? Fauré and the Great War," *Journal of the American Musicological Society* 52, no. 3 (1999): 596ff, regarding associations of "race" with the concept of "nationalism" as opposed to connotations of affection inherent in the word "patriotism."

18. Regarding the perception of composers as intellectuals see Fulcher, *French Cultural Politics*, 15–20.

19. See Hanna, *The Mobilization of Intellect*, 2–3.

20. Claude Debussy, *Correspondance, 1884–1918*, ed. François Lesure (Paris, 1993), 343–344; English translation in Edward Lockspeiser, *Debussy*, 3d ed. (London, 1951), 102, and *Debussy Letters*, ed. François Lesure and Roger Nichols, trans. Roger Nichols (London, 1987), 291.

21. See Ernest Closson, *L'élément flamand dans Beethoven* (Brussels, 1928). On the question of Flemish identity vis-à-vis the Germans see de Schaepdrijver, "Occupation, propaganda and the idea of Belgium," 281ff.

22. Letter to Nicola Coronio in *Debussy Letters*, 293. For a detailed assessment of the Wagner-Debussy relationship see Robin Holloway, *Debussy and Wagner* (London, 1979).

23. Debussy, *Correspondance*, 344–345.

24. Ibid.

25. As a result it has been observed that only four French wartime works ever aspired to a position in the literary canon: Apollinaire's *Calligrammes*, Paul Valéry's *Civilisations*, Barbusse's *Le feu*, and Marcel Proust's *À la recherche du temps perdu*, published between 1913 and 1927. See Marc Ferro, "Cultural Life in France, 1914–1918," in *European Culture in the Great War*, ed. Aviel Roshwald and Richard Stites (Cambridge, U.K., 1999), 304.

26. A *pièce d'occasion* written in June 1915, titled *Page d'album:* "Pour l'oeuvre du vêtement du blessé." The organization approached Debussy for a manuscript page to be offered at a fund-raising auction, and Debussy obliged not only with the requested autograph page but also a newly composed waltz for piano. The work is not without its subtleties and is of special interest for its metric and accentual shifting. Regarding the flirtation with the waltz by Paris-based composers in the second decade, see Messing, *Neoclassicism*, 90–91.

27. Originally written in 1830 during the struggle with Holland for Belgian independence, the music for "La brabançonne" was by François van Campenhout (1779–1848), but the original text by Hippolyte Louis Alexandre Dechet ("Jenneval," 1801–1830) was replaced in 1860 with another by Charles Rogier. See also E. Closson, *Pourquoi la Brabançonne n'est pas devenue un chant populaire* (Brussells, 1928). The French national anthem, on the other hand, had been composed in 1792, and only three years later, when it was officially adopted as France's national anthem, it appeared in Salieri's opera, *Palmira, regina di Persia*. Composers of various nationalities adopted it in succeeding decades, including Schumann in *Faschingsschwank aus Wien* and "Die beiden Grenadieren," Wagner in "Les deux grenadiers," Liszt in *Héroïde funèbre*, and Tchaikovsky in his *1812 Overture*.

28. See Charles-Henry Coombe, "Les citations d'hymnes nationaux chez Debussy," *Revue musicale de Suisse romande* 39, no. 1 (1986): 19–27.

29. Ernest Newman, "Elgar's 'Fourth of August,'" *The Musical Times* 58 (1 July 1917): 297.

30. Debussy, *Correspondance*, 344f.

31. Debussy, *Letters*, 295.

32. Debussy, *Correspondance*, 365–366; Debussy, *Letters*, 313.

33. Debussy, *Correspondance*, 361–363. Translated in Igor Stravinsky and Robert Craft, *Conversations with Igor Stravinsky* (Garden City, N.Y., 1959), 57–59.

34. Ibid.

35. Debussy, *Correspondance*, 365.

36. Léon Vallas, *Achille-Claude Debussy* (Paris, 1944), 251.

37. Letter of 22 July 1915. See Debussy, *Correspondance*, 351–352. Debussy hardly need have apologized for the inclusion of the Lutheran hymn in light of the introduction and verification of its symbolism by a group of French penitents in Meyerbeer's *Les Huguenots* as early as 1836.

38. See Jonathan Dunsby, "The Poetry of Debussy's *En blanc et noir*," in *Analytic Strategies and Musical Interpretation: Essays on Nineteenth- and Twentieth-Century Music*, ed. Craig Ayrey and Mark Everist (Cambridge, 1996), 164 n. 28; but also see Juren Vis, "Debussy and the War: Debussy, Luther, and Janequin," *Cahiers Debussy* 15 (1991): 36–38, 42, for a deft deciphering of Debussy's claims for a "foreshadowing" of "La Marseillaise."

39. Liner notes to Elektra Nonesuch 979161–2 (1987).

40. *Debussy on Music*, 315; originally in *Bulletin de SIM*, 1 March 1914.

41. J. M. Nectoux, ed., *Camille Saint-Saëns et Gabriel Fauré: Correspondance, soixante ans d'amitié* (Paris, 1973), 107–108.

42. Kenneth Silver's *Esprit de corps: The Art of the Parisian Avant-garde and the First World War, 1914–1925* (Princeton, 1989), reviews this issue at length.

43. The Action Française, which reached its zenith following World War I, suffered a severe blow when it was condemned by the papacy in 1926. Its association with the German collaborationist Vichy government (1940–1944) brought further discredit and ultimate dissolution following World War II. The rise and fall of the career of Charles Maurras, one of the founders of the Action Française in 1899, mirrors this trajectory in his support of the Pétain government followed by arrest and sentence to life imprisonment in 1944. See also Silver, *Esprit de Corps*, 102–103. For more on the intrigue of the various leagues and societies see Michel Duchesneau, "La musique française pendant la Guerre 1914–1918: Autour de la tentative de fusion de la Société Nationale de Musique et de la Société Musicale Indépendante," *Revue de Musicologie* 82, no. 1 (1996): 123–153.

44. See Fulcher, *French Cultural Politics*, 153ff.

45. *Le monde musical*, 30 October 1909.

46. See Duchesneau, "La musique française," 133–141.

47. Andrew Thomson, *Widor* (Oxford, 1987), 77. In 1917 a similar protest had been raised against Rodin's candidature. Widor campaigned for Rodin's admission and had garnered sufficient votes, when fate and nature once again conspired to settle the matter. "On Saturday, 24 November, the day fixed for the election," Widor said, "I had the sad honour to stand before Rodin's coffin and announce his success." Charles-Marie Widor, *Académie des Beaux-Arts: Fondations, portraits de Massenet à Paladilhe* (Paris, 1927), 176.

48. Lockspieser, *Debussy*, 103.

49. Hanna, *The Mobilization of Intellect*, 11; and Jane Fulcher, "The Composer as Intellectual: Ideological Inscriptions in French Interwar Neoclassicism," *The Journal of Musicology* 17, no. 2 (1999): 200ff.

50. See especially Silver, *Esprit de Corps*, 200–205, regarding Matisse, 110–145 for Picasso.

51. See Émile Boutroux, "L'Allemagne et la guerre; lettre de M. Émile Boutroux," *Revue des deux mondes* 23 (1914): 390–394.

52. Hanna, *Mobilization of Intellect*, 10, 144.

53. Pierre Imbart de la Tour, "Le Pangermanisme et la philosophie de l'histoire: Lettre à M. Henri Bergson," *Revue des deux mondes* 30 (1915): 485, as cited in Hanna, *Mobilization of Intellect*, 145. For an endorsement of this sentiment by Henri Focillon see Silver, *Esprit de Corps*, 101.

54. See especially Potter, *Most German of the Arts*, 201ff., for a rich discussion of the issue of "Germanness" in music.

55. See chapter 14 for a further discussion of Schoenberg's nationalist views.

56. Victor Basch, *Revue de métaphysique et de morale* (1915), as paraphrased in Hanna, *Mobilization of Intellect*, 159.

57. See Camille Saint-Saëns, *Germanophilie* (Paris, 1916), regarding the debate between the author and d'Indy over German music. Two of the cofounders of the Schola Cantorum were equally important for the French classic revival: Alexandre Guilmant, organist and editor of the works of French Baroque keyboard composers like Daquin and Clerambault; and Charles Bordes, whose choral ensemble, the *Chanteurs de Saint-Gervais*, performed widely across France. For an appreciation by Debussy of Bordes's work with the Chanteurs de Saint-Gervais, see his article, "At the Schola Cantorum," *Gil Blas*, 1 February 1903; reprinted in *Debussy on Music*, 110.

58. The cyclic idea was a formal principle based on the repetition of musical materials between movements clearly observable in the cantus-firmus, paraphrase, and parody masses of the Renaissance as well as more recently in the works of Beethoven, Schubert, Berlioz, and especially the symphony of César Franck and the music-dramas of Wagner.

59. Rolland, *Musicians of Today*, 317.

60. See Fulcher, "The Composer as Intellectual," 206, 348–349. For Debussy's article, "German Influence on French Music," originally published in *Mercure de France* (January 1903), see *Debussy on Music*, 83.

61. The edition of François Couperin's *pièces de clavecins*, for example, which had been achieved in 1871 by the Germans Brahms and Chrysander, had already been partly, if belatedly, supplanted by a French version in 1905 with the publication by Durand of the complete keyboard works. And a complete edition of the works of Rameau had been launched in 1895 with Malherbe and Saint-Saëns as general editors. Over the next decade and a half the project continued with versions of Rameau's operas *Les indes galantes, Dardanus,* and *Les fêtes de Polymnie* edited by Dukas (1902), d'Indy (1905), and Debussy (1908), respectively. For more on Debussy's view of Rameau's operas see his "Àpropos *Hippolyte et Aricie*," *Le Figaro,* 8 May 1908; reprinted in *Debussy on Music,* 228–231; on the importance of Rameau, "Jean Philippe Rameau" (November 1912), solicited by André Caplet for an American magazine, see *Debussy on Music,* 254–255.

62. Debussy, *Gil Blas,* 19 January 1903; reprinted in *Debussy on Music,* 86.

63. Debussy's first piano teacher and the most important early influence in his turn to music was Mme. Mauté de Fleurville, a former pupil of Chopin, and Debussy's continuing admiration for the latter during the war years was understandably enhanced by Allied concerns for a postwar Poland—an issue for which another pianist, Ignacy Paderewski, stood as an increasingly potent symbol.

64. It was a keyboard perspective previously adopted by Florent Schmitt in his *Sur cinq notes* of 1907 and that Stravinsky would adopt in his *Cinq doigts* of 1920–1921, both of which were the opposite of virtuoso keyboard writing and corroborated the growing affiliation between children's pieces and the revival of French classical traditions.

65. For a discussion of Satie's cabaret-style parody of Clementi in his *Sonatine bureaucratique* and its relation to Neoclassicism see Steven M. Whiting, *Satie the Bohemian: From Cabaret to Concert Hall* (Oxford, 1999), 484–488.

66. Letter to Stravinsky, October 24, 1915, in Debussy, *Correspondance,* 361–363. Translation in Stravinsky and Craft, *Conversations,* 57–59.

67. See Fulcher, *French Cultural Politics,* 184ff., regarding Debussy's views on the German approach to form and d'Indy's teachings at the Schola.

68. See Messing, *Neoclassicism in Music,* 46, for comparative examples.

69. Roger Nichols, "Debussy," *The New Grove Dictionary of Music and Musicians,* 20 vols. (London, 1980), 5: 300.

70. See Glenn Watkins, *Soundings* (New York, 1988), 183–184.

71. "Why are we so indifferent toward our own great Rameau?" Debussy wrote. "And toward Destouches, now almost forgotten? And to Couperin, the most poetic of our harpsichordists, whose tender melancholy is like that enchanting echo that emanates from the depths of a Watteau landscape, filled with plaintive figures? When we compare ourselves to other countries—so mindful of the glories of their pasts—we realize that there is no excuse for our indifference. The impression with which we are left is that we scarcely care at all for our fame, for not one of these people is ever to be seen on our pro-

grams . . . On the other hand, we do find *Parsifal.*" Text originally appeared in *Bulletin de SIM*, 15 January 1913; reprinted in *Debussy on Music*, 273.

72. Ibid., 322–323. Originally in *L'intransigeant*, 11 March 1915. About the same time Debussy privately related the following description of his new sonata to the cellist Louis Rosoor that suggests other perspectives: "Pierrot [Harlequin] wakes with a start, shakes off his torpor. Abruptly he serenades his sweetheart, who, in spite of his entreaties, remains unmoved; he consoles himself for his lack of success by singing a song of liberty." Could the "song of liberty" have held dual connotations? See Ellwood Derr's notes to the CD recording of the cello sonata on Music Masters, MMD 60146.

73. "You are an astonishing man . . . as daring as a lion, you find the means to have a piano, a cellist, and a sonata all brought together only a few meters from the *boches.* . . . [I]t is, indeed, this elegant bravura which is and always will be 'truly French.'" Debussy, *Correspondance*, 368. Regarding the possibility of hearing "Bizet's arias played on café pianos or on violins and cellos in the trenches" see Regina Sweeney, "Harmony and Disharmony: French Singing and Musical Entertainment during the Great War," Ph.D. diss., University of California, Berkeley, 1992, p. 335.

74. Debussy, *Correspondance*, 279; translated in Debussy, *Letters*, 327.

75. Despite Debussy's claim that there was no call for "tetralogical auditory efforts"—with obvious reference to the use of cyclical leitmotifs in Wagner's *Ring*, it is well worth noting that the violin sonata adopts recall of the first two movements in the sonata's finale.

76. Much like Fauré's Second Violin Sonata of 1916, which was dedicated to Queen Elizabeth of Belgium, who was a fine violinist. See Carlo Caballero, "Patriotism or Nationalism?" *Journal of the American Musicological Society* 52, no. 3 (1999): 609.

77. Labels notwithstanding, the collective evidence suggests that the intellectual foment among French wartime artists proved to be a more decisive cultural determinant in the postwar France than it did in Great Britain. See Hanna, *Mobilization of Intellect*, 23.

CHAPTER 6. WAR AND THE CHILDREN

1. Eleanor Dwight, *Edith Wharton: An Extraordinary Life* (New York, 1994), 189.

2. Shari Benstock, *No Gifts from Chance: A Biography of Edith Wharton* (New York, 1994), 316.

3. The impressive list of Wharton's contributors included General Joffre, Theodore Roosevelt, Sarah Bernhardt, Eleonora Duse, Jacques-Émile Blanche, Léon Bakst, Charles Dana Gibson, Claude Monet, Pierre-Auguste Renoir, Auguste Rodin, John Singer Sargent, Rupert Brooke, Paul Claudel, Jean Cocteau, Joseph Conrad, John Galsworthy, Thomas Hardy, Henry James, Maurice Maeterlinck, the Comtesse de Noailles, Vincent d'Indy, and Igor Stravinsky.

4. For more on the issue see Judith L. Sensibar, "Edith Wharton as Propa-

gandist and Novelist: Competing Visions of 'The Great War,'" in *A Forward Glance: New Essays on Edith Wharton*, ed. Clare Colquitt, Susan Goodman, and Candace Waid (Newark, N.J., 1999), 149–171.

5. Roosevelt's concerns regarding America's responsibilities and tardy response to the European conflict were expressed at length in print as early as 1915 in *America and the World War* (New York, 1915). He continued to agitate for America's entry into the war, and when it finally came, his patriotic zeal escalated, as he proudly sent his four sons off to the service. See Edward J. Renehan Jr., *The Lion's Pride: Theodore and His Family in Peace and War* (New York, 1998).

6. The second of three stanzas, for example, finishes with the victims shouting at the enemy, "May thy dearest ones be blighted and forsaken, and thy children beg their bread!" Hardy's poem is followed by a portrait of the author painted by Jacques-Émile Blanche.

7. The poem was written expressly for Edith Wharton's *Le livre des sans-foyer* (The Book of the Homeless) (London, 1916).

8. Haste, *Keep the Home Fires Burning*, 90–91.

9. Dwight, *Edith Wharton*, 203.

10. Reproduced in Audoin-Rouzeau, *Men at War*, 32. See also Lacombe, *Les chants de bataille*, 257. Amongst the various contributions to the anthology none excelled the sheer bathos of Edith Wharton's own poem, "The Tryst." For other French poets who wrote extensively of the war and music see Ian Higgins, ed., *Anthology of First World War French Poetry* (Glasgow, 1996), for examples by Guillaume Apollinaire, Louis Aragon, Paul Claudel, Jean Cocteau, André Martel ("Concert," 73), Albert-Paul Granier ("Musique," 54), and Marcel Martinet ("Musique militaire," 74).

11. Claude Debussy, "Noël des enfants qui n'ont plus de maisons" (Paris, 1916).

12. "Noël des enfants qui n'ont plus de maisons" was initially published in 1916, and it was arranged for two-voiced children's chorus with piano in the same year.

13. Blanche, *Cahiers d'un artiste*, 2d ser. (Paris, 1916), November 1914–June 1915, 240. That "Tipperary" was a familiar tune to Parisians is suggested by Blanche in his *Cahiers d'un artiste*, 3d ser. (Paris, 1917), 26 October, midi, 1915, where he speaks of hearing a group of marching Canadians sing this song as they climbed the banks of a river.

14. Debussy, *Correspondance*, 374.

15. Walton H. Rawls, *Awake America! World War I and the American Poster* (New York, 1988), 130.

16. I am grateful to Martin Katz for this observation.

17. That the French knew their Schubert is made touchingly clear in the wartime diaries of the portrait artist Jacques-Émile Blanche. There in an entry made at Christmastime 1914 he cites a letter just received from a soldier at the front: "The Germans, in the adjacent trenches, celebrate their God in song. Just now a tenor sings 'Death and the Maiden'. They have Schubert, they have

Schumann, and the Bible with them. I have a Bible, also, in my sack which I found in the ruins, and I re-read Ezechiel and the Book of Job." See Blanche, *Cahiers d'un artiste*, 2d ser., November 1914–June 1915, 137–138.

18. A copy exists in the Special Collections of the Sibley Music Library, Rochester, N.Y.

19. "Papa Noël, je t'écris cette lettre, du coin du feu, comme on est bien chez nous! Dans mon sabot, tu la prendra peut-être, En apportant tes bonbons tes joujoux. C'est que, vois tu, mon papa chasse au Boche; Il est soldat, il en tua plus d'un. Si tu voulais, tu mettrais dans sa poche. Tous mes bonbons, là bas, prés de Verdun." See also Silver, *Esprit de corps*, 95 and fig. 64.

20. Stéphane Audoin-Rouzeau, *La guerre des enfants, 1914–1918: Essai d'histoire culturelle* (Paris, 1993), offers an especially rich study of this topic.

21. British magazines such as *Chums*, and others like it that had traditionally exploited both military and imperialist glory in the 1890s, fed naturally into another kind of children's war literature that was to find support in Baden-Powell's popular scouting movement. See Field, *British and French Writers*, 160.

22. Ibid., 129, 139. In 1916 a book titled *Boy of My Heart* was also published in New York with the explicit warning "that this is not a work of fiction, but the exact record of the short years of an English boy who died at the front, in France, December, 1915."

23. See Schmidt, ed., *Chansons de la revanche*, 45–46.

24. For more on the artist see Lillian Browse, *William Nicholson* (London, 1956).

25. See especially Stéphane Audoin-Rouzeau, *L'enfant de l'ennemi, 1914–1918: Viol, avortement, infanticide pendant la Grande Guerre* (Paris, 1995).

26. Audoin-Rouzeau, *La guerre des enfants*, 102–103, 124, 129.

27. P. Fortuny, *Graine de héros*, n.p., n.d., p. 2. Evidence that recruitment of young children as soldiers continued in 2000 was reported by United Nations officials who were charged with trying to halt the use of an estimated 300,000 child soldiers worldwide. See Celia W. Dugger, "Rebels without a Childhood in Sri Lanka War," *The New York Times*, 11 September 2000, p. A21.

28. It has been argued, for example, that a flashback to the childhood nursery by the English poet Robert Graves was not so much a symptom of his neurasthenia, for which he was being treated, as a pointed desire to distance himself from incidents at the front. A memorable example appears in "The Adventure," where Graves takes the report of a machine-gun team that had annihilated an "enemy wire party" whose bodies then disappeared and transforms the story "into a childhood fantasy of killing tigers with stones." See Patrick Quinn, *The Great War and the Missing Muse: The Early Writings of Robert Graves and Siegfried Sassoon* (Selinsgrove, 1994), 35, 53, 58. See also William David Thomas, "The Impact of World War I on the Early Poems of Robert Graves," *Mahalat Review* 35 (1975): 121.

29. See Audoin-Rouzeau, *La guerre des enfants*, caption no. 2, facing p. 65.

30. Ibid., 44.

31. Other similar titles included *Our Allies' ABC War Book* and *The Allies' Alphabet of the ABC of the War.*

32. Steven Beller, "The Tragic Carnival: Austrian Culture in the First World War," in *European Culture in the Great War: The Arts, Entertainment, and Propaganda, 1914–1918,* ed. Aviel Roshwald and Richard Stites (Cambridge, U.K., 1999), 132–133.

33. Other French titles included a richly illustrated *L'alphabet des petits français* published in 1917 and an *Aux petits alsaciens, alphabet,* of 1918.

34. Beller, "Tragic Carnival," caption no. 10, facing p. 33.

35. Maurice Montabré, "Claude Debussy Tells Us of His Theatrical Projects," in *Debussy on Music,* 311–312.

36. Ibid., 31.

37. The allusion to "Feux d'artifice" is prefigured by the use of its dissonating *acciacature* in conjunction with the dual habanera rhythms of "La puerta del vino," a companion prelude in Book Two.

38. Reproduced in Audoin-Rouzeau, *La guerre des enfants,* fig. 5, following p. 96.

39. Ibid., 55.

40. See Robert Orledge, *Debussy and the Theatre* (Cambridge, U.K., 1982), 182.

41. Audoin-Rouzeau, *La guerre des enfants,* 38.

42. Ibid., 38–40.

43. Ibid., 186. But see also Deborah Dwork, *War Is Good for Babies and Other Young Children: A History of the Infant and Child Welfare Movement in England, 1898–1918* (London, 1987).

44. For diaries and photographs see Jim Murphy, *The Boys' War: Confederate and Union Soldiers Talk About the Civil War* (New York, 1990).

45. See Audoin-Rouzeau, *La guerre des enfants,* 185.

46. Chantal Brunschwig, Louis-Jean Calvet, and Jean-Claude Klein, *100 ans de chanson française* (Paris, 1972), 119, as translated in Sweeney, "Harmony and Disharmony," 46. Regarding "Musical Entertainment in the Theaters of Wartime Paris" see Sweeney, *Singing Our Way to Victory,* chapter 5.

47. See Serge Dillaz, *La chanson française de contestation de la Commune à Mai 1968* (Paris, 1973), 206; and Sweeney, "Harmony and Disharmony," 49.

48. See Émile Huet, *Jeanne d'Arc et la musique: Bibliographie musicale,* 2d ed. (Orleans, 1909).

49. Recounted in Modest Tchaikovsky's biography of his brother, *Zhizn' Petra Ilicha Chaikovskago* (Moscow and Leipzig, 1903), 35–37.

50. Huet, *Jeanne d'Arc,* 223–224. For the text of a song, "Jeanne d'Arc," from the period of the Franco-Prussian war, see Schmidt, *Chansons de la revanche,* 103–104.

51. See *The Musical Times* 59 (1 January 1918): 28.

52. Griffiths and DeMille set the taste for a series of later films on the subject including Carl Dreyer's "La Passion de Jeanne d'Arc" of 1928 and numerous others by Victor Fleming, Roberto Rossellini, and Otto Preminger.

53. Along with the Virgin Mary and Saint Joan another prominent intercessor during the Great War was Thèrése de Lisieux, whose cause was introduced in 1914 followed by beatification in 1923 and canonization in 1925. See Annette Becker, *La guerre et la foi* (Paris, 1994), 72.

54. James Carroll's review of Mary Gordon, *Joan of Arc*, in *The New York Times Book Review*, 26 March 2000, p. 14. Joan's attraction was to many different quarters, however, for a host of different reasons. Bernard Shaw's *Saint Joan: A Chronicle Play in Six Scenes and an Epilogue*, with incidental music by John Foulds, appeared in 1924 shortly after her canonization (see *Masters of the English Musical Renaissance*, Forlane UCD 16725). Adaptations that followed in the next years included Bertolt Brecht's *The Trial of Joan of Arc at Rouen* and Paul Claudel's *Jeanne d'Arc au bûcher* of 1935, set to music by Arthur Honegger in 1938.

55. Published in the periodical *Musique* 1, no. 6 (1928): 245–249 and 254. See Deborah Priest, *Louis Laloy (1874–1944) on Debussy, Ravel, and Stravinsky*, trans. Deborah Priest (Aldershot, U.K., 1999), for a translation of the entire article.

56. Translation by Benjamin Broening.

57. Beyond his teaching posts at the École and the Sorbonne, Laloy was also founding editor of *Mercure musical*, which ultimately became the *Revue musicale S.I.M.* (Société Internationale de Musique). See Fulcher, *French Cultural Politics*, 136–138.

58. For Laloy's influence and direction in these matters see ibid., 152, 183–186.

59. Laloy acquainted Debussy with an adaptation of the story by his former teacher and medievalist, Joseph Bédlier.

60. Silver, *Esprit de corps*, 115–116.

61. For this Cocteau, not surprisingly, provided an answer in a talk which he gave to the students of the Collège de France in May 1923. See Jean Cocteau, *Cocteau's World: An Anthology of Writings*, ed. Margaret Crosland (London, 1972), 391–392.

62. See *The Cock and the Harlequin*, in Jean Cocteau, *A Call to Order*, trans. Rollo H. Myers (New York, 1974), 16, 24, 35; and Nancy Perloff, *Art and the Everyday: Popular Entertainment and the Circle of Erik Satie* (Oxford, 1991), 7–11.

63. Laloy wrote: "From the first blow of the cannon, shot by the Germans against the fortresses of Liége, the vibration overturned the balustrades of his terrestrial paradise . . . I do not believe that he took the time nor found the strength to ask which side was right or to search for those responsible. Violence was odious to him, and from the beginning his primary concern was with the victims. Neither Claude Debussy nor I had then the serenity of spirit which is necessary to rise to a point of impartiality, above the battle (*au'dessus de la mêlée*). I do not believe it necessary, even today, to look for excuses for a natural gesture of indignation and compassion." Translation by Benjamin Broe-

ning. For the complete article, translated by Deborah Priest, see Priest, *Louis Laloy*, 231–235.

64. This appears on the last page of Laloy's article.

65. In December 1916 a war album was planned, to be called "Unpublished Pages on Woman and the War." Reserved for a thousand subscribers and dedicated to Queen Alexandra, wife of King Edward VII of England, it was published in facsimile in Paris by Mme. Alexander Melor. Among the musicians whose contributions were solicited were Saint-Saëns and Debussy, with the latter ultimately forwarding a two-page manuscript of an *Élégie* for piano. The work was published by Editions Jobert only in 1978. Marked "Lent et douloureux," it is one of the most curious works that Debussy ever penned, and no extended critique can account for the unfocused nature of the piece that seems more like an abortive sketch than a completed composition.

66. Jean Cocteau, "Joan of Arc," in *Cocteau's World: An Anthology of Writings by Jean Cocteau*, ed. Margaret Crosland (London, 1972), 246. Cocteau was also drawn to the theme of the boy soldier in his wartime novel, *Thomas l'imposteur* (1923), written in 1918, where an underage French youth "lies his way into the army (posing as the son of a famous general) and . . . finally dies a hero's death at the front." See Silver, *Esprit de corps* (Princeton, 1989), 111.

67. Blanche, *Cahiers d'un artiste*, 2d ser., November 1914–June 1915, 223. For another Blanchian tale that forges the same national distinctions under the guise of an imaginary performance of Debussy's string quartet, see ibid., 224.

68. François Lesure, *Claude Debussy: Biographie critique* (Paris, 1994), 394.

69. J. G. Prod'homme, "Claude Achille Debussy," *The Musical Quarterly* 4, no. 4 (1918): 555.

CHAPTER 7. WAR GAMES, 1914–1915

1. Jacques-Émile Blanche, *Portraits of a Lifetime* (London, 1937), 259–260. Gertrude Stein also spoke of the direct relationship between World War I and Cubism and reported Picasso's recognition of the relationship of camouflage to the Cubist painters. See Stephen Kern, *The Culture of Time and Space* (Cambridge, Mass., 1983), 288, 302–303, and the whole of chap. 11, "The Cubist War"; and David Cottington, *Cubism in the Shadow of War* (New Haven, 1998).

2. Jean Cocteau, "Nous voudrions vous dire un mot," *Le mot*, 27 February 1915, p. 1; translated in Messing, *Neoclassicism*, 78. In 1989 Modris Eksteins also appropriated the title *Rites of Spring* for his book devoted to the Great War and the birth of Modernism.

3. Cited in Truman C. Bullard, "The First Performance of Igor Stravinsky's *Sacre du Printemps*," Ph.D. diss., Eastman School of Music, 1970, vol. 3, pp. 271–272.

4. See Richard Taruskin, *Defining Russia Musically* (Princeton, 1997), 386–387, "Stravinsky and the Subhuman."

5. For the details of the background and an analysis of the first piece, see Glenn Watkins, *Pyramids at the Louvre: Music, Culture, and Collage from Stravinsky to the Postmodernists* (Cambridge, Mass., 1994), chap. 10, "Stravinsky and the Cubists." With respect to the notion of the Great War as a Cubist War see especially Kern, *Culture of Time and Space*, chap. 11.

6. For a reproduction see Cork, *A Bitter Truth*, 48, pl. 40.

7. Graves's intended sermon, that of the Old Lie, is made clear in a marginal note appended to the poem, which reiterates the opinion that "War should be a sport for men above forty-five only." See Robert Graves, *Good-bye to All That* (London, 1929), 288–289. Graves, like many who participated in the Battle of the Somme, was never the same after that experience. "Everyone was mad," he said, "and this lunacy and expression were difficult to express in lyric or Skeltonic poetry." See ibid., 290; and Quinn, *The Great War*, 46.

8. For a detailed discussion see Watkins, *Pyramids at the Louvre*, 260.

9. Regarding *Le mot* perspectives see Silver, *Esprit de corps*, 44ff.

10. A review of this concert by Richard Aldrich in *Concert Life in New York, 1902–1923* (New York, 1941), 479, claims that Mason's lecture purported to explain the composer's intentions as follows: "a gathering of peasants on the desert steppe, singing a folksong accompanied by instruments, some kind of a bagpipe and some kind of a drum. It may be hoped that there are really no such instruments. In the second he had in mind a cathedral with a priest intoning Gregorian plain chant and the organ sounding. The last represents a Pierrot burdened with some private grief, but obliged to go through with his juggling tricks before the public." It is clear that Aldrich switched the descriptions for the second and third numbers.

11. Printed in *Some Imagist Poets: An Anthology*, 3 vols. (London, 1915–1917). For three extracts see Eric Walter White, *Stravinsky: The Composer and His Works*, 2d ed. (Berkeley, 1979), 233–234.

12. Igor Stravinsky, *Selected Correspondence*, 2 vols., ed. Robert Craft (New York, 1984), 1: 407 n. 1.

13. See Amy Lowell, "Some Musical Analogies in Modern Poetry," *Musical Quarterly* 6, no. 1 (1920): 127–157, for her extended views on the possibilities of reciprocity between the arts. About her own verses for Stravinsky's string quartet pieces she is noncommittal: "Could I reproduce the effect of the music in another medium? Could I? Did I? The reader must determine" (148–150).

14. By 1915 Lowell, who was the most publicity-driven of all the Imagists, had outdone Pound himself and left for America. Pound consequently disbanded his group, relabeling them "Amygists." See Greg Barnhisel, "Marketing Modernism in America during the Great War: The Case of Ezra Pound," in *World War I and the Cultures of Modernity*, ed. Douglas Mackaman and Michael Mays (Jackson, Miss., 2000).

15. *Musical Times*, 1 March 1919, p. 113. Later in a pre-performance lec-

ture given by Ansermet on 13 February 1919, he added: "This music is absolute music in the true sense of the word, that is to say, music innocent of any and all suspicion of a literary or philosophic program." See Ernest Ansermet, "The Man and His Work—Igor Stravinsky—His First String Quartet," *Musical Courier* 25 (1915): 41.

16. Such tactics naturally evoke suspicion, however, and this one was a classic act of dissimulation that could not be made to square with the David and Goliath scenario Cocteau had proposed directly to the composer for the first of the pieces, let alone the autobiographical element openly admitted by the composer in later years for the second of them. See Erik Aschengreen, *Jean Cocteau and the Dance* (Copenhagen, 1986), 61, as well as Jann Pasler, "New Music as Confrontation: The Musical Sources of Jean Cocteau's Identity," *Musical Quarterly* 75 (1991): 255–278.

17. As described by the editors of the complete works of Rameau begun in 1895, which included Saint-Saëns, d'Indy, Dukas, and Debussy. See Richard Taruskin, "Nationalism," in *New Grove Dictionary of Music and Musicians*, 2d ed., 29 vols. (New York, 2001), sec. 8, "The scene shifts."

18. Three statements of the motto rhythm also occur in duo textures, but they also avoid the lowest pitch of the ostinato.

19. On 13 February 1915, for example, only two months after the composition of the "March," Stravinsky played four-hand arrangements of excerpts from his own music with the Italian composer, including parts of *Le sacre*, in a salon of the Grand Hotel in Rome for an audience that included Rodin, Balla, Buccioni, and Respighi. The next day, on 14 February 1915, Casella "had a sensational success conducting *Petrushka*"; Vera Stravinsky and Robert Craft, *Stravinsky in Pictures and Documents* (New York, 1978), 152. Casella also arranged one of the early performances of the *Three Pieces for String Quartet* on 19 May 1915.

20. Casella's *Pupazzetti* were published by J. & W. Chester with a cover design by Larionov, the designer of stage sets and costumes for Stravinsky's *Renard*. The work is recorded on Connoisseur Society CD 4171.

21. In a postcard from Casella to Stravinsky dated September 3, 1915 the former announced completion of his "four *Films*, inspired by cinematographic views of the war" and inquired as to when he might be receiving Stravinsky's "March," which was dedicated to him. See Stravinsky, *Selected Correspondence*, 2: 127. Casella's slightly later *Pezzi infantili* (or *Children's Pieces*) of 1920, written at the time of Stravinsky's *Five Fingers*, further underscores the fascination of the two composers with reductive piano games.

22. Igor Stravinsky and Robert Craft, *Dialogues and a Diary* (New York, 1963), 72–73. The dating is inconsistent here, as Stravinsky had already completed the "March" on 19 December of the previous year.

23. In his posthumously published monograph, *Stravinski* (Brescia, 1947), 77–78, Alfredo Casella recognized and emphasized this very point. Stravinsky realized, in any event, that the "March" was more than a simple "vamping"

piece and that the residual techniques of his massive Cubist experience in the *Rite* were ready and waiting for application to a new task, albeit now tethered to a seeming *volte-face* that carried a potent message.

24. For a surviving sample of the stationery used by Francesco Cangiullo to sketch a portrait of Stravinsky at the piano at the time of the first Futurist auditions in Milan during the spring of 1915, see *Strawinsky: Sein Nachlass, Sein Bild* (Basel, 1984), 60. Another later sample of Marinetti's stationery shows a figure clearly drawn from Balla's sculpture, "Boccioni's Fist," just below the letterhead. See Rita Reif, "You Could Tell the 'Ism' by the Letterhead," *The New York Times*, 31 March 1996, for an illustration, and Cork, *A Bitter Truth*, 65, for a reproduction of the original sculpture. See chapter 11 for a description of a Futurist demonstration that Stravinsky attended at that time.

25. See Martin Gilbert, *Atlas of World War I*, 2d ed. (New York, 1994), 36, for a map that illustrates this geographical redistribution.

26. See Harold Osborne, ed., *The Oxford Companion to Twentieth-Century Art* (Oxford, 1981), "Severini."

27. Stravinsky was soon to collaborate on *Renard* with Larionov, who with the declaration of war had returned precipitously to Russia. An exhibition of his painting planned for Berlin was cancelled, and early in the conflict, in November and December, Larionov was seriously wounded on the German front and invalided out of the service. At the end of January, the Moscow press published a photo of him in a group of "Futurist heroes." See Mikhail Larionov, *La voie vers l'abstraction: Oeuvres sur papier 1908–1915* (Frankfurt, 1987), 191.

28. See Cork, *A Bitter Truth*, 51–54. Lentulov's use of a central figure on a rearing horse and a surface choked with details of conflict openly advertises that the work is modeled directly on the central panel of a series collectively known as *The Battle of San Romano* by Paolo Uccello, an early Florentine Renaissance painter. This panel is now housed in the National Gallery, London. See ibid., 52. The memory of Uccello's San Romano battle pieces also inspired a huge canvas by the American artist Man Ray (Cork, fig. 22) that was begun in the summer of 1914, titled *AD MCMXIV 1914*; it is now in the Philadelphia Museum of Art.

29. Aristarkh Lentulov, *Put' khudoznika, Khudoznika i vromia* (Moscow, 1990), 9, claims that Lentulov was highly musical, possessing a fine ear and an excellent voice.

30. Stravinsky and Craft, *Conversations*, 81–82. As Messing has put it, "The desire to stitch together diverse cultures into a single nationalist fabric was a common ploy in anti-German rhetoric; even before World War I it had been a popular theme attending the appearance of the term *nouveau classicisme*"; Messing, *Neoclassicism*, 119.

31. Rolland, *Journal*, 59.

32. The Beethoven issue vis-à-vis Stravinsky is complex and deserves to be examined in more critical detail; see chapter 8.

33. Rolland, *Journal*, 853.

34. For a formidable discussion of the Eurasian or "Turanian" component throughout this period, see Taruskin, *Stravinsky and the Russian Traditions*, 1128ff.

35. Stravinsky, *An Autobiography* (New York, 1936), 53.

36. Taruskin, *Stravinsky*, 1135.

37. Ibid., 1136.

38. P. Tchaikovsky, *Pique Dame* (Moscow, 1983), 27–32. Regarding Stravinsky's early familiarity with Bizet's *Carmen*, which contains a similar scene without the developing rhythmic feature, see *An Autobiography*, 12. Furthermore, Stravinsky's father (1843–1902) sang in the premieres of several Tchaikovsky operas, and during Stravinsky's youth in St. Petersburg *The Queen of Spades* was a staple of the opera repertoire. During the fifteen years following its premiere on 7 February 1890 to the end of 1905—a time that stretched from Stravinsky's eighth to his twenty-third year, the opera was performed 120 times in St. Petersburg alone. I am indebted to R. John Wiley for these statistics.

39. Quinn, *The Great War*, 35–36.

40. Stravinsky and Craft, *Stravinsky in Pictures and Documents*, 76. The page from P. W. Joyce, *Old Irish Folk Music and Songs* (Dublin, 1909), 269, is reproduced in Taruskin, *Stravinsky*, 1474.

41. For more on Ireland's role see Thomas Hennessey, *Dividing Ireland: World War I and Partition* (London, 1998); and Dungan, *They Shall Grow Not Old*.

42. The force of such simple marches with nationalistic connotations for the period can be judged from the fact that Casella, a practicing concert pianist at the time, was obliged to play the "Royal March," Italy's unofficial national anthem, in order to quell a fight that broke out between neutralists and interventionists in the middle of a piano recital that he gave in Rome in early 1915. Both Stravinsky and Diaghilev were in attendance. See Alfredo Casella, *Music in My Time: The Memories of Alfredo Casella*, trans. and ed. Spencer Norton (Norman, Okla., 1955), 125. The *Marcia reale d'ordinanza* by Giuseppe Gabetti was commissioned by King Carlo Felice in 1831 and served as Italy's most widely used anthem until the *Inno di Mameli* was adopted by the Italian Republic in 1946 at the conclusion of World War II.

43. See White, *Stravinsky*, 237.

44. See T. N. Dupuy, *Numbers, Predictions and War* (Indianapolis, 1979).

45. Johan Huizinga, *Homo Ludens: A Study of the Play Element in Culture* (Boston, 1970), 36. See Leed, *No Man's Land*, 54: "For Huizinga, play is 'an activity connected with no material interest and no profit can be gained by it. It proceeds within its own proper boundaries of time and space according to fixed rules and in an orderly manner.'"

46. Osbert Sitwell, *Great Morning!* (Boston, 1947), 199.

47. For more on the role of English public schools in promoting the notion of war as a game, see Ferguson, *The Pity of War*, 201ff., and Fussell, *The Great War*, 25–26.

48. Fussell, *The Great War*, 27.

49. Leed, *No Man's Land*, 56.

50. The compelling attraction of neoclassical order and clarity for prewar Parisian avant-garde painters beginning around 1915 has been protested in depth by art historians, and Picasso's three *Ingriste* portraits of Stravinsky serve only as a port of entry to a remarkable story. The Russian composer's gradual movement in this direction is thus attributable in no small measure to both the literary and visual evidence he would have encountered amongst non-musicians at the time. See particularly Silver, *Esprit de corps*, chap. 2, "The Rewards of War." Russia's own neoclassical revival in architecture, and its infatuation with Palladian models in particular, was already in evidence by the twentieth-century's first decade. This was especially true in the historically Italianate city of St. Petersburg, where Stravinsky grew to manhood.

51. Erik Svarny, *"The Men of 1914": T. S. Eliot and Early Modernism* (Philadelphia, 1988), 162.

52. Gino Severini, *Du cubisme au classicisme: Esthétique du compas et du nombre* (Paris, 1921), 34–37; translated by Scott Messing in *Neoclassicism*, 80.

53. The Golden Section was not discovered by artists and composers as a result of the war, going back as it does to the Pythagoreans and especially to its notable revival by Pacioli in the fifteenth century. But it was no doubt embraced with a new fervor by artists like Severini in the war period and after because of the sense of order it implied. Amongst the painters, a group known as the Section d'Or endorsed its principles in 1912, and among composers it has been argued that Stravinsky followed suit as early as 1914 in the first of his *Three Pieces for String Quartet*. See Watkins, *Pyramids at the Louvre*, 263.

54. Katharine Hodgson, "Myth-making in Russian War Poetry," in *The Violent Muse: Violence and the Artistic Imagination in Europe, 1910–1939* (Manchester, U.K., 1994), 75.

55. George L. Mosse, *Fallen Soldiers: Reshaping the Memory of the World Wars* (New York, 1990), 143. For more on the concept of war games, the child, and masculinity, see Jonathan Bignell, "The Meanings of War-Toys and War-Games," in *War, Culture, and the Media: Representations of the Military in 20th-Century Britain*, ed. Ian Stewart and Susan L. Carruthers (Madison, N.J., 1996), 165–184.

CHAPTER 8. CHARADES AND MASQUERADES

1. Stravinsky, *Selected Correspondence*, 2: 21, 61.

2. Ibid., 2: 81.

3. Reviewing her various efforts to raise money for war relief, Edith Wharton noted that " 'The Book of the Homeless,' and the subsequent auction of the original manuscripts and sketches that were submitted for inclusion, brought in a large sum." Edith Wharton, *A Backward Glance* (New York, 1934), 350. That Stravinsky's manuscript was sold at auction is corroborated by the fact

that the copy which remained in the composer's possession, although signed and dated by him, is not in the composer's hand. The reverse side of his copy also includes a description of Wharton's book. See White, *Stravinsky*, 601. The original manuscript was ultimately received as a gift by the Library of Congress from Nicolas Nabokov on 6 December 1941. I am grateful to Sam Perryman of the Library of Congress for verification of the donor.

4. White, *Stravinsky*, 238.

5. See Stravinsky and Craft, *Stravinsky in Pictures and Documents*, 610.

6. Stravinsky, *Selected Correspondence*, 2: 88.

7. See Cork, *A Bitter Truth*, 53–54, for a reproduction of some of Malevich's lithographs.

8. Charles Joseph, *Stravinsky and the Piano* (Ann Arbor, 1983), 60.

9. Taruskin, *Stravinsky*, 1475. For a clear prototype of the echoing dotted rhythms that characterize the Trio in Stravinsky's "Souvenir d'une marche boche," see Schubert, *Trois marches héroïques für Klavier zu 4 Händen*, op. 27, Deutsch 602, no. 3. Italicizing the connection is Stravinsky's claim that Rimsky-Korsakov frequently assigned him Schubert marches as orchestration assignments.

10. Taruskin calls it "the epitome of unabashed *oproshcheniye*" or primitive simplification.

11. Stravinsky and Craft, *Stravinsky in Pictures and Documents*, 243.

12. J. van Cotton reported the following in *Comoedia*, 21 January 1924: "In the same light mood I threw in the name Wagner, and suddenly the smile gave way to a grimace. 'Wagner . . . is certainly not a real musician. He has had recourse to the theater at every moment in his career, and this remains an obstacle to his musical ideas, whose progress is hindered by his philosophy. Every time Wagner was tempted by pure music, he was hit on the nose . . .'" See Stravinsky and Craft, *Stravinsky in Pictures and Documents*, 250.

13. As early as 1822 Glinka conducted a performance of the Second Symphony (a work later favored by Stravinsky), and seven of Beethoven's symphonies were performed privately at the Vielgorsky estate. The next decade brought a short story by V. F. Odoevsky, "The Last String Quartet of Beethoven" of 1831, and the St. Petersburg premiere of the Ninth Symphony in 1836. In the 1850s Balakirev played through the Beethoven sonatas at the request of Ulyabyshev in preparation for his book, *Beethoven, ses critiques et ses glossateurs*. And Mussorgsky made an arrangement of the second movement of the string quartet, op. 59, no. 3, an activity which he continued into the next decade by arranging movements from the late quartets.

14. In a letter from Tchaikovsky to Sergey Taneyev dated 27 March–8 April 1878 the composer admitted that his Fourth Symphony was programmatic, and added: "In essence my symphony is an imitation of Beethoven's Fifth; that is, I was imitating not his musical thoughts but his basic idea. What do you think? Is there a program in the Fifth Symphony? Not only is there one, but there can be no dispute regarding what it is striving to express." See

P. I. Tchaikovsky, *Polnoe sobranie sochinenii; literaturnie proizvedeniya i perepiska* (Collected Works; Literary Works and Correspondence), vol. 7: 200–201. I am grateful to Roland John Wiley for the translation.

15. Stravinsky and Craft, *Stravinsky in Pictures and Documents,* 50.

16. See Stravinsky, *Autobiography,* 115–119. For more on the Beethoven question see Comini, *The Changing Image of Beethoven;* and Mark Evan Bonds, *After Beethoven: Imperatives of Originality in the Symphony* (Cambridge, Mass., 1996).

17. Igor Stravinsky and Robert Craft, *Expositions and Developments* (Garden City, N.Y., 1962), 95.

18. Rolland, *Journal,* 61. Translated in Igor Stravinsky and Robert Craft, *Memories and Commentaries* (Garden City, N.Y., 1960), 74–76.

19. See Nicholas V. Riasanovsky, "Emergence of Eurasianism," *California Slavic Studies* 4 (1967): 43–45; and Taruskin, *Stravinsky and the Russian Traditions,* 1135, 1152.

20. Cocteau's opinion was registered in an article that appeared in *Le mot,* 27 March 1914.

21. See Robert Craft and Igor Stravinsky, "Eau de Vie: An Interview on Beethoven," in *The First Anthology: 30 Years of the New York Review of Books,* ed. Robert B. Silvers, Barbara Epstein, and Rea S. Hederman (New York, 1993), 104, 106.

22. Stravinsky, *Selected Correspondence,* 2: 179; Taruskin, *Stravinsky,* 1132; Robert C. Ridenour, *Nationalism, Modernism, and Personal Rivalry* (Ann Arbor, 1981), 176; Taruskin, "Some Thoughts on the History and Historiography of Russian Music," *Journal of Musicology* 3 (1984): 336.

23. Taruskin, *Stravinsky,* 1152.

24. Taruskin, *Stravinsky,* 1292.

25. Silver, *Esprit de corps,* 50; and Cork, *A Bitter Truth,* 60. For other images of Chanteclaire as the emblem of France see Lucien Métivet's "Marianne and Germania" of 1918, in Silver, *Esprit de corps,* 15; and R. Duchamp-Villon, *Rooster (Gallic Cock),* 1916, also in Silver, *Esprit de corps,* 44.

26. Regarding "The Initial Impact of World War I" on the story of the Wandering Jew see George K. Anderson, *The Legend of the Wandering Jew* (Providence, 1965), 344ff.; and George Mosse, *The Image of Man* (Oxford, 1996), 57–60, 69.

27. See Silver, *Esprit de corps,* 131, for a reproduction.

28. Here, however, Cocteau threw the baby out with the bath water. For not only were the Impressionists dismissed along with the Wagnerites, but the latest alternative to both, the Stravinsky of *Le sacre,* was momentarily relegated to the enemy. Although Cocteau soon made amends with the Russian, for the moment he mistakenly prophesied that in the world of music only Satie—who was soon to disappear in a Dada dead-end—showed the way to the future. See Perloff, *Art and the Everyday,* 12–18.

29. Stravinsky and Craft, *Expositions and Developments,* 102. See also Taruskin, *Stravinsky,* 1298–1301.

30. Hubertus F. Jahn, *Patriotic Culture in Russia during World War I* (Ithaca, 1995), 94. For more on activities in Russia in the first year of the war see Rosa Newmarch, "The Outlook in Russia," *The Musical Times*, 1 September 1915, pp. 521–523. Notice is given of Skriabin's death and Chaliapin's travels to Warsaw "for the benefit of the ruined and homeless Poles" at which time he also visited the front. Otherwise, claims are made that the musical season was much the same as the prewar years except for the fact that, Bach and Beethoven aside, no German music was likely to be tolerated.

31. Jahn, *Patriotic Culture*, 90–91.

32. Sassoon, *Collected Poems*, 139–140. In a poem purportedly aimed at moralizing against the classic fox-hunt of the landed gentry, Sassoon launched a diatribe against senseless killing in any form: "Refortified by exercise and air, / I, jogging home astride my chestnut mare, / Grow half-humane, and question the propriety / Of Foxes Torn to Bits in Smart Society." Sassoon's verses invite comparison with the closing lines of Stravinsky's own *Renard*, which suddenly introduce the human dimension with an announcement by the cat and the goat that "Our masters come with their hounds. / Their horns are sounding . . . Now Renard's life is done." Elsewhere in *Memoirs of a Fox-Hunting Man* (New York, 1929), pt. 10, "The Front," Sassoon speaks of pretending to be hunting an imaginary fox, and in a poem, "Break of Day," composed while under treatment at Craiglockhart, he compares fox-hunting to man-hunting.

33. Stravinsky believed that the text was to be understood and performed in the language of the production. The English version was confected in part and approved by Stravinsky himself.

34. Stravinsky and Craft, *Expositions and Developments*, 138.

35. Further evidence of the need for some respite from the horrors of the day could be found in the Parisian music-halls, café-concerts, and circuses where clowns poked fun at the Germans, and at the Folies Bergères where kicking chorus girls contrasted with torch singers mourning the loss of French youth on the battlefield. For more on the popularity of the "patriotic rouser" in the café-concert tradition from the time of the Franco-Prussian War through the period of World War I, see Whiting, *Satie the Bohemian*, 17–20.

36. Stravinsky and Craft, *Stravinsky in Pictures and Documents*, 548–549.

37. Jeffrey R. Smith, "The First World War and the Public Sphere in Germany," in *World War I and the Cultures of Modernity*, ed. Douglas Mackaman and Michael Mays (Jackson, Mississippi, 2000), 71.

38. "Gerüchte," *General Anzeiger der Münchner Neuste Nachrichten*, no. 399 (6 August 1914), recounted by Smith, "First World War," 71.

39. For an alternative perspective, see Taruskin, *Stravinsky*, 1264–1265, 1290.

40. Entertainments throughout the war period were variously received. For example, although proceeds of the premiere performance of *Parade* had been tagged for the War Benefit Fund, reaction to Cocteau's cabaret-inspired entertainment was largely negative. This was clearly inspired by the fact that the

war had hit a low point. As Robert Orledge has noted in *Satie the Composer* (Cambridge, U.K., 1990), 65–66, "Russia had just defaulted, and Allied morale was at a low ebb; and to be faced with a Russian ballet company performing such trivialities, with Russian soldiers in the audience (at Diaghilev's invitation), was an affront to any Frenchman."

41. Nothing could have more clearly dramatized the conjunction of Russian and cosmopolitan forces in Stravinsky's psyche at the time. In a front-page report of the work's premiere in the leading Paris newspaper, *Figaro*, Stravinsky offered an open letter in defense of Tchaikovsky, whose *Sleeping Beauty* with completions by Stravinsky had been performed on the same program. Downplaying the importance of the work's picturesque nationalism in favor of the composer's "more aristocratic and cosmopolitan tradition," Stravinsky announced that he felt much closer to the tradition traceable to Glinka, Dargomizhsky, and Tchaikovsky than to the Russian Five. The Russian character of The Five's music, he contended, "came out above all as opposition to the conventional Italianism that reigned in Russia at that time." The "picturesqueness" of their music "struck the imagination of foreign audiences," he announced. "But that day is gone. Opposition to Italianism no longer has any purpose." "Une Lettre de Stravinsky sur Tchaikovsky," *Le Figaro*, 18 May 1922. See Stephen Walsh, *Igor Stravinsky: A Creative Spring* (London, 1999), 349–350.

42. Stravinsky, *Expositions and Developments*, 33–34.

43. Even Petrushka was pressed into service in 1916 with a glove-puppet show at The Comedians' Shop in Petrograd. See Jahn, *Patriotic Culture*, 107.

44. Jahn, *Patriotic Culture*, 97.

45. White, *Stravinsky*, 270, reports the following: "'Royal March,' which is in the style of a Spanish pasodoble, was suggested to him by an incident he had witnessed in Seville during the Holy Week processions of 1916. He was standing in a street with Diaghilev "and listening with much pleasure to a tiny 'bullfight' band consisting of a cornet, a trombone, and a bassoon. They were playing a pasodoble, when suddenly a large brass band came thundering down the street in the Overture to *Tannhäuser*. The pasodoble was soon drowned out." The Anti-Wagner sentiment is obvious.

46. Taruskin, *Stravinsky*, 1298–1299. On violin imagery in painting and poetry see James H. Billington, *Icon and the Axe* (New York, 1966), 477.

47. Hodgson, "Myth-making," 67–68. Stravinsky's specific attraction to cards—which led in later years to the declaration "I have always been attracted to card games [and] I never spoof at cartomancy"—was one that was shared by any number of Russian writers in the 19th century, including Pushkin and Dostoevsky. It was a metaphor that Stravinsky would put to use again many years later in the climactic scene of his opera *The Rake's Progress*.

48. A corrosive and poignant commentary on Cézanne's several renowned versions of *The Card Players* as well as a potentially brutal commentary on one of the most popular German comic postcards about the war called "Gas At-

tack," Dix's *The Skat Players* commandeers a further deception: the work is not simply a painting but a collage. For more on the role of the German postcard during the Great War see Mosse, *Fallen Soldiers*, 135; and Smith, "First World War," 77.

49. Stravinsky and Craft, *Expositions and Developments*, 91; Taruskin, *Stravinsky*, 1301ff.

50. Taruskin, *Stravinsky*, 1302–1306; Aron Marko Rothmüller, *The Music of the Jews*, trans. H. S. Stevens (South Brunswick, N.J., 1967), 172; and Macy Nulman, *Concise Encyclopedia of Jewish Music* (New York, 1975), 140.

51. Alan M. Gillmor, *Erik Satie* (Boston, 1988), 182–183.

52. Taruskin, *Stravinsky*, 1310.

53. This was ultimately straightened out by the insertion of a measure in 2/4 followed by two more measures in 3/8.

54. Taruskin, *Stravinsky*, 1312.

55. Stravinsky and Craft, *Expositions and Developments*, 92.

56. For more on the latter work see Whiting, *Satie the Bohemian*, 406–407.

57. See Watkins, *Pyramids at the Louvre*, ch. 10, "Stravinsky and the Cubists," for a fuller discussion of the premise.

58. See White, *Stravinsky*, 280.

59. Y. Yastrebtzev, *Recollections of Rimsky-Korsakov*, vol. 2 (Moscow, 1962).

60. See Paul Morand, *Journal d'un attaché d'ambassade, 1916–1917* (Paris, 1948), 209. See also Walsh, *Igor Stravinsky*, 277.

61. For a reproduction of Balla's *Patriotic Hymn* see Caroline Tisdall and Angelo Bozzolla, *Futurism* (New York, 1978), 197, fig. 167; for his set to Stravinsky's *Fireworks* see Watkins, *Pyramids at the Louvre*, 312, fig. 12.1.

62. Morand, *Journal d'un attaché*, 258.

63. See Taruskin, *Stravinsky*, 1183–1189, which includes comparative examples from the settings by Balakirev and Stravinsky.

64. It is of no little interest that in this work Glazunov had turned the opening four notes of the familiar tune into a repeated timpani figure that remarkably forecast Stravinsky's introductory ostinato to the "Dance of the Adolescents," one of the signature passages in *The Rite of Spring*.

65. For more recent developments regarding the sensitivity of an appropriate national anthem for Russia see Patrick E. Tyler, "Putin Pushes Soviet Hymn, Creating Disharmony," *The New York Times*, 6 December 2000, p. A1.

66. Stravinsky and Craft, *Stravinsky in Pictures and Documents*, 550.

67. Robert Craft, program notes to *Stravinsky, the Composer*, vol. 7 (Music Masters CD 01612-67152-2).

68. Arthur-Vincent Lourié, "Muzika Stravinskogo," *Vyorsti*, no. 1 (1926): 124, 126, 134, as translated by Taruskin in *Stravinsky*, 1133–1134.

69. Robert Bernard, *Les tendances de la musique française moderne* (Paris, 1930). See Fulcher, "The Composer as Intellect," 228.

CHAPTER 9. CHURCH, STATE, AND SCHOLA

1. Edith Wharton, *The Letters of Edith Wharton*, ed. R. W. B. and Nancy Lewis (New York, 1988), 346. See also Alan Price, *The End of The Age of Innocence* (New York, 1996), 40–41.

2. See Prod'homme, "Music and Musicians in Paris," 139–142.

3. Marcel Casadesus had also written a Violin Concerto in D major ("Adelaïde") ascribed to Mozart that was later widely understood to have been faked.

4. Price, *End of The Age of Innocence*, 41.

5. Vincent d'Indy, *Histoire du 105ème Bataillon de la Garde Nationale de Paris, en l'année 1870–71* (Paris, 1872). For a photograph of d'Indy in his military uniform during the Franco-Prussian War, see Vallas, *Vincent d'Indy*, opposite p. 127.

6. See L. L. Farrar Jr., "Nationalism in Wartime: Critiquing the Conventional Wisdom," in *Authority, Identity and the Social History of the Great War*, ed. Frans Coetzee and Marilyn Shevin-Coetzee (Providence, R.I., 1995), 144.

7. See Fulcher, *French Cultural Politics*, 24ff. From 1880 through 1910 Catholic scholars were openly discriminated against by the Third Republic, and many "were removed from or denied access to positions of academic responsibility and prestige." See Hanna, *The Mobilization of Intellect*, 39.

8. See Vincent d'Indy, *Une école de musique répondant aux besoins modernes: discours d'inauguration de l'école de chant liturgique . . . fondée par la Schola Cantorum en 1896* (Paris, 1900). For a detailed examination of d'Indy's anti-Dreyfusard, anti-Republican biases in the formation of the Schola Cantorum see Fulcher, *French Cultural Politics*, 21–35.

9. Vallas, *Vincent d'Indy*, 2: 92. ("Je voudrais que ce fût du bon orchestre *solide* et pas du Stravinsky, que je trouve décidément bien mal orchestré.")

10. Andrew Thomson, "Vincent d'Indy," www.grovemusic.com.

11. "Et, durant de longues années, Auférus servit l'Esprit de Ténèbres / Et, peu à peu, le mal s'emparant de son coeur, / il employa sa force à opprimer les faibles / et à combattre les oeuvres divines. / Mais il était choisi par Dieu; / un miracle le sauva de l'éternel abîme, / et la Croix lui révéla l'Amour."

12. "O Sainte Croix qui portas le Salut du monde, / ta puissance immortelle / arrêta le pécheur sur la route du mal; et ton charme lui révèla le ciel, / le ciel, sa future patrie."

13. See especially Jacques Fontana, *Les Catholiques françaises pendant la Grande Guerre* (Paris, 1990).

14. Vincent d'Indy, *La schola cantorum; son histoire depuis sa fondation jusqu'en 1925* (Paris, 1927), 93–94.

15. Vincent d'Indy, "Une école d'art répondant aux besoins modernes," *La tribune de Saint-Gervais*, November 1900, p. 305.

16. Letter of 17 September 1903 to Pierre de Bréville. See Vallas, *Vincent d'Indy*, 2: 327. D'Indy's anti-semitic views had not been visible in his student days, when he had many Jewish friends who were in the same class taught by

César Franck. There his association with Jews was anything but casual, and, despite the voiced displeasure that such associations brought from his family, he served as choral director in numerous performances of an all-Jewish choir singing works by Mendelssohn and Meyerbeer. See Vallas, *Vincent d'Indy*, 1: 129. His later anti-semitic, anti-Protestant position, which hardened at the time of the Dreyfus Affair, was not yet in place, and in 1877 he had published a two-volume edition of psalms, hymns, and madrigals by the late-sixteenth-, early-seventeenth-century Jewish composer Salomone Rossi *(dit l'Ebreo)*. It is of no little interest, however, that later d'Indy never made mention of this publication in the catalog of his works, and that he even suppressed mention of it when speaking of Rossi in his *Cours de composition*.

17. Debussy recorded a highly positive assessment of *L'étranger* in *Gil Blas*, 12 January 1903; reprinted in *Debussy on Music*, 87–91.

18. Seven chants, which support the narrative, are taken from the Common of Martyrs and from the Common of Martyrs Who Are Not a Bishop. See Vallas, *Vincent d'Indy*, 2: 335–338, for a detailed discussion of the chant citations as well as other musical references.

19. Vallas, *Vincent d'Indy*, 2: 333.

20. An opinion expressed in a letter to Octave Maus of 22 July and 4 November 1911; cited by Andrew Thomson, *Vincent d'Indy and His World* (Oxford, 1996), 174. For Debussy's views on music and the church see "M. Claude Debussy and *Le Martyre de Saint-Sébastien*," *Excelsior*, 11 February 1911; reprinted in *Debussy on Music*, 245ff.

21. See Fulcher, *French Cultural Politics*, 26–27. When Fauré became director of the Conservatoire, he attempted a mediation not only between these two opposing attitudes of the Conservatoire and the Schola regarding counterpoint but also the idea of the symphony; see 145–146.

22. Thomson, *Vincent d'Indy*, 165–166.

23. Vallas, *Vincent d'Indy*, 2: 94–95.

24. Ibid., 2: 96.

25. See Vincent d'Indy, *Beethoven: A Critical Biography*, trans. Theodore Baker (Freeport, N.Y., 1970), 100–101.

26. Wharton, *Letters*, 265.

27. Chantavoine published a book on Beethoven in 1906. See Danièlle Pistone, "Beethoven et Paris: Repère historiques et évocations contemporaines," *Revue internationale de musique française* 12 (1987): 22.

28. See Schrade, *Beethoven in France*, 200–201; Vallas, *Vincent d'Indy*, 2: 83.

29. Vallas, *Vincent d'Indy*, 2: 101.

30. See Vallas, *Vincent d'Indy*, 2: 97.

31. Jean-Marie Mayeur, "Le Catholicisme français et la Première Guerre mondiale," in *Francia*, vol. 2 (1974), as cited in Annette Becker, "The Churches and the War," in *The Great War and the French People*, ed. Jean-Jacques Becker, trans. Arnold Pomerans (New York, 1986), 179. See also Becker, *La guerre et la foi*.

32. Quoted by Becker, "The Churches and the War," 179. See also James F. McMillan, "French Catholics: *Rumeurs Infâmes* and the *Union Sacrée*, 1914–1918," in *Authority, Identity and the Social History of the Great War*, ed. Frans Coetzee and Marilyn Shevin-Coetzee (Providence, 1995), 114, 116; and James F. McMillan, "Reclaiming a Martyr: French Catholics and the Cult of Joan of Arc, 1890–1920," in *Martyrs and Martyrologies: Studies in Church History*, vol. 30, ed. Diana Wood (Oxford, 1993).

33. See Silver, *Esprit de Corps*, 13ff., regarding the figure of Marianne.

34. See Alain Denizot, *Le Sacré Coeur et la Grande Guerre* (Paris, 1994), 175–193.

35. McMillan, "Reclaiming a Martyr," 118.

36. A number of such "infamous rumors," however, were clearly promoted by French anti-clericals and the forces of Bismarck alike. In response, the pope expressed sympathy over the mistreatment of Cardinal Mercier, the archbishop of Mâlines, and outrage over the destruction of religious buildings in France. The pope's appointment of three new French cardinals, which followed in 1916, was made in an effort to restore French confidence in the papacy and to pave the way for a resurgence of papal power in a post-war society. See ibid., 127.

37. Romaine Rolland, *Jean-Christophe* (Paris, 1903–1912), "La Foire sur la Place," 70–90.

38. Rolland, *Musicians of Today*, 118.

39. Ibid., 118–120.

40. Thomson, *Vincent d'Indy*, 139.

41. See Fulcher, *French Cultural Politics*, 145–146.

42. Ibid., 31; and Brian Hart, "The Symphony in Theory and Practice in France, 1900–1914," Ph.D. diss., Indiana University, 1994, pp. 82–89.

43. Vallas, *Vincent d'Indy*, 2: 261.

44. Ibid., 2: 335. A. Maariotte, writing in *Le ménestrel* 82, no. 25 (1920): 252–253, proclaimed *La légende de Saint-Christophe* "the most perfect and grandiose expression of the art of d'Indy." See also the review by Henri Pruniéres, "La légende de Saint-Christophe," *Revue musicale* 1 (1920): 60.

CHAPTER 10. NEOCLASSICISM, AVIATION, AND THE GREAT WAR

1. Maurice Ravel, *A Ravel Reader: Correspondence, Articles, Interviews*, ed. Arbie Orenstein (New York, 1990), 150. Original French in Maurice Ravel, *Lettres à Roland-Manuel et à sa famille* (Paris, 1986), 23: "Oui, je travaille et avec une sûreté, une lucidité de fou. Mais, pendant ce temps, le cafard travaille aussi et, tout-à-coup, me voilà à sangloter sur les bémols!"

2. Ravel, *Reader*, 151.

3. The Second International, a federation of working-class parties founded by a congress in Paris in 1889, had endorsed parliamentary democracy and pro-

moted the Marxist doctrine of class struggle and the inevitability of social revolution. Although one of its main concerns was the prevention of war, this was inevitably compromised during World War I when the Socialist agenda realized the potential threat of reactionary powers. With the exception of the Russians and Serbs, the Socialist parties supported their governments in the war effort, as international working-class solidarity took a back seat to national purpose. By 1917, however, when half of the French units contained mutinous troops, the main socialist anthem, the "Internationale," briefly supplanted "La Marseillaise" and "Chant du départ." Written by Eugène Pottier in 1871 and set to music in 1888, the opening of the "Internationale" states: "Peace between us, war to the tyrants! / Let us apply the strike to the armies / If they insist, these cannibals / On making us heros, / They will know soon enough that our bullets / Are for our own generals." For more on the role of the "Internationale" during the period of the Great War, see Sweeney, *Singing Our Way to Victory*, 37–40, 230–231; for the sociopolitical backgrounds see Georges Haupt, *Socialism and the Great War: The Collapse of the Second International* (Oxford, 1972); and Merle Fainsod, *International Socialism and the World War* (New York, 1966).

4. Letter of 20 August 1914. Ravel, *Reader*, 152.

5. Letter of 26 September 1914. See Ravel, *Reader*, 154; Ravel, *Lettres à Roland-Manuel*, 26.

6. Marnat, *Maurice Ravel*, 408 n. 8.

7. Ravel, *Reader*, 155 n. 6; original French in Ravel, *Lettres à Roland-Manuel*, 25. Erik Satie also expressed his horror at the bombardment of Rheims cathedral at this time. See Erik Satie, *Écrits*, ed. Ornella Volta (Paris, 1981), 161, 392.

8. Marnat, *Maurice Ravel*, 390.

9. Ravel, *Reader*, 155.

10. For the details surrounding Magnard's death see *Le ménestrel*, 14 May 1920, 203.

11. Ravel acknowledged not only his awareness of the work in his letter to Roland-Manuel but also, perhaps, Magnard's insatiable penchant for canon and fugue evident in the last movement of his Piano Trio.

12. The work was premiered at the Salle Gaveau on 28 January 1915 at a thinly attended S.M.I. (Société Musicale Indépendante) concert. The violin part was originally intended for Georges Enesco, although at this event it was performed by Gabriel Willaume. The piano part, however, was performed by Alfredo Casella, a fact that endorses his celebrated reputation as a virtuoso pianist.

13. See the discussion of this repertoire in chapter 5.

14. Included were editions of several pieces published in mid-sixteenth-century France: Janequin, "La guerre de Renty" (1555); Claude le Jeune, "La sortie des gendarmes" (1559); and "Le siège de Metz" (1559). See Julien Tiersot, "Souvenirs de cinq années (1914–1919)," *Le ménestrel* 82, no. 3 (1920):

25, where the author notes that, beyond the musical imagery, the fiery texts were especially appropriate to modern times.

15. Marnat, *Maurice Ravel*, 409, 654.

16. See Schmidt, ed., *Chansons de la revanche*, 102. Other French songs also invoked the symbol of the bird as "Les canaris de Verdun," with words by André Piédallu and music by Henry Février (Heugel & Cie, 1916). For a German soldier song, "Köln am Rhein," with a similar symbolism see Schuhmacher, *Leben und Seele*, 178.

17. The original words were by G. Soubise and the music by F. Boissière. See Schmidt, ed., *Chansons de la revanche*, 116. For a visual confirmation in German culture, see the title page of *Der Drahtverhau* for March 1917, reproduced in Johann, *Innenansicht eines Krieges*, opposite 272, which shows a dirigible floating above the figure of Icarus prepared for takeoff.

18. By this time Ravel was already engaged in volunteer war work. Despite his earlier remarks about its inappropriateness for the times, Ravel also recommenced work on "Wien" alongside his new keyboard set.

19. Ravel, *Reader*, 155; original French in Marnat, *Maurice Ravel*, 409. The reference to "La Marseillaise" no doubt alluded in part to the fact that Debussy had recently used it in the last of his piano preludes, "Feux d'artifice."

20. See René Chalupt, *Ravel au miroir de ses lettres* (Paris, 1956), 106. Avoidance of the tango held no appeal for either Satie or Stravinsky, however: the former had already incorporated a "perpetual tango" in his *Sports et divertissements* of 1914 and the latter would soon introduce it in a trio of dances (waltz, tango, ragtime) in his *Histoire du soldat* of 1918.

21. See Messing, *Neoclassicism*, 50–54. Further analytical considerations regarding the "Forlane" may be found in Martha M. Hyde, "Neoclassic and Anachronistic Impulses in Twentieth-Century Music," *Music Theory Spectrum* 18, no. 2 (1996): 206–210; and Carolyn Abbate, "Outside Ravel's Tomb," *Journal of the American Musicological Society* 52, no. 3 (1999): 497–511.

22. Ben Arnold, *Music and War: A Research and Information Guide* (New York, 1993), no. 453.

23. See Silver, *Esprit de corps*, 83–85. For a discussion of anti-modernist cartoons that supported the same perspective see Peppis, *Literature, Politics, and the English Avant-Garde*, 103–104.

24. Ravel, *Reader*, 180; original French in Ravel, *Lettres à Roland-Manuel*, 99.

25. John Horne, "Soldiers, Civilians and the Warfare of Attrition: Representations of Combat in France, 1914–1918," in *Authority, Identity and the Social History of the Great War*, ed. Frans Coetzee and Marilyn Shevin-Coetzee (Providence, 1995), 240–241. The insurrection was ultimately brought under control with 3,427 soldiers court-martialed, 554 condemned to death, 49 shot, and hundreds sentenced to life imprisonment. See Leonard V. Smith, *Between Mutiny and Obedience: The Case of the French Fifth Infantry Division during World War I* (Princeton, 1994), 206–207; and Keegan, *First World War*, 329–331.

26. The poem was published by Paul Vaillant-Couturier in 1919. See *The New York Times*, 8 November 1998, p. Y9.

27. See Theo Hirsbrunner, *Maurice Ravel* (Laaber, 1989), 282–290.

28. Some have also argued with some reason for references to Scarlatti's pungent acciaccature. See Manuel Rosenthal, *Ravel: Souvenirs*, ed. Marcel Marnat (Paris, 1995), 172.

29. See Silver, *Esprit de corps*, 138–145, 271–281, for a discussion of Picasso and Neoclassicism, and 76–88 for a similar evaluation of Severini.

30. See Ameri Wallach, "The Retreat of French Art Began in Flanders Fields," *The New York Times*, 6 February 2000, p. AR 1, 38. See, however, the response by William Rubin, "Challenging a Thesis," *The New York Times*, 20 February 2000, p. AR 4, as well as Ms. Wallach's rejoinder.

31. It should be noted that, its distinctive qualities aside, the "Toccata" periodically draws material from the "Rigaudon," m. 3ff.

32. For the army citation see "Note de l'éditeur" to Joseph de Marliave's *Études musicales* (Paris, 1917), v. De Marliave also wrote a study of the string quartets of Beethoven, published posthumously in 1925 and in an English edition in 1961. See Marnat, *Maurice Ravel*, 436–437, n. 8.

33. The premiere of *Tombeau de Couperin* was Ravel's first public appearance following the Armistice, and Long's performance was so enthusiastically received that she was obliged to encore the suite. See Marguerite Long, *At the Piano with Ravel*, trans. Olive Senior-Ellis (London, 1973), 94.

34. Silver, *Esprits de Corps*, 62–63.

35. See letters to Jean Marnold and Roland-Manuel in Marnat, *Maurice Ravel*, 410–414. To Roland-Manuel, then in the Dardanelles, Ravel wrote on 14 December 1915: "After more than a year of processing, I'm going to be steered into aviation. I've paid visit after visit: my heart and lungs are still fine. Let's hope the former will have enough elasticity to find its way into my stomach at the right moment."

36. Ursula Vaughan Williams, *RVW: A Biography of Ralph Vaughan Williams* (London, 1964), 118.

37. Ravel, *Reader*, 161.

38. Ibid., 163.

39. Marnat, *Maurice Ravel*, 410–414: "Il ne m'est plus permis de penser à l'aviation. Du reste, il n'y a pas que le carburateur qui soit attent. Le moteur lui-même ne marche que sur trois pattes." (I'm no longer allowed to think of aviation. Besides, there is only a carburator which requires my attention. And the motor itself limps along on three feet.)

40. Ibid. ". . . depuis près d'un mois, je n'aie presque rien à faire, je me sens de plus en plus faible, de plus en plus fatigué. Comme j'allais enfin pouvoir passer à l'aviation, le major m'en a dissuadé: hypertropie du coeur, pas beaucoup, mais enfin."

41. J. H. Lartigue, *Mémoires sans mémoire* (Paris, 1975), 75.

42. In *Fighting Airman: The Way of the Eagle*, ed. Stanley M. Ulanoff (Garden City, N.Y., 1968), first published in 1919, Major Charles J. Biddle, a

leading World War I ace, described the principle of the synchronized machine gun. The valves of a gasoline motor were timed so as to open and close at a given point in the revolution of the engine, and the machine gun was connected to it and timed to shoot according to the cyclic pattern.

43. Roger de la Fresnaye, whose *Conquest of the Air* of 1913 had already recorded a newly developing fascination of the French on the eve of the war, painted an idealized portrait of Guynemer based on a photograph. See Silver, *Esprit de corps*, 295, for a reproduction.

44. The figure of Winged Fame frequently appears with Pegasus.

45. Karl Vollmoeller, the German translator of D'Annunzio's poetry, introduced a new lyricism when he spoke of music in the flying machine "whose taut wires sang like a harp" and whose propeller roared forth "the song of the high flight." See Robert Wohl, *A Passion for Wings: Aviation and the Western Imagination, 1908–1918* (New Haven, 1994), 261–263. For the role of flight in Western literature see Walter Muschig, "Der fliegende Mensch in der Dichtung," *Neue Schweizer Rundschau* 8 (1939–1940): 311–320, 384–392, 446–453; for its iconography in Western art see Clive Hart, *Images of Flight* (Berkeley, 1988); and for its twentieth-century wartime role see Williamson Murray, *War in the Air, 1914–45* (London, 1999).

46. Including especially Albert Robida (1848–1926). See his *Le vingtième siècle: La vie électrique* (Paris, 1883); and *Fantastique et science-fiction / Robida*, ed. Phillip Brun (Paris, 1980). For a picture of Robida's fantasy airship station atop Notre-Dame Cathedral in Paris, see Wohl, *Passion for Wings*, 97, fig. 97.

47. Motion picture shots were made of this event and were shown in Paris's cinemas the same afternoon. See Wohl, *Passion for Wings*, 277, for a series of five film frames which recorded the crash. For another contemporary notice of this event see Lartigue, *Mémoires*, 103.

48. See *Discours prononcés à l'occasion de l'Inauguration de l'Institut Aérotechnique de Saint-Cyr l'École* (Paris, 1911), 6; Beril Becker, *Dreams and Realities of the Conquest of the Skies* (New York, 1967), 170–171; and Wohl, *Passion for Wings*, 41.

49. Wohl, *A Passion for Wings*, 133. With respect to music's connection to the prehistory of aviation it is interesting to note that Charles-Marie Widor, renowned organist and secretary of the Académie des Beaux-Arts, was the grandson of Joseph Michel Montgolfier, pioneer inventor of the hot-air balloon, and that Widor frequently appended the motto "Soar Above" to the title pages of his scores. See John Near, "The Life and Work of C.-M. Widor," D.M.A. diss., Boston University, 1985.

50. It was a fact that had been acknowledged by the War Department from the very beginning. See *Discours*, 8–10.

51. *Discours*, 17.

52. Two sets of *Mélodies* were published in 1900 and 1909. For a copy of "Vers les cieux" see Paris Bibliothèque nationale, Vma.570.

53. See Roman d'Amat and R. Limouzin-Lamothe, *Dictionnaire de biogra-*

phie française, vol. 11 (Paris, 1967), 163. Notices of Henry Deutsch de la Meurthe are notably rare, and he is mentioned in no encyclopaedias or dictionaries of music.

54. For a copy see Paris, Bibliothèque nationale: 4° Vm^8. 207.

55. The title page reads: *Icare, épopée lyrique en trois tableaux*. A rare copy of the piano-vocal score in the possession of the University of California, Berkeley, Department of Music Library, carries the name of Sigmund Romberg stamped in gold on the front cover binding. In 1917 the New York revue *Over the Top* also showcased the music of Sigmund Romberg along with dancers Fred and Adele Astaire.

56. See Thomas Forrest Kelley, *First Nights* (New Haven, 2000), 273–276.

57. Lynn Garafola, *Diaghilev's Ballets Russes* (New York, 1989), 173, 278.

58. "Toute la rude et noble armée des travailleurs en extase devant les exploits des navigateurs aériens, qui glissent dans le ciel étoilé," piano-vocal score, 95.

59. "Tu meurs mais cependant / Quelque jour ton génie ardent / Vers la solitude éternelle ouvrira de nouveau son aîle / Après des jours, des ans et des siècles sans nombre, / Ainsi qu'un nouvel astre il jaillira de l'ombre / Et montera vers la clarté! / *(désignant les aéronautes, les aviateurs)* / D'autres mortels suivront ta trace. / Ils iront parcourir les abimes sans fond / Du soir bleuté du matin blond. / Et seront cette fois les maîtres de l'espace! / Ce n'est pas aux oiseaux qu'ils raviront des aîles / Car pour leur donner libre essor / La Terre, douce et maternelle, / Laissera couler ses trésors / Elle pliera son âme au joug de leur puissance. / Le monde en t'acclamant / Pourra voir ses enfants / Briser les vieilles lois que les dieux lui donnèrent / Et dans de grands vols triomphants et sûrs / Planner en plain azur tout nimbés de lumière."

60. See Harry Paul, *The Sorcerer's Apprentice: The French Scientist's Image of German Sciences, 1840–1919* (Gainesville, 1972), 27; and Hanna, *The Mobilization of Intellect*, 228.

61. See Maurice Barrès, "La Réorganisation intellectuelle de la France, I," *Revue universelle* 2 (1920): 387, 404; and Hanna, *The Mobilization of Intellect*, 229.

62. Painlevé's board membership is recorded in the *Bulletin de l'Institut aérotechnique de l'Université de Paris (Fondation Henry Deutsch de la Meurthe)* no. 1–3 (Paris, 1911–13). Painlevé had supervised the creation of the *Direction des inventions intéressant la défense nationale* in 1915, and, in accord with French academic positions that charged German science as a huge enterprise devoted to "creating the most formidable killing-machine ever produced," proposed that French science remain committed to the "disinterested search for truth." See Paul, *The Sorcerer's Apprentice*, 27; and Hanna, *The Mobilization of Intellect*, 178, 228.

63. See Cork, *A Bitter Truth*, 50, for a further analysis of Goncharova's lithographs.

64. H. G. Wells, *The World Set Free* (London: Macmillan, 1914), 116.

65. Quoted by Louise Faure-Favrier in *Les chevaliers de l'air* (Paris, 1923), 164.

66. Satie, *Écrits*, 221–223.

67. See Higgins, *Anthology of First World War French Poetry*, 37, 122. Garros, who collaborated with Morane and Saulnier in the development of a synchronized machine-gun/propeller mechanism, took Cocteau for flights in 1914. Garros was shot down in 1915, interned in a prisoner-of-war camp, escaped, and was finally killed in October 1918 after Cocteau had written his poem but before it was published. The extent to which the World War I airplane pilot persists as an elite breed of warriors in the modern memory is underscored by the fact that the French Open tennis tournament is played to this very day at a stadium named after Roland Garros.

68. Cocteau, *Le coq et l'arlequin*, in *Le rappel à l'ordre*, 32. *Parade* also betrayed its war-time pedigree in other respects. Cocteau's scenario for "The Little American Girl" episode, for example, includes among other items, the following: "the sirens of Boulogne—submarine cables—airplanes—the declarations of President Wilson—typewriters—torpedo boats—mines—posters—advertising—Charlie Chaplin—the list of the victims of the Lusitania. . . ." In light of the fact that the premiere of *Parade* was organized as a benefit for the *mutilés de guerre*, there would appear to be another layer of reality beyond that of the confounding artist and his unaccepting public. Indeed, the inept but authoritarian barker-managers who vainly try to sell their message to an uncomprehending public may be seen as another of Picasso's and Cocteau's double faces concerning the use of various types of propaganda, including posters and music, invoked in war time.

69. In the opening address at the inauguration of the Aérotechnical Institut, vice-rector Liard praised Deutsch as a pioneer who had proposed the application of gasoline-propelled motors. See *Discours*, 6; and Henry Deutsch, *Le pétrole et ses applications* (Paris, 1891).

70. In an interview of 1912 Deutsch confirmed his devotion to music and its importance to him, stating that a piano adorned his laboratory and was always at the ready for his improvisations. He added: "I have predicted the automobile and the dirigible, these sportive manifestations of the human genius—one the symbol of vitality, and the other the symbol of flight . . . I try now only to bring nearer a little beauty, to direct my brain toward noble sensations and to set aside all ugliness. And in this respect music procures for me a profound and sane joy." Deutsch revealed that he had received some guidance and encouragement in his music studies from the sister of Ambroise Thomas, but that it was only at around the age of 50 that he undertook the serious study of music. See Georges Casella, "La Musique et le Sport, II: Henri Deutsch de la Meurthe," *Revue musicale, S.I.M.* 7, no. 6 (1912), 79.

71. See Abbate, "Outside Ravel's Tomb," 495, 496.

72. On f♯, B, F♯—dominant and secondary dominants to E, the key of the piece.

73. Because of its low-register here, it also suggests the opening gesture of the recent "Toccata" for piano of 1912 by Prokofiev, one of the most important composers of the Allied nations.

74. See Pisano et al., *Legend, Memory and the Great War,* 65.

75. Prokofiev, for example, had already advertised his specific indebtedness to Schumann's *Toccata,* op. 7, which had wedded their two main ingredients of the "toccata" to that time, namely Paganinian virtuosity and Baroque propulsion.

76. I am grateful to Gregory Vitarbo, historian of Russian aviation and officer culture, for his thoughts on a reading of the fermata as well as the notion of the air ace as "virtuoso."

77. Rawls, *Wake Up, America!* 98.

78. Cf. Abbate, "Outside Ravel's Tomb," 496.

79. For more on the history of the musical *tombeau* see Abbate, "Outside Ravel's Tomb"; Michel Brenet, "Les 'Tombeaux' en musique," *La revue musicale* 3 (1903): 568–575, 631–638; and Marie-Claire Mussat, "Le Tombeau dans la musique du XXième siècle," in *Tombeaux et monuments,* ed. Jacques Dugast and Michèle Touret (Remes, 1992), 133–144. Marnat, *Maurice Ravel,* 424, claims that Ravel's funerary urn design was visibly copied from a *vase directoire* "au Frêne." For examples of the type see the drawings of two tureens from the workshop of Henry Auguste after Jean-Guillaume Moitte in Mary L. Myers, *French Architectural and Ornament Drawings of the Eighteenth Century* (New York, 1991), 1, 6. For this citation, thanks to Perrin Stein, assistant curator of drawings and prints, Metropolitan Museum of Art, in a communication of 11 January 1999.

80. Wohl, *A Passion for Wings,* 38.

81. See Leed, *No Man's Land,* 135.

82. Cork, *A Bitter Truth,* 164.

83. Ibid., 102.

84. Wohl, *A Passion for Wings,* 156

85. Cork, *A Bitter Truth,* 69–70.

86. See Ravel, *Reader,* 165, 167; and Kern, *The Culture of Time and Space,* 7. For more on Ravel and the issue of time and space, see Watkins, *Pyramids at the Louvre,* chap. 9, "The Valley of the Bells." Also compare Ravel's highly energized although sanitized view of aerial combat with that of Rolland, Marinetti, and others as discussed in Wohl, *A Passion for Wings,* 154.

87. Ravel reports several close brushes with death with telling immediacy, but his most vivid description of the war, recorded in a letter of April 1916 (see Ravel, *Reader,* 162–163), was punctuated only by the ghostly residue of airborne shells, lacking in any reference to the dangers of aerial combat, and bereft of any terrestrial sound whatsoever.

88. See Edward Higginbottom, "Couperin, François le grand," grovemusic.com; and J. Clark, *François Couperin "Pièces de clavecin": The Background* (Oxford, 1992).

89. After William Shakespeare in five acts and twenty-three tableaux. Argument and choreographic plan by Jean Cocteau with music of popular English airs arranged and orchestrated by Roger Desormière.

90. *Dawn Patrol* of 1930 and remade in 1938 was an instant hit, and the World War I aviation film maintained its popularity well into the post–World War II period.

91. The original collaboration was eventually abandoned, and Weill later composed his own version of Brecht's radio play, *Der Ozeanflug.*

92. Interview in Paris, January 1930, "Maurice Ravel and His *Bolero*" by José André, published in *La nación,* a Buenos Aires newspaper, 15 March 1930; reprinted in Ravel, *Reader,* 467. The image of Icarus was also tapped by Pascal Forthuny in *Plus haut que l'amour: Icare l'as de coeur; roman d'aviation antique* (Paris, 1918), and later by the composer Jehan Alain, *Icare* (Paris, 1944).

93. See Ravel, *Reader,* 469 n. 4. Interestingly, a new ballet, *L'envol d'Icare,* was completed by one of Diaghilev's last proteges, Igor Markevitch, in 1932, premiered in 1933, and recast in 1943 as *Icare.* The sections of Markevitch's ballet were as follows: Prélude—Eveil de la connaissance—Icare et les oiseaux—Les ailes d'Icare—Envol d'Icare—Où l'on retrouve les ailes d'Icare—Mort d'Icare.

94. For Painlevé's speech honoring Lindbergh see Paul Painlevé, *Paroles et Écrits* (Paris, 1936), 369. Painlevé left the office of prime minister for the last time on 22 November 1925, after which he served as war minister under Briand and Raymond Poincaré and then air minister in 1930–1931 and again in 1932–1933. He died 29 October 1933.

95. Emphasis is mine. The article, "Finding Tunes in Factories," appeared in English in *New Britain* (1933), 367; reprinted in Ravel, *Reader,* 398–400. In World War II the American composer Marc Blitzstein, who served in the U.S. Army Air Force, registered a related perspective in his *"Airborne" Symphony* of 1946.

96. Debussy, *Correspondance,* 329.

97. Debussy argued that despite their claims to be true representationalists, painters and sculptors were capable of capturing only one aspect at a time, of preserving only one moment.

98. Review in *S.I.M.* (1 November 1913); reprinted in *Debussy on Music,* 295, 297.

99. See Lartigue, *Mémoires,* 150; Wohl, *A Passion for Wings,* 276; and Vicki Goldberg, *Jacques Henri Lartigue, Photographer* (New York, 1999). Lartigue was also enamoured of the great pianists whom he likened to champions, and during the first months of the war he claimed that, even though he had to settle for such vicarious thrills through the pianola, the instrument was specifically capable of opening up a celestial imagery for him. See the entry for 10 January 1914 and 13 January 1915 in Lartigue, *Mémoires,* 167, 213.

CHAPTER 11. THE WORLD OF THE FUTURE

1. The Futurist distaste for Puccini notwithstanding, during World War I the tenor solo from act 3 of *La fanciulla del West*, "Ch'ella me creda libero e lontano," was reported to have been sung by Italian troops as an equivalent to the English song "It's a Long Way to Tipperary." See "Puccini," *The New Grove Dictionary*, 2d ed. (London, 2001).

2. Nice and Savoy had been lost to France the previous year, and the Veneto was held by Austria and would not be united with Italy until 1866. Napoleon III still claimed Rome, which would become the nation's capital only in 1870.

3. Stefan Zweig, *Romain Rolland: The Man and His Work* (New York, 1921), 221–222.

4. Ambrose Bierce, *The Devil's Dictionary* (New York, 1935).

5. H. G. Wells, "The Discovery of the Future," lecture at the Royal Institute, London, 24 January 1902; published in *Nature*, no. 65 (1902).

6. Marinetti's tract, *War, The World's Only Hygiene*, was written between 1911 and 1915.

7. Already by 1899 D'Annunzio had written a political tragedy, *Glory*, that centered on the revolution of a young hero supported by armed peasants. And in 1906 D'Annunzio and Marinetti both wrote of super-heroes inspired by Italian colonialist ambitions in the "scramble for Africa."

8. See Alfredo Bonadeo, *D'Annunzio and the Great War* (London, 1995), 69.

9. Lockspeiser, *Debussy*, 228–229. A further problem centered on D'Annunzio's emphasis on the Emperor Diocletian's attraction to Sebastian's physical beauty, an attribute, incidentally, that was repeatedly tapped by the war poets. See Fussell, *The Great War*, 285; and also François Le Targat, ed., *Saint-Sebastien dans l'histoire de l'art depuis le XVe siècle* (Paris, 1979).

10. Spoken by the women of Byblos (chorus) and a solo voice in the Third Act or Mansion.

11. Bonadeo, *D'Annunzio*, 71.

12. See Vallas, *Vincent d'Indy*, 223; and Fulcher, *French Cultural Politics*, 190.

13. Several attempts at the revival of the work occurred in the 1990s, including a notable recording under the direction of M. T. Thomas and a telecast production with the New York Philharmonic under the direction of Kurt Masur. See Barbara Jepson, "This Music Befits a Saintly Legend," *The New York Times*, 30 March 1997, p. H 32.

14. For further details behind Italy's abandonment of a Triple Alliance with Germany and Austro-Hungary, see chapter 7; Anthony Alcock, "Trentino and Tyrol: From Austrian Crownland to European Region," in *Europe and Ethnicity: The First World War and Contemporary Ethnic Conflict*, ed. Seamus Dunn and T. G. Fraser (London, 1996), 67–72; and Wohl, *Generation of 1914*, 164, 168.

15. For the lyrics and a critical interpretation see Savona and Straniero, *Canti della Grande Guerra*, 421–425. In a reflection of Italy's bitter reaction to

Wilson's Fourteen Points, the ninth of which called for the Italian frontier to be drawn approximately along prewar lines, the first stanza ends with the following stinging sarcasm: "Vince in cielo, vince in terra, / per dare i mari all'Inghilterra!! / Volete Napoli? Roma? Venezia? / Tutta la Sicilia vi può bastare? . . . / *Tarantè, tarantì, tarantà!*" (You conquer the sky and the earth only to give the seas to England! / Do you want Naples, Rome, Venice? / Will all of Sicily be enough for you?) A considerable discography, which preserves Italian songs from the Great War, is also cited here.

16. There is no complete edition of Futurist manifestoes. For English translations of some of the principal ones see Apollonio, 1973.

17. They included "Manifesto of the Futurist Musicians" of 1910, followed by two additional tracts, the "Technical Manifesto of Futurist Music" and "The Destruction of Quadrature"; all three were published together in 1912.

18. An extract from "Gioia," which originally appeared in *Lacerba*, May 15, 1914, is reproduced in Mark A. Radice, "*Futurismo:* Its Origins, Context, Repertory, and Influence," *The Musical Quarterly* 73, no. 1 (1989): 11–12. See also *Francesco Balilla Pratella: Edizioni, scritti, manoscritti musicali e futuristi,* ed. Domenico Tampieri (Ravenna, 1995). For more on Futurism see Cinzia Sartini Blum, *The Other Modernism: F. T. Marinetti's Futurist Fiction of Power* (Berkeley, 1996); and Marjorie Perloff, *The Futurist Moment: Avant-garde, Avant-guerre, and the Language of Rupture* (Chicago, 1986).

19. Umbro Apollonio, ed., *Futurist Manifestos*, trans. Caroline Tisdall (London, 1973), 74, 88. Of the three excerpts presented here, only the first and third appear as is in Apollonio; the second is rephrased.

20. Their success cannot be fully judged because they were destroyed in World War II, and a single gramophone recording that survives is inconclusive. Several recent reconstructions, however, have provided us with a reasonable approximation.

21. See chapter 7 for Stravinsky's relation to these events, a complete report of which is given in Tisdall and Bozzolla, *Futurism*, 118.

22. See Watkins, *Soundings*, 240, for a sample of the notation.

23. Tisdall and Bozzolla, *Futurism*, 119. For Boccioni's *Caricature of a Futurist Evening*, see ibid., 93.

24. See Ferruccio Busoni, *Selected Letters*, ed. Antony Beaumont (London, 1987), 165.

25. Boccioni has left us a visual record of an earlier demonstration in the Galleria in 1910. See Tisdall and Bozzolla, *Futurism*, 40, 177.

26. See Messing, *Neoclassicism*, 65–74, for an articulate overview of Busoni's position in the Neoclassicist revival.

27. See Wohl, *Generation of 1914*, 61 and 205, regarding the *Jugendbewegung* in Germany and Austria, the nationalist revival in France, the revolt of young Socialists against the party leadership in Italy, and the mobilization of young intellectuals in Spain.

28. Messing, *Neoclassicism*, 65.

29. They ranged from re-readings of the virtuoso organ works like the Pre-

lude and Fugue in D major and "Toccata, Adagio, and Fugue" to the trio-textured Schubler Chorale-Preludes and the unaccompanied "Chaconne" for solo violin.

30. Busoni, *Selected Letters*, 224.

31. See letter to Egon Petri of 7 March 1916 in ibid., 232.

32. Edward Dent, *Busoni* (London, 1974), 230.

33. Rudyard Kipling, *For All We Have and Are* (London, [1914?]), stanza 1: "For all we have and are, / For all our children's fate, / Stand up and take the war. / The Hun is at the gate!"

34. In the same issue of *Le mot*, 15 June 1915, Cocteau joined Paul Iribe in hailing "with love a people who might have chosen to sleep on palm leaves under the olive trees of Latium, and who, with a tuft of feather from our cock over their ear, marries us"; translated in Cork, *A Bitter Truth*, 68.

35. Reported in the Vienna *Neue Freie Presse*, 4 May 1918; translated in Antony Beaumont, *Busoni the Composer* (Bloomington, 1985), 237.

36. Dent, *Busoni*, 234 suggests that it is "a distorted reminiscence of the march in *La Figlia del Reggimento*," a claim that has been refuted by others.

37. See Watkins, *Pyramids at the Louvre*, chap. 12, "Masks and Machines."

38. "Zu den Wachspuppen von Lotte Pritzel," published in *Die Weissen Blätter* the very week they met. See Beaumont, *Busoni the Composer*, 225.

39. See Sarah Boxer's report on the fear of puppets as reported at the annual meeting of the American Psychoanalytic Association in December 1997 in "Pulling Strings: The Geppetto Effect," *The New York Times*, 17 January 1998, pp. Y A13–15.

40. Tisdall and Bozzolla, *Futurism*, 85.

41. Reported by Busoni in a notice to the *Neue Zürcher Zeitung* along with the obituary that appeared in the *Corriere della sera*. The translation here is a conflation of the two versions offered by Dent, *Busoni*, 231–232, and Tisdall and Bozzolla, *Futurism*, 181.

42. Beaumont, *Busoni the Composer*, 244.

43. See, however, John M. Brereton, *The Horse in War* (New York, 1976). For a photo of Boccioni on a horse, see Tisdall and Bozzolla, *Futurism*, 181.

44. Tisdall and Bozzolla, *Futurism*, 179, 189. One of their ranks, however, the painter Carlo Carrà, had been called up in 1917, rejected as unfit, and sent to a mental hospital because the examining medical officer deemed that his *Guerrapittura* (Warpainting) of 1915 could only have been painted by a madman. Carrà had signed the *Guerrapittura* with a protracted "r" (Carrrà) just as Marinetti had done with the word *vibrrrare* in his renowned "Turkish Captive Balloon" from *Zang Tumb Tuum* (1914). Their orthography obviously served as a model for Stravinsky's "Marrrch" in the *Trois pièces faciles* of the same year.

45. Beaumont, *Busoni the Composer*, 247–48.

46. Earlier, when Busoni saw Boccioni's Futurist sculpture for the first time in Bologna in 1913, he had commented: "Compared to *this* sort of art and the incarnation of Mona Lisa as Gabriele's mistress, *Pierrot Lunaire* is mere tepid

lemonade!" Dent, *Busoni*, 203. From an early date Boccioni's style had been recognized as so quintessentially Futurist that Balla's sculpture titled *Boccioni's Fist* of 1915 showed up on Marinetti's own letterhead stationery. It is reproduced but not interpreted by Rita Reif, "You Could Tell the 'Ism' by the Letterhead," *The New York Times*, 31 March 1996, p. H 38. See chapter 7 for the relation of this Futurist stationery to Stravinsky.

47. See Dent, *Busoni*, 347–348, for a list of Busoni's Bach editions and transcriptions.

48. Letter to Philipp Jarnach of February 12, 1919; see Beaumont, *Busoni the Composer*, 301.

49. Casella's sponsorship of the latest trends as found in the music of Stravinsky, Schoenberg, and Bartók at the Liceo (later Conservatorio) di Santa Cecilia in Rome and the Venice Biennale, as well as his help in founding the *Settimane senesi* at the Accademia Chigiana, only corroborated his role in promoting an enriched basis for an Italian national musical identity.

CHAPTER 12. "DANCE OF DEATH"

1. Marsha Rozenblit, *Reconstructing a National Identity: The Jews of Habsburg Austria during World War I* (Oxford, 2001), 17. See also David Rechter, *The Jews of Vienna and the First World War* (London, 2001).

2. Beller, "Tragic Carnival," 127–130.

3. See Michael P. Steinberg, "In Salzburg, a Fresh Skirmish in the Culture Wars," *The New York Times*, 17 October 1999, p. 35; and Michael P. Steinberg, *Austria as Theater and Ideology: The Meaning of the Salzburg Festival* (Ithaca, 2000).

4. See Celia Applegate, "What Is German Music? Reflections on the Role of Art in the Creation of the Nation," *German Studies Review* (Winter 1992): 25, 29–30. See also Celia Applegate, *A Nation of Provincials: The German Idea of Heimat* (Berkeley, 1990).

5. See Peter Jelavich, "German Culture in the Great War," in *European Culture in the Great War*, ed. Aviel Roshwald and Richard Stites (Cambridge, U.K., 1999), 47–53.

6. See Friedrich von Bernhardi, *Germany and the Next War*, trans. Allen H. Powles (London, 1912), chap. 1. The book was instrumental in provoking anti-German sentiment both before and during World War I. See Eksteins, *Rites of Spring*, 90.

7. See Beller, "Tragic Carnival," 131–143; Carmen Ottner, "Hans Gregor; Direktor der Wiener Hofoper in schwerer Zeit (1911–1918)," in *Oper in Wien 1900–1925*, ed. Carmen Ottner (Vienna, 1991), 107, 115; and Andrea Seebohm, ed., *Die Wiener Oper: 350 Jahre Glanz und Tradition* (Vienna, 1986), 92.

8. See Scott D. Denham, *Visions of War: Ideologies and Images of War in German Literature Before and After the Great War* (Bern, 1992), 81–86; and Peter Jelavich, "German Culture," 32–57, particularly 47ff.

9. Nowhere was this more vividly portrayed than in Georg Heym's poem called "Krieg" (War) of 1912, where the cosmic vision of a German nation that was not to be stilled for long is prophetically identified. See Michael Minden, "Expressionism and the First World War," in *The Violent Muse*, ed. Jana Howlett and Rod Mengham (Manchester, 1994), 45. See also Rother, ed., *Die letzten Tage*, 59ff., for this and other texts on the war including "O Freunde, nicht diese Töne" (1914) by Hermann Hesse, "Kriegshymnen" (1915) by Peter Altenberg, and an excerpt from Hugo von Hofmannsthal's *Krieg und Kultur* (1915).

10. Seven hundred forty-one composers entered, including Alexander Zemlinsky and Arnold Schoenberg, neither of whom won. The prize winners were three unknowns: Hans Hermann, Heinrich Eckl, and Gustav Lazarus.

11. "Verlorene Haufen" was one of two *Ballades*, op. 12, which includes "Jane Grey," both of which were also set by Zemlinsky.

12. Arnold Schoenberg, "Verlorene Haufen," 1907.

13. Denham, *Visions of War*, 68.

14. Alan Bullock, *Hitler: A Study in Tyranny* (London, 1952), 45. See also Rawls, *Wake Up America!*, 88; and Alan Seeger, *Letters and Diary of Alan Seeger* (New York, 1917). The attitude is traceable, among other sources, to Schiller, who wrote in his *Reiterlied* that it was only the soldier, in his confrontation with death, who was free. Theodor Körner's proclamation that "happiness lies only in sacrificial death" was perhaps even more dramatic; see Theodor Körner, *Bundeslied vor der Schlacht*, 12 May 1813. See Mosse, *Fallen Soldiers*, 27, 70–71.

15. Karl Hammer, *Deutsche Kriegstheologie (1870–1918)* (Munich, 1971), 167; and Mosse, *Fallen Soldiers*, 77–78.

16. See Mosse, *Fallen Soldiers*, 167. Later on a group of such men—viewed as "fanatic" with respect to their willingness to fight—were identified by the Third Reich. See Victor Klemperer, *LTI: Notizbuch eines philologe* (Berlin, 1947), 54, 62.

17. See Ernst von Salomon, "Der verlorene Haufen," in *Krieg und Krieger*, ed. Ernst Jünger (Berlin, 1930), 111; and Mosse, *Fallen Soldiers*, 168. Klemperer later survived during World War II partly because he was married to an "Aryan" but also in part out of recognition of his service on the front lines in World War I. For his revealing diary of these years, see Viktor Klemperer, *I Will Bear Witness: A Diary of the Nazi Years, 1933–1941*, trans. Martin Chalmers (New York, 1998); and Richard Bernstein's review, "How the Little Things Add Up to Horror," *The New York Times*, 11 November 1998, p. B8. See also Klemperer's *I Will Bear Witness: A Diary of the Nazi Years, 1942–1945*, trans. Martin Chalmers (New York, 2000).

18. For the text and music to "Morgenrot" see Schuhmacher, *Leben und Seele*, 242. See also Mathias Eberle, *Der Weltkrieg und die Künstler der Weimarer Republik* (Stuttgart, 1989), 31–62, for a similar analogy with the Expressionist painters. See also Jalevich, "German Culture," 52.

19. A performance by Ruth Ziesak, soprano, appears on Sony CD SK

57960, Alexander Zemlinsky, *Lieder aus dem Nachlass*. English text translations by Eugene Hartzell.

20. See Alan Riding, "Sometimes the Player's the Thing," *The New York Times*, 22 November 1998, pp. AR 7, 33, for a report on the revival of Schnitzler's play in English translation as "The Blue Room." The play has also flourished in French translation as "La Ronde."

21. Schnitzler coined the widely adopted term *"das süsse Mädel"* for a sexually available young woman in an early play, "The Fairy Tale" (1891). Berg, who knew Schnitzler's writings well, had availed himself of the type in fathering an illegitimate child as a late teenager. See Peter Gay, "Sex and Longing in Old Vienna," *The New York Times Book Review*, 11 July 1999, p. 39, for an assessment of Schnitzler's position and importance. See also *Alban Berg: Letters to His Wife*, ed. and trans. Bernard Grun (New York, 1971), 309, where in a letter of 1 April 1923 Berg speaks of Alma Mahler phoning him, having just returned from the Schnitzlers.

22. Fifield Christopher, *Max Bruch: His Life and Works* (London, 1988), 306–307.

23. See Christopher, *Max Bruch*, 307, 313.

24. See Dennis, *Beethoven in German Politics*, 67, and, for a statistical breakdown, n. 121. He calculated that from the 1914–1915 season through that of 1918–1919 the Berlin Philharmonic Orchestra performed 526 different programs in Berlin, of which 201 included works by Beethoven.

25. A series of articles by R. Sternfeld, Wilhelm Klatte, and Hans Mersmann, all titled "Zu viel Beethoven?" appeared in *Allgemeine Musik-Zeitung* on 20 February 1917, 2 March 1917, and 9 March 1917, respectively.

26. The pianist was Augusta Cuttlow. See Peter Muck, ed., *Einhundert Jahre Berliner Philharmonisches Orchester: Darstellung in Dokumente*, 3 vols. (Tutzing, 1982), 3: 153.

27. See Gary D. Stark, "All Quiet on the Home Front: Popular Entertainments, Censorship and Civilian Morale in Germany, 1914–1918," in *Authority, Identity and the Social History of the Great War*, ed. Frans Coetzee and Marilyn Shevin-Coetzee (Providence, 1995), 74.

28. See Muck, ed., *Einhundert Jahre*, 1: 464, for a review of the first performance as it was reported in *Neue Zeitschrift für Musik*.

29. Victor Fuchs, a Viennese singing teacher who was with Schoenberg at this time, somewhat lightheartedly relayed something of this experience in "Arnold Schoenberg als Soldat im ersten Weltkrieg," an article published in *Melos* 33, no. 6 (1966): 178–180. And in a commemorative volume put together by Schoenberg's friends in 1924, Hanns Eisler registered an encounter in which Schoenberg, when asked if he were "that controversial composer" replied, "I have to admit that I am: but it's like this—somebody had to be, and nobody else wanted to, so I took it on myself." Quoted in Reich, *Schoenberg*, 95. Eisler (1898–1962) fought during World War I in the Austrian army as part of a Hungarian regiment and was wounded and hospitalized several times.

In 1917 he wrote an anti-war oratorio and a set of *Galgenlieder* (Gallows Songs), subtitled "Grotesques," on poems by Christian Morgenstern.

30. See H. H. Stuckenschmidt, *Arnold Schoenberg: His Life, World and Work* (London, 1977), 193, 239–244, regarding Schoenberg's openly patriotic contribution to the war in a setting of Otto Kernstock's poem "Der deutscher Michel" and in the composition in 1916 of a march, "The Iron Brigade," as his cultural contribution to the fight.

31. Schoenberg, letter to Busoni, 14 November 1916, in Busoni, *Selected Letters*, 419–420. The editor of the volume, Beaumont, notes, "The last two words are crossed out by Schoenberg; the letter was opened by the censors."

32. Busoni, letter to Schoenberg, 24 November 1916, in ibid., 420.

33. "A. Bönsch[r]eg"—only the "r" is missing (if, indeed, it was) for a complete anagram of Schönberg's name. Schoenberg's article, "Friedenssicherung" (Safeguarding of peace), is published in the 1977 German edition of Busoni's letters.

34. Busoni, *Selected Letters*, 422 n. 2.

35. Schoenberg added that he also wanted to finish his second chamber symphony, which he had begun almost ten years earlier, as well as a revised, second edition of his *Harmonielehre*. He also spoke of his need to oversee the engraving of *Erwartung* (1909) and *Die glückliche Hand* (1910–1913), which did, in fact, appear in 1916 and 1917.

36. "Isn't that terrible: 'the English.' 30 months ago I spoke with pride of my English, French and Russian friends and now these are my enemies? Do you believe that? I must say that, for me, no international value has ceased to exist, not even in the first few weeks. But it is terrible that most people have long since abandoned them!" Busoni, *Selected Letters*, 421–422.

37. Brown and Seaton, *Christmas Truce*, 6–7, reproduces the hymn; Rother, ed., *Die letzten Tage*, 66–67, gives the complete German text. See also Arlie J. Hoover, *God, Germany and Britain in the Great War: A Study in Clerical Nationalism* (New York, 1989), chap. 4, "The Sins of Britain—According to Germany."

38. See Jelavich, "German Culture in the Great War," 32–33; Matthew Stibbe, *German Anglophobia and the Great War, 1914–1918* (Cambridge, 2001); and more generally Roger Chickering, *Imperial Germany and the Great War, 1914–1918* (Cambridge, U.K., 1998). Soldier songs touched upon a similar range of issues, including parodies of the equally sensitive issue of "the rape of Belgium." One of the most blatant was "Ninette," which openly declared "Mad'moiselle? Oh, mad'moiselle! / I'll annex you, if you please. / We're in Belgium, after all, / Where such things are done with ease." The song, with music by Walter Kollo and Willi Bretschneider and text by Rudolf Bernauer and Rudolf Schanzer, appeared in *Extrablätter! Heitere Bilder aus ernster Zeit. Textbuch der Gesänge* (Berlin, 1914), 15; translated in Jelavich, "German Culture in the Great War," 34.

39. Reich, *Schoenberg*, 95.

40. Ibid., 96, based upon information in letters from Berg to Webern of 13 and 22 June 1915. The completed text for "Jacob's Ladder" was published in 1917 and again together with the "Dance of Death" in 1926.

41. For the complete poem see Rother, ed., *Die letzten Tage.*

42. The image and title appeared in numerous contexts throughout the 1920s, including a poem by Federico García Lorca following the crash of the New York Stock Exchange in 1929.

43. Reich, *Schoenberg,* 96–111, gives a detailed summary of the textual material of *Die Jakobsleiter.*

44. Alexander Ringer, *Arnold Schoenberg: The Composer as Jew* (Oxford, 1990), 38.

45. Ibid., 101.

46. Schoenberg aside, see Richard Taruskin, "Back to Whom? Neoclassicism as Ideology," *Nineteenth-Century Music* 26 (1993): 286–302, regarding the difficulties attendant to the term.

47. Yet Roger Sessions correctly noted the connection between Schoenberg's and Stravinsky's embrace of eighteenth-century forms as early as 1933, a proposition that Charles Rosen reiterated in 1975 with the conclusion that "the invention of serialism was specifically a move to resurrect an old classicism as well as to make a new one possible." See Charles Rosen, *Arnold Schoenberg* (New York, 1975), 73. For a fuller discussion see Messing, *Neoclassicism,* 151–154.

48. These include the *Suite* for string orchestra of 1934, which could only have been viewed by the public as retrograde. It was a perspective that Schoenberg continued to endorse through the 1940s in pieces such as the *Variations on a Recitative* for organ (1941) and the *Theme and Variations* for wind band (1942) as well as in a somewhat more ambivalent fashion in works like the *Ode to Napoleon* and the *Piano Concerto,* both from 1942. Auner has correctly argued, however, that in all of these pieces Schoenberg's main concern seemed to center on his need to "differentiate himself from others who had returned to tonality and to locate these works in his evolutionary historical framework." See Joseph Auner, "Schoenberg's Handel Concerto," *Journal of the American Musicological Society* 49, no. 2 (1996): 284–285; and Glenn Watkins, "Schoenberg and the Organ," in *Perspectives on Schoenberg and Stravinsky,* ed. Benjamin Boretz and Edward T. Cone (Princeton, 1968), 98.

49. The essays in Wagner's *Art and Politics* were written between 1864 and 1878.

50. See *Arnold Schoenberg Letters,* ed. Erwin Stein, trans. E. Wilkins and E. Kaiser (New York, 1965), 164; and Auner, "Schoenberg's Handel Concerto," 268–269.

51. Arnold Schoenberg, "National Music (I)," in *Style and Idea,* ed. Leonard Stein, trans. Leo Black (New York, 1975), 169. See Auner, "Schoenberg's Handel Concerto," 280–281 and passim, for more on this intricate issue.

52. "The question is simply whether, and in whose interest, this historical parallel is bound to produce similar results: that is to say, whether the com-

poser's way of writing must again alter from now on, in as unexpected and un-foreseeable a way as after J. S. Bach." Schoenberg, "National Music (I)," 171. The same question had already been asked in a slightly different context by Egon Wellesz in an article "Schoenberg and Beyond," *The Musical Quarterly* 2, no. 1 (1916): 89. Regarding Schoenberg's historically based but radical turn to an art of polyphony, see Ringer, *Arnold Schoenberg*, 18–19.

53. Schoenberg's antagonism toward Debussy was not newly sprung. Al-though he had understood the importance of the Frenchman's music, Schoen-berg had bristled at some of his chauvinistic remarks made during the war, and as a consequence had refused a request made by Egon Wellesz to contribute to a Debussy memorial issue of *Revue musicale* in 1922. See Stuckenschmidt, *Schoenberg*, 268.

54. Arnold Schoenberg, "National Music (II)," in *Style and Idea*, ed. Leonard Stein, trans. Leo Black (New York, 1975), 172–173. Schoenberg pro-ceeds to describe in detail the strictly German lineage of his musical style: Bach (counterpoint); Mozart (phraseology); Beethoven (development, varia-tion, rhythmic displacement); Wagner (expressiveness, tonal relationships, motivic work); Brahms (extension and abbreviation of phrases; economy with richness; systematic notation)

55. For a rich discussion of "Germanness" in music and a review of Ger-many's earlier awareness of its dependence on foreign models, see Potter, *Most German of the Arts*, 201ff. For an expansion of the reasons behind Germany's escalating xenophobia see Hans Belting, *The Germans and Their Art: A Troublesome Relationship* (New Haven, 1998); and Joachim Köhler, *Nietzsche and Wagner*, trans. Ronald Taylor (New Haven, 1999).

56. For further perspectives regarding the role of music during the Third Reich, see Potter, *Most German of the Arts*; and Dennis, *Beethoven in German Politics*.

CHAPTER 13. "THE LAST DAYS OF MANKIND"

1. Kennedy, *Richard Strauss*, 58.

2. For a discussion of Strauss's preoccupation with Nature in the writing of the *Alpine Symphony*, see Charles Youmans, "The Twentieth-Century Sym-phonies of Strauss," *The Musical Quarterly* 84, no. 2 (2000): 238–258.

3. See Keegan, *First World War*, 283. For a map of the broad deployment of the *Alpenkorps* from Serbia and the Southern Tyrol to Verdun and the Somme, see the map following p. 246 in Martin Breitenacher, *Das Alpenkorps, 1914–18* (Berlin, 1939).

4. Mosse, *Fallen Soldiers*, 114ff.

5. See Michael P. Steinberg, "Mirrors, Steel, and Smoke for a Fairy Tale of Shadows," *The New York Times*, 9 December 2001, AR 35, 40.

6. The youthful and Romantic *Im Sommerwind* of 1904 gives full evidence of the tradition whence Webern emerged. Julian Johnson persuasively for-wards the thesis in *Webern and the Transformation of Nature* (Cambridge,

U.K., 1999) that the nature motif is persistent throughout Webern's music, regardless of program or text.

7. Quoted in Hans Moldenhauer, *Anton von Webern: A Chronicle of His Life and Work* (New York, 1979), 210.

8. It is not an anonymous folksong, however, both stanzas having appeared in Peter Rosegger's novel *Peter Mayr* and the first also as a simple evening prayer in volume two of the same author's *Waldheimat*. See Peter Andraschke, "Webern und Rosegger," in *Opus Anton Webern*, ed. Dieter Rexroth (Berlin, 1983), 108–112.

9. See Watkins, *Soundings*, 41, for a complete reproduction of the vocal part of "Der Tag ist vergangen."

10. Quoted in Moldenhauer, *Anton von Webern*, 212.

11. Ibid., 213. By the end of August, Webern was awaiting release from the service, a time that coincided exactly with Schoenberg's call to duty. Overwhelmed by guilt that he was about to be mustered out, Webern sought Schoenberg's release and his own reenlistment, both to no avail.

12. The texts of the middle two songs of opus 13 are taken from Hans Bethge's *Chinesische Flöte*. "Die Einsame" speaks of a lonely girl weeping for her friend who is far away; and "In der Fremde" is set in "a strange land" where a drowsy (soldier?) sees his home country from afar. See also the notes to Boulez's recording of Anton Webern's complete works (Sony SM3K 45845), 25.

13. Anonymous translations after Sony CD SM3K 45845.

14. See Rother, ed., *Die letzten Tage*, 79–80, for an extensive excerpt; Karl Kraus, *Schriften*, 20 vols. (Frankfurt, 1986–), 10: 724ff., for the complete text. See also Winter, *Sites of Memory*, 186ff.

15. See Beller, "Tragic Carnival," 146.

16. Minden, "Expressionism," 49ff.

17. Shreffler, *Webern*, 197.

18. See ibid., 199.

19. For more on this complex metaphor, see Mosse, *Fallen Soldiers*, 75ff.

20. See Erasmo Leiva-Merikakis, *The Blossoming Thorn: Georg Trakl's Poetry of Atonement* (Lewisburg, Pa., 1987), 136–139. See also Anne C. Shreffler, *Webern and the Lyric Impulse: Songs and Fragments on Poems of Georg Trakl* (Oxford, 1994), 197–199; and Martin Zenck, "Indifferenz von Ausdruck und Konstruktion in Anton Weberns Traklied 'Gesang einer gefangenen Amswel' (Op. 14, nr. 6)," in *Kunst als begriffslose Erkenntnis: Zum Kunstbegriff der ästhetischen Theorie Theodor W. Adornos* (Munich, 1977), 215.

21. Ibid., 217.

22. Adorno, feeling that Webern had musically misinterpreted Trakl's poem at the end, suggested that "the musical soul crashes in on itself" instead of portraying the redemption of a dying man. See Theodor Adorno, "Anton von Webern," in *Klangfiguren* (Berlin and Frankfurt am Main, 1959), 119; and a complementary interpretation by Zenck in "Indifferenz von Ausdruck und Konstruktion," 221. For a more balanced interpretation see Shreffler, *Webern*, 217–218.

23. George Perle, *The Operas of Alban Berg: Wozzeck* (Berkeley, 1980), 12, states that "the date, 'August 23, 1914,' that stands at the conclusion of the published score of the *Three Pieces* evidently refers to the completion of the scoring of the last movement rather than to the completion of the work as a whole." See also Mark DeVoto, "Alban Berg's 'Marche Macabre,'" *Perspectives of New Music* 22, nos. 1–2 (1983–1984): 386–447; and Stravinsky and Craft, *Conversations*, 80.

24. Perle, *Operas of Alban Berg*, 18.

25. See chapter 12 for a discussion of the term *Reigen* in this context.

26. Douglas Jarman, *The Music of Alban Berg* (Berkeley, 1978), 7.

27. This is evident from the fact that the earliest surviving sketches of the opera (act 2, scene 2, dated May or June 1914) are interspersed with sketches for the "Marsch."

28. The first sketches were for act 2, scene 2, as well as fragments for Andres's song in act 1, scene 2, and Marie's Lullaby of act 1, scene 3. See Jarman, *Music of Alban Berg*, 8.

29. See David P. Schroeder, "Opera, Apocalypse, and the Dance of Death: Berg's Indebtedness to Kraus," *Mosaic* 25 (1992): 91–105.

30. *Alban Berg: Letters to His Wife*, 247.

31. See Schroeder, "Opera, Apocalypse, and the Dance of Death," 97.

32. Beller, "The Tragic Carnival," 151–154. See also David Rechter, *The Jews of Vienna and the First World War* (London, 2001).

33. Stark, "All Quiet on the Home Front," 76.

34. Gerald Stieg, "*Die letzten Tage der Menschheit:* Eine negative Operette?" in *Oesterreich und der Grosse Krieg*, ed. Klaus Amann and Hubert Lengauer (Vienna, 1989), 180–181; and Franz Field, *The Last Days of Mankind: Karl Kraus and His Vienna* (London, 1967), 88.

35. For an example, see Beckmann's *Mustering* of 1914 in Cork, *A Bitter Truth*, 108, plate 136.

36. It is interesting that Berg's "Gavotte" in *Wozzeck* (act 1, scene 1) centers on the question of morality. See Perle, *Operas of Alban Berg*, 46.

37. *Alban Berg: Letters to His Wife*, 177. Berg's outburst against the operetta composers Leo Fall and Oscar Straus is striking in light of the fact that Berg had formerly expressed his appreciation for them. Berg may have attempted his own "Gavotte for (two) cripples" in the very first scene of *Wozzeck*, where a designated "Gavotte" with two doubles (variations) accompanies Wozzeck's first encounter with the Captain.

38. Stark, "All Quiet on the Home Front," 62–63; and John Williams, *The Other Battleground: The Home Fronts: Britain, France and Germany 1914–1918* (Chicago, 1972), 31. An attempt in Breslau to ban a performance of a Tchaikovsky opera was rebuffed, and a policy was ultimately established in Berlin that allowed the performance of works by authors from enemy nations who had died before 1914. See Stark, "All Quiet on the Home Front," 74.

39. Such as Kálmáan's *Gold gab ich für Eisen* (I Gave Gold for Iron) and *Komm' deutscher Bruder!* (Come, German Brother).

40. *Alban Berg: Letters to His Wife*, 168–169.

41. Such events, their initial impact and the ease with which they were typically forgotten, made Berg realize that "they are only tiny fractions in this piece of world history"; ibid., 170.

42. For the health report see ibid., 189–190.

43. Ibid., 183; 178–244 contains intermittent references to Berg's experiences in the army.

44. Ibid., 199–200.

45. Ibid., 224.

46. Ibid., 229. Perle, *Operas of Alban Berg*, 56, offers a detailed analysis of the degree to which the composer's self-identification with the title character surfaced in numerous revisions of Büchner's texts.

47. I am indebted to Prof. Robert Mueller for pointing out Messiaen's citation.

48. For Berg's own refutation of any and all resemblances to the old dance forms see the citation in George Perle, *Wozzeck* (Berkeley, 1980), 46.

49. See Perle, *Operas of Alban Berg*, 47.

50. See Schroeder, "Opera, Apocalypse, and the Dance of Death," 98–99.

51. Schroeder, "Opera, Apocalypse, and the Dance of Death," 99.

52. See Watkins, *Soundings*, 57–59, for discussion and illustration.

53. The constituents of Berg's pattern can also be viewed as embedded in some of the more typical polka rhythms. See *The Norton/Grove Concise Encyclopedia of Music*, ed. Stanley Sadie (New York, 1988), 587, "Polka," for two prominent figures.

54. See Schroeder, "Opera, Apocalypse, and the Dance of Death," 98.

55. For the music see Schuhmacher, *Leben und Seele*, 233–234.

56. See Perle, *Operas of Alban Berg*, 40, 42.

57. Karen Monson, *Alban Berg* (Boston, 1979), 140.

58. Furthermore, it clearly transcended Otto Weininger's restricted view of feminine hysteria exposed in his *Sex and Character* of 1906 and in part echoed the troubling view of Schnitzler's eternal sexual "roundelay" promoted in his play *Reigen* of 1900. *Ewartung's* text could now be read as transgendered and reflective of a society-at-large that had lost its moorings.

59. See Leonard V. Smith, "Masculinity, Memory, and the French First World War Novel," in *Authority, Identity and the Social History of the Great War*, ed. Frans Coetzee and Marilyn Shevin-Coetzee (Providence, 1995), 252. See also Showalter, *Female Malady*, chap. 7; Pat Barker, *Regeneration* (New York, 1991), and *The Ghost Road* (New York, 1995).

60. Hans Binneveld, *From Shell Shock to Combat Stress: A Comparative History of Military Psychiatry*, trans. John O'Kane (Amsterdam, 1997), 84–87.

61. Carol Tavris, review of Elaine Showalter's *Hystories* (New York, 1997), *The New York Times Book Review*, 4 May 1997, p. 28. See also Peter Gay, *Freud: A Life for Our Time* (New York, 1988), passim.

62. Jay Winter, "Shell-shock and the Cultural History of the Great War," *Journal of Contemporary History* 35, no. 1 (2000): 7ff.

63. See the essays in Mark Hussey, ed., *Virginia Woolf and War: Fiction, Reality, and Myth* (Syracuse, 1991), including Massami Usui, "The Female Victims of the War in Mrs. Dalloway," 152; Elaine Showalter, *The Female Malady* (New York, 1985), 171; and Elizabeth L. Keathley, "*Erwartung's* New Woman: Musical Modernism and Feminist Consciousness in Fin-de-Siècle Vienna," in *Abstracts of Papers Read* at the 61st Annual Meeting of the American Musicological Society, New York, 2–5 November 1995, p. 26. The "crisis of masculinity" was to be pursued further by Berg in his next and last opera, *Lulu*. Regarding Wedekind's relation to this issue and the larger question of Modernism, see Gerald N. Izenberg, *Modernism and Masculinity: Mann, Wedekind, Kandinsky through World War I* (Chicago, 2000).

64. Rainer Maria Rilke, *Wartime Letters of Rainer Maria Rilke, 1914– 1921*, trans. M. D. Herter Norton (New York, 1940), 32. Letter from Munich to Princess Marie von Thurn und Taxis-Hohenlohe, 9 July 1915.

65. "Stravinsky was magnificent. These songs are wonderful. This music moves me completely beyond belief. I love it especially. The cradle songs are something so indescribably touching. How those three clarinets sound! And 'Pribaoutki.' Ah, my dear friend, it is something really glorious." Moldenhauer, *Webern*, 229.

66. Ibid., 228–229.

67. Ibid., 233.

CHAPTER 14. "THE YANKS ARE COMING"

1. The vivid footage on the video film "The Lusitania: Murder on the Atlantic" (Cat. No. AAE 17129, 1998), which shows civilians watching the sinking from shore, would appear sufficient to confirm Roosevelt's judgment. Yet, more recent research has proposed two alternatives to the generally accepted theory that the ship was sunk as a result of a sustained torpedo attack: a) the sinking was caused by the direct hit of a single shell that ignited the dusty remains of a dwindling coal supply as the vessel neared the end of its voyage, or b) the so-called passenger ship may have been carrying munitions that blew up.

2. Lyons, *World War I*, 249.

3. The first of these is recorded on New World Records NW 222. The imagery of the sinking of the Lusitania did not immediately disappear: "Lost on the Lusitania" appeared in 1917, and two songs of 1918 and 1919 were titled simply "Lusitania." See Vogel, *World War I Songs*, 38, 206, 273.

4. Rawls, *Wake Up, America!* 56.

5. Vogel, *World War I Songs*, 43. The Gershwin song was never published. Caesar wrote songs during all of America's successive wars through the Vietnam conflict, including a setting of the Pledge of Allegiance to the Flag. For Ford's Peace Papers, 1915–1917, see University of Michigan Library, Labadie Holt Collection.

6. Rawls, *Wake Up, America!*, 67. Another celebrity in Addams's and Ford's philosophical camp was the remarkable Helen Keller, who undertook an un-

successful Chatauqua tour in the name of pacifism in 1916. See Dorothy Hermann, *Helen Keller: A Life* (New York, 1998).

7. Henry F. May, *The End of American Innocence: A Study of the First Years of Our Own Time, 1912–1917* (Chicago, 1964), 363.

8. David M. Kennedy, *Over Here: The First World War and American Society* (New York, 1980), 179. For the original text see John Grier Hibben, *The Higher Patriotism* (New York, 1915), which includes essays on "The Higher Patriotism," "Preparedness and Peace," "Might or Right," and "Martial Valor in Times of Peace."

9. On the issue of propaganda in every form see especially Stewart Halsey Ross, *Propaganda for War: How the United States Was Conditioned to Fight the Great War of 1914–1918* (Jefferson, N.C., 1996).

10. See Frances Early, *A World Without War: How U.S. Feminists and Pacifists Resisted World War I* (Syracuse, N.Y., 1997).

11. Al Bryan and Al Piantadosi, "I Didn't Raise My Boy to Be a Soldier" (New York, 1915).

12. Harvey's recording of this song from the fall of 1916 is included on New World Records, NW 222, side one, band two.

13. Carl H. Scheele, notes to *Songs of World Wars I & II* (New World Records, NW 222).

14. Vogel, *World War I Songs*, 15–21.

15. See William McBrien, *Cole Porter* (New York, 1998); and the review by Alexander Chancellor in *The New York Times Book Review*, 29 November 1998, p. 9.

16. See Friedrich Katz, *The Life and Times of Pancho Villa* (Stanford, 1998).

17. Gilbert, *First World War*, 308.

18. See Michael Lind, "Mr. Wilson Goes to Washington," review of Louis Auchincloss's *Woodrow Wilson* (New York, 2000), *The New York Times Book Review*, 9 April 2000, p. 8.

19. See Katz, *Life and Times of Pancho Villa*, 615.

20. Vogel, *World War I Songs*, 12–13.

21. See Walter Kellogg, *The Conscientious Objector* (New York, 1970); Norman Thomas, *Is Conscience a Crime?* (New York, 1972); John Rae, *Conscience and Politics* (Oxford, 1970); Gerlof D. Homan, *American Mennonites and the Great War, 1914–1918* (Waterloo, Ontario, 1994); and H. C. Peterson, *Propaganda for War: The Campaign Against American Neutrality, 1914–1917* (Norman, Oklahoma, 1939).

22. For the text to "Angelo" see Irving Berlin, *Early Songs III. 1913–1914*, ed. by Charles Hamm (Madison, 1994), 217. See also Richard K. Spottswood, "Commercial Ethnic Recordings in the United States" and Mick Maloney, "Irish Ethnic Recordings and the Irish-American Imagination," both in *Ethnic Recordings in America: A Neglected Heritage* (Washington: American Folklife Center, Library of Congress, 1982), 55–58.

23. See the publication by the American Civil Liberties Union, *War-time Prosecutions and Mob Violence Involving the Rights of Free Speech, Free Press*

and *Peaceful Assemblage (From April 1, 1917 to May 1, 1918)* (New York, 1918), including *The President on Mob Violence*, 8. See also the rich study by Frederick C. Lubke, *Bonds of Loyalty: German-Americans and World War I* (DeKalb, Ill., 1974).

24. The text for this song printed in Vogel, *World War I Songs*, 337, omits any reference to Germany, but the version recorded by the American Quartet on *Praise the Lord and Pass the Ammunition* (New World Records, NW 222, 1977) includes it. I am grateful to Suzanne Camino for this as well as other observations in "Turning the Dark Clouds Inside Out: Diversity, Denial and Desperate Optimism in American Songs of World War I," paper presented at a seminar at the University of Michigan, April 1996.

25. Lewis Paul Todd, *Wartime Relations of the Federal Government and the Public Schools 1917–1918* (New York, 1945), 73, as cited in Kennedy, *Over Here*, 54.

26. The author's mother, who was born in 1900 and attended high school in McPherson, Kansas, during this time, studied German during her freshman, sophomore, and junior years. In her senior year, however, when America joined the war, German instruction was outlawed even in this most inland state, and she was obliged to take a course in beginning French.

27. Hanna, *Mobilization of Intellect*, 162.

28. Kennedy, *Over Here*, 68. See also Otto Hermann Kahn, *Americans of German Origin and the War* (New York, 1917).

29. For example, "All Together, We're Out to Beat the Hun" of 1918, which warns that "German ways in our days are trech'rous and unfair."

30. I am grateful to Capt. Frank Byrne, USMC, for making many of these programs and scores available to me. He also noted that the conductor's part for the U.S. Marine Band's orchestral version of "Treu zu Kaiser und Reich" "has the title covered over with glue on cloth tape, and all the instrumental parts have the title lopped off, leaving only the English subtitle/translation." Capt. Byrne also notes that "the band parts appear to be missing. My guess? Someone trashed them during one of the wars."

31. The acoustic recordings from this date of Blankenburg's "German Fidelity," Wacek's "Krupp March," and Friedemann's "Grand Duke of Baden" are preserved on CD in *The Bicentennial Collection: Celebrating the 200th Anniversary of 'The President's Own' United States Marine Band: CD 1*, Band 30. The original recording of Warnken's "Treu zu Kaiser und Reich" was Victor Cat. 17731-A; the Blankenburg, Wacek, and Friedemann recordings were Victor Cat. 17577-B, Mx.B-14606–2; 17656-A, Mx. B-14609–2; and 17656-B, Mx. B-14603–2.

32. The complete lyrics are in Vogel, *World War I Songs*, 319.

33. In February 1918 the Lafayette Escadrille of 1916 became the 103rd U.S. Pursuit Squadron of the U.S. Army Air Service. The 94th Pursuit Squadron founded in March included U.S. pilot Eddie Rickenbacker, age 27.

34. Ezra Bowen, *Knights of the Air* (Alexandria, Va., 1980), 99.

35. These verses obviously could be sung to any number of tunes, includ-

ing "My Bonny Lies Over the Ocean." See Rawls, *Wake Up America!* 101–103, which also informs us that "of the original seven Americans in *L'Escadrille Américaine,* only three survived the war." For other songs of the aviators, including "The Passing Pilot," "A Handsome Young Airman," "Look at the Ears on Him," and "Kelly Field Air-Service Song" (to the tune of "Dixie"), see Dolph, ed., *"Sound Off!"* 113–121.

36. Pisano et al., *Legend, Memory and the Great War,* 93.

37. Georges Auric, "Bonjour Paris!" *Le coq* 1 (1920). See Perloff, *Art and the Everyday,* 109.

38. Numerous songs were written as a take-off on "It's a Long, Long Way to Tipperary," including "It's a Long, Long Way Back to the Good Old U.S.A.," ". . . to Old Broadway," ". . . to Somewhere in France," ". . . to the Battlefields of France," ". . . from Berlin to Broadway," ". . . to Europe but Teddy [Roosevelt] Knows the Way," and especially ". . . to Berlin But We'll Get There," with lyrics by Arthur Fields and music by Leon Flatow, which Fields recorded to popular acclaim. See Vogel, *World War I Songs,* 197.

39. Nora Bayes's performance of this piece, recorded on 3 March 1918, can be heard on *Music from the New York Stage, 1890–1920,* vol. 4: 1917–1920 (Pearl CDS 9059–61).

40. See Craig Campbell, *Reel America: A Comprehensive Filmography and History of Motion Pictures in the United States, 1914–1920* (Jefferson, N.C., 1985), 136 (unfolioed), for a still from the film short.

41. For more on the influenza epidemic see Rawls, *Wake Up America!* 222–225; Eileen Lynch, "The Flu of 1918," *The Pennsylvania Gazette* 97, no. 2 (1998): 28ff; and PBS Video A3081, "Influenza 1918." My father, dedicatee of this book, was a victim of this same flu epidemic, and as a small boy I remember him telling me of his hospitalization at Camp Fulton, Kentucky, where the two soldiers bedded on either side of him were removed, dead, shortly after his arrival. The flu epidemic in America took the lives of some 675,000 people, young and old, a number larger than the number of Americans killed in all the wars of the twentieth century combined.

42. Vogel, *World War I Songs,* 101–102.

43. Music by Isham Jones and lyrics by Tell Taylor and Ole Olssen.

44. Leo Feist advertised "K-K-K-Katy" as "a simple song simply irresistible!" and claimed that "Everybody sings it from California to France—and then some! It's the song of the doughboy—a real Yankee melody the Boys sing over and over again. You've got to stammer the chorus because Katy's beau was tongue-tied, but that's where the fun comes in."

45. Howard Johnson and George W. Meyer, "Just Like Washington Crossed the Delaware" (New York, 1918).

46. A seventy-two-minute videorecording, *America Over There* (Venice, CA: TMW Media Group, 1996), advertises the following on its container: "*America Over There* is the first officially released motion picture record of America's part in World War I. Every frame is genuine, taken under actual

combat conditions in France. All footage was shot by the U.S. Army Signal Corps."

47. John McCabe, *George M. Cohan: The Man Who Owned Broadway* (New York, 1973), 137–138. "Over There" later carried a symbolic meaning for the Viennese composer Erik Korngold, who came to America in 1934. In 1950 he completed his last symphony, the Fourth Symphony in F♯ major, which he dedicated to the memory of President Franklin Delano Roosevelt, who had died in 1945. By that time Korngold had become an American citizen, and in the final movement of his new symphony he entered an unmistakable citation of Cohan's rousing chorus, "Over There." The reference carried numerous potential inferences, of course, including not only America's role in World War II but also Korngold's reverse migration to America.

48. See chapter 6.

49. Ballard MacDonald, Edward Madden, and James F. Hanley, "War Babies" (New York, 1916).

50. For the cover of "War Babies" with Al Jolson's picture see Vogel, *World War I Songs*, 378.

51. Calvin Elliker, "Sheet Music Special Issues: Formats and Functions," *Notes* 53, no. 1 (1996): 12–13.

52. Not to be confused with "The Bravest Heart of All," with lyrics by Raymond Egan and music by Richard Whiting, written two years later. See Vogel, *World War I Songs*, 59, 300. Cavell's story was retold in the 1928 film *Dawn*, starring Sybil Thorndike, and later in *Nurse Edith Cavell*, starring Anna Neagle.

53. The covers are reproduced in Wenzel and Binkowski, *I Hear America Singing*, 72; and Vogel, *World War I Songs*, 327.

54. See Vogel, *World War I Songs*, 333 and 315, for the respective lyrics; also Marina Warner, *Joan of Arc: The Image of Female Heroism* (New York, 1981).

55. Becker, *La guerre et la foi*, 74.

56. The music was by Theodore Morse and the lyrics by Howard Johnson; it was popularized in vaudeville by Sophie Tucker.

57. The playwrights were Ernest Ball, Chauncey Olcott, and Rida Johnson Young. McCormack, an Irish tenor who sang regularly at Covent Garden and the Metropolitan Opera in New York, virtually personified the early cross-over artist by continuing to feature popular songs in recital throughout the 1920s.

58. Leo Feist published this song in a "patriotic war-size edition" and advertised it with the following words: "Boy, howdy! Here's the greatest little song-hit that has tickled the keys of the piano since Uncle Sam went 'over there.' Humor, love and a whack at the Kaiser—set to a rollicking, marching tune—why shouldn't it be sung by every son and daughter of the U.S.A. morning, noon and night?"

59. For more on the role of American women in war see Lettie Gavin, *American Women in World War I: They Also Served* (Niwot, Colo., 1997);

Dorothy Schneider, *Into the Breach: American Women Overseas in World War I* (New York, 1991); Ida Clyde Gallagher Clarke, *American Women and the World War* (New York, 1918).

60. The words are by Howard Rogers, the music by James Monaco, and it was published by M. Witmark and Sons, 1917.

61. Kimberly Jensen, "Women, Citizenship, and Sacrifice," in *Bonds of Affection: Americans Define Their Patriotism*, ed. John Bodnar (Princeton, 1996), 143.

62. Fairfax D. Downey, "I Loved an Amazon," *Stars and Stripes* 1 (1918): 2.

63. See Jensen, "Women, Citizenship, and Sacrifice," 140, 150.

64. See Gavin, *American Women in World War I.*

65. See Nart Van Kleeck, "After-War Status of Women Workers," in *Reconstructing America: Our Next Big Job*, ed. Edwin Wildman (Boston, 1919), 259–263. See also Gavin, *American Women in World War I.*

66. "New Songs of War," *New York Evening Post*, August 1918, as cited in Guillermo M. Tomas, *Invincible America: The National Music of United-States in Peace and at War* (Havana, 1919), 135.

67. Leonard Liebling, *Musical Courier*, August 1918, p. 136.

68. A list of war songs published in America is given in part 2 of Vogel's invaluable *World War I Songs.*

69. See ibid., 45ff.

70. Cleveland, *Dark Laughter*, 13. See also Les Cleveland, "Singing Warriors: Popular Songs in Wartime," *Journal of Popular Culture* 28 (1994): 155–175.

71. Cleveland, *Dark Laughter*, 60–61.

72. The last word of the French title was frequently misspelled "fini." See Dolph, *"Sound Off!"* for the music, multiple texts, and background information for these and many more soldier songs.

73. See Dolph, *"Sound Off!"* 131–133.

74. See Dolph, *"Sound Off!"* 76–80; and Paul E. Bierley, *John Philip Sousa, American Phenomenon* (Columbus, 1986), 77–78.

75. See Vogel, *World War I Songs*, 195, for a complete list. See Howard Pollack, *Skyscraper Lullaby: The Life and Music of John Alden Carpenter* (Washington, 1995), 158. Regarding J. A. Carpenter and the "Star-Spangled Banner" see Pollack, *Skyscraper Lullaby*, 158–159.

76. By British Major F. J. Ricketts, a.k.a. Kenneth Alford.

77. See Dieter Hildebrandt, *A Social History of the Piano*, trans. H. Goodman (New York, 1988).

78. Wenzel and Binkowski, *I Hear America Singing*, 62. The practice was in vogue in America from around 1895 to 1920, and the music supplement was also familiar to many European publications, including especially *The Musical Times* of London.

79. Such events shaped some of the earliest recollections of my childhood.

CHAPTER 15. "ONWARD CHRISTIAN SOLDIERS"

1. A congregation's unspoken prayer verbalized by an aged stranger claiming to be God's messenger in Mark Twain, "The War Prayer," dictated 1904–1905, published in *Complete Essays of Mark Twain*, ed. Charles Neider (Garden City, N.Y., 1963). The English poet laureate, John Betjeman, composed an update with a new twist in 1940 with *In Westminster Abbey*. I am grateful to Kevin March for numerous perspectives in this chapter.

2. Randolph Bourne, "The War and the Intellectuals," in *World War I at Home: Readings on American Life, 1914–1920*, ed. David F. Trask (New York, 1970), 73–80. See also Leslie J. Vaughan, *Randolph Bourne and the Politics of Cultural Radicalism* (Lawrence, Kan., 1997); Kennedy, *Over Here*, 49–53; and Lawrence W. Levine, *The Opening of the American Mind* (Boston, 1996), 114–116.

3. Bourne, "The War and the Intellectuals," 74, 79.

4. Karl Kraus, *Pro Domo et Mundo* (Munich, 1912), chap. 7.

5. Walter A. McDougall, *Promised Land, Crusader State* (Boston, 1997), 128. See also Gaines M. Foster, "A Christian Nation: Signs of a Covenant," in *Bonds of Affection: Americans Define Their Patriotism*, ed. John Bodnar (Princeton, 1996), 120–138.

6. For a set of sermons preached by the Archbishop of Canterbury, the Bishops of Winchester and London, the Dean of St. Paul's and other clergymen in wartime England, see Basil Mathews, ed., *Christ: And the World at War* (London, 1917).

7. E. Hershey Sneath, ed., *Religion and the War* (New Haven, 1918), 151–152; the essays are by the members of the faculty of the School of Religion, Yale University.

8. Ray H. Abrams, *Preachers Present Arms: A Study of the War-time Attitudes and Activities of the Churches and the Clergy in the United States, 1914–1918* (Philadelphia, 1933), xvi–xvii. See also John F. Piper, Jr., *The American Churches in World War I* (Athens, Ohio, 1985), for an attempt to balance some of the opinions offered by Abrams.

9. Jacques Rivière, *À la trace de Dieu* (Paris, 1925), 37.

10. For additional perspectives on the role of the church during the Great War see especially Annette Becker, "Les dévotions des soldats catholiques pendant la grande guerre," in *Chrétiens dans la première guerre mondiale: Actes des journées tenues à Amiens et à Péronne, les 16 mai et 22 juillet 1992*, ed. Nadine-Josette Chaline (Paris, 1993), 15–34; Annette Becker, *War and Faith: The Religious Imagination in France, 1914–1930* (Oxford, 1998); Hoover, *God, Germany and Britain in the Great War*; Shailer Mathews, *Patriotism and Religion* (New York, 1918); Piper, *American Churches*; Ross, *Propaganda for War*; and Ronald A. Wells, ed., *The Wars of America: Christian Views* (Macon, Ga., 1991).

11. See Robert Speer, *The Christian Man, the Church and the War* (New York, 1918), 64.

12. Regarding a commission of the Churches of Christ in America, which attempted in 1917 to lay out various spiritual, moral, and social forces of the nation in time of war, see Ernest R. May, *The World War and American Isolation, 1914–1917* (Cambridge, Mass., 1959); and Federal Council of the Churches of Christ in America, Dept. of the Church and Social Service, *Christian Duties in Conserving Spiritual, Moral and Social Forces of the Nation in Time of War* (New York, 1917).

13. George Bedborough, *Arms and the Clergy (1914–1918)* (London, 1934), 21, 31.

14. Ibid.

15. R. H. McKim, *For God and Country or the Christian Pulpit in War Time* (Dutton, N.Y., 1918), 116–117.

16. Evelyn Cobley, *Representing War: Form and Ideology in First World War Narratives* (Toronto, 1993), 43. See also Lisa Sowle Cahill, *Love Your Enemies: Discipleship, Pacifism, and Just War Theory* (Minneapolis, 1994); and James Turner Johnson, *Just War Tradition and the Restraint of War: A Moral and Historical Inquiry* (Princeton, 1981).

17. Bedborough, *Arms and the Clergy*, 100.

18. *The Mudhook*, 5 May 1918, p. 12; cited in Fuller, *Troop Morale*, 156.

19. Bedborough, *Arms and the Clergy*, 101.

20. For examples of hymns of hatred for the Germans by both the English and French see Johann, *Innenansicht eines Krieges*, 7–8.

21. Bedborough, *Arms and the Clergy*, 101. Similar sentiments spilled from the pulpits of Catholics, Episcopalians, Congregationalists, Mormons, and Methodists alike, and Henry Churchill King, president of Oberlin College, summarized what must have been on the minds of many Americans: "It is neither a travesty nor exaggeration to call this war on the part of America, a truly Holy war"; ibid., 104.

22. When Russia's Catherine the Great annexed the Crimea in 1783 she expelled the Turks and offered large land grants to the Mennonites, promising them religious freedom, exemption from military service, and the right to speak their native German. In 1872, when Czar Alexander II threatened to cancel these privileges, a group of well-to-do farmers from the Crimea came to America to explore the possibilities of settling there. Traversing the country from Pennsylvania to Wyoming and Texas to the Dakotas, they wrote letters home persuading their friends to join them. A majority settled in Manitoba because of liberal military service laws there, but many also settled in Kansas.

23. Abrams, *Preachers Present Arms*, 186. See also Homan, *American Mennonites and the Great War*, 182; and Elshtain, *Women and War*, 139ff. There were some 21,000 conscientious objectors in World War I, and of the 4,000 who stood their ground approximately half were Mennonites.

24. Bedborough, *Arms and the Clergy*, 108.

25. The movement had experienced its first wave in the 1850s and had received additional impetus from the formation of a National Prohibition Party

in 1872 and the Women's Christian Temperance Union (WCTU) in 1874. In the 1880s Kansas became the first state in the Union to ban the sale of spirits completely and was joined in 1890 by Maine, North Dakota, South Dakota, New Hampshire, and Vermont.

26. Recorded on GEMM CDS 9059–61.

27. William G. McLoughlin, *Billy Sunday Was His Real Name* (Chicago, 1955), 256. For John Philip Sousa's views on the subject see the papers of Wayne Bidwell Wheeler, Superintendent of the Anti-Saloon League of America, 1918–1926, University of Michigan, Bentley Historical Library, 86245 Aa 1.

28. McLoughlin, *Billy Sunday*, 257.

29. "Billy Sunday," *Encyclopaedia Brittanica*, vol. 21 (1968), 419–420.

30. Quoted in Heywood Broun, "Dramatizing Billy Sunday," *Literary Digest* 51 (1915): 713.

31. See Lyle W. Dorsett, *Billy Sunday and the Redemption of Urban America* (Grand Rapids, 1991), 97.

32. Ibid., 98.

33. McLoughlin, *Billy Sunday*, 273ff.

34. McPherson relied heavily upon patriotic-religious music played by a fifty-piece band before her fundamentalist sermons; she began preaching in Los Angeles in 1918.

35. The renowned singers Marion Talley and Gladys Swarthout both attended and were touched by the music in Billy Sunday's evangelistic meetings before going on to the Metropolitan Opera. And the Westminster Choir School was founded by John Finley Williams together with Homer Rodeheaver in Dayton, Ohio, where Williams served as chairman of Sunday's music committee before it was moved, first to Ithaca, N.Y., and then to Princeton, N.J. See Homer Rodeheaver, *Twenty Years with Billy Sunday* (Winona Lake, Ind., 1936), 80–81, 83–84.

36. The section designated for male voices carried titles such as "Let God Use You" and "My Anchor Holds," while a group of children's songs sported titles like "Pure White Ribbons!" and "Song to the Flag." A concluding selection of "Devotional Hymns" began with "Onward, Christian Soldiers," followed by a host of familiar favorites ready to serve a troubled world: "My Faith Looks Up to Thee," "Jesus, Lover of My Soul," Thomas Arne's "Am I a Soldier?" "Nearer My God to Thee," "The Son of God Goes Forth to War," and "When the Roll Is Called Up Yonder."

37. McLoughlin, *Billy Sunday*, xix.

38. Ibid., xxii.

39. See Campbell, *Reel America*, 87.

40. McLoughlin, *Billy Sunday*, 89.

41. Luther Wilson, *America—Here and Over There* (New York, 1918), 35–36.

42. Regarding its role in the services held at the National Cathedral in

Washington, D.C., following the events of 11 September 2001, see Sage Stossel, "The Battle Hymn of the Republic," *Atlantic Monthly*, 18 September 2001.

43. See Georg Goens, *Gott mit uns! Feldpredigten im Grossen hauptquartier gehalten* (Berlin, 1914), as well as the drawings by the Dutch cartoonist Louis Raemaeker, one of which shows a green German-helmeted devil sneering at the foot of Christ crucified over the slogan "Gott mit uns." See also Heinrich Missalla, *Gott mit uns; die deutsche katholische Kriegspredigt 1914–1918* (Munich, 1968).

44. Isabel Parker Semler, *Horatio Parker* (New York, 1942), 282. That Parker's patriotic piece was remembered early in World War II was confirmed by the following entry: "It is with a sense of almost fearful foreboding that I hear again, after more than twenty years, of the forthcoming performance of this song to be sung at the American Academy of Art and Letters' annual meeting, in memory of John Finley."

45. In her memoirs Parker's daughter relayed how her father took a perverse pleasure in speaking German to her mother when they were at the cinema and at other times, pronouncing "not all Germans have horns and hoofs." Ibid., 279–280.

46. Ibid., 295. In the spring of 1919 Parker composed his last work, which has sometimes been referred to as his own Requiem. The lengthy ode, titled *A.D. 1919*, was composed to commemorate those Yale students and alumni who had been killed in the war, but was little known outside of New Haven following its premiere.

47. William Kearns, *Horatio Parker, 1863–1919: His Life, Music, and Ideas* (Metuchen, N.J., 1990), 192. Arthur Farwell and W. D. Darby, eds., *Music in America*, vol. 4 of *The Art of Music*, ed. Daniel Gregory Mason, 13 vols. (New York, 1915–1916), 357.

48. The title page and copyright notice carry the date 1916: *A Hymnal of the Protestant Episcopal Church in the United States of America in the Year of Our Lord 1916* (New York, 1916). The preface's claim of 1918 seems the more likely date, however, in light of America's entrance into the war in April 1917. Parker, who was a member of the editorial committee, was represented by sixteen hymns including several from the 1903 edition which now particularly suited the temper of the times: "Go Forward Christian Soldiers" (1894), "The Royal Banners Forward Go" (1894), and "Fight the Good Fight" (1895). "God of the Nations" (Who hast led thy children since the world began), however, was newly composed (1918) and concludes with a call for truth and an end to the strife. The new hymnal, one of the first such to include a collection of patriotic songs during the war, also contained a section for men's voices, obviously suitable for soldiers' use.

49. Cleveland, *Dark Laughter*, 31.

50. The checkered history of "La Marseillaise" reveals that it was by turns hated, banned, and retexted. See Sweeney, *Singing Our Way to Victory*, 164–165.

CHAPTER 16. THE 100% AMERICAN

1. "The Great Nation of Futurity," *The United States Magazine and Democratic Review* 6 (1839). For the appropriate excerpt see Thomas G. Paterson, ed., *Major Problems in American Foreign Policy*, vol. 1: *To 1914* (Lexington, Mass., 1989), 255–256; and for a discussion, McDougall, *Promised Land*, 76 ff.

2. Cecilia Elizabeth O'Leary, "'Blood Brotherhood': The Racialization of Patriotism, 1865–1918," in *Bonds of Affection: Americans Define Their Patriotism*, ed. John Bodnar (Princeton, 1996), 53.

3. O'Leary, "'Blood Brotherhood,'" 53. Dialogue over the "Problem of Americanization" was to continue well into the postwar period. See especially the 1919 proclamation by Franklin K. Lane, secretary of the interior, "The Need of a Definite Program of Americanization of Our Foreign-Born Peoples," in *Reconstructing America: Our Next Big Job*, ed. Edwin Wildman (Boston, 1919), 386–395.

4. See O'Leary, "'Blood Brotherhood,'" 57–58, 72–73.

5. See Vogel, *World War I Songs*, 306–307, for the complete lyrics.

6. Raymond Zirkel, "Dixie Doodle: You're the Land for Me," published by Buckeye Music Pub. Co. in 1918; see O'Leary, "'Blood Brotherhood,'" 79.

7. D. G. Mason, *Contemporary Composers* (New York, 1918), 231. See also Jay Winter, "Propaganda and the Mobilization of Consent," in *The Oxford Illustrated History of the First World War*, ed. Hew Strachan (Oxford, 1998), 216–226.

8. See Richard Crawford, "Edward MacDowell: Musical Nationalism and an American Tone Poet," *Journal of the American Musicological Society* 49, no. 3 (1996): 528–560, for a rich assessment of the issue.

9. A singular early performance of Schoenberg's *Five Pieces for Orchestra* was given by the Chicago Symphony Orchestra in 1913. For a perspective of Schoenberg in New York, see the review of his *Kammersinfonie*, which appeared in *The New York Times*, 15 November 1915. See Aldrich, *Concert Life in New York*, 455–457.

10. For a review of a Futurist concert given by Ornstein on 6 December 1915 see Aldrich, *Concert Life in New York*, 481–482.

11. See Henry Gilbert, *The Musical Quarterly* 1, no. 2 (1915): 172. Also included in this issue was an article, "Tower Music of Belgium and Holland," by William Gorham Rice, who in 1914 had published a book, *Carillons of Belgium and Holland*. The article included notice that the study had been completed before the outbreak of the war, and the hope was expressed that this turn of events would not bring damage to the carillons.

12. Vincent d'Indy, "D'Indy Calls on America to Free Itself from German Musical Domination," *Musical Courier*, April 1916.

13. Ibid.

14. Hugo Leichtentritt, "The Renaissance Attitude towards Music," *The Musical Quarterly* 1, no. 2 (1915): 615. His view of Gesualdo undoubtedly re-

flected his awareness of Ferdinand Keiner's Berlin dissertation on this composer, published only the year before.

15. Egon Wellesz, "Schoenberg and Beyond," *The Musical Quarterly* 2, no. 1 (1916): 89.

16. Alfred Einstein, *The Italian Madrigal*, 3 vols. (Princeton, N.J., 1949).

17. Wellesz, "Schoenberg and Beyond," 89.

18. See Carol Oja, *Making Music Modern: New York in the 1920s* (New York, 1999), "Appendix. Programs of Modern-Music Societies in New York, 1920–1931."

19. A complete modern edition of Gesualdo's music was not achieved until 1966, and several projected series for Marenzio are still in progress. Regarding the perception of Gesualdo's continuing relevance for the contemporary scene, see Glenn Watkins, "Gesualdo, Stravinsky, Schnittke e la musica contemporanea," *Convegno Gesualdo: "Il fuoco nella Mente,"* Potenza e Venosa, 22–25 October 1997. Maurizio Pollini's *Perspectives* concerts at Carnegie Hall and the 92nd St. Y on 20–30 March 2000 also featured music of Schoenberg, Boulez, and Nono alongside Monteverdi and Gesualdo.

20. The argument is akin to that later expressed by Schoenberg regarding genius in his articles of 1930 on "National Music (I), (II)."

21. T. Carl Whitmer, "A Post-Impressionistic View of Beethoven," *The Musical Quarterly* 2, no. 1 (1916): 15–16. The author then repeated the story that Beethoven's grandfather was born in Antwerp in 1712 and concluded, "So we have a German of close Flemish ancestry living most of his life in Austria. Tut, tut! There *is* hope for us."

22. Duncan, "Music and War," 572–574. See chapter 4 for a further discussion of the issue.

23. Colles, "National Anthems," 609–611.

24. M. Montagu-Nathan, "The Composer of the Russian National Anthem," *The Musical Times* 56 (1915): 82.

25. *The Musical Times* (1 June 1915): 362.

26. Frank Kidson, "The 'Star-Spangled Banner': An Exhaustive Official Inquiry," *The Musical Times* (1915): 148.

27. Oscar George Theodore Sonneck, *"The Star-Spangled Banner" (revised and enlarged from the "Report" on the above and other airs, issued in 1909)* (Washington, D.C., 1914). See also William Lichtenwanger, *The Music of The Star-Spangled Banner from Ludgate Hill to Capitol Hill* (Washington, D.C., 1977); reprinted from the July 1977 *Quarterly Journal of the Library of Congress.*

28. Puccini's opera in turn inspired several popular songs, including "Poor Butterfly" of 1916 and "There's a Little Butterfly in Normandy" of 1918. For the text and cover to the sheet music for the former of these, see Vogel, *World War I Songs*, 355.

29. A few American composers had tapped it as the basis for original compositions in the period of the Civil War. John Knowles Paine, later a highly respected Harvard professor, composed a set of "Concert Variations on 'The Star-

Spangled Banner'" for organ as early as 1861, and Dudley Buck, one of America's most visible organist-church composers, composed a similarly named set in 1868, which he turned into a *Festival Overture* a decade later. But prior to the Great War several other tunes, including "America" (to the tune of "God Save the King"), had made periodic attempts to depose "The Star-Spangled Banner" from its favored position—a situation clearly reflected in Charles Ives's "Variations on 'America'" for organ (1891).

30. However, for an example of a German march in triple meter, where the shifting placement of left and right on the down beat is specifically indicated with the symbols "l" and "r" beneath the notes, see "Wenn wir marschieren" in Schuhmacher, *Leben und Seele*, 245.

31. Vogel, *World War I Songs*, 31–32. For Sousa's role in sponsoring "The Star-Spangled Banner" as the national anthem, see Edward S. Delaplaine, *John Philip Sousa and the National Anthem* (Frederick, Md., 1983), 70–83.

32. Kitty Cheatham, *Words and Music of "The Star-spangled Banner" Oppose the Spirit of Democracy which the Declaration of Independence Embodies* (n.p., 1918), 3.

33. Ibid., 17.

34. Campbell, *Reel America*, 89.

35. See Kennedy, *Over Here*, 143.

36. Commissioned by the Parliamentary Recruitment Committee from the London Film Company. See Ine van Dooren and Peter Krämer, "The Politics of Direct Address," in *Film and the First World War*, ed. Karl Dibbets and Bert Hogenkamp (Amsterdam, 1995), 98.

37. Published in New York in 1920.

38. Stephen Vaughn, *Holding Fast the Inner Lines: Democracy, Nationalism, and the Committee on Public Information* (Chapel Hill, 1980), 83.

39. See George Creel, *How We Advertised America* (New York, 1920), 200–205.

40. James R. Mock and Cedric Larson, *Words That Won the War: The Story of the Committee on Public Information, 1917–1919* (Princeton, 1939), 118.

41. See Ross, *Propaganda for War*, 262.

42. Ibid., 262; and Creel, *How We Advertised America*, 117.

43. See Mock and Larson, *Words That Won the War*, 124; and Kennedy, *Over Here*, 62.

44. Quoted in Leslie Halliwell, *Halliwell's Filmgoer's Companion* (New York, 1984).

45. The nine-hour CBS television series on World War I and the 1996 six-hour PBS series, *The Great War and the Shaping of the 20th Century*, testify to the considerable footage that was shot and preserved both behind the lines and in the trenches. See also the companion volume with the same title by Jay Winter and Blaine Baggett.

46. Ross, *Propaganda for War*, 263.

47. See Gillian B. Anderson, *Music for Silent Films, 1894–1929: A Guide*

(Washington, D.C., 1988), xiv, 40. See also Martin M. Marks, *Music and the Silent Film: Contexts and Case Studies, 1895–1924* (New York, 1997).

48. Campbell, *Reel America*, 41.

49. Ibid., 44–45.

50. See Anderson, *Music for Silent Films*, 24.

51. See ibid., xiv and xxxiv. Griffiths and Breil argued over accommodations that the former wanted to make in Wagner's "The Ride of the Valkyries," which accompanied the Klan call in *The Birth of a Nation*.

52. Ross, *Propaganda for War*, 264–265.

53. *Joan the Woman* (1916) and *Carmen I* (1915), both featuring Farrar, were re-released in home video versions in 1997. See Albert Innaurato, "When Opera Singers Mattered, These Mattered More Than Most," *The New York Times*, 31 August 1997, p. H 25; and Campbell, *Reel America*, 47.

54. *Moving Picture World*, 30 December 1916. See Leslie Midkiff De-Bauche, *Reel Patriotism* (Madison, 1997), 5–34.

55. Anderson, *Music for Silent Films*, 64.

56. Campbell, *Reel America*, 51, 54.

57. Ibid., 51.

58. Stuart McConnell, "Reading the Flag," in *Bonds of Affection: Americans Define Their Patriotism*, ed. John Bodnar (Princeton, 1996), 106–107; and Cecilia O'Leary, "'Americanize the Allied Child': Flags over the Public Schools," in *To Die For: The Paradox of American Patriotism* (Princeton, 1999), 176ff.

CHAPTER 17. "PROOF THROUGH THE NIGHT"

1. Reinhold Niebuhr, "The Failure of German-Americanism," *The Atlantic Monthly*, 118 (1916): 13–18; reprinted in David F. Trask, ed., *World War I at Home: Readings on American Life, 1914–1920* (New York, 1970), 145–149. See also United States Committee on Public Information, *American Loyalty by Citizens of German Descent* (Washington, Government Printing Office, 1917).

2. See Lubke, *Bonds of Loyalty*, 146; and *The Public Papers of Woodrow Wilson*, ed. Ray Stannard Baker and William E. Dodd (New York, 1925–1927), 3, 423–424. Wilson reiterated this position numerous times, although perhaps never in more slippery terms than in a "Tribute to the Foreign Born," which prefaced a publication by the Committee on Public Information titled *American Loyalty by Citizens of German Descent*, War Information Series No. 6 (Washington, D.C., August, 1917), 3, and which advertised its availability in German translation.

3. See Nancy G. Ford, "Drafting Foreign-born Doughboys into the American Army," in *Americans All! Foreign-born Soldiers in World War I* (College Station, 2001).

4. Weber, Overture to "Euryanthe"; Beethoven, Fifth Symphony; Strauss, *Don Juan;* Wagner, "Forest Murmurs" from *Siegfried* and the finale from *Die Götterdämmerung*.

5. During the war years the Beethoven "Eroica" was performed by the Chicago Symphony in 1914, 1915, 1917, 1918; the Fifth Symphony in 1914, 1915, 1916, 1918; the Ninth Symphony was never performed. For a comparison with the Boston Symphony Orchestra and the New York Philharmonic see note 31 below.

6. It was a claim that ultimately carried even more potent implications in light of the fact that Hitler perished with the *Rienzi* manuscript in his possession, having "refused to relinquish it to Bayreuth for safekeeping." See Joseph Horowitz, "The Specter of Hitler in the Music of Wagner," *The New York Times*, 8 November 1998, pp. 1, 38.

7. Philo Adams Otis, *The Chicago Symphony Orchestra: Its Organization, Growth and Development, 1891–1924* (Chicago, 1972), 302. I am grateful to the staff of the Archive Office of the Chicago Symphony Orchestra for assistance in determining program dates and repertoire.

8. See Dena J. Epstein, "Frederick Stock and American Music," *American Music* 10, no. 1 (1992): 24.

9. See Epstein, "Frederick Stock," 24–26; and Otis, *Chicago Symphony Orchestra,* 312. During the interim, Eric DeLamarter, organist and composer, made his first appearance as assistant conductor of the orchestra.

10. "Philip Hale, Selections from His Columns in the *Boston Home Journal, 1889–1891,*" in *Music in Boston: Music of the First Three Centuries,* ed. John C. Swan (Boston, 1977), 93.

11. Philip Hale in the *Boston Herald;* cited in M. A. DeWolfe Howe, *The Boston Symphony Orchestra, 1881–1931* (Boston, 1931), 131. Muck's wartime story with the Boston Symphony Orchestra is recounted in the *Life and Letters of Henry Lee Higginson,* ed. Bliss Perry (Boston, 1921), and it has been generously treated in two articles: Lowens, "L'Affaire Muck"; and Tischler, "One Hundred Percent Americanism and Music in Boston during World War I," *American Music* (Summer 1986): 164–176. See also J. J. Badel, "The Strange Case of Dr. Karl Muck, Who Was Torpedoed by *The Star-Spangled Banner* during World War I," *High Fidelity* 10, no. 10 (1970): 55.

12. "Threat to Disband Boston Symphony," *The New York Times,* 1 November 1917, p. 10; cited in Tischler, "One Hundred Percent Americanism," 168. See also "Dr. Muck Leaves for Copenhagen," *Boston Globe,* 21 August 1919, p. 10; cited in Tischler, *An American Music,* 82.

13. "Ex-Governor Warfield Would Mob Muck," *The New York Times,* 5 November 1917, p. 13; cited in Tischler, "One Hundred Percent Americanism," 168.

14. "Declares Muck Must Not Lead in Baltimore," *Boston Globe,* 5 November 1917, p. 3; cited in Tischler, "One Hundred Percent Americanism," 169, and *An American Music,* 80.

15. Howe, *Boston Symphony Orchestra,* 134.

16. "Threat to Disband Boston Symphony," *The New York Times,* 1 November 1917, p. 10.

17. Cited in Barbara L. Tischler, "World War I and the Challenge of 100%

Americanism," in *An American Music: The Search for an American Musical Identity* (New York, 1986), 79; and taken from the Boston Symphony Orchestra Archives scrapbook collected by Marcus Carroll. Tischler speculates that the article, "Colonel Would Intern Dr. Muck as Alien," although undated, may come from the *Boston Herald and Journal* of 3 November 1917. Irving Lowens, "L'affaire Muck: A Study in War Hysteria (1917–1918)," *Musicology* 1 (1947): 267, attributes the same statement to *The New York Times* of the same date.

18. *The Musical Times*, 1 January 1918, p. 28.

19. Tischler, "One Hundred Percent Americanism," 169.

20. Lowens, "L'Affaire Muck," 270–271.

21. For a review of the 9 November 1917 concert in Carnegie Hall see Aldrich, *Concert Life in New York*, 550–551.

22. I am grateful to Joseph Horowitz for alerting me to these details.

23. See the epigraph to this chapter.

24. Lowens, "L'Affaire Muck," 272–274.

25. See "Music World Agog over Question of Muck's Successor," *Musical America* 27 (1918): 1.

26. For a comparison of national repertoires performed by the Boston and New York orchestras from 1916 to 1922 see Tischler, "One Hundred Percent Americanism," 172.

27. See Howe, *Boston Symphony Orchestra, 1881–1931*, 183ff., appendix B, which provides the complete repertoire of the orchestra during this period.

28. For a more tempered discussion of the issue by one of New York's most widely read critics, see Aldrich, *Concert Life in New York*, 546–550, "The Case of Dr. Muck."

29. For a recounting of Muck's claim to Swiss citizenship, see Walter Damrosch, *My Musical Life* (New York, 1926), 225–226.

30. Ibid., 342–343.

31. A comparison of Damrosch's and Muck's attention to Beethoven's Third, Fifth, and Ninth Symphonies during the war years is instructive: Third Symphony: BSO, 1914, 1916, 1917, 1918; NYP, 1914, 1915, 1916; Fifth Symphony: BSO, 1914, 1917, 1918; NYP, 1914, 1915, 1917, 1918; Ninth Symphony: BSO, 1917; NYP, 1915, 1917. See Kate Hevner Mueller, *Twenty-Seven Major American Symphony Orchestras: A History and Analysis of Their Repertoires, Seasons 1842–43 through 1969–70* (Bloomington, 1973).

32. See notes by Denis Hall to Rachmaninoff's recording on London/Decca CD D 1005619.

33. Twenty-two years later a similar scenario was repeated when Igor Stravinsky offered his arrangement of "The Star-Spangled Banner" as a gesture of homage to his newly adopted country. As fate would have it, both musicians settled in Los Angeles where they occasionally saw each other in Rachmaninoff's last years. Both became American citizens, and neither communicated again with his native land to any appreciable degree.

34. I am indebted to Capt. Frank Byrne, U.S. Marine Band, for providing

me with the programs played at all three sites during the period 1914–1918 and for bringing this notice to my attention.

35. United States War Department, *Home Reading Course for Citizen-Soldiers*, War Information Series No. 9 (Washington, D.C., 1917), 51.

36. Stanley Coben, "A Study in Nativism: The American Red Scare of 1919–1920," in *Causes and Consequences of World War I*, ed. John Milton Cooper Jr. (New York, 1972), 180–181. e. e. cummings, who served in the ambulance corps, delivered one of the most decimating commentaries on the jingoism surrounding the national anthem in "next to of course god america," from e. e. cummings, *Is 5*, ed. George James Firmage (New York, 1985); reproduced in Fussell, ed., *Norton Book of Modern War*, 203–204.

37. Hussey, *Virginia Woolf and War*, 8.

38. Sousa wrote a fantasy of national airs for the International Congress in 1876. Undertaken at the request of Jacques Offenbach, who directed the orchestra for the Centennial Exhibition in Philadelphia, the work began with a fugue on "Yankee Doodle" and concluded with "The Star-Spangled Banner" amazingly arranged in the style of Wagner's Overture to *Tannhäuser*. An arrangement of this work was made for the use of the U.S. Marine Band in 1882. While bandmaster of the U.S. Marine Band, Sousa was also commissioned to make an arrangement of the anthems of numerous nations, which were published as a book, "The National, Patriotic, and Typical Airs of All Lands," in 1890. It included in addition to the national tunes of the principal nations a group of favorite songs in such remote places as Samoa, Lapland, and the Fiji Islands. See Delaplaine, *John Philip Sousa*, 10.

39. See Jon Pareles, "Listeners Ask Radio Stations for Songs that Sustain a Weary Soul," *The New York Times*, 1 October 2001.

40. Elise K. Kirk, *Music at the White House: A History of the American Spirit* (Urbana, 1986), 193–194. Wilson's second wife, whom he married on 18 December 1915, had studied music at Martha Washington College, and his daughter Margaret, who was 27 years old at the time of her father's inauguration, studied singing at the Baltimore Peabody Conservatory and made a recording of "The Star-Spangled Banner" for the benefit of the International Board of Relief in 1915. Just four White House musicales were scheduled before April 1916, and the only singer to be presented alone in solo recital was Ernestine Schumann-Heink on 8 February 1916. Eleven volumes of recordings preserved along with the Victrola from the White House during Wilson's tenure include Schumann-Heink's renowned "Stille Nacht" as well as recordings of Caruso, Sembrich, Melba, McCormack, and the violinist Efrem Zimbalist.

41. For a review see Aldrich, *Concert Life in New York*, 495.

42. The sinking of the *Sussex* took on an especially sad note in light of the fact that Granados had changed his return passage in order to accept the White House invitation.

43. I am grateful to Capt. Frank Byrne, USMC, for providing programs of the U.S. Marine Band during the period 1914–1918.

44. "Umberto Giordano," *The New Grove Dictionary of Music,* 20 vols. (1980), 7: 395–396; and Irving Kolodin, *The Metropolitan Opera, 1883–1966: A Candid History* (New York, 1967), 268–269. A similar event happened during World War II when on the opening night of the 1942 season the coloratura soprano Lily Pons demonstrated her patriotism for her native France by waving a French flag and interpolating "La Marseillaise" into an aria of Donizetti's French-language *Fille du Régiment.*

45. This was a replacement project (1914–1932) for an original 1829 canal that bypassed Niagara Falls and linked Lakes Erie and Ontario.

46. Kolodin, *Metropolitan Opera,* 269; and "Johanna Gadski," *The New Grove Dictionary of Music,* 20 vols. (1980), 7: 75.

47. Kolodin, *Metropolitan Opera,* 276.

48. Ibid., 276; John Dizikes, *Opera in America: A Cultural History* (New Haven, 1993), 407, incorrectly states that it was Rosa Ponselle who sang rather than Louise Homer.

49. Michael Scott, *The Great Caruso* (London, 1988), 165.

50. Ibid., 168–169.

51. Kolodin, *Metropolitan Opera,* 277, 282.

52. Ibid., 299.

53. Romola Nijinsky, *Nijinsky* (London, 1933), 283, 288, 299. During their detention Nijinsky was questioned by the police about a dance notation that he was developing and which they took to be some sort of military code. Stravinsky experienced a similar confrontation with the authorities over a Picasso portrait of him.

54. Ibid., 318.

55. Ibid., 332, 338.

CHAPTER 18. "ON PATROL IN NO MAN'S LAND"

1. See Curtis Morrow, *What's a Commie Ever Done to Black People? A Korean War Memoir of Fighting in the U.S. Army's Last All Negro Unit* (Jefferson, N.C., 1997).

2. W. Allison Sweeney, *History of the American Negro in the Great World War* (New York, 1969), 89.

3. Sweeney, *History of the American Negro,* 95ff.

4. Negro National Guard units had also increased in number since the Spanish-American War, though they were far from numerous at the time of America's entry into the European conflict. See Sweeney, *History of the American Negro,* 74–75.

5. Cited on The History Channel Video, A&E 40384, *As It Happened: The Spanish-American War.*

6. For more on the Battle of Las Guasimas see Carl Ploense III, "Ready and Forward Again. . . . A Unit History of the 10th Cavalry Regiment" at http://www.spanam.simplenet.com/10thcavhist.htm.

7. For the details of James Reese Europe's life see Reid Badger's compre-

hensive *A Life in Ragtime: A Biography of James Reese Europe* (New York, 1995).

8. Attaching himself to the Castles' rising star and to foxtrot interpretations of W. C. Handy's "Memphis Blues," Europe found his career catapulting upward, and recordings of turkey trots, waltzes, tangos, rags, and one-steps followed. For a listing of Europe's Society Orchestra recordings from 1914 see Badger, *A Life in Ragtime*, 236. For Gunther Schuller's recording of Europe's "Castle House Rag," see GM3018CD.

9. Quoted in Badger, *A Life in Ragtime*, 142.

10. Badger, *A Life in Ragtime*, 144.

11. Byron Farwell, *Over There* (New York, 1999), 153. For further background see chapter 15, "Blacks and Indians in the American Army."

12. Ibid., *A Life in Ragtime*, 154.

13. "Fear Negro Troops in Spartanburg," *The New York Times*, 13 August 1917, p. 4. Regarding other efforts to make military service appealing to African Americans see also Thomas Winter, "The Training of Colored Troops: A Cinematic Effort to Promote National Cohesion," in *World War I: Motion Picture Images*, ed. Peter C. Rollins and John E. O'Connor (Bowling Green, 1997).

14. Bierley, *John Philip Sousa*, 17, 67, 167.

15. See James P. Daughton, "Sketches of the *Poilu*'s World: Trench Cartoons from the Great War," in *World War I and the Cultures of Modernity*, ed. Douglas Mackaman and Michael Mays (Jackson, 2000), 47–49.

16. Winter, "Propaganda and Mobilization of Consent," 219–220.

17. Arthur West Little, *From Harlem to the Rhine: The Story of New York's Colored Volunteers* (New York, 1936), 185. See Irvin S. Cobb, "Young Black Joe," *The Saturday Evening Post*, August 1918, pp. 7–8, 77–78. See also Anita Lawson, *Irvin S. Cobb* (Bowling Green, 1984), 164. Cobb's article was widely reprinted in the black press and suddenly made its author, who had previously been noted for his capacity for demeaning caricature of blacks, something of a hero amongst this very group.

18. Sissle, "Memoirs," 168–169; see Badger, *A Life in Ragtime*, 304 n. 39.

19. Quoted in "A Negro Explains 'Jazz,'" 29; reprinted in Southern, *Readings in Black American Music* (New York, 1972), 240.

20. For Welton's report along with Europe's interview see Badger, *A Life in Ragtime*, 194–195.

21. For more on this issue, see the chapters on "Primitivism" in Watkins, *Pyramids at the Louvre*.

22. Badger, *A Life in Ragtime*, 196.

23. An attempt to remedy the official posture toward the black soldier in the Civil War was made only in 1998 with the erection of a monument in a historic black neighborhood at Vermont and U Street in the nation's capital. See *The Washington Post* for 19 July 1998.

24. The complete text of the *World*'s lengthy account of the reception is recorded in Sweeney, *History of the American Negro*, 267–274.

25. James Reese Europe's "On Patrol in No Man's Land" was apparently never published, only recorded by Pathé.

26. A report from *The Sun* of New York on 4 November 1917 carried the following description of jazz that centered on a series of pronounced wartime metaphors: "The clarinet wheedles and whines, the trombone chokes and gargles, the violins snicker and shriek, the piano vibrates like a torpedo boat destroyer at high speed in an endeavor to make itself heard above the tumult, and the drum, belabored by a drummer who is surrounded by all the most up-to-date accessories and implements of torture, becomes the heavy artillery of the piece and makes the performance a devastating barrage."

27. See Tim Gracyk's informative notes that accompany the reissue of all of these songs on Memphis Archives CD MA 7020, 9. See also Gracyk's multimedia site, http://www.redhotjazz.com/europe.html.

28. Included in *Music from the New York Stage*, vol. 4: *1917–1920* (Pearl CDS 9059–61).

29. See Vogel, *World War I Songs*, 233–234; Gracyk, notes, 17; and Howard Pollack, *Skyscraper Lullaby* (Washington, D.C., 1995), 161.

30. Gracyk, notes, 14.

31. Ernest Ansermet, "Sur un orchestre nègre," *La revue romande* (Lausanne) 3, no. 10 (1919): 10–13. See Watkins, *Pyramids at the Louvre*, 148.

32. Cornet, trombone, clarinet, two violins, banjos, piano and percussion. See Andrew Lamb, "Popular Music: Europe to World War II," in *The New Grove Dictionary of Music and Musicians*, 20 vols. (London, 1980), 15: 94.

33. Watkins, *Pyramids at the Louvre*, 164.

34. A. Philip Randolph and Chandler Owens, editors of the *Messenger* founded in 1915, were prominent amongst the dissenters. Following an anti-war demonstration in Cleveland in 1918, Randolph was arrested and jailed. See Sean Dennis Cashman, *America Ascendant* (New York, 1998), 153.

35. In W. E. B. Du Bois's *The Souls of Black Folk* (Chicago, 1903); reprint, New York, 1961, the author proposed that African Americans continue their demand for civil rights guaranteed by the Constitution, which translated into a call for the right to vote, civic equality, and access to an education. See also Ross Posnock, *Color and Culture: Black Writers and the Making of the Modern Intellectual* (Cambridge, Mass., 1998); and Cashman, *America Ascendant*, 104–112. David Levering Lewis, *W. E. B. Du Bois: The Fight for Equality and the American Century, 1919–1963* (New York, 2000), the second volume of a Du Bois biography, deals particularly with the post-Armistice issue of the returning black soldier and his expectations of recognition.

36. See Mark Ellis, "W. E. B. DuBois and the Formation of Black Opinion in World War I: A Commentary on the Damnable Dilemma," *The Journal of American History* 81 (1995): 1584–1590; and William Jordan, "'The Damnable Dilemma': African-American Protest and Accommodation During World War I," *The Journal of American History* 81 (1995): 1562–1590.

37. Sam Dennison, *Scandalize My Name: Black Imagery in American Popular Music* (New York, 1982), 381.

38. For the complete lyrics see ibid., 383.

39. See Wenzel and Binkowski, *I Hear America Singing*, 75; and Vogel, *World War I Songs*, 77.

40. See Vogel, *World War I Songs*, 78. I am grateful to Suzanne Camino for observations on many of these issues in "Turning the Dark Clouds Inside Out: Diversity, Denial and Desperate Optimism in American Songs of World War I" (seminar paper, University of Michigan, April 1996).

41. John Jacob Niles, *Singing Soldiers* (New York, 1927), vii–viii.

42. "I want to go home / I don't want to go in the trenches no more / Where hand-grenades and whiz-bangs they roar . . . [where] / It's always a raining, the mud is knee-deep / The lice are so active, I never can sleep . . . / Oh, my I'm too young to die / I want to go home"; ibid., 2–3.

43. Cited in Adrian Gregory, *The Silence of Memory: Armistice Day, 1919–1946* (Oxford, 1994), 82.

44. Niles, *Singing Soldiers*, 19–22.

45. Ibid., 49–50.

46. Dennison, *Scandalize My Name*, 383.

47. Quoted in Robert Kimball and William Bolcom, *Reminiscing with Sissle and Blake* (New York, 1973), 64. For a revisionist view of the racial component in the early history of jazz see Richard M. Sudhalter, *Lost Chords: White Musicians and Their Contribution to Jazz, 1915–1945* (New York, 1999); and the review by Jason Berry, "White Men Can Jam," *The New York Times Book Review*, 11 July 1999, p. 32.

48. Damrosch, *My Musical Life*, 223.

49. Léonie Rosenstiel, *The Life and Works of Lili Boulanger* (London, 1978), 114–115.

50. Damrosch, *My Musical Life*, 259. When Lili Boulanger returned to the Villa Medici in Rome in 1916, her health continued to decline. See Rosenstiel, *Life and Works of Lili Boulanger*, 119.

51. Rosenstiel, *Life and Works of Lili Boulanger*, 204–205. Lili's wartime compositions also include *De profundis* (Psalm 120, "Du fond de l'abîme) and *Vieille prière bouddhique* (1916). Nadia composed a song, "Soir d'hiver," that speaks of the mother of a baby boy, waiting for her husband to return from the front, who speaks of her child as having *"un coeur d'homme."* See Caroline Potter, "Nadia and Lili Boulanger: Sister Composers," *Musical Quarterly* 83, no. 4 (1999): 549.

52. Damrosch, *My Musical Life*, 249.

53. Ibid., 251.

54. D. Royce Boyer, "The World War I Army Bandsman: A Diary Account by Philip James." *American Music* 14 (1996): 200–201.

55. See D. Royce Boyer, "The American Expeditionary Forces, General Headquarters Band, Victory Loan Tour—1919," *Journal of Band Research* 26, no. 1 (1990): 44–51. In 1948 James wrote an overture for orchestra titled "Chaumont."

56. Damrosch, *My Musical Life*, 311.

57. Léonie Rosenstiel, *Nadia Boulanger: A Life in Music* (New York, 1982), 154.

58. See Tischler, *American Music*, 132–133, "The National Government and National Music," and 99–100, "Modernists in Search of an Audience."

59. George Antheil, "The Negro on the Spiral or a Method of Negro Music," in *Negro*, ed. Nancy Cunard (New York, 1970), 114.

60. The letter is dated 8 March 1928. See Watkins, *Pyramids at the Louvre*, 211.

61. Letter dated 24 November 1924, quoted by Jérôme Spycket, *Nadia Boulanger* (Stuyvesant, N.Y., 1992), 64.

62. See Andrew Ward, *Dark Midnight When I Rise: The Story of the Jubilee Singers Who Introduced the World to the Music of Black America* (New York, 2000).

CHAPTER 19. COMING OF AGE IN AMERICA

1. As Michael Howard, *Causes of War* (Cambridge, Mass., 1982), 26–28, has put it, "France *was* Marengo, Austerlitz and Jena. . . . Britain *was* Trafalgar. . . . Russia *was* the triumph of 1812. . . . Could a Nation, in any true sense of the word, really be born without war?"

2. In the world of operetta the whirlwind popularity accorded the works of Viennese composer Franz Lehar during the century's first two decades or similar offerings by Rudolf Friml and Victor Hugo did little to resolve the issue. More potent was the escalating attention and favor accorded such repertoires as African-American ragtime by Scott Joplin ("Maple Leaf Rag") and the imitative but more fashionable tunes by the Russian-Jew Irving Berlin ("Alexander's Ragtime Band"). See Richard Crawford, *America's Musical Life: A History* (New York, 2001), chap. 26, "Come On and Hear: The Early Twentieth Century," for a detailed parsing of the issue.

3. Charles Hamm, *Music in the New World* (New York, 1983), 412.

4. Alan Howard Levy, *Musical Nationalism: American Composers' Search for Identity* (Westport, Conn., 1983), 18–19.

5. Regarding the paradox surrounding the search for an American music see especially Crawford, "Edward MacDowell," 528–560.

6. Walter Spalding, "The War in its Relation to American Music," *The Musical Quarterly* 4, no. 1 (1918): 1–11.

7. Ibid., 9–11.

8. For a further discussion of the "melting-pot" idea and its implications for an American sense of identity see Levine, *Opening of the American Mind*, chap. 6, "From the Melting Pot to the Pluralist Vision."

9. See Pollack, *Skyscraper Lullaby*, 158.

10. Ibid.

11. For the role played by John Alden Carpenter and others in the U.S. Committee on Music for the Army and Navy see "To Standardize All Music

for Army and Navy," *Musical America* 26 (1917): 1, and "Making Singing Sailors for Uncle Sam's Navy," *Musical America* 27 (1918): 3. See also May Stanley, "Wanted: Singing Leaders for Army Camps," *Musical America* 26 (1917): 3.

12. See Pollack, *Skyscraper Lullaby*, 159.

13. At the top of the first page of the printed score the other members of the Committee of Twelve were identified as "John Alden Carpenter, Frederick Convere, Wallace Goodrich, and Walter R. Spalding, representing the War Department Commission on Training Camp Activities; Peter W. Dykema, Hollis Dann, and Osbourne McConathy, representing the Music Supervisors' National Conference; C. C. Birchard, Carl Engel, William Arms Fisher, Arthur Edward Jonstone, and E. W. Newton, representing Music publishers."

14. John Alden Carpenter, "The Home Road" (New York, 1917).

15. Victrola 831-A.

16. "Khaki Sammy" (New York, 1917).

17. An English translation by Tita Brand-Cammaerts, the poet's wife, was provided on the opening page of the original Schirmer publication, although there was no English textual underlay in the musical score.

18. Pollack, *Skyscraper Lullaby*, 153. Carpenter's orchestration is for a chamber ensemble of oboe, clarinet, bassoon, piano, harp, percussion, and strings.

19. Carpenter also tapped Siegfried Sassoon with "Slumber-Song," the first of *Two Night Songs*, in a ruminative post-war reflection characterized by a quiet nobility. That the composer was in contact with the English poet is verified by a photo-reproduction of the text in Sassoon's hand, dated and designated for the express use of Carpenter, that was included as a frontispiece to the printed edition.

20. In addition to a familiar parade of Spalding's German composers of the "first rank," plus Haydn, Schumann, and Schubert, there were intermittent performances of Liszt, Elgar, Grieg, and Dvořák; the Russian composers Tchaikovsky, Glazunov, Liadov, Rimsky-Korsakov, and Rachmaninov; the Frenchmen Berlioz, Bizet, Massenet, Chabrier, Delibes, Saint-Saëns, d'Indy and Dukas; and a smattering of conservative American works by MacDowell, Foote, Carpenter, Parker, Powell, De Lamarter, Sowerby, and Mrs. H. H. A. Beach.

21. Other orchestral works of Ravel received their Chicago Symphony Orchestra premieres in the following seasons: *Rapsodie espagnole*, 1909; *Tombeau de Couperin*, 1927; Piano Concerto in D major, 1944; Piano Concerto in G major, 1950. I am grateful to the Archive Division of the Chicago Symphony Orchestra for allowing me access to their records.

22. Chicago premieres of Stravinsky's works appeared in the following seasons: *Fireworks*, 1914; *Firebird Suite*, 1920; *Song of the Volga Boatmen*, 1924; *Le sacre du printemps*, 1924 and 1925 (and not again until 1948); *Petrushka Suite*, 1930; and *Pulcinella Suite*, 1934.

23. Otis, *Chicago Symphony Orchestra*, 312.

24. With performances of Debussy's *Nocturnes, La Mer,* and *Images* and Ravel's *Daphnis et Chloë, Mother Goose,* and *Rapsodie espagnole.* See Richard Schickel, *The World of Carnegie Hall* (New York, 1960), 171–172; H. Earle Johnson, *Symphony Hall, Boston* (Boston, 1950), 332; Richard Aldrich, *Concert Life in New York, 1902–1903* (New York, 1941), 619.

25. See Carol J. Oja, *Making Music Modern: New York in the 1920s* (New York, 2000), chap. 17, "The Advent of European Modernism Before and After the War."

26. Howe, *Boston Symphony Orchestra,* 149; and Johnson, *Symphony Hall,* 93–94.

27. See Oja, *Making Music Modern,* 28–29, 93, 204.

28. For a report on the Slonimsky concerts see Paul Griffiths, "American Music That Rattled Berlin," *The New York Times,* 14 January 2001, sec. 2, p. 35; and Anthony Tommasini, "Revisiting a Homage to American Composers," *The New York Times,* 23 January 2001, sec. E, p. 5. For an in-depth study of the period, the personalities, and the repertoire, see Oja, *Making Music Modern.*

29. See Tischler, *American Music,* chap. 1, "Perceptions of Concert Music in the United States."

30. Edward Rothstein, "Seeking a Home in the Brave New World," *The New York Times,* 1 January 2000, p. C21.

31. Frederick H. Martens, *Leo Ornstein* (New York, 1975), 24.

32. Both of the "Impressions de Notre-Dame," op. 16, nos. 1 and 2, are recorded on Hat Art CD 6144 by Steffen Schleiermacher, piano, along with "Danse Sauvage" and "Suicide in an Airplane."

33. The titles were not included in the Carl Fischer publication of 1918.

34. They include such well-known Heine texts set by Schumann as "Du bist wie eine Blume" (1897) and "Ich grolle nicht" (1898), or Brahms's beloved "Wiegenlied" ("Guten Abend, gute Nacht," 1908).

35. J. Peter Burkholder, *All Made of Tunes: Charles Ives and the Uses of Musical Borrowing* (New Haven, 1995), 34; H. Wiley Hitchcock, "Ives's *114 [+15] Songs* and What He Thought of Them," *Journal of the American Musicological Society* 52, no. 1 (1999): 115–116; and Watkins, *Soundings,* 434.

36. "Feldeinsamkeit" is one of Ives's most captivating early songs—a setting whose natural fluency of movement and harmony courts Impressionism and whose melodic rhythms owe much to Brahms, but whose accompanimental figure is patently modeled after the opening C-major prelude of the first volume of J. S. Bach's *Well-Tempered Clavier.*

37. For a thorough accounting of the various editions of Ives's songs, see Hitchcock, "Ives's *114 [+15] Songs,*" 97–144. An edition of the complete songs of Ives is in preparation by Hitchcock.

38. See J. Peter Burkholder, "Ives and the Four Musical Traditions," in *Charles Ives and His World,* ed. J. Peter Burkholder (Princeton, 1996), 3–34; and J. Peter Burkholder, "Ives and the European Tradition," in *Charles Ives and*

the Classical Tradition, ed. Geoffrey Block and J. Peter Burkholder (New Haven, 1996), 11–33.

39. Complete text in Charles Ives, *Memos,* ed. John Kirkpatrick (New York, 1972), 92–93.

40. See Burkholder, *All Made of Tunes,* 262–266, for a comprehensive description of the piece.

41. Hanna, *The Mobilization of Intellect,* 148.

42. Leon Botstein, "Innovation and Nostalgia: Ives, Mahler, and the Origins of Twentieth-Century Modernism," in *Charles Ives and the Classical Tradition,* ed. Geoffrey Block and J. Peter Burkholder (New Haven, 1996), 50.

43. Tischler, *American Music,* 33.

44. Burkholder, *All Made of Tunes,* 306–311.

45. McCrae's text was set in 1918 by at least eight composers including John Philip Sousa, and in 1919 by fifteen composers including Arthur Foote. See Vogel, *World War I Songs,* 195.

46. Ives, *Memos,* 271; and Frank Rossiter, *Charles Ives and His America* (New York, 1975), 153–154.

47. For more on the Debussy-Ives relationship see John Jeffrey Gibbens, "Debussy's Impact on Ives: An Assessment," D.M.A. diss., University of Illinois, 1985, p. 53; and David Michael Hertz, *Angels of Reality: Emersonian Unfoldings in Wright, Stevens, and Ives* (Carbondale, Ill., 1993), 93–113. Ives's setting of "Grantchester" (1921), on a text of Rupert Brooke, also includes a striking quotation (noted along with the title) from the opening two staves of Debussy's *Prélude à l'après-midi d'un faune.*

48. See Burkholder, *All Made of Tunes,* 276, regarding a similar counterpointing of "La Marseillaise" against "America" in the last of *Three Quartertone Pieces* for two pianos, which dates from 1923–1924. Here Ives seems to provoke an assessment of the avant-garde through a demonstration of new techniques in conjunction with readily recognizable national materials.

49. See Alan Houtchens and Janis P. Stout, "'Scarce Heard Amidst the Guns Below': Intertextuality and Meaning in Charles Ives's War Songs," *The Journal of Musicology* 15 (1997): 68–80. The authors conclude, I think rightly, that there is "no reason to believe that Ives consciously meant to be parodically jingoistic" through his use of a martial style in the third stanza.

50. The text would ultimately serve as the impetus for a familiar postwar tradition, Poppy Day. It was an American woman, Moina Michael, who initially suggested that American ex-servicemen adopt the poppy as their emblem, and that artificial poppies "be manufactured in the devastated areas of Northern France, by women, for the benefit of children." Soon thereafter the idea was taken up throughout all the Allied countries. See Gregory, *Silence of Memory,* 99.

51. John McCrae, *In Flanders Fields and Other Poems* (New York, 1919).

52. "Of the tunes suggested above," Ives wrote in his edition of *144 Songs,* "'Tenting tonight' was written and composed by Walter Kittredge, in 1862, a

farmer and soldier, from Merrimack, N.H.; the 'Battle Cry of Freedom' was also composed during the Civil war by Geo. F. Root, a composer and publisher in Boston; Henry Clay Work, the composer of 'Marching through Georgia' was born in Middletown, Ct. in 1832."

53. Ives Collection, John Herrick Jackson Music Library, Yale University, manuscript (frame number) f5775, as cited in Burkholder, *All Made of Tunes*, 314–315.

54. Tom C. Owens, "Selected Correspondence, 1881–1954," in *Charles Ives and His World*, ed. J. Peter Burkholder (Princeton, 1996), 252. *Charles Ives, the 100th Anniversary* (Columbia Records 432504) includes "They Are There" at the very end of Bonus Record, side 1, in two renditions by Ives himself that give the impression that he was in a most jovial, perhaps inebriated, state.

55. Charles Ives, "Tom Sails Away," in *144 Songs* (Redding, Conn., 1922).

56. Hitchcock, "Ives's 114," 115, 134.

57. Houtchens and Stout, "'Scarce Heard Amidst the Guns Below,'" 7–8.

58. Vivian Perlis, *Charles Ives Remembered* (New Haven, 1974), 12.

59. Charles Ives, "Nov. 2, 1920," in *144 Songs* (Redding, Conn., 1922).

60. Michael Broyles, "Charles Ives and the American Democratic Tradition," in *Charles Ives and His World*, ed. J. Peter Burkholder (Princeton, N.J., 1996), 120.

61. Charles Ives, "Lincoln, the Great Commoner," in *144 Songs* (Redding, Conn., 1922).

62. Charles Ives, *Essays Before a Sonata and Other Writings*, ed. Howard Boatwright (New York, 1962), 47–48.

63. Ives, *Memos*, 44. Ives also obviously took pleasure in recognizing that the first four notes of the hymn tune "Martyn" ("Jesus, Lover of My Soul") resemble the opening of Beethoven's Fifth Symphony.

64. Ibid.

65. Hamm, *Music in the New World*, 437.

CHAPTER 20. "GOIN' HOME"

1. The article appeared in the *British Music Society Bulletin* in June 1919 under the title "Starved Arts Mean Low Pleasures"; it was reprinted in *The Outlook*, 19 and 26 July 1919, as "The Future of British Music." See *The Bodley Head Bernard Shaw: Shaw's Music*, vol. 3: *1893–1950*, ed. Dan H. Laurence (London, 1981), 714–721.

2. Shaw, "The Future of British Music," 7–11.

3. *Bodley Head Bernard Shaw*, 723–724.

4. Quinn, *The Great War*, 230–233.

5. In Michael Thorpe, *Siegfried Sassoon: A Critical Study* (London, 1966), 50; and Quinn, *The Great War*, 231.

6. Sassoon, "Concert Interpretation," in *Collected Poems.*

7. Ibid., 158–159. See also Thorpe, *Siegfried Sassoon,* 50; and Quinn, *The Great War,* 231.

8. Oliver Wendell Holmes, Sr., *The Complete Poetical Works* (Boston, 1912), "The Music Grinders," st. 10, ll. 57–58.

9. Charles D. Isaacson, "A New Musical Outlook—and the War," *The Musical Quarterly* 6, no. 1 (1920): 1–11.

10. Raymond Poincaré, *Messages, discours, allocutions, lettres et télégrammes de Raymond Poincaré* (Paris, 1919–1920), 51.

11. For a description see Jean-Pierre Bois, *Histoire des 14 juillet: 1789–1919* (Rennes, 1991), 258. For a drawing of the destroyed figure that was placed overnight under the Arc du Triomphe before joining the parade the next day see Cork, *Bitter Truth,* 237. For a photograph see Rother, *Die letzten Tage,* 404. A lone pilot, signaling the collective dismay of the air corps at not having been included in the victory parade, swooped down the Champs-Élysées and threaded his aircraft like a needle through the Arc de Triomphe.

12. J. Vidal, *Marches et chansons des soldats de France* (n.p., 1919), 10.

13. It was ultimately decided that all headstones would be identical and carry no mention of rank, and that each cemetery would have a Cross of Sacrifice and a Great War Stone. The inscription for the latter was chosen by Kipling, whose son was reported missing at Loos and never found. Taken from Ecclesiastes, it read "Their Name Liveth for Evermore." See Hynes, *A War Imagined,* 271.

14. Modris Eksteins, "War, Memory, and the Modern: Pilgrimage and Tourism to the Western Front," in *World War I and the Cultures of Modernity,* ed. Douglas Mackaman and Michael Mays (Jackson, Miss., 2000), 154, 157.

15. See Becker, *La guerre et la foi;* Nadine-Josette Chaline, *Chrétiens dans la première guerre mondiale* (Paris, 1993); Annette Becker and Philippe Rivé, *Monuments de mémoire, monuments aux morts de la Grande Guerre* (Paris, 1991); Gregory, *Silence of Memory;* and Winter, *Sites of Memory.*

16. See Becker, *La guerre et la foi,* 132–133; and Denizot, *Le Sacré-Coeur.* Father Jacques Benoist, archivist at Sacré-Coeur, notes (private communication, 3 June 2000): "On Monday the 14th of July 1919 there was no special liturgical program at Sacré-Coeur Montmartre, as in the other churches of France. There were only celebrations for the feast of Saint Bonaventure. As there was no official government Te Deum, patriotic and Catholic ceremonies were celebrated at Sacré-Coeur on Friday June 27, 1919, and certainly at the consecration of the church from Thursday October 16 through Sunday October 19, 1919. The musical programs of these festivities can be reconstructed only with great effort and hypotheses. I have listed a variety of pieces played at Sacré-Coeur at the beginning of the century in my book, *Le Sacré-Coeur de Montmartre* (Paris, L'Atelier, 1992), volume 1, 612–613."

17. *The Musical Times,* 1 January 1918, p. 27.

18. See also Adrienne Fried Block, "Dvořák's Long American Reach," in

Dvořák in America, 1892–1895, ed. John C. Tibbetts (Portland, 1993), 158–159, who forwards the stylistically questionable hypothesis of an American Indian connection for this melody. Fisher's preface to the 1922 publication of "Goin' Home" does speak of the impression that Longfellow's *Hiawatha* had made on Dvořák, however.

19. A testimony recorded in William Arms Fisher's preface to "Goin' Home," published by the Oliver Ditson Co. in 1922.

20. Thomas A. Britten, *American Indians in World War I: At Home and at War* (Albuquerque, 1997), 116ff.

21. Ibid., 100–101.

22. Ibid., 152–153; Severt Young Bear and R. D. Theisz, *Standing in the Light: A Lakota Way of Seeing* (Lincoln, 1994), 84.

23. See chapter 2, n. 72, of Diane Camurat, "American Indians in the Great War: Real and Imagined," Master's thesis, University of Paris VII, 1993; online at raven.cc.ukans.edu/~kansite/ww_one/comment/camurat1.hml.

24. William K. Powers, *War Dance: Plains Indian Musical Performance* (Tucson, 1990), 155. See also Peter Nabakov, ed., *Native American Testimony: A Chronicle of Indian-White Relations from Prophecy to the Present, 1492–1992* (New York, 1991); Diane Glancy, *War Cries* (Duluth, 1997); and Fred Gaffen, *Forgotten Soldiers* (Penticton, B.C., 1985). Tara Browner has informed me that the Lakota word for German (*iyasica* with a dot over the *s*) means "bad mouth" or "bad language."

25. For other examples see "World War I Veteran's Song" recorded on *Songs from Porcupine: Honoring Irving Tail* (Turtle Island Music); *New Years at Porcupine* and *Sioux Songs of War and Love,* sung by William Horn Cloud (Canyon Records No. 6150).

26. Bear and Theisz, *Standing in the Light,* 83. See also the discussion on the Lakota warrior, 78–86. At home, an Osage Mother's War Song, recorded on *American Indian Music for the Classroom,* LP Canyon C 3001–3004, would have been available earlier in the war.

27. See Jeff Todd Titon, ed., *World of Music: An Introduction to the Music of the World's Peoples* (New York, 1996), 39–42, for a musical example. I am grateful to Tara Browner for her counsel on this matter. For additional discussion on this topic see David P. McAllester, *Enemy Way Music: A Study of Social and Esthetic Values as Seen in Navaho Music* (Cambridge, Mass., 1954), and *Indian Music in the Southwest* (Colorado Springs, 1961).

28. Britten, *American Indians,* 165. See also Nabakov, *Native American Testimony,* 279–282; Thomas E. Mails, *Fools Crow* (Garden City, N.Y., 1979), 110, and *Fools Crow: Wisdom and Power* (Tulsa, 1991); and especially Camurat, "American Indians," chap. 4, "Consequences of the War."

29. Britten, *American Indians,* 170.

30. See Camurat, "American Indians."

31. See Niles, *Singing Soldiers,* 1–2, and the discussion and text in chapter 14. For other songs that spoke to the same sentiment see those of the Royal Welch Fusiliers recorded by Robert Graves in *Good-bye to All That,* including

two that begin "I want to go home," reproduced in Paul Fussell, ed., *Norton Book of Modern War*, 95.

32. The preface to *The Spirituals of H. T. Burleigh* (Melville, N.Y., 1984), written by the composer's son, contains the following claim: "Burleigh played and sang the old melodies for Dvořák such as 'Swing Low Sweet Chariot,' which is mirrored in the second theme of the first movement of Dvořák's New World Symphony."

33. Words and adaptation by William Arms Fisher, © 1922 by Oliver Ditson Co.

34. Robeson's recordings of all of these songs have been reissued on Vanguard VCD-72020.

35. Vogel, *World War I Songs*, 105. Chapter 8 provides a rich review of the popular war-related songs that were written between 1919 and 1939.

36. *American War Songs*, published under the supervision of the National Committee for the Preservation of Existing Records of the National Society of the Colonial Dames of America (Philadelphia, 1925), 183.

37. See Dolph, *"Sound Off!"* 146–148.

38. The American Legion was initially called together by a committee headed by Lt. Col. Theodore Roosevelt, Jr., and the organization was granted a national charter the following September.

39. Among the most sentimental, if also the most forceful, of Patton's war poems was one called "The War Horses."

40. See especially Antoine Prost, *In the Wake of War: 'Les Anciens Combattants' and French Society, 1914–1919* (Providence, 1992), chap. 4, "Veterans' Patriotism."

41. Smith, "Masculinity, Memory, and the French First World War Novel," 253. Smith analyzes two highly popular French war novels, Henri Barbusse's *Le feu* (Under Fire, 1916) and Roland Dorgelès's *Les croix de bois* (Wooden Crosses, 1919), both of which speak directly to this condition.

42. "The New Army and Its Musical Needs," *The Musical Times*, 1 March 1915, p. 147.

43. See Wohl, *Generation of 1914*, 220. For Noel Coward on comradeship see "Post Mortem," reprinted in *Play Parade* (London, 1934), 1, 632, 617.

44. Virginia Woolf, *Three Guineas* (London, 1977), 197. See also Karen L. Levenback, *Virginia Woolf and the Great War* (Syracuse, 1998).

45. See Hynes, *A War Imagined*, 84–86; and Erin G. Carlston, *Thinking Fascism: Sapphic Modernism and Fascist Modernity* (Stanford, 1998), 144ff.

46. See Carlston, *Thinking Fascism*, 145, 150–151, 157, 168–169, and especially 177, 180–181. It was a perspective that Woolf had previously pursued in *The Voyage Out* of 1915. See Mark Hussey, "Living in a War Zone," in *Virginia Woolf and War: Fiction, Reality, and Myth*, ed. Mark Hussey (Syracuse, 1991), 8, 25.

47. See Nancy Topping Bazin and Jane Hamovit Lauter, "Woolf's Keen Sensitivity to War," in *Virginia Woolf and War: Fiction, Reality, and Myth*, ed. Mark Hussey (Syracuse, 1991), 25.

48. Fussell, *The Great War*, 272. For a more recent perspective on the issue see George Chauncey, "Christian Brotherhood or Sexual Perversion? Homosexual Identities and the Construction of Sexual Boundaries in the World War I Era," in *Same Sex: Debating the Ethics, Science, and Culture of Homosexuality*, ed. John Corvino (Lanham, Md., 1997); A. D. Harvey, "Some Queer Goings-on in the Trenches: Many British Soldiers Court Martialled for Homosexual Offenses in World War I," *New Statesman* 128, no. 4419 (1999): 30; and Martin Taylor, *Lads: Love Poetry of the Trenches* (London, 1989). See also Patrick Campbell, *Siegfried Sassoon: A Study of the War Poetry* (Jefferson, N.C., 1999), 31–41, 65–66, 77, 82, 103–4, 156, 182, 184; and for a more metaphorical consideration of killing as "intimacy," see Joanna Bourke, *Dismembering the Male: Men's Bodies, Britain, and the Great* War (London, 1996), and *An Intimate History of Killing: Face-to-Face Killing in Twentieth-Century Warfare* (London, 1999); as well as Jean Elshtain's review, "War in Person," *The New York Times Book Review*, 5 March 2000, p. 28. Regarding the career of Robert d'Humières, author of the scenario for Florent Schmitt's *Salomé*, who was ordered to sacrifice himself in an attack at the front or face dishonor and court-martial, see Christian Gury, *L'honneur retrouvé d'un officier homosexuel en 1915* (Paris, 2000).

49. For a first-hand viewpoint on the issue, see the excerpt from Eric Hiscock's *The Bells of Hell Go Ting-a-ling-a-ling*, in the *Norton Book of Modern War*, 145–163. Cf. with the World War II perspective in *Coming Out Under Fire*, videorecording by Zeitgeist Films (Fox Lorber Films, 1995).

50. Bourke, *Dismembering the Male*, 170.

51. Caleb Crain, "The Ties that Bound in America," *The New York Times Book Review*, 17 December 2000, p. 39.

52. See Russell, "We Carved Our Way to Glory," 65–66.

53. Stephane Audoin-Rouzeau, "Brotherhood in the Trenches?" in *Men at War, 1914–1918: National Sentiment and Trench Journalism in France during the First World War*, trans. Helen McPhail (Providence, 1992), 52.

54. Regarding the fiction of social classes and the dreams for a postwar world, see Wohl, *Generation of 1914*, 208.

55. © 1922 Copyright Renewed 1949, Donaldson Publishing Company and Gilbert Keyes Music Co. Kahn also wrote the lyrics to "It Had To Be You," "Orchids in the Moonlight," "Toot Toot Tootsie (Good-Bye)," and "Yes Sir, That's My Baby." Donaldson was also the composer of such tunes as "Carolina in the Morning," "Georgia," "Where'd You Get Those Eyes," and "My Blue Heaven."

56. The *Random House Dictionary of English Usage*, unabridged ed. (New York, 1967).

57. Another song hit, "My Buddies," from the musical play *Buddies*, was published by M. Witmark & Sons in 1919.

58. It is well to recall that while the song "M-o-t-h-e-r (a Word That Means the World to Me)" of 1915 was also popularized in vaudeville by Sophie Tucker, its voice increasingly came to reflect a specifically male soldier's nos-

talgia for home and mother left behind. Similarly, "My Buddy" of 1922 was promoted in vaudeville by ballad singers like Jeanne LaCrosse, and decades later Chet Baker sang it in a memorable performance, reissued on CD as *Chet Baker Plays and Sings the Great Ballads* (EMI-Capitol, Special Products ASIN: B00001T14).

59. See Pisano et al., *Legend, Memory and the Great War*, 62; and Peter Simkins, *PBS, The Great War:* "Interviews–Simkins: 'Pals' Battalions" at http://www.ww1.html.

60. The American Eddie Rickenbacker, for example, who had served for only a short period, reported that pilots' requests for missions increased markedly in the final week of the war, in part out of sheer vengeance and the desire for a last parting shot. See Eddie V. Rickenbacker, *Fighting the Flying Circus* (New York, 1967), 314.

61. Ibid., 319–321. See also Michael C. C. Adams, *The Great Adventure: Male Desire and the Coming of World War I* (Bloomington, 1990), 114.

62. *Legion Airs, Songs of "Over There" and "Over Here,"* compiled by Frank E. Peat, ed. Lee Orean Smith (New York, 1926), 143.

63. The French version of Donaldson's new piece, "Mais où est ma Zouzou?" was recorded in 1926 by Maurice Chevalier and the duo-piano team of Wiéner and Doucet. See Denise Pilmer Taylor, "*La musique pour tout le monde:* Jean Wiéner and the Dawn of French Jazz," Ph.D. diss., University of Michigan, 1998, p. 193.

64. *Legion Airs*, 143.

CHAPTER 21. CEREMONIALS AND THE WAR OF NERVES

1. In London's Whitehall, near the Old War Office, a Cenotaph, or "empty tomb," the symbolic last resting place of Britain's war dead, was also unveiled. Within two days 100,000 wreaths had been laid there, and between 500,000 and a million people paid homage in the first week.

2. See www.ebs.hw.ac.uk/edc/cac/m100/2tip.html for more on the development of the gramophone during World War I.

3. Sassoon, *Collected Poems*, 153–154.

4. See Quinn, *The Great War*, 230. For another lengthy poem that speaks of cross-bearers, prominent officials, and the choir's all "exalting Faith" in an abbey service see Sassoon's "Memorial Service for an Honest Soldier," in *Collected Poems*.

5. For more on this event see Gregory, *Silence of Memory*, 24–31.

6. Ibid., 79. Gregory notes that this "festival broadcast led directly 'to the eventual formation of the Empire Service' in 1932, and therefore marks the ultimate origin of the BBC World Service."

7. Cited in ibid., 82.

8. BBC Written Archives Centre, Caversham, Memo: A. D. M. to Herbage and Reybould, 21 August 1936, R 34/227/2, as cited in Gregory, *Silence of Memory*, 85, 113.

9. Ibid., 184–191. To the present day virtually all of church-going England sings Parry's "Jerusalem" on Remembrance Day. Elgar orchestrated the hymn, and it is his arrangement which has traditionally closed the Last Night at the Proms since 1953.

10. Ibid., 138.

11. "Arrondissement," *L'avenir de Verdun*, 20 November 1924; cited in Daniel J. Sherman, *The Construction of Memory in Interwar France* (Chicago, 1999), 243.

12. See Master Gunnery Sergeant D. Michael Ressler, *Historical Perspective on the President's Own U.S. Marine Band: 200th Anniversary* (Washington, D.C., 1998), 26. The details of the ceremony are contained in a printed program, "Ceremonies Attending the Burial of an Unknown and Unidentified American Soldier Who Lost His Life During the World War."

13. Chief Plenty Coups had not fought in the Great War but had been a Crow scout for the U.S. Army during the "Indian Wars." Tara Browner has in a personal communication informed me that "the Eagle feathers on a War Bonnet are powerful symbols (rather than the bonnet itself). A War Bonnet is just another way to wear more Eagle feathers. One rule about Eagle feathers is that they are a special gift from Eagles, and as such should not touch the ground. A dropped feather is a cultural metaphor for a fallen warrior. Putting an entire War Bonnet on the ground probably symbolized a 'large number' of fallen warriors." Marshal Foch, commanding general of the Allied Forces, later traveled to Montana where he met Chief Plenty Coups and smoked a traditional pipe of peace. See Michael L. Tate, "From Scout to Doughboy: The National Debate Over Integrating American Indians into the Military, 1891–1918," *Western Historical Quarterly* 17, no. 4 (1986): 417.

14. Steven Lee Myers, "Laying to Rest the Last of the Unknown Soldiers," *The New York Times*, 3 May 1998, p. WK5.

15. Copyright 1926 by Leo Feist.

16. John H. Cushman Jr., "Remains of Vietnam Unknown are Disinterred," *The New York Times*, 15 May 1998, p. A17.

17. Dos Passos, *USA: 1919* (Boston, 1946), 408.

18. See Nicholas Jenkins's review of T. S. Eliot, *Inventions of the March Hare: Poems, 1909–1917* (New York, 1997), in *The New York Times Book Review*, 20 April 1997, pp. 14–15. More recently the issue served Pat Barker's 1990s review of the Great War in her trilogy, *Regeneration, The Eye in the Door,* and *The Ghost Road*. Many of Barker's perspectives are based upon the wartime clinical reports of nervous disorders, including especially those in Dr. W.H.R. Rivers's "The Repression of War Experience" (*Lancet*, 2 February 1918) and his posthumously published book, *Conflict and Dream* (London, 1923). See also Herbert James Hall, *War-time Nerves* (Boston and New York, 1918).

19. See also Janet Oppenheim, *"Shattered Nerves": Doctors, Patients, and Depression in Victorian England* (New York, 1991). For more on music's role in defining the fast pace of modern society, see Kern, *Culture of Time and Space,*

123–125; and Werner Sombart, "Technik und Kultur," *Archiv für Sozialwissenschaft und Sozialpolitik* 23 (1911): 342–347.

20. Of whom Gertrude Stein said, "All of you young people who served in the war. You are a lost generation. . . . You have no respect for anything. You drink yourselves to death." Actually it was a remark attributed to Gertrude Stein by Ernest Hemingway, who used it as an epigraph in *The Sun Also Rises* (1926).

21. See Cashman, *America Ascendant,* chap. 7, "Tales of the Jazz Age"; G. H. Knoles, *The Jazz Age Revisited: British Criticism of American Civilization During the 1920s* (New York, 1968); and Malcolm Cowley, *Fitzgerald and the Jazz Age* (New York, 1966).

22. See Watkins, *Pyramids at the Louvre,* chaps. 6 and 7.

23. See A. E. Gallatin, *Art and the Great War* (New York, 1919), for a reproduction.

24. See Brophy and Partridge, eds., *Long Trail,* 216, for more about the tune from *The Bing Boys* that was sounding on Sassoon's phonograph; and *The Great War: An Evocation in Music and Drama Through Recordings Made at the Time,* Pearl GEMM CD 9355, Track 13, for a recording of "Another little drink." A "Blighty one" was slang for "a wound that secured return to England." See the glossary in *The Wipers Times,* 358.

25. Siegfried Sassoon, "Dead Musicians: III," in *Collected Poems,* 92–93. Sassoon offers further testimony to the power of the gramophone at the front in *Memoirs of a Fox-Hunting Man,* 344, 352.

26. George Antheil, *Bad Boy of Music* (Garden City, N.Y., 1945), 5.

27. Antheil Collection, Library of Congress, Washington, D.C. For more on Antheil's dreams of a post-Armistice world, see Antheil, *Bad Boy of Music,* 20–21.

28. Note especially the haiku-like brevity of the second of a group of *Five Songs, 1919–1920, after Adelaide Crapsey.* Titled "Triad," it reads: "These be three silent things, / the falling snow, / the hour before the dawn, / the mouth of one just dead."

29. See Kerns, *Culture of Time and Space,* 297.

30. All of Antheil's quotations are taken from his unpublished letters and typescripts in the Library of Congress, as reported in Linda Whitesitt, *The Life and Music of George Antheil, 1900–1959* (Ann Arbor, 1983).

31. That Antheil had a strong sense of theater as well as a predilection for danger and disaster had already been signaled by a piano "sonata" called "The Sinking of the *Titanic,*" which he had composed at the tender age of thirteen and which he had premiered for the kids of a neighborhood club shortly after the tragic events of 14–15 April 1912.

32. Honegger's score served as the musical accompaniment to Abel Gance's film *La roue,* of 1920–1921.

33. See Whitesitt, *Life and Music of George Antheil.*

34. See Tim Mathews, "The Machine: Dada, Vorticism and the Future," in *The Violent Muse: Violence and the Artistic Imagination in Europe, 1910–*

1939, ed. Jana Howlett and Rod Mengham (Manchester, 1994); also Ezra Pound, *Antheil, and the Treatise on Harmony* (Chicago, 1927).

35. George Antheil, *Bad Boy of Music*, CD Albany Records, Troy 146, notes by Joseph Fennimore.

36. For a review of a 1998 revival of *Transatlantic* see Anthony Tommasini, "An Opera of Yesterday with the Cynicism of Today," *The New York Times*, 3 May 1998, p. AR23.

37. Antheil, "The Negro on the Spiral," 214. Stravinsky composed three ragtime pieces, *Piano Rag, Ragtime for Eleven Instruments*, and another as part of a set of three dances in *Histoire du soldat*.

38. Modris Eksteins, "The Cultural Legacy of the Great War," in *The Great War and the Twentieth Century*, ed. Jay Winter, Geoffrey Parker, and Mary R. Habeck (New Haven, 2000), 344.

39. See Oja, *Experiments in Modern Music*, especially chap. 11, "Organizing the Moderns," for a rich review.

CHAPTER 22. THE PERSISTENCE OF MEMORY

1. Its author had been killed in action shortly after the outbreak of hostilities, and his 1913 novel centering on the adventures of a seventeen-year-old boy became a literary sensation. The work haunted Ravel for years, and his reaction to it was conveyed in a letter to Lucien Garban, October 8, 1916; reprinted in Ravel, *Reader*, 178.

2. Ricciotto Canudo, *S.P. 503 Le Poème du Vardar suivi de la Sonate à Salonique* (Paris: Les Poètes de la Renaissance du Livre, 1923).

3. *Les feuillets d'art*, no. 2 (1919).

4. Ricciotto Canudo, *Music as a Religion of the Future* (London, 1913), 53. Here he boldly and unfavorably compared his native Italian music to the art of Claude Debussy; ibid., 40–41. See also Giovanni Dotoli, *Paris ville visage-du-monde chez Ricciotto Canudo et l'avant-garde italienne* (Fasano, 1984). Canudo, a friend of Abel Gance and Blaise Cendrars, was also one of the earliest dreamers for the cinema, which he felt offered a solution that only music had previously been able to suggest. See Steven Kramer and James Welsh, *Abel Gance* (Boston, 1978), 43.

5. See Giovanni Dotoli, ed., *Lo scrittore totale: Saggi su Ricciotto Canudo* (Fasano, 1986), 88.

6. The privately owned manuscript from which Arbie Ornstein made his edition utilized a 5/4 metric signature in the secondo part.

7. Constructions of this kind recall the war poets' "game of structure," Stravinsky's number games, Schoenberg's contemporary *Jakobsleiter* (1916–1917, which was to lead to his "Method of Composing with 12 Tones"), and Berg's fixation on the agency of Fliess numbers in setting a musical proportion. See chapter 22 for a possible Ravel-Berg-Fliess connection. Regarding numerology in *Frontispice* see Deborah Mawer, "Musical Objects and Machines,"

in *The Cambridge Companion to Ravel*, ed. Deborah Mawer (Cambridge, U.K., 2000), 52–53.

8. From the sixth century B.C. Pythagoras, a religious zealot, had sponsored the belief that numbers were divine with distinct ethical and psychological qualities. But the notion had also flourished in Islamic culture, and the Jewish mystical tradition of the Kabbala had delighted in assigning numbers to each letter of the Hebrew alphabet in the late Middle Ages, with the implication that the world's organization could be reduced to such numerologies. See Margaret Wertheim, "When 1 Plus 1 Makes Neither 2 Nor 11," *The New York Times*, 22 October 1995, 2E.

9. Ravel and Canudo's friendship spanned the period from 1905 to well into the 1920s. Ravel's awareness of Canudo's writing is attested to by the composer's library at Montfort l'Amaury, which contains several works by the poet with personal dedications, including *Le Livre de l'évolution* (1908), and *Combats d'Orient: Dardanelles-Salonique (1915–1916)* (Paris, 1917)· see Arbie Orenstein, *Ravel: Man and Musician* (New York, 1975), 17, n. 12. Like Ravel, Canudo had been intent on joining up from the moment that war broke out, but as he was an Italian citizen and Italy had not yet declared either war or its allegiance, Canudo was obliged to join the French Foreign Legion, where he organized an entire Italian regiment. This unit left for the French Argonne in late 1914, where Canudo was wounded in March 1915. When Italy finally entered the war shortly afterward on 24 May, Canudo's French regiment dissolved, but the Italian philosopher-poet, still flush with a sense of mission, joined the First Algerian Infantry Regiment, known as the "Zouaves," which left for the Vardar region in the Balkans in September 1915. See Michel Décaudin, *Canudo* (Rome, 1976), "Chronology," for the details of Canudo's wartime experience.

10. The movements were identified thus: "Volontés" [Capricious Actions] (1st movement—Allegro), "Atmosphères" (2nd movement—Andante), "Chevauchées" [Excursion on Horseback] (3rd movement— Allegretto), and "Défaillances" [Extinction] (4th movement—Scherzo).

11. Décaudin, *Canudo*, 13.

12. Luke Howard, "Canudo's Poetry and the War-Wounded Symbolism of Ravel's *Frontispice*," a seminar report, University of Michigan, April 1996, offered the suggestion that the first to enter may signify the meandering of the Vardar River itself.

13. Furthermore, a brand of sonic Cubism, evident from the time of Ravel's "La vallée des cloches," was at the ready to serve Ravel's symbolist purpose as well as Canudo's avid commitment to the concept of simultaneity in music. It was a topic, interestingly enough, that Canudo had lucidly promoted as editor of *Montjoie!* as early as 1913. See Watkins, *Pyramids at the Louvre*, chap. 9, for a discussion of parallels between analytic Cubism and developments in music and literature at this time.

14. Canudo, *Combats d'Orient*, 228; translation by Luke Howard.

15. "*La barre-à-mine est aussi puissante que la baguette de Moïse. / Et l'on a vu l'eau gicler / soudain, si haute si haute que les yeux / voyaient son sommet*

*resplendir dans le soleil. / En bas, elle rugissait dans ses mouvantes frises /
comme autour d'une vasque. / Elle encerclait le rocher sanglant de vermeil /
sous la fureur liquide, / offerte aux feux crépusculaires des cieux."* (The mine-
drill is as mighty as the rod of Moses. / And the water began to spurt, / suddenly, so high so high that the eyes / saw its crest glitter in the sun. / And below, it roared in its swirling motion as around the pool of a fountain. / It
encircled the rock, bloodied with vermillion / under the liquid fury, /offered to
the twilight fires of the sky.) *"Nous vivions sur une nappe d'EAU / souffrant
dans des journées en FEU. / Nous ne la savions pas. / Nous ne connaissions que
notre tourment / dans la fournaise macédonienne, / la soif et la chaleur des
fièvres paludéennes. / Dans l'immobilité vibrante d'ardeur, / un vain désir
d'eau ou de vent. / Et l'on s'acharnait sur la terre, en la frappant. Nous écar-
tions sa chair, pour nous en faire des tranchées, / sexe et matrice, pour y en-
gouffrer notre virilité."* (We lived on a sheet of WATER / suffering during the
days by FIRE. / We did not know it. / We were aware only of our torment / in
the Macedonian furnace, / the thirst and swelter of malarial fever. / In the
shimmering immobility of heat, / a vain desire for water or wind. / And we
toiled desperately at the ground, striking it. / We pushed aside its flesh, to make
trenches in it for us, / sex and womb, for this place swallows our virility.)
Translation by Luke Howard in "Canudo's Poetry."

16. Rex Lawson, "Maurice Ravel: *Frontispice* for Pianola," *The Pianola
Journal* 2 (1989): 35–38.

17. Ravel's remark brings to mind the fact that during the war years
Bartók's folk tune researches were drastically curtailed. It is one of the few observations that can be made regarding Bartók's relation to the war, since neither his music nor his correspondence during the period offer significant insight on the matter.

18. Complete original in *La revue musicale* (December 1938): 70–71;
reproduced in Marnat, *Maurice Ravel,* 416–417. English translation of the
league's notice is from Ravel, *Reader,* 169–174, which also includes the relevant correspondence. For another letter to Jean Marnold of 2 June 1916 regarding the league see *La revue musicale* (December 1938), translated in Ravel,
Reader, 69.

19. On 8 July 1916 Ravel wrote Florent Schmitt asking if he had yet read
the statutes of the league, advising him to read them for a good laugh; see Ravel,
Reader, 171 n. 2. See Marnat, *Maurice Ravel,* 418, for the original French.

20. On 16 August he wrote Marnold, relaying his caution in a related matter: "From the rue François Ier where I tried in vain to contact Schmitt, I was
in telephone communication with Lieutenant Cortot, chief of musical propaganda. He apprised me of the reshuffling of the *Société nationale* and urgently
requested that I take part on the board. I hesitated, believing that this society
was too . . . national. He completely understood my reluctance but assured me
that: Gabriel Fauré is the president; d'Indy is no more than a board member
with Schmitt, Roussel, Vuillermoz, etc. I therefore accepted, and we will see
how things work out." Original French in Marnat, *Maurice Ravel,* 418–419.

21. For more concerning the Wagner question in France see Prod'homme, "Music and Musicians," 157–159; translated by Otto Kinkeldey.

22. Cocteau, *Cocteau's World*, 310.

23. Perle, *Operas of Alban Berg*, 18, has correctly and explicitly compared *La valse* to Berg's treatment of the idea of the march in the last of his *Three Pieces for Orchestra:* "In spite of the fundamental differences in their respective musical idioms, the emotional climate of Berg's pre-war 'march macabre' is very similar to that of Ravel's post-war 'valse macabre.'"

24. See Donald Harris, "Ravel Visits the *Verein:* Alban Berg's Report," *Journal of the Arnold Schoenberg Institute* 3, no.1 (1979): 75–82.

25. The program was listed as follows: Ravel, *Gaspard de la nuit* (Edward Steuermann); Schoenberg, 5 songs, *The Book of the Hanging Garden*, op. 15 (Lindberg, Steuermann); Schoenberg, *Two New Piano Pieces* (from op. 23?; Steuermann); Webern, *Four Pieces for Violin and Piano* op. 7, no. 1 (Rudolf Kolisch, Steuermann); Berg, *Four Pieces for Clarinet and Piano*, op. 5 (K. Gaudriot, Steuermann); Ravel, *Valses nobles et sentimentales*, 2 pf, 4 hands (Maurice Ravel and Alfredo Casella); Schoenberg, "Jane Grey" (from op. 12; Bauer Pilecka, Bachrich); Ravel, *String Quartet in F major* (Feist Quartet). *The Valses nobles et sentimentales* listed on the program is surely a mistake, as we know that Ravel had fashioned a four-hand version of *La valse*, an orchestral work, for its first reading with Diaghilev, while the former was a work for solo piano with no need of a four-hand arrangement.

26. *Revue musicale* (December 1938): 70–71; translated in Orenstein, *Ravel*, 74.

27. "An Interview with Ravel," *La revue musicale* (March 1931): 193–194.

28. Fulcher, "Composer as Intellectual," 216.

29. Pierre-Daniel Templier, *Erik Satie* (Paris, 1932), 76; Gillmore, *Erik Satie*, 175; and Whiting, *Satie the Bohemian*, 412–413.

30. Francis Poulenc, *Mes amis et moi* (Paris, 1963), 179. This event signaled a breach between Ravel and Diaghilev that was never to heal despite a later commission, which eventually came to naught, for a ballet after a text by the Italian Futurist poet Francisco Cangiullo. See Marnat, *Maurice Ravel*, 422, for the terms that Ravel spelled out regarding this enigmatic commission.

31. Regarding the appeal of the waltz during this period see Messing, *Neoclassicism*, 90–93. Some half dozen waltzes can be attributed to Satie and eight to Stravinsky.

32. "The French Music Festival: An Interview with Ravel," *De Telegraaf*, 30 September 1922; reprinted in Ravel, *Reader*, 423–425.

33. See pp. 397–401 for a discussion of the Piano Concerto for the Left Hand.

34. Julien Tiersot, "La Musique française après la guerre," *Le ménestrel* 82, no. 53 (1920): 517–519.

35. For the text and a recording of this work in an accompanying cassette see Taylor, *"Musique pour tout le monde,"* 102–105.

36. In 1925 the music publisher Jacques Durand reviewed the Parisian concert scene during the war years, and especially the joint productions of the

Colonne and Lamoureux orchestras which had given a place of honor to French composers. He observed that during this period the public had been obliged to familiarize itself not only with works of the younger school of French composers but also those of the fin-de-siècle, which the rage for Wagner and the Russian school had driven from view. "It is evident," he said, "that one of the lessons of the war has been to increase the understanding and to appreciate the true musical values present in our country." See Jacques Durand, *Souvenirs d'un éditeur de musique* (Paris, 1925); cited in Marnat, *Maurice Ravel*, 440.

37. For more about Wiéner's career see Taylor, *"Musique pour tout le monde."*

38. Taylor, *"Musique pour tout le monde,"* 85.

39. Joining the testimonials for a fresh start were Constantin Brancusi's *Beginning of the World*, from about 1920, and Joan Miró's *Birth of the World*, from 1923–1924. Regarding Mihaud's ballet see Watkins, *Pyramids at the Louvre*, 130–131.

40. For more on Ravel and Beethoven see Orenstein, *Ravel*, 122–123.

41. Marnat, *Maurice Ravel*, 414. Continuing the comparison with his beloved Mozart, Ravel was also reported as saying that "Beethoven, who was less perfect, was also less dry." The reporter in the same interview of 1911 also had Ravel venturing the opinion that "there is more musical substance in Debussy's *Après-midi d'un faune* (which M. Ravel considers a masterpiece) than in the wonderfully immense Ninth Symphony by Beethoven." Ravel registered his view that one of the major faults of d'Indy's teaching was the fact that it was based on Beethoven, and he even went so far as to call the *Missa solemnis* an "inferior" work; see "Maurice Ravel's Opinion of Modern French Music," unsigned interview in *The Musical Leader* 21, no. 11 (1911): 7. See also Ravel, *Reader*, 409–410, for the complete text.

42. Between rehearsal numbers 63 and 66.

43. C. D. Jung, *Memories, Dreams, Reflections*, ed. Aniela Jaffé, trans. Richard and Clara Winston (New York, 1963), 203.

44. Marnat, *Maurice Ravel*, 457.

45. Cited in ibid., 604 n. 4.

46. Cited in ibid., 609.

47. For a broad consideration of the issue of collective and cultural memory see Jay Winter and Emmanuel Sivan, eds., *War and Remembrance in the Twentieth Century* (Cambridge, U.K., 1999), 23ff., "Setting the Framework," by Jay Winter and Emmanuel Sivan, and "Forms of Kinship and Remembrance in the Aftermath of the Great War," by Jay Winter.

48. Wittgenstein gave the first performance in Vienna. Both Marguerite Long and the Durand catalogue give the date as 27 November 1931, while Orenstein, *Ravel*, 239, cites 5 January 1932. See Marnat, *Maurice Ravel*, 776.

49. The reaction occurred despite the fact that Wittgenstein, who had exclusive rights for five years, had made several modifications to the original text. Ravel was infuriated from the start with the licenses taken by the pianist, and following a private performance in Vienna shortly after the premiere he de-

clared to Wittgenstein, "But that's not it at all." For more on the contentious exchange between Wittgenstein and Ravel see Long, *At the Piano with Ravel*, 58–59.

50. Marnat, *Maurice Ravel*, 652–653, offers the debatable assertion that Liszt's *Totentanz (Danse macabre)* for piano and orchestra provided an even more direct model in light of Ravel's opening and later pervasive bassoon motif, which he claims to be a rhythmicized inversion of the "Dies irae."

51. A sympathetic survey, "The Jazz Age in Paris 1914–1940," was organized in 1998–1999 by the Smithsonian Institution Exhibition Service and the American Library Association with the support of the National Endowment for the Humanities.

52. Cf. Fulcher, "Composer as Intellectual," 217.

53. Review by Henry Prunières in *La revue musicale* (February 1933): 128.

54. For an appreciation of this film and its imagery see Kramer and Welsh, *Abel Gance*, chap. 3, "Gance's Accusations Against War: *J'Accuse* (1919), *La Fin du Monde* (1929), *J'Accuse* (1938)." Gance explained that he had originally been inspired to make this film by Woodrow Wilson's message to the American Senate, and at the film's gala premiere at the Ritz Carlton in New York on 10 May 1921, Gance told his audience that he was dedicating the work to President Harding. See René Jeanne and Charles Ford, *Abel Gance* (Paris, 1963), 28 n. 24. Thus the film is more than an indictment of German culpability, embracing as it does pacifism, Wilsonian idealism, and a degree of French nationalism. See Kramer and Welsh, *Abel Gance*, 67.

55. The recapitulation brings with it recall of material from halfway through the opening cadenza, and if the material cited from the earlier *unbarred* cadenza is approximated as having initially occurred at measure 46, then the recapitulation also appears precisely at measure 460.

56. See Jarman, *Music of Alban Berg*, 228–230. The number 23 has been demonstrated to play an especially significant role in *Wozzeck*, the *Lyric Suite*, the *Chamber Concerto*, and *Lulu*. In a letter of 10 June 1915, for example, Berg had written to Schoenberg of his almost morbid fascination with the number "23" and commented upon a few examples from the recent past: "I received your first telegram (to go back to the beginning) on 4/6 (46 = 2 × 23). The telegram contained the number Berlin Südende 46 (2 × 23) 12/11 (12 + 11 = 23)." See Douglas Jarman, "Alban Berg, Wilhelm Fliess and the Secret Programme of the Violin Concerto," *The International Alban Berg Society Newsletter* 12 (1982): 5–11.

57. In one scene Gance's ironic juxtaposition of shots of the dead, crosses in cemeteries, and parades is accompanied by the sound of the "Marseillaise" and the "Chant du départ." See Kramer and Welsh, *Abel Gance*, 75; and especially Winter's *Sites of Memory*, chap. 1, "Homecomings: The Return of the Dead," for a telling critique of Gance's *J'accuse*.

58. See Claude Leroy, ed., *Blaise Cendrars et la guerre* (Paris, 1995), for a collection of essays.

59. Erich Korngold was the first composer to respond to a request fro

Wittgenstein in 1923 with a substantial concerto that lasts nearly twenty-eight minutes on the recent recording by Howard Shelley, piano, and the BBC Philharmonic (Chandos 9508). It is a brilliant and difficult work with occasional and extraordinary flashes of dissonance that enrich the typical Romantic landscape, familiar from Korngold's youth, whose influence extended to his career as a film composer in Hollywood. In light of Wittgenstein's later "revisions" of the Ravel concerto to accommodate his technical limitations, one can only imagine how Wittgenstein negotiated this challenging concerto, which he premiered in Vienna on 22 September 1924 with Korngold conducting. In 1939, with war clouds forming once again, Wittgenstein joined the mass exodus of musicians, artists, and scholars to the United States and settled in New York, where he became an American citizen in 1946 and died in 1961.

60. See Winter and Baggett, *The Great War*, 315, for a reproduction of Picasso's portrait.

61. Erich Maria Remarque, *All Quiet on the Western Front*, trans. A. W. Wheen (London, 1929).

62. Dreyer stated a preference for silence to the Baroque music supplied for his *La passion de Jeanne d'Arc* in the 1950s, though it cannot be determined that the film was screened silent in the late 1920s. See Anderson, *Music for Silent Films*, xlix n. 100. The film was re-released in both tape (Home Vision) and DVD (Criterion Collection) formats in fall 1999; see Peter M. Nichols, "In a Joan of Arc Season, One Telling is Timeless," *The New York Times*, 24 October 1999, p. AR32. Regarding Ravel's proposed project see "A Visit With Maurice Ravel," *De Telegraaf*, 31 March 1931, unsigned; reprinted in Ravel, *Reader*, 474.

63. M. D. Calvocoressi, "M. Ravel Discusses His Own Work," *Daily Telegraph*, 11 July 1931; reprinted in Ravel, *Reader*, 476. About *Jeanne d'Arc* see Ravel, *Reader*, 480–481.

64. Hélène Jourdan-Morhange, *Ravel et nous: L'homme, l'ami, le musicien* (Geneva, 1945); cited in Marnat, *Maurice Ravel*, 641.

65. See José Bruyr, "An Interview with Maurice Ravel," *Le guide du concert* 18 (1931): 39–41; reprinted in Ravel, *Reader*, 479–483.

66. Sherman, *Construction of Memory*, 331.

CHAPTER 23. PROPHECIES AND ALARMS

1. See the letter dated "Whitsun holidays 1916" and those of 6 February and 21 March 1918 in *Selected Letters of Paul Hindemith*, ed. and trans. Geoffrey Skelton (New Haven, 1995), 9–11, 17–19.

2. For Hindemith's views of his commanding officer see Hindemith, *Selected Letters*, 21.

3. Undated text signed by Hindemith. See Andres Briner, Dieter Rexroth, and Giselher Schubert, *Paul Hindemith: Leben und Werk in Bild und Text* (Zurich, 1988), 36. In a letter written on 5 September 1918, Hindemith angrily

offered a new perspective and a way station in the discovery of a theme that he was later to pursue: "By rights the eager warmongers and Vaterland party members should now be sent to hold the front themselves for a change. Of course I know nothing at all about politics, and for that reason have in the past few days become a keen social democrat. When the war ends, I too shall be inscribing Liberté, Égalité, Fraternité on my banner"; Hindemith, *Selected Letters*, 23.

4. Hindemith returned to his former position as concertmaster of the Frankfurt Opera, rejoined the Rebner String Quartet, and composed a cycle for mezzo soprano and string quartet titled *Melancholie*, which he dedicated to a friend, Karl Vöhler, who had fallen in battle.

5. For more on *Das Nusch-Nuschi* see Watkins, *Pyramids at the Louvre*, 313–314. See also Dennis Crockett, *German Post-Expressionism: The Art of the Great Disorder, 1918–1924* (University Park, Pa., 1999).

6. For a detailed discussion of the ramifications of the term "Neue Sachlichkeit" see Stephen Hinton, "Aspects of Hindemith's Neue Sachlichkeit," *Hindemith-Jahrbuch 1985* 14 (1985): 22–80; and Kurt Grosh, *Die Musik der Neuen Sachlichkeit* (Stuttgart, 1999).

7. Although Hindemith admitted that he had never visited an art gallery prior to a combined art and music evening on 8 December 1915 in which he participated, he was introduced at that time to Grünewald's masterpiece through an illustrated lecture delivered by Dr. Fried Lübbecke. Lübbecke was a Frankfurt art historian whose pianist wife would later perform in several Hindemith premieres, and he recorded in his book *Der Muschelsaal* the interest which the young violinist took in his slides at the time. Geoffrey Skelton, *Paul Hindemith: The Man Behind the Music* (London, 1975), 45–46.

8. Andrée Hayum, *The Isenheim Altarpiece: God's Medicine and the Painter's Vision* (Princeton, 1989), 3, 119.

9. Hayum, *Isenheim Altarpiece*, 125ff, 140.

10. Cork, *A Bitter Truth*, 303; and Hayum, *Isenheim Altarpiece*, 17–20. See also Dieter Scholz, "Das Triptychon *Der Krieg* von Otto Dix," in *Otto Dix: Bestandskatalog: Gemälde, Aquarelle, Pastelle, Zeichnungen, Holzschnitte, Radierungen, Lithographien* (Galerie der Stadt Stuttgart, 1991), 261–267. St. Sebastian, one of Christianity's earliest martyrs, "had long been invested with power to protect against the plague" and "came to be associated with the repelling and warding off of bodily harm and of sudden, devastating, and epidemic disease in the broad sense." In Owen's "Asleep" and Sassoon's "The Dug-out" St. Sebastian is actually to be found transposed to the trenches and dressed in khaki.

11. For more on early views of music's power to heal see Hayum, *Isenheim Altarpiece*, 44–47.

12. Siglind Bruhn, *The Temptation of Paul Hindemith: Mathis der Maler as a Spiritual Testimony* (Stuyvesant, N.Y., 1998), 289–290. For a comprehensive discussion of other musical citations and their symbolism within the context of the opera see 288–303.

13. Matthias Eberle, *World War I and the Weimar Artists: Dix, Grosz, Beckmann, Schlemmer* (New Haven, 1985), 52.

14. Two studies that centered on the rediscovery of the historical Grünewald were in preparation during this very period, and the author of one of them, Wilhelm Fraenger, director of the Institute of Art History at Heidelberg, whose *Matthias Grünewald in seinen Werken; ein physiognomischer Versuch* was published in 1936, was a personal friend of Hindemith. Another landmark study, Walter Zülch's *Der historische Grünewald*, was published in 1938.

15. "Otto Dix," in *The Oxford Companion to Twentieth-Century Art*, ed. Harold Osborne (Oxford, 1988).

16. Winter, *Sites of Memory*, 163. See also L. Tittel, *Zur Sache 8 — Der erste Weltkrieg, Käthe Kollwitz, Ernst Barlach, Wilhelm Lehmbruck, Otto Dix* (Hamburg, 1978).

17. An expression used by G. F. Hartlaub in 1923 to describe his newly coined term "Neue Sachlichkeit." For an informative investigation of the term see Jost Hermand, *"Neue Sachlichkeit:* Ideology, Lifestyle, or Artistic Movement?" in *Dancing on the Volcano: Essays on the Culture of the Weimar Republic*, ed. Thomas W. Kniesche and Stephen Brockmann (Columbia, S.C., 1994), 57–67.

18. Cork, *A Bitter Truth*, 272. For an extensive investigation of Dix's relation to the term see Brigid Barton, *Otto Dix and die Neue Sachlichkeit, 1918–1925* (Ann Arbor, 1981). For an informative discussion of the term in historical context with particular reference to music see Stephen Hinton, *"Neue Sachlichkeit,* Surrealism, *Gebrauchsmusik,"* in *A New Orpheus*, ed. Kim Kowlake (New Haven, 1986), 61–82.

19. Beyond the more obvious references to the Isenheim altarpiece, Dix relies upon a rich memory of historical prototypes from Cranach the Elder (for the left panel) and the post-Hellenistic Pasquino group (for the right panel) to more contemporary descriptions out of Remarque's *All Quiet on the Western Front*. See Scholz, "Triptychon *Der Krieg,"* 263, 266.

20. Cork, *A Bitter Truth*, 273.

21. See Stephanie Barron, ed., *Degenerate Art: The Fate of the Avant-Garde in Nazi Germany* (Los Angeles and New York, 1991).

22. Cork, *A Bitter Truth*, 273. Ultimately *The Trench* and Dix's equally disturbing *War Cripples* disappeared, and it is thought that both were burned the following year by the Nazis. See Dieter Schmidt, *Otto Dix im Selbstbildnis* (Berlin, 1981), 262.

23. For Furtwängler's open letter to the press of 4 December 1934, see James E. Paulding, "Mathis der Maler—The Politics of Music," *Hindemith-Jahrbuch* 5 (1976): 104–108.

24. The original German is reproduced along with an English translation by John P. Thomas and W. Richard Rieves in the program notes to the complete recording of the opera on Wergo 6255–2.

25. Dix was not the only artist who was drawn to the Isenheim Altarpiece at this time. Picasso affirmed that a suite of drawings made in the fall of 1932

on the subject of the *Crucifixion* were directly inspired by it. See Hayum, *Isenheim Altarpiece*, 141–143. Others indebted to Grünewald's example with respect to subject matter include Max Ernst's *Temptation of St. Anthony*. See Bruhn, *Temptation of Paul Hindemith*, 123–125.

26. See Keegan, *First World War*, 5–6; and Winter, *Sites of Memory* 92–93.

27. Max Beckmann became increasingly involved with the triptych form, producing nine in his later years. Yet none of his triptychs demonstrates an ascertainable affinity for the Isenheim altarpiece, and none includes a predella. See Peter Selz, *Max Beckmann* (New York, 1996), 8, 25–26, 56–57.

28. Otto Dix, interview in *Neues Deutschland*, December 1964, quoted in Schmidt, *Otto Dix*, 262, translated in Cork, *A Bitter Truth*, 305–306. For further discussion of Dix's remarks see Scholz, "Triptychon *Der Krieg*," 261.

29. See Klaus Lankheit, *Das Triptychon als Pathosformel* (Heidelberg, 1959), 84. For two twentieth-century triptychs by Wilhelm Sauter and Adolf Eiermann that invite comparison with Otto Dix, see ibid., plates 36 and 37. Sauter's triptych, a propaganda piece that stands as a clear retort to the defeatism of Dix, carries the following citation above its predella: "'Vergesset Sie nicht – Sie geben ihr Bestes für Deutschland." (Do not forget—They give their best for Germany.) Eiermann's figures, which date from the post-Hiroshima period, are skeletons in the triptych and predella alike, stripped of all flesh and intended as a memorial to the tragedy of 1945.

30. In 1946 Hindemith once again registered the residual impact of the Great War in his *When Lilacs Last in the Dooryard Bloom'd: A Requiem "For Those We Love."* It taps the hymn "For the Departed," whose text had been written in 1915 by the British Congregational minister William Charter Piggott and which had been adapted to a traditional Jewish melody in 1919. For the fascinating details behind this story see Kim H. Kowalke, "For Those We Love: Hindemith, Whitman, and 'An American Requiem,'" *Journal of the American Musicological Society* 50, no. 1 (1997), 133–174.

31. William Bolcom, "His Songs Were a Soundtrack for the Jazz Age," *The New York Times*, 27 September 1998, pp. AR34, 38, on the occasion of Youmans's centennial.

32. Shortly thereafter Dmitri Shostakovitch served up Youmans's "Tea for Two" in his own "Tahiti Trot."

33. Adding to the impact of Dix's *Metropolis* was the release of Fritz Lang's classic film of the same name only shortly before in January 1927, following two years of a vigorous pre-release advertising campaign. See Dietrich Neumann, "The Urbanistic Vision in Fritz Lang's *Metropolis*," in *Dancing on the Volcano: Essays on the Culture of the Weimar Republic*, ed. Thomas W. Kniesche and Stephen Brockmann (Columbia, S.C., 1994), 143–144. Regarding the relationship of old German masters to the *Metropolis* triptych see Hanne Bergius, "Dix-Dionysos in der Kälate. Spuren von Mythen und Alten Meistern im Großstadt-Triptychon," in *Otto Dix: Bestandskatalog*, 219–227; and Birgit Schwarz, "'Otto Hans Baldung Dix' malt die Großstadt: Zur Rezeption der altdeutschen Malerei," in *Otto Dix: Bestandskatalog*, 229–238.

34. See chapter 13.

35. See Beeke Sell Tower, "'Ultramodern and Ultraprimitive': Shifting Meaning in the Imagery of Americanism in the Art of Weimar Germany," in *Dancing on the Volcano: Essays on the Culture of the Weimar Republic,* ed. Thomas W. Kniesche and Stephen Brockmann (Columbia, S.C., 1994), 93–95; and Cornelius Partsch, "Hannibal ante Portas: Jazz in Weimar," in *Dancing on the Volcano: Essays on the Culture of the Weimar Republic,* ed. Thomas W. Kniesche and Stephen Brockmann (Columbia, S.C., 1994), 110–111.

36. The emphasis given to the mythic trumpet- or trombone-like instrument on the left side of the central panel also reminds us that its essential sonority and style was one that Hindemith not only used in the 1920s but also was never to forget. Many years later, in 1943, newly arrived in America and ensconced as a professor of composition at Yale University, Hindemith recalled its seductive voice as a jazz inflection in his *Symphonic Metamorphosis on Themes of Carl Maria von Weber.* In a movement with a convoluted cultural pedigree titled "Turandot," Hindemith provided a gloss on a Chinese tune previously used by a German compatriot, Weber, and subjected it to an American stylization.

37. Tower, "Ultramodern and Ultraprimitive," 92–95.

38. See Susan C. Cook, "*Der Zar lässt sich photographieren:* Weill and Comic Opera," in *A New Orpheus: Essays on Kurt Weill,* ed. Kim Kowalke (New Haven, 1986), 83–101; and Susan C. Cook, *Opera for a New Republic: The Zeitopern of Krenek, Weill, and Hindemith* (Ann Arbor, 1988).

39. That the Great War remained a timely issue on numerous fronts in 1927 is corroborated by the fact that the motion picture *America Over There* was also produced in that year. Shot by the U.S. Army Signal Corp, it was the first officially released motion picture record of America's part in World War I. The claim was made that every frame was genuine and taken under actual combat conditions in France.

40. Gershwin's *Strike Up the Band!* (1927) includes "The Man I Love," "Oh, This Is Such a Lovely War," "Come-Look-at-the-War Choral Society," "Military Dancing Drill," "Homeward Bound," "The Girl I Love (reprise)," "The War That Ended War." It has been recorded on Elektra Nonesuch CD 79273–2.

41. Ben Brantley, "Jingoism Parodied: Gershwins' War of '27," *The New York Times,* 14 February 1998, p. A22.

42. Even the black soldiers of the 369th Regiment, who suffered constant humiliation from white American officers and soldiers and whose considerable success on the battlefield was ignored by almost everyone except the French government, who awarded them the Croix de Guerre, never wavered in their determination to fight for Old Glory and to lift the morale of all soldiers by playing their hearts out.

43. In the postwar period propaganda efforts attempted to adjust realities on numerous fronts. Between 1923 and 1927, for example, the German Foreign Ministry launched a campaign to enlist the aid of the United States in creating

a favorable public opinion on reparation, disarmament, and especially the so-called war-guilt question contained in Article 231 of the Treaty of Versailles. See Herman Wittgens, "Senator Owen, the Schuldreferat, and the Debate over War Guilt in the 1920s," in *Forging the Collective Memory,* ed. Keith Wilson (Providence, 1996), 128–150.

44. The latter had been composed in 1924, sung by Adele Astaire in the pre-Broadway tryout for the Broadway musical, *Lady, Be Good!,* and removed because the show was too long. "The Man I Love" had been published separately, however, and had already become a hit in London and Paris before being reintroduced in *Strike Up the Band!* Tommy Krasker, "Two Strikes, Two Hits, and One 'Man' Out," notes to Elektra Nonesuch CD 79273-2.

45. For the complete text of the British soldier's song "Oh, It's a Lovely War," see Dolph, *"Sound Off!"* 143–144; and for a recording see Pearl GEMM CD 9355. A British musical "Oh What a Lovely War," by Joan Littlewood, which includes vintage songs from the Great War, premiered 19 March 1963 at the Theatre Workshop at Theatre Royal in London.

46. With respect to talk of those at home who were knitting sweaters and stitching shirts. For the text of "Sister Susie's Sewing Shirts for Soldiers," see Vogel, *World War I Songs,* 361.

47. In "Homeward Bound," the references are to "Gee, But It's Great to Get Back Home Again" (1919), "Oh How I Hate to Get Up in the Morning" (1918), "There's a Long, Long Trail A-Winding" (1914), and "Little Grey Home in the West" (1911).

48. Vera Krasovskaya, *Nijinsky,* trans. John E. Bowlt (New York, 1979), 347.

CHAPTER 24. UNFINISHED BUSINESS

1. Quoted in the *New York Times,* 16 February 1930.

2. Hans Moser, *Geschichte der deutschen Musik,* 2d ed., 3 vols. (Stuttgart, 1920–1930), 3: 467, 469–470; cited and translated in Potter, *Most German of the Arts,* 3–4.

3. Fussell, ed., *Norton Book of Modern War,* 23.

4. Wallach, "Retreat of French Art," pp. AR1, 38. See, however, the response by Rubin, "Challenging a Thesis," AR4, and Wallach's rejoinder.

5. Francis M. Naumann, "New York Dada: Style with a Smile," in *Making Mischief: Dada Invades New York,* ed. Francis Naumann and Beth Venn (New York, 1996), 11.

6. See Oja, *Experiments in Modern Music,* chap. 11, "Organizing the Moderns," for a rich discussion of the events of this period.

7. See Howard Pollack, "Copland's Hope for American Music," *Institute for Studies in American Music Newsletter* 29, no. 1 (1999): 1, 2, 12, as well as the same author's *Aaron Copland: The Life and Work of an Uncommon Man* (New York, 1999); and David Denby, "The Gift to Be Simple," *The New Yorker,* 13 December 1999, pp. 102–111.

8. Note the argument in Rosen, *Schoenberg*, that, despite the composer's denials, Schoenberg's music of the 1920s was in its essentials a part of the Neoclassicist movement. See also Messing, *Neoclassicism*.

9. See Rosa Newmarch's preview, "A Requiem for the Allied Heroes," *The Musical Times*, 1 November 1917, pp. 496–497.

10. The work invoked quarter-tones, *Klangfarben* techniques borrowed from Schoenberg's *Five Orchestral Pieces*, and occasional proto-Minimalist gestures. In the main, however, the work was based on conservative, pandiatonic, chordal harmonies that were compared to Vaughan Williams. See Malcolm MacDonald, *John Foulds and His Music* (White Plains, 1989), 30–31, 36.

11. MacDonald, *John Foulds*, 28–37; and Samuel Hynes, *A War Imagined* (London, 1990), 275–276.

12. Jay Winter, "Britain's 'Lost Generation' of the First World War," *Population Studies* 31, no. 3 (1977): 457–465.

13. Jelavich, "German Culture in the Great War," 54.

14. See Calvin Tomkins, *Marcel Duchamp: A Biography* (New York, 1996). Back in Europe Hugo Ball recorded that the specific appeal of the mask for the Dada theater resided in "the fact that they embodied not human, but over-life-size characters and passion. The horrors of the day, the paralyzing background of things, were made visible." Hennring Rischbieter, *Art and the Stage in the Twentieth Century* (Greenwich, Conn., 1968), 164.

15. See also Francis M. Naumann and Beth Venn, eds., *Making Mischief: Dada Invades New York* (New York, 1996), for evidence of Dada's embrace of humor and laughter in America as an escape from the reality of the European conflict.

16. For lively readings of these pieces as Surrealist art see Albright, *Untwisting the Serpent*, chap. 11, "Surrealism (Music)."

17. See Annette Becker, "The Avant-garde, Madness and the Great War," *Journal of Contemporary History* 35, no. 1 (2000), 71.

18. Albright, *Untwisting the Serpent*, 199.

19. Poulenc approached the sonata idea from the last year of the war through the decade of the 1920s with what can only be judged as a grand compulsion. See Carl B. Schmidt, *The Music of Francis Poulenc (1899–1963): A Catalogue* (Oxford, 1995), 525–28, appendix 2, "Chronological list of compositions."

20. See Watkins, *Pyramids at the Louvre*, 104–108, regarding Poulenc's *Rapsodie nègre*.

21. Despite ongoing examples from Russia in the symphonies of Shostakovich, whose retro posture was typically explained away at the time by pointing to restrictive socio-political forces. See Joseph Horowitz, "A Moral Beacon Amid the Darkness Of a Tragic Era," *The New York Times*, 6 February 2000, p. AR1.

22. Or the anonymous fifteenth-century "Dirge" ("Fire and fleet and candle-lighte, / And Christe receive thy saule") and William Blake's "Elegy" on England's royal house ("O Rose, thou art sick! / The invisible worm / That

flies in the night, / In the howling storm, / Has found out thy bed / Of crimson joy: / And his dark secret love / Does thy life destroy.").

23. See Mervyn Cooke, *Britten: War Requiem* (Cambridge, U.K., 1996), 49–52; and Malcolm Boyd, "Britten, Verdi and the Requiem," *Tempo* 86 (1968): 2–6.

24. The legendary instability of the tritone and its struggle to find or resist resolution had once again become the concern of many composers in the postwar years, and its potential for encouraging dialectic along both formal and narrative paths had already been dramatically demonstrated in Hindemith's symphonic extracts from *Mathis der Maler* and theoretically argued in his *The Craft of Musical Composition*, trans. Arthur Mendel (New York, 1942). See Watkins, *Soundings*, 342–347, for a discussion.

25. Skriabin's use of C and F♯ as antipodal symbols of earth and heaven come to mind, especially in light of Britten's final resolution on F, which Skriabin associated with blood red!

26. Owen, *Collected Poems*.

27. Fussell, *The Great War*, 298.

28. The larger manifestations of the question are, of course, complex and differ from society to society and age to age. For some relevant perspectives see Robert A. Nye, *Masculinity and Male Codes of Honor in Modern France* (New York, 1993); Harry Oosterhuis, "Introduction," in *Homosexuality and Male Bonding in Pre-Nazi Germany: The Youth Movement, the Gay Movement, and Male Bonding before Hitler's Rise: Original Transcripts from "Der Eigene," the First Gay Journal in the World*, ed. Harry Oosterhuis, trans. Hubert Kennedy (New York, 1991); and Harry Oosterhuis, "Male Bonding and Homosexuality in German Nationalism," *Journal of Homosexuality* 22, no. 1 (1991), 241–263.

29. For a comprehensive and articulate study of the whole issue of modern masculinity, both as societal mirror and its specific relation to war, see George L. Mosse, *The Image of Man: The Creation of Modern Masculinity* (Oxford, 1996), particularly chap. 6, "Warriors and Socialists," and the same author's *Nationalism and Sexuality* (New York, 1985), particularly chap. 6, "War, Youth, and Beauty."

30. As a young composer Britten had wanted to go to Vienna to study with Alban Berg, although this never came to pass.

31. Ernest Hemingway, *A Farewell to Arms* (New York, 1929), chap. 27.

32. Winter, *Sites of Memory*, 227. It is an argument readily applicable to war memorials that were constructed in the post-Armistice period. See also Mosse, *Fallen Soldier*, 100ff.

33. Mosse, *Image of Man*, 107, placed the issue in rare focus by observing: "The crisis of masculinity at the fin de siècle had not changed but stiffened the ideal of normative manhood. Whatever challenge remained, it was temporarily drowned out by the August days of 1914 as European youth rushed to the colors. The Great War was a masculine event, in spite of the role it may h played in encouraging the greater independence of women"; see also 110–

Also see Mosse, *Nationalism and Sexuality;* Wohl, *Generation of 1914,* 100ff; and Ferguson, *Pity of War,* 462, passim.

34. From "The Parable of the Old Man and the Young," in Wilfred Owen, *Collected Poems,* 42. Regarding Owen's further indebtedness to Biblical metaphors, see Wilfred Owen, *Collected Letters,* ed. Harold Owen and John Bell (New York and Toronto, 1967), 534.

35. Leed, *No Man's Land,* 58. On the issue of "Soldiers Bathing" see Fussell, *Great War,* 199ff.

36. A similar imagery following death can be found in Elgar's *Dream of Gerontius* at the beginning of Part Two, where the Soul of Gerontius speaks: "I went to sleep; and now I am refreshed. A strange refreshment; for I feel in me an inexpressive lightness, and a sense of freedom, as I were at length myself. And ne'er had been before. How still it is! I hear no more the busy beat of time; No, nor my fluttering breath, nor struggling pulse; Nor does one moment differ from the next."

37. See Fussell, *The Great War,* 21–22, for an extended glossary of equivalents.

Selected Bibliography

Abbate, Carolyn. "Outside Ravel's Tomb." *Journal of the American Musicological Society* 52, no. 3 (1999): 465–530.

Abrams, Ray H. *Preachers Present Arms: A Study of the War-time Attitudes and Activities of the Churches and the Clergy in the United States, 1914–1918.* Philadelphia, 1933.

Adams, Michael C. *The Great Adventure: Male Desire and the Coming of World War I.* Bloomington, 1990.

Albright, Daniel. *Untwisting the Serpent: Modernism in Music, Literature, and Other Arts.* Chicago, 2000.

Aldrich, Richard. *Concert Life in New York, 1902–1923.* New York, 1941.

Anderson, Gillian B. *Music for Silent Films, 1894–1929: A Guide.* Washington, D.C., 1988.

Anderson, Robert. *Elgar.* London, 1993.

Ansermet, Ernest. "The Man and His Work—Igor Stravinsky—His First String Quartet." *Musical Courier,* 25 November 1915, p. 41.

Antcliffe, Herbert. "The Effect of the War on English Choral Music." *The Musical Quarterly* 6, no. 3 (1920): 342–353.

Antheil, George. *Bad Boy of Music.* Garden City, N.Y., 1945.

———. "The Negro on the Spiral or a Method of Negro Music." In *Negro,* edited by Nancy Cunard. New York, 1970.

Apollonio, Umbro, ed. *Futurist Manifestos.* Translated by Caroline Tisdall. London, 1973.

Applegate, Celia. "How German Is It? Nationalism and the Idea of Serious Music in the Early Nineteenth Century." *Nineteenth-Century Music* 21, no. 3 (1998): 274–296.

———. *A Nation of Provincials: The German Idea of Heimat.* Berkeley, 1990.

Arnold, Ben. *Music and War: A Research and Information Guide.* New York, 1993.

Aschengreen, Erik. *Jean Cocteau and the Dance.* Copenhagen, 1986.

Aubitz, Shawn, and Gail F. Stern. "Americans All! Ethnic Images in World War I Posters." *Prologue* 19 (1987): 41–45.

Auclert, Jean Pierre. *La Grande guerre des crayons: Les nois dessins de la propagande en 1914–18.* Paris, 1981.

Audoin-Rouzeau, Stéphane. "Brotherhood in the Trenches?" In *Men at War, 1914–1918: National Sentiment and Trench Journalism in France during the First World War,* translated by Helen McPhail. Providence, 1992.

———. *L'enfant de l'ennemi, 1914–1918: Viol, avortement, infanticide pendant la Grande Guerre.* Paris, 1995.

———. *La guerre des enfants, 1914–1918: Essai d'histoire culturelle.* Paris, 1993.

———. *Men at War, 1914–1918: National Sentiment and Trench Journalism in France during the First World War.* Translated by Helen McPhail. Providence, 1992.

Auner, Joseph. "Schoenberg's Handel Concerto." *Journal of the American Musicological Society* 49, no. 2 (1996): 284–285.

Badel, J. J. "The Strange Case of Dr. Karl Muck, Who Was Torpedoed by *The Star-Spangled Banner* during World War I." *High Fidelity* 10, no. 10 (1970).

Badger, Reid. *A Life in Ragtime: A Biography of James Reese Europe.* New York, 1995.

Bantock, Granville. *HB: Aspects of Havergal Brian.* Edited by Jürgen Schaarwächter. Aldershot, 1997.

Barber, Cecil. "Battle Music," *The Musical Times* 4, no. 1 (1918): 25–26.

Barnhisel, Greg. "Marketing Modernism in America During the Great War: The Case of Ezra Pound." In *World War I and the Cultures of Modernity,* edited by Douglas Mackaman and Michael Mays. Jackson, Miss., 2000.

Barton, Brigid. *Otto Dix and die Neue Sachlichkeit, 1918–1925.* Ann Arbor, 1981.

Baudelaire, Charles. "The Painter of Modern Life." In *L'art romantique.* Paris, 1869. Reprinted in *Selected Writings on Art and Artists.* Translated by P. E. Charvet. Harmondsworth, 1972.

Bazin, Nancy Topping, and Jane Hamovit Lauter. "Woolf's Keen Sensitivity to War." In *Virginia Woolf and War: Fiction, Reality, and Myth,* edited by Mark Hussey. Syracuse, 1991.

Beaumont, Antony. *Busoni the Composer.* Bloomington, 1985.

Becker, Annette. "The Avant-garde, Madness and the Great War." *Journal of Contemporary History* 35, no. 1 (2000): 71–84.

———. "The Churches and the War." In *The Great War and the French People,* edited by Jean-Jacques Becker, translated by Arnold Pomerans. New York, 1986.

———. "Les dévotions des soldats catholiques pendant la grande guerre." In *Chrétiens dans la première guerre mondiale: Actes des journées tenues à Amiens et à Péronne, les 16 mai et 22 juillet 1992,* edited by Nadine-Josette Chaline. Paris, 1993.

————. *La guerre et la foi: De la mort à la mémoire, 1914–1930*. Paris, 1994.

————. *War and Faith: The Religious Imagination in France, 1914–1930*. Translated by Helen McPhail. Oxford, 1998.

Becker, Annette, and Philippe Rivé. *Monuments de mémoire, monuments aux morts de la Grande Guerre*. Paris, 1991.

Becker, Jean-Jacques, ed. *The Great War and the French People*. Translated by Arnold Pomerans. New York, 1986.

Becker, Jean-Jacques, and Stéphane Audoin-Rouzeau, eds. *Les Sociétés européenes et la guerre de 1914–1918: Actes du colloque organisé à Nanterre et à Amiens du 8 au 11 décembre 1988*. Nanterre, 1990.

Bedborough, George. *Arms and the Clergy, 1914–1918*. London, 1934.

Bellaigue, Camille. *Propos de musique et de guerre*. Paris, 1917.

Beller, Steven. "The Tragic Carnival: Austrian Culture in the First World War." In *European Culture in the Great War: The Arts, Entertainment, and Propaganda, 1914–1918*, edited by Aviel Roshwald and Richard Stites. Cambridge, U.K., 1999.

Belting, Hans. *The Germans and Their Art: A Troublesome Relationship*. New Haven, 1998.

Benstock, Shari. *No Gifts from Chance: A Biography of Edith Wharton*. New York, 1994.

Berg, Alban. *Alban Berg: Letters to His Wife*. Edited and translated by Bernard Grun. New York, 1971.

Bergius, Hanne. "Dix-Dionysos in der Kälate. Spuren von Mythen und Alten Meistern im Grosstadt-Triptychon." In *Otto Dix: Bestandskatalog: Gemälde, Aquarelle, Pastelle, Zeichnungen, Holzschnitte, Radierungen, Lithographien*. Galerie der Stadt Stuttgart, 1991.

Berlin, Irving. *Early Songs III: 1913–1914*. Edited by Charles Hamm. Madison, 1994.

Bernhardi, Friedrich von. *Germany and the Next War*. Translated by Allen H. Powles. London, 1912.

Bernstein, Richard. "How the Little Things Add Up to Horror." *The New York Times*, 11 November 1998, p. B8.

Berry, Jason. "White Men Can Jam." *The New York Times Book Review*, 11 July 1999, p. 32.

Bierce, Ambrose. *The Devil's Dictionary*. New York, 1935.

Bierley, Paul E. *John Philip Sousa, American Phenomenon*. Columbus, 1986.

Binneveld, Hans. *From Shell Shock to Combat Stress: A Comparative History of Military Psychiatry*. Translated by John O'Kane. Amsterdam, 1997.

Blakey, George T. *Historians on the Homefront: American Propagandists for the Great War*. Lexington, 1970.

Blanche, Jacques Émile. *Cahiers d'un artiste*. 6 vols. Paris, 1915–1917.

————. *Portraits of a Lifetime*. London, 1937.

Blanche, Jacques-Émile, and Jean Cocteau. *Correspondance*. Paris, 1993.

Block, Adrienne Fried. "Dvořák's Long American Reach." In *Dvořák in America, 1892–1895*, edited by John C. Tibbetts. Portland, 1993.

Blum, Cinzia Sartini. *The Other Modernism: F. T. Marinetti's Futurist Fiction of Power.* Berkeley, 1996.

Bodnar, John. *Remaking America: Public Memory, Commemoration, and Patriotism in the Twentieth Century.* Princeton, 1992.

Bodnar, John, ed. *Bonds of Affection: Americans Define Their Patriotism.* Princeton, 1996.

Bois, Jean-Pierre. *Histoire des 14 juillet 1789–1919.* Rennes, 1991.

Bolcom, William. "His Songs Were a Soundtrack for the Jazz Age." *The New York Times,* 27 September 1998, pp. AR34, 38.

Bonadeo, Alfredo. *D'Annunzio and the Great War.* Madison, N.J., 1995.

Bonds, Mark Evan. *After Beethoven: Imperatives of Originality in the Symphony.* Cambridge, Mass., 1996.

Bonnaud, Dominique. *Chants de Bataille.* Paris, 1914.

Boorman, Derek. *At the Going Down of the Sun: British First World War Memorials.* York, 1988.

Botrel, Théodore. *Les chants du bivouac.* Paris, 1915.

Botstein, Leon. "Innovation and Nostalgia: Ives, Mahler, and the Origins of Twentieth-Century Modernism." In *Charles Ives and the Classical Tradition,* edited by Geoffrey Block and J. Peter Burkholder. New Haven, 1996.

Bourke, Joanna. *Dismembering the Male: Men's Bodies, Britain and the Great War.* London, 1996.

———. *An Intimate History of Killing: Face-to-Face Killing in Twentieth-Century Warfare.* London, 1999.

Bourne, Randolph. "The War and the Intellectuals." In *World War I at Home: Readings on American Life, 1914–1920,* edited by David F. Trask. New York, 1970.

Boutroux, Émile. "L'Allemagne et la guerre; lettre de M. Émile Boutroux." *Revue des deux mondes* 23 (1914): 390–394.

Boxer, Sarah. "Pulling Strings: The Geppetto Effect." *The New York Times,* 17 January 1998, pp. YA13–15.

Boyd, Malcolm. "Britten, Verdi and the Requiem." *Tempo* 86 (1968): 2–6.

Boyer, D. Royce. "The American Expeditionary Forces, General Headquarters Band, Victory Loan Tour—1919." *Journal of Band Research* 26, no. 1 (1990): 44–51.

Boyer, Nicole Lucien. *La chanson des poilus: Recueil des chansons et poémes dits par l'auteur en France et en Macédoine aux armées de la République.* Paris, 1918.

Brancour, René. *La Marseillaise et Le chant du départ.* Paris, 1916.

Brantley, Ben. "Jingoism Parodied: Gershwins' War of '27." *The New York Times,* 14 February 1998, p. A22.

Breitenacher, Martin. *Das Alpenkorps, 1914–18.* Berlin, 1939.

Brenet, Michel. "Les 'Tombeaux' en musique." *La revue musicale* 3 (1903): 568–575, 631–638.

Briner, Andres, Dieter Rexroth, and Giselher Schubert. *Paul Hindemith: Leben und Werk in Bild und Text.* Zurich, 1988.

Britten, Thomas A. *American Indians in World War I: At Home and at War.* Albuquerque, 1997.

Brophy, John, and Eric Partridge, eds. *The Long Trail: What the British Soldier Sang and Said in the Great War of 1914–18.* London, 1965.

———. *Songs and Slang of the British Soldier: 1914–1918.* London, 1930.

Brown, Malcolm. *The Imperial War Museum Book of the Somme.* London, 1996.

———. *Tommy Goes to War.* London, 1978.

Brown, Malcolm, and Shirley Seaton. *Christmas Truce.* London, 1984.

Broyles, Michael. "Charles Ives and the American Democratic Tradition." In *Charles Ives and His World*, edited by J. Peter Burkholder. Princeton, 1996.

Bruhn, Siglind. *The Temptation of Paul Hindemith: Mathis der Maler as a Spiritual Testimony.* Stuyvesant, N.Y., 1998.

Brunschwig, Chantal, Louis-Jean Calvet, and Jean-Claude Klein. *100 ans de chanson française.* Paris, 1972.

Bruntz, George G. *Allied Propaganda and the Collapse of the German Empire in 1918.* New York, 1938.

Buitenhuis, Peter. *The Great War of Words: British, American, and Canadian Propaganda and Fiction, 1914–1923.* Vancouver, 1987.

Bullard, Truman C. "The First Performance of Igor Stravinsky's *Sacre du Printemps*," Ph.D. diss., Eastman School of Music, 1970.

Burkholder, J. Peter. *All Made of Tunes: Charles Ives and the Uses of Musical Borrowing.* New Haven, 1995.

———. "Ives and the European Tradition." In *Charles Ives and the Classical Tradition*, edited by Geoffrey Block and J. Peter Burkholder. New Haven, 1996.

———. "Ives and the Four Musical Traditions." In *Charles Ives and His World*, edited by J. Peter Burkholder. Princeton, 1996.

Burleigh, H. T. *The Spirituals of H. T. Burleigh.* Melville, N.Y., 1984.

Busoni, Ferruccio. *Ferruccio Busoni: Selected Letters.* Edited by Antony Beaumont. London, 1987.

Caballero, Carlo. "Patriotism or Nationalism? Fauré and the Great War." *Journal of the American Musicological Society* 52, no. 3 (1999): 593–625.

Cadogan, Mary. *Women and Children First: The Fiction of Two World Wa* London, 1978.

Caesar, Adrian. *Taking It Like a Man: Suffering, Sexuality, and the War Po Brooke, Sassoon, Owen, Graves.* New York, 1993.

Cahill, Lisa Sowle. *Love Your Enemies: Discipleship, Pacifism, and Just Theory.* Minneapolis, 1994.

Calude, Ribouillot. *La musique au fusil avec les poilus dans la grande g* Paris, 1996.

Calvocoressi, M. D. "M. Ravel Discusses His Own Work." *Daily Tele* 11 July 1931.

Campbell, Craig. *Reel America and World War I: A Comprehensive Fil phy and History of Motion Pictures in the United States, 1914–1920.* Jefferson, N.C., 1985.

Campbell, Patrick. *Siegfried Sassoon: A Study of the War Poetry.* Jefferson, N.C., 1999.

Camurat, Diane. "American Indians in the Great War: Real and Imagined." Master's thesis, University of Paris VII, 1993. (Online at raven.cc.ukans.edu/ ~kansite/ww_one/comment/camurat1.hml.)

Canudo, Ricciotto. *Combats d'Orient: Dardanelles-Salonique (1915–1916).* Paris, 1917.

————. *Music as a Religion of the Future.* London, 1913.

Carlston, Erin G. *Thinking Fascism: Sapphic Modernism and Fascist Modernity.* Stanford, 1998.

Carter, Joseph. *1918: Year of Crisis, Year of Change.* Englewood Cliffs, N.J., 1968.

Casella, Alfredo. *Music in My Time: The Memories of Alfredo Casella.* Translated and edited by Spencer Norton. Norman, Okla., 1955.

————. *Stravinski.* Brescia, 1947.

Casella, Georges. "La Musique et le Sport, II: Henri Deutsch de la Meurthe." *Revue musicale, S.I.M.* 7, no. 6 (1912): 79ff.

Cashman, Sean Dennis. *America Ascendant.* New York, 1998.

Chaline, Nadine-Josette. *Chrétiens dans la première guerre mondiale.* Paris, 1993.

Chalupt, René. *Ravel au miroir de ses lettres.* Paris, 1956.

Chauncey, George. "Christian Brotherhood or Sexual Perversion? Homosexual Identities and the Construction of Sexual Boundaries in the World War I Era." In *Same Sex: Debating the Ethics, Science, and Culture of Homosexuality,* edited by John Corvino. Lanham, Md., 1997.

Cheatham, Kitty. *Words and Music of "The Star-spangled Banner" Oppose the Spirit of Democracy which the Declaration of Independence Embodies.* N.p., 1918.

Chevalier, Maurice. *Ma route et mes chansons.* Paris, 1950.

Chickering, Roger. *Imperial Germany and the Great War, 1914–1918.* Cambridge, U.K., 1998.

Child, Peter. *Modernism.* London, 2000.

Christian, Shirley. "In Kansas City, Few Trains, but New Life in the Station." *The New York Times,* 15 November 1999, p. B1.

————. "World War I Museum's New Drive on the Home Front." *The New York Times,* 31 March 1998, p. B2.

Clarke, Ida Clyde Gallagher. *American Women and the World War.* New York, 1918.

Cleveland, Les. *Dark Laughter: War in Song and Popular Culture.* Westport, Conn., 1994.

————. "Singing Warriors: Popular Songs in Wartime." *Journal of Popular Culture* 28 (1994): 155–175.

Closson, Ernest. *L'élément flamand dans Beethoven*. Brussels, 1928.

Cobb, Irvin S. "To War in a Taxicab." In *Paths of Glory: Impressions of War Written At and Near the Front*. New York, 1915.

———. "Young Black Joe." *The Saturday Evening Post*, August 1918, pp. 7–8, 77–78.

Coben, Stanley. "A Study in Nativism: The American Red Scare of 1919–1920." In *Causes and Consequences of World War I*, edited by John Milton Cooper Jr. New York, 1972.

Cobley, Evelyn. *Representing War: Form and Ideology in First World War Narratives*. Toronto, 1993.

Cocteau, Jean. *A Call to Order*. Translated by Rollo H. Myers. New York, 1974.

———. *Cocteau's World: An Anthology of Writings*. Edited by Margaret Crosland. London, 1972.

———. "Nous voudrions vous dire un mot." *Le mot*, 27 February 1915, p. 1.

———. *Le rappel à l'ordre*. Paris, 1926.

———. *Thomas l'imposteur*. Paris, 1923.

Coetzee, Frans, and Marilyn Shevin-Coetzee, eds. *Authority, Identity and the Social History of the Great War*. Providence, 1995.

Coetzee, Marilyn. *World War I and European Society: A Sourcebook*. Lexington, Mass., 1995.

Cohan, George. *Twenty Years on Broadway and the Years It Took to Get There*. New York, 1925.

Colles, H. C. "National Anthems: Their Birth and Parentage." *The Musical Times* 55 (1 October 1914): 609–611.

Comini, Alessandra. *The Changing Image of Beethoven: A Study in Mythmaking*. New York, 1987.

Committee on Public Information. *American Loyalty by Citizens of German Descent*. War Information Series No. 6. Washington, D.C., 1917.

Cook, Susan C. *Opera for a New Republic: The Zeitopern of Krenek, Weill, and Hindemith*. Ann Arbor, 1988.

———. "*Der Zar lässt sich photographieren:* Weill and Comic Opera." In *A New Orpheus: Essays on Kurt Weill*, edited by Kim Kowalke. New Haven, 1986.

Cooke, Mervyn. *Britten: War Requiem*. Cambridge, U.K., 1996.

Coombe, Charles-Henry. "Les citations d'hymnes nationaux chez Debussy." *Revue musicale de Suisse romande* 39, no. 1 (1986): 19–27.

Cooper, Henry, et al. *World War I and Its Consequences*. Milton Keynes, U.K., 1990.

Cork, Richard. *A Bitter Truth: Avant Garde Art and the Great War*. New Haven, 1994.

Corn, Wanda M. "Identity, Modernism, and the American Artist after World War I: Gerald Murphy and Americanisme." *Studies in the History of Art* (1991): 148–169.

Cornebise, Alfred E. *Art from the Trenches: America's Uniformed Artists in World War I.* College Station, Tex., 1991.

—, ed. *Doughboy Doggerel: Verse of the American Expeditionary Force, 1918–1919.* Athens, Ohio, 1985.

Cottington, David. *Cubism in the Shadow of War.* New Haven, 1998.

Coupe, William. "German Cartoons of the First World War." *History Today* 42 (1992): 23–30.

Cowley, Malcolm. *Fitzgerald and the Jazz Age.* New York, 1966.

—. *A Second Flowering: Works and Days of the Lost Generation.* New York, 1973.

Crain, Caleb. "The Ties that Bound in America." *The New York Times Book Review,* 17 December 2000, p. 39.

Crawford, Fred D. *British Poets of the Great War.* Selinsgrove, Pa., 1988.

Crawford, Richard. *America's Musical Life: A History.* New York, 2001.

—. "Edward MacDowell: Musical Nationalism and an American Tone Poet." *Journal of the American Musicological Society* 49, no. 3 (1996): 528–560.

Creel, George. *How We Advertised America.* New York, 1920.

Crockett, Dennis. *German Post-Expressionism: The Art of the Great Disorder, 1918–1924.* University Park, Penn., 1999.

—. "The Most Famous Painting of the 'Golden Twenties'? Otto Dix and the Trench Affair." *Art Journal* 51 (1992): 72–80.

Cross, Tim, ed. *The Lost Voice of World War I: An International Anthology of Writers, Poets, and Playwrights.* Iowa City, 1989.

Crowell, Benedict. *How America Went to War. An Account from Official Sources of the Nation's War Activities, 1917–1920.* New Haven, 1921.

Cruickshank, John. *Variations on Catastrophe: Some French Responses to the Great War.* Oxford, 1982.

Cushman, John H., Jr. "Remains of Vietnam Unknown are Disinterred." *The New York Times,* 15 May 1998, p. A17.

Damrosch, Walter. *My Musical Life.* New York, 1926.

Daughton, James P. "Sketches of the *Poilu's* World: Trench Cartoons from the Great War." In *World War I and the Cultures of Modernity,* edited by Douglas Mackaman and Michael Mays. Jackson, Miss., 2000.

Davies, Norman. *God's Playground: A History of Poland.* Vol. 2. Crakow, 1981.

DeBauche, Leslie Midkiff. *Reel Patriotism.* Madison, 1997.

Debussy, Claude. *Correspondance, 1884–1918.* Edited by François Lesure. Paris, 1993.

—. *Debussy Letters.* Edited by François Lesure and Roger Nichols. Translated by Roger Nichols. London, 1987.

—. *Debussy on Music: The Critical Writings of the Great French Composer Claude Debussy.* Selected by François Lesure. Edited and translated by Richard Longham Smith. New York, 1977.

ᴀudin, Michel. *Canudo.* Rome, 1976.

ᴦoot, Gerard. *Douglas Haig, 1861–1928.* London, 1988.

Delany, Paul. *D. H. Lawrence's Nightmare: The Writer and His Circle in the Years of the Great War.* New York, 1978.

Delaplaine, Edward S. *John Philip Sousa and the National Anthem.* Frederick, Md., 1983.

de Marliave, Joseph. *Etudes musicales.* Paris, 1917.

Denby, David. "The Gift to Be Simple." *The New Yorker,* 13 December 1999, pp. 102–111.

Denham, Scott D. *Visions of War: Ideologies and Images of War in German Literature Before and After the Great War.* Bern, 1992.

Denizot, Alain. *Le Sacré Coeur et la Grande Guerre.* Paris, 1994.

Dennis, David B. *Beethoven in German Politics, 1870–1989.* New Haven, 1996.

Dennison, Sam. *Scandalize My Name: Black Imagery in American Popular Music.* New York, 1982.

Dent, Edward. *Busoni.* London, 1974.

de Schaepdrijver, Sophie. "Occupation, Propaganda and the Idea of Belgium." In *European Culture in the Great War: The Arts, Entertainment, and Propaganda, 1914–1918.* Edited by Aviel Roshwald and Richard Stites. Cambridge, U.K., 1999.

Deutsch, Henry. *Le pétrole et ses applications.* Paris, 1891.

Deutsch, Otto Erich. "Dichterische Freiheiten in Rollands Beethoven: Ein kritisches Nachwort." *Zeitschrift für Musik* 9 (1926): 490ff.

DeVoto, Mark. "Alban Berg's 'Marche Macabre.'" *Perspectives of New Music* 22, nos. 1–2 (1983–1984): 386–447.

Dibbets, Karel, and Bert Hogenkamp, eds. *Film and the First World War.* Amsterdam, 1995.

d'Indy, Vincent. *Beethoven: A Critical Biography.* Translated by Theodore Baker. Freeport, N.Y., 1970.

———. *La schola cantorum; son histoire depuis sa fondation jusqu'en 1925.* Paris, 1927.

———. *Une école de musique répondant aux besoins moderns: Discours d'inauguration de l'école de chant liturgique . . . fondée par la Schola Cantorum en 1896.* Paris, 1900.

Dizikes, John. *Opera in America: A Cultural History.* New Haven, 1993.

Dolph, Edward Arthur, ed. *Sound Off! Soldier Songs from Yankee Doodle to Parley Voo.* New York, 1929.

Dorsett, Lyle W. *Billy Sunday and the Redemption of Urban America.* Grand Rapids, 1991.

Dotoli, Giovanni, ed. *Lo scrittore totale: Saggi su Ricciotto Canudo.* Fasano, 1986.

———. *Paris ville visage-du-monde chez Ricciotto Canudo et l'avant-garde italienne.* Fasano, 1984.

Drozdowski, Marian. *Ignacy Jan Paderewski: A Political Biography.* Warsaw 1981.

Du Bois, W. E. B. *The Souls of Black Folk.* Chicago, 1903.

Duchesnau, Michel. "La musique française pendant la guerre 1914–1918. Autour de la tentative de fusion de la Société Nationale et de la Société Musicale Indépendante," *Revue de musicologie* 82, no. 1 (1996): 123–153.

Duncan, Edmonstoune. "Music and War." *The Musical Times* 55 (1 September 1914): 571–574.

Dungan, Myles. *They Shall Grow Not Old: Irish Soldiers and the Great War.* Dublin, 1997.

Dunsby, Jonathan. "The Poetry of Debussy's *En blanc et noir.*" In *Analytic Strategies and Musical Interpretation: Essays on Nineteenth- and Twentieth-Century Music*, edited by Craig Ayrey and Mark Everist. Cambridge, U.K., 1996.

Durand, Jacques. *Souvenirs d'un éditeur de musique.* Paris, 1925.

Dwight, Eleanor. *Edith Wharton: An Extraordinary Life.* New York, 1994.

Early, Frances. *A World Without War: How U.S. Feminists and Pacifists Resisted World War I.* Syracuse, 1997.

Eberle, Matthias. *Der Weltkrieg und die Künstler der Weimarer Republik.* Stuttgart, 1989.

———. *World War I and the Weimar Artists: Dix, Grosz, Beckmann, Schlemmer.* New Haven, 1985.

Edwards, Paul. *Wyndham Lewis: Art and War.* London, 1992.

Eksteins, Modris. "The Cultural Legacy of the Great War." In *The Great War and the Twentieth Century*, edited by Jay Winter, Geoffrey Parker, and Mary R. Habeck. New Haven, 2000.

———. *Rites of Spring: The Great War and the Birth of the Modern Age.* Boston, 1989.

———. "War, Memory, and the Modern: Pilgrimage and Tourism to the Western Front." In *World War I and the Cultures of Modernity*, edited by Douglas Mackaman and Michael Mays. Jackson, Miss., 2000.

Elgar, Edward. *Edward Elgar: Letters of a Lifetime.* Selected by Jerrold N. Moore. Oxford, 1990.

Elliker, Calvin. "Sheet Music Special Issues: Formats and Functions." *Notes* 53 (1996): 9–17.

Ellis, Mark. "W. E. B. Du Bois and the Formation of Black Opinion in World War I: A Commentary on the Damnable Dilemma." *The Journal of American History* 81 (1995): 1584–1590.

Elshtain, Jean Bethke. *Women and War.* New York, 1987.

Epstein, Dena J. "Frederick Stock and American Music." *American Music* 10, no. 1 (1992): 20–52.

Fainsod, Merle. *International Socialism and the World War.* New York, 1966.

Farrar, L. L., Jr., "Nationalism in Wartime: Critiquing the Conventional Wisdom." In *Authority, Identity and the Social History of the Great War*, edited by Frans Coetzee and Marilyn Shevin-Coetzee. Providence, 1995.

Farwell, Arthur, and W. D. Darby, eds. *Music in America.* Vol. 4 of *The Art of Music.* 13 vols. Edited by Daniel Gregory Mason. New York, 1915–1916.

deral Council of the Churches of Christ in America. *Christian Duties in*

Conserving Spiritual, Moral and Social Forces of the Nation in Time of War. New York, 1917.

Ferguson, John. *The Arts in Britain in World War I.* London, 1980.

Ferguson, Niall. *The Pity of War.* New York, 1999.

Ferro, Marc. "Cultural Life in France, 1914–1918." In *European Culture in the Great War,* edited by Aviel Roshwald and Richard Stites. Cambridge, U.K., 1999.

Field, Frank. *British and French Writers of the First World War: Comparative Studies in Cultural History.* Cambridge, U.K., 1991.

Field, Franz. "Karl Kraus, Bernard Shaw and Romain Rolland as Opponents of the First World War." In *Karl Kraus in neuer Sicht,* edited by Sigurd Paul Scheichl and Edward Timms. Munich, 1986.

———. *The Last Days of Mankind: Karl Kraus and His Vienna.* London, 1967.

Fink, C., ed. *Neue Kriegslieder.* Shanghai, 1915.

Fischer, David Hackett. *Historians' Fallacies: Toward a Logic of Historical Thought.* New York, 1970.

Fisher, David James. *Romain Rolland and the Politics of Intellectual Engagement.* Berkeley, 1987.

Fontana, Jacques. *Les Catholiques françaises pendant la Grande Guerre.* Paris, 1990.

Ford, Nancy Gentile. *Americans All! Foreign-born Soldiers in World War I.* College Station, Tex., 2001.

Foreman, Lewis, ed. *Oh, My Horses! Elgar and the Great War.* London, 2001.

Forthuny, Pascal. *Graine de héros.* N.p., n.d.

———. *Plus haut que l'amour: Icare l'as de coeur; roman d'aviation antique.* Paris, 1918.

Foster, Fay. *The Americans Come!* New York, 1918.

Foster, Gaines M. "A Christian Nation: Signs of a Covenant." In *Bonds of Affection: Americans Define Their Patriotism,* edited by John Bodnar. Princeton, 1996.

Fuchs, Victor. "Arnold Schoenberg als Soldat im ersten Weltkrieg." *Melos* 33, no. 6 (1966): 178–180.

Fulcher, Jane F. "The Composer as Intellectual: Ideological Inscriptions in French Interwar Neoclassicism." *The Journal of Musicology* 17, no. 2 (1999): 197–230.

———. *French Cultural Politics and Music: From the Dreyfus Affair to the First World War.* New York, 1999.

———. "Speaking the Truth to Power: The Dialogic Element in Debussy's Wartime Compositions." In *Debussy and His World,* edited by Jane F. Fulcher. Princeton, 2001.

Fuller, J. G. *Troop Morale and Popular Culture in the British and Dominion Armies, 1914–1918.* Oxford, 1990.

Fussell, Paul. *The Great War and Modern Memory.* New York, 1975.

———, ed. *The Norton Book of Modern War.* New York, 1991.

Gallatin, A. E. *Art and the Great War.* New York, 1919.

Garafola, Lynn. *Diaghilev's Ballets Russes*. New York, 1989.

Gavin, Lettie. *American Women in World War I: They Also Served*. Niwot, Colo., 1997.

Gay, Peter. "Sex and Longing in Old Vienna." *The New York Times Book Review*, 11 July 1999, p. 39.

Giddings, Robert. "Delusive Seduction: Pride, Pomp, Circumstance and Military Music." In *Popular Imperialism and the Military, 1850–1950*. Manchester and New York, 1992.

Gide, André. *Journal 1889–1939*. Paris, 1939.

Gilbert, Martin. *Atlas of World War I*. 2d ed. New York, 1994.

———. *The First World War: A Complete History*. New York, 1994.

Gilbert, Sandra M. "'Unreal City': The Place of the Great War in the History of Modernity." In *World War I and the Cultures of Modernity*, edited by Douglas Mackaman and Michael Mays. Jackson, Miss., 2000.

Gillmor, Alan M. *Erik Satie*. Boston, 1988.

Glancy, Diane. *War Cries*. Duluth, 1997.

Goens, Georg. *Gott mit uns! Feldpredigten im Grossen hauptquartier gehalten*. Berlin, 1914.

Goldberg, Nancy Sloan. "French Pacifist Poetry of World War I." *Journal of European Studies* 21 (1991): 239–258.

Goll, Yvan. *Für den Gefallenen von Europa*. Zurich, 1917.

Gramophone Company. *Gramophone Records of the First World War: An HMV Catalogue, 1914–1918*. Introduced by Brian Rust. Newton Abbot, 1975.

Graves, Mark A. "A World Based on Brotherhood: Male Bonding, Male Representation, and the War Novels of John Dos Passos." *CLA Journal* 38 (1994): 228–246.

Graves, Robert. *Good-bye to All That*. London, 1929.

Grayzel, Susan R. *Women's Identities at War: Gender, Motherhood, and Politics in Britain and France during the First World War*. Chapel Hill, 1999.

Green, Paul. *Paul Green's War Songs: A Southern Poet's History of the Great War, 1917–1920*. Rocky Mount, N.C., 1993.

Gregory, Adrian. *The Silence of Memory: Armistice Day, 1919–1946*. Oxford, 1994.

Grey, Edward. "Viscount of Falloden." In *Twenty-five Years, 1892–1916*. 2 vols. New York, 1925.

Griffith, Llewelyn Wyn. *Up to Mametz*. Norwich, Norfolk, 1988.

Griffiths, Paul. "American Music That Rattled Berlin." *The New York Times*, 14 January 2001, sec. 2, p. 35.

Grimm, Rheinhold, and Jost Herman, eds. *1914/1939: German Reflections of the Two World Wars*. Madison, 1992.

Grosh, Nils. *Die Musik der Neuen Sachlichkeit*. Stuttgart, 1999.

̄ury, Christian. *L'honneur retrouvé d'un officier homosexuel en 1915*. Paris, 2000.

Habeck, Mary R. "Technology in the First World War: The View from Below." In *The Great War and the Twentieth Century*, edited by Jay Winter, Geoffrey Parker, and Mary R. Habeck. New Haven, 2000.

Hale, Philip. "Philip Hale, Selections from His Columns in the *Boston Home Journal*, *1889–1891*." In *Music in Boston: Music of the First Three Centuries*, edited by John C. Swan. Boston, 1977.

Hall, Herbert James. *War-time Nerves*. Boston and New York, 1918.

Hamm, Charles. *Music in the New World*. New York, 1983.

Hammer, Karl. *Deutsche Kriegstheologie (1870–1918)*. Munich, 1971.

Hanna, Martha. *The Mobilization of Intellect: French Scholars and Writers during the Great War*. Cambridge, Mass., 1996.

Hardie, Martin. *War Posters Issued by Belligerent and Neutral Nations 1914–1919*. London, 1920.

Harrington, Peter. *British Artists and War: The Face of Battle in Paintings*. London, 1993.

Harris, Donald. "Ravel Visits the *Verein*: Alban Berg's Report." *Journal of the Arnold Schoenberg Institute* 3, no. 1 (1979): 75–82.

Harris, John. *Silent Cities 1914–1919: An Exhibition of the Memorial and Cemetery Architecture of the Great War*. London, 1977.

Hart, Brian. "The Symphony in Theory and Practice in France, 1900–1914." Ph.D. diss., Indiana University, 1994.

Harvey, A. D. "Some Queer Goings-on in the Trenches: Many British Soldiers Court Martialled for Homosexual Offenses in World War I." *New Statesman* 128, no. 4419 (1999): 30.

Haste, Cate. *Keep the Home Fires Burning: Propaganda in the First World War*. London, 1977.

Hatcher, John. *Laurence Binyon: Poet, Scholar of East and West*. Oxford, 1995.

Haupt, Georges. *Socialism and the Great War: The Collapse of the Second International*. Oxford, 1972.

Hayum, Andrée. *The Isenheim Altarpiece: God's Medicine and the Painter's Vision*. Princeton, 1989.

Hemingway, Ernest. *A Farewell to Arms*. New York, 1929.

Hennessey, Thomas. *Dividing Ireland: World War I and Partition*. London, 1998.

Hermand, Jost. "*Neue Sachlichkeit*: Ideology, Lifestyle, or Artistic Movement?" In *Dancing on the Volcano: Essays on the Culture of the Weimar Republic*, edited by Thomas W. Kniesche and Stephen Brockmann. Columbia, S.C., 1994.

Herter, Joseph. "*Polonia*, op. 76, by Edward Elgar." *Journal of the Elgar Society* 2, no. 2 (1999): 97–109.

Hess, Paul. *La vie à Reims pendant la guerre de 1914–1918: Notes et impressions d'un bombardé*. Paris, 1998.

Hesse, Hermann. *If the War Goes On: Reflections on War and Politics*. Translated by Ralph Manheim. New York, 1971.

———. "O Freunde, nicht diese Töne." *Neue Zürcher Nachrichten*, September 1914.

Hexamer, Charles John. *Address of Dr. C. J. Hexamer, President of the National German American Alliance: Mass Meeting at the Academy of Music*. Philadelphia, 24 November 1914.

Hibben, John Grier. *The Higher Patriotism*. New York, 1915.

Hibberd, Dominic. *Wilfred Owen: The Last Year 1917–1918*. London, 1992.

Higgins, Ian, ed. *Anthology of First World War French Poetry*. Glasgow, 1996.

Higginson, Henry Lee. *Life and Letters of Henry Lee Higginson*. Edited by Bliss Perry. Boston, 1921.

Hindemith, Paul. *Selected Letters of Paul Hindemith*. Edited and translated by Geoffrey Skelton. New Haven, 1995.

Hinton, Stephen. "Aspects of Hindemith's Neue Sachlichkeit." *Hindemith-Jahrbuch 1985* 14 (1985): 22–80.

———. "*Neue Sachlichkeit*, Surrealism, *Gebrauchsmusik*." In *A New Orpheus*, edited by Kim Kowlake. New Haven, 1986.

Hirsbrunner, Theo. *Maurice Ravel*. Laaber, 1989.

Hirshfield, Claire. "Musical Performance in Wartime: 1914–1918." *The Music Review* 53, no. 4 (1992): 294–298.

Hitchcock, H. Wiley. "Ives's *115 [+15] Songs* and What He Thought of Them." *Journal of the American Musicological Society* 52, no. 1 (1999): 115–116.

Hobsbawm, E. J. *The Age of Extremes: A History of the World, 1914–1991*. New York, 1994. Published in the United Kingdom as *Age of Extremes: The Short Twentieth Century, 1914–1991*. London, 1994.

Hodgson, Katharine. "Myth-making in Russian War Poetry." In *The Violent Muse: Violence and the Artistic Imagination in Europe, 1910–1939*. Manchester, 1994.

Homan, Gerlof. *American Mennonites and the Great War, 1914–1918*. Waterloo, Ontario, 1994.

Hoover, Arlie J. *God, Germany and Britain in the Great War: A Study in Clerical Nationalism*. New York, 1989.

Horne, John. "Soldiers, Civilians and the Warfare of Attrition: Representations of Combat in France, 1914–1918." In *Authority, Identity and the Social History of the Great War*, edited by Frans Coetzee and Marilyn Shevin-Coetzee. Providence, 1995.

Horowitz, Joseph. "A Moral Beacon Amid the Darkness of a Tragic Era." *The New York Times*, 6 February 2000, p. AR1.

———. "The Specter of Hitler in the Music of Wagner." *The New York Times*, 8 November 1998, sec. 2, pp. 1, 38.

Houtchens, Alan, and Janis P. Stout. " 'Scarce Heard Amidst the Guns Below': Intertextuality and Meaning in Charles Ives's War Songs." *The Journal of Musicology* 15 (1997): 66–97.

Howe, M. A. DeWolfe. *The Boston Symphony Orchestra, 1881–1931*. Boston, 1931.

Howlett, Jana, and Rod Mengham, eds. *The Violent Muse: Violence and the Artistic Imagination in Europe, 1910–1939.* New York, 1994.

Huet, Émile. *Jeanne d'Arc et la musique: Bibliographie musicale.* 2d ed. Orleans, 1909.

Hughes, Matthew. *Allenby and British Strategy in the Middle East, 1917–1919.* London, 1999.

Huizinga, Johan. *Homo Ludens: A Study of the Play Element in Culture.* Boston, 1970.

Hussey, Mark. "Living in a War Zone." In *Virginia Woolf and War: Fiction, Reality, and Myth,* edited by Mark Hussey. Syracuse, 1991.

———, ed. *Virginia Woolf and War: Fiction, Reality, and Myth.* Syracuse, 1991.

Hyde, Martha M. "Neoclassic and Anachronistic Impulses in Twentieth-Century Music." *Music Theory Spectrum* 18, no. 2 (1996): 206–210.

Hynes, Samuel. *The Soldier's Tale: Bearing Witness to Modern War.* New York, 1997.

———. *A War Imagined: The First World War and English Culture.* London, 1990.

Imbart de la Tour, Pierre. "Le Pangermanism et la philosophie de l'histoire: Lettre à M. Henri Bergson." *Revue des deux mondes* 30 (1915).

Isaacson, Charles D. "A New Musical Outlook—and The War." *The Musical Quarterly* 6, no. 1 (1920): 1–11.

Isenberg, Michael T. *War on Film: The American Cinema and World War I, 1914–1941.* Rutherford, 1981.

Ives, Charles. *Essays Before a Sonata and Other Writings.* Edited by Howard Boatwright. New York, 1962.

———. *Memos.* Edited by John Kirkpatrick. New York, 1972.

Izenberg, Gerald N. *Modernism and Masculinity: Mann, Wedekind, Kandinsky through World War I.* Chicago, 2000.

Jahn, Hubertus F. *Patriotic Culture in Russia During World War I.* Ithaca, 1995.

Jarman, Douglas. "Alban Berg, Wilhelm Fliess and the Secret Programme of the Violin Concerto." *The International Alban Berg Society Newsletter* 12 (1982): 5–11.

———. *The Music of Alban Berg.* Berkeley, 1978.

Jay, Martin. "Against Consolation: Walter Benjamin and the Refusal to Mourn." In *War and Remembrance in the Twentieth Century,* edited by Jay Winter and Emmanuel Sivan. Cambridge, U.K., 1999.

Jeanne, René, and Charles Ford. *Abel Gance.* Paris, 1963.

Jelavich, Peter. "German Culture in the Great War." In *European Culture in the Great War,* edited by Aviel Roshwald and Richard Stites. Cambridge, U.K., 1999.

Jensen, Kimberly. "Women, Citizenship, and Sacrifice." In *Bonds of Affection: Americans Define Their Patriotism,* edited by John Bodnar. Princeton, 1

Johann, Ernst. *Innenansicht eines Krieges; Bilder, Briefe, Dokumente 1914–1918*. Frankfurt, 1968.

Johnson, H. Earle. *Symphony Hall, Boston*. Boston, 1950.

Johnson, James Turner. *Just War Tradition and the Restraint of War: A Moral and Historical Inquiry*. Princeton, 1981.

Johnson, Julian. *Webern and the Transformation of Nature*. Cambridge, U.K., 1999.

Jones, Barbara, and Bill Howell. *Popular Arts of the First World War*. London, 1972.

Jones, Gilbert J. *Apollinaire, la poésie de guerre: Voyage d'aventure pour poéte et lecteur*. Geneva, 1990.

Jordan, William. "'The Damnable Dilemma': African-American Accommodation and Protest During World War I," *The Journal of American History* 81 (1995): 1562–1590.

Joseph, Charles. *Stravinsky and the Piano*. Ann Arbor, 1983.

Jourdan-Morhange, Hélène. *Ravel et nous: L'homme, l'ami, le musicien*. Geneva, 1945.

Jouvin, Georges J. D., and Joseph Vidal, eds. *Marches et chansons des soldats de France*. Paris, 1919.

Joyce, P. W. *Old Irish Folk Music and Songs*. Dublin, 1909.

Kahn, Otto Hermann. *Americans of German Origin and the War*. New York, 1917.

Katz, Friedrich. *The Life and Times of Pancho Villa*. Stanford, 1998.

Kavanagh, Gaynor. *Museums and the First World War: A Social History*. London, 1994.

Kearns, William. *Horatio Parker, 1863–1919: His Life, Music, and Ideas*. Metuchen, N.J., 1990.

Keathley, Elizabeth L. "*Erwartung*'s New Woman: Musical Modernism and Feminist Consciousness in Fin-de-Siècle Vienna." Paper presented at the 61st Annual Meeting of the American Musicological Society, New York, 2–5 November 1995.

Keegan, John. *The First World War*. New York, 1999.

———. *The Illustrated Face of Battle*. New York, 1989.

Keene, Jennifer. *Doughboys, the Great War, and the Remaking of America*. Baltimore, 2001.

Kelley, Thomas Forrest. *First Nights*. New Haven, 2000.

Kellogg, Walter. *The Conscientious Objector*. New York, 1919.

Kennedy, David M. *Over Here: The First World War and American Society*. New York, 1980.

Kennedy, Michael. *The Works of Ralph Vaughan Williams*. Oxford, 1980.

Kennett, Lee B. *The First Air War, 1914–1918*. New York, 1991.

Kern, Stephen. *The Culture of Time and Space*. Cambridge, Mass., 1983.

Ketchum, J. Davidson. *Ruhleben: A Prison Camp Society*. Toronto, 1965.

an, Nosheen. *Women's Poetry of the First World War*. New York, 1988.

Kidson, Frank. "The 'Star-Spangled Banner': An Exhaustive Official Inquiry." *The Musical Times* 56 (1 March 1915): 148.

Kimball, Robert, and William Bolcom. *Reminiscing with Sissle and Blake.* New York, 1973.

Kirk, Elise K. *Music at the White House: A History of the American Spirit.* Urbana, 1986.

Klemperer, Victor. *I Will Bear Witness: A Diary of the Nazi Years, 1933–1941.* Translated by Martin Chalmers. New York, 1998.

Knoles, G.H. *The Jazz Age Revisited: British Criticism of American Civilization During the 1920s.* New York, 1968.

Kollwitz, Käthe. *The Diaries and Letters.* Edited by Hans Kollwitz. Translated by Richard and Clara Winston. Chicago, 1955.

Kolodin, Irving. *The Metropolitan Opera, 1883–1966: A Candid History.* New York, 1967.

Kowalke, Kim H. "For Those We Love: Hindemith, Whitman, and 'An American Requiem,'" *Journal of the American Musicological Society* 50, no. 1 (1997): 133–174.

Kramer, Lawrence. "Chopin at the Funeral: Episodes in the History of Modern Death." *Journal of the American Musicological Society* 54, no. 1 (2001): 97–125.

Kramer, Steven, and James Welsh. *Abel Gance.* Boston, 1978.

Krasovskaya, Vera. *Nijinsky.* Translated by John E. Bowlt. New York, 1979.

Kraus, Karl. *In These Great Times: A Karl Kraus Reader.* Edited by Harry Zohn. [Montreal,] 1976.

Kredel, Fritz. *Wer will unter die Soldaten: Deutsche Soldatenlieder mit farbigen Bildern.* Leipzig, 1934.

Kreisler, Fritz. *Four Weeks in the Trenches. The War Story of a Violinist.* Boston, 1915.

Lacombe, Nicole. *Les chants de bataille: La chanson patriotique de 1900 à 1918.* Paris, 1992.

Landrieux, Maurice. *The Cathedral of Reims; The Story of a German Crime.* London, 1920.

Lane, Franklin K. "The Need of a Definite Program of Americanization of Our Foreign-Born Peoples." In *Reconstructing America: Our Next Big Job,* edited by Edwin Wildman. Boston, 1919.

Lankheit, Klaus. *Das Triptychon als Pathosformel.* Heidelberg, 1959.

Larionov, Mikhail. *La voie vers l'abstraction: Oeuvres sur papier 1908–1915.* Frankfurt, 1987.

Lartigue, J. H. *Mémoires sans mémoire.* Paris, 1975.

Lawson, Anita. *Irvin S. Cobb.* Bowling Green, 1984.

Lawson, Rex. "Maurice Ravel: *Frontispice* for Pianola." *The Pianola Journal* 2 (1989): 35–38.

Lebovics, Herman. *True France: The Wars over Cultural Identity.* Ithaca, N.Y., 1992.

Leed, Eric J. *No Man's Land: Combat and Identity in World War I*. Cambridge, U.K., 1979.

Legion Airs, Songs of "Over There" and "Over Here." Compiled by Frank E. Peat. Edited by Lee Orean Smith. New York, 1926.

Leichtentritt, Hugo. "The Renaissance Attitude towards Music." *The Musical Quarterly* 1, no. 2 (1915): 615.

Leiva-Merikakis, Erasmo. *The Blossoming Thorn: Georg Trakl's Poetry of Atonement*. Lewisburg, Pa., 1987.

Lemmerman, Heinz. *Kriegesziehung im Kaiserreich: Studien zur politischen Funktion von Schule und Schulmusik, 1890–1918*. Lilienthal, 1984.

Leroy, Claude, ed. *Blaise Cendrars et la guerre*. Paris, 1995.

Lesure, François. *Catalogue de l'oeuvre de Claude Debussy*. Geneve, 1977.

———. *Claude Debussy: Biographie critique*. Paris, 1994.

Le Targat, François, ed. *Saint-Sebastien dans l'histoire de l'art depuis le XVe siècle*. Paris, 1979.

Levenback, Karen L. *Virginia Woolf and the Great War*. Syracuse, 1998.

Levine, Lawrence W. *The Opening of the American Mind*. Boston, 1996.

Levy, Alan Howard. *Musical Nationalism: American Composers' Search for Identity*. Westport, Conn., 1983.

Lewis, David Levering. *W. E. B. Du Bois: The Fight for Equality and the American Century, 1919–1963*. New York, 2000.

Lichtenwanger, William. "The Music of The Star-Spangled Banner from Ludgate Hill to Capitol Hill" (Washington, D.C., 1977). Reprinted from the *Quarterly Journal of the Library of Congress* (July 1977).

Little, Arthur West. *From Harlem to the Rhine: The Story of New York's Colored Volunteers*. New York, 1936.

Lockspeiser, Edward. *Debussy*. 3d ed. London, 1951.

Long, Marguerite. *At the Piano with Ravel*. Translated by Olive Senior-Ellis. London, 1973.

Lowell, Amy. "Some Musical Analogies in Modern Poetry." *Musical Quarterly* 6, no. 1 (1920): 127–157.

Lowens, Irving. "L'affaire Muck: A Study in War Hysteria (1917–1918)." *Musicology* 1 (1947): 265–274.

Lubke, Frederick C. *Bonds of Loyalty: German-Americans and World War I*. DeKalb, Ill., 1974.

Lyons, Michael. *World War I: A Short History*. Englewood Cliffs, 1994.

Macdonald, Lyn. *1915, The Death of Innocence*. New York, 1995.

MacDonald, Malcolm. *John Foulds and His Music*. White Plains, 1989.

MacGill, Patrick. *The Great Push; an Episode of the Great War*. New York, 1916.

Mackaman, Douglas, and Michael Mays. "The Quickening of Modernity, 1914–1918." In *World War I and the Cultures of Modernity*, edited by Douglas Mackaman and Michael Mays. Jackson, Miss., 2000.

———, eds. *World War I and the Cultures of Modernity*. Jackson, Miss., 2000.

MacKenzie, John M., ed. *Popular Imperialism and the Military: 1850–1950.* New York, 1992.

Maier, Charles S. "Slaughterhouse Jive." Review of Niall Ferguson's *The Pity of War. The New Republic,* 28 June 1999, p. 51.

Mails, Thomas E. *Fools Crow: Wisdom and Power.* Tulsa, 1991.

Maine, Basil. *Elgar: His Life and Works.* Portway, 1933.

Malorey, Henri. *L'Arc de Triomphe de l'Étoile.* Toulouse, 1942.

Marinetti, F. T. *Teoria e invenzione futurista.* Edited by L. De Maria. Milan, 1968.

Maritain, Jacques. *Art and Poetry.* London, 1945.

Marks, Martin M. *Music and the Silent Film: Contexts and Case Studies, 1895–1924.* New York, 1997.

Marnat, Marcel. *Maurice Ravel.* Paris, 1986.

Martens, Frederick H. *Leo Ornstein.* New York, 1975.

Mason, D. G. *Contemporary Composers.* New York, 1918.

Mathews, Basil, ed. *Christ: And the World at War.* London, 1917.

Mathews, Shailer. *Patriotism and Religion.* New York, 1918.

Mathews, Tim. "The Machine: Dada, Vorticism and the Future." In *The Violent Muse: Violence and the Artistic Imagination in Europe, 1910–1939,* edited by Jana Howlett and Rod Mengham. Manchester, 1994.

Mawer, Deborah. "Musical Objects and Machines." In *The Cambridge Companion to Ravel,* edited by Deborah Mawer. Cambridge, U.K., 2000.

May, Henry F. *The End of American Innocence: A Study of the First Years of Our Own Time, 1912–1917.* Chicago, 1964.

McAllester, David P. *Enemy Way Music: A Study of Social and Esthetic Values as Seen in Navaho Music.* Cambridge, Mass., 1954.

———. *Indian Music in the Southwest.* Colorado Springs, 1961.

McCabe, John. *George M. Cohan: The Man Who Owned Broadway.* Garden City, N.Y., 1973.

McConnell, Stuart. "Reading the Flag." In *Bonds of Affection: Americans Define Their Patriotism,* edited by John Bodnar. Princeton, 1996.

McCrae, John. *In Flanders Fields and Other Poems.* New York, 1919.

McDougall, Walter A. *Promised Land, Crusader State.* Boston, 1997.

McKim, R. H. *For God and Country or the Christian Pulpit in War Time.* Dutton, N.Y., 1918.

McLoughlin, William G. *Billy Sunday Was His Real Name.* Chicago, 1955.

McMillan, James F. "French Catholics: *Rumeurs Infâmes* and the *Union Sacrée,* 1914–1918." In *Authority, Identity and the Social History of the Great War,* edited by Frans Coetzee and Marilyn Shevin-Coetzee. Providence, 1995.

———. "Reclaiming a Martyr: French Catholics and the Cult of Joan of Arc, 1890–1920." In *Martyrs and Martyrologies: Studies in Church History,* vol. 30, edited by Diana Wood. Oxford, 1993.

Messing, Scott. *Neoclassicism in Music: From the Genesis of the Concept through the Schoenberg/Stravinsky Polemic.* Ann Arbor, 1988.

Messinger, Gary S. *British Propaganda and the State in the First World War.* Manchester, 1992.

Michel, André, and M. Baudrillart. *The Martyred Towns: Rheims, Soissons, Senlis, Arras and Louvain.* Paris, 1915.

Minden, Michael. "Expressionism and the First World War." In *The Violent Muse: Violence and the Artistic Imagination in Europe, 1910–1939,* edited by Jana Howlett and Rod Mengham. Manchester, 1994.

Missalla, Heinrich. *Gott mit uns; die deutsche katholische Kriegspredigt 1914–1918.* Munich, 1968.

Mock, James R., and Cedric Larson. *Words That Won the War: The Story of the Committee on Public Information, 1917–1919.* Princeton, 1939.

Moldenhauer, Hans. *Anton von Webern: A Chronicle of His Life and Work.* New York, 1979.

Monson, Karen. *Alban Berg.* Boston, 1979.

Montabré, Maurice. "Claude Debussy Tells Us of His Theatrical Projects." In *Debussy on Music,* edited by François Lesure. New York, 1977.

Montagu-Nathan, M. "The Composer of the Russian National Anthem." *The Musical Times* 56 (1915): 82.

Moore, Jerrold N. *Edward Elgar: A Creative Life.* Oxford, 1984.

Morand, Paul. *Journal d'un attaché d'ambassade, 1916–1917.* Paris, 1948.

Morrow, John Howard. *The Great War in the Air: Military Aviation from 1909 to 1921.* Washington, D.C., 1993.

Moser, Hans. *Geschichte der deutschen Musik.* 2d ed. 3 vols. Stuttgart, 1920–1930.

Mosse, George L. *Fallen Soldiers: Reshaping the Memory of the World Wars.* New York, 1990.

———. *The Image of Man: The Creation of Modern Masculinity.* New York, 1996.

———. *Nationalism and Sexuality: Respectability and Abnormal Sexuality in Modern Europe.* New York, 1985.

Muck, Peter, ed. *Einhundert Jahre Berliner Philharmonisches Orchester: Darstellung in Dokumente.* 3 vols. Tutzing, 1982.

Mueller, Kate Hevner. *Twenty-Seven Major American Symphony Orchestras: A History and Analysis of Their Repertoires, Seasons 1842–43 through 1969–70.* Bloomington, 1973.

Murdoch, Brian. *Fighting Sons and Warring Words: Popular Lyrics of Two World Wars.* London, 1990.

Murphy, Jim. *The Boys' War: Confederate and Union Soldiers Talk About the Civil War.* New York, 1990.

Murray, Williamson. *War in the Air, 1914–45.* London, 1999.

Muschig, Walter. "Der fliegende Mensch in der Dichtung." *Neue Schweizer Rundschau* 8 (1939–1940): 311–320, 384–392, 446–453.

'ussat, Marie-Claire. "Le Tombeau dans la musique du XXième siècle." In *'ombeaux et monuments,* edited by Jacques Dugast and Michèle Touret. mes, 1992.

Myers, Steven Lee. "Laying to Rest the Last of the Unknown Soldiers," *The New York Times*, 3 May 1998, p. WK5.

Nabakov, Peter, ed. *Native American Testimony: A Chronicle of Indian-White Relations from Prophecy to the Present, 1492–1992.* New York, 1991.

National Society of the Colonial Dames of America. *American War Songs.* Philadelphia, 1925.

Naumann, Francis M. "New York Dada: Style with a Smile." In *Making Mischief: Dada Invades New York,* edited by Francis Naumann and Beth Venn. New York, 1996.

Neumann, Dietrich. "The Urbanistic Vision in Fritz Lang's *Metropolis.*" In *Dancing on the Volcano: Essays on the Culture of the Weimar Republic,* edited by Thomas W. Kniesche and Stephen Brockmann. Columbia, S.C., 1994.

Newman, Ernest. "The Artist and the People." *The Musical Times* 55 (1 October 1914): 605–607.

———. "Elgar's 'Fourth of August.'" *The Musical Times* 58 (1 July 1917): 295–297.

———. "Mr. Ernest Newman on French and English Music." *The Musical Times* 59 (1 October 1918): 471–472.

———. "The New French Recipe." *The Musical Times* 58 (1 October 1917): 441.

———. "The Spirit of England." *The Musical Times* 58 (1 November 1917): 506.

———. "The Spirit of England: Edward Elgar's New Choral Work." *The Musical Times* 57 (1 May 1916): 235–239.

———. "The War and the Future of Music." *The Musical Times* 55 (1 September 1914): 571–572.

Newman, William. "The Beethoven Mystique in Romantic Art, Literature, and Music." *The Musical Quarterly* 69, no. 3 (1983): 354–387.

Newmarch, Rosa. "The Outlook in Russia." *The Musical Times* 56 (1 September 1915): 521–523.

———. "A Requiem for the Allied Heroes." *The Musical Times* 58 (1 November 1917): 496–497.

Nichols, Robert, ed. *Anthology of War Poetry, 1914–1918.* London, 1943.

Nichols, Roger. *Debussy Remembered.* London, 1992.

Nietzsche, Friedrich. *Götzendämmerung.* Munich, 1988.

———. *Twilight of the Idols.* Translation by R. J. Hollingdale. London, 1990.

Nijinsky, Romola. *Nijinsky.* London, 1933.

Niles, John Jacob. *Singing Soldiers.* New York, 1927.

———, ed. *The Songs My Mother Never Taught Me.* New York, 1929.

Norris, John. "The Spirit of Elgar." In *Oh, My Horses! Elgar and the Great War,* edited by Lewis Foreman. Rickmansworth, Herts, 2001.

Nye, Robert A. *Masculinity and Male Codes of Honor in Modern France.* New York, 1993.

O'Brien-Twohig, Sarah. "Imminent Explosion." In *The Great War and the Shaping of the Twentieth Century*, www.pitt.edu/~novsel/ww1.html.

Oja, Carol. *Making Music Modern: New York in the 1920s*. New York, 2000.

O'Leary, Cecilia Elizabeth. "'Blood Brotherhood': The Racialization of Patriotism, 1865–1918." In *Bonds of Affection: Americans Define Their Patriotism*, edited by John Bodnar. Princeton, 1996.

Olt, Reinhard. *Krieg und Sprache: Untersuchungen zu deutschen Soldatenliedern des Ersten Weltkriegs*. Giessen, 1980–1981.

Oosterhuis, Harry. "Male Bonding and Homosexuality in German Nationalism." *Journal of Homosexuality* 22, no. 1 (1991): 241–263.

Oppenheim, Janet. *"Shattered Nerves": Doctors, Patients, and Depression in Victorian England*. New York, 1991.

Orenstein, Arbie. *Ravel: Man and Musician*. New York, 1975.

Otis, Philo Adams. *The Chicago Symphony Orchestra: Its Organization, Growth and Development, 1891–1924*. Chicago, 1972.

Ottner, Carmen. "Hans Gregor; Direktor der Wiener Hofoper in schwerer Zeit (1911–1918)." In *Oper in Wien 1900–1925*, edited by Carmen Ottner. Vienna, 1991.

Owen, Wilfred. *Collected Letters*. Edited by Harold Owen and John Bell. New York and Toronto, 1967.

———. *The War Poems*. Edited by Jon Silkin. London, 1994.

Owens, Tom C. "Selected Correspondence, 1881–1954." In *Charles Ives and His World*, edited by J. Peter Burkholder. Princeton, 1996.

Painlevé, Paul. *Paroles et Écrits*. Paris, 1936.

Palmer, Roy. *What a Lovely War: British Soldiers' Songs from the Boer War to the Present Day*. London, 1990.

Parker, Peter. *The Old Lie: The Great War and the Public School Ethos*. London, 1987.

Parks, Richard. *The Music of Claude Debussy*. New Haven, 1989.

Parmée, Margaret A. *Ivan Goll: The Development of His Poetic Themes and Their Imagery*. Bonn, 1981.

Partsch, Cornelius. "Hannibal ante Portas: Jazz in Weimar." In *Dancing on the Volcano: Essays on the Culture of the Weimar Republic*, edited by Thomas W. Kniesche and Stephen Brockmann. Columbia, S.C., 1994.

Pasler, Jann. "New Music as Confrontation: The Musical Sources of Jean Cocteau's Identity." *The Musical Quarterly* 75 (1991): 255–278.

Paul, Harry. *The Sorcerer's Apprentice: The French Scientist's Image of German Science, 1840–1919*. Gainesville, 1972.

Paulding, James E. "Mathis der Maler—The Politics of Music." *Hindemith-Jahrbuch* 5 (1976): 104–108.

Peat, Frank E., and Lee Orean Smith, eds. *Legion Airs: Songs of "Over There" and "Over Here."* New York, 1932.

Peppis, Paul. *Literature, Politics, and the English Avant-garde: Nation and Empire, 1901–1918*. Cambridge, U.K., 2000.

Perle, George. *The Operas of Alban Berg: Wozzeck.* Berkeley, 1980.

Perlis, Vivian. *Charles Ives Remembered.* New Haven, 1974.

Perloff, Marjorie. *The Futurist Moment: Avant-garde, Avant-guerre, and the Language of Rupture.* Chicago, 1986.

Perloff, Nancy. *Art and the Everyday: Popular Entertainment and the Circle of Erik Satie.* Oxford, 1991.

Perris, Arnold. *Music as Propaganda: Art to Persuade, Art to Control.* Westport, Conn., 1985.

Peterson, H. C. *Propaganda for War: The Campaign against American Neutrality, 1914–1917.* Norman, Okla., 1939.

Piper, John F., Jr. *The American Churches in World War I.* Athens, Ohio, 1985.

Pirie, Peter J. *The English Musical Renaissance.* London, 1979.

Pisano, Dominick A., et al. *Legend, Memory and the Great War in the Air.* Seattle, 1992.

Poincaré, Raymond. *Messages, discours, allocutions, lettres et télégrammes de Raymond Poincaré.* Paris, 1919–1920.

Pollack, Howard. *Aaron Copland: The Life and Work of an Uncommon Man.* New York, 1999.

———. "Copland's Hope for American Music," *Institute for Studies in American Music Newsletter* 29, no. 1 (1999).

———. *Skyscraper Lullaby: The Life and Music of John Alden Carpenter.* Washington, D.C., 1995.

Posnock, Ross. *Color and Culture: Black Writers and the Making of the Modern Intellectual.* Cambridge, Mass., 1998.

Potter, Caroline. "Nadia and Lili Boulanger: Sister Composers." *Musical Quarterly* 83, no. 4 (1999): 536–556.

Potter, Pamela. *Most German of the Arts.* New Haven, 1998.

Poulenc, Francis. *Mes amis et moi.* Paris, 1963.

Pound, Ezra. *Antheil, and the Treatise on Harmony.* Chicago, 1927.

Pound, Reginald. *The Lost Generation.* London, 1964.

Powell, Anne, ed. *A Deep Cry: First World War Soldier-Poets Killed in France and Flanders.* Stroud, 1998.

Powers, William K. *War Dance: Plains Indian Musical Performance.* Tucson, 1990.

Pratella, Francesco Balilla. *Francesco Balilla Pratella: Edizioni, scritti, manoscritti musicali e futuristi.* Edited by Domenico Tampieri. Ravenna, 1995.

Prescott, John F. *In Flanders Fields: The Story of John McCrae.* Erin, Ont., 1985.

Price, Alan. *The End of The Age of Innocence.* New York, 1996.

Priest, Deborah. *Louis Laloy (1874–1944) on Debussy, Ravel, and Stravinsky.* Translated by Deborah Priest. Aldershot, 1999.

Prior, Robin. *Passchendaele.* Chicago, 1996.

Prod'homme, J. G. "Claude Achille Debussy." *The Musical Quarterly* 4, n (1918): 555.

————. "Music and Musicians in Paris During the First Two Seasons of the War." Translated by Otto Kinkeldey. *The Musical Quarterly* 4, no. 1 (1918): 135–160.

Prost, Antoine. *In the Wake of War: 'Les Anciens Combattants' and French Society, 1914–1919.* Providence, 1992.

Pruniéres, Henri. "La légende de Saint-Christophe." *Revue musicale* 1 (1920): 60.

Quinet, Edgar. *Allemagne au-dessus de tout!* Commentary by Paul Gautier. Paris, 1917.

Quinet, Mme. Edgar. *Ce que dit la musique.* Paris, 1894.

Quinn, Patrick J. *The Great War and the Missing Muse: The Early Writings of Robert Graves and Siegfried Sassoon.* Selinsgrove, 1994.

Quinn, Tom. *Tales of the Old Soldiers: Ten Veterans of the First World War Remember Life and Death in the Trenches.* Dover, N.H., 1993.

Radice, Mark A. "*Futurismo:* Its Origins, Context, Repertory, and Influence." *The Musical Quarterly* 73, no.1 (1989): 11–12.

Raskin, Richard. "Le chant des partisans: Functions of a Wartime Song." *Folklore* 102, no. 1 (1991): 62–76.

Ravel, Maurice. *Lettres à Roland-Manuel et à sa famille.* Paris, 1986.

————. *A Ravel Reader: Correspondence, Articles, Interviews.* Edited by Arbie Orenstein. New York, 1990.

Rawls, Walton H. *Wake Up, America! World War I and the American Poster.* New York, 1988.

Rayfield, Donald. "The Soldier's Lament: World War One Folk Poetry in the Russian Empire." *The Slavonic and East European Review* 66 (1988): 66–90.

Rearick, Charles. "Madelon and the Men—In War and Memory." *French Historical Studies* 17 (1992): 1001–1034.

Rechter, David. *The Jews of Vienna and the First World War.* London, 2001.

Reeves, Nicholas. *Official British Film Propaganda During the First World War.* London, 1986.

Reich, Willi. *Schoenberg: A Critical Biography.* Translated by Leo Black. London, 1968.

Reif, Rita. "You Could Tell the 'Ism' by the Letterhead." *The New York Times,* 31 March 1996, p. H38.

Reinhard, Olt. *Krieg und Sprache: Untersuchungen zu deutschen Soldatenliedern des Ersten Weltkriegs.* Vol. 1. Giessen, 1981.

Remarque, Erich Maria. *All Quiet on the Western Front.* Translated by A. W. Wheen. London, 1929.

Renehan, Edward J., Jr. *The Lion's Pride: Theodore and His Family in Peace and War.* New York, 1998.

Renzi, Renzo, ed. *Il cinematografo al camp: L'arma nuova nel primo conflitto mondiale.* Ancona, 1993.

....ler, D. Michael. *Historical Perspective on The President's Own U.S. Ma.... Band: 200th Anniversary.* Washington, D.C., 1998.

Rice, William Gorham. "Tower Music of Belgium and Holland." *The Musical Quarterly* 1, no. 2 (1915): 198–215.

Richardson, Matthew. *The Tigers.* London, 2000.

Rickenbacker, Eddie. *Fighting the Flying Circus.* New York, 1919.

Rilke, Rainer Maria. *Wartime Letters of Rainer Maria Rilke, 1914–1921.* New York, 1940.

Ringer, Alexander. *Arnold Schoenberg: The Composer as Jew.* Oxford, 1990.

Rischbieter, Hennring. *Art and the Stage in the Twentieth Century.* Greenwich, Conn., 1968.

Robida, Albert. *Le vingtième siècle: La vie électrique.* Paris, 1883.

Robinson, J. Bradford. "Learning the New Ropes: Kurt Weill and the American Theater Song." *Kurt Weill Newsletter* 15, no. 2 (1997): 7.

Rockwell, John. "At the Salzburg Festival, the Sting of a Gadfly May Endure." *The New York Times,* 22 July 2001, sec. 2, p. 1.

Rodeheaver, Homer. *Twenty Years with Billy Sunday.* Winona Lake, Ind., 1936.

Rolland, Romain. *Above the Battle.* Translated by C. K. Ogden. Chicago and London, 1916.

———. *Au-dessus de la mêlée.* Paris, 1915.

———. *Chère Sofia. Choix de lettres de Romain Rolland à Sofia Bertolini Guerrieri-Gonzaga (1909–1932).* In *Cahiers Romain Rolland.* Paris, 1960.

———. *Jean-Christophe.* Paris, 1904–1912.

———. *Journal des années de guerre, 1914–1919.* Paris, 1952.

———. *Mémoires, et fragments du journal.* Paris, 1956.

———. *Musicians of To-Day.* Translated by Mary Blaiklock. New York, 1914.

———. *Musiciens d'aujourd'hui.* Paris, 1908.

———. "L'opéra en Angleterre." In *Les origines du théâtre lyrique moderne.* Paris, 1895.

———. "Réponse à l'enquête de Paul Landormy: l'État actuel de la musique française," *Revue bleue,* 2 April 1904, p. 424.

———. *Le voyage intérieur.* Paris, 1959.

Roosevelt, Theodore. *America and the World War.* New York, 1915.

Roper, John H., ed. *Paul Green's War Songs: A Southern Poet's History of the Great War, 1917–1920.* Rocky Mount, N.C., 1993.

Rosen, Charles. *Arnold Schoenberg.* New York, 1975.

Rosenstiel, Léonie. *The Life and Works of Lili Boulanger.* London, 1978.

———. *Nadia Boulanger: A Life in Music.* New York, 1982.

Roshwald, Aviel, and Richard Stites, eds., *European Culture in the Great War: The arts, entertainment, and propaganda, 1914–1918.* Cambridge, U.K., 1999.

Ross, Stewart Halsey. *Propaganda for War: How the United States Was Conditioned to Fight the Great War of 1914–1918.* Jefferson, N.C., 1996.

Rossiter, Frank. *Charles Ives and His America.* New York, 1975.

Rother, Rainer, ed. *Die letzten Tage der Menschheit: Bilder des Ersten Weltkrieges.* Berlin, 1994.

Rothstein, Edward. "Must People Lie? Yes, Absolutely. Or Is That a Lie?" *The New York Times*, 18 August 2001, sec. B, p. 7.

————. "Seeking a Home in the Brave New World." *The New York Times*, 1 January 2000, p. C21, sec. B, p. 7.

Rozenblit, Marsha L. *Reconstructing a National Identity: The Jews of Habsburg Austria during World War I.* Oxford, 2001.

Rubin, William. "Challenging a Thesis." *The New York Times*, 20 February 2000, p. AR4.

Russell, Dave. "'We Carved Our Way to Glory': The British Soldier in Music Hall Song and Sketch, c. 1880–1914." In *Popular Imperialism and the Military, 1850–1950*, edited by John M. MacKenzie. Manchester, 1992.

Salomon, Ernest von. "Der verlorene Haufen." In *Krieg und Krieger*, edited by Ernst Jünger. Berlin, 1930.

Sarabianov, Dmitrii Vladimirovich. *Russian Art: From Neoclassicism to the Avant-garde, 1800–1917: Painting — Sculpture — Architecture.* New York, 1990.

Sassoon, Siegfried. *Collected Poems, 1908–1956.* London, 1961.

————. *Memoirs of a Fox-Hunting Man.* New York, 1929.

————. *Siegfried Sassoon's Long Journey: Selections from the Sherston Memoirs.* Edited by Paul Fussell. New York, 1983.

Satie, Erik. *Écrits.* Edited by Ornella Volta. Paris, 1981.

Savona, A. V., and M. L. Straniero, eds. *Canti della Grande Guerra.* 2 vols. Milan, 1981.

Schaarwächter, Jürgen, ed. *HB: Aspects of Havergal Brian.* Aldershot, 1997.

Schama, Simon. "Afterword." In *Dead Certainties: Unwarranted Speculations.* New York, 1991.

Schickel, Richard. *The World of Carnegie Hall.* New York, 1960.

Schinz, Albert. *French Literature of the Great War.* New York, 1920.

Schmidt, Carl B. *The Music of Francis Poulenc (1899–1963): A Catalogue.* Oxford, 1995.

Schmidt, Madeleine, ed. *Chansons de la revanche et la Grande Guerre.* Paris, 1985.

Schneider, Dorothy. *Into the Breach: American Women Overseas in World War I.* New York, 1991.

Schoenberg, Arnold. *Arnold Schoenberg Letters.* Edited by Erwin Stein, translated by E. Wilkins and E. Kaiser. New York, 1965.

————. "National Music (I), (II)." In *Style and Idea,* translated by Leo Black and edited by Leonard Stein. New York, 1975.

Scholz, Dieter. "Das Triptychon *Der Krieg* von Otto Dix." In *Otto Dix: Bestandskatalog: Gemälde, Aquarelle, Pastelle, Zeichnungen, Holzschnitte, Radierungen, Lithographien.* Galerie der Stadt Stuttgart, 1991.

Schrade, Leo. *Beethoven in France.* New Haven, 1942.

Schroeder, David. "Opera, Apocalypse and the Dance of Death: Berg's Indebtedness to Kraus." *Mosaic* 25 (1992): 91–105.

Schuhmacher, Wilhelm. *Leben und Seele unseres Soldatenlieds im Weltkrieg.* Frankfurt am Main, 1928.

Schwarz, Birgit. "'Otto Hans Baldung Dix' malt die Grossstadt: Zur Rezeption der altdeutschen Malerei." In *Otto Dix: Bestandskatalog: Gemälde, Aquarelle, Pastelle, Zeichnungen, Holzschnitte, Radierungen, Lithographien.* Galerie der Stadt Stuttgart, 1991.

Schwertfeger, Bernhard, and Erich Otto Volkmann, eds. *Der deutsche Soldatenkunde.* Leipzig, 1937.

Scott, Michael. *The Great Caruso.* London, 1988.

Seebohm, Andrea, ed. *Die Wiener Opera: 350 Jahre Glanz und Tradition.* Vienna, 1986.

Seeger, Alan. *Letters and Diary of Alan Seeger.* New York, 1917.

Segel, Harold B. "Culture in Poland during World War I." In *European Culture in the Great War: The Arts, Entertainment, and Propaganda, 1914–1918.* Edited by Aviel Roshwald and Richard Stites. Cambridge, U.K., 1999.

Segond, Joseph Louis Paul. *La Guerre mondiale et la vie spirituelle.* Paris, 1918.

Selz, Peter. *Max Beckmann.* New York, 1996.

Semler, Isabel Parker. *Horatio Parker.* New York, 1942.

Sensibar, Judith L. "Edith Wharton as Propagandist and Novelist: Competing Visions of 'The Great War.'" In *A Forward Glance: New Essays on Edith Wharton,* edited by Clare Colquitt, Susan Goodman, and Candace Waid. Newark, 1999.

Severini, Gino. *Dal cubismo al classicismo e altri saggi sulla divina proporzione e sul numero d'oro.* Edited by Piero Pacini. Florence, 1972.

———. *Du cubisme au classicisme: Esthétique du compas et du nombre.* Paris, 1921.

Shaw, George Bernard. *The Bodley Head Bernard Shaw: Shaw's Music,* vol. 3: *1893–1950.* Edited by Dan H. Laurence. London, 1981.

———. "The Future of British Music." *Music and Letters* 1, no. 1 (1920): 7–11.

Sherman, Daniel J. *The Construction of Memory in Interwar France.* Chicago, 1999.

Short, Michael. *Gustav Holst.* Oxford, 1990.

Showalter, Elaine. *The Female Malady.* New York, 1985.

Shreffler, Anne C. *Webern and the Lyric Impulse: Songs and Fragments on Poems of Georg Trakl.* Oxford, 1994.

Sices, David. *Music and the Musician in Jean-Christophe: The Harmony of Contrasts.* New Haven, 1968.

Silver, Kenneth. *Esprit de Corps: The Art of the Parisian Avant-Garde and the First World War, 1914–1925.* Princeton, 1989.

———. "Purism: Straightening Up after the Great War." In *Modern Art and Society: An Anthology of Social and Multicultural Readings,* edited by Maurice Berger. New York, 1994.

Skelton, Geoffrey. *Paul Hindemith: The Man Behind the Music.* London, 1

Slater, David. "Locating the American Century: Themes for a Post-Colonial Perspective." In *The American Century: Consensus and Coercion in the Projection of American Power,* edited by David Slater and Peter J. Taylor. Oxford, 1999.

Smith, Jeffrey R. "The First World War and the Public Sphere in Germany." In *World War I and the Cultures of Modernity,* edited by Douglas Mackaman and Michael Mays. Jackson, Miss., 2000.

Smith, Leonard V. *Between Mutiny and Obedience: The Case of the French Fifth Infantry Division during World War I.* Princeton, 1994.

————. "Masculinity, Memory, and the French First World War Novel." In *Authority, Identity and the Social History of the Great War,* edited by Frans Coetzee and Marilyn Shevin-Coetzee. Providence, 1995.

————. "Narrative and Identity at the Front: '*Theory and the Poor Bloody Infantry.*'" In *The Great War and the Twentieth Century,* edited by Jay Winter, Geoffrey Parker, and Mary R. Habeck. New Haven, 2000.

Sneath, E. Hershey, ed. *Religion and the War.* New Haven, 1918.

Sombart, Werner. "Technik und Kultur." *Archiv für Sozialwissenschaft und Sozialpolitik* 23 (1911): 342–347.

Sonneck, Oscar. *"The Star-Spangled Banner" (revised and enlarged from the "Report" on the above and other airs, issued in 1909).* Washington, D.C., 1914.

Spalding, Walter. "The War in its Relation to American Music." *The Musical Quarterly* 4, no. 1 (1918): 1–11.

Speer, Robert. *The Christian Man, the Church and the War.* New York, 1918.

Spycket, Jérôme. *Nadia Boulanger.* Stuyvesant, N.Y., 1992.

Stanford, Charles Villiers. *Interludes, Records and Reflections.* London, 1922.

Stanley, May. "Wanted: Singing Leaders for Army Camps." *Musical America* 26 (1917): 3.

Stanzel, Franz Karl, and Martin Loschnigg, eds. *Intimate Enemies: English and German Literary Reactions to the Great War, 1914–1918.* Heidelberg, 1993.

Stark, Gary D. "All Quiet on the Home Front: Popular Entertainments, Censorship and Civilian Morale in Germany, 1914–1918." In *Authority, Identity and the Social History of the Great War,* edited by Frans Coetzee and Marilyn Shevin-Coetzee. Providence, 1995.

Starr, William. *Romain Rolland and a World at War.* Evanston, Ill., 1956.

Steinberg, Michael P. "In Salzburg, a Fresh Skirmish in the Culture Wars." *The New York Times,* 17 October 1999, sec. 2, p. 35.

Sternlicht, Sanford V. *Siegfried Sassoon.* New York, 1993.

Stibbe, Matthew. *German Anglophobia and the Great War, 1914–1918.* Cambridge, 2001.

Stieg, Gerald. "*Die letzten Tage der Menschheit:* Eine negative Operette?" In *Oesterreich und der Grosse Krieg,* edited by Klaus Amann and Hubert Lengauer. Vienna, 1989.

Stradling, R. A., and Meirion Hughes. *The English Musical Renaissance 1860–1940: Construction and Deconstruction.* London, 1993.

Strauss, Richard, and Romain Rolland. *Correspondence.* Edited by Rollo Myers. Berkeley, 1968.

Stravinsky, Igor. *An Autobiography.* New York, 1936.

———. *Selected Correspondence.* 2 vols. Edited by Robert Craft. New York, 1984.

———. *Strawinsky: Sein Nachlass, Sein Bild.* Basel, 1984.

Stravinsky, Igor, and Robert Craft. *Conversations with Igor Stravinsky.* Garden City, N.Y., 1959.

———. *Dialogues and a Diary.* New York, 1963.

———. "Eau de Vie: An Interview on Beethoven." In *The First Anthology: 30 Years of the New York Review of Books,* edited by Robert B. Silvers, Barbara Epstein, and Rea S. Hederman. New York, 1993.

———. *Expositions and Developments.* Garden City, N.Y., 1962

———. *Memories and Commentaries.* Garden City, N.Y., 1960.

Stravinsky, Vera, and Robert Craft. *Stravinsky in Pictures and Documents.* New York, 1978.

Stuckenschmidt, H. H. *Arnold Schoenberg: His Life, World and Work.* Translated by Humphrey Searle. London, 1977.

Sudhalter, Richard M. *Lost Chords: White Musicians and Their Contribution to Jazz, 1915–1945.* New York, 1999.

Svarny, Erik Michael. *"The Men of 1914": T. S. Eliot and Early Modernism.* Philadelphia, 1988.

Swan, Alfred J. *Music 1900–1930.* New York, 1929.

Sweeney, Regina. "Harmony and Disharmony: French Singing and Musical Entertainment during the Great War." Ph.D. diss., University of California, Berkeley, 1992.

———. "*La Pudique Anastasie:* Wartime Censorship and Bourgeois Morality." In *World War I and the Cultures of Modernity,* edited by Douglas Mackaman and Michael Mays. Jackson, Miss., 2000.

———. *Singing Our Way to Victory: French Cultural Politics and Music during the Great War.* Middletown, Conn., 2001.

Sweeney, W. Allison. *History of the American Negro in the Great World War.* New York, 1969.

Taruskin, Richard. "Back to Whom? Neoclassicism as Ideology." *Nineteenth-Century Music* 26 (1993): 286–302.

———. *Defining Russia Musically.* Princeton, 1997.

———. "Nationalism." In *New Grove Dictionary of Music and Musicians.* 2d ed. 29 vols. London, 2001.

———. *Stravinsky and the Russian Traditions.* Berkeley, 1996.

Tate, Michael L. "From Scout to Doughboy: The National Debate Over Integrating American Indians into the Military, 1891–1918." *Western Historical Quarterly* 17, no. 4 (1986): 417–437.

Tavris, Carol. Review of Elaine Showalter's *Hystories*. *The New York Times Book Review*, 4 May 1997, p. 28.

Taylor, Denise Pilmer. *"La Musique pour tout le monde:* Jean Wiéner and the Dawn of French Jazz," Ph.D. diss., The University of Michigan, 1998.

Taylor, Martin. *Lads: Love Poetry of the Trenches*. London, 1989.

Tchaikovsky, Modest. *Zhizn' Petra Il'icha Chaikovskago*. Moscow and Leipzig, 1903.

Templier, Pierre-Daniel. *Erik Satie*. Paris, 1932.

Terry, Richard R. "Sidelights on German Art." *The Musical Times* 56 (1915): 457–461.

Thom, Deborah. *Nice Girls and Rude Girls: Women Workers in World War I*. London, 1998.

Thomas, Norman. *Is Conscience a Crime?* New York, 1927.

Thomson, Andrew. *Vincent d'Indy and His World*. Oxford, 1996.

———. *Widor*. Oxford, 1987.

Thorpe, Michael. *Siegfried Sassoon: A Critical Study*. London, 1966.

Tiersot, Julien. "La Musique française après la guerre."*Le Ménestrel* 82, no. 53 (1920): 517–519.

———. "Souvenirs de cinq années (1914–1919)." *Le Ménestrel* 82, no. 3 (1920): 25.

Tischler, Barbara L. *An American Music: The Search for an American Musical Identity*. New York, 1986.

———. "One Hundred Percent Americanism and Music in Boston during World War I." *American Music* 4 (1986): 164–176.

Tisdall, Caroline, and Angelo Bozzolla. *Futurism*. New York, 1978, 1992.

Tittel, L. *Zur Sache 8—Der erste Weltkrieg, Käthe Kollwitz, Ernst Barlach, Wilhelm Lehmbruck, Otto Dix*. Hamburg, 1978.

Todd, Lewis Paul. *Wartime Relations of the Federal Government and the Public Schools 1917–1918*. New York, 1945.

Tomas, Guillermo M. *Invincible America: The National Music of United-States in Peace and at War*. Havana, 1919.

Tomkins, Calvin. *Marcel Duchamp: A Biography*. New York, 1996.

Tommasini, Anthony. "An Opera of Yesterday with the Cynicism of Today." *The New York Times*, 3 May 1998, p. AR23.

———. "Revisiting a Homage to American Composers." *The New York Times*, 23 January 2001, sec. E., p. 5.

Tonnet-Lacroix, Eliane. *Après-guerre et sensibilités littéraires, 1919–1924*. Paris, 1991.

Tower, Beeke Sell. "'Ultramodern and Ultraprimitive:' Shifting Meaning in the Imagery of Americanism in the Art of Weimar Germany." In *Dancing on the Volcano: Essays on the Culture of the Weimar Republic*, edited by Thomas W. Kniesche and Stephen Brockmann. Columbia, S.C., 1994.

Trask, David F., ed. *World War I at Home: Readings on American Life, 1914–1920*. New York, 1970.

Trend, Michael. *The Music Makers: Heirs and Rebels of the English Musical Renaissance, Edward Elgar to Benjamin Britten*. London, 1985.

Trowell, Brian. "The Road to Brinkwells: The Last Chamber Music." In *Oh, My Horses! Elgar and the Great War*, edited by Lewis Foreman. Rickmansworth, Herts, 2001.

Tuchman, Barbara. *The Guns of August*. New York, 1962.

Tulloch, Donald. *Songs and Poems of the Great World War*. Worcester, Mass., 1915.

Turbet, Richard. "A Monument of Enthusiastic Industry: Further Light on Tudor Church Music." *Music and Letters* 81, no. 3 (2000): 433–436.

Twain, Mark. *Complete Essays of Mark Twain*. Edited by Charles Neider. Garden City, N.Y., 1963.

Tyler, Patrick E. "Putin Pushes Soviet Hymn, Creating Disharmony." *The New York Times*, 6 December 2000, sec. A, p. 1.

United States Committee on Public Information, *American Loyalty by Citizens of German Descent*. Washington, Government Printing Office, 1917.

United States War Department. *Home Reading Course for Citizen-Soldiers*. War Information Series No. 9. Washington, D.C., 1917.

Vallas, Leon. *Achille-Claude Debussy*. Paris, 1944.

———. *Vincent d'Indy*. 2 vols. Paris, 1946–1950.

van Dooren, Ine, and Peter Krämer. "The Politics of Direct Address." In *Film and the First World War*, edited by Karl Dibbets and Bert Hogenkamp. Amsterdam, 1995.

Van Kleeck, Nart. "After-War Status of Women Workers." In *Reconstructing America: Our Next Big Job*, edited by Edwin Wildman. Boston, 1919.

Vaughan, Leslie J. *Randolph Bourne and the Politics of Cultural Radicalism*. Lawrence, Kan., 1997.

Vaughn, Stephen. *Holding Fast the Inner Lines: Democracy, Nationalism, and the Committee on Public Information*. Chapel Hill, 1980.

Vaughan Williams, Ralph, and Gustav Holst. *Heirs and Rebels: Letters Written to Each Other*. New York, 1974.

Vaughan Williams, Ursula. *RVW: A Biography of Ralph Vaughan Williams*. London, 1964.

Vis, Juren. "Debussy and the War: Debussy, Luther, and Janequin." *Cahiers Debussy* 15 (1991): 36–38, 42.

Vogel, Frederick. *World War I Songs: A History and Dictionary of Popular American Patriotic Tunes, With Over 300 Complete Lyrics*. Jefferson, N.C., 1995.

Wallace, Stuart. *War and the Image of Germany: British Academics, 1914–1918*. Edinburgh, 1988.

Wallach, Ameri. "The Retreat of French Art Began in Flanders Fields." *The New York Times*, 6 February 2000, pp. AR1, 38.

Walsh, Stephen. *Stravinsky: A Creative Spring*. New York, 1999.

Ward, Andrew. *Dark Midnight When I Rise: The Story of the Jubilee Sing ers Who Introduced the World to the Music of Black America.* New York, 2000.

Ward, Larry Wayne. *The Motion Picture Goes to War: The U.S. Government Film Effort During World War I.* Ann Arbor, 1985.

Warner, Marina. *Joan of Arc: The Image of Female Heroism.* New York, 1981.

Watkins, Glenn. *Pyramids at the Louvre: Music, Culture, and Collage from Stravinsky to the Postmodernists.* Cambridge, Mass., 1994.

———. *Soundings: Music in the Twentieth Century.* New York, 1988.

Weintraub, Stanley. *Silent Night: The Story of the World War I Christmas Truce.* New York, 2001.

Wellesz, Egon. "Schoenberg and Beyond." *The Musical Quarterly* 2, no. 1 (1916): 89.

Wells, H. G. *The World Set Free: A Story of Mankind.* London: Macmillan, 1914.

Wells, Ronald A., ed. *The Wars of America: Christian Views.* Macon, Ga., 1991.

Wenzel, Lyn, and Carol J. Binkowski. *I Hear America Singing: A Nostalgic Tour of Popular Sheet Music.* New York, 1989.

Wetta, Frank Joseph. *Celluloid Wars: A Guide to Film and the American Experience of War.* New York, 1992.

Wharton, Edith. *A Backward Glance.* New York, 1964.

———. *Fighting France, from Dunkerque to Belfort.* Toronto, 1915.

———. *The Letters of Edith Wharton.* Edited by R. W. B. and Nancy Lewis. New York, 1988.

———, ed. *The Book of the Homeless (Le livre des sans-foyer).* London, 1916.

White, Eric Walter. *Stravinsky: The Composer and His Works.* 2d ed. Berkeley, 1979.

Whitesitt, Linda. *The Life and Music of George Antheil, 1900–1959.* Ann Arbor, 1983.

Whiting, Steven M. *Satie the Bohemian: From Cabaret to Concert Hall.* Oxford, 1999.

Whitmer, T. Carl. "A Post-Impressionistic View of Beethoven." *The Musical Quarterly* 2, no. 1 (1916): 15–16.

Wiegand, Wayne A. *An Active Instrument for Propaganda: The American Public Library During World War I.* New York, 1989.

Wilder, Amos Niven. *Armageddon Revisited: A World War I Journal.* New Haven, 1994.

Williams, John. *The Other Battleground: The Home Fronts: Britain, France and Germany 1914–1918.* Chicago, 1972.

Williams, Lee E. *Post-War Riots in America, 1919 and 1946: How the Pressures of War Exacerbated American Urban Tensions to the Breaking Point.* Lewiston, N.Y., 1991.

Wilson, Keith. *Decisions for War, 1914.* London, 1995.

Wilson, Louis. *Posters and Pictures Relating to the European War.* Worcester, Mass., 1917.

Wilson, Luther. *America—Here and Over There*. New York, 1918.

Wilson, Woodrow. *The Public Papers of Woodrow Wilson*. Edited by Ray Stannard Baker and William E. Dodd. New York, 1925–1927.

Wilton, S. T. H. "World War I." In *Encyclopaedia Britannica*, vol. 23. Chicago, 1968.

Winter, Jay. "Britain's 'Lost Generation' of the First World War." *Population Studies* 31, no. 3 (1977): 457–465.

———. "Popular Culture in Wartime Britain." In *European Culture in the Great War: The Arts, Entertainment, and Propaganda, 1914–1918*. Edited by Aviel Roshwald and Richard Stites. Cambridge, U.K., 1999.

———. "Propaganda and the Mobilization of Consent." In *The Oxford Illustrated History of the First World War*, edited by Hew Strachan. Oxford, 1998.

———. "Shell-shock and the Cultural History of the Great War." *Journal of Contemporary History* 35, no. 1 (2000). 7–11.

———. *Sites of Memory, Sites of Mourning: The Great War in European Cultural History*. Cambridge, U.K., 1995.

Winter, Jay, and Blaine Baggett. *The Great War and the Shaping of the Twentieth Century*. New York, 1996.

Winter, Jay, and Emmanuel Sivan, eds., *War and Remembrance in the Twentieth Century*. Cambridge, U.K., 1999.

Winter, Jay, Geoffrey Parker, and Mary R. Habeck, eds. *The Great War and the Twentieth Century*. New Haven, 2000.

Winter, Thomas. "The Training of Colored Troops: A Cinematic Effort to Promote National Cohesion." In *World War I: Motion Picture Images*, edited by Peter C. Rollins and John E. O'Connor. Bowling Green, 1997.

The Wipers Times; a Complete Facsimile of the Famous World War One Trench Newspaper, Incorporating The "New Church" Times, The Kemmel Times, The Somme Times, The B.E.F. Times, and The "Better Times." Edited and introduced by Patrick Beaver. London, 1973.

Wittgens, Herman. "Senator Owen, the Schuldreferat, and the Debate over War Guilt in the 1920s." In *Forging the Collective Memory*, edited by Keith Wilson. Providence, 1996.

Wohl, Robert. *The Generation of 1914*. Cambridge, Mass., 1979.

———. *A Passion for Wings: Aviation and the Western Imagination, 1908–1918*. New Haven, 1994.

Woolf, Virginia. *Three Guineas*. London, 1938.

Yastrebtzev, Y. *Recollections of Rimsky-Korsakov*. Vol. 2. Moscow, 1962.

Youmans, Charles. "The Twentieth-Century Symphonies of Strauss." *The Musical Quarterly* 84, no. 2 (2000): 238–258.

Young Bear, Severt, and R. D. Theisz. *Standing in the Light: A Lakota Way of Seeing*. Lincoln, 1994.

Zohn, Harry, ed. *In These Great Times: A Karl Kraus Reader*. Montreal, 1976.

Zweig, Stefan. *Romain Rolland, the Man and His Work*. Translated by Eder and Cedar Paul. New York, 1921.

Index

Compositor: G & S Typesetters, Inc.
Text: 10/13 Aldus
Display: Aldus
Printer and Binder: Edwards Brothers, Inc.

List of CD Contents

1. Edward Elgar, "To Women," from *The Spirit of England,* 1915–1917. Teresa Cahill, soprano; Scottish National Orchestra and Chorus, conducted by Sir Alexander Gibson. Recorded by Chandos (CHAN 6574). © 1917 by Chester Music and Novello, London. Mechanical License by G. Schirmer, Inc., on behalf of Novello & Co., Ltd. (Licensor) (Maestro #00009387). Master Recording License by Chandos Records Ltd. Length: 2:14.

2. Etienne-Nicolas Méhul, "Chant du départ," 1794. Arranged for wind ensemble in 1799. Arizona State University Harmonie Ensemble, conducted by Jeffrey Lyman. Length: 2:23.

3. Claude Debussy, "Berceuse héroïque," 1914. David Gompper, piano. Music © 1915 Durand, Paris. Length: 3:06.

4. Claude Debussy, *En blanc et noir,* second movement (excerpt), 1915. David Gompper and Réne Lecuona, piano. Music © 1915 Durand, Paris. Length: 1:26.

5. Claude Debussy, "Noël des enfants qui n'ont plus de maisons," 1915. Frederica von Stade, mezzo-soprano; Martin Katz, piano. Music © 1916 by Durand, Paris. Length: 2:40.

6. Igor Stravinsky, "March," from *Trois pièces faciles,* 1914. David Gompper and Réne Lecvona, piano. Music © 1919, 1991 Chester Music, Ltd., London. Mechanical License by G. Schirmer, Inc. (Licensor). Length: 1:07.

7. Igor Stravinsky, "Souvenir d'une marche boche," 1915. David Gompper, piano. Music © 1916 Boosey & Hawkes Music Publishers Ltd. Copyright renewed. Reprinted by permission. Mechanical License by Boosey & Hawkes, London. Length: 1:27.

8. Maurice Ravel, "Trois beaux oiseaux du Paradis," 1916. University of Michigan Chamber Choir, conducted by Thomas Hilbish. Music © 1916 Durand, Paris. Product License by SDRM, France. International rights secured. Length: 3:08.

9. Maurice Ravel, "Toccata," from *Tombeau de Couperin,* 1917. John Browning, piano. Originally recorded prior to 1972 (RCA Victor LSC 3028).

Music © 1918 Durand, Paris. Master Recording License: All rights reserved by BMG Entertainment. Recording courtesy the RCA Records Label. Product License by SDRM, France. International rights secured. Length: 3:34.

10. Henry Deutsch de la Meurthe, "O toi qui le premier osas quitter la terre," from *Icare*, 1911. Susan Jones, soprano; David Gompper, piano. Music © 1911 Gabriel Astruc, Paris. Length: 4:55.

11. Arnold Schoenberg, "Der verlorene Haufen," 1907. Leslie Guinn, baritone; Martin Katz, piano. Permission granted by Belmont Publishers, Pacific Palisades, California. Length: 4:19.

12. Anton Webern, "Der Tag ist vergangen," 1915. Kristie Tiggers, soprano; David Gompper, piano. Music © 1925 Universal Edition. Mechanical License by Universal Edition. Length: 1:09.

13. Noble Sissle, Eubie Blake, and James Reese Europe, "On Patrol in No Man's Land," 1919. Noble Sissle with the 369th Infantry Regiment "Hellfighters," conducted by James Reese Europe. Recorded in 1919 by Pathé. Length: 2:20.

14. John Alden Carpenter, "The Home Road," 1917. John Muriello, baritone; David Gompper, piano. Music © 1917 G. Schirmer, New York (Maestro #0021816). Mechanical license by G. Schirmer, Inc. (Licensor). Length: 2:57.

15. Charles Ives (music) and John McCrae (lyrics), "In Flanders Fields," 1917. John Muriello, baritone; David Gompper, piano. Music © 1917 Peer International Corporation / BMI. Mechanical License by Peer International. Length: 2:23.

16. Charles Ives (music and lyrics), "Tom Sails Away," 1917. John Muriello, baritone; David Gompper, piano. Music © Merion Music, Inc. / BMI. Mechanical License by Merion Music, Inc. Length: 2:47.

17. Maurice Ravel, *Frontispice*, 1919. David Gompper, Réne Lecuona, and Chin-Chu Hu, piano. Music © Salabert, 1975. Product License by SDRM, France. International rights secured. Length: 1:30.